IMAGINATION AND REFLECTION: INTERSUBJECTIVITY FICHTE'S: *GRUNDLAGE* OF 1794

MARTINUS NIJHOFF PHILOSOPHY LIBRARY
VOLUME 8

Series ISBN 90-247-2344-2

IMAGINATION AND REFLECTION: INTERSUBJECTIVITY FICHTE'S *GRUNDLAGE* of 1794

by

T.P. HOHLER

1982

MARTINUS NIJHOFF PUBLISHERS

THE HAGUE/BOSTON/LONDON

Distributors:

for the United States and Canada

Kluwer Boston, Inc.
190 Old Derby Street
Hingham, MA 02043
USA

for all other countries

Kluwer Academic Publishers Group
Distribution Center
P.O. Box 322
3300 AH Dordrecht
The Netherlands

Library of Congress Cataloging in Publication Data
Hohler, T. P.
    Imagination and reflection.

    (Martinus Nijhoff philosophy library ; v. 8)
    Includes index.
    1. Fichte, Johann Gottlieb, 1762-1814. Grundlage
der gesammten Wissenschaftslehre. 2. Knowledge, Theory
of. 3. Imagination. 4. Intersubjectivity. I. Title.
II. Series.
B2824.H63 1982   193   82-17333

ISBN 90-247-2732-4 (this volume)
ISBN 90-247-2344-2 (series)

For André Schuwer,

dedicated scholar,

inspiring teacher,

lasting friend

TABLE OF CONTENTS

PREFACE

This work resulted from my interests in several fundamental issues of contemporary phenomenology. Originally, their focal point was 1) the role and importance of the subject in philosophical activity and 2) the subject's finitude. To gain a perspective on these issues, a possible approach seemed to lie in the direction of the transcendental imagination and its relation to time. This focus on the imagination, of course, led to Fichte's egological philosophy that explicitly centers on the imagination. Here both issues are raised together. The reader of the Fichtean texts cannot for long hesitate to pose the question of intersubjectivity. These three issues--imagination, reflection, and inter-subjectivity—formed the basis of the present work.

Since such a work could never be completed if it were not for those numerous discussions and friendly conversation with friends and colleagues with whom philosophy is always alive, I wish to acknowledge my gratitude specifically to the following people:

Professor Andre Schuwer, of Duquesne University, for his encouragement, critical reading of the work, and his comments that have greatly aided me in the writing of the present work;

Professor John Sallis, Chairman of the Philosophy Department of Duquesne University, whose interest in Fichte provided invaluable insights and approaches to the issues;

Professor Paul Ricoeur, University of Paris and University of Chicago, whose reading and encouragement greatly helped in the work's publication;

Professor Samuel Ijsseling, University of Leuven, who introduced me to Martinus Nijhoff Publishers;

Professor G. A. De Brie, President of *Tijdschrift voor Filosofie*, who granted me permission to use my article "Intellectual Intuition and the Beginning of Fichte's Philosophy" that had been previously published in *Tijdschrift voor Filosofie*;

Ms. Phyllis McLaughlin, whose secretarial and editing assistance made a difficult and tedious task much easier.

All translations from German and French are my own. The German text that I have followed is *Johann Gottlieb Fichte's Sämmtliche Werke* edited by I. H. Fichte (Berlin, 1845–46) that is readily available in individual volumes from Felix Meiner Verlag and has been reissued as *Fichtes Werke* by Walter de Gruyter & Co. (Berlin, 1971). Although the recent English translation of Peter Heath and John Lachs, *Fichte: Science of Knowledge with First and Second Introductions* (New York, 1970), has been occasionally consulted, my translation differs considerably in key points and terms.

T.P.H.

Pittsburgh, PA

INTRODUCTION

> *There are only real men. With the*
> *emergence of philosophical questioning*
> *there concurrently emerges a subject*
> *who gives orientation to the whole field*
> *of experience; therefore "the" world*
> *becomes world-for-me. But with this re-*
> *orientation of the world into a world for*
> *me, an asymmetrical situation also*
> *obtains within the field of experience;*
> *there is I and there is the Other.*
>
> -Ricoeur

Reflection, imagination, and intersubjectivity—these three issues arose and have re-arisen throughout modern philosophy. Their irresolution and significance have had an impact on the contemporary philosophical issues. With the radical doubt and with the turning inwards in the search for certainty, Descartes began to philosophize. With *that* beginning are rooted the issues of reflection and inter-subjectivity.

The "*cogito, ergo sum*" opens up the possibility of transcendental philosophy along with the issues inherent in that philosophy. Since "the proposition: *I am, I exist,* is necessarily true every time that I pronounce it or conceive it in my mind"(1), thinking is necessarily and exclusively inseparable from the nature of the I or of the self.

To this *res cogitans* is opposed a *res extensa* that is absolutely different. Since each is a substance that is characterized by being what the other is absolutely not, the problem of the communication between different substances arises. How can one substance—a thinking substance—relate to and communicate with another substance—an extended one? With the *cogito,* with thinking of thinking, the problem of solipsism and the need to overcome it emerge because certitude is required and used as the grounding criterion.

The Cartesian philosophy is not only reflective, but also tries to ground itself in that reflection. Such a philosophy begins with a separation and an affirmation. It begins with the separation of oneself from the contingencies and vicissitudes of life and with the affirmation of the steadfastness of the I in its thoughtfulness. Such a beginning, undertaken with a doubt (whether methodical or otherwise), involves the problematic of solipsism. Of course, the problematic of solipsism which arises from self-reflection includes the issue of intersubjectivity.

Since the problematic of solipsism must include the issue of intersubjectivity, any interrogation of an I must also give an account of how this I is able to encounter the Other. Within my own consciousness, I should be able to ascertain the grounds that allow me to distinguish myself from others.

Though reflection and intersubjectivity were issues already implicit in the Cartesian doubt, it was not until Kant that the imagination was given a prominent place in a reflective philosophy. Although with Kant, the imagination took a subordinate role to the universal power of reason, its centrality with regard to understanding can hardly be questioned. In this latter case, the imagination mediated sensibility and spontaneity. Kant's young admirer Johann Gottlieb Fichte first recognized the central importance of imagination.

The three issues—reflection, imagination, and intersubjectivity—converge as a central concern in Fichte's philosophy. Fichte, within the tradition of reflective philosophy, concentrates these issues in a philosophy of the I. His philosophy, more than any other, is the first full-fledged egology. With Fichte's faithfulness to his Kantian roots, the imagination is a central dimension of this egology. No longer will it mediate between sensibility and understanding, but becomes the originary unity and possibility for self-reflection and experience.

By taking up the reflection on the I with the imagination's centrality in that reflection, the present work will focus on the issue of intersubjectivity. It will be shown that intersubjectivity is an essential aspect of the I. The aim of the study is to show that the transcendental I is essentially and inherently intersubjective. The thesis of this work is: the intersubjective dimension of the I is essential for the I to be an I.

This, however, does not mean that the I is and must *actually* be related to another I. The issue is a transcendental one. Whether the I has or does not have actual concrete relations with another I is not the issue: it is whether intersubjectivity is a transcendental constituent of the I-hood of the I. In other words, *why* does an I necessarily have to meet another I to be an I; not *does* the I actually meet another one?

Intersubjectivity is both a problem and an answer to reflective philosophy. If philosophy must be reflective, i.e., transcendentally reflective, and yet not be a subjectivistic philosophy, then, as one author notes, the

> issue is nowhere more decisive than in that area of problems that concern the subject's experience of another subject, for what we discover in this regard is a fundamental inherent reciprocity between the problematic of the subject's relation to its other and that of the essential possibilities of reflection as such. . . . This situation suggests that the problem of the other is an appropriate dimension in which to confront the project of total reflection(2).

It is the issue of intersubjectivity that brings to light the problem of philosophical reflection and also a possible direction for understanding that problem.

The central thesis of this work will also have an impact on Fichte's relationship to German Idealism. No longer can Fichte be understood as the initial step on the way to Hegel. Fichte's philosophy will no longer be considered an absolute idealism which fell short of its mark. In fact, finitude will be more strongly affirmed than the infinite or absolute and will take a central position.

The present approach to the three issues of reflection, imagination, and intersubjectivity will focus in general on Fichte's early writings (those prior to 1800) with special attention to the *Grundlage* of 1794. Our reasons for this are twofold.

First, we are not concerned with the over-all development and evolution of Fichte's thought, but only with that part of the early philosophy which immediately pertains to our thesis of the intersubjective character of the I. In this regard, our concern with these early writings is a concern for the essential insight and thought of Fichte. In our reflection, we do not want to be prejudiced by that which later developed from these writings. Whether Fichte's later writings are a mere development or a radical change from the earlier position is a question that needs to be postponed. Our task is to clarify and to interpret insightfully the early philosophy which Fichte himself did not hesitate to publish.

Secondly, since a horizonal concern is Hegel's interpretation of Fichte, it would seem appropriate to rely only on those texts on which Hegel's own understanding had been based. These are the texts of the early philosophy because Hegel was not familiar with the speculative writings after 1800(3). These are our two reasons for limitng ourselves to only the early writings. We will not be concerned with either the transitional writings (1800-1808) or the much later ones (1810-1813)(4). Our concern will primarily be those writings of 1794-1798, especially the *Grundlage* of 1794.

The centrality of the intersubjective aspect of the I in the interpretation of the *Grundlage* will develop through several steps. That the transcendental I is necessarily and essentially intersubjective can only be considered by first presenting Fichte's notion of reflective philosophy and by understanding that the unity of the I is the imagination.

Chapter One will present Fichte's notion of reflective philosophy as a systematic ideal. Within this context the meaning of Wissenschaftslehre and the methodology proper to it will be elaborated. In brief, this first chapter will primarily be concerned with how and what Fichte conceives philosophy to be.

Because the systematic ideal of philosophy does not guarantee its actuality, we will have to investigate the nature of the one who will attempt to realize such an ideal, such a Wissenschaftslehre. In Chapter Two, the "I am" that is necessarily presupposed in any philosophical activity will be discussed. What will come to the fore will be the I's essential, originary structure: the transcendental imagination. Although the intersubjective element must already be part of the imagination, the essential structure of the I, the *explicit* elaboration and justification is postponed to Chapter Three.

This most important chapter on intersubjectivity is based on and necessarily needs the previous chapter, for it makes explicit what had merely been implicit in the imagination. In this third chapter, we will first follow Fichte's own deduction of the Other—a deduction that can only take place because the I is as it had been described in the previous chapter. How can this explicit deduction be related to its implicit presence in the structure of the I? This question will be answered when we show how the *Naturrecht* can proceed out of the *Grundlage*. It is here that we will focus on the "Deduction of Representation" of the *Grundlage*. This merely presents explicitly what had already been presupposed and contained in our previous discussion. This circularity, however, is not empty.

The problematic of Chapter Four does not directly follow from the three preceding chapters, but is a problem that always lies on the periphery of our entire discussion. This is the problematic of the intellectual intuition and what it means for Fichte's reflective philosophy. We must come to some understanding both as to its nature and as to its position or role in reflection—if our thesis of the intersubjective character of the I is to have any plausibility. The manner in which this chapter refers back to all that had been previously discussed will entail an answer to some of the questions posed by the intellectual intuition and an indirect rebuttal of the Hegelian interpretation.

Through these four steps, the unique interconnectedness of reflection, imagination, and intersubjectivity will have been presented.

CHAPTER ONE

PHILOSOPHY AS A SYSTEMATIC IDEAL

*Let anyone try to give us a definite
concept of the philosopher, without first
having given us a definition of philosophy, that is a definite philosophy itself!*

-Fichte

To conceive philosophy as a systematic ideal must have a
prephilosophical root. Not only is this prephilosophical ground
the consciousness of freedom, but the consciousness of human
freedom within a social milieu. Fichte was highly motivated to
establish and to achieve a humanly free society. In his letter to
Kant of April, 1793, Fichte wrote that his soul was ardently
yearning to realize (in the words of Kant) "a constitution
allowing *the greatest possible human freedom* in accordance
with laws by which *the freedom of each is made to be
consistent with that of all others*"(1). Philosophy was to play an
essential role in this concern and goal.

The present chapter will be devoted to a preliminary
understanding of Fichte's notion of philosophy and its
methodology. This will enable us to enter his philosophical
question and thereby gain an appropriate insight into the
problem of self-consciousness. Besides clarifying Fichte's
response to this question, we also desire to understand how he
initially poses the question and how he proceeds. In the brief
text of 1794, entitled "On the Concept of Wissenschaftslehre,"
Fichte, in a very straightforward way, describes and
articulates his notion of philosophy. The interpretation of this
text will prepare the way for a discussion of the transcendental
imagination by showing the systematic ideal of philosophy and
its methodology.

Philosophy as Wissenschaftslehre

As a starting point, we will quote three texts that occur
in this essay. We will interpret these texts in light of the essay
and in light of the implications raised therein.

      1)   "Philosophy is *a science*"(2). More specifically,
philosophy is *"the science of a science in general"*(3).
      2)   "We are not the lawgivers of the human spirit,
but its historiographers; of course, not journalists, but
pragmatic writers of its history"(4).
      3)   Finally, the

> I as philosophizing *subject* is unquestionably only
> representing; the I as *object* of the philosophizing
> could still be something more. The act of
> representing is the highest and absolutely first
> activity of the philosopher as such; the absolutely
> first activity of the human spirit could well be
> another(5).

Contained in these three statements is the interconnectedness of philosophical reflection and experience as
well as the role each plays in terms of the other. There is also
contained the distinguishing characteristics between philosophy
and the other types of sciences.

For Fichte science means a systematic or structural form
which is certain. That which characterizes any science is its
fundamental proposition which roots the science in its
apodicticity. The absence of such a proposition destroys its
very scientific character and creates a relativism and an
uncertainty. Science as uncertain can hardly be called science.

On the other hand, we must pay close attention to what
Fichte is concerned with in this essay. He is not discussing an
actually existing science, but only a hypothetical one. The
paragraph headings concern themselves with the *concept* of
Wissenschaftslehre(6). He is not talking about an actually
existing, systematic science called Wissenschaftslehre, but is
concerned with what the concept implies. In other words, he is
concerned with its possibility—whether real or not—not with
its actuality. In fact, he notes "its possibility is till now
merely problematic"(7).

In this essay Fichte describes philosophy as an ideal, as
an idea in its most pure and certain mode. This idea of

philosophy contains the mark of certainty and absoluteness. This is its scientific character, but philosophy is a science of science or a Wissenschaftslehre. In other words, philosophy's foundational proposition in its absolute and unconditioned character is different from that foundational proposition of those other sciences, which are also characterized by certainty and apodicticity.

What is the relation of Wissenschaftslehre to science itself? How is a Wissenschaftslehre a science of science? The Wissenschaftslehre is the ground, and science is grounded in it. The foundational proposition of the Wissenschaftslehre is the absolute and unconditioned ground of all knowledge. Wissenschaftslehre is a science which has no higher grounding and, therefore, is the absolute foundation of science as such. This means that the Wissenschaftslehre not only exhibits the possibility of grounding the fundamental proposition itself, but it also shows that the specific foundational proposition(s) is(are) for *all* possible sciences. The certainty of the foundational proposition must be certain *in* and *through* itself as it is unprovable and ungrounded. This is its circularity and its grounding element.

We have seen that each is characterized by its systematic form or by its principle of interrelatedness and interdependence. With the Wissenschaftslehre as the ground, there must be a difference that accounts for this absolute character and that guarantees it. This grounding is that which distinguishes the one from the other. The fundamental proposition of any particular science is itself not contained therein, but is grounded in the Wissenschaftslehre. Although it is absolute and certain as a foundational proposition for that particular science, it is not for *all* knowledge. Since any system is characterized by the foundational proposition in that it contains both the form and the matter together for the whole system, we only have to discover the essential differences between the foundational proposition of the Wissenschaftslehre and those of the sciences in general.

Circularity characterizes the foundational proposition of the Wissenschaftslehre as opposed to its progressive character in the sciences. Since the Wissenschaftslehre is an absolute totality, it is a closed system in its being limited and finite whereas any science in general is an infinitely open-ended system that always leads away from the foundational proposition. Concerning the science of science, Fichte writes that "the foundational proposition necessarily leads to all asserted propositions, and all asserted propositions lead again back to it"(8). Or further, "the foundational proposition itself, from which we have departed, is also at the same time the final result"(9).

We have mentioned that the Wissenschaftslehre, due to its circularity, is a closed system. By this, we do not mean that nothing new can occur and that everything is already present and predetermined. By closed system, we merely mean that the Wissenschaftslehre gives the ground for the totality of experience and, therefore, is channeled by experience. Also closed system means that within the system the content and the form are inseparable. Each determines the other: the form is the content, and the content is the form.

This completeness designates the Wissenschaftslehre as such. It is an absolute totality in contrast to the unending and never-to-be-completed character of the sciences in general. It is a circle "out of which the human spirit can never escape"(10), but whose borders constantly move back. In other words, the Wissenschaftslehre is a finite totality that encompasses the totality of human experience and of the human spirit as the apodictic ground.

Philosophy as Wissenschaftslehre is considered as an ideal which is absolutely certain. This ideal has a circular determination due to its being all encompassing. Its apodicticity gives the foundation and the scientific character to all other kinds of human knowledge. We have also seen from those quotations that the human spirit is related to the ideal of philosophy. In fact, the human spirit might be more extensive than the limits of the Wissenschaftslehre even though philosophy is the science of science. Philosophy, it seems, must enter into the human spirit; to the extent it does, this ideal can be realized. Thus, philosophy becomes a project, a possibility, to be realized in and through the human spirit.

In the conception of philosophy as an ideal with absolute and apodictic certainty, Fichte thereby achieves the opening of this science to experience. The absolute character is both the justification for and the possibility of human experience. Not only does Fichte want to show the condition for the possibility of experience, but also wants to show its genesis in revealing the source. Philosophy as a Wissenschaftslehre is transcendental. Transcendental here means to trace the conditions of possibility of experience back to the ground in the I, but it also means that these structures of the I define and determine the Being of the beings of experience. These entities or beings are the I itself (or intelligence) as well as those beings independent of this intelligence. Yet, we are not lawgivers; *and* the I as the object of philosophizing might also be more.

If we were the lawgivers of the human spirit, this would imply that all experience is grounded in reflection and that philosophy would be subjective immanence. What is said here seems to be quite the contrary. Philosophy as an ideal with its apodicticity's demanding immanence seems to open up human experience to the very character of being *human*. The ideal that philosophy projects is a motivating one as well as a justification of experience. Experience seen as totally transitory and fleeting can now be seen as meaningful. In other words, experience is and becomes human because it has meaning. It is structured according to laws.

What Fichte wants to say at this point is that meaning is disclosed and revealed in and through philosophical reflection, through the apodictic and absolute science of science. It is philosophy as transcendental that allows this meaning to emerge, yet its source lies beyond the representation, beyond an exclusively theoretical concern. Philosophical reflection cannot be seen as the end and the completeness of human activity, but must always return to its origin in the human experience. Theory is not the last court of appeal, but rather finds its very possibility elsewhere.

Philosophy's disclosure of meaning signifies that it is concerned with the structural ground of all experience. This is the sense of its character as a founding or grounding of experience rather than its being founded or grounded as the other sciences. This is the meaning of Fichte's statement that philosophy has to give the ground for all experience with this ground's being outside all experience and not lying at all within experience(11). Thus, neither philosophical reflection is what is real nor can reflection be separated from and have nothing to do with the lived experience. Philosophy is a transcendental reflection on experience or the human spirit.

We now want to clarify Fichte's conception of philosophy through a discussion of dogmatism (or realism) and of idealism—the two philosophizing modes of which Fichte is critical. Positively this leads to a discussion of Fichte's critical idealism. Within this discussion the methodology of dialectical argumentation that characterizes all of Fichte's writings will be presented.

Since the task of philosophy is to furnish the ground for all experience, through an act of freedom one can approach this ground by means of the two necessary constituents of experience—the thing and the intelligence or consciousness. There are two possible ways of proceeding: the way of dogmatism and that of idealism. The dogmatist's way leaves consciousness out of consideration and "retains a thing-in-itself, i.e., abstracted from the fact that it [thing-in-itself] occurs in experience as ground of experience"(12). Idealism, however, proceeds in the exact opposite way: it leaves out the thing and "retains an intelligence in itself, i.e., abstracted from its relation to experience"(13).

The dogmatist or empirical realist accounts for experience by means of the affectivity that the thing-in-itself has upon anyone or anything. "According to him, everything that is present in our consciousness, along with our presumed determinations through freedom and the very belief that we are free—is a product of a thing-in-itself"(14). Thus, every understanding or explanation of experience must ultimately refer to this thing-in-itself. The dogmatist affirms the absolute and necessary character of the being of a thing.

More emphatically, the dogmatist cannot explain the very freedom that he has used to philosophize. His philosophy maintains that all is determined by this thing-in-itself—even the feeling of freedom that a subject might have. According to dogmatism all reality, all experience can only be accounted for by the mechanical laws of causality. To be aware of the mechanical laws of causality as such presupposes that one has already gone beyond those very causal laws, i.e., it presupposes freedom. Yet, the philosophical explanation can give no account for this.

> For in *presupposing* mechanism, they arise above it; their thinking of it is something extraneous to it. Mechanism is unable to apprehend itself precisely because it is mechanism. Only the free consciousness can apprehend itself(15).

On the other hand, this thing-in-itself does not really occur in experience, but must be freely constructed. Thus, the dogmatist finds himself in a *lived* contradiction as well as a logical one.

This critique of dogmatism leads to an idealist position which begins with the feeling of freedom, and not with that of necessity(16). Idealism attempts to explain all by the activity of an intellect from which a deduction of specific representations can be made. The intellect acts in a determinate way, i.e., "the intellect acts, but owing to its nature, it can only act in a certain way"(17).

Yet this free activity of the intellect must also act in accordance with the necessary laws. This transcendental idealism maintains that it constitutes the world freely, but this free activity follows a system of laws. This system of laws the intellect gives to itself whereby experience is and can be an objective experience. The problem that Fichte sees with such a philosophy is that there is no way for it to show whether these necessary laws are in fact related to experience. Thus, the idealist "can in no way confirm that his postulated laws of thought are really laws of thought, really nothing else but immanent laws of the intellect"(18). Why can they not be laws of things rather than laws of the intellect? The idealist can be asked: "whence comes that which has these relations and dispositions; whence the stuff that is organized in these forms"(19)? Though the idealist surpasses the dogmatist by beginning with freedom, the idealist cannot account for the fact that his deduced and postulated laws are in fact the ground of experience or are already inherent in reality itself.

The Methodology

Fichte wants to overcome the one-sidedness of dogmatism and of idealism. The attempted synthesis of both positions is the focal point of the next chapter's treatment of the transcendental imagination. But first, it is important to present Fichte's dialectical methodology through a discussion of the first three principles articulated in the *Grundlage*. Three strategies are involved in such a treatment. An overall view of the matter will be followed by an explicit treatment of the methodology used. A discussion of the movement of the three propositions (or principles) of *reality, negation,* and *limitation* will prepare for an understanding of the act of freedom presupposed by and necessary for philosophizing.

The beginning of the *Grundlage* is concerned with the posing and the subsequent development of the "I am." Though the specific treatment of this follows in the next chapter, the more general and broader consideration of these thirty pages aims at an articulation of identity and difference. It might also be called the articulation of the unity within the difference and/or multiplicity within a unity.

Since we are looking for the fundamental ground for all human knowledge, i.e., the conditions for the possibility of all human knowledge, the ground itself cannot be proved within the sphere of that knowledge; to do so would involve that ground in the realm of human knowledge. This, then, would presuppose another ground. In other words, the ultimate ground can never become an object of consciousness, but must be *thought* as the ground of all consciousness(20). The unconditioned must be an accomplish*ing* fact (*Tathandlung*) and can never be an accomplish*ed* fact (*Tatsache*).

Even with this methodological problem at the very outset, this unconditioned must be disclosed. The very thinking of the ground is ordered and structured by the laws of thinking which also cannot be proved because every proof presupposes them. Within another context there is a similar problem, but the connection will ultimately let us proceed. There is needed an absolutely valid proposition that is given to reflection as a *Tatsache* of empirical consciousness. From this we hope to be led to a pure proposition that is absolutely valid and that, in its purity, will be admitted as the ground or as the accomplishing fact (*Tathandlung*) of all human knowledge. This is Fichte's circular method as outlined in his essay "On the Concept of the Wissenschaftslehre" where he notes that the "foundational proposition itself from which we would have proceeded is at the same time also the final result"(21).

The Principle of Reality

The first fundamental principle which is absolute and totally unconditioned is reached through two steps or syntheses: 1) a movement from a purely logical relation to the "I am" as an accomplished fact of empirical consciousness, but not yet as an accomplishing fact; 2) a deduction of the nature of the I as activity—the pure category of reality. Each of these steps is developed or synthesized from five propositions.

Before continuing, two terms that Fichte uses quite extensively need to be explained. A system has both a content and a form. The fundamental proposition along with everything that is derived from it makes up the inner *content* or *matter*; but the way of interconnection is called the *form*(22). "That about which one knows something is called the matter;

and that which one knows about it, the form of the proposition"(23). Since every proposition contains both a form and a matter, in the foundational proposition they mutually determine each other and are, therefore, absolute and unconditioned. There are two other possibilities: either the form or the matter is conditioned whereas the other is totally unconditioned. The conditioning is ultimately derived from or is dependent on the fundamental proposition.

The first step in the movement from a purely logical relation begins with the principle of identity or "A is A." Here one is not concerned with the actual existence or non-existence of A, but merely with a relation of if/then. The interest is with the form—the what—of the proposition rather than with the content—the about which. This relation expresses a necessity—what is necessary for a possible object(24).

The question is: when *is* A? When does A exist? This necessary relation (now called X) must be posed "*in* and *by* the I"(25) because the I is the ground for judging and for the rules of judging. This relation, grounded in the I, expresses a necessary relationship of a subject (A-s) to an object (A-o) with A-o's being conditioned by A-s. Since this second relation (subject and object) is also grounded in the I, the members of that relation (the two A's) must also be grounded in the I. X expresses the unity of the different members, A-s and A-o.

We can summarize the above paragraph:

1) since X (the form of the relation if/then) is grounded in the I,

2) since A-s is also in the I,

3) since A-s is the condition of A-o, therefore A-o *is*. Thus, A *is* because A is posed in the I. "If A is posed *in the I, so it is posed* or so *it is*"(26). A is posed absolutely through the I and through X's being in the I. A is for a judging I and is posed by the rules of the judging I. This points to the fact that "I=I," that "I am I"; a self-identity arises or is given as an accomplished fact (*Tatsache*) for the empirical consciousness through X. X as a fact for empirical consciousness expresses the identity of the original proposition "A=A." X is that identity—the form for any possible object. "I am I" is the same as the X, but this identity of "I am I" is still not an accomplishing fact, but an accomplished fact. The "I am" is given only to empirical consciousness.

In the above argument the movement has been from the logical proposition to that which is presupposed or contained

therein. The "I am" has been uncovered, but it is only for
empirical consciousness. The accomplishing fact as the ground
for all knowledge has not been reached. We must proceed in
the second step to the pure activity that lies as the ground for
all human knowledge.

The logical proposition that discloses the "I am" is
grounded in a judging activity that is pure.

> Thus the posing of the I by itself is the pure activity
> of that. —The I *poses itself*, and *it is*, according to
> this mere posing by itself; and conversely: the I *is*,
> and it *poses* its being, according to its mere
> being(27).

The proposition "I am I" expresses this connection of activity
and the product of activity. The first I is posing while the
second expresses its being. The essence of consciousness is to
be posing and the *positing* of its being. To say I is to express
the being of that which poses itself as being(28). This is the
absolute subject. This is the ultimate meaning of "I am"—I am
for myself in posing my being. This might be called
spontaneity, for "*the 'I' originally poses absolutely its very own
being*"(29).

From the certainty, not the truth, of the logical
proposition we have discovered the same certainty that it is
grounded in the "I am" whose active being consists in posing
itself as being. Now if we were to abstract all content and
express only the formal relation, we would have the Category
of Reality. This is a purely formal condition for all reality(30).

The Principle of Negation

With the first proposition both the content and the form
determined each other because it was absolutely unconditioned. The second fundamental proposition is conditioned
materially, but unconditioned as to its form. The first
principle can be designated as posing whereas the second as
opposing. The methodology of disclosure will be the same.

Since we previously began with the logical statement
"A=A," here we begin with "-A≠A," which can equally be posed
as freely as the first proposition. This second is also an
absolute posing. In the posing, this proposition is not grounded
in the first one because "-A≠A" is not the same as "-A=-A."
This latter's form is the same as X of the previous proposition.

In other words, this second fundamental proposition is materially conditioned, but formally unconditioned. Yet the question arises: when is -A possible? What are the formal conditions for -A's being? What is necessary for something to be opposed to an A, to be other than A?

The form of the opposing is not the same as the form of the posing and is, therefore, totally unconditioned. The form of both propositions ("-A≠A" and "A=A") are not the same. For "a condition of that cannot be at all derived from it ["A=A"] because the form of the opposing is so little contained in the form of the posing, that it is rather opposed to it"(31). Thus, to be formally unconditioned means the "-A is posed *as* such absolutely *because* it is posed"(32).

This opposing is, however, under the activity of the I; it is an accomplished fact of empirical consciousness. It is absolute and has no condition for its happening. Its logical form demands the identity of subject and predicate, i.e., the identity of the I or of consciousness. The procedure is from the merely logical to the transcendental ground of the purely logical. The transcendental unity of the I's activity, its accomplishing fact, can be expressed as "A=A" where A-s is absolutely posed and where A-o is the reflected. To A-o is opposed a -A by the activity of A-s whose absolute opposing is identical to A as posing. (Confer the sketch.) Therefore, "the passage from posing to opposing is only possible by the identity of the I"(33) or else -A would be equal to A.

The I:

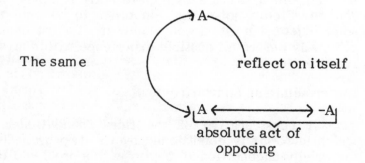

The same   reflect on itself

absolute act of
opposing

In summation, the being opposed is absolutely unconditionally posed by the I. Every opposite is in the I, and absolutely there. Fichte states that "the being-opposed in general is absolutely posed by the I"(34). This is the same as saying that the being-opposed is materially conditioned. A -A is opposed to an A and is conditioned by it. The activity of opposing is conditioned by another activity, that of posing. "It is an acting in reference to another acting"(35). The unity of consciousness of posing and opposing is the condition of the possibility of -A. Opposing can only be seen in reference to its counterpart, that of posing.

The -A's nature, the product, will be determined. In itself, it can be viewed both formally and materially. Formally it is determined to be an opposite of some X; while materially, in being opposed to a determined A, it is not something determined. It is not what A is; -A depends on A for its content(36).

Since only the I was originally posed, that which is opposed to the I must be the not-I. Just as previously it was certain that the I absolutely posed itself, so now it is certain that a not-I is absolutely opposed to the I. This opposing of the not-I to the I is formally unconditioned, but materially conditioned as was explained in the above discussion. Instead of A and -A, there is I and not-I. The pure form of the proposition expresses the Category of Negation.

For Fichte negation is not an absence or lack of the positive. It is not a concept arrived at by abstracting from some other fuller concept, but negation is intrinsically and intimately bound up with the positive. It is original, and not derived. In a passage that quite aptly reminds one of Plato's *Phaedo*, Fichte notes that "in order to be able to pose only some *object* I must already know it; it must consequently lie originally before all possible experience within myself—the one representing"(37).

The Principle of Limitation

A consideration of the third foundational proposition, which is formally conditioned by the two preceding ones, yet materially unconditioned, begins with a problematic that arises because of the results obtained in the first two fundamental propositions. A solution must take place.

The problematic arises if the two propositions are considered together. The posing of the not-I would seem to

deny the posing of the I, yet the not-I is posed in the I and is
opposed to it. It seems that the I is not posed in the I to the
extent that the not-I is posed there. On the other hand, the
not-I demands an identity of consciousness to which the not-I
can be posed. Thus, it seems that both the I and the not-I must
be posed in this identical consciousness. The second
foundational proposition both denies and affirms itself. If it is
to be at all related to the first, then the means of relating
would have to prevent the ensuing result of the I's being equal
to the not-I and vice versa(38). In other words, a mere
synthesis of the first two principles leads to reason's being in
conflict with itself.

Thus, the question is: "how A and -A, being and not-
being, reality and negation, are to be thought together without
denying and cancelling each other"(39)? The two must be
thought together; yet, the unity of consciousness must be
maintained. The very denial of the unity of consciousness
would make impossible the presence of such a conflict. This
synthesis X must be done within consciousness while both
members, the I and the not-I, are the products of an original
activity of the I—the posing of the I by itself which can be
called Y. X will be the result of Y's synthetic activity. Thus,
the conflict of reason is not seen as an absolute contradiction,
but as a conflict whose terms might be synthesized at a higher
level.

What must be the nature of this activity of Y to achieve
the desired synthesis and yet to maintain the differences
between the two members? This is achieved by a limiting. Y's
activity is one of limiting while X indicates the limits. By this
concept of limiting the unity is maintained with the
differences. This concept of limiting is a synthesis that
contains both the concepts of reality and negation.

To limit means to be divisible. Reality and negation only
partially deny each other. This concept of limitation expresses
the possibility of quantity, though not a determined quantity.
Thus, "the I as well as the not-I are absolutely posed as
divisible"(40). The acts of limiting and of opposing (Y and X)
are not two separate acts, but are one and the same, and are
distinguishable only by thought. "So as a not-I is opposed to an
I, accordingly the I to which it is opposed and the not-I which is
opposed are posed as divisible"(41).

The I can now be seen in two ways: 1) in its absolute
self-identity, and 2) in its relatedness to a not-I as both being
divisible. In one case the I is the principle ground for all

possible reality—a sort of unity-pole; in the other it is
something to which a negative magnitude is opposed. The I is
equal to itself and is in conflict with itself depending on the
perspective taken. Thus, *"the I opposes in the I a divisible
not-I opposed to the I"*(42). This, as a purely formal principle,
expresses the Category of Determination or, with Kant, of
Limitation.

This Dialectical Movement as a Whole

All three fundamental propositions must be examined as
a whole in order to understand the dynamics of the
interrelationship of the three.

With the third proposition's formulation, "an I opposes in
the I a divisible not-I opposed to a divisible I," the concept of
divisibility has been formulated. Fichte notes that no
philosophical activity can proceed beyond this knowledge; yet
fundamental philosophical thinking must return to it. This is
called the Wissenschaftslehre or knowledge of knowledge(43).
The concept of divisibility lays the ground for both relating *and*
distinguishing; it allows for the thinking of two opposed in a
unity.   More specifically, it allows for the possibility of
philosophical reflection in that it can mediate and articulate
the identity within difference, the unity of the totality *and*
that which is of the totality. The concept of divisibility is the
ground for the possibility of synthetic a priori judgments.
Fichte sees a judgment as a conceptual construction of relating
two distinct terms.

The distinction between analytic and synthetic is
comparable to the present distinction between an antithetic
procedure and a synthetic one. Fichte does not at all want to
oppose analytic to synthetic, but they are mutually related to
each other.   Analytic expresses the distinguishing whereas
synthetic expresses the relating(44).   Neither is possible
without the other. This is a crucial difference from Kant who
sees the need of an intuition for a synthetic a priori
judgment. Fichte believes such a judgment is grounded in the
concept of divisibility. Since a synthetic judgment is a relating
of difference, all further syntheses must depend on the concept
of divisibility. This will be further developed in the discussion
of the transcendental imagination. Fichte wants to begin with
the pure a priori to see the necessary condition for the world's
presence to me the subject, the condition for the constitution
of the world of experience.

To grasp the unity of these three fundamental propositions, their intimate interconnectedness as well as the foundational character of that interconnectedness must be seen. Fichte wants to describe the unity and the relation of a totality with that which is *of* that totality. This description must maintain both elements without reducing the one to the other. There are these two elements or aspects: 1) the totality or the absolute that is the ground or horizon, 2) that which is of the totality though in no way identical to the totality. The totality makes possible that which is of the totality, while at the same time the "that of" is not the same as the totality, but is grounded in the totality.

Fichte wants to express this relation between the totality and the "that of" in its unitary structure. The unity of the three propositions is the expression of this relation of identity and difference, which is ultimately the transcendental I of the "I am." As mentioned above, we will pursue this much more thematically in the forthcoming chapter. The entire *Grundlage*, then, is an attempt to disclose the meaning of this unity or the meaning of the I.

We have a thesis (the absolutely unconditioned), the antithesis (or the opposing), and the synthesis (or unity). We have seen that this synthesis is the ground for the unity of identity and difference, but yet no synthesis is possible without an antithesis which exhibits the opposition. These two, the synthesis as the relating of the difference and the antithesis as the differentiating, are in mutual reciprocity whose relation demands a thesis as the absolutely unconditioned. We have, so to speak, a circle with three phases of the same. In posing, there is an opposing which is synthesized in the unity that was already presupposed at the beginning. On the other hand, the synthesis presupposes an absolute ground for its very possibility. At the level of synthesis and antithesis a Wissenschaftslehre always seeks to bring the opposed into a unity to the point where the opposed can no longer be synthesized.

A conclusion will retrieve the entire movement that has been taking place. This will be done in order to understand it more fully, especially in terms of the philosophical activity. We have recently moved with Fichte from the thesis to the synthesis, or from the Principle of Reality to the Principle of Limitation. We now wish to reverse this order with the hope of getting a clearer insight into the very possibility and meaning of philosophy and reflection.

If we begin with what we might call the unity of experience, we can see how philosophy can proceed and what its necessary preconditions are. This unity of the totality with its differences is expressed by this unity of experience. A subject is experiencing his world and, in a sense, is lost in the every day and self-evident character of this world. This subject forgets and covers over those ties that connect him with his world. In his experiencing, he loses the sense of himself and is overwhelmed in that attitude that places priority on the self-evident objectivity of the objects. This situation, we think, is most concretely the synthetic relation that we have described above.

Conversely, one can by a free act negate or deny this being lost in experience and turn away from it. By the philosophical act one searches for the ground of all experience. This free act means that one directs his attention towards the ground and the conditions that make experience possible. Philosophy is transcendental. The philosophical act of reflection turns away from the unity of experience by means of this free act of negation. It turns away in order to see experience itself. In other words, the philosophical act is a free act whereby the philosopher turns away from his lostness in the world and thereby divides the pre-given unity of experience. It is essentially a negation, a negativity. This, of course, is related to the antithetic principle.

This negation is one not merely for the sake of negation, but is in function of a primary affirmation. What philosophy is concerned with is a self-understanding or self-knowledge. Fichte so clearly indicates this concern at the beginning of the *First Introduction*.

Pay attention to yourself: turn your attention from everything that surrounds you and towards that which is inner. This is the first demand that philosophy does to its disciple. The concern is of nothing outside yourself, but only with you yourself(45).

In other words, the very negation is negated with the primary affirmation of the self, of self-understanding. Philosophical reflection is not an activity that ends with negation, but travels through negation to affirm the self, to re-discover the meaning of the I. The negativity of the philosophical act is itself negated in order that reality, that being, that experience can be disclosed as meaningful. As Jean Nabert so pointedly and aptly states,

> Consciousness gathers itself in, loosens the ties which bind it to the world, refuses to confuse its being with the self which is made by its history, and attains, behind the self involved in effort or in friendship, a self which is for itself only the concrete and singular mode of an affirmation which affirms itself in this self, which is this self, but also surpasses this self absolutely(46).

Philosophical concern has as its task the affirmation of the identity of the I. This is the ground for the movement from the unity of experience through negation to itself. This is the thesis of the identity of the self—the first principle, the principle of reality.

We began this chapter with a discussion of Fichte's notion of philosophy—a Wissenschaftslehre, a science of science. This demanded that we confront the necessary methodology with its inherent problems and difficulties. We have in fact seen how Fichte concretely met these and proceeded. This has led to a deeper understanding of his philosophy and its essential concern. In our attempt to retrieve the entire discussion, we have returned to a point where philosophy in a reflective act affirms the self and attempts to understand the meaning of the I.

The discussion of philosophy as a systematic ideal (the content of this chapter) necessarily demands that the questioner himself be put into question. Philosophy returns on itself to ask "who?" of the one doing philosophy. We are led to the very condition of possibility of philosophy itself in its reflective activity. Even though Fichte has affirmed that any definition of a philosopher must be preceded by a definition of philosophy, he also seems to imply that to give a definition of philosophy means also to give a definite concept of the philosopher!

CHAPTER TWO

THE TRANSCENDENTAL IMAGINATION

Only for the imagination is there such a thing as time.

-Fichte

Philosophy considered as a systematic ideal requires that the questioner himself be placed in question. An attempt to discuss the nature of philosophy leads to the question of the self. The transcendental imagination will be in this chapter the access to understanding the self. The *Grundlage's* central theme is the transcendental imagination, and the latter expresses the I-character.

The conclusion of the last chapter showed that philosophy necessarily needs to turn inwards away from the world of experience in order to understand that world and the self. One's daily life is lived pre-reflectively and without explicitly turning inwards. In this world of experience certain features are certainly taken for granted and are overlooked. There is a certain continuity and unity in the lived world. Moments and things flow together. One lives through the world and fills its spaces. The world is not totally chaotic nor is it merely one's own subjective dream world. A certain commonality and sharability permeate this world. Objectivity is the name for that structural aspect that unifies this experiential world.

A brief descriptive analysis would show two predominant features. First, I see, perceive, am aware of objects and things that are *not* me; yet, secondly, it is *I* who am aware, who see, who perceive. The question is how to account for this objectivity of experience for the experiencing subject or how to account for an in-itself for us. An account must be given for the presence of passivity in the active I.

Within the last chapter the only feasible way was to turn inwards. The resolution of the issue can only be sought within the subject, within subjectivity. Only by interpreting the fullness of the "I am" will one be able to give the grounds for the objectivity of experience. This I to be interrogated, this "I am," is the synthetic unity of the three fundamental propositions.

This unity is expressed in the third principle that expresses the holding together of the I and the not-I. This can be expressed as two moments—the theoretical and the practical. The former asserts that the I poses itself as limited by the not-I whereas the latter affirms that the I poses the not-I as limited by the I. The task of this chapter is to interpret the third principle by showing the inherent structures of the I. This interpretative showing will show the centrality of the transcendental imagination. The primary concern will be with the theoretical dimension that accounts for the objectivity of the object or the in-itself for us.

This chapter will consist of three main divisions with a final section of interpretation. The first section will be devoted to what Fichte has called the independent activity. The issue here is that of the I-character of the I, of the I's reflective, spontaneous dimension. The subsequent section devoted to the relation or interplay is concerned with the I's capacity or power to relate to what is not itself. The transcendental imagination is the synthetic unity of both the independent activity and the relation. The presentation of these constitutive structures of the imagination lets the structures be seen as the conditions of the possibility for both human experience and philosophical reflection. The same structures will account for both experience and reflection and, yet, will maintain the differences between them.

The Independent Activity

Fichte describes the unity of this independent activity or the unity of the self-awareness in the following way:

> Because the I should exclude something from itself, a higher sphere must exist and be posed; and because a higher sphere exists and is posed, the I must exclude something from itself. More briefly, a not-I exists because the I opposes something to itself; and the I opposes something to itself because a not-I exists and is posed. Neither grounds the other, but both are one and the same act of the I(1).

In this unitary description of this awareness, two different ways describe the same activity. First, Fichte speaks of an exclusion *and* of a higher sphere. Secondly, he notes that the condition for the not-I is the fact that the I is *not* one with itself, i.e., it divides itself. In other words, the higher sphere is equivalent to the I's dividing itself; and the I can, therefore, exclude something from itself. The I can pose something other than itself. These are not two different acts, but *one* act.

When the I reflects on itself, looks back on itself, it thereby divides itself. To reflect is the same as to divide oneself. With this division, the I excludes something from itself and becomes, in a certain way, a non-self for itself. Again, both these moments are two aspects of the one activity of self-awareness. This act of reflection is related to that which it divides.

This fundamental unity can be understood by distinguishing its various constitutive moments. The formal moment would condition or make possible any type of relation; as the mode of interconnectedness, it is the principle of unity. The material moment is what is related. Thus, the task is to exhibit the form and the matter of the independent activity.

A clearer understanding of the independent activity can be realized by viewing its relational character. This relational character indicates how it relates to the interplay or the relation. In this context, what does *independent* mean? From what is it independent? It is an activity that is always related to, but independent of, the mutual reciprocity of activity-passivity. It is "the relational *ground* between action and passion in their being related"(2), i.e., the condition of possibility of the interplay or relation. It is essentially an activity that does not mutually relate to a passivity. "There is posed an activity in the I which is not at all opposed to a passivity in the not-I, and an activity in the not-I that is not at all opposed to a passivity in the I"(3). It is that I-character that renders experience possible. The independent activity is always related to, but independent of, experience or the consciousness of the object.

The unity of the independent activity consists of the interrelation of two moments. There is 1) the activity as independent from the form of the relation determining the activity as independent from the matter of the relation, 2) its converse determination, and 3) their mutual reciprocity(4). A fuller development of this consists of the two sides of the

synthetic unity of the independent activity as quoted at the
beginning of the chapter.

1. *The Formal Aspect or Quantitative Idealism*

This first section will discuss how the activity of the
form determines the activity of the matter; subsequently, how
the activity of the matter determines the activity of the form
will be discussed.   In the present context the activity is
characterized as an overflowing, a transference whereas in the
following case the activity is a middle term, a locus where
both components might be posed for the purpose of the one's
overflowing to the other.   It is the "X" that draws on
consciousness to pose both components, the positive *and* the
negative. It is that to which the unity of consciousness aspires
and which guides this consciousness(5).

This first case is "a non-posing by an absolute posing—a
posing of something as *not*-posed by the posing of another as
posed: negation by affirmation"(6). By affirming one sphere as
absolute and therefore filled up, this sphere must be filled in
terms of something else that is not being filled and which is
itself not posed, but is posed as *not*-posed.   Something is
excluded from the filled up sphere. This something else is not
negated, but merely excluded. Although this filled up sphere is
a determined or limited one, it is a totality. The other is only
a not-*this*; what it might be is not at all determined.

When this self-reflection affirms itself and its own
priority as the ground of experience, it does not negate
experience.   It only excludes that which cannot a priori be
encompassed by reflection. What that might be remains on
that other side, excluded from reflection. This reflective
awareness as the independent activity is related to experience
· as "*an exclusion from a sphere, determined and filled up, and
to that extent having a totality* (of what it contains)"(7).

This formal aspect is called a quantitative idealism in
which the I poses itself relatively or mediately to a not–I. This
is achieved through its own law: "*The I is finite absolutely
because it is finite*"(8).   The not–I is merely excluded, not
denied. The subject is posed with no definite predicates, but
only with possible ones because it is posed with everything
excluded from it. The subject affirms itself as having possible
determinations, i.e., as excluding, though not denying,
something from itself. The I is an I in reference to an excluded.

The subject is only a *formal* subject with empty predicates, i.e., with no predicates.

In the present formal aspect, self-awareness consists of an exclusion of all that is not itself; it abstracts from everything except itself. It affirms itself by returning to itself alone in its total purity. This subject has no predicates other than what it is not. Or, as Fichte says, "its sphere acquires absolutely no other predicate thereby, except a negative one"(9). All one can say is that the subject is.

2. *The Material Aspect or Qualitative Realism*

A return to the case where the matter of the independent activity determines its form concerns the posing of a higher sphere in which both components are encompassed. That which is excluded is also posed in that sphere which encompasses both components, A and B. The subject A is, in terms of itself, absolute, but in terms of B's being excluded is contingent. The independent activity materially poses this larger sphere wherein A and its excluded B are. This makes the act of exclusion possible.

A not-A is the ground and the possibility of any type of exclusion. The exclusion of B or not-A grounds the possibility of A's being able to pose itself absolutely with regard to itself; but, at the same time, this exclusion is possible because A is not only absolute, but is also related to B within this higher sphere. The independent activity of posing the higher sphere stems from the negativity of posing B, which is indeterminate.

In other words, this reflection on experience emerges because of its inherent dependence on experience. Reflection is dependent on what is not in itself, but is other than reflection. This is quite different from the first case (the formal aspect) in which the reflective activity was seen as the ground of experience. In the present case (the material aspect) experience provokes the reflective act to pose a higher sphere wherein and whereby the subject can then become itself. This latter situation in which experience provokes the posing of the higher sphere is the material condition for the former case. "The posing of such a *higher sphere, itself encompassing both, the determinate and the indeterminate,* would be that very activity whereby the previously established formal activity would become possible, thus, the activity of the matter"(10). Fichte had earlier called this a dogmatic or qualitative realism, a realism in which the not-I is a reality totally independent of the I. There is a *Ding-an-sich* that provokes or affects the I. The passivity of the I is understood by an activity in the object alone(11).

The subject can be seen from a certain perspective, but this perspective is not the only one. It is not an absolute perspective, but is a possible one among many other possibilities. These other possibilities can be other ones only because this subject has no definite predicate, but *can* have any predicate. If the subject *could not* have any predicate at all, it would make no sense to say that it has *no* predicates. Again negation is only because of affirmation. Abstraction from everyting is itself only possible and meaningful because abstraction is from something.

Although to a certain extent the unity of the whole synthesis is being expressed, rather than merely this particular moment in the synthesis, this is required to understand the meaning of this moment. The close interrelatedness of these two moments (the formal and the material) cannot be overlooked if a complete insight into the synthetic unity (as expressed in the first quotation) is to be obtained.

3. *The Synthetic Unity: Self-awareness as the I-character*

In the preceding two sections, the two extreme terms of the synthesis have been discussed. That discussion of their being interrelated requires a return to the synthetic unity of self-awareness. The return will complete one structural phase of the transcendental imagination.

The synthetic unity of the independent activity is a synthetic resolution of an issue. The issue is that of the compatible unity of self-awareness and experience or of consciousness and the consciousness of something. In Fichtean terms it is the issue of how to account for the passivity in the I. How can the I be active *and* passive at the same time?

Idealism or realism are two philosophical responses to the issue. Both attempt to account for the passivity in the I, but in a different way. Idealism explains the passivity of the I by means of exclusion whereas realism's account is based on an activity in the not-I that requires the passivity in the I. These positions have been called quantitative idealism and qualitative realism respectively.

In the idealistic position or in the formal determination the principle or ground of the interrelation is at stake. For the self to pose itself, to affirm itself, it must *exclude* everything that is not proper to itself. The posing of an excluded sphere immediately establishes that higher sphere that encompasses both the affirming and the excluded. Fichte aptly describes this:

> Posing an object is the same thing as not posing oneself. . .The I poses an object, or excludes something from itself simply because it excludes, and on no higher ground: by means of this exclusion, the higher sphere of *posing in general* (regardless of whether the I or not-I is posed) now first becomes possible(12).

This is the idealistic principle of consciousness whereby the self can discern itself as a self. By abstracting from everything or by excluding all, a not-I is posed. This can be possible only because there is a wider sphere. The I is both an absolute totality *and* a part of an indeterminate whole. It has this dual relation or aspect.

The self is only a self because it can discern itself. To be able to discern itself it must also in some way relate itself to an object. Here it excludes the object *without* saying what the object is or whether it is. Yet, what is possible for the I to experience is determined. In the affirmation of the I and the exclusion of the not-I, there is established the possibility of knowledge and experience. The I is posed in such a way for there to be a possible experience.

This quantitative idealism is inadequate. Idealism tries to explain the I's passivity or its relation to a not-I by means of a diminution. The I lessens some of its own activity or (as expressed here) excludes something from itself; but this cannot explain how the I "can refer this limitation to something in the not-I as the cause of it"(13). All that is explained is that the I does limit itself, but not that this limitation is because of a not-I. The limitation is only in the I; the I poses itself as finite in some way.

With the realist position where the matter does the determining, the situation is quite different. The grounds of any type of transition between the members of the relation is found not in the I, but in the wider sphere. The I's activity is grounded in that which is not itself. The "I is in general the posing; that under a specific condition, namely when it does *not* pose the not-I, it *poses* itself. . ."(14). In this realist position the ground of experience and knowledge is not in the self, but outside the self. The I's becoming itself, its possibility of self-affirmation, arises out of the fact of the higher sphere wherein the I and the not-I are posed.   The I is here a representing I which discovers itself according to things-in-themselves.   Since the former principle has been called the principle of consciousness, this present activity can be called the principle of experience.

Here the subject is dependent upon an object because the object provides the ground for experience and knowledge. Although the object to be an object is and must be related to this subject, the object is still *not* a subject. The abstraction of the subject is possible only because the subject's passivity is dependent on the independent object.

Realism in general fails to explain how the I is aware of its passivity that stems from the not-I. Realism sees the I as exclusively passive without the I's being aware of its passivity. This passivity could only be seen by a third party or an outside observer(15). This qualitative realism affirms a real presence of a not-I, of a *Ding-an-sich*, to explain the limitation of the I or the I's passivity.   It is a qualitative realism because the opposition between the I and the not-I is a radical one. The I has nothing to do with its own passivity or limitation. Here the I cannot explain how it is aware of its own passivity and limitation.

Consequently,   neither   idealism   nor   realism   can philosophically explain certain aspects of experience. Each's inadequacies   are   overcóme   by   the   further   synthesis—the synthetic unity of the independent activity. This return to that point of origin is a return to the mutual interdependence of both   the   principle   of   consciousness   and   the   principle   of experience. It is the unity of idealism and realism.

This synthetic unity of consciousness—a synthesis of self-awareness and of the consciousness of the object—expresses the possibility of experience. By one identical activity of the I, the self affirms itself while at the same time it opens up a field   of   experience.   This   activity   of   transferring,   of overflowing, is the ground for experience; it lets the self be opened to experience. Consciousness must divide itself and go beyond itself; it must overflow if its unity is to be maintained. This is grounded in consciousness itself. Self-awareness as the I-character is the unity within consciousness where the subject has divided itself. In this unified reflective act the philosopher lives related to the terms he unites(16). This is called critical idealism, which has reached its concluding point by merely explaining one term by the other. For "the I. . .is merely the opposite of the not-I and nothing more"(17). There is merely a subject and an object, but no means to distinguish one from the other. The basis of any explanation lies in neither one separately, but in both together. This synthetic unity of idealism and realism is accomplished on the side of the I, on the side of subjectivity. Since there is no basis for distinguishing, the I's fundamental finitude emerges within the I-character. This finitude forces further synthetic development that must appropriate the finitude and not leave it behind.

The emergence of finitude means that reflection must also take seriously into account its own path of movement. That the I gives an account of its own passivity and limitation means reflection must also provide a basis for methodology. With the present synthesis the importance of this insight is made explicit. Now the reflective subject is concerned not only with content, but also with methodology.

Subjectivity as the ground of experience includes the subject's self-affirmation as well as its self-division. The unity of the self as subject and the self as object within consciousness makes experience possible, but it is only one structural phase of the transcendental imagination. This phase has dealt only with the independent activity which reflects on reflection itself. The next task is to understand the reciprocal relation.

The Relation or Interplay

In this section the relation itself will be discussed. Since the members of the relation relate to each other, the mutual reciprocity of the relation in general will be first discussed. The second step will examine the substantiality of the I. Substantiality designates the interplay's reference to the I. The final step will prepare the way for the synthesis of the transcendental imagination. This whole process consists of two sets of five syntheses. From the exposition of the unity we will proceed to the constitutive elements of the synthetic unity.

1. The Relation in General

What is essential is the relation, and that alone. For, "the absolute and relative grounds for determination of the totality should be one and the same; the relative must be absolute, and the absolute should be nothing more than a relation"(18).   More explicitly, the members of the relation necesarily interact in movement because they are in movement in a relation(19).

The retrieval of the meaning of this synthetic unity involves three constitutive moments. The first and the second consist of the form of the relation and the matter of the relation respectively.   The final examination of their inter-dependence leads back to the unity that has just been expressed.

A. The Formal Aspect of the Relation

The form of the relation is the mutual exclusion of the members involved.   More specifically, each of the members is excluded from an absolute totality.   The members are related to each other in that both are excluded from an absolute totality.   This is the identity of the members with their differences.   The relation seen formally is one of exclusion; the content of this exclusion is the relation's material aspect.

B. The Material Aspect of the Relation

If one member is posed as absolute, then the other must necessarily be excluded from that sphere.   Yet, what the totality may consist of is unknown; it is completely undetermined, but determinable. Since the totality and what is to be excluded from it are unknown, a way or principle for determining the totality is required.   This principle would, then, enable us to state what is to be excluded. Thus, the principle or ground for completely determining the totality must be articulated.

There are two spheres: that of A and that of A+B. The former is an absolute activity whereas the latter is an activity related to something else. To say that each is a totality says nothing because there is no way to distinguish the one member from the other. This indeterminacy also makes it impossible to have a relation because a relation consists of two *different* discernible members. Thus, the matter of the relation consists of two things: 1) the necessity of two different members and 2) the need to be able to distinguish the one from the other. Since the matter articulates this difference, the matter is the principle of determinability which makes the relation possible.

"Hence the *determinability* of the totality, as such, is presupposed in order to make the postulated relation possible; it is presupposed that both totalities should be distinguishable in some particular; and this determinability is *the matter of the interplay.* . ."(20).

Let us try to get some insight into the issue at hand. We have repeatedly said that we are dealing with the interplay between two terms and are concerned only with that. We have been trying to understand the structures necessary for the consciousness of an object. How is it possible that a subject experience, encounter, or be related to an object? The form of such an interplay is the exclusion of each member from an absolute totality. This means that each is itself *not* an absolute totality, *if* they are to be related. The subject is not and cannot be an absolute subject, but is always related to its object. "The totality is a totality from two points of view"(21). There are not two separate totalities, but one totality from two points of view or perspectives. The absolute totality is neither the subject alone nor the subject and the object, but their interaction, their being together.

Experience is this totality that is continuous and all-encompassing, yet can be viewed from two perspectives. It can be seen from each of the members, the subject and the object. The real question is which member is the subject and which is the object. They are not the same, but are related. Thus, we need a ground for discerning the one from the other.

If the matter consists of an activity-passivity(22), it is not known which of the members is active and which is passive. Thus, there must be a ground that can account for their mutual exclusion (each of them *not* being an absolute totality) and also a ground that can account for the ways of distinguishability. Here the I's finitude that was mentioned earlier has important implications for reflective philosophy. Fichte seems to be denying an absolute supremacy of the subject. At the level of experience, the subject always seems to be tied to a relation with its other.

Fichte himself seems to indicate this in a text which describes his own critical idealism as being realistic. He also notes that philosophical reflection is and must be subordinated to life which philosophy tries to understand. In a comparison of the philosopher's reflective subjectivity with the perspective of living—a perspective that does not doubt the existence of any real world outside the subject, Fichte writes that the

first standpoint is that of pure speculation; the
second, that of life and of science (in a sense
contrasted with that of Wissenschaftslehre). The
second is only intelligible on the basis of the first;
moreover, realism indeed has grounds; for it is
forced upon us by our nature, but it has no *known*
and *comprehensible* ground: yet the first standpoint,
again, exists only for the purpose of making the
second intelligible. Idealism can never be a *way of
thinking*, but it is only *speculation*(23).

The intelligibility of this quotation will become more evident
as we disclose the very structures of the transcendental
imagination, whose structures are fundamental for experience
and reflection. This quotation points to Fichte's meaning of
transcendental as well as that of man's being the
"historiographer of the human spirit"(24). Fichte's philosophy
is not a philosophy that absolutely constitutes and poses reality
purely and exclusively from the subject. It is not an absolute
idealism, but is essentially a realism that is transcendental. It
is a transcendental realism(25).

C. The Synthetic Unity of the Relation

We wish now to return to our discussion of the syntheses
required in our consciousness of the object. The next
syntheses, which express the interrelation of the matter and
the form, are the foundational aspects of the whole unity that
we are striving for here. In the case where the form
determines the matter (the mutual exclusion determines the
totality) there is nothing new, but merely the affirmation that
neither an absolute subject nor the combination of subject and
object is absolutely the absolute totality. Therefore, "there is
absolutely no possible ground of determination except through
relation"(26). We cannot hope to find any principle of
discerning the subject from the object except by and within the
very relation itself. There is *no absolute* ground of
determination. There is only the interplay of a subject and an
object, and what is meant by subject or object entirely depends
on what point of view one might want to take. The ground is a
relative ground. All possibility of determining the one from the
other is not to be found outside the relation or outside of
experience.

Yet when we consider the matter's determining the form, we see that there is and must be a ground for distinguishing. The totality must be determined by some absolute ground. We must start somewhere, and that very starting point determines how we proceed. If we are to explain the mutual exclusion, we must necessarily have a principle of explanation. This is the same as saying that the mutual exclusion needs two different terms to be an exclusion. Experience has a meaning only if there are two aspects that are both related and also different. We must have both terms even though we can only start from one of them to come to an understanding of their interplay, their relation. We must be able to give a reason for starting our reflection from one term rather than from another if our explanation is to have any sense. Thus, "there is an absolute ground of the totality, and this is not purely relative"(27).

Thus, the unified synthesis with which we began expresses both this relative and absolute character. There is nothing outside of experience. There is not an absolute subject, yet the relativity must be explained, i.e., the starting point is posed as a ground (though it may only be tentative) if the relation is to be understood. The subject must have an object; and they must not be the same, but different. The synthesis expresses this activity that unifies two distinct members. In fact it is one and the same. In conclusion, there is a relation that "must be absolute; and the absolute must be nothing more than a relation"(28). It is this conclusion that becomes the object of reflection and constitutes the next series of syntheses. The relationship of the subject to its object must be seen from two points of view, from two starting points, from that of each.

2. *The I as Substance*

In the preceding synthesis, the subject's experiencing has been expressed in two ways. The synthetic unity of these two modes (the form's determination of the matter and vice versa) has been expressed: "the absolute and the relative grounds for determination of the totality should be one and the same; the relation should be absolute; and the absolute should be nothing more than a relation"(29). In the first case the act of excluding allows for the possibility of any interaction between subject and object, yet the grounds for distinguishing the one from the other are totally relative. In the latter case the

absolute ground of this distinguishability means that any
exclusion depends on the correlation of a subject and an object.

The totality is purely a relation between the two modes
of determination, between the relative and the absolute
ground. This totality is neither the subject nor the subject and
the object; it is the relation of these two. This relative
totality must be considered from both sides, from the side of
the subject and from that of the object. The designation of
this totality is determinability or substance, that is essentially
a relation. Determinability is a totality that is a unity of a
determinable and a determinate, i.e., it is a determinate
quantum.

These two points of view are themselves mutually
related. Within subjectivity the structural grounds for the
subject's consciousness of an object are to be made explicit.
Within subjectivity the experiential totality will be seen from
two points of view. On the side of the *subject*, it is formally
expressed as the mutual relation of "A determined by (A+B)"
and "(A+B) determined by A." On the side of the *object* it is
expressed as "B determined by (A+B)" and "(A+B) determined
by B"(30). As a dynamic, synthetic unity,

> the totality consists simply in the complete relation,
> and there is generally nothing stable in itself that
> determines this [relation]. The totality consists of
> the completeness of a *relationship*, but not of a
> reality(31).

An examination of the relationship between the absolute
and the relative modes of determination will present the
grounds of experience. From the perspective of the subject,
the mutual determination of A and (A+B) expresses the totality
or substance. The self poses itself absolutely and is thereby
the ground of the I's posing an object. In the subject's self-
affirmation, a sphere is complete; but completeness is only
meaningful if there is another sphere. Thus, there is the
sphere (A+B). In this latter sphere the subject is only in
reference to and dependent upon something other than itself—
an object.

The posing of the self can be seen from two perspectives.
To pose oneself means both the *absolute* positing of the self by
means of excluding the not-I and/or positing the not-I relative
to its exclusion from the I's sphere. The one is unconditioned;
the other, conditioned(32).

Substance is a relation of an absolute and a relation, of an unconditioned and a conditioned. The absolute affirmation of a subject in its total purity simultaneously includes a plurality of at least two—the self and the not-self. These two must be included in a wider sphere or totality. In terms of experience, there must be the absolute limits or the sphere of experience. It is an *I* who experiences, not just anything; yet, this experience of the I is relative to what is not itself, but is determined by its other.

The initial sections of the *Grundlage*(33) express the same thing. There Fichte had been concerned with the logic; now he is concerned with the transcendental principle of experience—that ground which makes experience possible. Again, the act of self-posing has two aspects. The subject is itself, but must also always be related to an object in order to be a subject. The determinability of a subject needs both, i.e., only through both can one ever understand the intrinsic character of a subject.

From the side of the object, the act of excluding the object from the subject (the unity within the relation) presupposes a more fundamental connection of the object with the subject. Prior to any exclusion, the excluded itself must be posed. Thus, it must be posed independently of the exclusion. It is absolutely posed, but the exclusion is contingently posed.

By means of exclusion the object is contingently related to a subject; but prior to any act of exclusion, the object is absolutely and unconditionally posited. The object must be related to a subject, but at the same time must be different. Thus, an object is an object from two points of view: as an object independent of a subject and as an object intimately related. It is in-itself, yet for us.

This duality expresses the circularity of the totality from the side of the object. It is the relating of the absolute mode and the relative mode of the determination which distinguishes the subject and the object. This relating articulates the structural possibility of experience. This relational totality is the transcendental ground for experience, for the possibility of an object's relating to a subject. Substance as the totality in circularity expresses the condition for the possibility of experience: an object is given *and* is not given to the self. At the level of logic, this is related to the antithetical principle(34).

A greater insight has been reached concerning the fact that the absolute is only a relation and what is related is absolute. Substance is only a relationship with nothing fixed. It is a continual movement between the members. These members consist of 1) the form of the relation (exclusion), 2) the matter of the relation (the distinguishability), 3) the form's determining the matter (the relative ground), and 4) the matter's determining the form (the absolute ground). This continual movement among the members of the relation expresses the consciousness of an object or experience. Through this synthetic unity a world is opened up for the subject. A subject can have a world, a world of experience, because of this originary synthetic unity.

3. Summation

In this final section some of the many threads of thought that have been implicitly winding their way through the discussion will be retrieved and brought together. We wish to make explicit what has for the most part been only implied in this totality whose absolute character consists only of a relation.

First, what at this level of discourse has been called the matter and the form is also an object of reflective consciousness. Distinguishability is the matter in the present context, but had been the form in the previous synthesis; the form in the present context (the excluding) had been the matter in the discussion of the independent activity. Thus, the previous series of syntheses are also carried over or are contained in this second series. What had been called the principles of experience (the matter) and of consciousness (the form) are now operative in the constitution of the totality. As transcendental principles, they functionally interrelate to condition the possibility of the givenness of an object. The following diagram exhibits this. The present syntheses of the relation become the object for a reflective consciousness, the first series of syntheses. These present syntheses form a basis for a self-awareness in that the reflective subject "abstracts" from them. Experiential consciousness is the necessary condition for the subject's self-awareness. Consciousness or the self must be interrelated with the world in order that the I might be able to reflect on or relate to this consciousness in a reflective act.

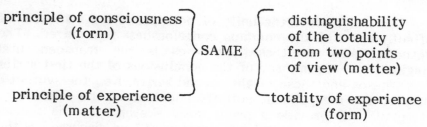

Independent Activity   Interplay (Relation)

Self-awareness: consciousness of. . . . . consciousness of the
object

principle of consciousness   distinguishability
(form)   of the totality
                              SAME   from two points
                                              of view (matter)

principle of experience   totality of experience
(matter)   (form)

Secondly, Fichte calls this totality substance. Substance
is not something that underlies or carries accidents, but
substance is a relation. The totality is substance whose
accidents are the members of the moving relation; for "in
substance nothing at all is to be thought fixed, but only a
relation"(35). Thus, for Fichte substance is a moving relation
in which "there is nothing *absolutely* fixed"(36). The members
of this relation constitute the accidents, with the totality in its
continual movement between the members as being substance.

Thirdly, this substance is a power. It is a power—a
possibility—uniting all the moments in their mutual opposition.
"This power it is—almost always misunderstood—which from
inveterate opposites knits together a unity—that intervenes
between moments that would mutually abolish (*aufheben*) each
other, and thereby preserves them both"(37). Substance is a
power and relation that unites opposites. This power will
eventually be identified as the transcendental imagination.

Fourthly, this relational power is the necessary condition
for the possibility of life and consciousness. Only because of
this can the subject be conscious at all, can be alive, and,
therefore, have experience. This substance and power in its
dynamic unity opens the subject to experience.

Finally, the nature of this movement can be more clearly
exposed. This dynamic unity that relates and distinguishes and,
thereby, opens up experience is the generation of time. It
generates the moments of time. Fichte says that "it is that
which alone makes possible life and consciousness as a
progressive temporal succession"(38). The generation of time
or temporalization is an aspect of substance and is a necessary
condition for conscious life and experience. The task of the

next section will be to focus on the synthetic unity of the reflective consciousness and the consciousness of the object.

The Transcendental Imagination: A Synthetic Unity

An insight into the unity of both preceding syntheses of reflection and of the common consciousness is required. The synthetic unity of those syntheses is the transcendental imagination. A summary of the conclusions of the first series of syntheses and those of the second series, i.e., the synthetic unity of the independent activity and that of the relation or interplay, will provide a preliminary sketch. In the second section the transcendental imagination will be discussed as the mutual reciprocity between those two previous syntheses. Finally, the third section will draw out in greater detail those important structural functions of the imagination. With this achieved, the I's structural significance will hopefully have been exposed.

1. Retrieval as a Preliminary Sketch for the Imagination

Within the synthesis of the synthetic unities of the independent activity and the relation there is exposed the fundamental unity that had been presupposed in the previous analyses. In fact, this unity makes possible the two activities as well as the present reflective discussions. This unity will exhibit the transcendental imagination as the fundamental meaning of the I.

First, a synoptic, general definition of the independent activity describes it "*as an absolute uniting and holding fast of opposites,* a subjective and an objective, *in the concept of determinability,* in which, however, they are also opposed"(39). This is similar to the description of the activity of the power or the imagination found in the synthetic unity of the relation. There that activity is also described as one that unites two absolutely *opposed* moments(40). Since these two moments must be absolutely opposed to each other, that which unites them together is their meeting, their interlocking and taking hold of each other. "A is not to be thought, and B is not to be thought; but the meeting, the *interlocking* of both is to be thought, and this alone is their point of unity"(41). This synopsis of the relation with neither A nor B's being absolute, but merely related, means that the relation itself is also determinability(42). As was noted, consciousness of an object is a relation between two entirely opposed members that are related.

Thus, both of these synthetic unities are in some way identical. They are the same activity from two points of view, i.e., the starting point of consideration is different. Since the concern is with this total activity that comprises both self-awareness and the consciousness of an object, it "can be said that according to the independent activity one starts from self-consciousness, from the subject; whereas according to the relation one starts from the consciousness of the object"(43). The synthetic unity is a *mutual* determination of these two points of view—that of self-awareness and of consciousness of the object. If it were only a unilateral determination, either idealism or realism would emerge.

The idealist position expresses the activity of the subject, its spontaneity, as the ground of the relation of subject and object, and consequently of experience. The problem is that one cannot account for the presence of objectivity because "that is something not posited by the absolute posing of the I"(44). This says that the I absolutely and spontaneously poses both the subject and object, and their unity. If this were so, then the objective side really originates in the subjective; and, therefore, the objective is not radically different. Since the object is not really independent of subjectivity, this idealism does not explain the objectivity of the object, the not-I.

The realist position maintains the need for a check, an encounter, in order that the spontaneity might take place. The spontaneity must be checked or clashed with. That which is objective does not have to be present, but merely the "presence of a check on the I, i.e., for some reason that lies outside the I's activity, the subjective must be extensible no further"(45). The status of this check is not presently an issue. It is not a not-I which exists independent of the I nor is it some type of determination intrinsic to the I. The check is only the I's determinability, its possible self-determination. There is merely "the requirement for a determination to be undertaken *within itself by that very self*(46). The posing of the check is achieved within and by the spontaneity of the I. The determination is a feeling that can only be explained in the practical sphere(47).

This realist position cannot explain how the self can be determinable in posing itself as determinable. This realism too is not sufficient by itself to explain experience because it does not show how this encounter is *for* the I, how the I is aware of its own limitation. Only the mutual reciprocity of the realist and the idealist positions, their synthetic unity, can fully explain and give the necessary conditions of possibility for either reflective consciousness or the consciousness of an object. This final synthesis allows the I to be opened to experience.

2. *The Transcendental Imagination*

The transcendental imagination as an active, synthetic unity articulates the intentionality of the subject; for it is the fundamental unity of consciousness whereby experience can be *my* experience. This synthetic unity is a synthesis of both the reflective consciousness and the consciousness of an object.

> The check (not posed by the posing I) occurs to the I to the extent it is active; and there is a check only to the extent there is activity in the I. Its possibility is conditioned by the I's activity: no activity of the I, no check. Conversely, the activity of the I's own determining would be conditioned by the check: no check, no self-determination.—Moreover, no self-determination, nothing objective, etc.(48).

This synthetic activity of the I, that maintains idealism and realism, accomplishes two things. First, it holds together opposites; and, secondly, these opposites are definitely opposed. The imagination is an activity of the I that holds together those things that are opposed while at the same time maintaining their opposition. The I has the capacity and power to encompass both the I and the not-I without reducing the one to the other.

This activity knows nothing of the not-I. The check does not depend on an independently existing not-I nor does the I realize whether the limitation is merely a self-determination. The I merely knows that it must set limits to its own activity if there is to be an encounter and that the check is at the same time a necessary condition for the I's activity. The I's activity has an infinite dimension and a finite one. The infinite activity is that dimension which limits itself so that there is a check; but the finite activity is that aspect that requires an encounter for the I's activity. In the most general terms, the infinite activity is the reflective dimension while the consciousness of an object is the finite side of the activity. Each are moments of that synthetic unity called the imagination. These moments in their unifying synthesis constitute a circular movement.

A second issue is concerned with the very possibility of this necessary synthesis. Its inherent necessity must be made manifest. The one reflecting must be able to see the unity and be able to present it. Since the reflective consciousness in its activity is only one moment, it must also be able to show its activity arising from the unity. Reflection must be able to show its activity as constitutive of that activity to which reflective consciousness is directing its attention. In other words, the possibility of reflection must be exhibited as being already in the unity of the I. The activity of encompassing and the encounter, though opposed, are the same act of the I.

The following quotation explains how the activity of combining and the check are the same act of the I. This one fundamental act with its various moments is the basis for conscious life because the unitary structure accounts for both the reflective consciousness and the consciousness of the object. Fichte writes that the independent

> activity returns into itself by way of the relation; and the relation returns into itself by way of the activity. Everything reproduces itself; and there can be no *hiatus* therein; from every component one is driven to all others. The activity of the form determines that of the matter; this, the matter of the relation which determines its form; this latter, the activity of the form and so on. They are all one and the same synthetic affair. The act returns into itself by way of a circle. But the whole circular rotation is absolutely posed. It is because it is, and no higher ground can be given for it(49).

The following diagram presents a summary of the synthetic unity. This unity will ultimately be called the transcendental imagination. The solid line in the diagram indicates the synthetic unity with the movement between the various constituents. These constituents ultimately make up the synthetic unities of the independent activity and the relation (the broken line). Each of these has been discussed, but now they are brought together in the unity that comprises them. This is the internal structure of intentionality whereby a world

can be experienced by a subject. It is the transcendental
imagination.

A.   Independent Activity:
       (reflective consciousness)

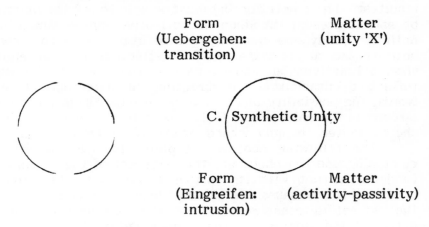

                        Form   Matter
                   (Uebergehen: (unity 'X')
                     transition)

                              C. Synthetic Unity

                        Form   Matter
                   (Eingreifen: (activity-passivity)
                     intrusion)

B.   The Relation:
        (consciousness of the object)

      This structure is a circularity in which all the moments
are never permanently fixed or stable, but only lead to the
next moment. This circular movement defines the subject and
the ground of all objectivity. A subject is never isolated nor
totally cut off from experience, but by this movement a world
is opened up.   In addition to subjectivity, the structure
indicates the meaning of objectivity and how the object can be
for the subject. The subject's ground for possible experience
has been exposed.

3. A Further Analysis of the Transcendental Imagination

      Along with Fichte, a further analysis of the imagination
can be made, especially with regard to its role as an ultimate
and foundational synthetic unity. The first issue concerns the
characterization of the I's activity as both infinite and finite.
The former is called a conjoining; and the latter, a limitation
because of the check.   The infinite activity, the reflective
consciousness, and the finite activity, because of which the
check is a necessary condition for consciousness of an object,

are absolutely opposed, yet are one and the same: *"no infinity, no limitation; no limitation, no infinity"*(50).

The synthetic unity is the unity of these two absolutely opposed dimensions. The I is defined by its infinite activity and by its possible relation to some object. Both are the results of the I's activity. Thus, "the activity of the I consists of unlimited self-posing: to this there occurs a resistance"(51). Both the unlimited activity *and* the resistance are required. To be a subject means to be able to extend oneself infinitely and *also* to limit oneself. The I necessarily poses itself as both finite and infinite. This is its intentional structure. To pose itself as finite means that it must be infinite. Thus,

> the I is only what it poses itself to be. That it is infinite means that it poses itself as infinite: it *determines* itself by the predicate of infinitude; thus, it limits itself (the I) as a substratum of infinitude. It differentiates itself from its own infinite activity (both of which, as such, are one and the same); and so it must comport itself if the I should be infinite(52).

The self in affirming itself divides itself, and thereby a limitation is posed. This limitation is not due to an external object nor to one intrinsic to the I itself. It is merely a limitation that the I poses upon itself in posing itself as infinite. The I is limited due to an encounter, a collision with itself. With regard to the nature of this encounter or its determination, nothing can be said at this point; this is the task of the practical dimension of the I. The theoretical dimension is unable to explain this check or limitation that occurs to the I.

The transcendental imagination is this activity of holding together both the infinite and the finite acts of the I. This unified movement holds together two absolutely opposed elements and also maintains their differences. Again it is the unitary movement of the mutual reciprocity of self-awareness and the consciousness of the object.

> This relation of the I, *in and with itself* [these italics added] whereby it poses itself at the same time as finite and infinite—a relation that consists, as it were, in a conflict with itself and thereby reproduces itself in that the I wants to unite the

irreconcilables, now attempts to receive the infinite in the form of the finite, now forced back, poses it again outside the latter, and in that very moment once more tries to entertain it under the form of finitude—this is the power of *imagination*(53).

This hovering between the two extremes is the imagination by which a world is opened up for the self.

A second issue considers this activity in terms of the triad thesis-antithesis-synthesis. The thesis of the imagination is the production of the I as limited. The I poses itself as limited, i.e., as a subject on the borders of possible experience. Yet, by this act there is also the antithesis: the infinite activity of production and the product are opposed to each other. The subject that is posed as product is not the I in its totality, but they are distinguished. Again this antithesis also presupposes or retains the thetic act of posing; this means that the antithetic act is reproductive: it must not deny the previous thetic act. This togetherness of the thesis and the antithesis is, of course, the synthesis of the imagination. Any one of these three at the same time includes all three. All three are interconnected in the affirmation of one(54).

The third issue considers this triadic structure as the production of the moments of time(55). The imagination is that power that holds all three together at the same time, that holds together those opposed elements. "It is this wavering of the imagination between irreconcilables, this conflict with itself, which. . .extends the condition of the I therein to a moment of time"(56). Fichte then notes that only for the imagination is there time. Thus, the temporal series of moments is the result of the imagination in its productive and reproductive aspects. Within this context, the triadic structure of thesis-antithesis-synthesis is viewed as temporality.

The connection between the triad and temporality can be clarified by elaborating on Fichte's notion of a temporal series. Earlier the imagination's unifying activity of hovering had been seen as producing a successive temporal series and, therefore, as making consciousness and life possible. In another text, Fichte describes a time series.

In that text, a series is that situation in which a given point is dependent upon a previous point even though the given point is opposed to the previous one. Fichte speaks of the synthetic unification of these points. Each point, though, is dependent upon the former; yet, the former, in terms of the present point, is not at all dependent. The *present* temporal moment is such a point which depends on another—the *past*—but which has nothing necessarily dependent upon it(57).

The past is a necessary condition for the present, with the present's being the necessary condition for consciousness. There are always these two moments: the present and the past. Consciousness must be both infinite and finite. The affirmation of the present can only be possible on the condition that something precedes it and is, therefore, opposed to it, viz. the past. The unity is a synthetic movement ad infinitum. Every "now" is only in terms of a "before." This expresses the continual movement of holding together the opposed—the infinite and the finite *and* the determined and undetermined—in whose circular movement nothing is fixed(58).

One moment includes all the other moments. This circle in which nothing is fixed and in which time is produced is that totality called both substance and the imagination. This relational activity called substance and imagination designates the activity of the I *qua* I. Because of this a subject opens itself to a world and thereby a consciousness is a consciousness *of.* Through and by time a world is disclosed for a subject. The objectivity of that world finds its roots in subjectivity's temporalizing—in the transcendental imagination as the source of time. Fichte quite strongly states:

> all reality...is brought forth solely by the imagination. . . . This act of the imagination forms the basis for the possibility of our consciousness, our life, our being for ourselves, i.e., our being as I(59).

Thus, to be a substance is to be a subject; to be a substance is to be temporal; and finally to be temporal is to be a subject(60).

Finally, for Fichte the I can never be an absolute and pure I removed from the world. The I is always in and directed towards an objective world. Through its own activity, objectivity is given to the I. Through the production of time the I opens itself to be outside itself and, thus, "poses itself as determined by the not-I"(61). The intentional consciousness is, as one author has noted,

> the opening to the world through and in time. The primordial act—founding all objectivity—is the

cogito known in the repetition of itself: "*ego sum, ego existo.*" In intentionality as the source of time, the otherness to itself is founded and by this is founded every form of possible otherness. Thus, in the movement by which the I poses itself, it poses itself in otherness, in the difference(62).

Striving and the Future

The treatment of the transcendental imagination has taken place within the theoretical syntheses of the *Grundlage*. These syntheses have consisted of a movement from a relation between the I and the not-I to a situation in which the I's unlimited activity is checked because of an indeterminate and indeterminable not-I. This interdependence of the I and the not-I has accounted for the intentionality of the subject. The imagination has been the center of these syntheses. Its structures have been considered the conditions of the possibility for reflection and for the consciousness of the object.

Several issues still remain. The most obvious one is that the practical side has never been discussed. Earlier the fundamental synthetic unity of the three principles had been considered. The I and the not-I are similar and/or opposed only *in part*. They are *partially* related. This means: 1) the I poses the not-I as limited by the I, and 2) the I poses itself as limited by the not-I. This articulates the practical and the theoretical divisions respectively. Only the theoretical dimension has been resolved. The practical side and its relation to the theoretical must now be discussed.

A second issue left unanswered is the issue of the *Anstoss*, the check or encounter. The imagination held together both the infinite and the finite activity of the I, but it never could provide a ground for the presence of the limitation. Although the object was produced by the imagination, this production was due to the fact that the I limited itself. But why must the I limit itself? What is the basis for the check that provokes the I to limit itself? The practical sphere takes up this issue in terms of the infinite and the finite activity of the I. It becomes the issue of feeling.

The final issue is that of temporality. The past and the present have been the only moments of time that have been mentioned in the grounding of objectivity. What has happened to the future moment? Is it not important?

In this section the future moment of time and its relation to the past and the present will be discussed, even though Fichte has not himself taken up this issue. It will be shown that the practical aspect is related to the future and that, consequently, the future is in fact the most important element. The past and the present moments of time are in function of the future and are guided by it. Thus, the task is to show the priority of the future in the practical dimension of Fichte's philosophy.

Secondly, the fundamental unity between the theoretical and the practical must be shown. This unity is the same as the unity of all three ecstasies of time. This unity comprises that of the I. The unity of time expresses the unity of the subject that is never an absolute subject.

There will first be a presentation of some of Fichte's statements concerning the priority of the practical over the theoretical. This will lead to a fuller discussion by way of the notion of striving. Although Fichte describes the genesis of this striving from its most rudimentary expression, the present concern will be its highest development—that of human striving as human. Finally, all of these will be brought together in light of the future moment of time(63).

The second part of the *Grundlage*, whose task is to understand how "the I poses itself as determining the not-I," attempts to determine the fundamentality of the practical sphere. Fichte writes that "reason cannot even be theoretical, if it's not practical: that there can be no intelligence in man if he does not possess a practical possibility; the possibility of all representation is founded on the latter"(64). In another place Fichte states just as clearly: "without a practical possibility in the I, no intelligence is possible"(65). Yet what immediately follows—"if the I is not intelligence, there is no consciousness of its practical possibility"(66)—can only be understood in retrospect to the development of the primacy of the practical.

For the present interpretation, these statements of Fichte must be taken seriously. How can the theoretical be grounded in the practical sphere? If the previous analyses of the transcendental imagination have shown the ground of the objectivity of any object, is it not now being asserted that the ground of all objectivity is rooted in the practical dimension of the self? Fichte's meaning and intent can only become clearer by developing his notion of striving. This must, however, be seen in the light of those concluding remarks of the theoretical part where Fichte described the tension between the I's infinite

and its finite activities. The tension resulted from the need
for the check. If there were only the infinite activity, then the
not-I would be exclusively produced by the I and would not be
opposed to the I. This was the inadequacy of idealism. The I
limits itself and posits itself as finite because of the
encounter. With this tension the theoretical part concludes.

The I is *infinite* in its activity. It poses itself, and such
activity is related exclusively to the I and to nothing else. It is
a *pure* activity without any conditions or limits. This pure and
infinite activity of the I is an activity "that has no sort of
object, but returns back on itself"(67). A *finite* activity, on the
other hand, is objective; it is an activity that is directed
towards an object and is, thereby, limited. An activity of
posing that "does not relate immediately to itself, but rather
to a not-I that is opposed to it"(68) is called an objective
activity.

The issue is how to ascribe these two divergent activities
to the same I. This tension constitutes the two sides of the
imagination, the reflective side and the intentional side. How
are the two maintained in the imagination in such a way as to
ground the objectivity of experience? The issue succinctly
stated is the possibility of the transcendental imagination in its
temporalizing of past and present.

An understanding of striving presents a possible
resolution. The results of the theoretical discussion leads to
the following point:

> in relation to a possible object, the pure self-
> returning activity of the I is a *striving*; and, indeed,
> as shown earlier, *an infinite striving*. This infinite
> striving is in its infinite extension the *condition of
> possibility of all objects*: no striving, no object(69).

The pure, infinite activity poses an object and thereby limits
itself(70).

The posing of an object is the posing of a resistance, a
"no" to the I's own activity. This resistance does not mean that
there is something present which blocks the I's activity. The I
limits its own activity, but this limit is not necessarily a
determined one. This self-limitation accounts for the not-I
that is opposed to the I.

The resistance, the "ob" of the object, or the opposing is
an activity posed outside and independent of the I's activity. In
fact, this new activity must be opposed to the posing activity.

Since this opposed activity is posed by the I, it must lie in the I; but since it is opposed to the I's activity, it must lie in the object. Within the I there is the posing activity and this other activity that Fichte has called "X". This latter is the condition "*of possibility of such a posing*"(71) and is different from it.

Though this activity is called "X", several features are evident. First, this unknown activity of the I cannot be eliminated by the object, but must be copresent and opposed to the resisting of the object. The being of such an activity is independent of the object and conversely so. Thus, there is a fundamental hiatus between the I and the not-I. Secondly, such an independent activity which serves as the condition of possibility of the posing activity must be grounded exclusively in the I, in the I's absolute activity of self-posing. It is independent of any objective activity. Thirdly, since the object can be posed on into infinity, the present activity of the I which goes against the object's activity must also proceed beyond any possible object into infinity. This accounts for the infinite dimension of this activity.

In summary, this unknown activity called "X" is an infinite, independent activity and is the condition of possibility for the objective activity. Without a *resistance* to the I's activity, there *is no* object; and if there is not present an *infinite activity* which is resisted, then there is no object. The resistance is the essential feature, not merely the opposition. The resistance grounds the posing of the object. "*Only in so far* as there is a resistance to this activity ["X"] can an object be posed; and in so far as it is not resisted, there is no object"(72).

These two activities are completely independent of and opposed to each other. There is the unknown activity in the I called "X"; and there is the activity of the object which is resisting and opposing the I. The hiatus between them prevents a relation; yet, both activities—that of the I and that of the object—must have some relationship if the object is to be posed by the I. If no relation, no posing of the object is possible. Both activities are related because an object *is posed.*

Since the object is posed absolutely and since the ground of possibility of that posing of the object is the relating, the relating too must be posed absolutely and without any ground. In other words, the *absolute* posing of an opposed not-I rests on the relation. To pose the opposed is to pose being-related. Therefore, this being-related means to pose something as similar to the posing—as *alike*. The fact that both these activities are absolutely related means they are posed as alike. *If* they are *not* alike, then they *should* be. As a matter of fact, the object by its very nature is not alike; but "they should be absolutely the same"(73).

At this point, Fichte introduces a new, but most crucial, dimension. The ideal, the ought, emerges in contrast to the actual (*Wirklichkeit*). The coincidence between the I's infinite activity and the not-I's resisting activity is *demanded*. What the I is and what it should be, confront each other. Everything *should* be dependent on the I. "Thus, there is demanded a conformity of the object with the I; and the absolute I, precisely because of its absolute being, is that which demands the conformity"(74).

With this demand for agreement, the unknown activity called "X" is identified. It is a *striving*, an infinite striving, that is the fundamental condition for the possibility of any possible object whatsoever. Striving is that which accounts for the presence of an object for a subject. Without the striving of the I, there would be no object. This striving is a demand on the I that it bring all into harmony with itself. This striving is practical, not theoretical; for it serves as the condition for the theoretical-representational intelligence. In terms of the foundational principles, the second and the third (the antithetic and the synthetic) are both related to the first principle (the thetic). The unity expressed in the first principle is not an actual one, but one that needs to be strived for. Reason is, therefore, fundamentally practical—a fact that serves as the possibility for all representation.

Fichte unequivocally affirms the primacy of practical reason. This primacy rests on the striving of the I. This thesis accentuates the finitude of the I. Finitude has emerged in the theoretical dimension of the I; for the I divides itself to have a world, to be in a world. The striving of the I necessarily involves finitude in that the I now negates the negation and strives to be itself; the I affirms itself. Because of the I's absolute character, it *should* encompass all reality. There is the demand on the I that it fulfill its infinity, that everything be in itself. This demand is an *ideal*; but the I as actual is finite. Since the I does *not* encompass all reality, it strives to achieve its ideal.

The finitude that appears with the notion of striving must also include negativity. This negativity is at the very core of the I, for there is always something still outstanding which needs to be included. The I as striving is directed or oriented towards that which is still outstanding. What is outstanding is the end or goal of the I. Striving introduces the realm of ends. The ultimate end, of course, is the I itself, i.e., the I strives towards a total self-consciousness of itself.

This end or goal must also be seen as a task. Striving is not only directed towards an end, viz. itself, but has that end as something to be accomplished. To strive is to struggle in order to accomplish and establish that end. This end, which is also a task, is an ideal and is, therefore, unattainable. This does not mean that the striving of the I is an exercise of futility and ultimately has no meaning for the I. The unattainable and infinite idea (*Idee*) gives the ground and the sense of the I's striving and its involvement in a world. This ideal task sets in motion one's *actual* concerns. More fundamental than the tension and/or opposition between the I and the not-I is the split between the ideal and the actual. Herein the I extends beyond the actual world to a world as it *might* be and become.

In my *desire*, in my drive and striving for harmony, in this interest to *be*, the I poses itself. This posing of itself allows there to be a world of involvement, a world of things. This world mediates the fulfillment of my desire to be myself. From and through this world the self attempts to overcome its inherent tensions and contradictions and becomes actualized, and no longer a mere possibility. Thus, the ground of the theoretical is the practical interest or desire that finds its possibility in the striving. This interest or drive of the I for absolute unity and completeness in itself is the condition for the I's posing and for the constitution of a world(75).

The task towards which the striving aims and the hiatus between the actual and the ideal presuppose the horizon of freedom. The primacy of the practical affirms a philosophy of freedom. It is a finite freedom which rests on a fundamental concern with the self: an interest to be free rather than unfree. It is an interest in what kind of man one *wants* to *be*(76). The I's relationship to the world is not primarily one of representing the world, but the world is a field of action. Since the I should be free, it strives to be free.

This striving must now be related to time, specifically to the future. In the earlier discussions of this chapter, only the past and the present moments of time had been connected with the imagination and its power to represent objects. The future moment and the practical sphere had not been discussed. In the present section striving has been seen always in terms of a goal or task. There was always something out-standing. In other words, striving has always been aimed towards the future because within the practical sphere the I strives for a complete unity with itself. The future moment explains the practical sphere.

Because of the primacy of the practical sphere and because of this sphere's connection with the future, the future moment of time has a certain priority over the other two moments even though the future can never be separated or isolated from the other two. The past and the present—the temporal moments of the theoretical—are in function of the future practical concerns of the I.

Temporality is the fundamental horizon for the unity of the I in its theoretical-practical dimension. This unity consists of the temporalizing imagination which is guided by the I's interest to be itself. Time as the fundamental unity of the I is the originary, horizonal unity whereby the I can *be* in its own meaningful world. The fundamental unity of the theoretical and the practical is the unity of the temporal ecstases of past, present, and future.

The I's intimate link to time reaffirms the finitude of the I in several ways. First, temporality is the *necessary perspective* from which the I can come to understand itself. Self-consciousness has its condition of possibility in temporality. In other words, the I can never escape time in order to have a divine perspective or divine understanding of itself or its world. Secondly, the temporal future of the I is limited and finite; for the future is the I itself. The I has an ultimate goal to be accomplished; its end is nothing but itself. Thirdly, the very accomplishing of this task must take place in time. The I's interest to *be* is an interest to *be in time*. The I's absolute character is not atemporal, but achieves itself in and through the temporal domain. Finally, the ultimate unattainability of this task, for the I to be one with itself, also shows the inherent negativity within the I itself. This negativity, too, is another expression of the I's finitude.

This dynamic, structural unity of the "I am" articulates the self that is and must be the condition of the possibility of a reflective philosophy and of a Wissenschaftslehre. Thus, reflection enunciates, elucidates, and explicates the I's structural unity, whereby the I can become conscious of itself. The reflective and/or the theoretical dimension allows the subject to become conscious of its practical possibility which, in turn, is the very ground of the theoretical. Reflection allows the subject to become aware of its lived experiential desire to be itself, i.e., I become aware of myself as a self, as an I. Self-consciousness is grounded in the practical, lived concern of temporal experience.

With the primacy of the practical sphere, with the predominance of finitude, with the presence of the *Anstoss*, the imagination of the theoretical part is not and cannot be completely adequate. The production of the imagination always will fall short of its intended goal, for the objective world can never fully be like the subjective. Not only finitude frustrates this task, but more importantly, the fact that what is most objective in the strict sense of the word, what is most unlike a subject and limits this production is *another* subject. Thus, the thrust of the present discussion on the imagination becomes the question of intersubjectivity.

CHAPTER THREE

THE I AS INTERSUBJECTIVE

No You, no I; no I, no You.

–Fichte

The imagination is the fundamental character of the I. The imagination's dynamism holds together the original interrelating of the I and the not-I without allowing the one to collapse into the other. This dynamic circling is a temporalizing that brings about conscious life and accounts for experience. As a reflective science, the Wissenschaftslehre attempts to articulate this continual hovering as the ground of experience. Without the independence of something outside the I, the I could never become conscious of its own self nor know how it determines the not-I; yet, with the I's production through the imagination there is a reality for the I. The Wissenschaftslehre is a *transcendental realism* because that which is independentof the I can only be understood because of the I(1).

To understand through the I what is independent of the I is to proceed by means of a transcendental deduction. Such a deduction implies circularity. In a deduction the foundation and/or justification is reflectively established for that which is given; yet, the justification is simultaneously the founding for that which is given. It is a circle: that which needs to be justified leads to the justification which, in turn, returns to justify that which had been in need of such a justification. This is not an empty, vicious circle that is purely formal and without reference to reality.

This chapter will take up the issue of intersubjectivity. A transcendental deduction of the Other is carried out within the context of a deduction of right. The Other will be seen as an essential aspect of right. Thus, the deduction of natural rights includes a justification of the Other. Such a deduction of the Other can take place only on the background of the transcendental realism of the *Grundlage*. The egological structures of the imagination in the *Grundlage* provide the conditions of possibility of the deduction in the *Naturrecht*.

As with any deduction, nothing new will be added; but only something will be made explicit. The deduction of the Other in the first section of this chapter can only be achieved on the basis of the "I am" as it has been understood and explicated in the previous chapter. The deduction of the Other is not a mere formal, conceptual undertaking, but is grounded in the "I am," that finite subject who is necessarily related to a world.

Such a deduction is to treat intersubjectivity *transcendentally*. This does not mean to prove the existence of the Other, but to explain, by the means of the laws of consciousness, what is not in consciousness, but independent of consciousness. Transcendental consciousness does not create the world, but explains it. Because of it the experiential world finds its structural intelligibility. In terms of intersubjectivity, the presence of the Other is explained and justified by and through consciousness, but consciousness in no way creates the Other. Because of the lawful structuring of consciousness, the Other becomes explicable and intelligible; but this justification does not reduce the Other to consciousness just as the not-I cannot be reduced to consciousness alone.

The thrust of the present chapter is that within the very structures of the I, not only is the Other transcendentally deducible, but, more importantly, the Other is an essential and necessary dimension for the I-hood of the I. Thus, the second section will explicitly show that the Other is inherently necessary and essential for the I's very character. The second section's reference to the structures of the *Grundlage* provides the foundation for the Other's deduction in the *Naturrecht*.

The second section justifies what had already been presupposed in the very carrying out of the deduction of the Other in the first section. That the Other *qua* Other is *essential* for the I to be an I is demonstrated by those sections of the *Grundlage* that had not been discussed in the previous chapter. It will be explicitly shown that the intersubjective dimension arrived at through the *Naturrecht* is an essential structure of the transcendental imagination's temporalizing activity. This chapter will establish that the I's intersubjectivity is a *sine qua non* for the objectivity of experience.

In summary, this chapter will discuss the intersubjective character of the I through three lengthy sections. In the first section, Fichte's deduction of the Other, as it occurs in the opening pages of the *Naturrecht*, will be exposed and explicated.   Secondly, the foundational character for this deduction will be connected with those structures of the imagination, as described in the last chapter.   Here intersubjectivity will be shown as an essential and necessary constitutive of the "I am." The final section will retrieve and systematically unify the insights of the first two sections.

The Deduction of the Other

The "reality of the world—that is, for us, for every finite reason—is the condition of self-consciousness"(2).   This reformulation of the central position of the last chapter needs to be understood. Through the interpretative analysis, reality will be disclosed as another self, another I.

A right designates that relationship between two selves. More specifically, a relationship based on right is a

> relationship between rational beings such that each limits his own freedom by the concept of the possibility of the freedom of the other on condition that the latter limit his own likewise by that of the former. . . .
> This relation is deduced out of the concept of the individual(3).

Four key notions are connected with this statement: rational being, freedom, limiting, and individual. These four, with their interconnection and within the context of right, will play an important role in the deduction of the Other for the intersubjective dimension of the I.

Since such a relation presupposes two individuals who are mutually related and since such a relation is essential for the I's character, the present task is to show that the nature of self-consciousness demands another subject as its condition. Although reflective consciousness is characterized by a self-returning activity—one that has its own self as its ground, this activity is finite and limited by a limiting activity. These are the conditions of self-consciousness:

> that a self-returning activity is, or such a one has its ultimate foundation in the rational being itself; that this [activity] is finite and limited, and that it is posed as limited, i.e., in opposition and reference to

the limiting which happens merely because it is
generally reflected on(4).

A reasonable being is necessarily related to a world, a sensible
world. Within this context, the I achieves its freedom. The
condition of its self-consciousness is the free activity of the
subject in relation to an object. This is a relation of causality.
In other words, because I freely act in a sensible world, I can
be recognized as a free being. Free action in the world allows
for recognition.

This is merely a reformulation of the transcendental
imagination. The subject poses an object, but this posing of an
object limits the free activity of the subject. To pose an
object means that the subject limits its own activity: it poses
itself as finite or limited. The paradoxical situation in which
there is a posing by means of a free, but limited, activity is
resolved by the notion of *self*-determination. The subject is
determined to determine itself; its task is to limit itself.

The allusion to the imagination will give a fuller
understanding of the I's free causality in the sensible world. In
the givenness of the object, the subject finds its own freedom
and independence. In the certainty of conceiving an object
outside itself, the subject

> has as certain the concept of its own freedom and
> autonomy, indeed as one given from outside. It
> obtains the concept of its own free efficacy, not as
> something that *is* in the present moment. . .but as
> something which *should* be in the future(5).

To be free means that the rational being realizes its free
activity, an activity that contains both a causing and a non-
causing.

The object does not *force* the subject to act, but
provokes it to realize its own freedom. Thus, the subject can
choose either to act or not to act. In either case, its freedom
is realized in the provocation by the object. Both causality and
counter-causality are required for self-consciousness. This
challenge or provocation (*Aufforderung*) presupposes an
understanding; otherwise the subject would be forced to act.
The subject must understand its *end*, its *goal*, viz. to act
freely.

An inherent aspect of the causality of a rational being is to have ends or goals. A goal is the subject's projection of that which guides the subject to act. The concept of end is that product that guides one's activity:

> a rational cause, as certain as it is this, projects for itself a concept of its product which should be realized by its own activity, and according to which it directs itself in acting, and likewise looks towards it incessantly(6).

Consequently, a rational being is a being who realizes his freedom by acting freely. This free activity depends upon a provocation. To act freely means the subject is aware of its limitation, of its being limited. The limitation provokes it to realize that it is free by establishing its goal to act such. Only a rational being can propose ends to itself because only such a being can have knowledge of something other than itself—of an object. To determine oneself to *act* freely—to propose a goal—means that this free activity is posed as limited. There is an object outside the subject.

Nature, on the other hand, is unfree and without ends precisely because nature is enclosed upon itself. It is not and can never be outside itself, yet transcendence is an essential aspect of rationality and freedom. A subject can go beyond itself; it has possibilities. Possibility, on the other hand, implies limitation or finitude. To be possible means that a subject is aware that it is not definite nor self-contained.

> A certain criterion of the efficacy of a rational being would, therefore, be this: the efficacy is only thought as possible under the condition of a knowledge of its object. But now knowledge itself can only be thought as possible by knowledge, not by the mere power of nature. Thus, if the object and, here also, the goal of the efficacy could only be to bring about knowledge, then it would be necessary to assume a rational basis for the efficacy(7).

The quotation, first of all, asserts that a rational being can have a free causality, can freely be in the world only if it has a knowledge of its goal or end. A subject can only act freely if it proposes ends to itself, if it sees and determines what will be the object of this action. Secondly, it follows that knowledge is a condition of free activity. Only a knowing or conscious being can have a free activity, a free causality. Finally, this knowledge which is the condition of free activity depends on the object which provokes the subject to act freely. I act freely because I recognize the object as a being that provokes me to act in that way.

If my free activity is conditioned by a recognition of something other than myself and if this being provokes me to act freely upon recognition, then it would seem that this object must be such a being that has as its goal the free activity of the subject. This would mean that the object too must have goals or ends for itself. Here it has the goal to provoke the subject to act freely. To have goals or ends is only the characteristic of a rational being. Thus it would seem that this object is really a rational being whose goal is to provoke the I to act freely. On the basis of the subject's analysis of its own activity, the subject realizes that *another* subject is responsible for that activity. The subject's free activity depends on an object that also has a goal—another subject. Thus, my freedom is based on the assumption of the presence of another rational being as the object that provokes me to act freely.

> The rational being cannot pose itself as such unless a demand to act freely is addressed to it. . . . But if such a demand to act is addressed to it, then it must necessarily pose a rational being outside itself as the reason for it(8).

This is a mutual reciprocity between two rational beings; it is the concept of right.

This concept of right depends on the notion of an individual. A rational being is not merely *one* individual, but is one among many; for individuality is significant only within a plurality(9). The individuality of a rational being includes the presence of a similar being outside itself. This can be more clearly understood on the basis of the previous chapter's insights on the imagination.

With the imagination the mutual interaction of the I and the not-I is ultimately one between the I and itself. Although the not-I is essential for the I to come to an awareness of itself as producing this not-I, the relation between the I and the not-I is that of an I with itself. In order for the I to pose itself it must limit itself by posing the not-I. This circularly structural movement of the imagination poses the subject as both infinite and finite; both are essential aspects of the I. In other words, the subject has its foundation within itself *and* also needs an object outside itself that is another subject. The ground of its identity is both inside and outside. This accounts for the I's being an individual. The form of its activity is the condition set by the object, whereas materially it has a general sphere of action. Being separated from the Other, the subject has its *own* sphere of free activity. The subject is an individual. It expresses its own freedom within the sphere of activity as being different and opposite to another. "That which chose exclusively in this sphere is *its* I, is the individual, the rational being determined by opposition with another rational being; and this is characterized by a determined manifestation of freedom, pertaining exclusively to it"(10).

There are two free individual beings, two I's, in mutual reciprocity. Each needs the other to be itself—to be an I. Mutual determination is possible only between equals that are in opposition(11). To consider these two as free and as individual means that the subject chooses its sphere and also chooses not to go beyond that sphere. The mutual reciprocity implies the same condition for the Other outside me. This recognition means that the one acts freely because the Other acts so. Acting freely also means that the subject limits itself to its own sphere, i.e., does not infringe upon the sphere of the Other. The

> being outside the subject has presumably required by its own activity that the latter [the subject] act freely; it has restricted its own freedom by a concept of goal in which the freedom of the subject is presupposed—if indeed only problematically. It has thus limited its freedom by the concept of the (formal) freedom of the subject(12).

With the subject's limitation of its own freedom, the subject thereby opens up the possibility of knowing the Other as free and rational. There is this mutual limitation and recognition of the Other whereby each is required to act freely. The subject acts freely because the Other demands it; yet, this demand can be heard only because the I recognizes the Other as a being who acts freely. This mutual determination results in a perpetual circle that Fichte admits to.

The recognition of the one individual by the other is
conditioned by the fact that the other treats the one
as a free [individual], (i.e., restricts his own freedom
by the concept of the freedom of the former). . . .
The relation of free beings on each other is thus a
relation of a mutual reciprocity through intelligence
and freedom.   The one cannot recognize the other
unless both recognize each other together: one
cannot treat the other as a free being unless both so
treat each other together(13).

This circularity of mutual reciprocity can be summarized
in three statements. They express the necessary conditions for
self-consciousness, i.e., that I recognize myself as such.   No
self-consciousness is possible without a consciousness of
individuality.   1) If I act freely, i.e., treat the Other as a
rational being, then I can expect to be recognized as a rational
being.   2) If I can be recognized by *a* rational being, I must be
able to be recognized by *all* rational beings.   This means that
there must be some universal characteristic that is the
condition for universal recognition.   Therefore, 3) I too must be
able to recognize the Other as rational because, according to
the second statement, a rational being must be universally
recognizable and because I am a free rational being.   This
means that I limit or restrict my freedom by the concept of
the possibility of his freedom, i.e., that I act freely and
therefore recognize the Other(14).   My very acting freely is a
recognition of the Other as a rational being. If I can recognize
the Other, then he is able to recognize me; for there can be no
mutual causality between two substantially different beings.

My being recognized depends on the fact that I must
really act in the sensible world and also that I can enter into a
mutual causality.   This causality is the only way I can affect or
encounter the Other.   He must be able to see me as another
self, as another rational being.   Mutual causality depends on
self-consciousness, i.e., that the I comes to know itself through
the mediation of a not-I. Though the mediation through a not-I
had been shown in the preceding chapter, how this not-I *as*
another I is the ground for self-consciousness is the present
issue. The relationship between two subjects must be extended
to a polysubjective context.   The extension to a universal
situation would mean: if I can be recognized by *an* other being,
then I must be recognizable by *all* other rational beings.

There must be some determination of the I that allows for its being universally recognized. Reason and freedom would allow the extension of this particular context to a universal one. I am an individual that is opposed to another. I can *pose* myself as free and rational in that I ascribe similar characteristics to the Other. In this mutuality each chooses his own sphere of free activity and respects that of the other's. This mutual recognition of treating the Other as free and rational is that whereby I pose myself as such. He treats me as such. To *act* as a free rational being is to *recognize* and *treat* the Other as such. Individuality is a reciprocal relationship.

Individuality and freedom are closely connected with each other. My individuality affirms itself in my freedom. Through freedom universal recognition will be established. The fact that I can be *universally* recognized by *all* rational beings grounds the principle of right. The establishment of universal recognition will be achieved because of freedom's relation to time.

To be free means to be able to realize one's projects and possibilities. It means that I can become myself—a free rational being. Within this context, such words as *realize, become, possibilities* are used. All of these indicate a future. The future dimension of time does not mean only one or two determined possibilities to be fulfilled, but necessarily *all* the future. In being free one does not limit himself to merely one moment in the future, but to the entire future.

Since being free means the realization of one's projects, freedom is futural and is concerned with *all* future possibilities. To be an individual is necessarily to be related to another; this individuality depends on the freedom to realize one's possibilities.

> Freedom is thus always posed in the future; and if it ought to constitute the character of a being, it is posed for *all* the future of the individual: it is posed in the future as far as the *individual itself* is posed in it(15).

This also accounts for the transition from mutual reciprocity with one Other to a universal recognition. This transition is dependent on the fact that the I is not concerned with any particular future moment, but with all future moments. This implies that the I is not limited to only one future with one individual besides himself, but the future implies an infinite

number—in fact all other rational beings. Since the future is
an entirety, the mutual recognition is universally extended and
is not limited merely to one Other and his future. Now I can
expect *all* reasonable beings to recognize me. This universal
extension depends on the fact that my freedom is concerned
with or is realized in *all* futures, not merely in this particularly
definite futute. Consequently,

> as certain as I pose myself as an individual, equally
> as certain do I expect all rational beings known to
> me—in all cases of the mutual activity—to recognize
> myself as a rational being(16).

This mutual relation has been called right. It is a
relation between rational beings that act freely. By the
mutual limitation of one's freedom, one is related to another
who has done the same. Thereby, one discovers his own self,
his identity. To be an I means to be related to other I's. Right
is an a priori concept deduced from the I—a concept that
expresses the relationship between myself and Others. This
Other has been deduced a priori to express this mutuality.

The Foundation of the Deduction of the Other

Since the preceding section has exposed Fichte's
deduction of the Other against the background of the insightful
results of the previous chapter, the present task is to show that
the Other is an essential aspect of the I and that its
essentiality had already been implicitly indicated in the
Grundlage. This will be made explicit by attending to the
"Deduction of Representation" of the *Grundlage*.

In the "Deduction of Representation" Fichte makes some
interestingly provocative statements in the description of the
necessary structures of objectivity as they are found in the
subject. Although in the context Fichte is concerned with the
not-I as an object, he strongly suggests that the not-I is
another I. These passages, quoted in their entirety, will serve
as an interpretative guide.

> The activity of the intuited in the mutual
> reciprocity, to the extent it goes to the intuiting, is
> similarly determined by an *activity that returns back
> upon itself*, whereby it determines itself to influence
> the intuit*ing*(17).

> No passivity in the intuiting, no original activity that returns back upon itself *in the object,* as a thought activity. No such activity *in the object,* no passivity in the intuiting. . . . The *inner activity of the object,* whereby it determines itself to causality, is a mere thought(18).

In a later section of the *Grundlage* in which Fichte describes the relationship of the objective activity and the pure activity, he writes that there is posed

> an object wherever. . . [the I] might pose it in infinity, and thereby poses an activity lying outside and independent of its own activity (of posing), but is opposed to its own. This opposed activity must *lie* to be sure in some sense (though we do not ask what) *in the I* to the extent it is posed there; but it must also *lie* in another sense (again we do not ask what) *in the object*(19).

The interpretative analysis of these texts will be done within the problematic of intersubjectivity. They must be seen within the context of the entire "Deduction of Representation" that serves as a bridge between the theoretical and the practical parts of the *Grundlage.* The first section will discuss the relationship between the deduction and the transcendental imagination of the previous chapter. This overall view of the "Deduction" will lead to a detailed explication in the context of intersubjectivity. Fichte's shorter work, the *Grundriss,* will provide an interpretative aid.

1. The "Deduction" and the Imagination

In the chapter on the imagination an interpretation of the two aspects of the "I am" had been given. The theoretical aspect was expressed in the formula "the I poses itself as determined by the not-I." The foundational meaning of this was articulated as the transcendental imagination. Although most of the time was devoted to this, the second part, the practical, was briefly discussed to give a full unitary description of the "I am" with temporality as the horizon. This dimension was formulated as "the I poses itself as determining the not-I." The imagination played the central role in the theoretical aspect, but its activity was guided by the practical desire and striving. The concluding section is the "Deduction of Representation."

The theoretical syntheses have shown how the opposed, the I and the not-I, can be thought together. The imagination keeps both of them together. The imagination, that point where all the tensions and conflicts are unitarily held together, achieves that structural unity whereby the three foundational principles can be thought together without destroying the unity of consciousness. The theoretical syntheses attempted to eliminate the nonessential and the contradictory so that the final synthesis is truly a fact of consciousness, but this fact must be exhibited as an original fact of the human spirit. In other words, the facts *as* facts have been grounded, and an "empty, formal philosophy"(20) has been avoided—a philosophy that would be an "appeal to facts that lie within the sphere of ordinary consciousness, unguided by philosophical reflection"(21). Now the grounding itself must be considered. Not only must there be consistency, but it must also be shown how "the conviction was arrived at that they [the facts] are present as facts"(22). The previously established insights must be exhibited as founded in the I.

What does "founded in the I" mean? If one recalls the first and the second foundational propositions, one would notice that they were posed absolutely by an act of freedom. The second one could not be derived from the first; it was unconditioned as to its form. The third one, as the unity of the first two, resulted in the theoretical and practical formulation. Throughout the theoretical sphere, all the contradictions were eliminated from these spontaneously and artfully produced facts. The artful production of these facts was accomplished and is only possible because of the laws of that which remains independent of any production. They were formed according to the laws of the I. It must be shown *how* the I comes to this production according to its own laws. The fact that the imagination is the central point of the "I am" is a fact that "the I must explain to itself, but this can be explained in no other way than according to the laws of its own nature which are the same laws by which our reflection up till now has also been undertaken"(23). Now the I must look at its own structures as an I. The I must present to itself *how* it came to produce those facts of the imagination. The I comes to the truth of its own being. The syntheses of the imagination are exactly the same as those of the "Deduction," but the direction of proceding is different and opposite.

Though both are the same, differences remain. Besides moving in the opposite direction, each reflection has a different correlate.   Previously the correlate was the possibility of thought. The "spontaneity of the human spirit was that which brought forth not only the object of reflection—even those possibilities of thought, though according to the rules of an exhausting synthetic system—but also the form of reflection, the activity of reflecting itself"(24). The previous object of reflection was a description of that structure of the "I am."

The following section will pay heed to the results obtained and articulated in the imagination. The "Deduction" is a reflection on a *reflection* itself. The latter (the italicized) produced its object by its spontaneity; the former (the unitalicized) will bring the latter to consciousness. "Thus, in the future series of reflection, the object of that reflection is not first *brought forth* by that same reflection, but is merely raised up *to consciousness*"(25).   There is now a genetic description of those same structures.   How consciousness comes to be conscious of itself is the concern of the "Deduction."

This genesis of consciousness' coming to be conscious of itself is indicated by the difference in the direction. The imagination or structural syntheses began with the self-posing of the I; its truth was subsequently exhibited. The "Deduction" proceeds in the opposite direction because it begins with and leads to a transcendental understanding of the most primitive. It is the process that moves from being lost in the object to the point where the I finally sees that the objects are *my* objects. The process proceeds

> from the child who leaves his cradle for the first time, and thereby learns to distinguish it from himself, to the popular philosopher, who still accepts the material idea-images and searches for the seat of the soul, till the transcendental philosopher who at least thinks to himself and demonstrates the rule to think a pure I(26).

In other words, the "Deduction" shows how the descriptions and the result of the last chapter had been possible.

2. The "Deduction of Representation" and Intersubjectivity

Since the relationship between the two series of syntheses has been indicated, the "Deduction" as a history of consciousness (a description of how consciousness comes to know and how it comes to know its own foundations) will be exposed in eight parts(27).

A. Sensation: the Immediacy with the Object

The structures of the imagination's activity give the ground for the subject's relating to an object. In order to make explicit what, for the most part, remains implicit, we begin with the I's first immediacy with an object. With this encounter with an object, the subject is forced to take account of itself. In *sensation*, i.e., in this contact with what is not itself, the I can distinguish various dimensions and aspects of its own activity.

At this point the I's activity is limited in that it can go no further than some point. This limitation indicates that the activity at the same time presupposes a passivity in itself. The passivity accounts for the activity's being limited; the activity has found a resistance. Intuiting names that situation of activity *and* passivity.

The three dimensions of this intuiting activity can be understood thetically, antithetically, and synthetically. The I poses something outside itself as a condition whereby the I can explain its own passivity, its own affective feeling. This does not imply that the I actually perceives something. This passivity can be such in terms of an activity posed outside the I, but it can also be viewed as a diminished activity. In the present context, sensation is not merely receptivity, not merely a passively absorbing sponge. No, it is a receptivity that is receiving what is not itself. This active passivity is a limited activity, one that is related to what is not itself. Consequently, the limited activity (passivity) is related to an unlimited activity within itself. Since there has been the movement from an I—not-I relation to an I's being related to itself, there are two opposed activities in the I: the limited activity and the unlimited, pure activity. It is the same activity of the same I. This same activity, seen now from within its relation to itself, poses the activity of the not-I as contingent on its own activity. Whereas previously the I needed the not-I to explain its own passivity, now it explains the passivity by its own activity. Although sensation is a passive receptivity, this sensation is an activity of the I that *goes out* by diminishing its own activity. Sensation is a thetic activity

> in as far as it poses an activity outside the I that is opposed and is by no means perceptible. . . . *Antithetically* in as far as it opposes to itself the one and the same activity of the I by posing or not posing the condition. *Synthetically*, in as far as it poses that activity as one and the same by posing the opposed activity *as* an accidental condition(28).

The fact that the I's activity goes only to a point indicates its passivity. The unity and ground of these two is the unlimited activity. At a given point intuiting is related to an intuited. Sensation is a pure activity of and in an I which needs and, therefore, poses something active external to itself; but what is external to the I is not affected by the I—it is excluded from the I. The I has both a pure activity *and* an objective or limited activity, both of which are held together. In other words, by sensation something foreign to the I is referred to the I; sensation is the immediacy of the I with an object.

B. Integration of Sensation in the I

Since intuiting is an activity conditioned by a passivity, it must be shown how the I appropriates this intuiting to itself. That "*the I should pose itself as intuiting*"(29) means that the I poses itself with an activity that is conditioned by a passivity or by a resisting activity. This intuiting of Section A is an activity related to a not-I or an intuited. In the previous section sensation was thetic, antithetic, and synthetic. The first activity whereby an activity was posed outside the I was a production in order to explain the passivity of the I. The I's passivity is explained by an external activity. Here the I is related to a not-I by an external intuiting, one that goes outwards. If, however, this passivity is viewed as a diminished activity, i.e., as an activity related to another activity that is not external, but internal, then a pure activity and a limited activity are seen as relating to each other. This situation is the original producing activity that posed the external activity *and* also the limited activity. This perspective on the two activities is *within* the I; it is an internal intuiting. Now the I intuits its own activity as a pure one producing and as a limited activity. The same I sees itself as producing and as being related to a not-I. Since this not-I was the product of the imagination, the activity of production is a pure activity or the I's activity of self-positing. In other words, to pose oneself as intuiting means that the I produces that whereby intuiting can take place. This production by the imagination is itself an intuiting that is active and passive; but its intuited is *its very self* and is, therefore, non-resistant. As prereflective, the I is not aware of these activities.

Two types or levels of intuiting can be indicated:

> The producing possibility is always the imagination; thus, this posing of the intuited takes place through the imagination and is itself an intuiting(30).

First, there is the intuiting that expresses the I's resisted activity; and, secondly, there is the imagination's intuiting that produces the intuited by absolute spontaneity. Since intuiting is both internal and external, there must be a means to distinguish the one from the other. "This is the question: how does the human spirit originally come to distinguish between a reflection of external activity from another that is internal"(31). How is the I able to distinguish an activity that goes outwards in its passivity and one that remains within? These activities of the same I have two different objects, two different *intuiteds*. The next section will attempt to distinguish the subject's activity that goes outside itself from the one that recoils back upon itself and thereby intuits its own intuiting. The intuition must be fixed, and the imagination's hovering between the two activities must be stabilized.

C. The Coagulation of the Intuition: Understanding

Since we have been unable to distinguish between the inner and the outer intuiting activity of the imagination, the ground of distinguishing must be established. Presently there is no way to determine whether the product of the imagination is merely a fantasy or reality. If the intuition can somehow be fixed and if the imagination's hovering can be stabilized, then a clearer insight into the nature of intuition with its necessary relation to the I might be obtained.

If this happens, however, then the imagination no longer hovers; yet its nature is to hover. Thus, any stabilization or fixing must not and cannot destroy the intuition and/or the imagination. Consequently, "in the intuition there must at least remain the product of the condition, a trace of the opposed directions, consisting of neither, but containing something of both"(32). The product alone preserves this opposition of activity and passivity when the intuition is fixed. The product results from the coagulation.

The coagulation of this intuition whereby something ideal becomes real is the understanding(33). This gives reality to the products of the imagination. The reality of the product which remains with the coagulating of the intuition results from the imagination's being limited by the free spontaneity of reason. The understanding is the mediating term between the free spontaneity of reason's determination and the imagination's production. The understanding is

> possibility wherein a changeable comes to *stand*, as if it were brought to a stand: is under-*stood*. . . . The understanding is simply such in so far as something coagulates in and by it; and everything coagulates in this coagulation of the understanding. The understanding can be described as the imagination structured by reason or as reason furnished with objects by the imagination(34).

The understanding is not an activity, but is that wherein the products of the imagination are preserved. Through the understanding something is given to the I because of the imagination's limitation. This is the next issue: how the imagination is limited or how to further determine the intuiting.

D. Further Determination of Intuiting: Intuiting and Intuited

The imagination is limited in its hovering while its product is being held in the understanding. That which has come to stand in the understanding is that unitary whole which had been produced by the imagination. That product comprises the intuiting or sensation of what is not the I. In addition to the limited activity that goes towards the object, there is also that infinite activity which has posed something outside the I and is opposed to the limited activity that is directly related to the not-I. This whole activity has come to stand; it is the product of the imagination as coagulated in the understanding.

By presently intuiting this entire intuiting activity as coagulated in the understanding, the ground of its accomplishment will be clarified. Although the "coming to stand" in the understanding—the coagulation—is the ground of objectivity, its specific mode of accomplishment has remained in obscurity. Within itself, the I sees its own activity in two perspectives: as an unlimited activity and as a limited one. The active I looks at its own activity as it has come to stand in the understanding, but this looking activity does not view itself as it is *presently* acting. Thus, there is the I's activity that has come to stand (called the intuited) and the I's activity that views its coagulated activity (the intuiting). In the I's intuiting of its own intuiting activity, "the *intuited* is the I in so far as it senses. The *intuiting* is equally the I, but does not reflect on its intuiting; yet in so far as it intuits, it can reflect on its intuiting"(35).

An intuiting activity goes towards an active intuited. Since the imagination is central in the intuiting activity, it must also now be the ground of encompassing. Yet, in the present case the object is itself an intuiting. Thus, the imagination merely *reproduces* what it had previously produced and had brought to stand in the understanding. "The imagination in its present function does not produce, but merely apprehends (for posing in the understanding, not indeed for conserving) what had already been produced and seized upon in understanding, and is, therefore, called reproductive"(36).

Since by description and definition intuiting has an active and a passive dimension(37), the opposed intuited is active in relation to the intuiting's passivity and is passive in relation to the intuiting's activity. Thus, there must be an activity opposed to the activity of intuiting. This opposed activity in the intuited serves as the basis for the passivity of the intuition, but is posed as the intuited preserved in the understanding. Thus, on the basis of the mutual reciprocity that defines intuiting, to determine the intuiting's content also determines the opposed intuited. The intuited is directly or mediately determined. Although the intuited has not been directly or immediately grasped, it is determined in virtue of the reciprocal relation that defines intuiting through the determination of intuiting. Yet the intuited as such has not been determined in that the intuition of it has not been explicitly brought to consciousness.

> To the extent that the content of the intuiting should thereby be determined, this opposed tendency must itself be intuited; and so, along with the determination of the intuiting, there is simultaneously present an intuition, though not reflected, of the *intuited*.
> But the intuited itself must be determined *as* an intuited if it should be opposed to the intuiting(38).

The intuiting activity is a limited activity in that it also is a passivity; and this intuiting is, therefore, dependent upon the I's infinite activity that had produced some activity as the ground for the passivity. This ground as an activity was produced by the infinite activity and is preserved in the understanding. This is the intuited and is grounded *in the nonintuited not-I* which is an "absolute product of the I's activity"(39). It is the noumenal aspect of the not-I.

The attempt to determine an intuition has led only to a mutual reciprocity between intuiting and intuited.

> They are reciprocally related as activity and passivity (reality and negation) and are, therefore, united by mutual reciprocity. No intuited, no intuiting; and vice versa. Moreover, if and in so far as an intuited is posed, an intuiting is posed and vice versa(40).

What constitutes an intuition by itself has not been determined. The attempt must now be made to determine the intuition, not by its relation to an intuited, but by and from itself.

E. Determination of the Intuition by Itself

The distinction between the two intuiting activities is each's direction—one directed externally and one directed internally. There is the activity of intuiting that must be determined and an activity related to an external intuited that has been preserved in the understanding. Both must be determined if there is to be the possibility of distinguishing the intuiting from the intuited. Although the intuiting—intuited have been reciprocally related, a way must be found to determine the one by itself. "But one of the two must be determined out of the same ground *by itself*, and not by the other"(41). The intuition must be determined by itself within the I and not by a relation.

The I has an objective activity in that a passivity is found in its opponent, but this objective activity is also determined by a pure activity. This objective activity corresponds to that finite activity discussed in the last chapter whereas the pure activity corresponds to the infinite activity. The imagination keeps both together. This objective activity (the intuiting) and the intuited are under the condition of a passivity—the condition whereby the absolute and pure activity comes to be objective and vice versa. This condition as the unity of their mutual reciprocity, as "the borderline of the pure and the objective activity is intuited by the imagination, fixed in the understanding"(42). The previous chapter on the imagination has discussed these two aspects of the I's own activity, the infinite and the finite. The former dimension limits itself in order that a check (*Anstoss*) might take place whereas the latter requires and necessitates the check for its own activity. In terms of the imagination the two aspects are the reflective consciousness and the intentional consciousness respectively. The unity of the imagination is the circularity of the two perspectives.

Thus, there is a unity of the I's pure activity and its objective activity. This unity as the ground and condition of the two must be exhibited. That the pure activity becomes objective means that the absolute cancels itself or that passivity is the basis of every objective activity. The I "feels itself limited, or there is present in it a feeling of limitation, of impossibility, or of force"(43). There is the feeling of necessity. Within the I, the I feels *itself* as not being the ground for that feeling. It must be related to something other than itself; it is limited in its activity(44).

Conversely, the I is also aware of its own freedom and spontaneity. Since the imagination hovers and is not fixed, but only its products are, the imagination can act or not act. There are an infinite number of possibilities(45) for the I, and the I is not limited to any particular one(46). The I is both infinite and finite. The not-I as the ground of passivity is a product of the I even though the I, in its being lost in the objects, is not conscious of its own activities. The I always needs the check to provoke itself to reflect on this infinite activity. The object is required for the absolute spontaneity to be able to view itself.

There is this mutual reciprocity between a necessary and a free act. The free act limits itself—it poses a passivity in itself whereby it can be objective; yet the spontaneity of its free activity depends on the check that causes the I to reflect. This unity of self-affection and external affection distinguishes intuition from the intuited: "Mutual reciprocity of self-affection of the intuiting and an affection from without is the condition under which intuiting is an intuiting"(47). This fundamental unity of the two aspects is within subjectivity. On the one side, there is the affectivity and/or receptivity of the I in its being related to what is not itself. This had been called the presence of the check. On the other side, there is the self-orientation of the I's pure activity. By this latter the I determines itself, orients itself for a possible affection. This was the I's proposing to itself a self-limitation. This self-orientation opens up the possibilities for the I, opens up a world for it. This can be called "self-affection," for the I determines itself to act in a determinate way. The I, so to speak, gathers itself together and thereby orients itself towards what is not itself. The mutual reciprocity between these two sides articulates the fundamental unity of the I's intuiting. This, of course, is the transcendental imagination.

The I is limited to an infinite number of possibilities within determined limits. The mutual reciprocity between the self-returning activity and an objective activity is the imagination's circularity of the independent activity and the relation. The intuition has been determined.

F. Judgment

The subject's grounding unity, which consists of the unity between the pure activity and the objective activity, explains the I's posing itself as limited. The I freely poses itself as being related to a not-I. The ground for distinguishing the subject from the object is discovered in and through the subject itself. That the I needs to pose itself as related to a not-I points to its finite character. The I is both infinite and finite.

This pure activity—the infinite activity whereby the I affects itself and orients itself towards what is not itself—is called a "self-returning activity." Since it is the condition for

the objective activity, it must now be more clearly
determined. The self-returning activity is in the intuiting
subject and, as will be seen, is *thought* in the intuited object.
Since such an activity constitutes the character of a subject, it
will be investigated within this section from two perspectives:
1) from the perspective of the pure activity and the objective
activity, and 2) from the perspective of image and thing.

    In the first five sections above, the possibility and the
significance of intuiting an object have been presented. The
possibility was found to be the self-returning activity which is
in the subject and projectedly thought in the object.   This
"activity for self-determination is the determination, by
reason, of a fixed product of the imagination in the
understanding: thus, a *thinking*"(48). Since in understanding
the products of the imagination's freedom are coagulated,
understanding would include a self-determination that is for
the sake of an object projected as a noumenon. This grounds
the intuiting objective activity.

    This pure activity can direct its attention on itself and
fix that as its object. In so doing, the subject abstracts from
any object and would focus on the possibility of such an object.
This is the act of judgment:

> the till now, free possibility to reflect on the objects
> already posed in the understanding or to abstract
> from them, and to pose them in the understanding
> with more determination on the basis of this
> reflection or abstraction(49).

In judgment, there is the unity of the free hovering of the
imagination and the coagulation of the understanding.

    Since judgment is the possibility of a subject to look at
itself, to look at the fixing of objects in understanding, there is
a mutual relationship between judgment and understanding.
Understanding supplies the objects that are produced by the
imagination, but from which judgment can abstract.
Understanding thinks or projects a noumenon. On the other
hand, judgment furnishes the possibility for an object in
general.   Judgment presents the condition for the
understanding's projection of an object. Both condition each
other.   "Nothing in the understanding, no judgment; no
judgment, nothing in the understanding *for the understanding*,
no thinking of the thought as such"(50).

In the preliminary discussion, the I was lost in the object and did not realize that the object was its own product. The I presently focuses on this product of its productive imagination, on the image. An image always refers to what is not an image, to an original which "is the *actual thing* in virtue of which the imaging I directs itself in the projection of its image; and that [actual thing] must necessarily thereby hover before the I with its image"(51). In contrast to an image, a thing directs the productive hovering I. This contrast is not an absolute opposition, for both must somehow be related. There must be a ground of compatbility.

The relatability between the image and the thing is a "pre-reflective intuition of the thing"(52). This pre-reflective intuition is a first production of the object; as such, it founds the relation between the image and the thing. Since an intuition is an activity and a passivity, the passivity consists of the I's being directed by the object. Since the I, though pre-reflectively intuiting, is active in its intuiting, the intuition is "referable to the I that is acting in the imaging"(53).

> This intuition is without consciousness, exactly for the same reason it is present, because the I cannot act doubly, cannot, therefore reflect on two objects at the same time. In the present connection, it is examined as posing its product *as* such, or as imaging; it cannot at the same time be posed, thus, as directly intuiting the thing(54).

Both an image and a thing are needed. Each is explained by the other; they are in mutual reciprocity.

Each is distinguishable from the other even though the referring of the image to the thing happens in and by the I. The I must be involved in this referring even though it might not be conscious of it. "The I must, therefore, come at least indirectly forward in consciousness, and so a distinction of the image from the thing would become possible"(55). The pre-reflective of the I is considered less important here than the posing of the thing. The completely determined image is characteristic of a thing. "But the thing in its contingent condition is disclosed precisely as a presupposed product of the I to which nothing is ascribed except being"(56). The founding unity of the thing's being is judgment. Since what is thinkable and thinkability itself are objects of judging, the being of the thing is a thought noumenon. "Only what is judged as thinkable can be thought as the ground of intuition"(57). The ground of objectivity, the condition of possibility that "something *is* such and such," is the unity of freedom and necessity, of the substantial and the accidental. The judging dimension of the active I is the ground by which there is a possible object or an object in general for the subject.

Fichte's description of judging had noted two important aspects: 1) abstraction from what was given by and in the understanding, and 2) a further determination. That further determination judgment ascribes to the object is the ontological status, the *is* dimension. The *is* now needs to be more clearly articulated. First, the being of the thing has been seen as a *thought* noumenal which serves as the ground for the limited intuiting activity. The ontological determination is intimately connected to the being of the I. Secondly, this *is* is an *is* of the thing in opposition to an image. This distinction must constantly be kept in mind. An image is *not* a thing; a thing is *not* an image. On the other hand, this thing is the pre-reflective product of a pre-reflective intuiting of the I; in a sense it, too, is an image. If we are to maintain both of these—1) the absolute distinction between image and thing and 2) that the thing is an image in a sense, then the circle of idealism and realism again emerges. The not-I is a *thought* ground for the intuition of that which *is* a not-I. This circle of the theoretical dimension of the I affirms the finitude of the I, but the finitude cannot be understood or explained within this context.

> The result of this investigation would be that for all eternity we could not indicate to our opponent any single moment at which the independent reality outside the I would not be present for the striving of the I; but to us, he could not indicate where this independent not-I could not be represented and thereby be made dependent in some way on the I. Where does our opponent's independent not-I or thing-in-itself lie. . . ? *Obviously nowhere and everywhere at the same time. . . .*This relation of the thing-in-itself to the I forms the basis for the entire mechanism of the human and all finite minds. To want to change this would entail the elimination of all consciousness, and with it all existence(58).

Again the circle can only be broken by the striving of the practical dimension of the I.

Judgment grounds the being of that not-I. This *is* which is rooted in judgment points towards that which is essentially independent of the I, but which can be thought *and* strived for. The being of the not-I emerges because of this judging I, yet this judging activity does not create the not-I. By the judgment the thing and the image are brought together. The being of the I is such that the being of the not-I is disclosed as a practical determination. The seemingly endless circle of finitude-infinitude can only be broken by the practical imperative of the I.

One fundamental issue might be raised in connection with Fichte's conception of judgment. The traditional conception of judgment considered judgment as a connection of a subject and a predicate. Kant decisively broke with the tradition through his distinction between analytic judgment and synthetic judgment. The central issue that distinguishes analytic judgment from a synthetic one is the latter's necessary reference to an object. With this radical split between the two and with synthetic judgment's necessary reference to an object, Kant understood the meaning of judgment in a new way(59). Since Fichte conceived analytic and synthetic judgments as the same, but from two different points of view, does he then fall back into a traditional conception of judgment?

Not only did Fichte not overlook this distinction and did not conceive judgment in a traditional way(60), but his conception of the *is* is based on an understanding of the priority of the practical sphere over the theoretical—a priority he had found in Kant. The distinction synthetic-analytic is related by Fichte to the synthetic and the antithetic foundational propositions respectively. Yet, both need the thetic proposition, the first foundational proposition, whose fundamentality can only be understood in a practical sense(61).

Judgment for Fichte must make reference to an object that is posed in the sense of being *thought*—a theoretical concern, but is not posed and is independent in a practical sense. Thus, the Kantian distinction, in that it is theoretical, is not appropriate within the present context. The thing is not completely and exclusively an image; if it were, then the subject would know nothing, a Wissenschaftslehre would be impossible, and the I would no longer be finite nor infinite. The thing's character, the not-I, can only emerge within the practical dimension of the I.

In the present section a clearer insight into the meaning of a subject has been achieved: that the grounding of objectivity lies in judgment. The subject is a *thinking* subject(62). In the next section, a thinking subject will be determined by its relationship to another subject. A world of experience emerges because a subject is transcendentally related to another subject.

G. Intersubjectivity

The reciprocal relation between intuiting and the intuited has been established. Because of this mutual reciprocity between the intuiting and the intuited, the determination of the one is also a determination of the other. The intuition's mutual reciprocity consisted of a reciprocity between self-determination and its objective activity. Self-determination was determined as a self-returning activity or as the free spontaneity of the I. This self-returning activity served as the basis for any objectivity and ultimately defined the I's subjectivity as an intuiting.

Since 1) intuiting is *reciprocally* related to an intuited, 2) since this intuiting has been determined as a self-returning activity, and 3) since the intuited is also determined to the extent that intuiting has been determined, there, therefore, must be *in the intuited* a mutual reciprocity of the pure and the objective, of the free and the necessary acts. The intuited also has a self-returning activity similar to the intuiting; but this is *thought,* not intuited. This self-returning activity of the intuited is thought by the activity of the I. The I *thinks* this similar activity in the intuited.

In the previous section judgment was such an activity. In that context the ground of that limited activity which intuits an object was the pure activity's diminishing itself or excluding something from itself. The I *thinks* an activity in the object in order to account for its own passivity. Judgment grounds the ontological status of the object, but it does this by thinking an activity—a self-returning activity within the object, within the intuited. Intuition is grounded in a thought activity in the object. Thus, because of the mutual reciprocity between the intuiting and the intuited, *both* have a self-returning activity.

Since self-returning activity is that which determines the subject's subjectivity and since the same activity is thought in the intuited because of the mutual reciprocity, the object thought in intuition is similar to the I; the intuited is like the intuiting. The intuited is another I; the not-I is similar to the I in that both have a self-returning activity—that which characterizes the I's I-hood. An earlier quoted statement had already asserted this.

> The activity of the intuited in the mutual reciprocity, to the extent it goes to the intuiting, is similarly determined by a self-returning activity, whereby it determines itself to effect the intuiting. . . .No passivity in the intuiting, no original self-returning activity in the object as a thought activity. No such activity in the object, no passivity in the intuiting(63).

The object has a self-returning or self-determining free activity just as the subject; but this self-returning activity in the object is not intuited, but only thought. An aspect of the object is totally other than the subject and is projected by the subject to found the relationship between the subject and the object. This thought inner activity, however, is not merely any activity, but is a free spontaneous self-determination. The object, the not-I, is another subject similar to the subjectivity that has been interrogated all along. It is a self-affecting or self-orienting activity.

Earlier this self-affecting activity had been described. Within the mutual reciprocity of the I's own activity, the I freely determines itself to act in a determinate way. This self-orientation opens up the world for the I. This is the fundamental unity of the I's intuiting: the pure activity's reciprocal relationship with the objective activity. This is the self-returning activity of the imagination, but now this same activity is also determined in the intuited. This situation served as the basis for the deduction of the Other in the *Naturrecht*.

The I as well as the not-I have two dimensions to their interrelationship. Both have a dimension that directly relates to the other, and each has an aspect that is thought in the other and thus founds the former relation. Each thinks, but does not intuit, the noumenal aspect whereby the intuition can occur. "The inner activity of the object whereby it is determined for causality is a mere thought (a *noumenon*, if one gives a substratum to this activity by the imagaination, as one must)"(64). That aspect that is not grasped, but only thought, is the free or self-returning activity. These two dimensions— the immediate relation through intuition and the thought dimension—can be distinguished as the phenomenal and the noumenal respectively.

The noumenal, characterized as a thought self-returning activity, is the necessary condition for the phenomenal. Since this not-I has an activity similar to the I, the I and the not-I are alike. This similarity guarantees the objectivity of experience. This similarity consists of the *free* self-returning activity, which characterizes intelligence. Thus, the ground of the objectivity of experience must be this mutual relation between an I and a not-I that are alike. The not-I must be another I, or the ground of the objectivity of experience is an intersubjective relationship. Intersubjectivity or the mutual reciprocity of two free subjects with their respective activities is the basis for any objectivity of experience.

The noumenal, that self-returning activity thought in the object, is only succinctly and obliquely discussed in the *Grundlage*, but is explicitly elaborated in the later work *Wissenschaftslehre 1798 nova methodo.*

> A necessary free activity is accordingly thought as the ground of a demand occurring in ourselves. This determining and determinable is really a free being outside me. That which is determining is necessarily free, since that which is discovered should be an acting. But from this perspective, as acting, it can be explained only by a free intelligence. Man's common understanding similarly concludes in this case: "I am questioned, thus there must be something there questioning." This common sense is completely correct here because it is at the level of appearance. But if that conclusion is drawn in other cases, it is incorrect. In scholarly terms, there is here a transference from determinability to determinacy. There is in the middle the determining which makes the transference. Thus, from the demand to act freely, a free intelligence is concluded, according to the laws of thought, to be outside me. The acting appears to me, but not the intelligence from which it comes. The free intelligence is only thought; it is a *noumenon*. The free intelligence outside me is thus

entirely determined as the counterpart to myself; only I come to it in another way than to myself (viz. by ascent). With myself, I go outside myself and first act freely by having previously projected a goal concept. But in the case of the free being outside me, I proceed from the activity that appears to its reason, to a free being outside me which I do not find, but only conclude or think. This is why I am not You, and You are not I. I am that which is immediately a *noumenon* for myself and will act sensibly. You are that which does not occur to me directly as a *noumenon*, but is shown to me only in an appearance from which I proceed to the *noumenon*(65).

Although this free self-returning activity is projected or thought, it is that aspect of the subject which only knows itself.

Although this latter point of self-knowledge had been developed in the preceding chapter, it has now been shown that the I is essentially and necessarily intersubjective. This intersubjective dimension accounts for the I's character as an I and for its inherent finitude. The I is related to Others and thereby can *be* itself and *become* aware of itself. The I cannot be self-conscious until the Other addresses itself to the I; yet, the very foundation of this address is and must be constituted by the inherent essential structures of the I. The Other is the necessary condition for the I's self-consciousness, its experience of the objective world, and for the Other's being *thought* in and by the I. This paradox constantly permeated the discussion: it is the finite and the infinite aspect of the I.

The ground for distinguishing a subject from an object has still not been determined, but only the mutual reciprocity between the intuiting and the intuited has been indicated. This has led to the insight that this mutual reciprocity is between two subjects. A clearer understanding of subjectivity, i.e., a clearer insight into the terms of the relation, must be exhibited. The subject must become aware of its being, of its own activity. It must become aware of the fact that these are products of its transcendental imagination. Such an awareness sees reason as the ultimate ground.

H. Reason: The Foundation of Subjectivity

In judgment abstraction had been made from any determinate object, and the ground had been exhibited. Now abstraction will be made from every object in general in order to discover the ultimate meaning of the subject. If such an abstraction would be impossible, then the ground for distinguishing subjectivity from objectivity could never be disclosed. Such abstraction must be possible if self-awareness and the consciousness of an object are to be possible.

By abstracting from the judging activity and by focusing on its fundamental unity the central character of the I and the ultimate ground of objectivity would be disclosed. The law of self-determination is disclosed: "nothing remains except the rule of reason in general to abstract, the mere law of an unrealizable determination (through imagination, and for clear consciousness, through understanding)"(66). Reason remains; the subject is "that which *determines itself* and is *determined* by *itself*—the I"(67). This is the point of pure activity at which the I's own activity comes back on itself. Although this was first seen in judgment, now the subject is aware of determining itself to determine an object. The subject is self-thinking thought.

> That which thinks should determine itself to think something as thinkable, and to that extent the thinkable would be passive; but again the thinkable should determine itself to be thinkable, and to that extent that which thinks would be passive(68).

In reason there is the mutual reciprocity of thinking and thought, of the subject and the object; but there is also a standpoint of distinguishability.

Reason is the ultimate possibility to abstract from every object whatsoever. The I alone, as subjectivity, remains after the elimination of everything else; the object is that which is eliminated.

> But the I is now determined as that which remains over after the cancellation of all objects by the absolute possibility of abstraction; and the not-I as that from which abstraction can be made by the possibility of abstraction(69).

Reason is where the I, the subject, is totally transparent to itself and knows that the object is its own product. It is the point of unity where the I relates to itself, a relation of itself with itself, an intersubjective relation.

A Reflective Retrieve

This present section will reflectively retrieve some important themes of this chapter and will highlight the essentially intersubjective character of the I.

The importance of the I's finite character has emerged. Since the I must necessarily relate to what is not itself, to a not-I, the I cannot be interpreted as an absolute subject that has escaped and is removed from all contingencies and situations. Although the I's infinite and absolute dimension is an important element, finitude cannot be overlooked. Since the I's unity is an ideal harmony to be strived for, negativity is immediately present: the I's negativity in the form of its not-yet. The I thereby requires the not-I for self-knowledge.

The discussion of finitude has also led to the I's essentially, intersubjective character. Although the harmonious I in its intersubjective dimension is not a "we," a community of other I's, finitude requires an intersubjective dimension as a condition for the realization of the absolute and infinite dimension. Although Fichte's concern and philosophical question was to question the self and to interrogate self-consciousness as the ground, the ground of objectivity, the response to this question showed that the I's need for a not-I (as Fichte has shown in the *Grundlage*) is really a need for another subject. The I is essentially intersubjective.

The objective mode of experience is only possible to the extent that the I is intersubjective. An inherent and constitutive structure of the I is its relational structure with another subject. The ground of objectivity leads to the question of subjectivity; from this latter question issues the intersubjective concern. Thus, the real significance and justification of the objective world of experience is to be found in intersubjectivity.

The centrality of intersubjectivity stems from the finite dimension of the I which has an infinite, lived task and possibility of self-realization. The I's aim is total awareness of itself as it is, total transparency of itself to itself. If achieved, the I would see everything as its *own*; the world of experience would be *my* world. Since the not-I would mirror the I, the not-I would also mirror the I's freedom and self-knowing. This is only possible between subjects. A fixed, non-conscious object can never mirror me as a subject. Even though it might be mine in its having been produced by me, it would be *reduced* to my world. Thus, there emerges the requirement for an absolute *difference* between the I and the not-I.

This difference must be considered in the relation of the subject with what the subject is not. Although an object is not a subject and there also is no thing-in-itself, the object as such is not absolutely different, but is only so by me, the subject. The object can never be totally independent of the subject, but must always be related to it. In fact, it is produced by the I. On the contrary, this is not the case with another subject; for another subject is both an object *and* a subject. Another subject has its own autonomy and freedom. Only another subject is totally other and always remains other and unknown to the I because it is another consciousness and another will. Only another subject is absolutely transcendent to the I and can bring out and reveal my finitude whereas an object reveals my infinite possibility and activity. The object, not the other subject, can come under my dominion.

The role of finitude can be seen in the two formulations that comprise the unity of the "I am." These formulations—the theoretical and the practical—implicitly bring out the finite character of the I. In the case of the theoretical the I poses itself as determined by the not-I. Here the I is fundamentally determined and affected by the not-I; the I is not in control, but feels and is affected. With the practical sphere in which the I poses itself as determining the not-I, the finite character is not so clear because the not-I is determined here by the I. Yet, this practical goal or task of the I has been shown to be an ideal and unattainable goal. The complete harmony strived for is always something that is ahead of and before the I; it is something the I is not yet.

An objection might be raised that the I poses itself in both situations and that, therefore, the infinite and absolute dimension of the I has the priority. A response could be made that the freedom found in the I's absolute, infinite dimension cannot be considered alone and by itself. Although the I strives and desires to be one with itself and with all, the striving is always in relation to and is provoked by the not-I. Still one must not overemphasize the finite character of the I at the expense of the infinite as the traditional interpretation had overstressed the absolute posing of the I and had interpreted the I as an absolute subjectivity(70).

In the preceding paragraph, it has been argued that the absolute difference between the I and the not-I is essential for justifying the intersubjective character of the I. Now the argument will be made for the need of *similarity*. Since mutual reciprocity requires some kind of similarity between the members of the relation, even an object would have to have some kind of similarity to the I for the relation. The similarity between two subjects is a much closer similarity than that between the subject and the object, even though the differences are also greater. This mutual reciprocity between equals has been clearly discussed in the deduction of the Other in the *Naturrecht*.

In the case of right, no right is possible unless both members of the relation are and act as rational beings. A relation between equals is required so that the mutual reciprocity can be the foundation of right. Again the intersubjective element enters as a fundamental constituent of the I: the I needs to be related not to any not-I, but to one that is another subject like itself. This is the condition for the I's being itself and realizing itself. Mutual reciprocity, a central notion throughout the entire series of deductions, can only be fully understood when there is a relationship between similar terms, in this case, between two subjects. This need for similarity is the reverse side of that need for absolute difference.

The subject can only achieve itself in cooperation with others. Objects or things can only serve as a means for this self-realization, but another rational being cannot serve only as a means. He is also an end. In the mutual cooperation and commitment, each subject finds itself as a subject.

This intersubjective element has been approached from the transcendental perspective. No such subject must concretely and in every case be related to an actual Other. Only the transcendental conditions of possibility for the I's being an I have been shown. Fichte is doing, as he clearly indicates, transcendental philosophy. Again too, his descriptions always arise within the context of a subject who has become aware of his own freedom and free possibilities. The philosopher's perspective is one of self-awareness and of freedom.

This transcendental perspective recalls the discussion and the place of philosophical reflection in the imagination's intentionality previously articulated. This transcendental perspective not only allows the I to understand its possibilities, but also lays bare the ground of all experience. This is what Fichte had conceived the task of philosophy to be.

These comments form the context in which one can come to an understanding of the intellectual intuition. They will offer a strong basis for a discussion of the Hegelian interpretation. Since this Hegelian interpretation has been central for most interpretations of Fichte, it must be dealt with because the interpretation of the I as intersubjective puts into question that absolute subjectivity of the I that is maintained by Hegel.

CHAPTER FOUR

THE INTELLECTUAL INTUITION

> *The Wissenschaftslehre goes out from an intellectual intuition, that of the absolute self-activity of the I.*
>
> –Fichte

In his *Differenzschrift* of 1801 Hegel asserts that the

> foundation of *Fichte's system* is the intellectual intuition, pure thinking of itself, pure self-consciousness, I=I, I am; the absolute is subject-object, and the I is this identity of subject and object(1).

These words which identify the intellectual intuition with the first principle of Fichte's *Grundlage* of 1794 were decisive for every interpretation of Fichte from that time to the present. This interpretation had the greatest impact on situating Fichte as the very first and necessary stage of German Idealism whose culmination is Hegel himself.

The aim of this chapter is to call this interpretation into question and to suggest a new understanding of Fichte—an understanding that will save Fichte from the clutches of Hegel and will justify the I's intersubjective character. The inherent intersubjectivity of the I seriously undermines the possibility of an absolute reflection; yet, the intellectual intuition not only grounds such an interpretation, which stems from Hegel, but also questions the I's intersubjective character. If such an intuition is the foundation and the cornerstone of the Wissenschaftslehre, then it seems that the I could never be essentially intersubjective. The thrust of this chapter is two-fold: to present and interpret the intellectual intuition and to show how and why it does not affect the interpretation of the essentiality of the I's intersubjective character.

The strategy will be to direct our fullest attention on Fichte himself without being distracted by a direct confrontation with Hegel and without becoming engaged in a discussion of Schelling's notion of the intellectual intuition. The first part will consist of a descriptive treatment of the intellectual intuition, especially as it is discussed in *Die Zweite Einleitung* of 1797. This will lead to a consideration of the intellectual intuition as a starting point of the Wissenschaftslehre. At this point the *Wissenschaftslehre 1798 nova methodo* where Fichte does explicitly begin with the intellectual intuition will be discussed. This later work will then be related back to the *Grundlage* of 1794. The third section will focus on the actual beginning of the *Grundlage*, on the first principle. Finally the *Grundlage* will be considered explicitly as a Grundlage.

Description of the Intellectual Intuition

In this section Fichte's arguments for the intellectual intuition and the function it serves will be presented. As is indicated in the *Erste Einleitung*, Fichte's concern is to account for those representations which are accompanied by the feeling of necessity. In other words, how are there *objects* there *for me*? This question implies that there *are* objects there for a consciousness; and consequently, this means that consciousness must also be aware of itself as being different from objects. Thus, the question of the ground of the existence of objects for me becomes the fundamental question.

One might wonder why or how such a question arises in the first place, for these are not ordinary questions. These are not questions that are asked in one's daily concerns and occupations. Fichte would maintain that this "why?" which is so necessary for philosophy emerges from the horizon of a *practical* independence and autonomy of the questioner. These philosophical questions come to the fore from a person who feels the need to ask questions and to secure answers. They arise out of an act of freedom. Freedom is the indemonstrable ground for philosophy in that freedom is the context wherein there issues forth a doubt, a question. In this act of freedom whereby the individual puts into suspension his concernful absorption in the objects of his concern, he comes to an awareness of himself. Only on the basis of an act of freedom can any individual follow the Fichtean dictum:

> Attend to yourself; turn your attention from all that surrounds you and turn it towards your inner; this is the first demand philosophy does to its disciples. It is not concerned with anything outside yourself, but only with you yourself(2).

Thus, the reflecting individual is aware of two things in his reflection: 1) he is aware of himself *and* 2) he is aware of himself as investigating and being investigated. In turning inwards the I not only grasps itself, but also is simultaneously aware that the I is both being watched and doing the watching. This turning away from the world reveals two dimensions of the I: it is an activity whose correlate is its very self. Here the inward return to the self is thereby a dividing of itself, i.e., a going outside itself. This double dimension expresses the fundamental unity of the I: that "self-consciousness and the consciousness of something that is to be—not ourselves—are necessarily connected"(3).

The I's activity of turning inwards is a self-returning activity. Only in this act *is* the I; it is its activity. Since this returning-activity is the primordial point where the I is for itself, the I is not a concept because a concept is possible only in opposition to a not-I and through a determination of the I. This self-returning act whereby and in which the I immediately knows something, viz. itself, because it is that which does the acting, is called the intellectual intuition. I am that which I enact(4).

The self-returning activity is the first characteristic of the intellectual intuition. It is the most eventful act, but it is *not* consciousness nor self-consciousness(5). By this primordial act whereby the I grasps itself, "the I is merely transplanted into the possibility of self-consciousness and with it the possibility of all remaining consciousness"(6).

This first characteristic presents a textual ambiguity concerning the intellectual intuition. In subsequent passages Fichte relates this intuition to self-consciousness. Although that activity whereby the I immediately grasps itself had been identified as the intellectual intuition, and although that activity was not self-consciousness nor a consciousness of an object, Fichte writes that

> self-consciousness is immediate, in it the subjective and the objective are inseparably joined and are absolutely one.

> Such an immediate consciousness is called with
> the expression of the Wissenschaftslehre an
> *intuition*(7).

This passage identifies the intellectual intuition with self-consciousness; but, in terms of the *Grundlage*'s practical part, this self-consciousness is a demand, a practical task, an unattainable ideal.   Although self-consciousness as a transcendental ideal that lies in infinity is never realizable because of the inherent limitation and finitude of the I, this transcendental ideal finds its possibility in the consciousness of the moral law wherein the I alone can ever grasp itself. This consciousness of the moral ideal too is the intellectual intuition.   "Only through this medium of the moral law do I catch sight of *myself*; and in catching sight of myself, do I necessarily see myself as self-active"(8).

This would indicate that the intellectual intuition should not be construed as a starting point, but is related to an ideal. If philosophy were to begin with the intellectual intuition, then philosophy would have to begin with the consciousness of the moral law; yet this identity of the I with itself is a *practical task*. "I *should* proceed in my thinking from a pure I and *should* think of that as absolutely self-active"(9).   Here philosophy begins with an ought, a demand for unity, but not with an actual unity. To achieve this unity is the task of philosophy in its practical dimension.

The notion of Fichte's intellectual intuition contains an ambiguity. On the one hand, it is an immediate awareness of the I in its activity; yet, on the other hand, it is a consciousness of the moral/practical ideal never to be attained. Fichte does not seem to distinguish a methodological unity of the I with itself from an absolute, ideal unity that is always ahead of the finite I—even though he does make a distinction between the I as intuition and the I as ideal. There is the confusion

> of the I as intellectual intuition from which the
> Wissenschaftslehre sets out, and of the I as the ideal
> with which it ends. In the I as intellectual intuition
> lies merely the form of the I-hood, the self-returning
> activity which also, of course, becomes the content
> of that(10).

In the first case, the self-returning act of the I is seen as the form of the I-hood or as the intellectual intuition.   In contradistinction to this, there is the I which "as ideal is the rational being in so far as it has partly exhibited universal reason perfectly within itself, is indeed rational throughout, and nothing else but rational"(11).

This ambiguity between a methodological unity or an ideal unity for the intellectual intuition might be clarified if the intuition is seen as being passive and active.

Above, the intellectual intuition was considered an activity that enacts itself. It is a knowing that is grounded on the fact that I am the one that does the acting. It is a posing in which the posing itself is disclosed. This is the active side of the intellectual intuition: in the very acting the I discovers that it is itself acting, and its ideal thereby emerges. On the passive side, this intuition is an awareness—an awareness of the ideal to be realized. This ideal, of course, is total harmony or unity of the I with itself. This is the harmony that the passivity expresses as the I's relationship to its ideal, to its task to be realized. This ideal serves as the fundamental unity without which no other act of the I would be possible.

What has been called the methodological unity of the I would be related to the active side of the intellectual intuition whereas the absolute ideal unity would be related to the passive side of the same intuition. The intellectual intuition can be seen from two perspectives: as an active posing or as a passive awareness. This dual perspective accounts for the ambiguity of the intellectual intuition.

This ambiguity is not made any clearer with Fichte's reference to Kant's intellectual intuition whose possibility Kant had denied.   Fichte's occasional blending of the distinctions mentioned above results in the problem of the proper locus of the intellectual intuition. Besides the fact that Fichte's intuition intuits an activity and is thereby distinct from Kant's position, the latter denies the very possibility of any such intellectual intuition in an entity which is not the primordial one, viz. God. This primordial being that has an intellectual intuition would be such an entity that *gives existence* to beings. Since such an intellectual intuition in a being that is ontologically and epistemologically dependent is contradictory,

such intellectual intuition seems to belong solely to the primordial being, and can never be ascribed to a

> dependent being, dependent in its existence as well
> as in its intuition, and which through that intuition
> determines its existence solely in relation to given
> objects(12).

Furthermore, such an intellectual intuition would mean that
such a being would *know* itself as it immediately is without any
sensible intuition. For Kant, such a thing is impossible because
that being is only conscious of its own synthetic powers that
need the inner sense of time. "Such an intelligence, therefore,
can know itself only as it appears to itself in respect to an
intuition which is not intellectual and cannot be given by the
understanding itself, not as it would know itself if its *intuition*
were intellectual"(13). Its object is non-sensible; it is
noumenal. Kant says that there cannot be such a non-sensible
intuition of the noumenal; one cannot even comprehend its
possibility.

Besides Kant's denial of such intuition's possibility, the
ambiguity is in no way clarified when Fichte relates it to
Kant's categorical imperative and to the unity of apperception.
"The intellectual intuition, of which the Wissenschaftslehre
speaks, goes not at all to a being, but to an act, and simply
finds no mention in Kant (unless one wants under the title of
pure *apperception*)"(14). This pure apperception is called that I
which must accompany all representations.

Kant's highest principle of human knowledge, the
principle of apperception, grounds all representations as mine.

> I am conscious of the self as identical in respect to
> the manifold of representations that are given to me
> in an intuition, because I call them one and all *my*
> representations, and so apprehend them as
> constituting *one* intuition. This amounts to saying
> that I am conscious to myself a priori of a necessary
> synthesis of representations—to be entitled the
> original synthetic unity of apperception—under
> which all representations that are given to me must
> stand, but under which they have also first to be
> brought by means of synthesis(15).

For Kant as well as for Fichte, this unity of apperception is
self-consciousness. This identity Fichte affirms when he refers
to Kant's own text:

At B 132 he says: "But this representation ('I think') is an act of spontaneity, i.e., it cannot be regarded as belonging to sensibility." . . ."I call it pure apperception, in order to distinguish it from empirical apperception (just mentioned) because it is that self-consciousness which, while generating the representation: 'I think' (a representation which must be capable of accompanying all others and which *in all consciousness is one and the same*), cannot be accompanied by any further ones." Here the nature of pure self-consciousness is clearly described. . . .

According to the Wissenschaftslehre, all consciousness is determined by self-consciousness, i.e., all that is present in consciousness is founded, given, and introduced by the conditions of self-consciousness(16).

Consequently, Fichte can say that the intellectual intuition is the I, is self-consciousness in its absolute unity. "I am this intuition and absolutely nothing more, and this intuition itself is the I"(17).

In summary, the intellectual intuition is the I's activity that returns back on itself. This is the way philosophy must begin and proceed, but it is not clear whether this is a total consciousness of the self or whether it is merely a methodological procedure. The question might be posed in another way: is reflection intuition or vice versa? Is the I immediately given as such or is it given as a task of concrete reflection? Is the thetic posing of the I the beginning or the task of philosophical reflection? Or finally, does *setzen* in the *Grundlage* mean *intuition*?

To these questions one might get an access if one tries to discover the locus of the intellectual intuition both in terms of the Wissenschaftslehre in general and the *Grundlage* in particular. This leads to the discussion in the next section where the intellectual intuition as a starting point will be investigated.

The Intellectual Intuition as a Starting Point

Fichte writes that the "Wissenschaftslehre proceeds . . . from an intellectual intuition, that of the absolute self-activity of the I"(18). With such a statement, the question is whether the *Grundlage* of 1794 begins with the intellectual intuition or whether the intuition should be placed elsewhere in respect to the *Grundlage*. This question becomes most serious and most critical in the light of the fact that in the *Grundlage* one cannot find any reference to an intellectual intuition. Let us repeat: in the *Grundlage* of 1794 *no* reference is *ever* made to any intellectual intuition. What exactly does this all mean if a Wissenschaftslehre must proceed from an intellectual intuition, which is the only firm philosophical perspective?

If both of these are true—if the Wissenschaftslehre must begin with the intellectual intuition and if the *Grundlage* makes no mention of it, then it would seem, if consistency is to be maintained, that the *Grundlage* is *not* a Wissenschaftslehre. This is not as shocking if the title of the work of 1794 is recalled: *Grundlage der gesamten Wissenschaftslehre*. For something to be a Grundlage means that it *shows the foundation*, that it is a propaedeutic to the Wissenschaftslehre. It is suggested that the *Grundlage* is not yet a Wissenschaftslehre, but only an introduction to it.

What takes place in the *Grundlage*, as it has been shown in Chapter II, is a description of the transcendental imagination, which is the essence of the I and its activity. The unity of this I, the "I am," is the unity of theory and practice, of necessity and freedom, and of finitude and infinitude. This unity of the "I am," of finitude and freedom, is a practical and ideal unity in which the I in its freedom finitely strives to appropriate itself in order to achieve this fundamental unity of itself with itself. This is the I's practical ideal with freedom as its basis.

It would consequently seem that only at the end of the *Grundlage*, when all the syntheses have been gone through, has the point been reached where the described I could perform an act of freedom. Only at this point has the I along with its necessary conditions and structures been described. Only at the end of the syntheses could such an I begin to philosophize, because only then has the I come to be aware of its own freedom as free. This is the necessary condition for the birth of philosophy, for the birth of the Wissenschaftslehre. "If this potentiality of freedom is not already there and exercised, the Wissenschaftslehre can do nothing with man"(19).

Since consciousness of its freedom has just emerged at the end of the *Grundlage*, the I can now turn inwards and intuit itself. All the while that it does this, it must also be aware of its limitation and rootedness in the "I am." Philosophy thus becomes an unfolding of what had remained only implicit. When philosophy makes more explicit the free, finite I, it also lays bare the total and necessary conditions of the I as a whole. It attempts to give the grounds for and the justification of its ultimate task—total self-consciousness. With the use of the intellectual intuition a further understanding and insight into the "what" of the I is obtained.

The implications of what has been said are that the *Grundlage* does not begin with the intellectual intuition, but that this intuition emerges at the end of the text. The present task is to clarify how the intellectual intuition can still be said to be the beginning of philosophy, even though the *Grundlage* actually does not so begin, but begins differently. This clarification will be achieved by examining the *Wissenschaftslehre 1798 nova methodo* which actually does begin with the intellectual intuition. In this text Fichte begins with the *feeling* whereas the *Grundlage* ended there.

On the introductory page before the introduction of the *Wissenschaftslehre 1798 nova methodo* can be found the following statements:

> And indeed according to any entirely opposed procedure of his compendium of 1794. Where he moves from the theoretical, i.e., from that which should be explained, to the practical part of philosophy, by which that [theoretical] should be explained. But in his lectures the till now usual division of philosophy into theoretical and practical does not take place. But he expounds philosophy in general, theoretical and practical joined; he begins according to a far more natural procedure with the practical; or he transfers, where clarity demands it, the practical over into the theoretical in order to explain the former out of the latter. A freedom which the author at that time still did not feel confident to venture when he gave his Wissenschaftslehre to print(20).

Three remarks contrast this new text of 1798 with that of 1794. First, the *Grundlage* of 1794 begins with the theoretical and subsequently moves to the practical sphere. The relationship between the theoretical and the practical is important. Concerning the 1794 text, the introductory comment says that the theoretical should be and is explained by the practical. The 1794 text indicates this:

> why reflection must proceed from the theoretical part; nevertheless it will be subsequently shown: that the theoretical possibility does not indeed make possible the practical, but that conversely the practical possibility first makes the theoretical possible (that reason in itself is purely practical and that it first becomes theoretical in the application of its laws to a not-I that limits it). This is so because the *thinkability* of the practical principle depends on the thinkability of the theoretical principle(21).

At that time reason's practical dimension was most fundamental even though reason needed the theoretical to be aware of this priority of the practical. Secondly, this quite obviously contrasts with the Wissenschaftslehre of 1798 where the theoretical explains the practical sphere. The ground of explanation in the *Wissenschaftslehre 1798 nova methodo* is the theoretical. Thirdly, Fichte maintains in the *Grundlage* the distinction between the theoretical and the practical whereas at its end the distinction seems to break down; any new beginning will begin with the "theoretical and the practical joined." Consequently, in this new text of 1798 Fichte presents a structure of the Wissenschaftslehre that does not follow the necessary path laid out in the *Grundlage*. Why can it proceed in this different fashion? A preliminary answer can be the intellectual intuition.

From another perspective, the new Wissenschaftslehre of 1798 begins not with the first principle, which states that the I poses itself absolutely, but begins with the third principle of the *Grundlage*, the principle that states that everything opposed is *partially* the same, and that everything the same is *partially* opposed. The *Wissenschaftslehre 1798 nova methodo*'s beginning and its relationship to the intellectual intuition will be shown. Since this new beginning rests on the foundation laid in the *Grundlage*, it will be related to the earlier work, especially in reference to the third fundamental principle.

As it has been indicated, the intellectual intuition is an activity whereby the I grasps its own activity, where the subject and the object are the same. In essence it is an activity that turns back on itself. In the very first pages of this new text of 1798, the same phenomenon is found. In distinguishing the philosophical act from the activity that goes to the object, Fichte notes the difference:

> with the representation of my I, the thinking and the thought are the same—in the concept of the I. *I am the thinking and the thought*. . .but here the activity returns back on itself(22).

This is an immediate intuition whereby

> in that I act on my very self, in that I pose myself, that my activity returns back on myself, the I comes forth, I think my I; and both: I am I and I pose myself as I, both mutually exhaust each other(23).

Here the subject and object are one, or there is an identity of posing and being posed.

Though this intuiting of an activity is the starting point, it is important to realize that this activity must be a posed one, i.e., it must also be a non-activity, a resting. In focusing on the activity, one forgets that this activity has ceased to be active; but in the observation it has come to stand, has come to be posed: it is *objective*. In both the Wissenschaftslehre of 1798 and in the published *Versuch einer neuen Darstellung der Wissenschaftslehre* (1797), Fichte describes this situation. This is the movement from the intuition of the I to the concept of the I. In the latter work, Fichte requests:

> Think yourself; and having understood the last word, you enacted *in the act of understanding* the self-returning activity by which the thought of the I comes to pass only without knowing it because you were not particularly attentive to it; thus what you found in consciousness came to you. Take note on how you make it, I said to you; now you enact, only with attention and consciousness, the same activity that you had already enacted.
>   The inner activity encompassed in its equanimity is definitely called the *concept*(24).

Consequently in the intuition of the I there is necessarily a rest along with the activity. Both activity and rest or both posing and being posed are there together. Therefore, the intuition and the concept of the I are intimately and necessarily connected. They both fall together into one; the I is both subject and object. Such is the beginning of the new Wissenschaftslehre of 1798(25).

With such a beginning Fichte notes that it is the opposite of the *Grundlage*'s of 1794 where the movement was from an accomplishing fact (*Tathandlung*) to an accomplished fact (*Tatsache*). Here in 1798 the method is reversed because it begins with the determinacy of the I which is the middle term of the I and not-I. In brief, this new Wissenschaftslehre begins with the third foundational principle as understood at the end of the *Grundlage*, and not with the first principle.

In the *Grundlage* the third principle is third because it is formally conditioned, but materially unconditioned. It needs the first two principles for its own form. The two preceding principles assign the third its task, but the way in which this task is to be achieved is completely unconditioned(26).

What is this task? It is to find some point of unity between the I and the not-I where both could be maintained as they are without canceling each other and without destroying the unity of consciousness. This is achieved by means of the concept of divisibility. Mutual limitation is what maintains both the unity of consciousness and the togetherness of what is opposite. Limitation is only partial denial or negation. There is a third act which partially unites the opposed. To limit is to set limits between things. Thus, every synthesis is also an analysis in that "as a not-I is opposed to an I, accordingly the I *which* is opposed and the not-I *which* opposes are partially posed"(27).

Consequently, all the opposed are alike in *one* way and all the alike are opposed in *one* way. This is true only of part of knowledge, not of the whole. It is a principle that grounds all syntheses and antitheses. This is the third foundational principle of the *Grundlage*: the I and the not-I are partially opposed to each other.

> Granted that the logical rules under which all antithesis and synthesis stand are derived from the third principle of the Wissenschaftslehre, so in general the authority over all antithesis and synthesis is derived from it. But we have seen in the exposition of that principle that the original act which it expresses—that of uniting the opposed in a third was not possible without the activity of

opposing and that this equally was not possible without the activity of uniting: that consequently both are inseparably bound in the act and are only distinguishable in reflection(28).

Any situation where opposites are joined together or where likes can be separated is governed by this third principle, i.e., all syntheses and all antitheses are exclusively under the principle of limitation. This principle alone grounds the possibility of synthetic and analytic judgments. This principle allows the I and the not-I to be thought together and contains all other syntheses. It is the *form* of the Wissenschaftslehre. All content returns to this form; and the whole form of all propositions, regardless of content, is so determined. In other words, the form is the content, and the content is the form.

This is the third principle of the *Grundlage*. If the previous suggestion is meaningful, then this must also be the starting point of the *Wissenschaftslehre 1798 nova methodo*. Thus, the 1798 work must start with the unity of opposites or with a situation wherein opposites are contained together. Since the third principle of the *Grundlage* was arrived at through the other two principles, the question is then how does the new Wissenschaftslehre actually begin and proceed.

It has already been mentioned that the movement of the 1798 work is the reverse of that of 1794. The later work begins with an accomplished fact and proceeds to an accomplishing fact(29). Fichte describes this *Tatsache's* beginning:

> One must infer from the being to the self-posing and vice versa—from the concept to the intuition and vice versa—both must be at the same time; there must be a rest connected with the intuition of activity. I acquire the concept only by the intuition and intuition only by the concept—the two are found at the same time together in the free act of the self-returning activity(30).

This accomplished fact is the intuiting of the activity *and* also seeing *how* the I emerges.

This "how" is bringing the activity to stand or it is looking on the activity as resting. Both are needed, both an intuition and the concept—as was indicated earlier. The activity must be limited; and in so doing, how the I emerges is

disclosed. "Thus, we became conscious of our own activity by
the undetermined's flowing over, or, in other words, by the
transference from the determinable to the determined, from
the unlimited to the limited; we maintained intuition of our
activity"(31). Both activity and rest are intuited at the same
time; and only because of this can the Wissenschaftslehre
begin. This, of course, is the intellectual intuition(32).

The I emerges only when there is a limited activity, i.e.,
an activity contrasted with rest. Since this self-returning
activity is determined, it is limited. The beginning is a
situation where there is a posing and an opposing or where
there is an I and a not-I posed together. Thus, the
Wissenschaftslehre of 1798 begins with the I and the not-I
being partially opposed to each other; it begins with the third
principle of the *Grundlage*. This Fichte affirms when he
writes: "Critical idealism—the Wissenschaftslehre and with it
fully the Kantian system—proceeds from the absolutely joined
accidents of both—or from the mutual working of the I and the
not-I"(33).

The Wissenschaftslehre does begin with the intellectual
intuition, but this is only possible because this intuition is
related to the third principle as that principle is understood at
the end of the *Grundlage*. The intellectual intuition is not
related to the first principle; consequently, this first principle
must be reinterpreted as the starting point of the *Grundlage*.

The First Principle as a Starting Point

In this section it must be shown that the *Grundlage*
begins in a different way: different from the writing of 1798
and from the intellectual intuition. A detailed analysis and
interpretation of the first principle as first will be given. In
the very first paragraph Fichte begins by stating that he wants
"to *look for* the absolutely first, absolutely unconditioned
fundamental proposition of all human knowledge"(34). He
wants to find and express the fundamental proposition that
serves as the basis for all knowledge. This proposition
expresses an activity, a *Tathandlung*.

Immediately Fichte notes that an accomplishing fact
must be distinguished from an accomplished fact. This latter,
this *Tatsache*, is the result of the former; the activity must be
the ground, and not that which is dependent on an activity. In
other words, the relation between *Tathandlung* and *Tatsache* is
similar to the one between the founding and the founded. This

first principle is to express this founding or grounding that necessarily cannot be among the founded or the grounded. This fundamental activity would be expressed in the fundamental principle. How then is this primordial activity to be arrived at?

Since this activity is the absolute condition for any state of consciousness and must be presupposed in the case of any *Sache*, one can *think* this activity as this ground. In other words, from a state of consciousness one can proceed to the necessary condition for that state. The ground can be thought from the grounded, but in order to think anything the laws of logic must be used. This leads to the question whether there is any state of consciousness that is indubitable. Indubitability, of course, is found in the highest or the most fundamental proposition of logic: A=A.

With this logical proposition the *Grundlage* begins. A *is* A. Fichte makes it quite clear what this "is" means. It is an "is" as a logical copula in contradistinction to an existential meaning "to be" or "to exist." Being can have two entirely different meanings: a purely relational or connective meaning between a subject and a predicate, e.g., "A is A" or "The mountain is picturesque." Or there can be the existential meaning where there is no predicate to be connected to the subject, e.g., "There is an A" or "A exists" or "A is." The present situation is not at all concerned with the existential meaning, but only with the copula meaning where the two terms are related. Fichte maintains this distinction, but does not presently develop it.

Another important feature that is present in the proposition is that it is certain, but there is no further ground for this certainty other than that it is such in and by itself. This certainty is self-evident and without doubt. For "this proposition is *absolutely* certain, i.e., *without any further reason*: and in saying this, undoubtedly with general approval, one ascribes to himself the possibility *to pose something absolutely*"(35). Here Fichte indicates the possibility of posing something *absolutely*. Man's freedom means that man can pose something absolutely. To be free means to be able to pose something without any ground or justification other than itself. This emerges here in the merely logical statement. Fichte, however, is not speaking about anything existing, but only about a logical relation.

Since the concern is not whether A exists or not, but only with the formal relation between the two members, the search is made for that which can account for the transition, for the passing over from A on the left (A-l) to A on the right (A-r). In other words, what is it that holds the two together in the "is"? This Fichte calls "X."

The *Grundlage* begins conspicuously with a merely logical assertion, but this logic contains more and implies more. It immediately presents the possibility of freedom, an act of posing something absolutely. This leads to investigate this "X" further.

Thus, by beginning with "A is A" (A=A), it was shown that the issue was not that of the existence of the A. This "is" was merely a relation. The focusing on the formal aspect alone led to this: "if A, then A is." This was based on "X"; but here, in the expression "A is," the "is" is without a predicate and consequently expresses an existential meaning. With the givenness of A as existing (A-r), under what conditions does or can this givenness take place? By beginning with A's existing the intention is to trace back to the conditions of possibility. When and how can there *be* an A? No longer is it a merely logical connection, but now it is an existential condition. This logical proposition that had been asserted in the judgment leads back to the source or root of judging. The unity that is the ultimate condition for the being of A—the unity called "X"—is also traced back. It must somehow or other be *in* the I and *posed by* the I because the I is that which judges and from which, consequently, the "is" in both meanings springs.

The logical movement of the relation between subject and predicate is the condition of A's being, only because this logical movement is expressed in the unity of "X" and is related to a judging. Why does judgment ground the existential A?

"X" accounts for the connection between A-l and A-r and is the rule of unification. This rule, accounted for in "X," gives the condition under which A can *be*. This rule accounts for the self-identity of A and, therefore, its existence. This rule is posed and is applicable because it is posed by a judging I. That an I judges means that an I follows the rule of connection called "X" according to which A is identical to itself and therefore exists. The judging one in posing "X" also poses himself as bound to this "X" whereby there can be a possible A. Again it ultimately goes back to the I that judges.

Consequently, there is posed by the I with the help of X: *A exists for the judging I absolutely and*

simply because of its being posed in the I in general;
this means: it is asserted that in the I—it might now
be specifically posing or judging, or whatever it may
be—there is something that is continually like itself,
is continually one and the same; and the absolutely
posed X is also so expressed: I=I, I am I(36).

A exists by virtue of the rule that expresses the *unity* between
A-l and A-r. This rule, posed in the judging I, affirms the self-
sameness or self-identity of A. A is like itself or is equal to
itself because of the rule of identity. Since this rule "X" has
its source in the posing of it by the judging I, what the rule
affirms—self-identity—has its source in the posing of the
judging I. In other words, the rule of identity expressed in "X"
is grounded in the "I=I" or in the "I am I."

The source of the identity in the posing of the I has been
reached. The validity of the proposition "A=A" is grounded in
the "I=I." There is, however, a difference between the
proposition "A=A" and that of "I=I." This difference is that in
the case of the former, its entire content is conditioned by
something other than itself. It depends at least on the "X" or
on the identity derived from "I=I." Conversely, "I am I" is
posed absolutely and is unconditioned. It is posed as identical
to itself absolutely and not on condition of anything else. The
"I am" is disclosed through and by means of the logical
proposition "A=A." The latter is only a *Tatsache*, but not yet
an ultimate *Tathandlung*. Any posing of anything in the I
requires that the I must also be posed before hand. This has
not yet been seen as an absolute *act* that grounds all.

It is not required to go from a judging activity to an
absolute self-posing activity, from a particular activity to a
pure activity. This posing activity is one that expresses its
own being. .To pose is its very being; and to be is its posing:
"the *I poses itself,* and it *is* according to this mere posing by
itself; and vice versa, the I *is,* and it *poses* its being according
to its mere being"(37). The *am* of the "I am" means a posing or
an affirming of itself, that the I poses or affirms its being.
The being of the I is self-affirmation, self-assertion; it is a
necessary and essential character of the being of the I or of
the I-hood of the I. This is to say that the I is to be understood
as absolute subject. *"That whose being or essence merely
consists of posing itself as being* is the I as absolute
subject"(38).

Thus the I-hood of the I has been indicated; this "I am" which is a pure activity, a *Tathandlung*, consists of a self-posing. This determines the I as an absolute subject: its being is to affirm or pose itself; and in so doing, it *is*. What does Fichte mean by *absolute* subject? One important dimension of this absolute character is that it is a subject without any predicate, an "is" that expresses an existential meaning rather than a relational one. The "I am" has this existential meaning for its "is," but in a unique way: it is the completely unconditioned. In other words, since the "I am" originally does not have a predicate, but *is*, this subject has the possibility of having predicates.

Expressed differently, the I-hood of the I is the posing or the affirming of itself. The self-posing of its being designates the I as absolute subject. This self-posing implies that the I is necessarily and originally an I that has only possible predicates. In and by this self-posing of its being a world can open up for it. This thetic self-posing opens up for the I a whole realm of possibility, but this posing must take place in the desert. It must be absolute; but in this self-posing of itself in a desert without predicates, the I's absolute character emerges as a necessity to move from itself, outside itself, and beyond itself. The first principle--*because it is* the first principle--moves on to a second principle.

With this positive meaning of the absolute character of the subject so articulated, the negative sense can now be seen. At this point, this absolute dimension does not mean that all that is, can be found in the subject and by the subject. This may be the case, but it has not been shown at this point in the *Grundlage*. In other words, Fichte has *not* indicated that to be an absolute subject means to have a vision of the absolute or to have absolute knowledge. There is not a vision nor an intellectual intuition of the I's identity with itself. The absolute subject does not know itself *absolutely* as might be the case for Schelling or for Hegel's understanding of Fichte. Here there is the I's being for itself; but by this, Fichte merely wants to express the identity of the self-affirmation of the I and its being. This had already been indicated a little while ago. The for-itself does not mean an intuition or a vision of itself; this is not the meaning of the absolute subject. That the "*I originally poses its own being absolutely*"(39) means that the I is a self and not a thing; but this distinction between the self and a thing already leads beyond the first principle. There is no way for determining the difference between that whose being is to affirm that being, and *that* which is opened up for that being. What is affirmed, however, is that the I is an identity from which all identity must spring.

This last sentence is most thought provoking because of the light it sheds on the notion of absolute subject. As Fichte has so emphatically indicated, the certainty of a logical proposition as a beginning has shown that this too is derived from and grounded in the self, in its self-identity. Fichte pursues this through two abstractions until he arrives at the category of reality. In and by this category, what is real emerges as that to which the identity expressed in "A=A" can be applied. "Everything to which the proposition A=A is applicable has reality *in so far as this proposition is applicable to it*"(40). This category defines what is real; and this is defined in terms of the applicability of identity. What does this mean?

An insight into the meaning of the real can be found in the very next sentence in which Fichte conjoins it with essence (*das Wesen*). What Fichte suggests is an identity of reality and the essence. "That which is posed by the mere posing of some thing (that which is posed in the I), is its reality, its essence"(41). This recalls the Kantian notion of real(42). By reality Fichte does not mean actuality, for reality is more closely related to essence.

Reality is related to the whatness of something, to that which constitutes something to be *this* unity as opposed to *that* unity. The issue is not the actual existence of something, but *what* something essentially is. It is a determination of something as to its thing-character and is that precondition which is demanded prior to any discussion of its actuality or non-existence. It is that unity which as an object over against me must confront me as a subject. In other words, reality is the determination of the object, is that aspect which guarantees the self-sameness necessary to speak even of existence or non-existence. Since this category of reality is founded on the identity of the I, there is necessarily presupposed and demanded a unity, a self-sameness, if anything as an object is to confront a subject. This has its ground in the subject. Only what is a unity, is a subject, can serve as the unity and identity of anything else. Thus, the subject is an absolute subject, i.e., one which is the ground of unity and identity. This subject is the ground for the real, but not necessarily the actual. Thus, the I is for itself: an identity of self-posing and being. Only because of the I as subject can there be an awareness of the real and what is not real; but again, this immediately leads to the second principle.

Nowhere in this present discussion has an intuiting vision of the identity of subject and object been encountered. Fichte does not begin the *Grundlage* with the intellectual intuition, i.e., with the I's grasping its own activity as its own; but he rather begins with the thinking of a *Tathandlung* as ground. A glimpse of the *Tathandlung* is obtained because the movement was from its derivative to the activity needed as ground. In the course of the text, this ground becomes the absolute I as an infinite task. In no place in the first principle is there an immediate vision of this activity. Since the *Grundlage* is a progressive reinterpretation of the "I am," the first principle is a thetic posing that takes place in a desert; and yet, the fullness of this will not have been regained until the practical sphere. Though the first principle is first, it is not immediately and intuitively last, but is mediated by the next two principles. Only then can philosophy begin, only then can a Wissenschaftslehre begin and proceed. At this point the act of freedom that asserts itself in the self-posing is not yet a freedom that is conscious of itself, that is conscious of its own being. This total self-consciousness is an infinite task and is the essential meaning of the absolute I; for the

> I demands that it encompass all reality in itself and that it fulfill the infinite. On this demand the idea of the absolutely posed infinite I necessarily lies as ground; and this is the *absolute* I of which we have been speaking. (Here the meaning of the proposition: *the I poses itself absolutely,* first becomes completely clear. . .)(43).

The *Grundlage* as a Grundlage

With the development of the two previous sections, it is now necessary to articulate the meaning of the *Grundlage* as a Grundlage. This articulation results from an understanding of Fichte's intellectual intuition. The discussion of that intuition presented an ambiguity between a methodological understanding and one that identifies the intuition with self-consciousness. This implies that the intellectual intuition should not be introduced until the very end of the *Grundlage*. This was justified by examining the Wissenschaftslehre of 1798 which begins with the intellectual intuition. The possibility of such a beginning is very closely related to the third principle of the *Grundlage*, i.e., to the *Grundlage's* conclusion.

In contrast to this, the *Grundlage* begins with the first principle which is not an intuition. It commences with a logical formula and reflectively thinks its necessary condition. It thinks an activity. This discussion led to a better understanding of the absolute subject, not as an intuition, but as an infinite and unattainable ideal.

The present task is to show how the *Grundlage* of 1794 can be understood, not as the whole system, but as an introduction to the system. Fichte's own division of his system or *Wissenschaftslehre* with particular emphasis on the *Grundlage* will be considered. Any conclusions or implications will then be drawn out(44).

In the last pages of the *Wissenschaftslehre 1798 nova methodo* the necessary divisions of the Wissenschaftslehre are described. Without giving a detailed analysis of the divisions, let us note that there are two main divisions: the Wissenschaftslehre of theory and the one of praxis. The former is an empirics that tries to show how the world is and must be, i.e., how the world is given. The latter is concerned with the individual in his moral concerns and dimensions. Here the question is how the world *should* be for rational beings. Further distinctions and divisions are made: logic, philosophy of religion, aesthetics.

The essential issue is how Fichte himself relates the *Grundlage* to the entire system.

> This Wissenschaftslehre must be contained in our *Grundlage*; and it is so contained, but only according to its main features. The particular science is distinguished from the whole in that the particular science proceeds to the determination of the individual which is contained in the main concept; and the universal science, on the contrary, remains situated within the main concept and its determinacy.
> ...Only the fundamental concepts belong in the *Grundlage*—not everything that emerges in consciousness; and so it has been. But all that is in consciousness must be found there by analysis of the fundamental concepts contained in the *Grundlage*(45).

Here Fichte explicitly makes a distinction between a *Grundlage* and the Wissenschaftslehre as a whole. A *Grundlage* would contain the main features and principles that the individual sciences take over and appropriate. In the *Grundlage* the fundamental concepts are developed and exposed in order that they might be further developed and analysed in the particular parts of the Wissenschaftslehre.

It can be said that the *Grundlage* articulates the *formal* dimensions for the Wissenschaftslehre whereas the individual parts or sciences furnish the *material* aspect. Consequently, one cannot identify the *Grundlage* with the entirety of the Wissenschaftslehre. This purely formal dimension of the *Grundlage* lays the foundation according to which any further deduction might be able to proceed. What is the foundation that is laid in the *Grundlage* for the other divisions of the Wissenschaftslehre?

As has been indicated, the *Grundlage* begins with the certainty of a logical proposition. It begins with discourse or language which can reflectively be traced back to its ground. With the first principle is discovered the ground for such a principle. From another perspective, it can be said that the *Grundlage* begins with an act of freedom. It begins with the posing of something. Both of these threads wind their way through the entire *Grundlage* towards more self-understanding and justification.

This dual aspect of language as logic and of the necessity of freedom can be seen in the I which is under explicit study throughout the *Grundlage*. Gradually in the dynamism of that work there comes an understanding that this I needs a check (*Anstoss*) for its own self-understanding. This I, seen essentially as the imagination, more and more comes to appropriate itself and its first act of freedom which had been exhibited at the outset in the posing of A=A. Within the movement of the *Grundlage*, the I comes to see its own freedom and its necessary conditions and limitations. As one author has pointed out, with the certainty from which the *Grundlage* begins and constantly tries to maintain and attain, there accompanies it a precarious situation where fallibility is as present as any certainty(46). *"So infallibel das Wissen ist, so fallibel ist dessen Nachkonstruktion"*(47). The *Grundlage* presents the reasons, or better yet, the necessary situation of every philosophical reflection.

Thus, in the development of the various parts of the system, there is always this precarious background. Each of the deductions, e.g., those of the *Naturrecht*, always stems from and returns to what has been laid down in the *Grundlage*. Consequently, the *Grundlage* is both an introduction and a foundation. One cannot enter the Wissenschaftslehre without going through the *Grundlage*, nor can one leave it behind. Thus, the Wissenschaftslehre is a continual beginning and re-beginning pragma of the charting of that movement toward self-understanding and self-consciousness; for, as philosophers, we are "pragmatic writers of the history" of the human spirit(48).

INTERSUBJECTIVITY AND REFLECTION

> *The positing of the self is not a given, it is a task; it is not* gegeben, *but* aufgegeben.
>
> -Ricoeur

The three issues of reflection, imagination, and intersubjectivity have become centralized in Fichte's philosophy. Within this full-fledged egology, however, the I in its transcendentality is essentially intersubjective. The task of this work has been to show that this intersubjective dimension is an essential constitutive of the I's I-hood.

The dynamics from reflection through the imagination to intersubjectivity can now be reversed. The initial innocence, which began merely with a descriptive discussion of the nature of philosophy, soon discovered philosophy's foundational character by which the ground of experience is laid bare. The issue of philosophy's foundational character recoiled onto the questioner himself. The questioner as questioned provokes an egological concern for exhibiting those necessary and essential structures. The I's structural unity of the transcendental imagination is also discovered as intersubjective. In this reversal, intersubjectivity will no longer be seen as emerging from the problematic of reflection, but now its centrality in the I-character will have shown the possibility and necessity for a finite reflection.

The problematic of intersubjectivity is situated between two apparently irreconcilable requirements. The first of these asserts and maintains an irreducibility between the I and the Other. Since both the I and the Other cannot be reduced to each other, an absolute chasm exists; and reflection cannot totally incorporate the Other in itself. The otherness of the Other must be respected by the I. The Other and the I can never meet nor exchange positions; each's interiority always remains an interiority that can never be penetrated by the other.

The concern for the Other *qua* Other is equally matched by the transcendental question of the presence of the Other. This is the question of the transcendental constitution of the Other. How does the I come to know this Other, come to encounter and to recognize the Other as an Other? A transcendentally reflective philosophy seeks the ground for the recognition of the Other in the very structures of the I.

Fichte's reflective philosophy has attempted a response to these two demands without becoming solipsistic nor absolutely idealistic. Fichte's response has shown that the I, in order to be itself, must transcend itself and go outside itself. That the I is essentially intersubjective has meant that the Other is essential for the I's I-hood; yet, this intersubjectivity cannot be taken up into the I's own subjectivity.

The essentially intersubjective dimension of the I came to the fore within the context of the imagination. Within that context, the I's necessary relatedness to a not-I had been discovered. The I's rootedness in a not-I was the condition for the I's realizing itself. The intersubjective character finds its possibility and necessity here in the imagination, which also shows the I's radical finitude. There must always remain a dimension which the I can never totally reach.

It was shown that the I's harmony with itself can never be reached. This finitude and negativity within the I brings together those two demands found in the problematic of intersubjectivity. With the intimations in the *Grundlage* and their subsequent explication in the *Wissenschaftslehre 1798 nova methodo*, the argument and interpretation reach culmination and even fruition. Both sides of the problematic are held together, yet distinguished, in that pertinent passage that unites the phenomenal and the noumenal. This dual dimension or perspective affirmed that You are You and that I am I.

The I's radical finitude is an essential feature of the I. Although the I's infinitude plays an important role, the finite character and its effect on reflection prevent Fichte's philosophy from becoming an absolute idealism. Within that reflective context of the imagination several connotations or aspects of the I's finitude emerged.

The various aspects come together in the notion of the I's *striving* and its connection with the primacy of the practical sphere. The I's striving is an unlimited activity of the I whereby the I incessantly attempts to overcome its lack and to attain harmony with itself. Within this context, finitude designates that lack to be contrasted with the infinite striving. Yet, this striving arose because the I has a *limited* or *checked* activity. The checked activity points to the I's *dependence*. For the I to be itself, it requires something other than itself; the I is dependent upon the not-I.

In addition to designating the striving's priority, the lack of harmony, the checked activity, and dependence on a not-I, the I's finitude is also an index of the I's radically temporal character. Temporality is the fundamental horizon for the unity of the I in its theoretical-practical dimension. This unity consists of the temporalizing imagination which is guided by the I's interest to be itself. Time as the fundamental unity of the I is the originary, horizonal unity whereby the I can *be* in its own meaningful world. The fundamental unity of the theoretical and the practical is the unity of the temporal ecstases of past, present, and future.

The I's activity, the imagination, is a temporalizing one in which and by which the I constitutes itself. This self-constitution is accomplished in terms of the I's tasks that have been projected from its "was." The I's activity is one of extending itself between these two horizons of past and future, neither of which can become a reified object. This temporal dimension is another account for the I's dependence and finitude.

The I's intimate link to time reaffirms the finitude of the I in several ways. First, temporality is the necessary perspective from which the I can come to understand itself. Self-consciousness has its condition of possibility in temporality. In other words, the I can never escape time in order to have a divine perspective or divine understanding of itself or of its world. Second, the temporal future of the I is limited and finite; for the future is the I itself. The I has an ultimate goal to be accomplished; its end is nothing but itself. Third, the very accomplishing of this task must take place in time. The I's interest to *be* is an interest to *be in time*. The I's absolute character is not atemporal, but achieves itself in and through the temporal domain.

Consequently, the *Grundlage* cannot begin with the intellectual intuition. If the I's inherently intersubjective character means that the I is thereby challenged and/or provoked to go outside itself to appropriate the meaning of its desire to be, then the problematic of the intellectual intuition remains. If reflection is not intuition, then the issue of such an intuition must be resolved. In the course of the last chapter, several related issues emerged. The intellectual intuition cannot be introduced at the beginning of the *Grundlage*, but is best located at the end where the I's unity becomes prominent. This prominence depends on the absence of a radical distinction between the theoretical and the practical spheres or on the fundamental unity that underlies the distinction. At this point the ambiguity of the intuition as active and passive can be best understood. The third foundational principle probably best articulates this unity of the I. This unity also indicates that the intellectual intuition is best located at the end of the *Grundlage*. This interpretation contrasts with those that locate the intuition at the beginning of the work and refer it to the first principle.

In another context, this intuition is not an envisioning nor a seeing that immediately grasps the totality or the absolute. Thus, reflection is permeated with finitude—a finitude that an intellectual intuition cannot eliminate. The philosophical act of reflection, always finite, but never absolute, is in the midst of the totality and never outside it.

NOTES

INTRODUCTION

1. Rene Descartes, *Meditations* (New York: Bobbs-Merrill, 1960), p. 19 according to the first French edition.

2. John C. Sallis, "On the Limitation of Transcendental Reflection or Is Intersubjectivity Transcendental?", *The Monist*, 55 (April, 1971): 314.

3. Ludwig Siep, *Hegels Fichtekritik und die Wissenschaftslehre von 1804* (Freiburg: Verlag Karl Alber, 1970), pp. 14-15.

4. Here we are following the more detailed division of Fichte's writings according to Julius Drechsler, *Fichtes Lehre vom Bild* (Stuttgart: Kohlhammer Verlag, 1955), pp. 31-37, but especially pp. 34-36.

CHAPTER ONE

1. Immanuel Kant, *Critique of Pure Reason* (New York: St. Martin's Press, 1965), B 373. Henceforth CPR with page number. Fichte's letter can be found in J.G. Fichte, *Ruf zur Tat. Sein Leben in Briefen und Berichten* (Berlin: Verlag der Nation, 1956), p. 62.

2. J.G. Fichte, *Sämmtliche Werke* (Berlin: Veit, 1845), I, 38. "Die Philosophie ist *eine Wissenschaft*." Henceforth S.W. with volume and page number.

3. S.W., I, 45: "*die Wissenschaft von einer Wissenschaft überhaupt.*"

4. S.W., I, 77: "Wir sind nicht Gesetzgeber des menschlichen Geistes, sondern seine Historiographen; freilich nicht Zeitungsschreiber, sondern pragmatische Geschichtsschreiber."

5. S.W., I, 80. "Das Ich als philosophirendes *Subject* ist unstreitig nur vorstellend; das Ich als *Object* des Philosophirens könnte wohl noch etwas mehr sein. Das Vorstellen ist die höchste und absolut-erste Handlung des Philosophen als solchen; die absolut-erste Handlung des menschlichen Geistes könnte wohl eine andere sein."

6. For this whole discussion confer the illuminating article of Jean Hyppolite, "L'idée fichtéene de la Doctrine de la science et le projet husserlien," *Husserl et la Pensée Moderne* (Den Haag: Martinus Nijhoff, 1959), pp. 173-82.

7. S.W., I, 44: "deren Möglichkeit bis jetzt bloss problematisch ist."

8. S.W., I, 58: "der Grundsatz notwendig auf *alle* aufgestellten Sätze führt, und *alle* aufgestellten Sätze notwendig wieder auf ihn zurückführen."

9. S.W., I, 59: "der Grundsatz selbst, von welchem wir ausgegangen wären, zugleich auch das letzte Resultat sei."

10. S.W., I, 61: "aus dem der menschliche Geist nie herausgehen kann."

11. S.W., I, 423-25.

12. S.W., I, 426: "so behält er ein Ding an sich, das heisst, abstrahiert davon, dass es in der Erfahrung vorkommt, als Erklärungsgrund der Erfahrung übrig." Our discussion relies heavily on the *Erste und Zweite Einleitung* even though there is mention of it throughout the *Grundlage*, esp. S.W., I, 171-91.

13. S.W., I, 426: "so behält er eine Intelligenz an sich, das heisst, abstrahiert von ihrem Verhältnis zur Erfahrung."

14. S.W., I, 430: "Nach ihm ist alles, was in unserem Bewusstsein vorkommt, Produkt eines Dinges an sich, sonach auch unsere vermeinten Bestimmungen durch Freiheit, mit der Meinung selbst, dass wir frei seien."

15. S.W., I, 510: "Nämlich, indem sie den Mechanismus *voraussetzen*, erheben sie sich über ihn; ihr Denken desselben ist etwas ausser ihm Liegendes. Der Mechanismus kann sich selbst nicht fassen, eben darum, weil er Mechanismus ist. Sich selbst fassen, kann nur das freie Bewusstsein."

16. S.W., I, 509 in footnote.

17. S.W., I, 441: "die Intelligenz handelt; aber sie kann vermöge ihres eigenen Wesens, nur auf eine gewisse Weise handeln."

18. S.W., I, 442: "kann daher durch nichts erhärten, dass seine postulierten Denkgesetze wirklich Denkgesetze, wirklich nichts als immanente Gesetze der Intelligenz sind."

19. S.W., I, 443: "Aber woher denn das, welches diese Verhältnisse und Beschaffenheiten hat; woher denn der Stoff, der in diese Formen aufgenommen wird?"

20. S.W., I, 91 f.

21. S.W., I, 59: "der Grundsatz selbst, von welchem wir ausgegangen wären, zugleich auch das letzte Resultat sei."

22. S.W., I, 43.

23. S.W., I, 49: "Dasjenige, von dem man etwas weiss, heisse indess der Gehalt, und das, was man davon weiss, die Form des Satzes."

24. S.W., I, 93-94.

25. S.W., I, 93: "*im* Ich, und *durch* das Ich."

26. S.W., I, 94: "Wenn A *im* Ich gesetzt ist, so *ist es gesetzt*; oder-so *ist es*."

27. S.W., I, 96: "Also das Setzen des Ich durch sich selbst ist die reine Tätigkeit desselben. —Das *Ich setzt sich selbst*, und es *ist*, vermöge dieses blossen Setzens durch sich selbst; und umgekehrt: Das Ich *ist*, und es *setzt* sein Sein vermöge seines blossen Seins."

28. S.W., I, 97.

29. S.W., I, 98: *"Das Ich setzt ursprünglich schlechthin sein eigenes Sein."*

30. S.W., I, 99.

31. S.W., I, 102: "Bedingung kann sich aus ihm gar nicht ergeben, da die Form des Gegensetzens in der Form des Setzens so wenig enthalten wird, dass sie ihr vielmehr selbst entgegengesetzt ist."

32. Ibid.: "-A ist *als* solches gesetzt schlechthin *weil* es gesetzt ist."

33. S.W., I, 103: "Mithin ist auch der Übergang vom Setzen zum Entgegensetzen nur durch die Identität des Ich möglich."

34. Ibid.: "Das Entgegengesetztsein überhaupt ist schlechthin durch das Ich gesetzt."

35. Ibid.: "es ist ein Handeln in Beziehung auf ein anderes Handeln."

36. S.W., I, 104.

37. S.W., I, 105: "um nur irgendeinen *Gegenstand* setzen zu können, muss ich es schon wissen; es muss sonach ursprünglich vor aller möglichen Erfahrung in mir selbst, dem Vorstellenden, liegen." This is only mentioned in the third edition of 1802.

38. S.W., I, 106-07.

39. S.W., I, 108: "wie lassen A und -A, Sein und Nicht-Sein, Realität und Negation sich zusammendenken, ohne dass sie sich vernichten und aufheben?"

40. S.W., I, 109: *"schlechthin das Ich sowohl als das Nicht-Ich teilbar gesetzt."*

41. Ibid.: "So wie dem Ich ein Nicht-Ich entgegengesetzt wird, wird demnach das Ich, *dem* entgegengesetzt wird, und das Nicht-Ich, *das* entgegengesetzt wird, teilbar gesetzt."

42. S.W., I, 110: *"Ich setze im Ich dem teilbaren Ich ein teilbares Nicht-Ich entgegen."*

43. Ibid.

44. S.W., I, 112-14.

45. S.W., I, 422: "Merke auf dich selbst: kehre deinen Blick von allem, was dich umgibt, ab, und in dein Inneres; ist die erste Forderung, welche die Philosophie an ihren Lehrling tut. Es ist von nichts, was ausser dir ist, die Rede, sondern lediglich von dir selbst."

46. Jean Nabert, *Elements for an Ethic* (Evanston: Northwestern University Press, 1969), p. 53. Also confer Paul Ricoeur, "Negativity and Primary Affirmation," *History and Truth* (Evanston: Northwestern University Press, 1965), pp. 305-28.

CHAPTER TWO

1. S.W., I, 194-95: "Weil das Ich einiges von sich ausschliessen soll, soll eine höhere Sphäre sein und gesetzt werden, und weil eine höhere Sphäre ist, und gesetzt ist, muss das Ich einiges von sich ausschliessen. Kürzer: es ist ein Nicht-Ich, weil das Ich sich einiges entgegensetzt; und das Ich setzt einiges entgegen, weil ein Nicht-Ich ist, und gesetzt wird. Keins begründet das andere, sondern beides ist eine und ebendieselbe Handlung des Ich."

2. S.W., I, 152: "der *Beziehungsgrund* zwischen Tun und Leiden im Wechsel."

3. S.W., I, 149: "Es wird eine Tätigkeit in das Ich gesetzt, der gar kein Leiden im Nicht-Ich entgegengesetzt wird, und eine Tätigkeit in das Nicht-Ich, der gar kein Leiden im Ich entgegengesetzt wird."

4. S.W., I, 166-67.

5. S.W., I, 167.

6. S.W., I, 191: "ein Nicht-Setzen durch ein absolutes Setzen;
    —das Setzen eines Etwas als *nicht gesetzt*, durch das
    Setzen eines andern als *gesetzt*:   Negation durch
    Affirmation."

7. S.W., I, 192: *"ein Ausschliessen von einer bestimmten,
    erfüllten, und insofern Totalität* (des darin enthaltenen)
    habenden Sphäre."

8. S.W., I, 184: *"Das Ich ist endlich, schlechthin weil es
    endlich ist."*

9. S.W., I, 191: "seine Sphäre bekommt dadurch schlechthin
    kein anderes Prädikat, als ein negatives."

10. S.W., I, 192: "Das Setzen einer solchen *höhern, beide, die
    bestimmte und unbestimmte, in sich fassenden Sphäre* wäre
    diejenige Tätigkeit, durch welche die soeben aufgestellte
    formale Tätigkeit möglich würde; mithin die Tätigkeit *der
    Materie."*

11. Confer S.W., I, 172 and 185.

12. S.W., I, 193: "ein Objekt setzen, und—sich nicht setzen,
    ist gleichbedeutend. . . .das Ich setzt ein Objekt, oder es
    schliesst etwas von sich aus, schlechthin weil es
    ausschliesst, und aus keinem höhern Grunde: durch dieses
    Ausschliessen nun wird erst die höhere Sphäre des *Setzens
    überhaupt* (davon abstrahiert, ob das Ich oder ein Nicht-Ich
    gesetzt werde) möglich."

13. S.W., I, 147: "diese Einschränkung auf etwas im Nicht-Ich,
    als die Ursache derselben, beziehen könne."

14. S.W., I, 194: das Ich ist überhaupt *setzend*; dass es unter
    einer gewissen Bedingung, wenn es nämlich das Nicht-Ich
    nicht setzt, *sich setzt."*

15. Confer S.W., I, 146.

16. S.W., I, 167-68.

17. S.W., I, 188: "das Ich...ist bloss das Gegenteil des Nicht-Ich und nichts weiter."

18. S.W., I, 199: "absoluter und relativer Grund der Totalitätsbestimmung sollen Eins und ebendasselbe sein; die Relation soll absolut, und das Absolut soll nichts weiter sein, als eine Relation."

19. S.W., I, 169. Although this is a freer rendering of the German text, what we have in mind is the following. "Sie *wechseln* notwendig und sie wechseln nur auf Eine mögliche schlechthin dadurch, *dass* sie wechseln, bestimmte Art."

20. S.W., I, 196: "Mithin wird zum Behuf der Möglichkeit des postulierten Wechsels die *Bestimmbarkeit* der Totalität, als solcher, vorausgesetzt; es wird vorausgesetzt, dass man beide Totalitäten an irgend etwas unterscheiden könne; und diese Bestimmbarkeit *ist die Materie des Wechsels.*"

21. Ibid.: "Die Totalität in beider Rücksicht ist Totalität."

22. S.W., I, 168.

23. S.W., I, 455: "Der erstere Standpunkt ist der rein spekulative, der letztere der des Lebens und der Wissenschaft (Wissenschaft im Gegensatze mit der Wissenschaft*lehre* genommen). Der letztere ist nur vom ersteren aus begreiflich; ausserdem hat er Realismus zwar Grund, denn er nötigt sich uns durch unsere Natur auf, aber er hat keinen *bekannten* und *verständlichen* Grund: der erstere ist aber auch nur lediglich dazu da, um den letzteren begreiflich zu machen. Der Idealismus kann nie *Denkart* sein, sondern er ist nur *Spekulation.*"

24. S.W., I, 77.

25. Confer S.W., I, 279-80.

26. S.W., I, 198: "es ist überhaupt gar kein Bestimmungsgrund möglich, als durch Relation."

27. Ibid.: "es gibt einen absoluten Grund der Totalität, und dieselbe ist nicht lediglich relativ."

28. S.W., I, 199: "die Relation soll absolut, und das Absolut soll nichts weiter sein, als eine Relation."

29. Ibid. Confer footnote 18 above in the present chapter for text.

30. Confer S.W., I, 199-204.

31. S.W., I, 204:   "die Totalität besteht bloss in der vollständigen Relation, und es gibt überhaupt nichts an sich Festes, was dieselbe bestimme. Die Totalität besteht in der Vollständigkeit eines *Verhältnisses*, nicht aber einer Realität."

32. S.W., I, 202.

33. S.W., I, 91-123, especially I, 91-101. Also confer this text of Chapter One, pp. 13-20 above.

34. S.W., I, 101-05.

35. S.W., I, 204:   "in der Substanz gar nichts Fixiertes zu denken ist, sondern ein blosser Wechsel."

36. Ibid.: "es ist nicht *absolut* fixiert."

37. S.W., I, 204 f.: "Dieses fast immer verkannte Vermögen ist es, was aus steten Gegensätzen eine Einheit zusammenknüpft, —was zwischen Momente, die sich gegenseitig aufheben müssten, eintritt, und dadurch beide erhält."

38. S.W., I, 205: "es ist dasjenige, was allein Leben und Bewusstsein, und insbesondere Bewusstsein als eine fortlaufende Zeitreihe möglich macht."

39. Ibid.:   "*durch ein absolutes Zusammenfassen und Festhalten Entgegengesetzter*, eines Subjektiven und Objektiven, *in dem Begriffe der Bestimmbarkeit*, in welchem sie doch auch entgegengesetzt sind."

40. Confer S.W., I, 204-05.

41. S.W., I, 207: "A ist nicht zu denken, und B ist nicht zu denken; aber das *Zusammentreffen, —Eingreifen* beider ist zu denken, und bloss dieses ist ihr Vereinigungspunkt."

42. Ibid.

43. Alexis Philonenko, *La Liberté humaine dans la philosophie de Fichte* (Paris: J. Vrin, 1966), pp. 291. Original is in italics. "On peut dire que selon l'activité indépendante on part de la conscience de soi, du sujet, tandis que selon le relation on part de la conscience de l'objet."

44. S.W., I, 209: "ein solches ist durch das Setzen des Ich schlechthin nicht gesetzt."

45. S.W., I, 210: "ein Anstoss für das Ich vorhanden sein, d.h. das Subjektive muss, aus irgendeinem nur ausser der Tätigkeit des Ich liegenden Grunde, nicht weiter ausgedehnt werden können."

46. S.W., I, 210-11 with italics added: "die Aufgabe für eine durch dasselbe selbst in sich vorzunehmende Bestimmung."

47. This important issue will be discussed in the last part of the present chapter in the section called "Striving and the Future." There the practical sphere of Fichte's *Grundlage* will be seen in relation to the imagination and to those comments in Section III.

48. S.W., I, 212: "Der (durch das setzende Ich nicht gesetzte) Anstoss geschieht auf das Ich, insofern es tätig ist, und er ist demnach nur insofern ein Anstoss, als es tätig ist; seine Möglichkeit wird durch die Tätigkeit des Ich bedingt: keine Tätigkeit des Ich, kein Anstoss. Hinwiederum wäre die Tätigkeit des Bestimmens des Ich durch sich selbst, bedingt durch den Anstoss: kein Anstoss, keine Selbstbestimmung. —Ferner, keine Selbstbestimmung, kein Objektives, usw."

49. S.W., I, 170-71: "Tätigkeit geht in sich zurück vermittelst des Wechsels; und der Wechsel geht in sich selbst zurück vermittelst der Tätigkeit. Alles reproduziert sich selbst,

und es ist da kein *Hiatus* möglich; von jedem Gliede aus wird man zu allen übrigen getrieben. Die Tätigkeit der Form bestimmt die der Materie, diese die Materie des Wechsels, diese seine Form; die Form dieses die Tätigkeit der Form usf. Sie sind alle ein und ebenderselbe synthetische Zustand. Die Handlung geht durch einen Kreislauf in sich zurück. Der ganze Kreislauf aber ist schlechthin gesetzt. Er ist, weil er ist, und es lässt sich kein höherer Grund desselben angeben."

50. S.W., I, 214:   *"keine Unendlichkeit, keine Begrenzung; keine Begrenzung, keine Unendlichkeit."*

51. Ibid.:   "Die Tätigkeit des Ich besteht im unbeschränkten Sich-Setzen: es geschieht gegen dieselbe ein Widerstand."

52. S.W., I, 214-15: "Das Ich ist nur das, als was es sich setzt. Es ist unendlich, heisst, es setzt sich unendlich: es *bestimmt* sich durch das Prädikat der Unendlichkeit: also es begrenzt sich selbst (das Ich), als Substrat der Unendlichkeit; es unterscheidet sich selbst von seiner unendlichen Tätigkeit (welches beides an sich eins und ebendasselbe ist); und so musste es sich verhalten, wenn das Ich unendlich sein sollte."

53. S.W., I, 215.   This description reminds one of the quotations on pages 44 and 45 above. "Dieser Wechsel des Ich in und mit sich selbst, da es sich endlich und unendlich zugleich setzt—ein Wechsel, der gleichsam in einem Widerstreite mit sich selbst besteht, und dadurch sich selbst reproduziert, indem das Ich Unvereinbares vereinigen will, jetzt das Unendliche in die Form des Endlichen aufzunehmen versucht, jetzt, zurückgetrieben, es wieder ausser derselben setzt, und in dem nämlichen Momente abermals es in die Form der Endlichkeit aufzunehmen versucht—ist das Vermögen der *Einbildungskraft.*"

54. Ibid.

55. Confer my article "Fichte and the Problem of Finitude," *The Southwestern Journal of Philosophy,* 7 (1976): 21-23.

56. S.W., I, 217:   "Dieses Schweben der Einbildungskraft zwischen Unvereinbaren, dieser Widerstreit derselben mit sich selbst ist es, welcher, ...den Zustand des Ich in demselben zu einem *Zeit*-Momente ausdehnt."

57. S.W., I, 409.

58. Confer S.W., I, 408-11.

59. S.W., I, 227:   "alle Realität...bloss durch die Einbildungskraft hervorgebracht werde.... auf jene Handlung der Einbildungskraft die Möglichkeit unsers Bewusstseins, unsers Lebens, unsers für uns, d.h. unsers Seins, als Ich, sich gründet."

60. Confer Philonenko, p. 287 footnote 139.

61. S.W., I, 127: "das Ich setzt sich, als bestimmt durch das Nicht-Ich." Confer S.W., I, 127-131.

62. Philonenko, p. 300. "L'intentionalité est donc ouverture au monde par et dans le temps. L'acte originaire, fondement de toute objectivité, est le Cogito, saisi dans la répétition de soi: *'ego sum, ego existo.'* Dans l'intentionalité comme source du temps, l'alterité à soi est fondée et par là est fondée toute forme d'alterité possible. Ainsi dans le mouvement par, lequel il se pose, le Moi se pose dans l'alterité dans la différence."

63. Confer my article "Fichte and the Problem of Finitude," pp. 16-21.

64. S.W., I, 264: "die Vernunft könne selbst nicht theoretisch sein, wenn sie nicht praktisch sei: es sei keine Intelligenz im Menschen möglich, wenn nicht ein praktisches Vermögen in ihm sei; die Möglichkeit aller Vorstellung gründe sich auf das letztere."

65. S.W., I, 277: "Ist kein praktisches Vermögen im Ich, so ist keine Intelligenz möglich."

66. S.W., I, 278: "ist das Ich nicht Intelligenz, so ist kein Bewusstsein seines praktischen Vermögens."

67. S.W., I, 256: "die gar kein Objekt hat, sondern in sich selbst zurückgeht."

68. Ibid.: "nicht unmittelbar auf sich selbst, sondern auf ein entgegenzusetzendes Nicht-Ich."

69. S.W., I, 261-62: "die reine in sich selbst zurückgehende Tätigkeit des Ich ist *in Beziehung auf ein mögliches Objekt ein Streben*: und zwar, laut obigen Beweise, *ein unendliches Streben*. Dieses unendliche Streben ist ins Unendliche hinaus die *Bedingung der Möglichkeit alles Objekts*: kein Streben, kein Objekt."

70. Confer my article "Fichte and the Problem of Finitude," pp. 16-21.

71. S.W., I, 259: "*der Möglichkeit eines solchen Setzens*."

72. Ibid.: "Nur *inwiefern* jener Tätigkeit widerstanden wird, kann ein Gegenstand gesetzt werden; und inwiefern ihr nicht widerstanden wird, ist kein Gegenstand."

73. S.W., I, 260: "sie *sollen* schlechthin gleich sein."

74. Ibid.: "Also, es wird die Übereinstimmung des Objekts mit dem Ich gefordert; und das absolute Ich, gerade um seines absoluten Seins willen, ist es, welches sie fordert."

75. Confer S.W., I, 326.

76. Confer S.W., I, 434.

CHAPTER THREE

1. Confer S.W., I, 279-81 for Fichte's development of this: "Der letzte Grund aller Wirklichkeit für das Ich ist demnach nach der Wissenschaftslehre eine ursprüngliche Wechselwirkung zwischen dem Ich und irgendeinem Etwas ausser demselben, von welchem sich weiter nichts sagen lässt, als dass es dem Ich völlig entgegengesetzt sein muss. In dieser Wechselwirkung wird in das Ich nichts gebracht, nichts Fremdartiges hineingetragen; alles was je bis in die Unendlichkeit hinaus in ihm sich entwickelt,

entwickelt sich lediglich aus ihm selbst nach seinen eignen
Gesetzen; das Ich wird durch jenes Entgegengesetzte bloss
in Bewegung gesetzt, um zu handeln, und ohne ein solches
erstes Bewegendes ausser ihm würde es nie gehandelt, und,
da seine Existenz bloss im Handeln besteht, auch nicht
existiert haben. Jenem Bewegenden kommt aber auch
nichts weiter zu, als dass es ein Bewegendes sei, eine
entgegengesetzte Kraft, die als solche auch nur gefühlt
wird.

Das Ich ist demnach abhängig seinem Dasein nach;
aber es ist schlechthin unabhängig in den Bestimmungen
dieses seines Daseins. Es ist in ihm, kraft seines absoluten
Seins, ein für die Unendlichkeit gültiges Gesetz dieser
Bestimmung, und es ist in ihm ein Mittelvermögen, sein
empirisches Dasein nach jenem Gesetze zu bestimmen.
Der Punkt, auf welchem wir uns selbst finden, wenn wir
zuerst jenes Mittelvermögens der Freiheit mächtig werden,
hängt nicht von uns ab; die Reihe, die wir von diesem
Punkte aus in alle Ewigkeit beschreiben werden, in ihrer
ganzen Ausdehnung gedacht, hängt völlig von uns ab.

Die Wissenschaftslehre ist demnach *realistisch*. Sie
zeigt, dass das Bewusstsein endlicher Naturen sich
schlechterdings nicht erklären lasse, wenn man nicht eine
unabhängig von denselben vorhandene, ihnen völlig
entgegengesetzte Kraft annimmt, von der dieselben ihrem
empirischen Dasein nach selbst abhängig sind. Sie
behauptet aber auch nichts weiter, als eine solche
entgegengesetzte Kraft, die von dem endlichen Wesen
bloss *gefühlt*, aber nicht *erkannt* wird. Alle möglichen
Bestimmungen dieser Kraft, oder dieses Nicht–Ich, die in
die Unendlichkeit hinaus in unserem Bewusstsein
vorkommen können, macht sie sich anheischig, aus dem
bestimmenden Vermögen des Ich abzuleiten, und muss
dieselben, so gewiss sie Wissenschaftslehre ist, wirklich
ableiten können.

Ohnerachtet ihres Realismus aber ist diese
Wissenschaft nicht transzendent, sondern bleibt in ihren
innersten Tiefen *transzendental*. Sie erklärt allerdings
alles Bewusstsein aus einem unabhängig von allem
Bewusstsein Vorhandnen; aber sie vergisst nicht, dass sie
auch in dieser Erklärung sich nach ihren eignen Gesetzen
richte, und so wie sie hierauf reflektiert, wird jenes
Unabhängige abermals ein Produkt ihrer eignen Denkkraft,
mithin etwas vom Ich Abhängiges, insofern es für das Ich

(im Begriff davon) da sein soll. . . .Alles ist seiner Idealität nach abhängig vom Ich, in Ansehung der Realität aber ist das Ich selbst abhängig; aber es ist nichts real für das Ich ohne auch ideal zu sein; mithin ist in ihm Ideal- und Realgrund Eins und ebendasselbe, und jene Wechselwirkung zwischen dem Ich und Nicht-Ich ist zugleich eine Wechselwirkung des Ich mit sich selbst."

English translation: "The last ground of all reality for the I is, then according to the Wissenschaftslehre, an original inter-working between the I and something other, outside the I, of which nothing more can be said than it must be completely opposed to the I. In this mutual reciprocity nothing is brought into the I, nothing foreign is imported; everything that is developed in it, is infinitely developed out of itself according to its own laws. By that opposed, the I is merely set in motion in order to act; and without such a first external moving, it would never have acted. Since its existence consists only in acting, it would have not existed. But to that moving, nothing is ascribed to it except that it is a mover, an opposed force that is only felt as such.

The I is, therefore, dependent as to its existence; but it is absolutely independent in the determination of its own existence. Because of its absolute being, the I contains an infinitely valid law for these determinations, and a mediating power to determine its empirical existence according to this law. The point where we find ourselves when we first become the master of the mediating power of freedom does not depend on ourselves; considered in its full extension, the series which, from this point onwards, we will describe to all eternity, is completely dependent on ourselves.

The Wissenschaftslehre is, therefore, *realistic*. It shows that the consciousness of those things finite is absolutely inexplicable if one does not presume a force existing independent of and completely opposed to them. On this force, they are themselves dependent according to their empirical existence. But the Wissenschaftslehre affirms nothing more than such an opposed force, which is merely *felt* by the finite being, but not *known*. All possible determinations of this force or this not-I, which can come infinitely into our consciousness, the Wissenschaftslehre undertakes to derive from the determining capacity of the I, and must really be able to derive them—as certain as it is a Wissenschaftslehre.

Nowithstanding its realism, this science, however, is not transcendent, but remains in its innermost depths *transcendental.* It accounts, of course, for all consciousness out of something present that is independent of all consciousness; but it does not forget that it is also guided in this explanation according to its own laws; and so as it reflects on this, that independent becomes a product of its own thought-force, therefore, becomes something dependent on the I in so far as it should be there for the I (in the concept of it). ...Everything is according to its ideality dependent on the I; but in view of its reality, the I itself is dependent; but there is nothing real for the I unless it is also ideal. Therefore, in it the ideal and the real ground are one and the same; and that mutual reciprocity between the I and the not-I is at the same time an inter-working of the I with itself."

2. S.W., III, 40: "Die Realität der Welt—es versteht sich für uns, d.h. für alle endliche Vernunft—ist Bedingung des Selbstbewusstseins."

3. S.W., III, 52: "Das deduzierte Verhältnis zwischen vernünftigen Wesen, dass jedes seine Freiheit durch den Begriff der Möglichkeit der Freiheit des anderen beschränke, unter der Bedingung, dass das erstere die seinige gleichfalls durch die des anderen beschränke, heisst das *Rechtverhältnis.* . . .

Dieses Verhältnis ist aus dem Begriffe des Individuums deduziert."

4. S.W., III, 20: "dass nämlich eine in sich zurückgehende Tätigkeit sei oder eine solche die ihren letzten Grund im Vernunftwesen selbst habe, dass diese endlich sei, und begrenzt, und dass sie als begrenzte, d.h. im Gegensatze und Beziehung mit dem Begrenzenden gesetzt werde, als welches bloss dadurch, dass überhaupt über sie reflektiert wird, geschieht."

5. S.W., III, 33: "so gewiss hat es den Begriff von seiner eigenen Freiheit, und Selbstständigkeit, und zwar als einer

von aussen gegebenen. Es bekommt den Begriff seiner freien Wirksamkeit, nicht als etwas das in gegenwärtigen Moment *ist*, . . .sondern als etwas, das im künftigen sein *soll*."

6. S.W., III, 37: "eine vernünftige Ursache, so gewiss sie dies ist, entwirft sich den Begriff von Produkte, das durch ihre Tätigkeit realisiert werden soll, und nach welchem es sich im Handeln richtet, und gleichsam auf denselben unablässig hinsieht."

7. S.W., III, 38: "Ein sicheres Kriterium der Wirkung eines vernünftigen Wesens wäre demnach dieses, dass die Wirkung sich nur unter Bedingung einer Erkenntnis des Objekts derselben als möglich denken liesse. Nun aber ist nichts, was sich nicht durch blosse Naturkraft, sondern lediglich durch Erkenntnis, als möglich denken lässt, als die Erkenntnis selbst. Wenn sonach das Objekt, und hier, auch der Zweck einer Wirkung nur der sein könnte, eine Erkenntnis hervorzubringen, dann wäre notwendig eine vernünftige Ursache der Wirkung anzunehmen."

8. S.W., III, 39: "Das vernünftige Wesen kann sich nicht setzen, als ein solches, es geschehe denn auf dasselbe eine Aufforderung zum freien Handeln. . . .Geschieht aber eine solche Aufforderung zum Handeln auf dasselbe, so muss es notwendig ein vernünftiges Wesen ausser sich setzen als die Ursache derselben. . . ."

9. Ibid.

10. S.W., III, 42: "Das, was ausschliessend in dieser Sphäre wählte, ist *sein* Ich, ist das Individuum, das durch Entgegensetzung mit einem anderen vernünftigen Wesen bestimmte Vernunftwesen; und dasselbe ist charakterisiert durch eine bestimmte, ihm ausschliessend zukommende Ausserung der Freiheit."

11. This will be dealt with more specifically and in greater detail in the subsequent section based on the *Grundlage* of 1794.

12. S.W., III, 43: "Das Wesen ausser dem Subjekte hat, vorausgesetztermassen, das letztere durch seine Handlung

zum freien Handeln aufgefordert; es hat demnach seine
Freiheit beschränkt durch einen Begriff vom Zwecke, in
welchem die Freiheit des Subjekts—wenn auch etwas nur
problematisch—vorausgesetzt wurde; es hat sonach seine
Freiheit beschränkt durch den Begriff von der (formalen)
Freiheit des Subjektes."

13. S.W., III, 44: "Die Erkenntnis des Einen Individuums, vom
anderen, ist bedingt dadurch, dass das andere es als ein
freies behandele, (d.i. seine Freiheit beschränke durch den
Begriff der Freiheit des ersten). . . .Das Verhältnis freier
Wesen zueinander ist daher das Verhältnis einer
Wechselwirkung durch Intelligenz und Freiheit. Keines
kann das andere anerkennen, wenn nicht beide sich
gegenseitig anerkennen: und keines kann das andere
behandeln als ein freies Wesen, wenn nicht beide sich
gegenseitig so behandeln."

14. Confer S.W., III, 44-56.

15. S.W., III, 51-52: "Die Freiheit wird daher immer in die
Zukunft gesetzt; und wenn sie den Charakter eines Wesens
ausmachen soll; für *alle* Zukunft des Individuums; sie wird
in der Zukunft gesetzt, soweit das *Individuum selbst* in ihr
gesetzt wird."

16. S.W., III, 51: "so gewiss ich mich als Individuum setze, so
gewiss mute ich allen mir bekannten vernünftigen
Wesen, in allen Fällen des gegenseitigen Handelns an, mich
selbst für ein vernünftiges Wesen anzuerkennen."

17. S.W., III, 240 with italics added. "Die Tätigkeit des
Angeschauten in der Wechselwirkung, insofern sie auf das
Anschauende geht, wird gleichfalls bestimmt durch eine *in
sich selbst zurückgehende Tätigkeit*, durch die es sich zur
Einwirkung auf das Anschauende bestimmt."

18. S.W., III, 241 with italics added. "Kein Leiden im
Anschauenden, keine ursprüngliche und in sich
zurückgehende Tätigkeit *im Objekte*, als gedachte
Tätigkeit. Keine solche Tätigkeit *im Objekte*, kein Leiden
im Anschauenden. . . . Die *innere Tätigkeit des Objekts*,
wodurch es sich bestimmt zur Wirksamkeit, ist ein bloss
Gedachtes."

19. S.W., III, 258: ". . .einen Gegenstand, wohin auch in der Unendlichkeit es ihn setzen möge, und setzt dadurch eine ausser ihm liegende und von seiner Tätigkeit (des Setzens) nicht abhängende, sondern vielmehr ihr entgegengesetzte Tätigkeit. Diese entgegengesetzte Tätigkeit muss allerdings in einem gewissen Sinne (ununtersucht in welchem) *im Ich liegen*, insofern sie darin gesetzt ist; sie muss aber auch in einem anderen Sinne (gleichfalls ununtersucht in welchem) *im Gegenstande liegen*."

20. S.W., I, 220: "leeren Formular-Philosophie."

21. S.W., I, 220-21: "Berufung auf Fakta, die innerhalb des Umfangs des gemeinen, durch kein philosophische Reflexion geleiteten Bewusstseins liegen."

22. S.W., I, 221: "man zu der Überzeugung gelangt ist, dass sie als Fakta vorhanden."

23. Ibid.: "das Ich muss sich jenes Faktum erklären; aber es kann dasselbe sich nicht anders erklären, als nach den Gesetzen seines Wesens, welches die gleichen Gesetze sind, nach denen auch unsere bisherige Reflexion angestellt worden."

24. Ibid.: "Die Spontaneität des menschlichen Geistes war es welche den Gegenstand der Reflexion sowohl—eben jene Denkmöglichkeiten, jedoch nach dem Regeln eines erschöpfenden synthetischen Systems—, als die Form der Reflexion, die Handlung des Reflektierens selbst, hervorbrachte."

25. S.W., I, 222: "Mithin wird in der künftigen Reflexionsreihe der Gegenstand der Reflexion nicht erst durch die gleiche Reflexion selbst *hervorgebracht*, sondern bloss *zum Bewusstsein* erhoben."

26. S.W., I, 244-45: "vom dem Kinde an, das zum ersten Mal seine Wiege verlässt, und sie dadurch von sich selbst unterscheiden lernt, bis zum popularen Philosophen, der noch materielle Ideen-Bilder annimmt, und nach dem Sitze der Seele fragt, und bis zum transzendentalen Philosophen, der wenigstens die Regel, ein reines Ich zu denken, sich denkt, und sie erweist."

27. Confer the following: Philonenko, pp. 317-332; Balduin Noll, *Kants und Fichtes Frage nach dem Ding* (Frankfurt am Main: Klostermann, 1936), pp. 157-211; Martial Guéroult, *L'évolution et la Structure de la Doctrine de la Science chez Fichte* (Paris: Société d'Édition, 1930), I, 225-38.

28. S.W., I, 337-38: "*Thetisch*, inwiefern sie, eine, schlechterdings nicht wahrzunehmende, entgegengesetzte Tätigkeit ausser dem Ich setzt. . . .*Antithetisch*, inwiefern sie durch Setzen oder Nicht-Setzen der Bedingung eine und ebendieselbe Tätigkeit des Ich ihr selbst entgegensetzt. *Synthetisch*, inwiefern sie durch das Setzen der entgegengesetzten Tätigkeit *als* einer zufälligen Bedingung, jene Tätigkeit als eine und ebendieselbe setzt."

29. S.W., I, 229: "*das Ich soll sich setzen, als anschauend.*"

30. S.W., I, 230: "Das produzierende Vermögen ist immer die Einbildungskraft; also jenes Setzen des Angeschauten geschieht durch die Einbildungskraft, und ist selbst ein Anschauen."

31. S.W., I, 232: "Es ist die Frage, wie der menschliche Geist ursprünglich zu einer Unterscheidung zwischen einer Reflexion der Tätigkeit von aussen, und einer andern von innen komme."

32. S.W., I, 233: "muss wenigstens das Produkt des Zustandes in der Anschauung, die Spur der entgegengesetzten Richtungen, welche keine von beiden, sondern etwas aus beiden Zusammengesetztes ist, bleiben."

33. Confer S.W., I, 233-34.

34. S.W., I, 233: "das Vermögen, worin ein Wandelbares besteht, gleichsam verständigt wird (gleichsam zum Stehen gebracht wird). . . .Der Verstand ist Verstand, bloss insofern etwas in ihm fixiert ist; und alles, was fixiert ist, ist bloss im Verstande fixiert. Der Verstand lässt sich als die durch Vernunft fixierte Einbildungskraft oder als die durch Einbildungskraft mit Objekten versehene Vernunft beschreiben."

35. S.W., I, 349: "Das *Angeschaute* ist das Ich, inwiefern es empfindet. Das *Anschauende* gleichfalls das Ich, das aber über sein Anschauen nicht reflektiert, noch insofern es anschaut, darüber reflektieren kann."

36. S.W., I, 235: "Die Einbildungskraft in ihrer gegenwärtigen Funktion produziert nicht, sondern fasst bloss auf (zum Setzen im Verstande, nicht etwa zum Aufbehalten) das schon Produzierte und im Verstande Begriffene, und heisst daher reproduktiv."

37. Confer S.W., I, 229.

38. S.W., I, 236: "Diese entgegengesetzte Richtung muss, insofern die im Anschauen vorhandene dadurch bestimmt werden soll, selbst angeschaut werden; und so ist denn mit der Bestimmung des Anschauenden zugleich eine, aber nicht reflektierte, Anschauung des *Angeschauten* vorhanden.

Aber das Angeschaute selbst muss *als* ein Angeschautes bestimmt werden, wenn es dem Anschauenden entgegengesetzt werden soll."

39. Ibid.: "absolutes Produkt der Tätigkeit des Ich."

40. S.W., I, 237: "Sie verhalten sich gegenseitig wie Tätigkeit und Leiden (Realität und Negation), und sind demnach vereinigt durch Wechselbestimmung. Kein Angeschautes, kein Anschauendes, und umgekehrt. Hinwiederum, wenn und inwiefern ein Angeschautes gesetzt ist, ist ein Anschauendes gesetzt und umgekehrt."

41. Ibid.: "Eines von beiden aber muss aus dem gleichen Grunde *durch sich selbst*, und nicht durch das andere, bestimmt werden."

42. S.W., I, 238: "Grenze der reinen und der objektiven Tätigkeit, wird angeschaut durch die Einbildungskraft, fixiert im Verstande."

43. S.W., I, 367: "fühlt sich begrenzt, oder es ist in ihm ein Gefühl der Begrenztheit, des Nichtkönnens oder des Zwanges vorhanden."

44. In addition to S.W., I, 237-39 also confer S.W., I, 367-69.

45. The word *infinite* will be used in two different senses. In the one case, infinite understood as free and spontaneous is contrasted with finite understood as limited. Within this finite or definite sphere, there is also a great number of possibilities—an infinite number that cannot be counted. In this latter connotation, the infinite number of possibilities is always already determined by the boundaries outlined by the finite. In this case, the finite and the infinite are not opposed notions whereas in the former case, these two notions are completely opposite because in that case, infinite means unbounded, free, and completely open-ended.

46. Confer S.W., I, 369-71.

47. S.W., I, 239: "Wechselwirkung der Selbstaffektion des Anschauenden, und einer Affektion von aussen ist die Bedingung, unter der das Anschauende ein Anschauendes ist."

48. S.W., I, 240: "ist die Tätigkeit zur Selbstbestimmung Bestimmung eines fixierten Produkts der Einbildungskraft im Verstande durch die Vernunft: mithin ein *Denken*."

49. S.W., I, 242: "das bis jetzt freie Vermögen, über schon im Verstande gesetzte Objekte zu reflektieren, oder von innen zu abstrahieren, und sie, nach Massgabe dieser Reflexion oder Abstraktion, mit weiterer Bestimmung im Verstande zu setzen." Also confer S.W., I, 373.

50. S.W., I, 242: "Nichts im Verstande, keine Urteilskraft; keine Urteilskraft, nichts im Verstande *für den Verstand*, kein Denken des Gedachtes, als eines solchen."

51. S.W., I, 375: "Dies ist das *wirkliche Ding*, nach welchem das bildende Ich in Entwerfung seines Bildes sich richtet, und das ihm daher bei seinem Bilden notwendig vorschweben muss."

52. Ibid.: "bewusstseinlos Anschauung des Dinges."

53. Ibid.: "beziehbar auf das im Bilden handelnde Ich."

54. S.W., I, 376-77: "Diese Anschauung ist ohne Bewusstsein, gerade aus dem gleichen Grunde, aus welchem sie vorhanden ist, weil das Ich nicht doppelt handeln, mithin nicht auf zwei Gegenstände zugleich reflektieren kann. Es wird im gegenwärtigen Zusammenhange betrachtet, als setzend sein Produkt, *als* solches, oder als bildend; es kann sich demnach nicht zugleich setzen, als unmittelbar das Ding anschauend."

55. S.W., I, 379: "Das Ich müsste demnach wenigstens mittelbar im Bewusstsein vorkommen, und so würde eine Unterscheidung des Bildes vom Dinge möglich werden."

56. S.W., I, 380: "Das seiner Beschaffenheit nach zufällige Ding aber entdeckt sich eben dadurch als ein vorausgesetztes Produkt des Ich, dem nichts zukommt, als das Sein."

57. S.W., I, 243: "Nur das als denkbar Beurteilte kann als Ursache der Anschauung gedacht werden."

58. S.W., I, 282-83 with italics added: "Das Resultat dieser Untersuchung würde sein, dass wir unserm Gegner in die Unendlichkeit hinaus keinen einzigen Moment würden aufzeigen können, in welchem nicht für das Streben des Ich eine unabhängige Realität ausser dem Ich vorhanden wäre; er aber auch uns keinen, in welchem nicht diese unabhängige Nicht-Ich vorgestellt, und auf diese Art von dem Ich abhängig gemacht werden könnte. Wo liegt nun das unabhängig Nicht-Ich unsers Gegners, oder sein Ding-an-sich. . .? *Offenbar nirgends und allenthalben zugleich.* . . .Auf dieses Verhältnis des Dinges an sich zum Ich gründet sich der ganze Mechanismus des menschlichen und aller endlichen Geister. Dieses verändern wollen, heisst, alles Bewusstsein, und mit ihm alles Dasein aufheben."

59. In this connection confer Martin Heidegger, *What is a Thing?* (Chicago: Gateway Edition, 1967), pp. 153-65.

60. Confer Noll, pp. 195-202.

61. Confer S.W., I, 277. The relationship of the first principle to the practical sphere is discussed in Chapter Four, "The First Principle as a Starting Point."

62. Confer S.W., I, 242-43.

63. S.W., I, 240-1. Confer footnote 17 and 18 of this chapter
for the German text.

64. S.W., I, 241: "Die innere Tätigkeit des Objekts wodurch es
sich bestimmt zur Wirksamkeit, ist ein bloss Gedachtes
(ein *Noumen*, wenn man dieser Tätigkeit durch die
Einbildungskraft ein Substrat gibt, wie man es muss)."

65. J.G. Fichte, *Wissenschaftslehre 1798 nova methodo,
Nachgelassene Schriften* (Berlin, 1937), II, 596.
Henceforth N.S. with volume and pagination. "Es wird
sonach ein notwendig freies Handeln gedacht als der Grund
einer in uns vorkommenden Aufforderung. Dieses
Bestimmende und Bestimmbare ist wirklich ein freies
Wesen ausser mir, denn das bestimmende ist notwendig
frei, da das Gefundene ein Handeln sein soll. Aber als
Handeln wird es auf diesem Gesichtspunkte lediglich aus
einer freien Intelligenz erklärt. Der gemeine
Menschenverstand schliesst hier gleich so, er sagt: Ich
werde gefragt, es muss also ein fragender da sein. Der
gemeine Menschenverstand hat hier ganz recht, weil er
hier in der Sphäre der Erscheinung steht. Wenn er aber
auch in andern Fällen so schliessen will, so hat er
unrecht. Scholastisch ausgedrückt ist hier ein Übergehen
von Bestimmbarkeit zur Bestimmtheit. In der Mitte ist
das Bestimmende, welches den Übergang macht. Also von
der Aufforderung zur freien Tätigkeit wird nach den
Gesetzen des Denkens geschlossen auf eine freie
Intelligenz ausser mir. Das Handeln erscheint mir, aber
die Intelligenz, von der es kommt, erscheint mir nicht.
Die freie Intelligenz wird also nur gedacht, sie ist ein
Noumen. Die freie Intelligenz ausser mir ist daher ganz
bestimmt das Gegenstück von mir selbst; nur komme ich
zu ihr auf einem andern Wege (nämlich durch Aufsteigen)
als zu mir selbst. Bei mir gehe ich aus von mir selbst und
steige dadurch, dass ich bevor den Zweckbegriff entwerfe,
erst hinab zu meinem freien Handeln. Hier aber bei dem
freien Wesen ausser mir steige ich von der Handlung, die
erscheint, zu der Ursache derselben, zu einem freien
Wesen ausser mir, welches ich nicht finde, sondern nur
schliesse, denke. Dieses ist der Grund, warum Ich nicht
Du bin, und Du nicht Ich. Ich bin derjenige, der sich selbst

unmittelbar *Noumen* ist und versinnlicht handeln wird. Du bist derjenige, der mir als *Noumen* nicht unmittelbar vorkommt, sondern sich mir nur in einer Erscheinung zeigt, von der ich erst fortschliesse auf das *Noumen*."

66. S.W., I, 244: "Bleibt demnach nichts übrig, als überhaupt die blosse Regel der Vernunft, zu abstrahieren, das blosse Gesetz einer nicht zu realisierenden Bestimmung (durch Einbildungskraft, und Verstand für das deutlich Bewusstsein)."

67. Ibid.: "das sich *selbst Bestimmende*, und durch sich *selbst Bestimmte*, das Ich."

68. S.W., I, 243: "Das Denkende soll sich selbst bestimmen, etwas als denkbar zu denken, und insofern wäre das Denkbare leidend; aber hinwiederum soll das Denkbare sich selbst bestimmen, ein Denkbares zu sein; und insofern wäre das Denkende leidend."

69. S.W., I, 244: "Das Ich aber ist jetzt als dasjenige bestimmt, welches, nach Aufhebung alles Objekts durch das absolute Abstraktionsvermögen, übrig bleiben; und das Nicht-Ich als dasjenige, von welchem durch jenes Abstraktionsvermögen abstrahiert werden kann."

70. In this connection confer the next chapter as well as my two articles "Fichte and the Problem of Finitude," pp. 15-33 and "Intellectual Intuition and the Beginning of Fichte's Philosophy: A New Interpretation," *Tijdschrift voor Filosofie*, 37 (maart, 1975): 52-73.

CHAPTER FOUR

1. G.W.F. Hegel, *Differenz des Fichte'schen und Schelling'schen Systems der Philosophie, Werke in zwanzig Bänden* (Frankfurt am Main: Suhrkamp Verlag, 1970), II, 52. "Die Grundlage des *Fichteschen Systems* ist intellektuelle Anschauung, reines Denken seiner selbst, reines Selbstbewusstsein Ich=Ich, Ich bin; das Absolute ist Subjekt-Objekt, und Ich ist diese Identität des Subjekts und Objekts."

2. S.W., I, 422: "Merke auf dich selbst: kehre deinen Blick von allem, was dich umgibt, ab, und in dein Inneres; ist die erste Forderung, welche die Philosophie an ihren Lehrling tut. Es ist von nichts, was ausser dir ist, die Rede, sondern lediglich von dir selbst."

3. S.W., I, 457-58: "Selbstbewusstsein und Bewusstsein eines Etwas, das nicht wir selbst—sein solle, sei notwendig verbunden."

4. S.W., I, 463.

5. S.W., I, 459.

6. Ibid.: "Das Ich wird durch den beschriebenen Akt bloss in die Möglichkeit des Selbstbewusstseins, und mit ihm alles übrigen Bewusstseins versteht."

7. S.W., I, 528: "Also das Selbstbewusstsein ist unmittelbar; in ihm Subjektives und Objektives unzertrennlich vereinigt und absolut Eins.
Ein solches unmittelbares Bewusstsein heisst mit dem wissenschaftlichen Ausdrucke eine *Anschauung*."

8. S.W., I, 466: "Nur dieses Medium des Sittengesetzes erblicke ich *mich*; und erblicke ich mich dadurch, so erblicke ich mich notwendig, als selbsttätig."

9. S.W., I, 467: "Ich *soll* in meinem Denken vom reinen Ich ausgehen, und dasselbe absolut selbsttätig denken."

10. S.W., I, 515: "des Ich, als intellektueller Anschauung von welchem die Wissenschaftslehre ausgeht, und des Ich, als Idee, mit welchem sie schliesst. Im Ich, als intellektueller Anschauung, liegt lediglich die Form der Ichheit, das in sich zurückgehende Handeln, welches freilich auch selbst zum Gehalte desselben wird."

11. Ibid.: "als Idee, ist das Vernuftwesen, inwiefern es die allgemeine Vernunft teils in sich selbst vollkommen dargestellt hat, wirklich durchaus vernünftig, und nichts als vernünftig ist."

12. Kant, *CPR*, B 72.

13. Ibid., B 159.

14. S.W., I, 472: "Die intellektuelle Anschauung, von welcher die Wissenschaftslehre redet, geht gar nicht auf ein Sein, sondern auf ein Handeln, und sie ist bei Kant gar nicht bezeichnet (ausser, wenn man will, durch den Ausdruck *reine Apperzeption*)."

15. Kant, *CPR*, B 135-36.

16. S.W., I, 476-77: "S. 132 sagt er: 'Diese Vorstellung: Ich denke, ist ein Aktus der Spontaneität, d.i. sie kann nicht als zur Sinnlichkeit gehörig, angesehen werden.' ...'Ich nenne sie die reine Apperzeption, um sie von der empirischen (soeben angeführten) zu unterscheiden, weil sie dasjenige Selbstbewusstsein ist, was, indem es die Vorstellung: Ich denke, hervorbringt, die alle andern muss begleiten können, *und in allem Bewusstsein, ein und dasselbe ist*, von keiner weiter begleitet werden kann.' Hier ist die Natur des reinen Selbstbewusstseins klar beschrieben. ...

     Nach der Wissenschaftslehre ist alles Bewusstsein durch das Selbstbewusstsein bestimmt, d.h. alles, was im Bewusstsein vorkommt, ist durch die Bedingungen des Selbstbewusstseins begründet, gegeben, herbeigeführt."

17. S.W., I, 529: "Ich bin diese Anschauung und schlechthin nichts weiter, und diese Anschauung selbst ist Ich."

18. S.W., I, 471: "Die Wissenschaftslehre geht...aus von einer intellektuellen Anschauung, der absoluten Selbsttätigkeit des Ich."

19. S.W., I, 506: "Wenn dieses Vermögen der Freiheit nicht schon da ist, und geübt ist, kann die Wissenschaftslehre nichts mit dem Menschen anfangen."

20. N.S., II, 343: "Und zwar nach einem ganz entgegengesetzten Gange seines Kompendiums von 1794. Wo er vom theoretischen, das ist dem, was erklärt werden soll, zum praktischen Teil der Philosophie, das ist, woraus jenes erklärt werden soll, übergeht. In seinen Vorlesungen findet aber die bisher gewöhnliche Abteilung der Philosophie in theoretische und praktische nicht statt.

Sondern er trägt Philosophie überhaupt vor, theoretische und praktische vereinigt, fängt nach einem weit natürlicheren Gange vom praktischen an, oder zieht da, wo es zur Deutlichkeit was beiträgt, das praktische ins theoretische herüber, um aus jenem dieses zu erklären. Eine Freiheit, die der Verfasser sich damals, als er seine Wissenschaftslehre in Druck gab, sich noch nicht herauszunehmen getraute."

21. S.W., I, 126: "warum die Reflexion vom theoretischen Teile ausgehen müsse; ohngeachtet sich im Verfolg zeigen wird, dass nicht etwa das theoretische Vermögen das praktische, sondern dass umgekehrt das praktische Vermögen erst das theoretische möglich mache, (dass die Vernunft an sich bloss praktisch sei, und dass sie erst in der Anwendung ihrer Gesetze auf ein sie einschränkendes Nicht-Ich theoretisch werde). —Sie ist es darum, weil die *Denkbarkeit* des praktischen Grundsatzes sich auf die Denkbarkeit des theoretischen Grundsatzes gründet."

22. N.S., II, 355: "bei der Vorstellung meines Ichs ist das Denkende und Gedachte ebendasselbe—im Begriffe des Ichs. *Ich* bin das Denkende und Gedachte. . .hier aber geht die Tätigkeit auf mich selbst zurück."

23. Ibid.: "indem ich auf mich selbst handle, mich selbst setze, dass meine Tätigkeit in mich selbst zurückgeht, kommt das Ich hervor, denke ich mein Ich; und beides: Ich bin Ich und ich setze mich als Ich, erschöpft sich gegenseitig."

24. S.W., I, 533: "denke dich; und du das letztere Wort verstandest, vollzogst du *im Akte des Verstehens selbst* die in sich zurückgehende Tätigkeit, durch welche der Gedanke des Ich zustande kommt, nur ohne es zu wissen, weil du darauf nicht besonders aufmerksam warst; und daher kam dir das, was du in deinem Bewusstsein vorfandest. Merke auf, wie du das machst, sagte ich dir ferner; und nun vollzogst du dieselbe Tätigkeit, die du schon vollzogen hattest, nur mit Aufmerksamkeit und Bewusstsein.

Man nennt die innere Tätigkeit, in ihrer Ruhe aufgefasst, durchgängig den *Begriff*."

25. Confer N.S., II, 355-60 for a more complete discussion.

26. S.W., I, 105-06.

27. S.W., I, 109: "wie dem Ich ein Nicht-Ich entgegengesetzt
     wird, wird demnach das Ich *dem* entgegengesetzt wird, und
     das Nicht-Ich, *das* entgegengesetzt wird, teilbar gesetzt."

28. S.W., I, 113: "Sind die logischen Regeln, unter denen alle
     Antithesis und Synthesis steht, von dem dritten
     Grundsatze der Wissenschaftslehre abgeleitet, so ist
     überhaupt die Befugnis aller Antithesis und Synthesis von
     ihm abgeleitet. Aber wir haben in der Darstellung jenes
     Grundsatzes gesehen, dass die ursprüngliche Handlung, die
     er ausdrückt, die des Verbindens Entgegengesetzter in
     einem Dritten, nicht möglich war ohne die Handlung des
     Entgegensetzens; und dass diese gleichfalls nicht möglich
     war, ohne die Handlung des Verbindens: dass also beide in
     der Tat unzertrennlich verbunden und nur in der Reflexion
     zu unterscheiden sind."

29. Confer N.S., II, 359.

30. N.S., II, 360: "Man muss von sein auf das sich setzen und
     umgekehrt schliessen—von Begriff auf die Anschauung und
     umgekehrt—beide müssen zugleich sein, es muss mit der
     Anschauung der Tätigkeit eine Ruhe verknüpft werden. Ich
     erlange den Begriff nur durch Anschauung, und
     Anschauung nur durch den Begriff, das beides in dem
     freien Akt der zurückgehenden Tätigkeit mit einander
     zugleich sich findet."

31. Ibid.: "Also durch das Übergehen von dem Unbestimmten
     oder, mit einem andern Worte, von dem Bestimmbaren zu
     dem Bestimmten, von dem Unbeschränkten zu dem
     Beschränkten wurden wir dieser unsrer Tätigkeit bewusst,
     erhielten wir Anschauung unsrer Tätigkeit."

32. Confer S.W., I, 463 and also N.S., II, 357.

33. N.S.,   II,   384:   "Der   kritische   Idealismus—die
     Wissenschaftslehre und mit ihr im Ganzen auch das
     kantische System—geht von dem absolut vereinigten

Accidens beider—oder von der Wechselwirkung des Ich und Nicht-Ich aus."

34. S.W., I, 91: "den absolut-ersten, schlechthin unbedingten Grundsatz alles menschlichen Wissens *aufzusuchen*."

35. S.W., I, 93: "jener Satz sei *schlechthin, d.i. ohne allen weitern Grund*, gewiss: und indem man dieses, ohne Zweifel mit allgemeiner Bestimmung, tut, schreibt man sich das Vermögen zu, *etwas schlechthin zu setzen*."

36. S.W., I, 94: "Es wird demnach durch das Ich vermittelst X gesetzt; *A sei für das urteilende Ich, schlechthin, und lediglich kraft seines Gesetztseins im Ich überhaupt*; das heisst: es wird gesetzt, dass im Ich, —es sei nun insbesondere setzend, oder urteilend, oder was es auch sei- -etwas sei, das sich stets gleich, stets Ein und ebendasselbe sei; und das schlechthin gesetzte X lässt sich auch so ausdrücken: Ich=Ich; Ich bin Ich."

37. S.W., I, 96. Confer Chapter One, footnote 27 for German text.

38. S.W., I, 97: "*Dasjenige, dessen Sein (Wesen) bloss darin besteht, dass es sich selbst als seiend, setzt* ist das Ich, als absolutes Subjekt."

39. S.W., I, 98: "*Das Ich setzt ursprünglich schlechthin sein eigenes Sein*."

40. S.W., I, 99: "Alles, worauf der Satz A=A anwendbar ist, hat, *inwiefern derselbe darauf anwendbar ist*, Realität."

41. Ibid.: "Dasjenige, was durch das blosse Setzen irgendeines Dinges (eines im Ich Gesetzten) gesetzt ist, ist in ihm Realität, ist sein Wesen."

42. In this connection confer Heidegger, pp. 206-22. Also confer Kant, *CPR*, A 166-76, B 207-18 and A 595-603, B 623-31.

43. S.W., I, 277: "Das Ich fordert, dass es alle Realität in sich fasse, und die Unendlichkeit erfülle. Dieser Forderung liegt notwendig zum Grunde die Idee des schlechthin

gesetzten, unendlichen Ich; und dieses ist das *absolute* Ich, von welchem wir geredet haben. (Hier erst wird der Sinn des Satzes: *das Ich setzt sich selbst schlechthin*, völlig klar. . .)."

44. Confer the excellent article of Reinhard Lauth, "Le problème de l'interpersonnalité chez J.G. Fichte," *Archives de Philosophie*, 25 (juillet-decémbre, 1962): 336-44.

45. N.S., II, 606: "Diese Wissenschaftslehre muss auch in unsrer Grundlage enthalten sein, und sie ist es auch wirklich, aber nur ihren Grundzügen nach. Die besondere Wissenschaft unterscheidet sich von dem ganzen nur so, dass die besondere Wissenschaft zur Bestimmung des einzelnen im Hauptbegriffe enthaltenen fortgeht und die allgemeine Wissenschaft hingegen bei dem Hauptbegriffe und seiner Bestimmtheit stehen bleibt.

   . . .In die Grundlage gehören nur die Grundbegriffe, nicht alles was im Bewusstsein vorkomnt: und so haben wir es auch getan. Es muss sich aber alles, was im Bewusstsein ist, durch Analyse der in der Grundlage enthaltenen Grundbegriffe finden lassen."

46. Hans Radermacher, *Fichtes Bergriff des Absoluten* (Frankfurt am Main: Klostermann, 1970), pp. 39-66.

47. Ibid., p. 44.

48. Confer S.W., I, 77.

BIBLIOGRAPHY

I. Editions of Fichte's Writings

Gesamtausgabe. Edited by Reinhard Lauth and Hans Jacob. Stuttgart: Friederich Frommann Verlag, 1964 ff.

Nachgelassene Schriften. Edited by H. Jacob. Berlin, 1937. Bd. II.

Nachgelassene Werke. Edited by I.H. Fichte. Bonn: Adolph-Marcus, 1834-35. 3 volumes.

Sämmtliche Werke. Edited by I.H. Fichte. Berlin: Veit, 1845-46. 8 volumes.

Science of Knowledge with First and Second Introdutions. Translated by Peter Heath and John Lachs. New York: Appleton-Century Crofts, 1970.

II. Literature on Fichte's Philosophy

Baumanns, Peter. *Fichtes Wissenschaftslehre*. Bonn: Bouvier Verlag Herbert Grundmann, 1974.

Bracken, Ernst von. *Meister Eckhart und Fichte*. Würzberg: Konrad Triltsch Verlag, 1943.

Coreth, Emrich. "Vom Ich zum absoluten Sein. Zur Entwicklung der Gotteslehre Fichtes," *Zeitschrift für katholische Theologie*, LXXIX (1957), 257-303. In French: "Le développement de la Théologie de Fichte," *Archives de Philosophie*, XXV (juillet-décembre, 1962), 484-540.

Drechsler, Julius. *Fichtes Lehre vom Bild*. Stuttgart: Kohlhammer Verlag, 1955.

Duesberg, Hans. *Person und Gemeinschaft*. Bonn: H. Bouvier, 1970.

Duyckaerts, F. "L'imagination productrice dans la logique transcendentale de Fichte," *Revue philosophique de Louvain*, 50 (1952): 233-50.

Flach, W. "Fichte über Kritizismus und Dogmatismus," *Zeitschrift für philosophische Forschung,* 18 (1964): 585-96.

Girndt, H. *Die Differenz des Fichteschen und Hegelschen Systems in der Heglschen "Differenzschrift."* Bonn, 1965.

Guéroult, Martial. *L'évolution et la structure de la Doctrine de la Science chez Fichte.* Paris, 1930.

Gurwitsch, Georg. *Fichtes System der konkreten Ethik.* Tübingen, 1924.

Hammacher, K. "Der Begriff des Wissens bei Fichte," *Zeitschrift für philosophische Forschung,* 22 (1968): 345-68.

Hartmann, Nicholai. *Die Philosophie des deutschen Idealismus.* Berlin, 1929.

Heimsoeth, H. *Fichte.* München, 1923.

Henrich, Dieter, "La découverte de Fichte," *Revue de Métaphysique et de Morale,* 72e année, no. 2 (1967): 154-69.

_____. *Fichtes ursprüngliche Einsicht.* Frankfurt am Main: Klostermann, 1967.

Hohler, Thomas. "Fichte and the Problem of Finitude," *The Southwestern Journal of Philosophy,* VII (1976): 15-33.

_____. "Intellectual Intuition and the Beginning of Fichte's Philosophy: A New Interpretation," *Tijdschrift voor Filosofie,* 37 (maart, 1975): 52-73.

Hyppolite, Jean. "L'idée de la Doctrine de la Science et le sens de son évolution chez Fichte," *Études sur l'histoire de la philosophie. Festschrift für Martial Guéroult.* Paris, 1964. pp. 93-108.

_____. "L'idée fichtéene de la Doctrine de la Science et le projet husserlien," *Husserl et la Pensée Moderne.* Den Haag: Martinus Nijhoff, 1959. pp. 173-82.

Inciarte, Fernando. *Transzendentale Einbildungskraft.* Bonn: H. Bouvier u. Co. Verlag, 1970.

Janke, Wolfgang. "Das empirische Bild des Ich—zu Fichtes *Bestimmung des Menschen,*" *Philosophische Perspektiven* herausgegeben von Rudolph Berlinger und Eugen Fink. Frankfurt am Main: Klostermann, 1969. I, 229-46.

_____. *J.G. Fichte. Wissenschaftslehre von 1804 Wahrheits--und Vernunftslehre, I-XV Vortrag.* Frankfurt am Main: Quellen der Philosophie, 1966.

_____. *Fichte. Sein und Reflexion. Grundlagen der kritischen Vernunft.* Berlin: de Gruyter und Co., 1970.

_____. "Leben und Tod in Fichtes 'Lebenslehre'," *Philosophisches Jahrbuch,* LXXIV (1966): 78-98.

Julia, Didier. "Phénoménologie, Ontologie ou Logique? Apropos de la Théorie de la Science de Fichte," *Revue philosophique de Louvain,* LVII (1959): 184-96.

_____. "La question de l'homme et le fondement de la philosophie," *Collection Analyses et Raisons.* Paris, 1964.

_____. "Le savoir chez Fichte et la problème de la philosophie," *Archives de Philosophie,* XXV (1962), 345-70.

Kabitz, Willy. *Studien zur Entwicklungsgeschichte der Fichteschen Wissenschaftslehre aus der Kantischen Philosophie.* Darmstadt: Wissenschaftliche Buchgesellschaft, 1968.

Kroner, Richard. *Von Kant bis Hegel.* Tübingen: Mohr, 1961.

Lauth, Reinhard. *Begriff, Begründung und Rechtfertigung der Philosophie.* München, 1967.

_____. "Die erste philosophische Auseinandersetzung zwischen Fichte und Schelling 1795-97," *Zeitschrift für philosophische Forschung,* 21 (1967): 341-67.

_____. "Fichtes Gesamtidee der Philosophie," *Philosophische Jahrbuch,* 71 (1964).

_____.　"Genèse du *Fondement de toute la Doctrine de la Science* de Fichte," *Archives de Philosophie*, 34 (1971): 51-79.

_____.　"L"interpersonnalité chez Fichte," *Archives de Philosophie*, XXV (1962), 325-44.

Leon, Xavier. *Fichte et son temps*. Paris, 1954.

Mader, Johann.　*Fichte, Feuerbach, Marx. Leib, Dialog, Gesellschaft*. Wien: Verlag Herder, 1968.

Marx, Werner. "Die Bestimmung der Philosophie im Deutschen Idealismus," *Vernunft und Welt. Zwischen Tradition und anderem Anfang*. Den Haag: Martinus Nijhoff, 1970. Pp. 1-20.

Mohanty, J.N.　"Fichte's *Science of Knowledge* and Husserl's Phenomenology," *The Philosophical Quarterly*, 25 (1952): 113-21.

Noll, Balduin.　*Kants und Fichtes Frage nach dem Ding*. Frankfurt am Main: Klostermann, 1936.

Philonenko, Alexis.　*La liberté humaine dans la philosophie de Fichte*. Paris: Vrin, 1966.

_____.　*Théorie et Praxis dans la pensée morale et politique de Kant et de Fichte en 1793*. Paris: Vrin, 1968.

Radermacher, Hans. *Fichtes Begriff des Absoluten*. Frankfurt am Main: Klostermann, 1970.

Sallis, John.　"Fichte and the Problem of System," *Man and World*, 9 (February, 1976): 75-90.

Schindler, Ingrid.　*Reflexion und Bilding in Fichtes Wissenschaftslehre*. Düsseldorf: Schwann, 1966.

Schuhmann, Karl.　*Die Grundlage der Wissenschaftslehre in ihrem Umrisse. Zu Fichtes "Wissenschaftslehre" von 1794 und 1810*. Den Haag: Martinus Nijoff, 1968.

Schulz, Walter. *Das Problem der absoluten Reflexion.* Frankfurt am Main: Klostermann, 1963.

_____. *Vernunft und Freiheit.* Stuttgart: Neske, 1962.

Schüssler, I. *Die Auseinandersetzung von Idealismus und Realismus in Fichtes Wissenschaftslehre.* Köln, 1969.

Siep. Ludwig. *Hegels Fichtekritik und die Wissenschaftslehre von 1804.* Freiburg: Verlag Karl Alber, 1970.

Tilliette, Xavier. "La Théorie de l'image chez Fichte," *Archives de Philosophie,* XXV (1962), 541-554.

Vuillemin, Jules. *L'héritage kantien et la révolution copernicienne.* Paris: Presse Universitaires de France, 1954.

Widmann, J. "La structure interne de la Doctrine de la Science de 1804," *Archives de Philosophie,* XXV (1962), 371-87.

III. Background Literature

Descartes, Rene. *Discourse on Method and Meditations.* Trans. by Laurence J. Lafleur. New York: Bobbs-Merrill, 1960.

Hegel, G.W.F. *Werke in zwanzig Bänden.* Frankfurt am Main: Suhrkamp Verlag, 1971.

Heidegger, Martin. *Due Frage nach dem Ding. Zu Kants Lehre von den Transzendentalen Grundsätzen.* Tübingen: Max Niemeyer Verlag, 1962. (English translation by W.B. Barton. *What is a Thing?* Chicago: Gateway edition, 1967.)

_____. *Kant und das Problem der Metaphysik.* Bonn: Cohen, 1929. (English translation by James S. Churchill. *Kant and the Problem of Metaphysics.* Bloomington: Indiana University Press, 1962.)

156   BIBLIOGRAPHY

_____.   *Sein und Zeit*. Tübingen: Max Niemeyer Verlag,
1967. (English translation by John Macquarie and Edward
Robinson, *Being and Time*. New York: Harper and Row,
1962.)

Kant, Immanuel. *Kants Gesammelte Schriften*.   Prussian
Academy Edition. Berlin: de Gruyter, 1900-42.

_____.   *Critique of Pure Reason*. Translated by Norman
Kemp Smith. New York: St. Martin's Press, 1965.

Levinas, Emmanuel. *Totality and Infinity*.   Translated by
Alphonso Lingis. Pittsburgh: Duquesne University Press,
1969.

Nabert, Jean. *Éléments pour une Éthique*. Paris: Presses
Universitaires de France, 1943. (English translation by
William Petrek.   *Elements for an Ethic*.   Evanston:
Northwestern University Press, 1969.)

Ricoeur, Paul.   *Le conflit des interprétations*.   *Essais
d'herméneutique*. Paris: Editions du Seuil, 1969. (English
translation by Don Ihde *et al*.   *The Conflict of
Interpretations*.   *Essays in Hermeneutics*.   Evanston:
Northwestern University Press, 1974.)

_____.   *Freud   and   Philosophy: An   Essay   on
Interpretation*. Translated by Denis Savage. New Haven:
Yale University Press, 1970.

_____.   *History and Truth*.   Transalted by Charles
Kelbley. Northwestern University Press, 1965.

_____.   *Husserl: An Analysis of His Phenomenology*.
Translated by Edward G. Ballard   and Lester Embree.
Evanston: Northwestern University Press, 1967.

Sallis, John C.   "On the Limitation of Transcendental
Reflection or Is Intersubjectivity Transcendental?" *The
Monist*, 55 (April, 1971): 312-333.

Schelling, F.W.J. *Schellings Werke*. München, 1958.

Spinoza, Benedict. *Ethics*. New York: Hafner, 1967.

INDEX

DIASPORAS OF THE MIND

DIASPORAS OF THE MIND
JEWISH AND POSTCOLONIAL WRITING AND THE NIGHTMARE OF HISTORY
BRYAN CHEYETTE

YALE UNIVERSITY PRESS
NEW HAVEN AND LONDON

For information about this and other Yale University Press publications, please contact:

U.S. office: sales.press@yale.edu   www.yalebooks.com
Europe office: sales@yaleup.co.uk   www.yalebooks.co.uk

Set in Minion Pro by IDSUK (DataConnection) Ltd
Printed in Great Britain by TJ International Ltd, Padstow, Cornwall

Library of Congress Control Number 2013952402

ISBN 978-0-300-09318-6

10 9 8 7 6 5 4 3 2 1

For Jacob, with love and respect

Contents

Acknowledgements

The forbearance of many individuals has enabled me to understand a great deal (not least the extent of my ignorance) during the preparation of this book. I have, over many years, moved between several academic institutions, which has allowed me to participate in a wide variety of wonderfully stimulating gatherings, both large and small. I have found this diasporic period deeply enriching and I am greatly in the debt of so many that I find myself overwhelmed with the memories of the help I have received. The book began at the University of Southampton in the Parkes Institute (under the wise directorship of Tony Kushner) and in the English Department, where I had a group of most supportive colleagues who understood from the beginning why I would be reckless enough to go on this exponential intellectual journey. I want to thank in particular David Glover, Lucy Hartley, Cora Kaplan, Elena Katz, Peter Lawson, Nicky Marsh, John McGavin, Peter Middleton, Stephen Morton, Nils Roehmer, Nadia Valman and Tony Kushner (who has been a comrade-in-arms since our postgraduate days together at the University of Sheffield). While at Southampton, I was kindly granted research leave in 2004 to take up the position of the Brownstone Visiting Professor in English and Jewish

Studies at Dartmouth College. I want to record my gratitude to Susannah Heschel, who was the most stimulating and unstinting colleague, and who has contributed more to this book than she could possibly know. I learned from Susannah both to be intellectually ambitious and to have the courage of my convictions, although I make no claims to match her courage. While at Dartmouth I also benefited greatly from the support of Jonathan Crewe, Marianne Hirsch, Donald Pease, Louis Renza and Leo Spitzer, who enabled me to give early versions of this book at various challenging symposia. Southampton granted me leave in 2005 to become a Steinhardt Research Fellow at the Herbert D. Katz Center for Advanced Judaic Studies, University of Pennsylvania, where I undertook much of the research for this project and benefited enormously from the weekly seminars and the end-of-year conference. My thanks go firstly to David Ruderman for inviting me to his centre and especially to Anita Norich, who was an ideal friend and colleague. I would also like to thank Marc Caplan, Amelia Glaser, Kathryn Hellerstein, Michael Kramer, Alan Mintz, Alan Rosen, Laurence Roth, Anita Shapira, Deborah Starr and Liliane Weissberg, my fellow fellows, who taught me a great deal.

I regard this project, more than a little foolishly, as a kind of spiritual autobiography, and I have profited from advice and inspiration given by friends and colleagues for many years. Susheila Nasta has been an intellectual confidante since our time at Queen Mary and Westfield College, and has done more than most to validate this project by inviting me to guest-edit her journal *Wasafiri* in 2009 and run a series of research seminars with the Open University at the University of London. Steve Zipperstein, over many, many years, has given and continues to give me the confidence, against all evidence to the contrary, that what I am doing is worthwhile; I am immensely grateful to him. David Feldman, at the Pears Institute at Birkbeck College, has inspired me to the heights of academic rigour and curiosity, which I know can only ever be a Pisgah sight. David Herman is my sternest critic but, if there is anything worthwhile here, I have no doubt that he will let me know in the kindest possible way. And David Cesarani remains a model of the best type of academic and intellectual engagement and is a source of undiminished friendship and generosity. Jonathan Freedman has shown me what is possible, and his imaginative and insightful scholarship, in particular, has been a constant stimulus. Three younger colleagues, Peter Boxall, Robert Gordan and Phiroze Vasunia, are models of both modesty and intellectual energy, and their help and advice have been invaluable.

This book is also for John Barnard, Shaul Bassi, Eitan Bar Yosef, Irena Bauman, Lydia Bauman, Murry Baumgarten, Haedee Becker, Michael Berkowitz, Ian Black, Sara Blair, Elleke Boehmer, Jonathan Boyarin, Alan Craig, Melanie Craig, Valentine Cunningham, Sidra DeKoven Ezrahi, Robert Eaglestone, Todd Endelman, Elaine Feinstein, Monika Fludernik, Eva Frojmovic, Sander Gilman, Paul Gilroy, Stephen Grabiner, Miriam Grabiner, Helen Harris, Robin Hilton, Alfred Hornung, Lynette Hunter, Maja Jaggi, Vivien Jones, Jonathan Judaken, Chana Kronfeld, Hermione Lee, Miriam Leonard, Tony Lerman, Peter Lichtenfels, Vivian Liska, Simon Louvish, Maurice Lyons, Mairi Macdonald, Laura Marcus, David Marriott, Tony Metzer, Aamer Mufti, Beate Neumeier, Adam Zachary Newton, Benita Parry, Griselda Pollock, James Porter, Jacqueline Rose, Michael Rothberg, John Schad, John Schwarzmantel, James Shapiro, Max Silverman, Clive Sinclair, Axel Staehler, Alistair Stead, Mark Stein, Lyndsey Stonebridge, Louise Sylvester, Sue Vice, Dawn Waterman, John Whale, Jonathan Wilson, Hana Wirth-Nesher, James Young and Froma Zeitlin. Zygmunt and the late Janina Bauman, Geoffrey Hartman and Gabriel Josipovici continue to have a transformative influence.

I would also like to acknowledge earlier versions of part of chapter 2 which appeared in Max Silverman, ed., *Frantz Fanon's 'Black Skin, White Masks'* (Manchester: Manchester University Press, 2005); early versions of part of chapter 3 which appeared in Bryan Cheyette and Laura Marcus, eds, *Modernity, Culture and 'the Jew'* (Stanford: Stanford University Press, 1998, and Cambridge: Polity Press, 1998); early versions of part of chapter 4 which appeared in Bryan Cheyette, *Muriel Spark* (Plymouth: Northcote House Press, 2000); and earlier versions of part of chapter 7 which appeared in Susheila Nasta, ed., *Reading the 'New' Literatures in a Postcolonial Era* (Cambridge: Boydell & Brewer, 2000).

At the University of Reading I am fortunate enough to work with supportive and generous colleagues who have, through many kindnesses, enabled me to complete this project. I want to thank, in particular, David Brauner (more than I can say), Alison Donnell, Christopher Duggan, Ronan McDonald, Andrew Nash, Patrick Parrinder and Peter Robinson while acknowledging, above all, that I am particularly fortunate to be part of a big-hearted department. While at Reading I have been awarded a matching Arts and Humanities Research Leave, which was absolutely essential in enabling me to complete this book. Another essential is Robert Baldock, the best possible publisher any academic author (especially one of my disposition) could have. Without him, and his equally gifted staff, such as Candida Brazil and Rachael Lonsdale, and my copy-editor Robert Shore, this book would not have come to fruition. I also want to thank Peter Herbert, Jan Montefiore, and Isabelle Travis without whom I would not have been able to get over the line.

But I could not have written a word without my family. Their emotional and practical support, and considerable sacrifices over many years, have given me the space to write and think (perhaps a little too much). My wife, Susan Cooklin, remains a source of strength and undiminished love despite the many provocations generated by this project. My mother's Irish-Jewish background is a model of diasporic fortitude, and the care she receives from my sister, and that both continue to give to me, is the epitome of love and kindness. They have been through a great deal while I have been writing this book and I am only sorry that it has, at times, taken me away from them. *Diasporas of the Mind* is dedicated to my son, Jacob, who has lived with it for most of his life. He is, like many of his generation, a diasporist down to his very bones. This gives me great hope for the future – and not just because he is a most wonderful son.

Preface

This book explores both the power and the limitations of the diasporic imagination after the Second World War. Rather than the disciplinary thinking of the academy, which confines different histories of diaspora to separate spheres, *Diasporas of the Mind* argues for a new comparative approach across Jewish and postcolonial histories and literatures. The book examines some of the most important novelists and thinkers since 1945 – including Hannah Arendt, Frantz Fanon, Primo Levi, Muriel Spark, Philip Roth, Edward Said, Salman Rushdie, Anita Desai, Caryl Phillips and Zadie Smith – as critical exemplars of a transcultural diasporic imagination. Where *Diasporas of the Mind* differs from earlier accounts of these figures is in understanding the extent to which they all cross disciplinary boundaries and identities, whether as supposedly 'Jewish', 'Catholic', 'postcolonial', 'black', 'Asian', 'postethnic', 'post-Holocaust' or 'Caribbean' writers. There should be no need for this book in an ideal world, but there seems to be an increased necessity to indicate the ways in which histories and cultures can be imagined across national and communal boundaries.

It is in these terms that the phrase 'diasporas of the mind' can be read dismissively: 'diasporas of the *mind*' rather than the real thing; or *imagined* diasporas rather than *actual* or *historical* diasporas. But the point of the book is precisely to show the ways in which the boundaries between historical reconstruction and the imagination are hardly distinct and the concept of diaspora, in particular, illustrates this. On the one hand, 'diaspora' is deeply conservative and imbricated in historical narratives concerning a timeless exile from an autochthonous 'homeland'. On the other, 'diaspora' is also commonly understood as a state of creatively disruptive impurity which imagines emergent transnational and postethnic identities and cultures. One definition moves in the direction of historicism, the other in the direction of the imagination, with the word 'diaspora' remaining unstable and elusive. All of the figures whom I discuss here work through and between these historical and imagined versions of diaspora – which are in turn elided with 'victim' or 'celebratory' diasporas – but none settles completely on one side of these competing versions.

In returning to the years immediately after the Second World War, the book proposes a new form of metaphorical thinking (defined as seeing 'similarities in dissimilars' after Aristotle) which Hannah Arendt first articulated as a means of bringing together the intertwined histories of fascism and imperialism. Immediately after the Second World War, anti-colonial thinkers naturally included the aftermath of Nazism in their analysis of colonialism and those who were imprisoned in the Nazi concentration camps looked in part to the victims of colonialism to understand their experiences. My argument, made in the first chapter, is that disciplinary thinking of all kinds – from nationalism to identity politics to academic specialization – has increasingly separated out these analogous histories. At the same time, there is a recognition that a sense of a new beginning at the end of the Second World War took very different forms after the death camps and at the dawn of decolonization. There are, in short, two very different narratives of cosmopolitanism that arose at this time. For Frantz Fanon, one narrative of cosmopolitanism was part of his vision of emergent transnational and postracial identities and cultures after colonialism. But, from a post-Holocaust perspective, as Arendt makes clear, a competing narrative of cosmopolitanism was largely associated with the destruction of the European Jewish diaspora embodied in the figure of the free-floating *luftmensch* (a vagrant or rootless cosmopolitan) who haunts all of the writers in this book, beginning with Fanon. *Diasporas of the Mind* revolves around the idea of the *luftmensch*, in origin a Yiddish word which constructed East European Jews as hapless 'air-people' in need of national salvation. But the word was also co-opted by the Nazis to characterize Jews as rootless cosmopolitans and essentially parasitic. The post-history of this word will be a preoccupation of the book.

There is always a risk in engaging in metaphorical thinking, which I have called the anxiety of appropriation, especially in relation to histories of racial victimization. There is an understandable fear that the objects of racial discourse, who were mere figurative beings in relation to this discourse, might once again descend into metaphor. But the alternative to such metaphorical thinking is a sense of disciplinary uniqueness, outside such imaginative connectedness, which results in an inability to embrace the dissimilar. That is why *Diasporas of the Mind* argues for more meta-phorical thinking rather than less. But this is not a straightforward matter. On the one hand, the imaginative works of Anita Desai, Caryl Phillips, Philip Roth, Salman Rushdie, Zadie Smith and Muriel Spark will be shown to engage imaginatively with the intertwined experiences of Fanon, Césaire, Memmi, Primo Levi and Jean Améry, discussed in Part One, in ways that are absent from specialist academic disciplines. But the novelists discussed in the second part of the book are also deeply suspicious of a limitless imagination, especially when personified as free-floating and otherworldly in the guise of the *luftmensch*. The period after the Second World War was a time when those who experienced the worst desired to reimagine the world beyond 'race' and the camps. This was a time when disciplinary thinking was dormant. *Diasporas of the Mind* aims to reclaim the ill-disciplined spirit of these times, well aware of the pitfalls of thinking 'without banisters' (in Arendt's felicitous phrase), and all too conscious that this is merely scratching the surface of a new comparative project.

1

Introduction
Diasporas of the Mind

'I always joke that my intellectual formation was through Jewish scholars and writers, even though I didn't know it at the time. Whether it was theologians or Philip Roth who helped shape my sensibility . . .'
Barack Obama/Jeffrey Goldberg Interview, *The Atlantic*, 2008.

'The enthusiastic Jewish intellectual dreaming of paradise on earth, so certain of his freedom from all national ties and prejudices, was in fact farther removed from political reality than his fathers, who had prayed for the coming of the Messiah and the return of the people of Palestine.'
Hannah Arendt, *The Origins of Totalitarianism* (1951), p. 74.

'I'm the last Jewish intellectual. You don't know anyone else. All your other intellectuals are now suburban squires. From Amos Oz to all these people here in America. So I'm the last one. The only true follower of Adorno. Let me put it this way: I'm a Jewish-Palestinian.'
Edward Said/Ari Shavit Interview, *Ha'aretz*, 18 August 2000. Reprinted in *Power, Politics, and Culture: Interviews with Edward Said*, ed. Gauri Viswanathan (2001), p. 458.

The Missing Apostrophe

At the end of May 2011, President Barack Obama visited his Irish 'ancestral home' in the village of Moneygall, County Offaly. In 2007, Irish genealogists had discovered that Obama's great-great-great-grandfather Falmouth Kearney had been raised in Moneygall before he emigrated, in the wake of the Great Famine, to New York in 1850 at the age of nineteen. During the visit Obama spoke of 'blood links' between the United States and the Republic of Ireland and of 'coming home' to Eire in search of his 'missing apostrophe'.[1] On one level, this was an entirely inconsequential visit. There are nearly forty million people in the United States who claim to have Irish ancestry and thirteen previous presidents of the United States have self-declared Irish roots, with most of them visiting Ireland, not unlike Obama, as part of a campaign for re-election. Given the influence of Irish-Americans on the politics of the Democratic Party in the United States, not least in Chicago, it would have been more noteworthy if Obama had decided to give Ireland a miss on his European tour.

But, needless to say, Obama's use of the language of blood and home in relation to his supposed Irishness has a different racial inflection from that of previous presidents. Deemed both 'too black' and not 'black enough', as he put it during his 2008 election campaign, Obama has been at pains to control the language of 'race' during his presidency (Remnick 2010: 512 and 583–85).[2] That this language is something that can be managed and shaped – and is ultimately a matter of choice – characterizes Obama's considered use of racial discourse which, as he showed in Ireland, can be both genetically freighted ('blood links') and pointedly emptied of meaning ('the missing apostrophe'). After reading *Dreams from my Father: A Story of Race and Inheritance* (1995), Zadie Smith characterized Obama as a quintessentially 'self-created man' who passes easily between 'culturally black and white voices' (Smith 2009: 138 and 141).[3] Not unlike the conversionist fiction of Muriel Spark, Obama eschews a 'simple linear inheritance' which implies a 'new, false voice' gained at the expense of a 'true one' (137). Instead, *Dreams from my Father* can 'speak' to the people as a whole in, as Smith puts it, a veritable plethora of voices: 'Obama can do young Jewish male, black old lady from the South Side, white woman from Kansas, Kenyan elders, white Harvard nerds, black Columbia nerds, activist women, churchmen, security guards, bank tellers, and even a British man called Wilkerson' (136). Smith is at pains to stress the moral authority of Obama's different voices – 'each man must be true to his selves, plural' (137) – and these many voices characterize the assumed 'new post-racial world' (141) of his presidency. My argument is that such multiple voices and plural selves (as a means of subverting 'race') remain a troubling aspect for the writers under discussion and clearly troubled Obama, who pointedly subtitled his memoir a 'story of race and inheritance'.[4] Hannah Arendt, not always on the side of cosmopolitan politics, noted in a similar spirit that 'the enthusiastic Jewish intellectual dreaming of . . . freedom from all national ties and prejudices' was far 'removed from political realities' in the interwar years (Arendt 1951: 74).

But the figure of Obama, whether the very personification of the postracial world or of racialized political realities, is clearly a touchstone of our age when attempting to go beyond received ways of understanding 'stories of race'. To put his Irish speech in perspective, it is worth remembering a very different black-Irish intersection, from the late 1980s, to show just how radical Obama's many voices could be today. Addressing the question of whether ethnicity is 'obsolete' (another version of the postracial), the poet and novelist Ishmael Reed noted the possibility of going beyond blackness as the epitome of ethnicity with regard to Alex Haley's bestselling *Roots: The Saga of an American Family* (1976): 'If Alex Haley had traced his father's bloodline, he would have travelled twelve generations back to, not Gambia, but *Ireland*'. Reed was at pains to note the extent to which African-Americans have a 'multi-ethnic heritage' and to show the 'absurdity' of reducing this to a single 'black' identity (Reed 1989: 227).[5] Nearly half a century after *Roots*, Barack Obama made another journey of discovery, but this time to play with, at least in one incarnation, the constructed nature of 'black' ethnicity.[6]

David Hollinger, writing in the mid-1990s, renamed Reed's multi-ethnic version of Haley's search for 'roots' as 'Haley's choice'. By the end of the twentieth century, the choice between Haley's Irish and African roots was deemed 'phony, of course, for the blackness of Haley's skin was understood to rule his white heritage inconsequential. Haley's choice is the Hobson's choice of ethno-racial identity in America because it is not a real choice at all' (Hollinger 1995: 8). The difference between a racially determined Hobson's choice and a postethnic Haley's choice structures Hollinger's argument. In this regard, Hollinger is right to note the exact parallel between the multicultural forms of 'race' (African-American, Asian-American, Euro-American, Indigenous, Latino) and its straightforwardly 'biological' forms (black, yellow, white, red and brown). This still-prevalent 'ethno-racial pentagon' (12), increasingly exported from the United States, shapes much contemporary race-thinking. But this is not a simple contrast between the single-voiced and the many-voiced; the cosmopolitanism of an Obama and the identity politics of a Haley. While Obama can be playfully postracial in his search for his missing apostrophe, he cannot avoid talk of the 'racial inheritance' and 'blood-lines' that gave Haley's *Roots* its importance in popularizing the history of slavery. At the same time, Haley's search for ethnoracial authenticity in discovering his ancestor's village in Gambia is no less constructed and, as is widely acknowledged, is also a form of artifice as it turns out to be partially based on Harold Courlander's novel *The African* (1967).[7] Such are the always blurred boundaries between what is imagined, or constructed, and what is authentic, or historical.

As a freshman, Obama remembers a 'multiracial' student called Joyce who refused to go with him to a Black Students' Association meeting. We are told that she had an Italian father and her mother '*happened* to be part African and part French and part Native American and part something else'. Joyce complains that it is '*black people* who always have to make everything racial. *They're* the ones making me choose'. Obama's youthful response to Joyce is quite scathing as the supposed 'richness' of her 'multicultural heritage' 'avoid[s] black people' (Obama 2004: 99). Her behaviour shows mistakenly that only 'white culture could be neutral and objective', which is an assumption that Obama has been at pains to counter, at some political cost, during his presidency and which Zadie Smith has made the subject of her latest novel.[8] At the same time, Obama is well aware of being 'too hard on poor Joyce', whom he casts as the caricature 'tragic mulatto', an emotional condition he must resist:

> The truth is that I understood her, her and all the other black kids who felt the way she did. In their mannerisms, their speech, their mixed up hearts, I kept recognising pieces of myself. And that's exactly what scared me. Their confusion made me question my own racial credentials all over again. ... To avoid being mistaken for a sellout I chose friends carefully. ... We smoked cigarettes and wore leather jackets. At night, in the dorms, we discussed neo-colonialism, Frantz Fanon, Eurocentrism and patriarchy. (100)[9]

That the confusions of a mixed-up Joyce made the young Obama question his own 'racial credentials', and that he resolved these confusions by embracing the supposedly authentic figure of 'Frantz Fanon', is a story that will be repeated throughout *Diasporas of the Mind*. David Remnick may be right in depicting Obama as a protean figure or 'shape-shifter' but he should surely also acknowledge that such a characterization, which has a long history when it comes to 'the Jews', can result in what Zygmunt Bauman calls 'proteophobia' or the 'anxiety caused by those who do not fall easily into any established categories' (Bauman 1998: 144).[10] The Obama who claimed that his 'intellectual formation' or sensibility was fashioned unconsciously through 'Jewish scholars and writers' such as Philip Roth certainly understands this crossover, which we will consider first of all in the figure of Fanon.[11] This is, in other words, another way of telling the story of the 'Jewish mind' (Roth, for example, as self-confessed 'walking text') and the 'black body' (Fanon reduced to the sign of irrational revolutionary violence), which is, even today, an all too frequent racial opposition.[12] Obama's cosmopolitanism has the power and the ability to make 'Haley's choice' a real choice that enables him both to claim, and disclaim, a variety of ethnoracial ancestries. This is to anticipate the argument for the imaginative power of the figures in this book who would similarly attempt to transform racial discourse. All of the stories and histories that are explored here place our shape-shifting imaginations (as in the case of Obama's many voices) next to lost histories of diaspora and exile (as in the case of Haley's maternal but not paternal racial inheritance in recovering the history of slavery). Whether the imagination is able to transform racial discourse, even under the sign of diasporic impurity, will remain open to question.

Hannah Arendt's Imagination

The Janus-faced history and experience of diaspora is both a blessing and a curse. At one end of the spectrum, diaspora is on the side of impurity and hybridity (and points in the direction of emergent or lost cultures) and, at the other end, diaspora is conservative and 'roots-defined' and has as its end point a return to an autochthonous (pure) space. The celebratory version of diaspora tends to foreground a transgressive imagination and precolonial histories made up of intertwined cultures (and is associated with Postcolonial and Diaspora Studies), whereas a victim-centred version tends to stress particular communities of exile with specific and unique histories of suffering (and is associated with Holocaust and Genocide Studies). As I will argue, one way of understanding these differing versions of diaspora is in relation to metaphorical thinking (after Hannah Arendt) and disciplinary thinking (after Frantz Fanon). Arendt, as we will see, defined metaphorical thinking (following Aristotle) as finding 'similarities in dissimilarities', which will help to characterize the importance of imaginative literature in this book (Arendt 1971: 102–03). Fanon, in contrast, thinks of the 'native intellectual' as being preoccupied with 'special disciplines' so that s/he loses sight of the 'unity of the [revolutionary] movement' (Fanon 1961: 38–39). Such unity, undermined by disciplinary thinking, prefigures a new humanism that was equally Fanon's and Arendt's response to colonialism and the death camps.[13] However well intentioned, disciplinary thinking, in these terms, divides people into separate spheres, and does not make the imaginative leap of seeing 'similarities in dissimilarities'.

Arendt especially has become a common point of reference for much new work aiming to bring together the histories of racism, fascism, colonialism and anti-Semitism, which, in one formulation, helps us to 'connect the presence of colonial peoples in Europe to the history of Europe's Jews and other vulnerable minorities' (Gilroy 2000: 77). This foundational status has been achieved not least because her best-known books, *The Origins of Totalitarianism* (1951) and *Eichmann in Jerusalem: A Report on the Banality of Evil* (1963), helped to give birth to two new disciplines – Postcolonial Studies and Holocaust Studies – while at the same time transcending these disciplinary boundaries.[14] Fanon, at the start of *The Wretched of the Earth*, speaks of 'the kind of tabula rasa which from the outset defines any decolonization' (Fanon 1961: 1); Arendt also has a sense of a new beginning, tentatively formulating a radical way of speaking about the world anew, from her position as a stateless refugee. It is the dissident comparative perspectives of Arendt and Fanon, after their experiences of fascism and colonialism, in contrast to our current disciplinary orthodoxies, that provide the starting point for this book and that locate such work beyond the more usual context of the Francophone tradition, which will be explored in Chapter 2.[15]

In her search for a new 'tentative' vocabulary, Arendt placed both the imagination and storytelling at the heart of much of her unclassifiable and idiosyncratic oeuvre, which has been rightly judged to contain 'very considerable works of art' (Canovan 1974: 47). Working somewhere between literature, history, philosophy and politics, Arendt not only refused to confine the imagination or storytelling to an individual consciousness but read novels and other narratives especially as an aid to understanding and articulating the horrors of the modern world.[16] I will follow her lead in this regard. Her work, which has been dismissed by some as overly aestheticized, takes from the German philosophical tradition a sense that metaphorical thinking is at the heart of the 'life of the mind' and connects the 'inward' individual to the 'world of appearances'

(Arendt 1971: 105). Arendt's political aesthetic is highlighted especially in *The Life of the Mind* (1971), where she defines the 'language of metaphor', after Aristotle, as 'an intuitive perception of similarity in dissimilars' (103) or, after Shelley, as the 'unapprehended *relations* of things' (102). Finding the 'unapprehended *relations* of things' or the 'similar' in 'dissimilars' is one way of describing *The Origins of Totalitarianism*, which is structured loosely around the historical 'crystallization' (Arendt 1951: 44) of anti-Semitism, colonialism and totalitarianism. Arendt took this form of metaphorical thinking from Walter Benjamin's sense of 'language as an essentially poetic phenomenon' and it is precisely these kinds of 'constellations' that shaped *The Origins of Totalitarianism* (Arendt 1968: 205).

In her 1959 lecture on Lessing, collected in *Men in Dark Times* (1968), Arendt argues that 'no philosophy, no analysis, no aphorism, be it ever so profound, can compare to the intensity and richness of meaning with a properly narrated story' (22). In this spirit of freewheeling storytelling, Arendt called for 'a new kind of thinking that needs no pillars and props, no standards and traditions to move freely without crutches over unfamiliar terrain'. Moving freely over unfamiliar terrain or 'thinking without a banister' characterized her risk-taking metaphorical thinking and was a consequence of her sense of living after a radical break with the past: 'we need only look around to see that we are standing in the midst of a veritable rubble heap of such pillars' (10).[17] In *The Human Condition* (1958), Arendt argues that storytelling is part of an 'already existing web of human relationships': 'the reason why each human life tells its story and why history ultimately becomes the storybook of mankind . . . is that both are the outcome of action' (Arendt 1958: 184). This intimate link between thought and action, or storytelling and the world, characterizes much of Arendt's 'multidimensional' work (Canovan 1974: 109).[18]

As a stateless person for more than a decade, and a Jewish refugee from Nazi-occupied Germany and France (escaping from Gurs internment camp in 1940), Arendt struggled to find a language to articulate what she called in her 1950 preface to *The Origins of Totalitarianism* (1951) 'homelessness on an unprecedented scale, rootlessness to an unprecedented depth' (Arendt

1951: xxv). Comprehension, she argues, does not mean 'deducing the unprecedented from precedents' (xxvi), and for this reason she is well aware of the limitations of the vocabulary that she is using: 'antisemitism (not merely hatred of Jews), imperialism (not merely conquest), totalitarianism (not merely dictatorship)' (xxvii). Her search for a new vocabulary to 'move freely' over the ruins of the nineteenth and twentieth centuries meant that she particularly valued the language of literature in helping her chart this 'unfamiliar terrain'. As I have shown elsewhere, literature can complicate Semitic discourse so that it is no longer regarded as 'eternal' or unchanging, in Arendt's acute formulation, and supposedly beyond political and historical contingencies.[19] What is more, Arendt rightly counters disciplinary responses to imaginative works that mistakenly provide them with 'banisters', or ideological certainties, whether in the name of identity, nation or 'race'.

Her stress on the centrality of metaphorical or poetic thinking is found most prominently in her essay 'The Jew as Pariah: A Hidden Tradition' (1944), which was, in a draft version, part of the opening chapter of *The Origins of Totalitarianism*.[20] The 'immediate impulse' behind *The Life of the Mind*, she explains in her introduction, was the experience of attending the Eichmann trial in Jerusalem and the '*thoughtlessness*' of Eichmann:

> The deeds were monstrous but the doer … was quite ordinary, commonplace and neither demonic nor monstrous. … Clichés, stock phrases, adherence to conventional, standardized codes of expression and conduct have the socially recognized function of protecting us against reality, against the claim on our thinking attention. … Eichmann differed from the rest of us only in that he clearly knew of no such claim at all. (Arendt 1971: 4)

Arendt first placed this banal thoughtlessness at the heart of Eichmann's 'monstrous' deeds (to show the enormous gap between his crimes and his consciousness) in the postscript to the 1965 edition of her 'report':

> It was precisely this lack of imagination which enabled [Eichmann] to
> sit for months on end facing a German Jew who was conducting the
> police interrogation, pouring out his heart to the man and explaining
> again and again how it was that he reached only the rank of lieutenant
> colonel in the SS and that it had not been his fault that he was not
> promoted. (Arendt 1965: 287)

Arendt characterized this 'thoughtlessness', without any further elucidation,
as Eichmann's 'word-and-thought-defying *banality of evil*' (252).[21] Earlier
in her account, she noted Eichmann's inability to 'think from the standpoint
of somebody else' (49), which is illustrated in the above-quoted passage in
relation to his 'lack of imagination' when speaking insensitively for months
to a 'German-Jewish' (in fact, Israeli) policeman about his career being
blocked in the SS. It was this lack of human empathy, and shameless narcissism, that enabled Eichmann to discount the 'superfluous' humanity of his
many victims. That is why Arendt routinely uses the language of literature,
such as spontaneity, irony and communal storytelling, to exemplify the
'human condition'. It is also why she foregrounds Eichmann's prosaic use of
stock phrases to characterize his dehumanizing consciousness.

There is, in other words, a spectrum in Arendt's work from the
thoughtlessness of the *génocidaire* to the poetic imagination of the writer
of literature. But where this spectrum breaks down is in relation to
the powerlessness of the diaspora, a troubling aspect of Arendt's work,
which contrasts with the power of storytelling. For Arendt, the diaspora
is inevitably associated with exile and victimhood, which paradoxically
is the source of her sense of an empowering pariah imagination. On
the one hand, Arendt was utterly dismissive of the diaspora, which, in its
utter victimization and self-delusion, was unable to give the imagination
a wider communal dimension that might lead to political action. At the
beginning of *The Origins of Totalitarianism* (1951), for instance, she
described the Jewish diaspora as a social condition that had 'avoided all
political action for two thousand years ... so that the Jews stumbled
from one role to the other and accepted responsibility for none' (Arendt

1951: 8). As David Biale has noted, this construction of an apolitical, passive diaspora is no different from more conventional Zionist historiography as articulated by David Ben-Gurion (usually taken as Arendt's opposite), who dismissed the Jewish diaspora in no less contemptuous terms (Biale 1986: 5). Both Ben-Gurion and Arendt, in other words, characterized the diaspora in terms of political powerlessness, although, to be sure, they eventually drew radically different conclusions from this belief. One went in the direction of an exclusive nationalism and state-building, the other in the direction of binationalism and the ideal of an inclusive political community.

Where Arendt differed from the Zionist 'negation' of the diaspora was in making the well-known distinction between 'parvenus' and 'pariahs', with the parvenu confined to the assimilating social realm and the pariah having the potential, at least, for political action and rebellion. Arendt took this distinction from the first Dreyfusard, Bernard Lazare, who inspired Emile Zola and who understood what it was to be labelled a 'déraciné' intellectual whose thinking could only ever be rootless and denationalized.[22] Not unlike Arendt, Lazare was a dissident Jewish nationalist and, as many commentators have noted, Arendt knowingly identified herself with Lazare, who was a 'self-conscious pariah' and who argued that 'the Jew should come out openly as the representative of the pariah, "since it is the duty of every human being to resist oppression"' (Arendt 1944: 284). But the assumption that the leaders of diaspora Jewish communities were self-serving parvenus led to her assertion (in a letter to Karl Jaspers before the Eichmann trial began) that to a 'huge degree the Jews helped organise their own destruction' (quoted Benhabib 179). In a statement that ignited a sustained attack on Arendt over many years she argued in *Eichmann in Jerusalem*:

> Wherever Jews lived, there were recognized Jewish leaders, and this leadership, almost without exception, cooperated in one way or another, for one reason or another, with the Nazis. The whole truth was that if the Jewish people had really been unorganized and leaderless,

there would have been chaos and plenty of misery but the total number of victims would hardly have been between four and a half and six million people. (Arendt 1965: 125)

The delusion of power of parvenu Jews, cut off from true political power, here reaches tragic proportions. As Arendt notes in *Eichmann in Jerusalem*, while this 'chapter of the story' (125) was not part of the Eichmann trial, it was included in her 'report' since she regarded the 'role of the Jewish leaders in the destruction of their own people' as 'undoubtedly the darkest chapter of the whole dark story' (117). But this characterization of the forced collusion of the victims of genocide as the 'darkest chapter' – surely that was the genocide itself – is, as others have argued, rather perverse.[23] Arendt's preoccupation with the iniquities of diaspora Jewish leadership led her to describe the diaspora, in her lecture on Lessing, as a form of 'worldlessness' and, equally, as a form of 'barbarism' (Arendt 1968: 13) or a 'loss of humanness' (23). It is in the context of such caustic dismissals, which compare poorly with Primo Levi's more nuanced understanding of the 'grey zone', that Arendt reclaims the Jewish diaspora, through the figure of the pariah, for both 'the world' and 'humanity'. The problem, however, is that in rejecting the experience and history of the diaspora *tout court*, with the exception of a few isolated pariahs, Arendt does not take the diaspora seriously as a context for creative or political action.

In her lecture on Lessing, Arendt argues that under the 'pressure of persecution the persecuted have moved so close together that the inter-space which we have called the world . . . has simply disappeared' (13). This is what Arendt meant by 'worldlessness', which confines an utterly victim-ized Jewish diaspora, in her thinking, to the social or private realm of the assimilating parvenus rather than the political and public realm of the resistant and free-thinking pariahs: 'Concentration on an artificially complicated inner life helped Jews to respond to the unreasonable demands of society, to be strange and exciting' (Arendt 1951: 7). But the worldless-ness of the Jewish diaspora also prefigured a more general 'world alienation' which characterizes the 'human condition': 'because Jews were a despised and oppressed people, they were . . . an even purer and more exemplary model of mankind' (57). That is why Arendt's 'enlarged mentality' famously moves from the rights of an oppressed minority in *Eichmann in Jerusalem* to 'human rights', and from the statelessness of 'the Jews' in *The Origins of Totalitarianism* to the 'right to have rights'.[24]

The universalization of the Jewish diaspora, in so far as she denies it a specific history beyond its destruction, exposes the limits of Arendt's metaphorical thinking. What is more, the pariah/parvenu distinction confines the Jewish diaspora to good/bad Jews, which is merely a continuation of prewar racial discourse.[25] Equally problematically, Arendt applies the pariah/parvenu distinction to the civil rights campaign to desegregate schools in the American South after the Supreme Court ruling in favour of the Eisenhower administration. 'Reflections on Little Rock', written in 1957 but not published until 1959, proved to be an extraordinarily combustible intervention and, as Ralph Ellison noted a few years later, was a 'dark foreshadowing of the Eichmann blow-up' (quoted Young-Bruehl 308).[26] The starting point of her essay is a photograph of a black schoolgirl being accompanied home from her recently integrated school by a white friend of her father as she is abused by a 'jeering and grimacing mob' (Arendt 1959: 203). Speaking from the imagined viewpoint of the schoolgirl, Arendt is scathing about this experience:

> The most startling part of the whole business was the Federal decision to start integration in, of all places, the public schools. It certainly did not require too much imagination to see that this was to burden children, black and white, with the working out of a problem which adults for generations have confessed themselves unable to solve. I think no one will find it easy to forget the photograph. . . . The girl, obviously, was asked to be a hero – that is something neither her absent father nor the equally absent representatives of the NAACP felt called upon to be. (203)

She concludes by asking: 'have we now come to the point where it is the children who are being asked to change or improve the world?' (204).

These inflammatory remarks are wholly predicated on the pariah/parvenu split between the social and the political which was eventually extended to characterize the 'modern age' in *The Human Condition*. As Young-Bruehl notes, the girl's absent father had done what, in Arendt's opinion, no parent ought to have done: 'he had asked his child to go where she was not wanted, to behave like a parvenu, to treat education as a means of social advancement' (Young-Bruehl 311).

Arendt believed that the social advancement of the Jewish diaspora was mistakenly conflated with racial equality and that the same confusion was being repeated in the campaign for the desegregation of schools in the American South. She therefore distinguished rigidly in the essay between the social and the political, and also defended the private realm against an encroaching mass society, as she argued in *The Human Condition*. That is why she insisted in 'Reflections on Little Rock': 'Segregation is discrimination enforced by law, and desegregation can do no more than abolish the laws enforcing discrimination; it cannot abolish discrimination and force equality within the body politic' (Arendt 1959: 204). Her conclusion is even starker: 'What equality is to the body politic – its innermost principle – discrimination is to society' (205). But, as Seyla Benhabib has rightly argued, 'Arendt cannot have it both ways: political equality and social discrimination cannot simply co-exist' (Benhabib 152). The fact that schools straddle the political/social/private divide in Arendt's thinking means that her distinctions, imposed on the events in Little Rock, finally fail her.

In a form of metaphorical thinking Arendt displaces her experience of the failed social assimilation of European Jewry onto the black/white 'racial divisions' in the United States (Benhabib 149). But this argument points in two contradictory directions. On the one hand, Arendt sees similarities in dissimilars and follows *The Origins of Totalitarianism* by refusing to reduce racial discourse to a black/white binary. This leads in the direction of new thinking to challenge what Arendt conceived of as the liberal consensus on these issues. But, at the same time, she wished to distinguish the United States, which granted her refuge, from the continent of Europe, which had banished her. That is why she notes that the 'colour question was created by the one great crime in America's history and is soluble only within the political and historical framework of the Republic', whereas the 'colour problem in world politics grew out of the colonialism and imperialism of European nations' (Arendt 1959: 198), which did not 'involve' the United States. As with her previous distinctions, the assumption that the American 'colour problem' (that is, the history of slavery) has nothing to do with European colonialism (a connection in fact made in *The Origins of Totalitarianism*) once again shows the limitations, as we will see in the fiction of Philip Roth, of making European anti-Semitism the master narrative for an understanding of racial politics in the United States.

Arendt helps us to understand the dangers of metaphorical thinking outside the context of diaspora, where there are different historical possibilities, which she replaces with a more abstract sense of a political community. Michael Rothberg speaks of Arendt's 'blindness and insight' (in a knowing reference to the rather more culpable Paul de Man) in so far as the 'figurative connection[s]' in *The Origins of Totalitarianism* are a product of metaphorical 'boomerang effects' that may 'silence one history of violence to convey another' (Rothberg 2009: 65). As in 'Reflections on Little Rock', Arendt has been accused of an insensitivity to the 'suffering of blacks', which has been used as a means of challenging her perception of the history of imperialism as part of the 'origins' of Nazi totalitarianism. Arendt understood European imperialism in Africa as a 'preparatory stage of the coming catastrophes' (Arendt 1951: 123), which is said to diminish the 'crimes of imperialism' in so far as they are deemed to be merely a prelude to the death camps.[27] Her supposedly uncritical reading of Joseph Conrad's *Heart of Darkness* (1899) as the 'most illuminating work on actual race experience in Africa' (185) has been deemed, in particular, to be her greatest act of miscomprehension. According to this argument, Conrad's racism and his Eurocentric flaws, exposed not least by Chinua Achebe, have been inherited, posthumously, by Arendt.[28] But I firmly believe that the risk-taking in Arendt's metaphorical thinking, with its comparative perspective, should not be dismissed out of hand in the name of disciplinary virtuousness.

To be sure, Arendt does have a naïve faith in the ability of *Heart of Darkness* to reproduce 'actual race experience in Africa'. But those who have castigated her for downplaying the 'crimes of imperialism' have tended to ignore her extraliterary accounts of 'race and bureaucracy' in Africa inspired by *Heart of Darkness*:

> 'Exterminate all the brutes'. This answer resulted in the most terrible massacres in recent history, the Boers' extermination of Hottentot tribes, the wild murdering by Carl Peters in German Southeast Africa, the decimation of the peaceful Congo population – from 20 to 40 million reduced to 8 million people; and, finally, perhaps worst of all, it resulted in the triumphant introduction of such means of pacification into ordinary, respectable foreign policies. (185)

The banalization of genocide (as part of 'ordinary, respectable foreign policies') is considered 'perhaps worst of all' by Arendt since it anticipates the bureaucratization of genocide in the death camps following its routine practice in Africa. In contrast to Arendt's always risky irony, the bare facts ('20 to 40 million reduced to 8 million') speak for themselves. At the same time, she does follow Conrad in presenting the Africans as mute black bodies who are incapable of speaking for themselves – who represent the limit case of dehumanized suffering – which enables her to explain the deployment of colonial genocide on the continent of Europe. But Arendt's metaphorical use of 'boomerang effects' has, since the decline of totalitarianism as an overarching concept, been particularly productive in generating a range of comparative work that has shown, in her words, the ways in which 'African colonial possessions became the most fertile soil for the flowering of the . . . Nazi elite' (206). While there is clearly not a single, coherent response to Arendt in this new work – and we will see that both Fanon and Aimé Césaire crucially speak from the position of the supposedly mute victim – her formulation of Nazism as a form of 'racial imperialism' has resulted in what has been rightly called the 'colonial turn in Holocaust studies' (Rothberg 2009: 70).[29]

But the decoupling of her metaphorical thinking from the history and experience of diaspora can lead to abstraction. Arendt conceived of the 'masses' in modern times as being either literal or metaphorical refugees, having the central experience of 'loneliness', and the sense of being uprooted and superfluous, of having no recognized place among a common community. According to Arendt, these conditions led to totalitarianism, not least because such 'world alienation' meant that 'the masses' could no longer distinguish between what was real and what was imagined (Canovan 1974: 25). But these characteristics of the 'modern age', which led to totalitarianism in Arendt's thinking, were not dissimilar to the condition of exile. For this reason, Arendt repeatedly stressed that human rights and ethnic and racial plurality could only exist within the protective realm of a political community in contrast to the utterly vulnerable 'natural' condition of humanity, such as sub-Saharan Africans at the turn of the twentieth century, who were outside such a community (Gilroy 2010: 82–83). But this validation of a political community (in contrast to a victimized diaspora) as a bulwark against what Giorgio Agamben calls 'bare life' (Agamben 1998) – when 'everything is possible' (Arendt 1951: 625) – finally acts as a brake on Arendt's metaphorical thought.[30]

Thinking 'without banisters' could lead to an overwhelming sense of rootlessness and alienation which Arendt had to limit so that her pluralistic and comparative imagination could be part of a wider 'comity of peoples', as she puts it at the end of 'We Refugees' (Arendt 1943: 274).[31] After all, as J. Middleton Murry argues in the opening chapter on 'Metaphor' in his *Countries of the Mind: Essays in Literary Criticism* (1931), the exploration of metaphor 'cannot be pursued very far without our being led to the borderline of sanity' (Murry 1). Murry wished to locate a *tertium quid*, a middle way between metaphor and reality, to retain his sense of sanity (1–17).[32] Arendt similarly wished to distinguish between reality and the imagination, which she felt had become increasingly eroded in the modern age, which is why she relied so heavily on rigid (not always helpful) binary distinctions throughout her corpus. The danger of pursuing the figurative in the name of historical understanding ('without banisters') is the loss of sanity or rationality. But the alternative to such risk-taking is to retain disciplinary boundaries and to be mired in what Fanon called, at the beginning of *The Wretched of the Earth*, the old forms, 'the rise of a new nation, the establishment of a new state' (Fanon 1961: 1). As I will now show, whereas Arendt can only think of diaspora as a passive and apolitical realm predestined for destruction, we will see that Edward Said (in the guise of the 'last Jew') was able to move from such Manichaeism to a sense of exile (but not, as I will show, diaspora) that could include the impure and disruptive as a value in and of itself.

Edward Said and Other 'Last Jews'

After being told by Ari Shavit that he 'sounds very Jewish', Edward Said, in a well-known *Ha'aretz* interview, described himself as the 'last Jewish intellectual'. This was an act of bravado which, in a not insensitive context, placed metaphorical thinking in explosive conjunction with the political and historical. As Said argued: 'You don't know anyone else. All your other intellectuals are now suburban squires. From Amos Oz to all these people here in America. So I'm the last one. The only true follower of Adorno. Let me put it this way: I'm a Jewish-Palestinian' (Viswanathan 2001: 458). This provocative declaration – which figuratively collapsed the distinction between 'Jew' and 'Palestinian' or, alternatively, 'Adorno' and 'Said' – made an enormous impact. It is the last word in a comprehensive volume of Said's interviews, with its various claims left hanging without a response.[33] The pregnant pause at the end of *Power, Politics and Culture* has been filled with countless citations and scholarly articles that refer to the now 'legendary' interview. One reason for the variety of interpretations that it has received (which range from the reductively nationalistic to the playfully postmodern) is that the three rather enigmatic elements in the statement – 'last Jewish intellectual', 'The only true follower of Adorno' and 'Jewish-Palestinian' – do very different kinds of cultural and political work for Said.[34]

Although Said chose Adorno as part of his imagined genealogy, he could also have chosen Arendt (who is a crucial influence on his early work) given her not dissimilar role as a 'last European', in Walter Benjamin's phrase, who has achieved iconic status in the Anglo-American academic culture.[35] Arendt is particularly relevant to Said as she was one of the early precursors of Postcolonial Studies who utterly rejected a celebratory version of the diaspora for, in Said's more qualified formulation, a more unremitting and irreconcilable version of 'exile'.[36] Both Arendt and Fanon engaged with the 'common enslavement' of the oppressed on the continent of Europe and within its colonies and spoke of a 'new beginning' for humanity as a whole after decolonization and the defeat of fascism (Fanon 1964: 43). In this worldly humanistic spirit, Said in the late 1970s acknowledges anti-Semitism and Orientalism as 'secret sharers' and has an 'ironic double vision' that comprehends equally (but not as equivalents) both Jewish and Palestinian suffering (Said 1979: xiii). In this context, Said quotes *The Origins of Totalitarianism*, which has rightly been described as 'one of the constitutive books of postcolonial studies', in the *Question of Palestine* (1979): 'the solution to the Jewish question merely produced a new category of refugees, the Arabs, thereby increasing the number of stateless and rightless by another 700,000 to 800,000 people. And what happened in Palestine ... was then repeated in India on a large scale involving many millions of people' (xiii).[37] This historical conjunction, at the point of decolonization, is the subject of Aamer Mufti's work, which expanded the 'constellation' of the European 'Jewish Question' onto the global stage and reads back this history from the perspective of the victims of nationalist partition in Southeast Asia. In recent years, there has been an increasing number of studies – across and outside disciplinary formations – that have tried to make connections between Jewish, colonial and postcolonial history.[38] These intertwined histories, however, have been largely dissipated by the growth of disciplinary fields – such as Diaspora Studies, Postcolonial Studies, Jewish Studies and Holocaust Studies – which tend to stress specific histories of victimhood and exile rather than a 'common enslavement' across Europe's minorities and the colonies. As Said noted in an interview in 1986: 'it is an inadmissible contradiction ... to build analysis of historical experience around exclusion ... only women can understand feminine experience, only Jews can understand Jewish suffering, only formerly colonial subjects can understand colonial experience' (Said 1986: 49). This is why Said in his *Representations of the Intellectual* (1994) defined the intellectual as an 'amateur', beyond any professionalized disciplinary formations, and an 'exile' outside all forms of identity politics or separate spheres.

But as many others have noted, there is a tension throughout Said's work between being 'simultaneously internationalist and nationalist' which places, for instance, his urbane and cosmopolitan readings of the Western literary and musical canon next to his championing of the Palestinian cause 'as a Palestinian' in exile (Young 2012: 27). Said's internationalism takes him in the direction of hybridity, the imagination and comparative thought, and his nationalism takes him in the direction of community, national renewal and the politics of conflict. There is, in other words, a simultaneous pull towards, and refusal of, national identity in Said's worldly humanism, which is both reinforced and undermined by his autobiographical turn. One way in which he resolves this contradiction is by characterizing his 'secular criticism' as a continuation of mainly German(-Jewish) philology whose 'work deals with humanity at large and transcends national boundaries', as Said puts it in *The World, the Text and the Critic* (Said 1984: 7). The figure of Erich Auerbach, as is well known, is crucial for this formulation; like Adorno, he was a 'last Jew', writing *Mimesis* (1946) while exiled in Istanbul. Said especially notes the places in *Mimesis* where 'Auerbach seems to be negotiating between the Jewish and European (hence Christian) components in his identity' (Said 2004: 102). His German-Jewish inbetweenness enables Said both to engage with a transnational humanism and to claim the analogous position of 'exile'. To this extent Said, who describes Auerbach's work as an 'exile's book' in his introduction to *Mimesis*, is rightly said to have read 'Auerbach in a rigorous sense as a Jewish figure, as a member of a minority' (Mufti 2000: 236).[39] But, as Emily Apter has shown, this version of Auerbach in splendid isolation is something of a self-construction on Said's part as Auerbach in fact joined a department in Turkey with Leo Spitzer and other German-Jewish refugees who had paved the way for the supposedly 'lone' author of *Mimesis*.[40]

As I have shown elsewhere, Said tends to portray his 'last Jews' in self-fashioned terms as isolated or exilic 'amateurs'.[41] This goes back to *Beginnings: Intention and Method* (1975), which starts with the foundational image of the exilic critic, after Matthew Arnold, as a 'wanderer, going from place to place for his material, but remaining a man essentially *between* homes' (Said 1975: 8).[42] This abiding inbetween figure, Said confirms, is taken from George Steiner's *Extraterritorial: Papers on the Literature and the Language Revolution* (1971):

> A great writer driven from language to language by social upheaval and war is an apt symbol for the age of the refugee. No exile is more radical, no feat of adaptation and new life more demanding. It seems proper that those who create art in a civilization of quasi-barbarism which has made so many homeless, which has torn up tongues and peoples by the root, should themselves be poets unhoused and wanderers across language. (Steiner 1971: 21)

This passage is quoted at the start of Said's formative essay 'Reflections on Exile' (1984) and makes the crucial connection between individuals and peoples in the 'age of the refugee'. Steiner's importance as a 'courier' between the lost world of Central European humanism (Prague, Vienna, Budapest and Berlin) and the parochialism of Great Britain and the United States is not dissimilar to Said's role in the 1970s and '80s (in relation to French theory in particular) when 'Reflections on Exile' was written. Here the characterization of a European 'civilization of quasi-barbarism' (after Benjamin) comes close to the spirit of Said in *Orientalism* and the rereading of the Western canon from the perspective of empire in *Culture and Imperialism* (1993). But where Said differs from Steiner is in his insistence on the dialectical 'interplay between nationalism and exile' as 'opposites informing and constituting each other' (Said 1993: 176). To this extent he understandably rejects Steiner's free-floating extraterritoriality ('my homeland the text') for a version of exile that is produced by nationalism.[43] But Steiner's influence, especially his suspicion of anything resembling nationalism, is not entirely absent from the rest of the essay:

> Palestinians feel that they have been turned into exiles by the prover-
> bial people of exile, the Jews. But the Palestinians also know that their
> own sense of national identity has been nourished in the exile milieu,
> where everyone not a blood-brother or sister is an enemy, where every
> sympathizer is an agent of some unfriendly power, and where the
> slightest deviation from the accepted group line is an act of treachery
> and disloyalty. (178)

Said's critique of an excessive Palestinian paranoia and homogeneity ('everyone . . . is an enemy'), a product of the 'exile milieu', recalls Arendt's fears of the consequences of an unthinking homogeneity on the eve of the pronouncement of the State of Israel (Bernstein 114–15). Both Said and Arendt, to this extent, are members of the 'loyal opposition' (quoted 11) in relation to their Palestinian or Jewish constituencies and, in their refusal to follow a party line, are both 'self-conscious pariahs'. In fact, Said's formulation of being the only 'true' intellectual, when compared to the 'other' intellectuals, who are 'now suburban squires', echoes almost exactly the distinction between Arendt's socially acculturated parvenus and singular pariahs.

One strand of postcolonial criticism, as Bruce Robbins has argued, invokes the pariah figure of the rootless cosmopolitan who is not part of 'the nation', a figure castigated by both Hitler and Stalin, and who origi-nated in the 'déraciné' intellectual (beginning with Lazare) so vilified during the Dreyfus Affair (Robbins 1997: 72).[44] This figure, I want to argue, is an unsung example of the repressed Jewish other within Postcolonial Studies, who, already apparent in Fanon's work, prefigures the contemporary vilification of those who are deemed to disavow nation-alist anti-colonialism and, in doing so, are said to disempower and disre-gard the wretched of the earth. Aijaz Ahmad, for instance, uses the

Orwellian distinction (in all senses) between the principled 'exile' and depthless 'vagrant' to portray Rushdie and Said as 'vagrants' (Ahmad 157). Only Said's public pronouncements on behalf of the Palestinian people, and the death threat looming over Rushdie, are said to redeem them from their 'political vagrancy' (157–58 and 198).

This line of argument was given prominence by Kwame Anthony Appiah in a much-quoted passage in which he argued that 'Postcoloniality is the condition of what we might ungenerously call a comprador intelligentsia: of a relatively small, Western-style, Western-trained, group of writers and thinkers who mediate the trade in cultural commodities of western capitalism at the periphery' (Appiah 149). In a notorious simplification of this passage, which nonetheless represents a key strand in Postcolonial Studies, Arif Dirlik wrote that 'postcoloniality is the condition of the intelligentsia of global capitalism' (Dirlik 329 and 356). In this argument, the rootless cosmopolitan – and by extension the focus on diaspora, minority histories and mixed or hybrid expressions of dissidence – are reduced to an expression of global capitalism. Said, of course, was well aware of these reductions, which he faced first of all as a Palestinian activist. After the publication of *The Question of Palestine* (1979), he was accused of frittering away Palestinian national rights by making 'unwarranted concessions to Zionism' and of committing the fatal error of defining the conflict as one 'between two peoples' rather than as an 'armed struggle' against the crimes of colonialism and imperialism. His 'bourgeois humanistic approach' was said to be apparent in the way he favoured a political solution to a tragic situation (a 'tragic symphony', as he puts it in the *Ha'aretz* interview), where both sides of the conflict have been victims (Hovsepian 12). This nationalist response to Said is exemplified by Joseph Massad who, in much recent work, is at pains to dissociate Jewish nationalism from the Holocaust (in stark contrast to Said) to avoid what he calls a 'Zionist ideological trap' that supposedly lessens the suffering of the Palestinians when juxtaposed with the Holocaust (quoted Hochberg 55).

One reason why Said calls himself a 'Jewish-Palestinian' (a knowing form of hybridity) is precisely to complicate this nationalist response where Palestinians are 'the new Jews', which denies any connection between Palestinian and Jewish suffering as two different peoples. Here is a typical response to such one-eyed nationalism:

> What Israel does to Palestinians it does against a background, not only of the long-standing Western tutelage over Palestine and the Arabs ... but also against a background of an equally long-standing and equally unflattering anti-Semitism that in this century produced the Holocaust of the European Jews. We cannot fail to connect the horrific history of anti-Semitic massacres to the establishment of Israel; nor can we fail to understand the depths, the extent and the overpowering legacy of suffering and despair that informed the postwar Zionist movement. (Said 1994b: 167)

In his much-cited 1997 essay 'Bases for Coexistence', Said argues memorably that Jews and Palestinians 'cannot coexist as two communities of detached and uncommunicatingly separate suffering' (Said 2000: 208). His sense of exile, in this formulation, is neither detached from 'the facts of material life' as 'metaphor' (Ahmad 86) nor is it merely 'postcolonial'. To this extent there is a relationship between Said's rejection of the term 'post-colonial' and his turn (or, more accurately, re-turn), in his late work, to such 'last Jews' as Freud in *Freud and the Non-European* (2003), Auerbach in *Humanism and Democratic Criticism* (2004) and Adorno in *On Late Style: Music and Literature against the Grain* (2006). In foregrounding these Jewish figures, all in the name of exilic singularity and dissidence, Said, I want to argue, highlights those aspects of Postcolonial Studies, especially the histories of fascism and anti-Semitism (and by implication their impact on the Palestinian people), that have been missing from its purview.

If all academic disciplines are defined by what they leave out – what Jonathan Boyarin calls 'discipline and exclude' (Jonathan Boyarin 1996: 172) and Gayatri Spivak calls 'disciplinary fear' (Spivak 19) – then it is clear that Postcolonial Studies at its foundation left out, in particular, any interconnections with Jewish history and the Holocaust, which, as I have

shown elsewhere, were expunged under the rubric of a dominant white
'Judeo-Christian' Western culture.[45] Aamer Mufti has done much to
redress these exclusions by articulating the 'paradigmatic narratives' of
minority existence within Western culture – 'assimilation, emancipation,
separatism, conversion, the language of state protection and minority
rights ... exile and homelessness' (Mufti 2007: 2–3) – as part of the
so-called 'Jewish Question' in modern Europe. These paradigms, he
argues, were 'disseminated globally' (2) under colonial and semi-colonial
conditions and were applied to the partitionary formation of nation-states,
such as India and Pakistan, after decolonization. His insistence on the
'metaphorical possibilities of Jewishness for contemporary postcolonial
culture' (6) is illustrated by many of the figures in this book, from Fanon
to Naipaul and Rushdie to Zadie Smith. But I will show that the writers
themselves, and not just cultural critics, as Mufti would have it, were
deeply suspicious of the 'metaphorical possibilities of Jewishness'.

Rushdie started to publish fiction at the moment when Postcolonial
Studies began to be institutionalized in the Western academy, and the
contrast between the imaginative and disciplinary approaches to this
history could not have been starker. After *Grimus* (1975) and *Midnight's
Children* (1981), Rushdie delivered his well-known literary manifesto in
1982 at a London conference on Indian writing held to mark the Festival
of India. He notes in the introduction to *Imaginary Homelands: Essays and
Criticism 1981–1991* (1991) that the conference tended to ignore minority
communities in India and to describe Indian culture in exclusive, and
excluding, Hindu terms. The focus is on the way in which Muslims, and
his own family, were transformed into a minority in post-partition India.
Rushdie's perspective is that of someone who had been part of a 'minority
group all my life', and it was from this standpoint that he delivered his
manifesto which proposed an alternative canon of Indian writing going
beyond any conception of a single national culture:

Let me suggest that Indian writers in England have access to a second
tradition, quite apart from their own racial history. It is the culture and

political history of the phenomenon of migration, displacement, life in a minority group. We can quite legitimately claim as our ancestors the Huguenots, the Irish, the Jews; the past to which we belong is an English past, the history of immigrant Britain. America, a nation of immigrants, has created a great literature out of the phenomenon of cultural transplantation, out of examining the ways in which people cope with a new world; it may be that by discovering what we have in common with those who preceded us into this country, we can begin to do the same. (Rushdie 1991: 20)[46]

What is interesting about this imagined genealogy – 'one of the more pleasant freedoms of the literary migrant [is] to be able to choose [one's] parents' (21) – is that it is not unlike Said's own imagined genealogy with his fellow Jewish exiles or, as we will see, Muriel Spark's imagined identity as a 'Gentile Jewess' and Roth's reimagining of Anne Frank in the United States. Rushdie includes 'the Huguenots, the Irish, the Jews' as part of this alternative transnational minority tradition. These imagined moments of identification with diasporic Jews (as the most troublesome and troubling of Rushdie's troika) is a largely unacknowledged feature of Rushdie's fiction (from *Grimus* to *Shalimar the Clown*), as we will see in Chapter 6, in stark contrast to the disciplinary formation of Postcolonial Studies. Rushdie, in his fiction, evokes the history of Spain (where Jews and Muslims lived together peacefully before they were expelled in 1492), the history of Jewish communities in India, and also compares border states in Europe and Southeast Asia where, respectively, Jewish and Muslim 'communities of suffering' have lived for centuries.

The danger is that Rushdie's 'imaginary homeland' merely aestheticizes the diaspora (indulging in too much imagination) so that it becomes another 'great tradition' of international writers beyond historical or political contingency. But we will see that in his metaphorical engagement with these lost cosmopolitan histories (what he calls 'Indias of the Mind') he is well aware, not least in his fiction, of the pitfalls of mere aestheticization. Starting with *Grimus*, Rushdie embraces a lost Central European

Jewish history and culture as a model of secular religious identity and, at the same time, as an example of the dangers of, in Arendtian terms, world-lessness. For Rushdie, the difference between exile and diaspora is equivalent to the difference between the individual and the masses. This contrasts with Said, who associates exile with Palestinian national narratives and diaspora with Jewish nationalism. These distinctions are discussed in the conversation between Rushdie and Said ('On Palestinian Identity') in *Imaginary Homelands*. Here Rushdie rejects the notion of exile as 'primarily literary and bourgeois' in contrast to 'the Palestinians' where 'exile is a mass phenomenon' (Rushdie 1991: 171). He also notes that Said demurs from the phrase 'Palestinian diaspora', which Said reinforces:

> I suppose there is a sense in which, as one man wrote to me from Jerusalem, we [Palestinians] are 'the Jews of the Arab world'. But I think our [Palestinian] experience is really quite different and beyond such attempts to draw parallels. Perhaps its dimension is much more modest. In any case the idea that there is a kind of redemptive homeland doesn't answer my view of things. (173–74)

At one point in the interview, Rushdie speaks of the false assumption that the Palestinian community who are 'inside Palestine' have, at one time, been deemed to be 'somehow contaminated by the proximity of the Jews' (169). As Patrick Williams has shown, Said consistently distinguishes between Palestinian and Jewish history and identity in relation to the difference between 'exile' and 'diaspora'.[47] In the interview immediately preceding 'My Right of Return' in *Power, Politics and Culture*, Said argues that 'I naturally reject the term "diaspora"' and goes on: 'But nothing can prevent the term being used. The Jews used it to fulfil their own imagination, but we are talking about a different situation for the Palestinian. The Palestinian situation and society Palestinians desire is peculiar to that nation' (Viswanathan 2001: 442). That Said validated 'exile' over 'diaspora' is perhaps due to the fear of being 'contaminated' by a more powerful historical narrative than his own which, by the time of his late work, he was attempting to remake in his own image as the exiled and isolated amateur intellectual (Said 2001: 174). As he puts it in the interview with Rushdie: 'To be a victim of a victim does present quite unusual difficulties. For if you are trying to deal with the classic victim of all time – the Jew and his or her movement – then to portray yourself as the victim of the Jew is a comedy worthy of one of your novels' (Rushdie 1991: 182). Unlike the term 'diaspora', 'exile' is supposedly disruptive and intransigent and not redeemed by a sense of nationalist return.[48] Rushdie in *The Satanic Verses* (1988), as if following Said's advice, structures the novel around the difference between migrant and exile, which is not dissimilar to Said's distinction between diaspora and exile (although in Rushdie's case it is exile that is the negative term). For Rushdie, the exile is a deeply conservative figure who sees history as continuous and always has a bounded and pure autochthonous 'homeland' to return to. The migrant, in stark contrast, is at home nowhere and is an impure presence who disrupts all certainties.[49]

Stuart Hall's foundational definition of 'diaspora' is relevant here precisely because the context of Israel/Palestine that he evokes makes this a highly contested term:

> I use [diaspora] here metaphorically, not literally: diaspora does not refer us to those scattered tribes whose identity can only be secured in relation to some sacred homeland to which they must at all costs return, even if it means pushing other people into the sea. This is the old, the imperialising, the hegemonising, form of 'ethnicity'. We have seen the fate of the people of Palestine at the hands of this backwards-looking concept of diaspora – and the complicity of the West with it. The diaspora experience as I intend it here is defined, not by essence or purity, but by recognition of a necessary heterogeneity and diversity; by a conception of 'identity' which lives with and through, not despite, difference; by *hybridity*. (Hall 235)

As in the case of Arendt, we can once again see the risks inherent in such 'metaphorical' thinking, although Hall is of course taking his notion

of hybridity from the diverse and mixed history of the Caribbean. But
Williams, writing from a Palestinian perspective, rejects Hall's 'classic' definition on the grounds that the stress on 'heterogeneity and diversity', or
'difference and hybridity', does not accord with the idea of a Palestinian
'return' to what Said calls, in 'Reflections on Exile', a 'true home' (Said 2001:
173). As Williams puts it: 'what is perhaps less certain [in Hall's definition
of diaspora] is [whether] Palestinians, even after so many years of dispersal,
might be – indeed should be – ready to give up the idea of return to their
homeland since that is allegedly not what modern diaspora is about'
(Williams 94). Said's critique of Postcolonial Studies, as has been argued,
was also on the grounds that the Palestinians had been refused entry into
the supposed postcolonial era.[50] At the same time, Said insists on what he
calls, in his conversation with Rushdie, the 'whole notion of crossing over,
of moving from one identity to another', as 'extremely important . . . being
as I am – as we all are – a sort of hybrid' (Viswanathan 2001: 182), which
became the subject of his memoir, *Out of Place* (1999).

But Hall's version of diaspora can be read completely differently
from a diasporic Jewish perspective. For Jonathan and Daniel Boyarin,
Jewishness in this account is identified '*only* with a lack, a neurotic attachment to a lost homeland'. In this reading, Hall fatally confuses Jewish
nationalism, which aimed to *negate* the diaspora, with 'Jewish diasporism',
which aims to preserve it. They conclude, in a not dissimilar argument to
Williams in relation to the Palestinians, that Hall 'banishes Jews from the
brave new world of hybridity. Hall's hybridity, as it would appear from this
quote, must be purified – of Jews' (Boyarin and Boyarin 13). For the
Boyarins, Hall has mistakenly negated the 'last' diasporic Jews by locating
them within a hegemonic imperium. By pushing the Palestinians 'metaphorically' into 'the sea' (Hall 235) – a threat initially applied to 'the
Jews' – he associates Palestinians exclusively with the timeless pantheon
of victimhood, not unlike Massad's 'new Jews'. Rooted in the past, and
unhoused everywhere as 'last Jews', means that the Jewish diaspora is
inevitably universalized. As Said puts it in *Freud and the Non-European*,
'the diasporic, wandering, unresolved, cosmopolitan consciousness of

someone who is both inside and outside his or her community' is no longer just a 'Jewish characteristic' (Said 2003: 53).

But the line between universalizing Jewish history and superseding it can be quite thin. In fact, much of this book explores the tension between those who construct Jews as 'world-historical victims' or the quintessential insider/outsider, enabling other victims of history or ambivalent others to speak, and those who wish to go beyond Jewish history in the name of more contemporaneous histories. Within Diaspora Studies, for instance, there is a strand of reductive thinking, inspired by Hall's foundational essay, that starts with the premise that Jews, having formed what is called the 'classic diaspora', have been transcended by newer, more contemporary, diasporic groups.[51] The problem with such disciplinary thinking is that it reinforces the narrative that diasporic Jewish history ended with the European Holocaust, which is, to compound the Boyarins' bitter irony (as anti-nationalists), also the narrative of Jewish nationalism. Such secular transcendence of 'last Jews' (mirroring Christian antecedents) discounts, above all, the history and reality of the contemporary Jewish diaspora and other 'minor' forms of Jewishness.[52]

While the work of Said as a 'Jewish-Palestinian' is on the side of hybridity, it also wants to distinguish between different kinds of 'classic' Jewish narratives which can be summarized as majoritarian or minoritarian. In the *Ha'aretz* interview he is quite blunt about this: 'the more interesting Jews I know – are not defined by their Jewishness. I think that to confine Jews to their Jewishness is problematic' (Viswanathan 452). Here the contrast between Disraeli and Marx, who provide epigraphs at the start of *Orientalism* (1978), is significant. One goes the way of empire, 'race' and myth-making; the other goes the way of internationalism, anti-imperialism and intellectual critique. There are always two Jews or two Semites (Said 1978: 307), and it is this binary narrative that Said finally overcomes in his late work as a 'Jewish-Palestinian'. The phrase 'last Jewish intellectual' obviously assumes a mass of non-intellectual, suburban Jews who remain untouched by a Marxian oppositionist tradition as championed by Isaac Deutscher in his essay 'The non-Jewish Jew'. This is, in the end, the problem with the distinction between 'pariah' and 'parvenu', which, as seen in the case of Arendt, can easily be reduced to a discourse of 'good' and 'bad' Jews, a racial discourse that Philip Roth spends much of his time dismantling in his fiction. But Said's late work, I want to argue, is no longer confined by such binaries. Rather than the 'last Jewish intellectual', shadowed by its 'secret (suburban) sharer', we have the 'Jewish-Palestinian' who comes closest to symbolizing the lost ideal of a binational state in Israel/Palestine as articulated by Arendt and the Brit Shalom group led by Judah Magnes.[53]

In describing a novel that could account for the variety of Palestinian experience, Said tells Rushdie that it would have to be 'the kind of crazy history in *Midnight's Children*, with all those little strands coming in and out', which Rushdie summarizes as 'a form which appears to be formlessness, and which in fact mirrors the instability of the situation' (Rushdie 1991: 179). As a self-proclaimed exilic and amateur intellectual, Said also wishes to think 'without banisters', beyond disciplinary thinking or, as he puts it, beyond our 'professional guilds' (Said 1994a: xvi). Seeing dissimilars in similarities accounts for the risk-taking in the modernist forms of expression in all of the works that I will discuss – from Fanon to Zadie Smith – which are nonetheless deeply imbricated in the racial discourses which did not end with either the death camps or decolonization. Said, following Terry Eagleton, who had long since characterized the instabilities of modernism as being constituted by 'exiles and émigrés', understood the centrality of diasporic German-Jewish refugees to his ideal of a new global humanism and of new, creatively disruptive ways of thinking and writing.[54] But when his Israeli interviewer made the appropriating comment (however innocent) that Said 'sounded Jewish', his interviewee was quick to reappropriate his own hybrid identity as an overdetermined mix somewhere between the 'last Jewish intellectual', a 'Jewish-Palestinian' and the 'only true follower of Adorno'. These appropriations and reappropriations continue in *Diasporas of the Mind* with the Saidian persona (George Ziad) at the heart of Roth's *Operation Shylock: A Confession* (1993) and the figure of Primo Levi reimagined in *The Satanic Verses*.

To be sure, Said's identification with the 'last Jewish intellectual' was an act of risk-taking not least because it illustrates the power of metaphorical thinking. The difficulties in deciding whether the work of metaphor is ethically suspect or not are, as James Young has shown, deeply embedded in those who, after Arendt, wished to protect the victims of the Holocaust from the figurative realm which was said to expunge 'actual' history (Young 1988: 84). As Cynthia Ozick put it most forcefully: 'Jews are not metaphors – not for poets, not for novelists, not for theologians, not for murderers, and never for antisemites' (Ozick 1975: 128). In *Metaphor and Memory* (1989), however, Ozick makes out a case for the all-encompassing ethical dimension of metaphor as the 'reciprocal agent, the universalizing force: it makes possible the power to envision the stranger's heart'. Metaphorical thinking, in these examples, seems to lie somewhere between the anxiety of appropriation (as I will call it) and a reciprocal engagement with the stranger (or dissimilarities). But it is not easy drawing the line between these two versions of metaphor (as threat or as ethical good), as can be seen in Ozick's typically brazen contradictions where metaphor can 'convey a leap of faith' which makes it 'so dangerous' (Ozick 1989: 279).[55] These anxieties and ethical possibilities, I have argued, can be found in Said's appropriation of the 'last Jew' and, as I will now show, in the founding instance of postcolonial mimicry.

The Anxiety of Appropriation: Naipaul's Shylock

On the first page of V.S. Naipaul's *The Mimic Men: A Novel* (1967), we have the following passage:

> I paid Mr Shylock three guineas a week for a tall, multi-mirrored, book-shaped room with a coffin-like wardrobe. And for Mr Shylock, the recipient each week of fifteen times three guineas, the possessor of a mistress and of suits made of cloth so fine I felt I could eat it, I had nothing but admiration. I was not used to the social modes of London or to the physiognomy and complexion of the North, and I thought

Mr Shylock looked distinguished, like a lawyer or business man or politician. He had the habit of stroking the lobe of his ear and inclining his head to listen. I thought the gesture was attractive; I copied it. I knew of recent events in Europe; they tormented me; and although I was trying to live on seven pounds a week I offered Mr Shylock my fullest, silent compassion.

There is much in *The Mimic Men* that anticipates the complex and often contradictory identification with Jews and Jewish history (evoking both the Holocaust and the racialized figure of Shylock in a single breath) in the writers whom we will discuss. Naipaul's Caribbean exile, Ralph Singh (born Ranjit Kripalsingh), admires his Jewish landlord and sees him as embodying ambiguously both Northern European civilization ('a lawyer or business man or politician') and the consequences of European barbarity ('recent events in Europe; they tormented me'). In copying Mr Shylock's mannerisms and dress, and enduring the high rents of his boarding house, Singh significantly gains a sense of identity, however provisional, in relation to his erstwhile prototype. The search for stability can be found in the 'multi-mirrored, book-shaped room with a coffin-like wardrobe' which combines mimicry or mirroring with literature and death. We are told that Mr Shylock died shortly after Singh had arrived in 1945 and, perhaps because of this swift and secret 'London death' (Naipaul 5), Naipaul frames his novel with Singh's memories of his erstwhile landlord.[56]

At the beginning of the novel we are told that Singh travelled from the Caribbean to the 'miraculous' city of London, shortly after the end of the war, in a bid to seek 'order' (the 'continuing consciousness of wholeness and sanity') and gain a singular, rather than a fractured, 'personality' (26). Instead of the dream of order, however, he finds himself in Mr Shylock's boarding house, which is akin to the 'shipwreck which all my life I had sought to avoid' (7). The human flotsam and jetsam of postwar and post-colonial London can be found in the hotel, including an Italian 'countess', a British fascist, several 'damp, macintoshed Maltese' (13), a girl from

Kenya, a 'Frenchman from Morocco', a Burmese student and a 'Jewish youth, tall and prophetic in black' (14). One critic has reduced these assorted figures to 'wandering Jews', descended from Shakespeare's 'quintessential outcast' (Greene 152), whereas others have read Singh's emulation of Shylock as prefiguring the mimicry that is said to 'destabilize colonial discourse' (Ashcroft et al. 126–27). But what is most interesting about this novel, for our argument, is that Naipaul reads these different 'Jewish', 'colonial' and 'postcolonial' histories in relation to each other so that Singh is able to mimic Shylock in order to give his fluid identity some kind of shape.

Singh experiences his first snowfall in the boarding house and comes to the realization that London does not represent the 'beginning of order' which he associates with the gods of his 'Aryan ancestors' (Naipaul 18). With Mr Shylock, 'one type of order had gone for good' and the world was no longer 'simple black and white' (30–31) or, we might add, Jew and Aryan. His 'double journey' between the 'landscapes of sea and snow', two distinct forms of tabula rasa, represents instead one of many new beginnings for Singh and the 'final emptiness' (8) or 'feeling of impermanence' (11) that he attempts to overcome. Looking back after fourteen months in his rather clichéd garret room, where he was to write his life-story, he takes solace in the order that the act of writing imposes on him: 'I re-created the climb up the dark stairs to Mr Shylock's attic. . . . By this re-creation the event became historical and manageable; it was given its place; it will no longer disturb me' (243). For Singh, the 'recording of a life' became a form of mechanical lifelessness: 'I . . . have grown to relish the order and constriction of hotel life. . . . Order, sequence, regularity' (244).

Singh's troubled memories of the death of Mr Shylock (victim and persecutor, double and other), and the estrangement caused by living in his boarding house after migrating to London, enable him to reconstruct his past and present lives imaginatively so that they become 'historical and manageable'. Exiled and isolated and utterly reliant on his imagination to 're-create the moment' (7), Singh allows the figure of Shylock to constitute his own identity. This is particularly astonishing when we note that Naipaul's Shylock was undoubtedly based on the notorious slum landlord Peter Rachman, a stateless Jewish refugee from Poland. Rachman exploited, in particular, Afro-Caribbean immigrants in London's Notting Hill in the 1950s and '60s, and has been the subject of numerous novels and plays largely because, as is implicit in Naipaul, he combines a history of victimhood with the exploitation of new migrants to Britain, which led to the term 'Rachmanism'.[57] But Singh's mirroring of Shylock, however ambiguous, avoids the gulf that, in other renderings, can come between Jewish and black histories in Britain and the United States. What is more, he anticipates a generation of British-Caribbean writers, such as Caryl Phillips, who not only have a 'fascination' with 'the Jews' but who regard Shakespeare's Shylock as their 'hero' (Phillips 1987: 55 and 66).

Phillips has written extensively on his experience of being the offspring of the Windrush generation of migrants to Britain's shores, arriving from St Kitts in 1958 at the age of twelve weeks, and his resultant loss of self during his formative years. He begins his travel book *The European Tribe* by looking back at his 'lack of a coherent sense of identity in 1970s Britain' (Phillips 1987: 1) which was highlighted by an English literature teacher in Leeds who attempted to explain his surname: 'So Greenberg was Jewish, Morely . . . Yorkshire . . . and McKenzie was a Scot. . . . Phillips . . . must be from Wales.' Humiliated by this exercise, he concludes: 'If the teaching of English literature can feed a sense of identity then I, like many of my black contemporaries in Britain, was starving' (2). Phillips, significantly, eventually inverts 'Haley's Choice' and claims his 'Jewish grandfather' as part of an imagined genealogy (Phillips 2001: 130). As Stephen Clingman has argued, Phillips in the subsequent chapters of *The European Tribe* goes on to find 'some coherence and perspective through a gathering awareness of the recent history of Jews' (Clingman 2009: 70), which, as we have seen, is a reprise of Naipaul's *The Mimic Men*.[58] The contrast in *The European Tribe* is provided by Phillips's experience of historical and cultural invisibility in Europe, and the invisibility of colonial genocide in Africa, as against the manifold visibility of 'the Jews' as Europe's acknowledged world-historical victims:

As a child, in what seemed to me a hostile country, the Jews were the only minority group discussed with reference to exploitation and racialism, and for that reason, I naturally identified with them. At that time, I was staunchly indignant about everything from the Holocaust to the Soviet persecution of Jewry. The bloody excesses of colonialism, the pillage and rape of modern Africa, the transportation of 11 million black people to the Americas, and their subsequent bondage were not on the curriculum, and certainly not on the television screen. As a result I vicariously channelled a part of my hurt and frustration through the Jewish experience. (Phillips 1987: 54)

Phillips is looking back at a naïve younger self who has not, as yet, been able to construct a black-British identity but can draw parallels, for instance, with Venetian Jews being confined in the proto-ghetto. Such identifications with 'the Jews', as Paul Gilroy also notes, confirm a sense in which public representations of the Holocaust enabled other minorities and histories of oppression to be articulated. Gilroy's *The Black Atlantic: Modernity and Double Consciousness* (1993) historicizes the black presence in Europe, which engages with Phillips's sense of exclusion and which also began a much larger project of articulating the 'knotted intersection of histories' which, in one example of comparative racial history, brings together black American soldiers as witnesses to the horrors of the Nazi death camps.[59] These intersections certainly became a feature of Phillips's fiction, which began with a reworking of the story of Anne Frank (anticipating Roth) and is characterized by his switching between Caribbean and (Jewish) diasporic histories. That is why the youthful Phillips – as a fellow 'black man living in Europe' – takes Frantz Fanon's Antillean philosophy professor at his word: 'Whenever you hear anyone abuse the Jews, pay attention, because he is talking about you' (54), although, as I will show, Fanon does not always abide by this guidance. At the same time, Phillips notes 'the virulent anti-Semitism that seems to permeate much black thought' (52–53) in the United States, which can be seen in the voice of Rudi in *Higher Ground*

(1989), published shortly after *The European Tribe*. Phillips was well aware of the anxiety and necessity of appropriating Jewish history in relation to his own writing.

To be sure, the attempt to imagine crossover black and Jewish histories in the United States has resulted, as we will see in the account of *The Plot against America* (2004), in the charge that black experience in the United States has been appropriated by Philip Roth. As David Biale has noted, in the United States the Holocaust has been overdetermined as a world-historical model of racism, with all forms of historical oppression expected to fit into this framework (Biale et al. 1998: 17–33). In *The European Tribe*, Phillips understands, in this context, that 'an American black might respond with contempt to an American Jew who told him, "I know what it is to be persecuted; I am a Jew"' (Phillips 1987: 53). Such is the anxiety of appropriation, with the fear being that one history of racism expunges other histories. The institutionalized presence of the Holocaust in the United States makes it a convenient filter through which other, more immediate American histories of oppression – such as the history of slavery and the genocide of Native Americans – can be under-played. What is more, the double-edged nature of Jewish victimhood in the United States produces a community that both insists on its victimized status and, at the same time, has the clout to place a Holocaust museum in the political heart of Washington, DC. As Biale notes, it serves American state interests to award the 'genocide of Europeans by Europeans ... canonical status' while the 'home grown mass sufferings of African and Native Americans' (Biale et al. 1998: 28) still remain largely outside the national canon.

The anxiety of appropriation accounts for the 'disciplinary fear' that constructs the 'classic' Jewish diaspora as a history of victimhood to be superseded. This anxiety is not unlike the anxiety of influence, although it is rather less creative and rather more polemical. This can be seen, for instance, in the reception of Phillips's *The Nature of Blood*, which mixes 'black' and 'Jewish' history in the guise of Shakespeare's Othello and Shylock. As Hilary Mantel argues:

it is demented cosiness that denies the differences between people,
denies how easily the interests of human beings become divided. It is
indecent to lay claim to other people's suffering: it is a colonial impulse,
dressed up as altruism. The heart may be pure, but more than the heart
is needed; good motives sometimes paralyse thought. We are not all
Jews. That is a simple fact. It is why the Holocaust happened. (Mantel 40)

Mantel's fear is that, by universalizing the Jewish experience, other
histories will be colonized; for this reason, distinct racial identities need to
be maintained to explain 'why the Holocaust happened'. Her argument
highlights the fear of 'the Jew' as metaphor from the other side, as it were,
with the phrase 'we are not all Jews' echoing uncannily a Hanif Kureishi
short story rather than the history of the Holocaust.[60] Mantel's polemic
indicates, above all, the anxiety of appropriation, as seen in her misguided
sense that the longevity and hegemony of Jewish history can deny the
'differences between people' by being such a compelling structural narrative. This fearful 'colonial impulse', however wrong-headed, may well
explain why self-designated 'new' disciplines – such as Diaspora Studies,
Postcolonial Studies and Ethnic and Racial Studies – defined themselves
as superseding a Jewish history that is constructed as age-old or 'classic'.
But, as Alain Finkielkraut has shown, the anxiety of appropriation need
not be merely a matter between Jews and non-Jews. As the son of an
Auschwitz survivor, he bridled at the May 1968 demonstration on behalf
of Daniel Cohn-Bendit (denied entry into France from Germany), with its
famous chant 'We are all German Jews!' (Finkielkraut 17). This chant is
described acutely as the 'sudden democratization' (135) of Jewish identity,
where 'every child of the postwar era could change places with the outsider
and wear the yellow star' (17): 'Born after the fact, exempted from Jewish
destiny by the kindness of time, the last minute martyrs made up for
their tardiness by being finicky about their Jewish sensitivity. Colonized
peoples fighting for their independence, Black Power, the Third World
reconquering its dignity: those were, for them, the new Jews of history.' In
looking back at May 1968, Finkielkraut remembers the fierce debates

about who were 'the legitimate heirs to the mantle of Jewish identity' (134) with the assumption that such identities were exhausted in the diaspora and had to take a national form in Israel or a 'new' historical form in the West. A few years before the May 1968 demonstration, intellectual manifestos had described the French military presence in Algeria as a 'Hitlerite order' and Simone de Beauvoir, an ardent supporter of these manifestos, wrote of ten thousand Algerians 'herded into the Vel' d'Hiv' like 'the Jews at Drancy once before' (Beauvoir 321).[61] But Finkielkraut tends to resist such analogical thinking as he understands that Jews were no longer the object of discourse (after they had entered history as nation-alists), which is why he argues that the demonstrators were not 'German Jews' but, instead, 'imaginary Jews' or metaphorical Jews. As he recog-nizes, the borderline between what is 'similar' and what is 'dissimilar' (in the language of metaphor) is policed with particular rigour by postwar Jews and Jewish organizations in the name of protecting the memory of Holocaust victims (as seen in the fierce criticisms of *Eichmann in Jerusalem*). The fear is that such metaphorical thinking – where the similar and dissimilar become blurred – will dilute Jewish particularity. Such is the baleful sense of 'uniqueness', beyond metaphor, where Jews and Jewish history become the very essence of dissimilarity.[62]

One response to such ill-disciplined metaphorical thinking ('we are all German Jews') has been called the 'particularization of the genocide' (from genocide to Holocaust) which is the 'alpha and omega of Jewish history' (Benbassi 148). In this reading, Finkielkraut is merely engaging in another form of appropriation (as he recognizes) in his role as 'imaginary Jew':

I thought I was living up to Israel's calling, and played the role of the Jew, the black, the colonized, the Indian, or the impoverished of the Third World. These were happy, boisterous years, when I stuck to my origins like glue. It doesn't work anymore: the drama's mainspring has unsprung. . . . Even the affirmation 'I am a Jew' quickly produces a painful sense that I'm *appropriating the Holocaust as my own*, draping myself with the torture that others underwent. (Finkielkraut 32)

Esther Benbassi questions whether a 'Jewishness that has become synonymous with victimhood can perpetuate itself indefinitely', and notes
cautiously that while the memory of the Holocaust in a global era has
become ever more cosmopolitan, the 'apparent cosmopolitanism of this
memory does not make its message universal' (Benbassi 147–49). The
challenge, as ever, is to aim for universality without expunging historical
specificity. But the fear, above all, is that universality will lead to vacuity.
That is why Finkielkraut dreads the figure of the *luftmensch*, 'a Jew without
substance . . . in a state of zero gravity, relieved of what could have been his
symbolic universe, his personal place' (Finkielkraut 38). A rarely understood after-effect of the Holocaust and of colonialism is the proteophobic
anxiety of being a *luftmensch* (literally an 'air-man'), which, I will show,
extends from Fanon to Rushdie in the colonial and postcolonial realm,
shapes the dispute between Levi and Améry after Auschwitz, and is the
starting point for Spark's and Roth's imaginary Jewishness beyond the
eternally suffering Jew. This figure, in its postethnic guise, will finally be
embraced and rejected in the fiction of Anita Desai and Zadie Smith. Go
too far in the direction of metaphorical thinking and the danger is that
you are left with nothing but the *luftmensch* ('of the *mind*') who invites, it
seems, the not so warm disciplinary embrace of nations, identities and
communities (sometimes in the guise of academic specialisms). But all
of the figures explored here negotiate between such metaphorical and
disciplinary thinking in the name of diaspora. The haunting figure of the
disembodied *luftmensch*, coupled with the overdetermined black body,
will now be examined in the resonant life and work of Frantz Fanon.

PART ONE

2

Diaspora and Colonialism
Frantz Fanon, Albert Memmi and the Cosmopolitan Jew

'The last shall be first and the first shall be last.' Matthew 20:16, cited in
Frantz Fanon, *The Wretched of the Earth* (1961), p. 2.

'This tearing away [from "the white man's culture"], painful and difficult though it may be, is, however, necessary. If it is not accomplished
there will be serious psycho-affective injuries and the result will be
individuals without anchor, without horizon, colourless, stateless, rootless – a race of angels.' Frantz Fanon, *The Wretched of the Earth* (1961),
p. 175.

'I was a sort of half-breed of colonization, understanding everyone
because I belonged completely to no one.' Albert Memmi, *The Colonizer
and the Colonized* (1957), p. 14.

There have been many Frantz Fanons since his untimely death in 1961 at
the age of thirty-six. He became a revolutionary figurehead of the Black
Power movement in the United States in the 1960s; was adopted as a
Third World leader of the 'wretched of the earth' in the 1970s; and was

reinvented as a postcolonial theorist – with reference to *Black Skin, White Masks* (1952) – in the 1980s and '90s.[1] The main problem with these various incarnations is that they tend to reinforce the image of a polarized figure whose first and last works are treated as mutually exclusive – as if one were on the side of Freud, the other on the side of Marx.[2] 'Postcolonial' Fanon, for instance, is no longer a revolutionary figure, theorizing violence and counterviolence and speaking for the oppressed, but is instead most concerned with questions of sexual and racial identity. Those who make this argument tend to cite Homi Bhabha's 'Remembering Fanon', the influential foreword to *Black Skin, White Masks*, whose subtitle – 'Self, Psyche and the Colonial Tradition' – indicates the distance travelled from a 'revolutionary' or 'Third World' perspective.[3] Bhabha is quite explicit about refiguring Fanon so that he can no longer be 'easily placed in a seamless narrative of liberationist history' (Bhabha 1986: viii). But this repositioning of Fanon has proved to be short-lived, with his biographer arguing convincingly, in a damning summary, that Bhabha's version of Fanon has transformed him into a free-floating figure 'outside of time and space and in a purely textual dimension' (Macey 27–28).

Henry Louis Gates was the first to contend that Fanon, by the 1990s, had become emptied of meaning as both 'totem and text' and was now a 'Rashomon-like' figure who could be interpreted and appropriated from radically different critical positions.[4] He concludes that the rewriting of Fanon as a 'transcultural, transhistorical Global Theorist' in the 1980s has resulted in a 'tableau of narcissism, with Fanon himself as the Other that can only reflect and consolidate the critical self' (Gates 465 and 470). This reading of Fanon, as 'icon' or 'screen memory' (470), contrasts starkly with the co-option of Fanon in the 1960s and '70s as the acme of authenticity. The Black Cat edition of *The Wretched of the Earth*, published in the United States in 1968, is described, for instance, as 'the handbook for the black revolution that is changing the shape of the world'.[5] The characterization of decolonization as a 'kind of tabula rasa', on the first page of *The Wretched of the Earth*, has returned to haunt a posthumous Fanon, who

has been inscribed from so many contradictory perspectives that he is in
danger of becoming an empty signifier or *luftmensch*.

By the end of the twentieth century, Fanon's sense of the world as a
tabula rasa after colonialism, which culminates in the call for a new
'species' of humanity, no longer defined by 'race', has resulted in another
kind of redemptive narrative where he is said to represent 'post-ethnicity
avant la lettre'.[6] According to this argument, Fanon's attempt near the end
of *Black Skin, White Masks* to 'reach out for the universal' (Fanon 1952:
197), beyond black and white, makes possible the cosmopolitan tradition
of 'black American intellectuals' (Posnock 1998: 99). This Americanized
version of Fanon, in stark opposition to his co-option by American black
nationalists, can be made in relation to Fanon's new universalism and also
his 'new humanism' which concludes *The Wretched of the Earth*: 'Let us try
to create the whole man, whom Europe has been incapable of bringing to
triumphant birth' (Fanon 1961: 198 and 252). What is stressed, in this
version of Fanon, is his disavowal of both origins and authenticity, which
takes him beyond race-thinking and thereby allows him to act as a
resource for the 'modern black intellectual'.

In his account of twentieth-century black American writers, Ross
Posnock rightly notes that 'intellectual' entered political discourse as a
term of abuse during the Dreyfus Affair. By invoking universal values, in
response to French nationalism and the Catholic Church, Emile Zola and
the Dreyfusards were branded as 'déracinés' (Posnock 1998: 2). For
Posnock, the Dreyfus Affair generated a cluster of alternatives to an essentialized belonging, such as the rootless cosmopolitan, which, he contends,
informed the work of modern black writers such as Fanon. What is
missing from this argument, however, is precisely the issue of Semitic
racial discourse and the figure of 'the Jew' which generated the Dreyfus
Affair in the first place. Where I differ from Posnock is in showing that the
'déraciné' or rootless cosmopolitan was most obviously imbricated in a
Semitic racial discourse in the first half of the twentieth century, not least
in France, which was the optic through which Fanon, and other black
writers, perceived the condition of diasporic rootlessness.

Between Fanon and Memmi

The universalization of the figure of the rootless cosmopolitan in the name of Fanon's postethnicity is, I believe, entirely ahistorical, although this is not the same as saying that one can draw easy or straightforward conclusions from Fanon's life experience. At the age of eighteen, Fanon volunteered to join de Gaulle's Free French and sailed from Martinique singing 'Hitler, we are going to knock you off your hilltop' (quoted Macey 92). By the end of his life, many of his comrades in the Free French were on the other side of the trenches after Fanon joined the Front de Libération Nationale (FLN) to liberate Algeria from colonial control. Such is Fanon's 'impossible life' in the phrase of Albert Memmi, his contemporary.[7] Those who have reclaimed Fanon for the twenty-first century have returned to the figure described by Memmi, whose influential portrait, according to Gates, was 'emphatically . . . not the Fanon we have recuperated for global culture' (Gates 468). In calling for a more 'provisional, reactive and local' (470) approach to Fanon, a narrative taken up in David Macey's biography, Memmi's version, in relation to both diaspora and colonialism, has proved to be most productive, if not, as we shall see, entirely uncontentious.

Memmi, a French-Tunisian-Jewish novelist and philosopher, who was educated in Tunis and Paris, published *The Colonizer and the Colonized* (1957) five years after *Black Skin, White Masks* and two years after Aimé Césaire's *Discourse on Colonialism* (1955). *The Colonizer and the Colonized*, which included a preface by Jean-Paul Sartre, was part of a canon of works that indicates the rise of the 'postwar French anti-colonial intellectual' who, in differing ways, searched for a new vocabulary to understand the period of decolonization.[8] *The Pillar of Salt* (1955), Memmi's autobiographical novel of this period, begins and ends with a rejection of the language of philosophy and the promise of an academic career in France. Instead, Memmi's persona becomes a storyteller, placing the imagination at the heart of his concerns, and returns to Tunisia so that he can 'see clearly into my own darkness . . . to find a way out'.[9] In this way, *The Pillar of Salt* combines an extraterritorial imagination with a sense of national belonging. It was from this paradoxical perspective that Memmi was to engage with Fanon.

The founding figures of French anti-colonialism were often in dialogue with each other (as we will see in the case of Fanon and Césaire), with Memmi, in a long essay and several shorter pieces, advocating an increasingly influential version of Fanon as a cosmopolitan exile. Memmi traces Fanon's various guises as an assimilated 'white' French Antillean, a black West Indian, a revolutionary Algerian nationalist, a pan-Africanist and a universalizing 'new humanist', and concludes that it is the very 'impossibility' of these serial transformations that has 'become the source of his far-reaching influence' (Memmi 1975: 39). For Memmi, it was the disavowal of his origins and of the people of Martinique in particular that characterizes a diasporic Fanon who 'broke with France, the French people and Europe' and thereby 'had to tear himself loose to the last fibre and eradicate what had constituted his life up to that point' (19). In this reading, Fanon's life becomes something of a family romance, with the surrogate fatherland of Algeria taking the 'place of Martinique' (24).

For Memmi, the disjunction between the Antilles, France and Algeria is only bridged in relation to a lifelong search for transcendence, or what he calls the coherence of Fanon's 'unshakeable belief in radical and final change' (39). 'The Impossible Life of Frantz Fanon' turns out to be a series of conversion stories, although, as David Marriott has rightly argued, Fanon's sense of liberation from racism as a 'difficult question that cannot be resolved' should not be reduced to a conventional redemptive narrative.[10] To this extent, Memmi rejects the idea of Fanon as the doyen of a transcendent postethnicity and instead thinks of him as a déraciné 'Jewish intellectual', which accounts for a series of invented guises culminating in his rejection of Algerian nationalism and his turn to pan-Africanism:

> I suspect that Fanon's sudden and intransigent Africanism roused new hostility against him. He might have shared the fate of those Jewish intellectuals who declare themselves universalists and are suspected of

cosmopolitanism and even treason; they are not considered sufficiently legitimate members of the community to be permitted such aloofness. For an Algerian so late in the making it was imprudent, to say the least, to put so recent a bond to the test. (Memmi 1973: 32)[11]

Rather than locating Fanon within the nation of Algeria or on the continent of Africa, Memmi tends to find commonalities in his life and work: 'oppressed people resemble each other. Their own particular features and individual history aside, colonized peoples, Jews, women, the poor show a kind of family likeness.'[12] It was for this reason that Memmi argued at length for the similarities between Negritude and Jewishness in *Dominated Man: Notes towards a Portrait* (1968). Not that these commonalities led to a transcendent postracial narrative: 'one cannot shed identity so easily. A Black man does not get rid of his Negritude by calling it a mirage: nor can anyone exchange his cultural, historical and social singularity for another, by a simple act of will – not even in the service of a revolutionary ethic' (Memmi 1975: 28). Fanon and Memmi have been aptly described as an 'imaginary interracial male couple' due to their similar experiences as French-educated racial and religious minorities in North Africa. My argument is that Memmi transforms Fanon into a 'family likeness', the only transformation permissible by Memmi, as an imagined double.[13]

While Memmi's version of Fanon may be considered to be an act of critical narcissism (*pace* Gates), it is worth remembering that Memmi was well aware that his reading of Fanon through the prism of a diasporic Jewishness was based on lived experience. Fanon was denounced by Memmi's acquaintance Dr Ben Soltan as a 'Zionist' (as well as a 'Black Doctor') after a conflict of interest at the Clinique Manouba in Tunis, where Fanon worked for three years following his exile from Algeria in 1956. Soltan, the director of the clinic, argued that Fanon was maltreating Algerian and Tunisian patients 'on Israeli orders' (Macey 317) or as a 'spy and ally of the Jews' (Memmi 1975: 26). Two of Fanon's closest colleagues at the clinic, as Macey notes, were Tunisian-Jewish (Macey 313). While the minister for health, Hammed Ben Saleh, did not take these accusations seriously, Fanon's position was made so uncomfortable that he moved his family out of the hospital grounds. After this episode, Memmi rightly stressed Fanon's discomfort as a black non-Muslim in Algeria and the fact that he needed an interpreter, although he was learning Arabic, to function as a psychiatrist at the Manouba clinic. The accusation of being an Israeli spy, three years after France's involvement in the Suez adventure to neutralize Egyptian influence in North Africa, both arose from and reinforced Fanon's status as an outsider or 'European interloper' (Gates 468). In the context of a nationalist anti-colonial struggle, the supposed dual loyalties of rootless cosmopolitans were clearly open to suspicion.[14]

As Aimé Césaire stated in his eulogy, Fanon 'chose. He became Algerian. Lived, fought and died Algerian.'[15] Such a figure, as Macey notes, is 'not easy to remember in France' (Macey 17). But he is also not easy to remember in Algeria. If Algerian nationalism is defined as 'Arab-Islamic', then it becomes almost impossible to 'absorb a black agnostic into that nationalism' who, soon after Algerian independence, was deemed both 'foreign to Islam' and to the 'Algerian nation' (8–9). Such concerns, which Memmi relates to prevailing and long-standing anxieties about supposed cosmopolitan Jews in French colonial culture, are apparent in much of Fanon's work, where 'the Jew' as secret sharer remains a particularly troubling figure.

Here I follow Daniel Boyarin, who argues in general terms, after Memmi, that 'the Jew' plays a 'powerful, disturbing and enigmatic role' in Fanon's thinking.[16] That 'the Jew' also remains a disturbing figure for contemporary critics working on Fanon can be seen in Homi Bhabha's more recent foreword to *The Wretched of the Earth*. In this, an implicit retraction of the earlier foreword (with its stress on 'the self' and the 'psyche'), the only repetition, a quotation from *Black Skin, White Masks*, has blacks 'overdetermined from without' (Fanon 1952: 115) and thereby embodying the 'racialized person'.[17] Except that the contrasting 'racialized person' in *Black Skin, White Masks* is the figure of 'the Jew' who is 'overdetermined from the inside' (Fanon 1952: 115), which Bhabha elides in the second, but not the first, foreword.[18] The indeterminate figure of 'the Jew' has disappeared in the second foreword as the certainties of *The Wretched of the Earth*, and what it is to be a racialized person, replace the uncertainties of *Black Skin, White Masks*.

At about the same time that Fanon was accused of being a Zionist agent, he argued in *Studies in a Dying Colonialism* (1959) that three-quarters of the 'native' Jewish population in Algeria were a 'floating, highly Arabized mass having only a poor knowledge of French'. The 'mass' of Jews in these terms were the equivalent, or 'homologues', of Tunisian or Moroccan Jews who tended to live in 'Jewish quarters'. Fanon concludes that 'for these Jews, there is no problem: they are Algerians' (Fanon 1959: 155). It is a paradox of Fanon's thought that Jewish assimilation ('they are Algerians') is a virtue in a decolonizing (but not a metropolitan) context. That Jews assimilate as Algerians by being located in a 'Jewish quarter' indicates something of the indeterminate diasporic condition of 'the Jew' within colonialism and Fanon's response to it. For Jews, living in a ghetto (or 'quarter') is a form of assimilation. But it is precisely this paradoxical form of assimilation, where Jews are both the same as the indigenous population ('homologues') and ghettoized, that points to the difficulties in locating (in all senses) Algerian Jews.

To be sure, Fanon was well aware that the 'attitude' of Algerian Jews (about a fifth of the non-Muslim population of Algeria) to the revolutionary struggle was 'not a homogenous one'. Along with the 'mass' of Jews, there were 'Jewish tradesmen' who were invested in French rule and to this extent were no different to 'European tradesmen of all origins' (153). At the same time, Fanon also notes that 'several Jewish tradesmen have been arrested for aiding and abetting the Algerian revolution'. Jewish civil servants, on the other hand, are said to 'look upon the prospect of the birth of an Algerian state with fear and trembling'. On these 'rare' occasions, it was possible for 'the Jew, despised and excluded by the European', to 'identify himself with those who humiliate him [and] to humiliate the Algerian in return' (154). To this extent, Jewish civil servants or tradesmen could move between European and Algerian identities. In the context of revolutionary struggle, however, Fanon is clear that such ambivalence needed to be resolved and urged Jews, 'within the framework of their professions', to become ' "the eyes and ears of the Revolution" inside the enemy apparatus' (155). In a line from Dreyfus to the present, Jews are deemed to be spies with dual loyalties (resonating in the charge that Fanon was an 'Israeli spy') – in this case, in the name of the struggle against colonialism.

Albert Memmi's account of the Tunisian Jewish community is close to Fanon's, especially when he notes that the ambivalent 'Jewish population identified as much with the colonizers as with the colonized':

> They were undeniably 'natives' as they were then called, as near as possible to the Moslems in poverty, language, sensibilities, customs, taste in music, odours and cooking. However, unlike Moslems, they passionately endeavoured to identify themselves with the French. To them the West was the paragon of all civilization and culture. The Jew turned his back happily on the East . . . For better or for worse, the Jew found himself one small notch above the Moslem on the pyramid which is the basis of all colonial societies. . . . My own relations with my fellow Jews were not made any easier when I decided to join the colonized, but it was necessary for me to denounce colonialism, even though it was not as hard on the Jews as it was on the others. (Memmi 1957: 12)

From a revolutionary perspective, the 'common fight' against colonialism meant that Muslims and Jews are deemed by Fanon, unlike Memmi, to be 'racial brothers' and both are said to have a 'deep and lasting attachment to the Algerian fatherland' (Fanon 1959: 157). According to the FLN, in August 1956, Jews showed their 'friendship to the revolution' by 'proudly proclaiming their Algerian nationality' as 'Algerians of Jewish origin' (156). Memmi, however, refuses this assimilationist Jewish identity: 'I was a sort of half-breed of colonization, understanding everyone because I belonged completely to no one' (Memmi 1957: 14). Sartre, as we will see, takes up the contrast between the uncertain cosmopolitan detachment of a Memmi (belonging to no one) and the certainties of a nationalist anti-colonialism where the 'Jewish lawyers and doctors . . . in the camps or in prison share the fate of millions of Algerians' and thereby signify the 'multiracial reality of the Algerian nation' (Fanon 1959: 157). As Martin Evans has shown, the leadership of the Algerian-Jewish community attempted a position of 'measured neutrality' in relation to the FLN which was met by violence on both sides of the conflict.[19] The response of the vast majority of the 130,000 Algerian Jews was to migrate mainly to France in 1962.

Memmi reads a diasporic ambivalence back into Fanon. This has proved to be both productive, as we have seen in the case of Gates and Macey, and quite contentious, as can be seen in the work of Posnock and Azzedine Haddour.[20] Posnock argues that Memmi judged Fanon in relation to the 'Cartesian terms of existential humanism'. By this he means that implicit in Memmi's reading of Fanon's 'impossible life' is the desire to resolve the 'identity logic' of 'identity/difference, inside/outside, native/stranger' (Posnock 1998: 96). He is quite right to argue that Fanon's life and work should be understood outside these binaries. And yet, by ignoring the figure of the 'half-breed' Jew, which structures Memmi's reading of Fanon, Posnock downplays the extent to which Memmi, in his version of Fanon as a 'Jewish intellectual' (Memmi 1975: 32), precisely challenges these binaries. Haddour, on the other hand, appreciates fully the extent to which Memmi's Jewishness inflects his reading of Fanon but maintains that Memmi 'criticises' Fanon 'on the basis of the Zionist idea of return to home or to self' (Haddour 2002: 35). But this is to ignore the explicitly socialist version (*pace* Sartre) of Memmi's Zionism, which included an acknowledgement of Palestinian rights including statehood.[21] The stress on Fanon's refusal to return to Martinique, and his voluntary exile, does not mean that Memmi belittles the version of his subject as irredeemably cosmopolitan or desires a more 'authentic' Fanon.

Haddour wrongly characterizes the 'Zionist project at the core of Sartre's work' (Haddour 2002: 35) in so far as this national project was understood as enabling Jews to re-enter history after the war. As in the case of Memmi, Sartre's avowed socialism and first-hand understanding of the suffering of the Palestinians meant that he also supported a Palestinian state, in the same terms as his 'Zionism' (Jewish nationalism), so that Palestinians could move from being the objects of history to its subjects.[22] But it was because of Sartre's support of Israel after the 1967 Six-Day War that Josie Fanon wished to publish *The Wretched of the Earth* without Sartre's preface and, in so doing, make clear her husband's posthumous distance from the supposed taint of 'Zionism' which had already been levelled at Fanon.[23] David Macey is only half-right when he claims that the similarity between Fanon and Memmi 'derived from their common debt to Sartre and, in particular, to the argument of his [*Anti-Semite and Jew*]: colonial racism creates the colonized, just as anti-Semitism creates "the Jew"' (Macey 422). It is now recognized increasingly that Fanon drew specifically, and in detail, on Sartre's *Anti-Semite and Jew* while formulating his work on the effects of colonial racism on himself and others.[24] What is less well understood is the extent to which the indeterminate figure of 'the Jew' became an essential self-image that Fanon both resisted and incorporated into his understanding of colonial racism.

To be sure, the history of fascism and Nazi anti-Semitism acted as an essential point of reference on which Fanon was especially influenced by his comrade and teacher Aimé Césaire. At the same time, Fanon distanced himself from his secret sharer, the diasporic cosmopolitan Jew, who does not always fit into Césaire's narrative of a colonizing European fascism. My argument is that the Sartrean reading of 'the Jew' and 'the colonized', as equivalent passive products of anti-Semitism and colonial racism, needs to be qualified and is in fact undermined by Sartre himself.[25] It is clear, for instance, that Sartre's prefaces to *The Colonizer and the Colonized* and *The Wretched of the Earth* reinforce the racialized differences between Memmi and Fanon. In the first preface, Memmi's indeterminacy as a member of an 'indigenous but non-Muslim' group is foregrounded: 'What is he exactly? Colonizer or colonized? He himself would say: neither one nor the other; you will say, perhaps: both one and the other; it comes down to the same thing. . . . since he is everybody at once, he is the best of witnesses' (Sartre

1957: 57). In stark contrast to the breadth of Memmi's thought or subject positions ('since he is everybody at once'), Sartre's preface to *The Wretched of the Earth*, as is well known, focuses mainly on a reductive reading of the first chapter, 'Concerning Violence': 'Read Fanon: you will learn how, in the period of their helplessness, their mad impulse to murder is the expression of the natives' collective unconscious' (Sartre 1961: 16). Memmi's 'non-Muslim' (that is, Jewish) identity clearly influences Sartre's version of him as a detached cosmopolitan (the 'best of witnesses'). What is more, Memmi's Jewishness also reinforces his universalism, which is not humanist (as 'Man . . . does not yet exist') but is a form of 'rigorous Reason which applies to all' (Sartre 1957: 57). As we will see, the supposed imperialism of a universalizing rationality is a 'Jewish' characteristic in *Anti-Semite and Jew*. But a 'rigorous Reason' here enables decolonization, and is in stark contrast to the 'violence' of the colonized, which Sartre places at the heart of Fanon's thought: 'read Fanon; for he shows clearly that violence is neither sound nor fury . . . it is man re-creating himself' (Sartre 1961: 19). Such is the opposition between the 'mad impulse to murder', which is located, tellingly, in the 'collective unconscious' of the colonized, and the conscious realm of rationality that is Memmi's mode as 'witness'. In *Black Skin, White Masks*, Fanon incorporates and resists, under the sign of Sartre, the Cartesian binaries of mind and body, conscious and unconscious, reason and emotion. But neither Memmi nor Fanon, as racialized minorities, is able to escape these dualities which are reinforced by Sartre, who reads Memmi as a diasporic 'Jew' on the side of reason and Fanon as a colonized 'black' on the side of irrationality.[26]

Between Fanon and Césaire

At one point in *Black Skin, White Masks*, Frantz Fanon describes Sartre's 'masterful' *Anti-Semite and Jew* as containing some of the 'finest [pages] that I have ever read. The finest, because the problem discussed in them grips us in our guts' (Fanon 1952: 160 and 181). This gut-wrenching response is the key to Fanon's understanding of the fraught link between

anti-Semitism and Negrophobia. The tension between whether racism
can be understood rationally rather than written on the body ('in our
guts') runs through *Black Skin, White Masks*. 'The Portrait of the
Antisemite', the first and best chapter of *Anti-Semite and Jew*, was initially
published in *Les Temps modernes* in November 1945 and was a key point
of reference for those who opposed the resurgence of French anti-
Semitism immediately after the war. Fanon had read this chapter and lived
through the Vichy-led discrimination against the handful of Jews in
Martinique, which was one of the main reasons why he had decided to
'knock Hitler off his hilltop' (Macey 83–84 and 92–97). His Martiniquean
experiences informed much of *Black Skin, White Masks* and are most
explicitly articulated in the essay 'West Indians and Africans' (1955),
collected in *Toward the African Revolution* (1964), which is something of
a postscript to his first book.

'West Indians and Africans' is best known for its account of Aimé
Césaire's arrival in Martinique and his subsequent celebration of Negritude
which persuaded Antilleans to celebrate their racial difference. What is
less often remarked is that Fanon narrates Césaire's shift in race consciousness in relation to the chronology of the Second World War.[27] The experience of being occupied by the racist pro-Vichy French forces ends the
illusion that French Antilleans are 'white' compared to African 'Negroes'.
After 1945, the Antillean 'changed his values. Whereas before 1939 he had
his eyes riveted on white Europe . . . in 1945 he discovered himself to be
not only black but a Negro, and it was in the direction of distant Africa
that he was henceforth to put out feelers' (Fanon 1964: 34–35). Such is the
overwhelming ambivalence – being 'haunted by impurity' (35) – that
engulfed his fellow Antilleans after the war. The well-known conclusion to
'West Indians and Africans' – 'the West Indian, after the great white error,
is now living the great black mirage' (27) – encapsulates this impure sense
of being neither black nor white. The Second World War contextualizes
such ambivalence – especially the 'impure' black Free French soldiers
within the metropolitan heartland – which juxtaposed Fanon with the
similarly indeterminate metropolitan Jew.

As with a great many black soldiers who fought for the Allies during the Second World War, Fanon's appreciation of the horrors of fascism arose from his understanding of European colonialism and the racism of the United States. Robert Young has argued that anti-colonial French thinkers especially understood the history of Nazism and fascism as 'European colonialism brought home to Europe'.[28] In *The Wretched of the Earth*, to be sure, Fanon argued: 'not long ago Nazism transformed the whole of Europe into a veritable colony' (Fanon 1961: 80). Sartre, in his preface, followed Césaire and Arendt in speaking of the metaphorical 'boomerang effect' of violence in Algeria and Angola: 'it comes back on us, it strikes us, and we [Europeans] do not realize any more . . . that it's we that have launched it' (Sartre 1961: 17). For Sartre, the boomerang effect is the closed hermeneutic circle between violence and counterviolence in French-controlled Algeria. Both Arendt and Césaire, in their radically different ways, wished to break this closed circle by thinking of the European 'occupation' of Asia and Africa as not unlike the Nazi 'occupation' of Europe.[29] Before the rise of Hitler, Nazi-like practices were tolerated in Europe because, as Césaire contends, they had 'been applied only to non-European peoples' (Césaire 1955: 36 and 41).

Césaire's political speeches and *Discourse on Colonialism*, which Fanon refers to throughout *Black Skin, White Masks*, are exemplary texts on the complicity of European humanism with colonialism and Nazism, a theme taken up by Sartre. As Sartre argued in his preface to *The Wretched of the Earth*: 'liberty, equality fraternity . . . all this did not prevent us [Europeans] from making anti-racial speeches about dirty niggers, dirty Jews and dirty Arabs' (Sartre 1961: 22). Césaire was saying much the same nearly two decades before Sartre's preface, and it was for this reason that Fanon in *Black Skin, White Masks* cited his teacher and compatriot:

> When I turn on my radio, when I hear that Negroes have been lynched in America, I say that we have been lied to: Hitler is not dead; when I turn on my radio, when I learn that Jews have been insulted, mistreated, persecuted, I say that we have been lied to: Hitler is not dead; when,

finally, I turn on my radio and hear that in Africa forced labour has been inaugurated and legalized, I say that we have certainly been lied to: Hitler is not dead. (Fanon 1952: 90)

Césaire's metaphorical thinking is here utilized as part of an extended critique of Octave Mannoni, who argued in his *Prospero and Caliban: The Psychology of Colonization* (1950) that colonial racism was essentially unique. Mannoni stated contentiously that those who are colonized are psychologically predisposed to this condition and therefore 'colonial exploitation is not the same as other forms of exploitation, and colonial racialism is different from other kinds of racialism' (quoted Fanon 1952: 88).[30] Following Césaire, Fanon, however, makes no distinction between different kinds of racism and his rebuttal is especially powerful:

Colonial racism is no different from any other racism. Anti-Semitism hits me head on: I am enraged, I am bled white by an appalling battle, I am deprived of the possibility of being a man. I cannot disassociate myself from the future that is proposed for my brother. Every one of my acts commits me as a man. Every one of my silences, every one of my cowardices reveals me as a man. (88–89)

Here the memory of being part of Vichy France, and therefore complicit with Nazism, means that Fanon 'cannot disassociate' himself from a blood-drenched European humanism. To this end, he cites the words of Maryse Choisy, who argues that all those who remained 'neutral' during the Nazi occupation of France 'felt that they were responsible for all the deaths and all the Buchenwalds' (89). Fanon's qualification of Mannoni's version of colonial uniqueness prefigures those who today wish to qualify the idea of the uniqueness of the Holocaust and for similar reasons. As Michael Rothberg has argued, the idea of uniqueness prevents a common understanding of racial suffering beyond the particularities of victimhood.[31] One strand of Fanon's thought wished to pursue such commonalities.

At the point where he feels most complicit with European anti-Semitism, Fanon confirms his common humanity or 'whiteness'. Those who did not oppose fascism and Nazism are 'white', in the same way that those who align themselves with colonialism (either passively or actively) are. To be sure, Fanon is initially responding to Mannoni's misguided belief that 'European civilization and its best representatives are not ... responsible for colonial racism' (90) by showing that racism and anti-Semitism are at the heart of European humanism. Césaire was particularly important for this argument. Fanon cites an extraordinary passage from *Discourse on Colonialism* which notes that those who did not oppose Nazism 'were responsible for it, and it drips, it seeps, it wells from every crack in Western Christian civilization until it engulfs that civilization in a bloody sea' (Césaire 1955: 36; Fanon 1952: 90–91). Césaire's potent mixture of Negritude and radical anti-humanism, both particularist and universalist, prefigured the hybrid vocabulary of *Black Skin, White Masks*, which veers between the mind and the body, reason and emotion, diaspora and colony. To this extent, the juxtaposition of the diasporic Jew (under the sign of the intellect and rationality) and the colonized black (under the sign of the body and irrationality) not only occurs on the level of history but also becomes the entwined style of the book.

Memmi, however, makes a rather too rigid distinction between Fanon and Césaire when he argues that Césaire 'reaffirmed' (Memmi 1973: 17) himself as a West Indian by returning to Martinique whereas Fanon reaffirmed himself by refusing to locate his politics within his originary homeland. As we have seen, Césaire's influence on Fanon was enormous, even after he eventually rejected Negritude and went into voluntary exile. In his essay 'Racism and Culture' (1956), for instance, Fanon follows Césaire's metaphorical thinking in making explicit the connection between the death camps and colonial experience. The 'common enslavement' of the victims of racism on the continent of Europe and within its colonies, according to this argument, has 'deeply modified the problem and manner of approaching' racial difference:

The memory of Nazism, the common wretchedness of different men, the common enslavement of extensive social groups, the apparition of 'European colonies', in other words the institution of a colonial system in the very heart of Europe, the growing awareness of workers in the colonizing and racist countries, the evolution of techniques, all this has deeply modified the problem and manner of approaching [racial difference]. (Fanon 1964: 33)

That the 'memory of Nazism' has 'deeply modified' the approach to an understanding of racial difference is a lesson, learnt from Césaire, that Fanon takes into all of his work, culminating, as we shall see, in *The Wretched of the Earth*. The 'memory of Nazism', in particular, qualifies a redemptive or transcendent narrative; a narrative which, according to Memmi, supposedly drove Fanon to reinvent himself constantly. In *Dominated Man* (1968), Memmi paraphrases Fanon by arguing that 'the day oppression ceases, the new man is supposed to appear before our eyes immediately'. He counters this 'romantic' notion with the following: 'the colonized lives on for a long time in the decolonized man, and we will have to wait longer still before we see a really new man' (Memmi 1968: 88). But that is to assume mistakenly that Fanon, even in the 1950s, did not understand that the lingering and traumatic effects of colonialism might well prevent such transfigurations.

That he was made 'white' by fighting against Nazism with the Free French is the central 'problem' of *Black Skin, White Masks*, as 'the Negro of the Antilles is proportionately whiter ... in direct ratio to his mastery of the French language' (Fanon 1952: 18). The first chapter of his first book ends with a French acquaintance telling Fanon enthusiastically, 'At bottom you are a white man' due to his mastery of the 'white man's language', which in turn gives him 'honorary [French] citizenship' (38). Antillean soldiers, Fanon notes, often acted as interpreters 'conveying the master's orders' to other black soldiers and so have a 'certain position of honour' (19). Fanon's position as one of a group of middlemen or interpreters in the Free French army enables him to understand what he later calls the 'racial distribution of guilt': 'The Frenchman does not like the Jew, who does not like the Arab, who does not like the Negro' (103). Fanon's free-floating role in the French army – between the colonizers and the colonized – means that he is positioned in the role of a Jewish middleman. Here Memmi's characterization of the Jewish population in Algeria as 'eternally hesitant candidates refusing assimilation' is relevant:

> Their constant and very justifiable ambition is to escape from their colonized condition, an additional burden in an already oppressive status. To that end they endeavour to resemble the colonizer in the frank hope that he may cease to consider them different from him. Hence their efforts to forget the past, to change collective habits, and their enthusiastic adoption of Western language, culture and customs. But if the colonizer does not always openly discourage these candidates to develop that resemblance, he never permits them to attain it either. Thus, they live in painful and constant ambiguity. (Memmi 1957: 81)

Robert Young has related this 'cultural inbetweenness' – Jews as both colonial and anti-colonial – to the Derridean roots of postcolonial theory, which arises out of the Algerian-Jewish community. Memmi, in these terms, becomes a premature Derridean, in the same way that Homi Bhabha's reading of Fanon turns him into a 'premature poststructuralist'.[32] Young, in fact, notes that Bhabha develops Memmi's argument that there 'is never a simple distinction between the colonizer and the colonized' because, in Memmi's words, the 'colonial relationship . . . chained the colonizer and the colonized into an implacable dependence' (Memmi 1957: 7). According to Young, this dialectic was undone by 'the spectral presence of all those liminal figures who slipped between these two categories' (Young 2001: 423). But here the question of Fanon's liminality, in relation to the figure of 'the Jew', becomes paramount, not least for Fanon himself. In *Black Skin, White Masks*, the extremity of his ambivalent identification with/differentiation from 'the Jew' is precisely bound up with whether he is able, finally, to embrace such ambivalence.

Between Fanon and Sartre

As David Marriott has rightly maintained, the rhetoric of war or 'perpetual conflict' is a key motif in *Black Skin, White Masks*. Marriott identifies Fanon's war rhetoric with both an internal struggle, the 'imago' of the black man which has to be defeated from within, as well as an external anti-colonial struggle between black and white.[33] This rhetoric is crucially carried over from the Second World War as Sartre demonstrates – 'The Jew of today is in full war' (Sartre 1946: 150) – and this struggle continues most obviously with the war of Algerian independence. The figure of the diasporic Jew is both the embodiment of ambivalence and increasingly, in relation to Algeria, a means by which Fanon can reinforce the certainties of revolutionary struggle. What Fanon will eventually attempt to resolve is the two incommensurable narratives in *Black Skin, White Masks* that are concerned with whether Jews should be regarded as 'black' or 'white', colonized or diasporic. Fanon, that is, simultaneously rewrites and resists Sartre's *Anti-Semite and Jew*, sometimes explicitly, often implicitly, in a bid to make a range of contradictory points about both the particularity of black anti-colonial struggle and the universality of racist and anti-Semitic discourse. The 'persistent instabilities' in Fanon's writings are therefore figured in terms of a competing discussion of Jews and anti-Semitism, with Fanon both identifying with diasporic Jews and giving voice to a Semitic discourse.[34]

The references to Jews and anti-Semitism in *Black Skin, White Masks* are, in these terms, part of a wider tension concerning the relationship between a particularist anti-colonial nationalism (which excludes 'the Jew') and more universalist or cosmopolitan theories of racial oppression (which include 'the Jew').[35] Sartre's *Anti-Semite and Jew* revealed, in part, a generalized anti-racism to complement his universalizing *Black Orpheus* (1948). Sartre's essay was famously resisted by Fanon until he published

The Wretched of the Earth since it 'destroyed black zeal' (Fanon 1952: 135) by placing black cultural nationalism or Negritude in the context of a supposedly all-encompassing Hegelian dialectic. This fear of being assimilated back into a set of 'pre-existing' (134) Eurocentric paradigms – however ostensibly progressive – also plays itself out in relation to Sartre's *Anti-Semite and Jew*. For this reason Fanon brings together the history of 'Negrophobia' with the history of 'anti-Semitism' while at the same time resisting a too easy assimilation between these two racisms which he dismisses as 'errors of analysis' (183). Here Fanon contrasts starkly with Memmi, who finds no difficulty in concluding that 'all the oppressed are alike in some ways' (Memmi 1957: 7).

In a famous scene in *Black Skin, White Masks*, taken up by both Paul Gilroy and Caryl Phillips, a drunken Frenchman on a train, after spouting anti-Semitic vitriol, turns to Fanon and states: 'let's face up to the foreigners . . . no matter who they are' (Fanon 1952: 121).[36] The author's conclusions from this incident are echoed throughout the following chapters:

> At first thought it may seem strange that the anti-Semite's outlook should be related to that of the Negrophobe. It was my philosophy professor, a native of the Antilles, who recalled the fact to me one day: 'Whenever you hear anyone abuse the Jews, pay attention, because he is talking about you'. And I found that he was universally right – by which I meant that I was answerable in my body and in my heart for what was done to my brother. Later I realized that he meant, quite simply, an anti-Semite is inevitably anti-Negro. (122)

The process of working through the acknowledged strangeness of associating anti-Semitism with Negrophobia – which culminates in the simplicity of his conclusion that anti-Semites are, inevitably, anti-Negro – is more troubled than at first appears. Fanon's philosophy professor also argued that 'what is happening in Europe is no concern of ours. When white men kill each other, it is a blessing for blacks' (Macey 88). Fanon was purportedly outraged by the latter claims, and his response to them, as we have seen, was to leave Martinique to fight for the Free French forces in 1943. These issues are equally conflicted in the pages of *Black Skin, White Masks*, and here my reading differs from those of Gilroy and Phillips. Does Fanon's final straightforward sentence ('Later I realized . . . an anti-Semite is inevitably anti-Negro') mean that he is no longer 'answerable in my body and in my heart for what was done to my brother'? That the question of anti-Semitism should be eventually disembodied and become a mere cerebral matter for the cosmopolitan intellectual ('Later I realized') is repeated on a larger scale throughout *Black Skin, White Masks*. Sartre's writing on anti-Semitism is 'masterful' precisely because it 'grips us in our guts' (Fanon 1952: 181). The shift towards a disembodied response to anti-Semitism is therefore significant as it lessens its importance for Fanon, shifting the issue of racism from the colonized body to the deracinated mind.

To be sure, there is an uneasy intimacy between Fanon and Sartre's *Anti-Semite and Jew*, and it is significant that the latter book ends with the following: 'what must be done is to point out . . . that the fate of the Jews is [our] fate' (Sartre 1946: 153). This statement clearly prefigures the Antillean philosophy professor when he warns Fanon that the anti-Semite is also 'talking about you'. And yet Fanon resisted both the universalizing dialectic of *Black Orpheus* and the particularizing gestures in *Anti-Semite and Jew*, especially with regard to the 'somatic characteristics' (Sartre 1946: 63) of Jews. Unlike Fanon, Sartre relies upon an all-embracing dialectic, and not particular acts of resistance, to defeat racism, and at the same time does not distinguish between the 'somatic characteristics' of blacks and Jews. As Jock McCulloch notes, Fanon pointedly chose to ignore the Marxist tenor of *Anti-Semite and Jew* in his early writings and therefore stressed increasingly the racial differences between blacks and Jews.[37]

But there are also times when Fanon makes it possible to run together both black and Jewish oppression in relation to the 'manicheism delirium' of Western metaphysics which divides the world into 'Good-Evil, Beauty-Ugliness, White-Black' (Fanon 1952: 183). Sartre's understanding of anti-Semitism as 'at bottom a form of Manichaeism' (Sartre 1946: 40) is relevant in this regard as it enables an understanding of all forms of race-thinking. There are a number of notable moments in *Black Skin, White Masks* when Fanon dramatically brings the implications of this broader, inclusivist analysis home. At his most inclusive, Fanon can argue, not unlike Memmi, 'what others have described in the case of the Jew applies perfectly in that of the Negro' (Fanon 1952: 183). Earlier in the same chapter, Fanon is quite explicit about what he calls the 'one point in common' that Jews and blacks have: 'both of us', he says, 'stand for Evil' (180). Once again, Sartre says much the same thing: 'anti-Semitism is a conception of the Manichaean . . . in which hatred for the Jew arises as a great explanatory myth' (Sartre 1946: 148). What racism and anti-Semitism have in common, in other words, is Manichaeism. But this facile point of identification is quickly qualified by Fanon as he goes on to state: 'the black man more so, for the good reason that he is black'. Fanon has gone back to his memory of the Vichy-led occupation of Martinique: ' "His body is black, his language is black, his soul must be black too". This logic is put into daily practice by the white man' (Fanon 1952: 180). Such is the somatic nature of anti-black racism.

The overarching logic of racial Manichaeism, which brings together blacks and Jews, is countered by the stark and ever-present fact of the black body in relation to the white racist. At this point, Fanon has a prevailing sense of being 'a body in the middle of a spatial and temporal world', which in turn 'creates a real dialectic between my body and the world' (111). His 'racial epidermal schema' (112), however, is precisely what makes it impossible for Fanon to identify fully with the suffering Jew, who is always 'white', that is disembodied, in his work. When placed in the context of Martinique, however, this equivocal identification with 'the Jew' is particularly fraught. The construction of 'the Jew' as being identified, at one and the same time, with both abused 'blacks' and 'white' oppressors clearly creates a good deal of anxiety which Fanon must eventually resolve in the name of a more disciplined revolutionary decolonization.

On the one hand, much of Fanon's experiential evidence, taken from his psychiatric case studies, explicitly echoes Sartre's *Anti-Semite and Jew*. Fanon's belief that the greatest fear of many of his patients is that they cannot escape being formed by the racial imagination reinforces Sartre's definition of the inauthentic Jew as someone who does not engage dialectically with the anti-Semitic image of them. In other words, as Fanon vehemently argues in response to Mannoni's *Prospero and Caliban*: '*it is the racist who creates his inferior*' (93) in whomever happens to be the object of his gaze. At this point of absolute identification with 'the Jew', in so far as he or she is created by racial discourse, Fanon most explicitly disrupts any too easy equivalence between black and Jewish victimhood and, most especially, the black and the Jewish body. This can be seen with regard to the incident on the train when Fanon, immediately after hearing the racist and anti-Semitic diatribe of a drunken passenger, comments as follows: 'An outrage! The Jew and I: Since I was not satisfied to be racialized, by a lucky turn of fate I was humanized. I joined the Jew, my brother in misery' (122). After Fanon is brought together with 'the Jew', as part of the brotherhood of the racially abused, there is a fateful, if limited, form of European humanization. This can only be because 'the Jew' in these terms is unequivocally 'white'. Such paradoxical humanization is opposed to the experience of being 'racialized', which is associated, in Fanon's mind, exclusively with Negrophobia. The main point of difference, that is, between Fanon and Sartre is with regard to the nature of the Jew's body. Sartre argues contentiously that 'we must envisage the hereditary and somatic characteristics of the Jew as one factor among others in his situation, not as a condition determining his nature' (Sartre 1946: 64). Later on, Sartre contends that 'the sole ethnic characteristics of the Jews are physical. The anti-Semite has seized upon this fact and has transformed Jews into a myth' (118). Sartre therefore speaks of the 'black and curly' hair and beard of the Jew in several places (62–63), and it is this aspect of Sartre's work – drawn from wartime anti-Semitic sources – that Fanon rightly rejects.[38] Rather than the ethnic blackness of the Jew, in Sartre's terms, Fanon argues:

the Jew can be unknown in his Jewishness. He is not wholly what he is. One hopes, one waits. His actions, his behaviour are the final determinant. He is a white man, and apart from some rather debatable characteristics, he can sometimes go unnoticed. He belongs to the race of those who since the beginning of time have never known cannibalism. What an idea, to eat one's father! Simple enough, one has only not to be a nigger. (Fanon 1952: 115)

It is the body or, to be precise, the lack of the Jewish body in *Black Skin, White Masks* that overdetermines the cosmopolitan Jewish mind. The key point for Fanon, as we will see, is that it is possible for Jews, in their essentialized whiteness, to assimilate or pass unnoticed in European society whereas it is impossible for blacks, in their essentialized blackness, to do so. Fanon spends much of his book recounting the failed assimilation of other black intellectuals such as the Antillean Jean Veneuse who was 'unable to be assimilated, unable to pass unnoticed' (65) in France. Like Fanon, Sartre also places the question of the body at the heart of European racism but notes that, given their self-evident ethnicity, some Jews 'deny the body that betrays them' and thus seek 'disincarnation' (Sartre 1946: 119 and 111). Here Fanon learned a great deal from Sartre in terms of his representation of the Jew. For Sartre argues: 'the rationalism to which the Jew adheres so passionately is first of all an exercise of asceticism and purification, an escape into the universal' (112). In other words, 'if reason exists, then there is no French truth or German truth; there is no Negro truth or Jewish truth. There is only one Truth' (111). In a passage that Fanon cites at length, Sartre calls this assimilatory logic the 'impassioned imperialism of reason':

For ['the Jew'] wishes not only to convince others that he is right; his goal is to persuade them that there is an absolute and unconditional value to rationalism. He feels himself to be a missionary of the universal; against the universality of the Catholic religion, from which he is excluded, he asserts the 'catholicity' of the rational, an instrument

by which to attain the truth and establish a spiritual bond among men.
(Sartre 1946: 112–13; Fanon 1952: 118–19)

There is a telling slippage throughout *Anti-Semite and Jew*. Sartre argues
that the characterization of 'the Jew' as a 'pure reasoner' is an aspect of
French anti-Semitism where 'the terms *abstract, rationalist, intellectual* . . .
take on a pejorative sense' (Sartre 1946: 109). But these terms also apply to
real Jews: 'what the Jew wishes to destroy is strictly localized'; 'he has a
taste for pure intelligence'; 'on a superior [intellectual] level he realizes that
accord and assimilation which is denied him on a social level' (112–14).
Sartre's overdetermined characterization of the disembodied Jewish mind,
eliding discourse and reality, is repeated by Fanon. In fact, Fanon utilizes
this model of deracinated or inauthentic Jewish universalism to see the
extent to which it can be applied to his own situation as a 'Negro' in metropolitan France. Soon after quoting Sartre, he attempts to 'rationalize the
world and to show the white man that he was mistaken', and to this end he
sets about 'cataloguing and probing his surroundings'. But he is quickly
disillusioned and has to 'change my tune' (Fanon 1952: 118–19). After this,
he encounters the drunkard on the train, whose irrational prejudices
taught him that 'since no agreement was possible on the level of reason, I
threw myself back toward unreason' (123).

The shift from reason to unreason and back again is figured crucially
in relation to the diasporic Jewish mind and the colonized black body.
Inauthentic Jewish universalism, the absolute promise of liberal assimilation, results in the denial of what is local and particular: 'my unreason was
countered with reason, my reason with "real reason". Every hand was a
losing hand. . . . I wanted to be typically Negro – it was no longer possible.
I wanted to be white – that was a joke. And, when I tried . . . to reclaim my
Negritude, it was snatched away from me' (132). Fanon's ambivalent posi-
tioning, somewhere between Sartre's 'white' dialectical reasoning and the
unreason of Negritude, leads to a contagion of disciplinary antitheses with
regard to Jews and blacks: 'In the case of the Jew, one thinks of money and
its cognates. In that of the Negro, one thinks of sex. Anti-Semitism can be

rationalized on a basic level. It is because he takes over the country that the Jew is in danger' (160). Or again:

> No anti-Semite would ever conceive of the idea of castrating the Jew. He is killed or sterilized. But the Negro is castrated. . . . The difference between the two attitudes is apparent. . . . [E]very time that a Jew is persecuted, it is the whole race that is persecuted in his person. But it is in his corporeality that the Negro is attacked. It is as a concrete person that he is lynched. It is as an actual being that he is a threat. The Jewish menace is replaced by the fear of the sexual potency of the Negro. (163–64)

In stating that black men are attacked bodily and as individuals, and Jews as a group or collective, Fanon, as Ann Pellegrini has noted, 'effectively denies Jewish men personality and particularity'.[39] That is why Fanon argues that 'the Jewish menace *is replaced* by the fear of the sexual potency of the Negro' (my emphasis). It is significant, in this regard, that Fanon notes elsewhere that 'there is no such thing as an African people. There is an African world. And a West Indian world as well. On the other hand, it can be said that there is a Jewish people; but not a Jewish race' (Fanon 1964: 28). That there is a Jewish 'people' but an African 'world' once again exacerbates the differences between the two and confines them to separate spheres. Jews, that is, are an abstraction as they are persecuted as part of a 'whole', whereas blacks are made concrete as an 'actual being' in their persecution. The disciplinary logic of Fanon's essentializing oppositions – that Jews are overdetermined from the inside and blacks from the outside – means that he is able, eventually, to reduce anti-Jewish and anti-black racism to the following formula: 'The Negro symbolizes the biological danger; the Jew, the intellectual danger' (Fanon 1952: 165).

At the same time as disembodying Jews in the name of black embodiment, Fanon also displaces the question of anti-Semitism onto the issue of repressed homosexuality: 'Fault, Guilt, refusal of guilt, paranoia – one is back in homosexual territory. In sum, what others have described in the case of the Jew applies perfectly in that of the Negro' (183). Here, the 'idea' of 'the Jew' is part of the guilt and paranoia supposedly inherent in 'homosexual territory'. As the Antilles is specifically discounted both from any 'overt presence of homosexuality' (180) and, by extension, from the Oedipus complex, it is the one place where anti-Semitism and Negrophobia can no longer be brought together:

> Granted, the Jews are harassed – what am I thinking of? They are hunted down, exterminated, cremated. But these are little family quarrels. The Jew is disliked from the moment he is tracked down. But in my case everything takes on a *new* guise. I am given no chance. I am over-determined from without. I am the slave not of the 'idea' that others have of me but of my own appearance. (115–16)

By reducing the Holocaust to 'little family quarrels' – such as the Oedipus complex – Fanon limits the 'memory of Nazism' to the boundaries of the continent of Europe. At the same time as creating distinct boundaries for understanding Jews and anti-Semitism, Fanon's approach can also be worryingly unbounded. When Fanon states that 'anti-Semitism can be rationalized on a basic level. It is because he takes over the country that the Jew is in danger' (160), he is referring, not unlike Sartre, *both* to the supposed actions of Jews and to the 'idea' of Jewish behaviour. At the same time, the first chapter of *Anti-Semite and Jew*, which Fanon read in *Les Temps modernes*, stresses that it is the '*idea* of the Jew that one forms for himself which would seem to determine history, not the "historical fact" that produces the idea' (Sartre 1946: 16). It is for this reason that Sartre argues that the 'hereditary' characteristics of 'the Jew' are not 'a condition determining his nature' (63). For much of his work, Fanon also emphasizes the determining impact of ideas and images on minority consciousness: 'But when we assert that European culture has an *imago* of the Negro which is responsible for all the conflicts that may arise, we do not go beyond reality' (Fanon 1952: 169).

On several occasions, Fanon pulls himself up short so as not to identify too closely with 'the Jew'. After understanding black identity in diasporic as opposed to colonial terms – 'the truth is that the Negro race has been scattered, that it can no longer claim unity' – he states tentatively: 'this in a way places [the Negro] besides the Jew'. But, immediately after making this statement, he notes categorically: 'against all the arguments I have just cited, I come back to one fact: *Wherever he goes, the Negro remains a Negro*' (173). The danger is that those in the diaspora, rather than the colony, can be universalized by an imperious rationality. Fanon is aware that Sartre, not unlike Memmi, makes no distinction between blacks and Jews: 'Sartre said: Here it is the Jew, somewhere else it is the Negro. What is essential is a scapegoat' (183). By creating a third category, that of 'scapegoat' or 'homosexual', to encompass both blacks and Jews, Sartre is engaging in a form of dialectical reasoning that destroys 'black zeal' (135). According to Fanon, 'assimilating anti-Semitism to Negrophobia' is an 'error . . . of analysis' (183) precisely because it universalizes difference and places it in a synthetic and feminized Eurocentric framework.

After Fanon rejects Sartre's dialectics, he argues, significantly, that 'black consciousness is immanent in its own eyes. I am not a potentiality of something, I am wholly what I am. I do not have to look for the universal' (135). Later on, he speaks about being 'drown[ed] in the universal' (186) and of valuing his own subjectivity in relation to a 'European unconsciousness' in which, as he emphasizes, '*the black man is the symbol of Evil*' (188–90). The figure of the Jewish psychologist, the embodiment of the cosmopolitan Jewish mind, has an overdetermined role in *Black Skin, White Masks* since the question of a specifically black unconscious is central to Fanon's concerns. As Fanon reminds us, 'Freud and Adler . . . did not think of the Negro in all their investigations' (151), and so these Jewish psychologists are unqualified (*pace* Daniel Boyarin) to restore a healthy black subjectivity.[40] Because 'a Negro is forever in combat with his own image' (194), this restorative work is particularly crucial to Fanon, who practised as a psychiatrist so as to help combat such deeply ingrained and damaging self-representations. Jewish psychologists, on the other hand, are dismissed with increased anger both as unworthy of combating Negrophobia and as part of 'homosexual territory'. Fanon's prime example of an unsuitable Jewish doctor, when it comes to treating black patients, is Michel Salomon:

> Although he defends himself against the charge, he stinks of racism. He is a Jew, he has had a 'millennial experience of anti-Semitism', and yet he is a racist. Listen to him: 'But to say that the mere fact of his skin, his hair, of that aura of sensuality that he [the Negro] gives off, does not spontaneously give rise to a certain embarrassment, whether of attraction or revulsion, is to reject the facts in the name of a ridiculous prudery that has never solved anything . . .' Later he goes to the extreme of telling us about the 'prodigious vitality of the black man'. (201)

To this extent, Fanon defines a specifically black psychoanalysis by opposing a 'racist' Jewish physician whom he confines explicitly to 'homosexual territory'. As he says of Salomon: 'I have never been able, without revulsion, to hear a *man* say of another man: "He is so sensual"' (201). In the case of one of the founders of European psychoanalysis, Alfred Adler, Fanon explicitly devises a strategy to 'shak[e] off the Adlerian leech' (215) from his thoughts. By assimilating 'the Negro' into an empty universalism at the deepest level, Jewish psychologists are said to 'leech' off their black counterparts, which is not unlike the critique of the deracinated cosmopolitan intellectual who is also said to 'leech' off the life blood of an authentic nation and religion. That such figures were regarded by Fanon as his 'secret sharers', from whom he needed to distance himself, can be seen with regard to his response to the Hollywood film *Home of the Brave* (1949), which positions the Jewish psychiatrist next to the traumatized black soldier.

Between Fanon, the United States and Algeria

Home of the Brave confirmed Fanon's distrust of the ways in which main-stream European psychoanalysis had been 'applied' (151) to blacks.[41] The film was based on a Broadway play by Arthur Laurents which originally had a Jewish soldier, Peter Coen, as the protagonist. As Michael Rogin has argued, *Home of the Brave* is a significant moment in the history of black-Jewish relations in the United States. The film's producer and writer, Stanley Kramer and Carl Foreman, decided to 'black up' Coen after the release of *Crossfire* (1947) and *Gentleman's Agreement* (1947), both of which exposed American anti-Semitism, as it would be better 'box office . . . to shift from Jews to blacks' (Rogin 1996: 228). Coen, therefore, was transformed into Peter Moss, a young black GI who in a series of flash-backs describes to a sympathetic doctor his emotional breakdown during the war. In a deviation from the facts of life in the segregated Jim Crow US army of the Second World War, Moss has suffered 'partial amnesia and a hysterical paralysis' after his best friend, who is white, is killed (Rogin 1996: 231–32; Marriott 2000: 75). As Rogin has shown, the film not only 'blacks up' the soldier character but turns his psychiatrist into a Jew by giving him a 'Jewish nose', photographing him so as to emphasize his 'facial look' and having him allude briefly to his own experience of anti-Semitism (Rogin 1996: 231–33). The unnamed psychiatrist's 'cathartic cure' (Marriott 2000: 72) takes the form of again subjecting Moss to the wartime racism that has traumatized him so that he can, paradoxically, finally overcome it.

Fanon objected principally to the ending of the film, which concluded on a note of mutual recognition between black and white. Moss leaves the military hospital fully cured. An easy-going white soldier called Mingo, whom Moss knew during the war, approaches him and asks him to become a partner in a bar-and-restaurant business that he wants to open. Mingo has lost an arm and a wife and, in the final scenes of the film, Moss asks him to 'take my coward's hand' (a constant refrain) in a 'powerful gesture of solidarity' (Marriott 2000: 76). After this homosocial gesture at the end of the film, Moss goes on to mouth the assimilatory liberalism of Kramer and Foreman: 'I am different,' he says. 'We all are. But underneath we're the same.'[42] As Fanon comments: 'The crippled veteran of the Pacific war says to my brother, "Resign yourself to your colour the way I got used to my stump; we're both victims"' (Fanon 1952: 140). This easy universalization of victimhood makes Fanon 'weep' (in an echo of Moss's abjection in the film) and relates back to his earlier rejection of blacks and Jews as undifferentiated 'scapegoats' (140 and 183). At this point in *Black Skin, White Masks* Fanon is most dismissive of any form of metaphorical thinking, which he considers a form of empty humanism.

In the end, the film undermines itself since the transcendence of difference between black and disabled, black and white, black and Jew, is only possible by 'the Negro' acting out his deep-seated racial inferiority. What is more, such contradictions are figured in terms of the mind/body binary: 'Assimilated to the Jew at the high level of the mind, Moss is made emotion-ridden and female at the level of the body' (Rogin 1996: 235). To adapt to the values of Jewish liberals such as Kramer and Foreman, and his unnamed doctor, Moss must parade his abject blackness in the name of a 'shared humanity'. The play of sameness and difference conforms to how his Jewish analyst sees him, which is, essentially, as a crippled victim. *Home of the Brave*, the first of the postwar Hollywood 'problem pictures' (Bogle 144), dissolves 'black rage' (Rogin 1996: 238) and represents the black psyche as nothing more or less than an extension of the white imago. But, as we will see when we discuss Philip Roth, the coming together of the black body and the Jewish mind in the decades after the Second World War was at the heart of American self-definitions of white liberalism.[43]

Fanon's rejection of a spurious Euro-American humanism reached its apogee in *The Wretched of the Earth*, where the Eichmann trial acted as a prism through which, as he argued, the processes of decolonization could be taken in a 'new direction' (Fanon 1961: 252). Fanon initially refers to the aftermath of the Second World War:

> Not long ago Nazism transformed the whole of Europe into a veritable
> colony. The governments of the various European nations called for
> reparations and demanded the restitution in kind and money of the
> wealth which had been stolen from them.... There was only one
> slogan in the mouths of Europeans on the morrow of the 1945 V-day:
> 'Germany must pay'. (80)

Here we have an exact comparison with the moment of decolonization.
Fanon quotes the West German chancellor, Konrad Adenauer commenting
on the opening of the Eichmann trial and asking for 'forgiveness from the
Jewish people' as he renews his promise to 'go on paying to the State of Israel
the enormous sums which are supposed to be compensation for the crimes
of the Nazis' (80). For Fanon, the parallel is with West Germany and newly
decolonized states, which should not be 'blinded by the moral reparation of
national independence' as the 'wealth of the imperial countries is our wealth
too' (81). Unlike West Germany, which has assimilated itself completely into
the 'anti-communist system' (80), the 'young nations of the Third World'
should recognize that they are strong in their 'own right, and in the justice
of our point of view' (81). Fanon was well aware of the selective nature of
Western concerns with regard to other racialized minorities such as Soviet
Jewry or the 'millions of Muslims oppressed by Communist dictatorship'
(63). What was needed was a form of justice that could account for all of the
oppressed. As Chancellor Adenauer was known for integrating former
National Socialists into West Germany, his grand gesture of reparation at the
Eichmann trial was deemed by Fanon a 'supposed compensation' (80) and,
by extension, an example of a partial form of European humanism that
decolonization would overcome.[44]

As Benita Parry has noted, Fanon in *The Wretched of the Earth* turned
away absolutely from Europe and the United States as a 'source and model
of meanings and aspirations'.[45] A blood-soaked Western humanism is
discounted as being utterly complicit with 'racial hatreds, slavery, exploitation and above all the bloodless genocide which consisted of the setting
aside of fifteen thousand million men' (Fanon 1961: 254). These

comparisons with the 'crimes of Nazism' resulted in Fanon calling for a 'new humanism' or a genuine universalism precisely because he did not want to 'imitate Europe' (252) with partial gestures such as the Eichmann trial. This is why he ends the section on 'Violence in an International Context', which begins with the genocide of the Jews, with the following: 'The Third World does not [need] to organize a great crusade of hunger against the whole of Europe. What it expects from those who for centuries have kept it in slavery is that they will help it to rehabilitate mankind, and make man victorious, once and for all' (84). Fanon's 'new humanism' would transcend European and American values and would be 'inventive' and 'make discoveries' (254) so as to include the world as a whole. What makes *The Wretched of the Earth* such an important book is precisely Fanon's wish to go beyond the immediate context of the Algerian War and the Manichaeism that was at the heart of the rhetoric accompanying this war. It was Sartre, rather than Fanon, who reinforced a conflict rhetoric with reference to the concentration camps, which, in addressing a European reader, refers pointedly to both the Nazis and the French military: 'you will have to fight or rot in concentration camps' (Sartre 1961: 26). But Fanon wanted to complicate such either/or thinking while recognizing that it was undoubtedly a product of the bloody conflict in Algeria, with up to one and a half million Algerians dying in their war for liberation. The role of the intellectual would, therefore, act as an 'awakener of the people' (Fanon 1961: 179) and enable the 'rebirth of the imagination' (197) so as not to be subsumed completely by the armed struggle.

Fanon did not want the European nation-state replicated in the Third World, which is why he conceived a national government not merely for and by the people but also 'for the outcasts and by the outcasts' (165). This minority consciousness preoccupied Fanon. For this reason, he continued to be haunted by the image of the deracinated cosmopolitan, which could all too easily bleed into the reborn intellectual, not unlike himself, who was always at risk of becoming a *luftmensch*: 'This tearing away [from "the white man's culture"], painful and difficult though it may be, is, however, necessary. If it is not accomplished there will be serious psycho-affective injuries and the result will be individuals without anchor, without horizon, colourless, stateless, rootless – a race of angels' (175). The deracinated intellectual – 'colourless, stateless, rootless' – is contrasted starkly with the organic intellectual who, in the words of Ahmed Sékou Touré, had to be 'a living part of Africa and her thought' (quoted 167). Just as the response to the 'Nazi crimes' was an example of a limited version of liberation and freedom, along Western lines, the figure of the cosmopolitan Jewish intellectual (one of a 'race of angels') needed to be transformed in a completely new and redeemed decolonized world.

In contrast to Sartre, as Arendt acknowledged, Fanon understood that 'Racialism and hatred and resentment – "a legitimate desire for revenge" – cannot sustain a war of liberation' (111).[46] As we shall see in the next chapter, Jean Améry, after his torture and imprisonment in Auschwitz, emphatically assumed the mantle of a vengeful Shylock in a bid to make the world understand that assimilating West Germany into the Western system meant that the victims of Nazism were denied justice. Améry, following Fanon, thought of violence as a form of negative transcendence, redeeming the oppressed, whereas Primo Levi, following Memmi and Arendt, rejected counterviolence in the name of the continuation of a radical tradition of European humanism.[47]

Fanon, more than anything else, wanted finally to transcend the Manichaeism of colonialism in the name of a 'new humanism' and a psychoanalytic practice that included all sides of the Algerian conflict. He agonized over the role of revolutionary violence, the limits of national spontaneity and the authenticity of the reborn 'intellectual' in the context of decolonization. While all of these formulations could be reduced to the certainties and disciplines of revolutionary struggle, Fanon also universalized his last work so that it was to transcend the immediacies of the bloody conflict that accompanied Algerian liberation. But, to achieve this imaginative transcendence, he replaced the deracinated mind of the impure and inauthentic cosmopolitan, which he associated with Europe and the United States, and which spoke most intimately, as Memmi proposes, to Fanon's diasporic journey away from Martinique. The figure of 'the Jew', in its enforced role as *luftmensch*, corresponded exactly to the fearful 'race of angels', somewhere between colonization and decolonization, who continued to haunt Fanon with their supposely emasculated selves (hence asexual angels) and utter detachment from 'the people'. As we will see in the next chapter, Fanon's struggle with the role of the 'Jewish intellectual' in the context of the bloodshed in Algeria, and the nature of European humanism after Nazism and colonialism, also spoke directly to the Auschwitz survivors Primo Levi and Jean Améry.

3

Diaspora and the Holocaust
Primo Levi, Jean Améry and the Art of Returning the Blow

'If you wish, I bear my grudge for reasons of personal salvation. . . . But no one wants to relieve me of it, except the organs of public opinion-making, which buy it. What dehumanized me has become a commodity, which I offer for sale.' Jean Améry, *At the Mind's Limits* (1966), p. 80.

'The Jews, enemies by definition, impure and sowers of impurity, destroyers of the world, were forbidden that most precious communication, contact with their country of origin and their family. Whoever has experienced exile, in any of its many forms, knows how much one suffers when this nerve is severed. This leads to a deadly impression of desertion, and also to unjust resentment.' Primo Levi, *The Drowned and the Saved* (1986), p. 81.

Shortly before he committed suicide in 1978, Jean Améry, who briefly shared a barracks with Primo Levi in Auschwitz-Monowitz, described his fellow 'intellectual in Auschwitz' to a mutual friend as 'the forgiver' (Levi 1986: 110). Améry, as a growing number of commentators have noted, is Levi's most significant interlocutor, the 'intellectual angel', in Alexander

Stille's felicitous phrase, with whom Levi, at the end of his life, struggled to clarify the meaning of the Holocaust.[1] But this was not a one-way street, and Levi also helped to shape, albeit unwittingly, Améry's account of his experience of Auschwitz. As his biographer notes, Améry felt that when Levi's *If This Is a Man* (1947) was published in German in 1961 it had 'stolen the show' from him to the extent that he decided not to publish his 'Auschwitz diaries' in their current form.[2] *At the Mind's Limits* (*Jenseits von Schuld und Sühne*) (1966) was published five years later, and responded in part to his fellow 'professional Auschwitz inmate' (Heidelberger-Leonard 65), in Améry's sardonic phrase. Within three pages of the opening of his memoir, Améry describes his 'barracks mate Primo Levi from Turin' as one of the camp's 'chosen', who, as a chemist, was 'employed in [his] profession' (Améry 1966: 3). This was in stark contrast to the 'intellectual in Auschwitz', such as the author of *At the Mind's Limits*, whose intellect pointedly remained outside any 'social reality that could support and confirm it' (6).

Born Hans Maier in Vienna in 1912, Améry was studying philosophy and education at the University of Vienna when the Nazis came to power in 1933. His Jewish father, whom he remembers pictured like 'a Tyrolean Imperial Rifleman' (83), died in the First World War when he was four, and his Roman Catholic mother raised him as a Catholic in the Alpine provinces of western Austria, until he returned to Vienna as a student. After the Anschluss in March 1938, he fled to France and then to Belgium, where he joined the Resistance. He was arrested and tortured by the Gestapo in 1943 and subsequently deported to Auschwitz. After the war, Levi had a home and family to return to in Turin, and a language and culture in which he was steeped, whereas Améry's immediate family were dead. On his return to Belgium in April 1945, he discovered that his wife, who had stayed hidden in the city, had also died. Whereas Levi had a strong sense of continuity after Auschwitz, Améry cultivated an abiding distrust of the Austro-German culture of his youth.

At the Mind's Limits is a collection of five autobiographical essays that reflect upon Améry's experience of being tortured in Fort Breendonk by the SS and incarcerated in Gurs (from where he, followed by Hannah

Arendt, escaped) and Auschwitz-Monowitz. The book, which Levi read with 'almost physical pain' (Levi 1978: 49), is also a philosophical meditation on Améry's identityless identity as a Sartrean 'Catastrophe Jew' or 'Non-non-Jew' (Améry 1966: 94), given his mixed Jewish-Christian background and his racialized Jewish identity which was wholly a product of the Nuremberg Laws. Through this consciously constructed identity, Améry, unlike Levi, wanted to understand how he became a specifically 'Jewish victim' given that he could also have claimed 'Aryan' status (Heidelberger-Leonard 45 and 71). Levi's *The Drowned and the Saved* (1986) has an essayistic form similar to *At the Mind's Limits*, mixing autobiography with more general philosophical and conceptual questions, and at times comes close to Améry's uncompromising despair which does not require the 'company' (71) of the reader. If *At the Mind's Limits* implicitly refigures Levi's *If This Is a Man*, then Levi returns the compliment in his last book, not exactly in a spirit of friendship, in his essay 'The Intellectual in Auschwitz' (1986).[3]

Soon after hearing of Améry's suicide in 1978, Levi began to translate *At the Mind's Limits* into Italian, although the translation remained incomplete. There is a strong sense in which this book haunted Levi long after its publication.[4] To this extent, Améry can be regarded as Levi's philosophical and emotional opposite, who was, unlike Levi, unable to adjust to life after the camps. This argument was first made in an obituary, 'Jean Améry: Philosopher and Suicide', where Levi described his subject as a 'cantankerous and solitary philosopher' (Levi 1978: 48). This rather ungenerous description of Améry, not least in an obituary, gives a sense of just how antagonistic Levi was to his rather troubling 'intellectual angel'. One reason for their mutual distrust was that their tentative relationship was mediated almost entirely through a third party, Hety Schmitt-Maas, who has an unusually honourable role in Levi's 'Letters from Germans', summarized in *The Drowned and the Saved*. Mrs Hety S, as Levi calls her, was a lifelong correspondent: 'It was she who gave me the address of Jean Améry and mine to him, but on one condition: that we both send her carbon copies of the letters we would exchange' (Levi 1986: 163). Although her aim was to bring her two correspondents together in a spirit of comradeship, her account of Levi to Améry – a man 'entirely free of resentment . . . standing above such things' (Heidelberger-Leonard 65) – inevitably provoked Améry, who described himself pointedly, after Nietzsche, as a 'self-confessed man of resentments' (Améry 1966: 69).[5]

My argument is that the differences between Levi and Améry are precisely to do with Levi's good fortune in returning to his family home and, conversely, Améry's sense of exile from home, language and culture. In other words, Levi enacted a rather conservative version of diaspora (exile and return), and Améry was forced into an uncompromisingly permanent, and unremitting, exile.[6] Unlike Levi, Améry was utterly bereft after the war; without parents or close relations, without a home or partner, and completely distrustful of the German language and culture that he had devoted himself to as a student of literature and philosophy in the early 1930s at the University of Vienna. In contrast, Levi returned to the home and culture of his parents in Turin where he was born and where he continued to live and work with his extended family. For this reason it is a little too neat (*pace* Eugene Goodheart) to reduce the differences between Levi and Améry to one of 'temperament': 'if Améry is the man of reason, Levi is the reasonable man.'[7] Their material circumstances, it seems rather too obvious to state, clearly shaped their contrasting characters, with one on the side of diasporic return, the other on the side of unremitting exile.

Between Levi and Améry

In comparison with Améry's exile and loss, Philip Roth has commented on the extent to which Levi 'voluntarily remained, over so many decades, intimately entangled and in such direct, unbroken contact with his immediate family, his birthplace, his region, the world of his forebears, and, in particular, with the local working environment'.[8] Levi agrees with this statement, and goes further in characterizing his life of 'communal interconnectedness':

It is true that I have deep roots and that I had the luck of not losing them. My family was almost completely spared by the Nazi slaughter, and today I continue to live in the very flat where I was born. The desk here where I write occupies, according to family legend, exactly the spot where I first saw light. When I found myself 'as uprooted as a man could be' certainly I suffered, but this was far more than compensated afterwards by the fascination of adventure, by human encounters, by the sweetness of 'convalescence' from the plague of Auschwitz. (Roth 2001a: 12)

As Robert Gordon argues, the values that Levi associates with *casa* or 'home' are an abiding counterweight to the 'no-place' of Auschwitz in his work. If Levi felt at home in the centuries-old humanist values of Italian culture, it is precisely to place these values next to the horror of the death camps.[9] To this extent, Levi's embrace of the quotidian and his rootedness has been characterized as a form of civilizing 'revenge' against the Lager.[10] He is utterly preoccupied with the notion of home, using the Italian word *casa* extensively throughout his corpus, precisely to create a sense of narrative and emotional order in his testimony in response to the horrors of the camps. It is no coincidence, as he informs Roth, that 'family legend' associates Levi's writing desk with the place in which he was born. The idea of writing as a form of rebirth has a tremendous resonance in Levi's work and is first expressed in the preface to *If This Is a Man*: 'The need to tell our story . . . had taken on for us, before our liberation and after, the character of an immediate and violent impulse, to the point of competing with our elementary needs. The book has been written to satisfy this need: first and foremost, therefore, as an interior liberation' (Levi 1947: 15).[11]

Améry, in one of the many ways in which he distinguished himself from Levi, argues specifically against any form of aesthetic 'transcendence' (Améry 1966: 7) both within and beyond the camps, as can be seen in his much-cited dictum: 'No bridge led from death in Auschwitz to *Death in Venice*' (16). He was to reject not only any sense of an 'interior liberation' after Auschwitz, but also the very notion, so crucial to Levi, of being at home: 'whoever has succumbed to torture can no longer feel at home in the world' (40). Améry devotes a chapter to the question 'how much home does a person need?', which, he argues, 'weighs the exile down' from the beginning and will 'never leave him again' (42). He characterizes 'home-sickness' as 'alienation from the self' and relates this especially to his becoming a racialized 'Jew' (43) under the Nuremberg Laws. In speaking about the 'Passover ritual' with its communal injunction – 'Next year in Jerusalem' – Améry notes that 'it wasn't at all a matter of getting to the Holy Land' and thereby detaches his notion of 'home' from a specific locus. Unlike Levi, he was a free-floating exile.

For this reason he was prepared to consider a 'transportable home' or an 'ersatz for home' (44), which is close to George Steiner's abstract diasporic ideal of an 'extraterritorial homeland' as a means of under-standing a non-national Jewish history.[12] At the same time as identifying Proust, Sartre and Beckett as his 'spiritual compatriots', in much the same way as Steiner, Améry also recognizes that 'one must have compatriots in village and city streets if the spiritual ones are to be fully enjoyed'. He was well aware how privileged Levi's position was after the war – 'One must have a home in order not to need it' (46) – but recognized equally, in an implicit reference to Levi, that a narrow focus on one's homeland 'can lead to desolation and to intellectual wilting in provincialism'. But, at the other extreme, an unremitting sense of homelessness leads to 'disorder, confu-sion, desultoriness' (47), and it is this sense of indeterminacy that threat-ened to overwhelm him during his years of exile. A 'second-rate cosmopolitanism' (56) cannot replace a sense of place since 'cultural inter-nationalism thrives only in the soil of national security' (46). For this reason, Améry, unlike Steiner, supported a Jewish national response to the Holocaust.[13] As W.G. Sebald has argued, whereas Levi's Jewishness was comprised of a 'framework of family traditions', Améry's Jewish identity was 'nothing but pure abstraction' as it was merely an extension of his sense of exile.[14]

Levi and Améry can be brought together on a number of grounds – not least their avowed secular humanism, their brief spells in the Resistance and their extended periods in the Auschwitz-Monowitz labour camp – although they draw radically different conclusions from their experiences. Their memoirs can be said to conform to Walter Benjamin's well-known distinction between the 'tribe of storytellers' who have 'come from afar' and those who 'stay at home' and know the 'local tales and traditions'.[15] Améry's sense of irredeemable exile meant that he could only recount his experiences as a 'unique' (80) victim from afar, whereas Levi's sense of diasporic return meant that he continually negotiates between the received values of Italian and European society at large (often in the guise of Ulysses) and his experiences far from home. As Levi notes:

> If I too had seen the world collapse upon me; if I had been sentenced to exile and the loss of national identity; if I had been tortured until I fainted and lost consciousness and beyond, I would perhaps have learned to return the blow, and would harbour, like Améry, those 'resentments' to which he dedicated a long essay full of anguish. (Levi 1986: 110)

Both camp survivors deployed competing and received versions of European humanism which, at times, could sound remarkably similar. Améry, for instance, characterizes his resentment as a victim of Nazism, after Nietzsche, as 'a matter neither of revenge on the one side nor a problematic atonement on the other' (Améry 1966: 77), and thereby situates himself, not unlike Levi, in the rational middle between revenge and forgiveness. To be sure, Améry's self-characterized 'radical humanism' was in fact much closer to Levi's sceptical liberal humanism than is often assumed.[16] Like Arendt, Améry continued to believe in the values of the '*classical* enlightenment' (Améry 1984: 136), which, he argued, remains our '*sole hope* of making history and . . . lending meaning to the meaningless' (140). These Enlightenment values were, in other words, a kind of ersatz home for Améry, saving him from the disorder and confusion that a nihilistic rejection of these values (another kind of exile) would have entailed.[17]

Their many similarities, rather than their renowned differences, meant that Améry and Levi were at pains to distance themselves from each other. By dubbing Levi 'the forgiver', Améry not only insulted his comrade but also dejudaized him so that he was no longer a 'Jewish victim'. But this was nothing more than a fabrication which Levi resisted throughout his life. As his biographer notes, the pressure on Levi to forgive had been 'exalted at thousands of school and church occasions [attended by Levi] as Catholic pupils raised on the virtue of forgiveness could not accept Levi's refusal to "pardon" his tormentors' (Thomson 345). Levi makes his views clear in Simon Wiesenthal's *The Sunflower: On the Possibilities and Limits of Forgiveness* (1969), which discussed whether Wiesenthal, a camp inmate, should grant a dying member of the SS absolution:

> What would this pardon have meant for the dying man and for you? Probably a great deal for the former; a kind of sacralization, a purification which would have freed his religious conscience, all too tardily aroused, from the terror of eternal punishment. But I think that, for you, it would have been meaningless. . . . On your part it would have been an empty formula and consequently a lie.[18]

Améry, in the same volume as Levi, is ironically rather less strident on the issue of forgiveness: 'My opinion is a private one . . . and is of no public importance whatsoever. . . . You didn't forgive and that was certainly right, and if you had said the words of forgiveness in a fit of emotion, that would have been legitimate too' (Wiesenthal 106–09). But the reasons for Améry's remarks are important. Assisted by Hety Schmitt-Maas, Levi corresponded with Dr Ferdinand Meyer, a relatively 'humane' German chemist in Auschwitz-Monowitz, who, by coincidence, was to be Levi's postwar supplier of chemical products. Meyer also wrote to Améry, who informed Schmitt-Maas that, unlike Levi, 'I am not a man to forgive, and I have no sympathy for the gentlemen who belonged to the "management staff" [*Fuhrungspersonnel*] of the I.G. Farben Auschwitz' (Heidelberger-Leonard 66).

The correspondence with the German chemist is also referred to in *The Periodic Table* (1975), where Levi revealed that Meyer, renamed Müller, detected a strand of 'Christian forgiveness' in *If This Is a Man*.[19] In the 'Vanadium' chapter of *The Periodic Table*, Levi responded to this by noting that a Dr Müller mistakenly 'perceived in my book an overcoming of Judaism, a fulfilment of the Christian precept to love one's enemies' (Levi 1975: 221). That both Müller and Améry, on either side of the divide at Auschwitz-Monowitz, should regard Levi as a 'forgiver' is an irony that Levi did not appreciate. His response is significant:

> I don't consider this either an insult or praise but an imprecision. I am not inclined to forgive, I never forgave our enemies of that time, nor do I feel I can forgive their imitators in Algeria, Vietnam, the Soviet Union, Chile, Argentina, Cambodia, and South Africa, because I know of no human act that can erase a crime. I demand justice, but I am not able, personally, to trade punches or return blows. (Levi 1986: 110)

As Berel Lang has demonstrated, it is notable that the 'place of revenge' in the aftermath of the Holocaust is characterized primarily by its absence or displacement.[20] Levi's call for justice as a witness is, in this context, symptomatic of a wider taboo with regard to the Shylockian stereotype of the vengeful Jew that Améry pointedly evokes in *At the Mind's Limits*. Améry, in the name of the ethics of victimhood, is on the side of Shakespeare's Shylock: 'the world, which forgives and forgets, has sentenced me, not those who murdered or allowed the murder to occur. I and others like me are the Shylocks, not only morally condemnable in the eyes of the nations, but already cheated of the pound of flesh too' (Améry 1966: 75). In stark contrast to Améry, Levi wished to expunge the vengeful and hysterical Jew and therefore aimed to narrate his camp experiences, with the exception of his 'bloody poems' (Levi 1975: 151), by replacing the ethics of victimhood with the ethics of witnessing (a distinction that will be explored in the final section of this chapter). This is why Levi's rejoinder to being called a 'forgiver' precisely situates the Holocaust in an 'endless chain' (Berel Lang 1999: 158) of injustice – Algeria, Vietnam, the Soviet Union, Chile, Argentina, Cambodia and South Africa – which, in Berel Lang's terms, displaces the desire for revenge onto the demand for justice. Levi articulates this idealized voice of reason most explicitly in the Afterword ('Appendice') to the popular 1976 schools edition of *If This Is a Man*, which is not insignificant given the continued injunction to forgive in the Catholic schools where he spoke frequently:

> I repress hatred even within myself: I prefer justice. Precisely for this reason, when describing the tragic world of Auschwitz, I have assumed the calm, sober language of the witness, neither the lamenting tones of the victim nor the irate voice of someone who seeks revenge. I thought that my account would be all the more credible and useful the more it appeared objective and the less it sounded overly emotional; only in this way does a witness in matters of justice perform his task, which is that of preparing the ground for the judge. The judges are my readers. (Levi 1976: 186)

In statements such as these, Levi uses the received values of Western humanism – law, science and reason – which provided him with a point of continuity between his time before and after the camps. But the use of this language has mistakenly led to Levi's appropriation, in Europe especially, as the iconic Auschwitz survivor who turns the other cheek.[21] This was a charge that haunted Levi for much of his life: 'to forgive is not my verb. It has been inflicted on me' (Belpoliti and Gordon: 111). In the conventional discourse, vengeance and forgiveness are fundamentally opposed since forgiveness 'erases the past' whereas revenge 'preserves it' (Berel Lang 1999: 158) in endless retribution. Far from being a 'forgiver', Levi wanted, not unlike Améry, to preserve the consequences of historic genocide for the present day.[22] That Levi includes the detention camps and torture chambers of Algeria, which are said to imitate the Nazis, is significant in this context as it echoes Améry's extended dialogue with Frantz

Fanon, which we will now explore. In the late 1960s, Levi noted that 'deportations and torture have reappeared in Algeria' and that in 'Vietnam an entire people is threatened with destruction'. He related these injustices to the refusal to prosecute known Nazis in the West and in South America (Levi 1968: 29). These views are quite similar to those of Améry, who notes: 'half the French nation rose up against the torture in Algeria. One cannot say too often and emphatically enough that by this the French did honour to themselves' (Améry 1966: 23). But, despite these commonalities, Améry and Levi were to extenuate their differences to the extent that they became each other's opposites.

Between Améry and Fanon

Levi's allusion to Algeria, which is said to imitate the Nazis, refers back to Frantz Fanon and Aimé Césaire, who similarly understood the Holocaust, as we have seen, as part of the colonial sphere of racial violence. But whereas Levi was prepared to compare metaphorically the injustices that he suffered with those suffered by the Algerian people under French rule, Améry regarded his resentment as essentially 'unique': 'Everything will be submerged in a general "Century of Barbarism"' the 'murder of millions . . . will be lumped . . . with the shameful acts of violence by the colonial French' (Améry 1966: 80). Améry's fear was that his past experience would be 'submerged' and would no longer be reclaimable as a 'negative possession' (77–78). To understand his 'unique' sense of victimhood, my argument is that, for Améry, Levi and Fanon became two poles in his thought. One extreme is deemed to transcend the violence of the death camps complacently as 'the forgiver'; the other is deemed to resist racial oppression actively and is thereby able to regain his humanity by making his ever-present 'resentment' concrete. It is in relation to the question of 'trading blows', highlighted in Levi's response to Améry, that the two figures most clearly distinguished themselves one from the other. Here the work of Fanon, a shadowy presence in Levi's writings, is singularly important since he provides Améry, as Paul Gilroy has argued, with 'a constant point of reference and dialogue' which is summarized in *At the Mind's Limits*.[23] Améry's characterization of the humanizing counterviolence that he needed to overcome his 'resentment' as a victim of Nazism is, as he notes, first articulated by Fanon:

> What I later read in Frantz Fanon's *Les damnés de la terre* [*The Wretched of the Earth*] ... I anticipated back then [in Auschwitz] when I gave concrete social form to my dignity by punching a human face. To be a Jew meant the acceptance of the death sentence imposed by the world as a world verdict. ... I became a person not by subjectively appealing to my abstract humanity but by discovering myself within the given social reality as a rebelling Jew and by realizing myself as one. (Améry 1966: 91)

Améry is referring here to his decision to 'hit back' at a brutal Kapo in Auschwitz, even though he was physically much weaker than his tormentor and was beaten severely because of this act. Only by hitting back could Améry cease to be a victim and regain his 'dignity' as a 'rebelling Jew'. Here Fanon's belief that the colonized recreate their humanity through counter-violence is given a particularly Jewish inflection. Améry, in an interview, is quite explicit about the 'redemptive character of revolt and violence' in both the context of Auschwitz and Treblinka and the 'counter-aggression' of Third World 'freedom fighters' in the 1960s.[24] Levi's response to this Fanonian perspective is unequivocal: 'I have never known how to "return the blow", not out of evangelic saintliness or intellectual aristocracy, but due to intrinsic incapacity – perhaps because of the lack of a serious political education' (Levi 1986: 109). The mocking reference to a 'serious political education' alludes to Améry's close alliance with Sartre after the war and also to Levi's left-of-centre political pragmatism.[25] Levi goes on: 'I admire Améry's ... decision to leave the ivory tower and enter the battle-field ... but I must point out that this choice ... led him to such positions of severity and intransigence as to make him incapable of finding joy in life, indeed of living' (110).

By the end of 'The Intellectual in Auschwitz', Levi diverges completely from Améry with regard to his unmitigated 'devot[ion] to death': 'Perhaps because I was younger . . . I almost never had the time [in Auschwitz] to devote to death . . . I had many other things to keep me busy. . . . The aims of life are the best defence against death: and not only in the Lager' (120). Sebald argues: 'it is as if Levi were primarily concerned, in view of Jean Améry's death, to assert himself – unlike Améry, who had long been preoccupied with possible ways of death – by attaching himself to life the importance of which, he hoped, would preserve him from the ultimate act that he too already sensed within himself.'[26] His biographer notes poignantly that Levi committed suicide at the same age as Améry and that he kept by his side a copy of Améry's *On Suicide: A Discourse on Voluntary Death* (1976), a staunch defence of those 'human beings in search of their own, freely chosen death' which defined suicide as a 'summing up of many humiliations' (Améry 1976: xxv and 19). But it would be a mistake to read Levi's final depression and suicide as a teleological 'key' to *The Drowned and the Saved*.[27]

Although Levi was deeply affected by Améry's suicide in 1978, he regarded it at the time as part of the culmination of the process of 'trading blows' with the world that would 'achieve dignity', but at a 'very high price' as Améry was 'sure to be defeated' (Levi 1986: 110). Sebald is right in regarding Améry as Levi's Other, on the side of death rather than life, but this case can also be made with respect to other survivors who committed suicide, such as Paul Celan. The extent to which Levi's work is constantly moving between 'life' and 'death' can be seen, for example, when he demurs from Celan for being only on the side of 'death'. His argument against Celan's 'obscure' poetry makes this position clear:

If [Celan's poetry] is a message, it gets lost in the 'background noise': it is not a communication, it is not a language, or at most it is a dark truncated language precisely like that of a person who is about to die and is alone, as we will be at the point of death. But since we are not alone, we must not write as if we were alone. As long as we live we have a responsibility: we must answer for what we write, word for word, and make sure that every word reaches its target. (Levi 1985: 161–62)

Writing in his *Other People's Trades* (1985), Levi argued that Celan's modernist 'obscurity' disabled him from communicating with an expansive readership – thus, Celan is deemed to have widened the gap between the living and the dead. A figure like Celan raises the issue for Levi of whether he should adopt the 'language of fear and chaos' or, alternatively, render his experience in language that is as 'accessible . . . as possible' (Gordon 2001a: 78–79). For Giorgio Agamben, the 'background noise' of Celan's poetry is equivalent to the 'non-language' of Auschwitz, which is why Levi included Celan's 'Death Fugue' in his *The Search for Roots* (1981).[28]

Early canonizers of Holocaust literature have characterized *If This Is a Man* as a 'death story' which mistakenly places Levi's experiences in an unknowable realm of extremity beyond ordinary ethical concerns.[29] Levi rejected such a one-dimensional response to his time in Auschwitz-Monowitz and negotiated, in stark contrast to Améry, between the death camps and the values of the world at large. Levi's greatest nightmare, the haunting climax to *The Truce* (1963), was that 'nothing is true outside of the Lager' (Levi 1963: 379). In his essay on Améry, Levi described Auschwitz-Monowitz as 'a university' (Levi 1986: 114), an idea that was completely anathema to Améry who wrote, as he argued, from the phenomenological perspective of the victim. By giving a 'concrete social form' to his dignity by 'punching a human face', Améry distinguished himself from Levi, who locates human dignity in the 'moments of reprieve' where his brief Lager friendships with Alberto and Lorenzo remind him of his humanity.

In an essay on 'The Birth of Man from the Spirit of Violence: Frantz Fanon the Revolutionary' (1971), published five years after *At the Mind's Limits*, Améry expands on his earlier references to *The Wretched of the Earth* and on the ideal of vengeful humanism. We are told that Fanon's account of colonialism was 'quite comparable' with the 'situation in which I found myself as a Jewish concentration camp inmate' to the extent that both situations constituted a 'force-field in which violence is bound to engender counter-violence' (Améry 1971: 15). But, unlike Fanon, Améry 'never fully got over the fact that I had not fought the oppressor weapon in hand' as 'freedom and dignity must be attained by way of violence, in order to be freedom and dignity' (16). Fanon, in this account, was able to shatter 'the prison of his black skin' and choose the 'freedom of battle' (14). In stark contrast to Levi, Fanon represented an authentic model for the 'rebelling Jew' (Améry 1966: 91), who could escape victimization, and thereby regain his/her humanity, by returning the blow.

Améry's 'implacable resentment' is maintained by his deeply felt inability, unlike the colonized who were liberated by their own hands, to free himself finally from his oppressors.[30] Rather than liberation by his own hands, Améry was granted freedom merely by 'English, American and Russian soldiers who fought for it' (Améry 1971: 16). But his argument, taken from Sartre, is that his resentment could only be ended by actualizing the 'unresolved conflict between victims and slaughterers' (Améry 1966: 77). After the war, Améry regarded this battle for freedom as still unfought and therefore demanded 'recognition of the *right* of resentment' in the consciousness of a German nation 'already rehabilitated by [linear] time' (Sebald 2003: 162). The counterviolence of the 'rebelling Jew' reverses linear time as it humanizes even the victimizer, who 'at the instant of his execution' would want 'exactly as much as I to turn back time, to undo what has been done' (Améry 1966: 70). What Améry and Fanon both take from Sartre is that 'the act of violence reverses time':

The oppressor, once pulled into the violence the oppressed inflicts upon him, becomes a brother in humanity. Do you know what it is like when you feel the cold steel of the barrel of a rifle on your warm skin? Now you know. You are now like me who was made to feel it. Thus in the moment in which I have turned from the receiver of violence to its bearer, you have become my fellow human. (Améry 1971: 16)

Written in the same year as his Fanon essay, Améry's 'In the Waiting Room of Death: Reflections on the Warsaw Ghetto' goes a stage further by replacing his 'resentment' with a sense of 'revenge' which he wants to understand from the victim's perspective outside the 'non-binding space of speculation' (Améry 1969: 16). Améry begins the essay by calling for a 'phenomenology of the victim's existence in the ghetto' that will reflect 'direct experience' rather than filtering it through the 'medium of thought' (Améry 1969: 21). This supposedly unmediated account, Améry argues, allows him to reconstruct the Warsaw Ghetto Uprising from the viewpoint of the victim, where the 'realization of *humane vengeance*' is given a concrete social reality. For Améry, the 'avenging violence' of the ghetto uprising aims to nullify the 'oppressor's violence' (26) and therefore enables those trapped in the ghetto to escape a 'two-thousand-year history' (24) of victimization and a diasporic solidarity based exclusively on suffering. But here the anti-colonial model of liberation, where the victim utilizes the 'redemptive power of violence in the context of colonialism' (Améry 1971: 16), can no longer be applied to rebelling Jews. The ghetto wall, Améry argues, was the 'demarcation line that separated the Jew from the *human being*', which resulted in the 'total solitude of the Ghetto Jew' (Améry 1969: 23). This radical solitude is the crucial difference between the colonized of Algeria and ghettoized Polish Jewry:

> To be sure, what Fanon said of the colonial slave holds true also for the Jew: that the master 'makes' the servant and thereby determines him in his entire being. However, the colonial master 'makes' his dehumanized human workhorse for the purpose of exploitation [which] demands in turn that everything be taken from the exploited but that his life be spared. For the Nazi, on the other hand, the death of the Jew, the Final Solution, took incontestable priority over exploitation. The Ghetto Jews were made to work until they died like dogs. Decisive, however, was not their work but their death. (23–24)[31]

Revolutionary violence is 'eminently *humane*' as it is 'not just the mid-wife of history, but the mid-wife of the human-being discovering and refashioning himself in history' (Améry 1971: 16). It is in these terms that the Warsaw Ghetto Uprising is characterized as '*humane vengeance*' since, in this revolutionary moment, the ghetto Jew finally 'became the hunter, not for the joy of hunting but from the will to remain who he was and at the same time to become another' (Améry 1969: 26). By overcoming the 'solidarity that extends only to suffering' (24), the ghetto fighters are able to point towards an entirely different future for 'the Jew'. Here the 'hopeless revenge' of the ghetto Jew is contrasted starkly with the 'comparatively simple "violence" of Fanon' (27). Unlike the liberatory 'violence and revolution of the Algerian', the only aim of the ghetto Jew was the 'reattainment of dignity' and the '*freedom of choosing death*' (28), however suicidal. This is why Améry argues that the 'untouchable and abjected concept of revenge' (Améry 1971: 16), which he associates primarily with a response to Nazism, does not, finally, apply to Fanon.

Améry aimed to make the Jewish victim the subject of his/her own history rather than the object of other people's machinations. In these terms, the figure of the victim became a site of interpretation, just as the camp itself was for Levi, rather than an object of pity. By moving from object to subject, Améry believed that the 'determination for revenge' enabled the Warsaw ghetto fighters to transfigure an age-old history of segregation and persecution. He is well aware of how contentious his argument is but insists that the inability of the majority of the victims of Nazism to 'rise in revolt' remains 'our very painful, constantly reopening wound' (Améry 1969: 27). As Berel Lang confirms, many wartime ghetto fighters or partisan units 'viewed resistance as a form of revenge' and even included the Hebrew word *nekamah* ('revenge') in the title of their group (Berel Lang 1999: 146). Although he does not cite Améry, Lang agrees with him that the 'instant revenge' of Jewish partisans is 'identical to resistance' and that the desire for revenge is a 'means of *creating* . . . memory as such' (158–59). Like Améry, Lang here is referring back to Nietzsche's 'man of resentments' (Améry 1966: 69) who constructs memory precisely *'to make revenge possible'* (Berel Lang 1999: 59).[32]

Between Améry, Levi and the Art of Returning the Blow

At one point in his essay on the Warsaw ghetto resistance, Améry argues that the ghettoized Jew had 'internalized the image of himself created by the Nazi; he had become the louse of Kafka's *Metamorphosis*' (Améry 1969: 24). Earlier he had described 'those who had tortured me and turned me into a bug' as akin to the 'dark powers' (Améry 1966: 64) that had transformed Kafka's protagonist. These literary references are in stark contrast to his dictum that 'No bridge led from death in Auschwitz to *Death in Venice*' (16). While the bridge between Kafka's 'louse' or 'bug' and the racialized Jew is obviously not a form of aesthetic transcendence, which Améry was arguing against, it does indicate that it is impossible to avoid metaphorical thinking in the supposedly unmediated or non-speculative account of the victims of Nazism.[33] After all, the very act of reversing time, so as to humanize the oppressor by 'returning the blow', is nothing if not an act of imaginative counterviolence.

As is well known, Améry was to dismiss completely Hölderlin's poetry in the camp because it 'no longer transcended reality' (7), whereas Levi was to draw solace from Dante's *Inferno* in the Lager. But, as with Améry, Levi's memory of the famous Ulysses canto in the *Divine Comedy* – 'you were made men, to follow after knowledge and excellence' (Levi 1947: 113) – also speaks to the Lager ('you were made men') and Levi's experience, not unlike Ulysses, of exile, return and testimony ('to follow after knowledge').[34] Levi agrees with Améry that 'reason, art, and poetry are no help in deciphering a place from which they are banned' (Levi 1986: 115) but he also argues with his usual pragmatism that 'culture could be useful even if only in some marginal cases and for brief periods' (114). The act of testimony resided for Levi in the dignity of the camp inmate who finds his or her humanity in 'brief periods' or 'moments of reprieve' outside the camp, whereas for Améry dignity was achieved by 'returning the blow'.

Human dignity, for Améry, is associated with 'the deed' of bodily resistance, hence his imagined transformation into a Kafkaesque bug and his desire, following Nietzsche, for a 'genuine reaction' (Améry 1966: 67) to alleviate his overwhelming resentment at his victimization. In stark contrast, Levi writes in his original preface to *If This Is a Man* that he does not want to 'formulate new accusations' but rather to 'furnish documentation for a quiet study of certain aspects of the human mind' (Levi 1947: 15).

That Améry (*pace* Fanon) is on the side of the body and Levi on the side of the mind can be seen in their differing versions of Kafka. To be sure, Levi's account of translating Kafka from German to Italian also reads the protagonist of *The Trial* through the optic of the camps: 'his dignity as a man is compromised right from the start, and then wilfully and determinedly demolished day by day' (Levi 1983: 140). It is not insignificant, in this regard, that Levi's German was perfected in the Lager, as he notes in his preface to the German edition of *If This Is a Man*. But, at the same time, Levi was at pains to moderate the 'sensation of a collision, a conflict' in Kafka and, in a 'middle path', to 'impose my own way of writing' (141), which, by extension, tempers the German language so that it is no longer completely subsumed by the experience of the camps. That Améry remains distrustful both of his mother tongue and of a humanism that does not speak from the perspective of the resentful victim finally separates the two survivors. Once again, the Benjaminian distinction between the exilic and homebound storyteller speaks to this difference, although it would be a mistake to assume that Levi does not, at times, capture the spirit of Améry's isolating vengeful humanism. Take, for instance, the last stanza of Levi's poem 'For Adolf Eichmann' (1960):

> Oh son of death, we do not wish you death.
> May you live longer than anyone ever lived.
> May you live sleepless five million nights,
> And may you be visited each night by the suffering of
>   everyone who saw,

Shutting behind him, the door that blocked the way back,
Saw it grow around him, the air fill with death.

At the beginning of his discussion of Holocaust memory and revenge, Berel Lang cites this stanza without comment as if the poem speaks straightforwardly to his topic (Berel Lang 1999: 142). But this version of humane vengeance, above all, blurs the boundaries between justice and vengeance as Levi resists the calls for the immediate death of Eichmann by channelling the passion for revenge into a form of (albeit merciless) justice. Levi consigns Eichmann to eternal life so that he can witness the sufferings of his victims in their entirety. As others have argued, the poem 'bespeaks a bitter yet rational message' as Eichmann's death alone could not 'avenge the deaths of those he murdered' (Ariella Lang 259). Paradoxically, the immortal Eichmann, in Levi's fantasy, becomes both the 'true witness' (Levi 1986: 63) of the Holocaust, unlike the camp survivors, and he also suffers the nightmares that haunt Levi at the end of *The Truce*. This version of Eichmann refuses the crude call of an 'eye for an eye', which, once again, contrasts with Améry who, in the context of the Warsaw Ghetto Uprising, fully embraces the figure of the vengeful Jew:

I already hear protests: No, that's not the way it was! An eye for an eye, a tooth for a tooth, *jus talionis*; for God's sake, that is by no means what the Jews wanted who were rousing themselves to resistance!

Yes, it is! I believe that is what they wanted. I myself . . . wanted just that; and countless comrades along with me. (Améry 1969: 27)

Despite its ironically dispassionate title and purposeful equivocations, the vengeful justice in 'For Adolf Eichmann', along with some of Levi's other early verse, is the closest that he comes to the humanizing vengeance of Améry. But while Levi could rage in his poetry, his prose aimed, with mixed results, to 'repress hatred even within myself' (Levi 1976: 186). Rather than answer violence with violence, Levi repeatedly states that he has 'never cultivated within myself hatred as a desire for revenge, or as a desire to inflict suffering on my real or reputed enemy.... [E]xactly because I am not a Fascist or Nazi, I refuse to give way to this temptation' (185–86). The association of vengeance with fascism, popularized in the schools edition of *If This Is a Man*, is reinforced in another much earlier account of Eichmann which differs markedly from 'For Adolf Eichmann': 'The Eichmann trial and historical documentation of Nazi crimes certainly have educational value, but they alone are not enough.... The moral restoration that we need can only come from schools. That Eichmann is guilty is clearly shown; but every citizen, from schooldays onwards, needs to learn the meaning of truth and lies' (Levi 1961: 182). Here the movement from the language of law and empiricism to that of a wider ethical community, beginning with educational institutions, speaks to Levi's sense of being part of a healing social realm. Améry, on the other hand, is particularly resentful about the sort of survivor who 'lazily and cheaply forgives' and thereby 'submerges his individuality in society' and becomes merely a 'function of the social' (Améry 1966: 71–72). For Améry, 'the experience of persecution was, at the very bottom, that of an extreme *loneliness*' (70), beyond the social, which is why Levi's obituary described him as a 'solitary philosopher' (Levi 1978: 48). As he notes in *The Periodic Table*, anyone who has experienced exile 'in its many forms' is 'forbidden that most precious communication, contact with their country of origin and their family'. This 'severed nerve' can lead to the 'deadly impression of desertion, and also to unjust resentment' (Levi 1986: 81). Not least in his fiction, Levi wished to counter this version of exile as personified by Améry's solitariness and all-consuming resentments.

Levi's novel *If Not Now, When?* (1982) locates the question of revenge in a wider social and communal frame, made up of a network of friendships, which is a telling point of comparison with Améry. Levi recreates imaginatively a group of wartime East European Jewish partisans who are hiding out in the Russian forests behind the front line but pointedly have a terrible sense of homelessness: 'their homes no longer existed: they had been swept away, burned by the war or by slaughter' (Levi 1982: 100). This is in stark contrast to the sense of diasporic return in *The Truce* and is Levi's fictive way of communing with the mass of East European Jews who did not return home.[35]

Although he eschews the lethal conditions of the Warsaw ghetto, Levi nonetheless represents historically similar groups to those whom Améry discusses in 'In the Waiting Room of Death'. What is more, his motivation for researching the 'Jewish resistance movement' was to confirm that such resistance was 'much more important – in scale and moral significance – than is commonly thought'. Just as Améry locates morality in the act of humanizing counterviolence, Levi finds 'moral significance' in challenging the unfounded 'accusation' that 'the Jews stood still, were passive, let themselves be led to the slaughter like sheep' (104). That both Améry and Levi were captured by the Nazis as partisans clearly speaks to their abiding preoccupation with Jewish resistance. Both writers belittled their resistance activities and both were eventually 'discovered' to be Jews (Améry under severe torture), even though neither belonged to a Jewish resistance group.

However, Levi, unlike Améry, does not confine Jewish resistance to humanizing vengeance, which is questioned in the novel by members of Jewish resistance groups in contrast to their Polish and Russian equivalents. This can be seen especially in relation to the divided Mendel the watchmaker, the central protagonist of *If Not Now, When?*, who is a 'peaceable, bookish, chess-loving man with a philosophic bent [who] becomes a strong and proficient partisan' (Levi 1982: 419). Levi, in an interview, describes Mendel as an idealized alter ego, not least in relation to his own short time as a partisan: 'he does what I would have done, or rather what I should have done if I had been able' (105). In *The Periodic Table*, he stresses that virtually all of his friends in 1942, who eventually went underground, were 'writing poetry' and that they were the 'most disarmed partisans in the Piedmont, and probably the most unprepared' (Levi 1975: 128). Although Levi claimed never to have fired a shot as a partisan, he was implicated in the case of two renegade compatriots who were both given the death sentence, which devastated him: 'we had come out of [the sentence] destroyed, destitute, waiting for everything to finish and to be finished ourselves' (132). It was shortly after this incident that Levi, seemingly without the heart to resist, was captured.[36]

Levi remained strangely fascinated with the 'pitiless justice' (Thomson 419) meted out to his compatriots, which found a fictional form in *If Not Now, When?* when a drunken Russian partisan is shot for revealing secrets to the enemy. In the novel, Mendel, a former Red Army soldier, continually debates the nature of killing, and the question of revenge, to the extent that by the end of the book he is defined, above all, by his 'doubt' (Levi 1982: 202). When his wife is shot, and all of the inhabitants in his village are destroyed, he argues that 'only by killing a German can I manage to persuade the other Germans that I'm a man', which is identical to Améry's vengeful humanism. But he qualifies this statement by arguing that this is German 'logic' and that 'Jewish partisans, and Jews in the Red Army' represent something other than killing. Piotr, the Russian partisan leader to whom he says this, responds: 'Shooting is one thing and reasoning another. If a man reasons too much, in the end he can't shoot straight, and you people always reason too much' (78). The Russian-Jewish partisan leader, Gedaleh Skidler, is Piotr's prime example of someone who could 'shoot' but who, like the Jewish intellectual, also 'made up poems' and 'carried a violin around with him' (79).

The distinction between reasoning and shooting is reproduced in the novel in a variety of forms and speaks to a larger set of oppositions, which invariably break down, between 'pure and impure, man and woman, Jew and goy ... the laws of peace and the laws of war' (142). These fragile oppositions, personified in Mendel's doubt, are addressed at length in *The Periodic Table*, which will be explored in the next section. Levi's narrator tells the reader that 'Gedaleh's Jews ... savoured vengeance, though at a high price', like 'animals whose cage had been opened' (111). But, by the end of the novel, Mendel, whose name literally means 'the consoler' (253), is clear that 'Blood isn't paid for with blood. Blood is paid for with justice' (243). Just as Levi 'the forgiver' does not actually forgive anybody, Mendel 'the consoler' does not 'console anybody, not even myself' (253). Other Jewish partisans go further and argue that 'killing is a sin always' (177) and distinguish themselves from the Germans as they 'don't enjoy killing' (75). Levi associates the question of vengeance primarily with the Germans who 'hungered' (183) for revenge and were 'drunk on blood', although, by the end of the war, most of the partisans also felt the 'barbaric joy of revenge' (244).

Much of the novel, as many commentators have noted, sets up received images of Ashkenazi East European Jewry, in memory of the majority of Jews who died in the camps, which Levi aimed to mediate for a largely Sephardic or Italian Catholic readership. To this extent, his characters are mainly one-dimensional and didactic; 'differences or conflicts between them are represented through lengthy exchanges of views more than through action'. For a picaresque historical novel covering the same terrain as *The Truce*, *If Not Now, When?* is a curiously disembodied work whose characters are 'marked not by their bodies but by their discourse'.[37] One reason for the discursive quality of the novel is that it was in part written to engage with the troubling assumption, which Levi first records in *The Truce*, that 'anyone who doesn't speak Yiddish isn't a Jew' (Levi 1963: 154). Levi, all too aware of being a minority non-Yiddish-speaking Jew in Auschwitz, adopts the Yiddish proverb *Ibergekumene tsores iz gut tsu dertseylin* ('Troubles overcome are good to tell') as the epigraph to *The Periodic Table* and repeats it several times in the novel. For Améry, overcoming the past could not be dissociated from the humanizing act of 'hitting back'; for Levi, as his novel dramatizes at some length, it was the disembodied act of storytelling that helped him and his characters to overcome their *tsores* or troubles.

The difference between the two survivors can be gauged by the fact that Levi confines the issue of revenge to the sphere of fantasy and imagination. Améry's ever-present resentment, on the other hand, remains seemingly unmediated and inscribed on the body. After torture, he is a living being who is 'transcribed so thoroughly into flesh' that he is made into a 'prey of death' (Améry 1966: 40). When he was 'painfully beaten' after hitting back, Améry again notes that 'there are situations in life in which our body is our entire self and our entire fate' (90–91). This negative transcendence, which can only restore the traumatized body by 'physical violence' (91), is articulated repeatedly in *At the Mind's Limits* and results in Améry's perverse 'purification' (77). The transcendence of suffering, beyond the purity of violence, is characterized by him as 'the masochistic conversion of a suppressed *genuine* demand for revenge'. That is why Améry is so scathing about German-Jewish victims of Nazism who, soon after the war, were 'already trembling with the pathos of forgiveness and reconciliation' (71). Levi, in contrast, wished to mediate in a self-consciously 'impure' manner between his tortured body in Auschwitz (his 'flesh') and the world at large.

Améry, Levi and the *Muselmann*

My argument is that Levi and Améry can be distinguished in relation to two different kinds of ethics and ways of achieving dignity which I have called the ethics of witnessing and the ethics of victimhood. Améry claims the ethics of victimhood, his right as a victim to resent a postwar German history that has diminished its complicity with what has gone before. He imagines a time when he could 'hit back' and restore a sense of genuine morality (as opposed to a Nietzschean slave morality) to German society and thereby reclaim his humanity. Levi, on the other hand, achieves dignity through the act of testimony which moves, however inadequately, from the babel of noise and the 'phantoms', barely glimpsed on arrival at Auschwitz, to those who are now evoked as memorable human beings. For this reason, both *If This Is a Man* and *The Truce* begin by recalling two children who died in the camps and who are now memorialized 'through these words of mine' (Levi 1963: 198). It is tempting, in this regard, to place Améry on the side of combative 'deeds' and Levi on the side of mere 'words'. But this would be an oversimplification. If Améry is only too aware that his resentment is caused by being able to do nothing more than write, which merely commodifies his memories, there are many times in

Levi's work when he acknowledges the inadequacy of 'these words of mine' and desires hopelessly to make them flesh.

Améry characterizes himself as a product of the Nuremberg Laws – a 'non-non-Jewish' Jew – who is, in Sartrean terms, an inauthentic product of anti-Semitism. For this reason, he can only overcome his racialized identity by 'hitting back' and being purified of that which has been imposed on him. He is alone in his 'unique' (Améry 1966: 80) fight against racialization: 'I was a person who could not say "we"' (44). Such a solitary figure 'excludes' the *Muselmann* or Muslim from 'our considerations' and characterizes these inmates who had lost the will to live, which made up the masses in the camps, as 'a staggering corpse, a bundle of physical functions in its last convulsions'. These figures are omitted by Améry ('as hard as it may be') as they are 'in the actual sense of the word dehumanized'. Always already dehumanized, the *Muselmann* lacks any humanity to retrieve and, in a telling slippage (revealed by its awkward grammar), is regarded as 'giving up and was given up by his comrades' (9). The problem, unaddressed by Améry, is that by claiming the ethics of victimhood he has to 'give up' on the *Muselmann* who, as the ultimate victim and mere object within the camp, exposes the limits of his ethical purity.

Améry attacked Levi for being too forgiving a victim, to which Levi responded by noting Améry's disregard for the *Muselmann*: 'his gaze is directed on high and rarely lingers on the vulgar populace of the Lager, and on its typical character, the "Muslim"' (Levi 1986: 114). As is well known, Levi makes no claims, as a survivor, to be one of 'the true witnesses' as he 'did not touch bottom' (63–64): 'Those who did so ... are the "Muslims", the submerged, the complete witnesses, the ones whose deposition would have a general significance' (64). Unlike Améry, Levi speaks on behalf of survivors in the plural and also recognizes the submerged rationality of the 'Muslims' in their potential deposition of 'general significance'. Giorgio Agamben has named as 'Levi's paradox' the insistence that the 'true witness' is the one who cannot bear witness given the fact that the 'non-human' cannot 'testify to the human' (Agamben 1999: 82). This reading (or misreading) of Levi has led to the charge of mystification on the grounds that Levi has endowed the 'witness in extremis with a nearly mystical quality, unknowable in its horrid essence'.[38] But if Levi's paradox is reversed and we ask whether 'the human' can testify for 'the non-human', then we get much closer to Levi's limited and impure perspective. It is in relation to this ethical uncertainty as a witness that Levi differs profoundly from the convictions of Améry, whose ceaseless victimization ultimately blocks the 'path of a radical scepticism that would put his moral convictions in doubt' (Goodheart 520).

Whereas Améry foregrounds his resentment as a victim, Levi foregrounds his ambiguity and doubt as a witness, in relation to his sense of self and Italian-Jewish background, which is articulated most explicitly in *The Periodic Table*. We learn in particular that Levi's scepticism grew out of his opposition to Mussolini's Italy, which gave it a considerable power. Being 'a Jew, excluded and made sceptical by recent upheavals' (Levi 1975: 57) meant, finally, that he did not simply embrace the language of reason as a form of purification, as Améry was to assume. From the very beginning of this deliberately indefinable 'chemical treatise ... autobiography ... micro-history' (224), he was at pains to remain uncategorizable, whether in relation to his Jewishness, his training as a chemist or his humanity. For this reason, he states from the outset that diaspora Jews reflect in microcosm the 'human condition' as Jews have been 'torn between their divine vocation and the daily misery of existence'. This fissure is 'inherent in the human condition' because 'man is a centaur, a tangle of flesh and mind, divine inspiration and dust' (9). In this impure spirit, Levi's chemistry is defined throughout as an uneasy mixture of the magic of alchemy and the exactness of physics.

As Marco Belpoliti notes, Levi's most consistent self-image, echoing *The Periodic Table*, was as a 'hybrid' or 'centaur', which 'does not only represent the presence of opposites, but also ... an unstable union destined to break down'. In these terms, Levi's fragile and shifting 'hybrid nature' is reflected in the precarious act of bridging the 'true witnesses' of Auschwitz and the world outside in his determinedly mixed memoir-stories.[39] Améry was quite explicit in rejecting the idea of a bridge between his experience in the camps and the world at large. Working in a German philosophical tradition, he opposed any form of Hegelian synthesis and instead held all sides of a contradiction in pristine opposition. His fight remained within the camps. Levi's least systematic work – ironically entitled in Italian *Il Sistema Periodico* – is, in stark contrast to Améry, his most explicit and thoroughgoing acknowledgement of the value of impurity and that which cannot be categorized. In the 'Zinc' chapter, for instance, Levi is a young student performing his first experiments and is drawn into broader areas of speculation by the element's resistance to chemical breakdown:

> One could draw from [this experiment] two philosophical conclusions: the praise of purity, which protects from evil like a coat of mail; the praise of impurity, which gives rise to changes, in other words, to life. I discarded the first, disgustingly moralistic, and I lingered to consider the second, which I found more congenial. In order for the wheel to turn, for life to be lived, impurities are needed. . . . Dissension, diversity, the grain of salt and mustard are needed: Fascism does not want them, forbids them, and that's why you're not a Fascist; it wants everybody to be the same. (Levi 1975: 33–34)

Levi's distrust of moralizing, which he associates with the 'praise of purity', was signalled from his earliest writings. In *If This Is a Man* he rejected what he called 'a moral system elaborated by others . . . is it really necessary to elaborate a system and put it into practice? Or would it not be better to acknowledge one's lack of a system?' (Levi 1947: 47). By the time of *The Truce* he was commenting that 'moral codes, all of them, are rigid by definition; they do not admit blurrings, compromises, or reciprocal contaminations. They are to be accepted or rejected *en bloc*' (Levi 1963: 219). For this reason, Levi always described himself as an unbeliever in the widest sense. He needed 'reciprocal contaminations' precisely for the 'wheel to turn, for life to be lived' and to go beyond fascist sameness. This fundamental link between 'impurity' and 'life' is crucial to an understanding of the power of Levi's sceptical humanism. At the same time, the figure of the *Muselmann* personified for Levi 'all the evil of our time in one image' (Levi 1947: 90) and thereby represented the limits of his scepticism and the transition from an empty moralizing to an uncertain ethics.

While Améry also characterizes the 'intellectual in Auschwitz' as 'sceptical and humanistic', he differs from Levi significantly:

> the problem of the confrontation of intellect and horror appeared in a more radical form and, if the expression is permitted here, in a *purer* form. In Auschwitz the intellect was nothing more than itself. . . . Thus the intellectual was alone with his intellect, which was nothing other than pure content of consciousness, and there was no social reality that could support and confirm it. (Améry 1966: 6)

This version of the disembodied intellectual, or *luftmensch*, is close to Sartre's characterization of diaspora Jews as socially dispossessed by anti-Semitism and left only with their rationalizing intellect (Sartre 1946: 112–13). Here 'the Jew' is pure mind and the *Muselmann* is pure 'de-intellectualized' (Améry 1966: 9) body. For Améry, the 'basic quality' of intellectual life – 'its transcendence' (7) – was lost in Auschwitz. Unlike true believing 'militant Marxists, sectarian Jehovah's Witnesses, or practicing Catholics' (12–13), there was no possibility of the political, religious or aesthetic transfiguration of death for the 'sceptic-humanistic' (13) intellectual. After the war, however, his embrace of Sartre (whom he first heard lecture in Brussels in 1945) is precisely associated with such life-giving transcendence: 'Existentialism became for me a wholly personal philosophy of the hunger for life which had gnawingly returned after so many deaths, so many provisional resurrections.'[40] This devotion to Sartre goes hand in hand with his eventual remarriage and his adoption of a Francophone nom de plume, an anagram of his given German name, Mayer. Looking back at his younger self, Améry concludes: 'The epoch was ripe for a new teaching. And what could accord better with the spirit of those days than Sartre's message of existence, of being sentenced to freedom' (Améry 1984: 120).

Levi, throughout his work, but most explicitly in *The Wrench* (1978), *The Search for Roots* (1981) and *The Periodic Table*, specifically counters the notion of a 'pure' intellect and prefers instead knowledge that is deeply embedded in relationships between friends and communities.[41] In summarizing the differences between Levi and Améry, Eugene Goodheart rightly notes that 'Améry's sense of extremity *tends* to divide the world sharply between victim and tormentor; he is less interested in the range of intermediate behaviour that occurs in what Levi calls the grey zone' (Goodheart 524). This is why Levi speaks of a 'typically grey human specimen' (Levi 1975: 221) in *The Periodic Table*. Acknowledging such imperfection means that when Levi's memory self-consciously fails him, he is at pains to bear witness to those moments of failure whenever they occur. Speaking of Resnyk, a Polish Jew whom he once briefly encountered, Levi states: 'he told me his story, and today I have forgotten it, but it was certainly a sorrowful, cruel and moving story' (Levi 1947: 71). Unlike Améry's essays, forged in the purity of violence and counterviolence, Levi is always aware of the limits of his own experience and of what it means to turn experience into knowledge after Auschwitz. His failure of memory at this point becomes Resnyk's story:

> it was certainly a sorrowful, cruel and moving story; because so are all
> our stories, hundreds of thousands of stories, all different and all full of
> a tragic disturbing necessity. We tell them to each other in the evening,
> and they take place in Norway, Italy, Algeria, the Ukraine, and are
> simple and incomprehensible like the stories of a new Bible. (71–72)

It is this refusal to make easy connections or straightforward narratives out of his experience that is always in self-conscious tension with Levi's absolute authority, as Améry would have it, as a victim. By relating Resnyk's unremembered 'sorrowful, cruel and moving story' to other stories which take place in 'Norway, Italy, Algeria, the Ukraine', he shows from the beginning his instinct to transcend his personal experience as an Italian Jew and make a new and disparate bible of suffering.

That he did not regard his suffering as unique, and aimed to move from the camps to other places and contexts of oppression and cruelty, has been characterized as a form of 'planetary humanism' by Paul Gilroy. But Gilroy, in his later work, does not distinguish between Levi and Améry, and wrongly assumes that they hold identical views.[42] Levi's references to Algeria in both his first and last works (part of Resnyk's untold story) are obviously not as systematic as Améry's sustained comparisons, but, by moving beyond the isolated survivor, they do represent a profound engagement with another kind of 'Muslim' such as the millions of emaciated and dying Muslims in Bengal from 1940 to 1943 or the Muslims of Algeria whom Fanon champions. Whereas Améry chooses Fanon, the fighter on behalf of Algerian Muslims, Levi is preoccupied with the non-stories of the camp 'Muslims': 'All the [*Muslims*] who finished in the gas chambers have the same story, or more exactly, have no story' (Levi 1947: 90). Agamben, with characteristic overstatement, replaces such 'no stories' with a 'ferocious irony': 'it is certain that . . . the Jews knew that they would not die at Auschwitz as Jews' (Agamben 1999: 45). While this is far from being historically accurate, Améry's displacement of the dehumanized Jewish victims of Auschwitz (under the sign of 'Muslim') onto the Algerian Muslims who fight back (under the sign of Fanon) can be said to speak to this irony.

For Agamben, the *Muselmann* is equally a figure of indeterminacy, between the human and non-human, as well as the personification of 'a new ethics, an ethics of a form and life that begins where dignity ends'. Levi, in this reading, bears witness to 'the drowned, speaking in their stead', as 'the cartographer of this new *terra ethica*, the implacable land-surveyor of *Muselmannland*' (Agamben 1999: 69). But, as Robert Eaglestone has rightly argued, Agamben's version of the *Muselmann* as embodying the Holocaust is not only reductive in itself but can also, as Levi and Améry demonstrate, be applied to the 'colony and colonial subject'.[43] That Agamben speaks for the *Muselmann*, through Levi, is made possible by constructing Auschwitz as a 'non-place in which all disciplinary barriers are destroyed' (Agamben 1999: 48). But whereas Agamben does not question his right to speak for the *Muselmann*, Levi is all too aware that in categorizing 'the drowned' as not quite human he is, to some degree, replicating the gaze of his persecutors. In *If This Is a Man* the 'Muslims' are, for Levi, 'an anonymous mass, continually renewed and always identical, of non-men who march and labour in silence, the divine spark dead within them, already too empty to really suffer. One hesitates to call them living: one hesitates to call their death death' (Levi 1947: 96).

By refusing the ethics of victimhood (*pace* Agamben), Levi was all too aware of how unsettling the 'anonymous mass' was when he wanted to go beyond camp slang ('Muslims') and account for the dehumanized. As he notes in his essay on Améry, Levi's training as a chemist resulted in a habit that can be 'judged' as either 'human or inhuman'. Those in the camps could be considered to be both 'human beings' and also ' "samples", specimens in a sealed envelope to be identified, analysed and weighed' (Levi 1986: 114). After all, Levi attempts to impose the language of dehumanizing rationality on his time in Auschwitz by regarding the camp as '*pre-eminently*, a gigantic biological and social experiment' (Levi 1947: 93; my emphasis). Levi's categorizing perspective is in response to the barbarism of the camps, which denies the inmates the capacity for thought, as he is told from the beginning by a guard: ' "*Hier ist kein warum*" (there is no why here)' (29). Levi's awareness of such simultaneous humanizing and dehumanizing systems – both within and without the law, as Agamben argues – goes to the heart of his ethical uncertainty. He understood, from the very beginning, that even he, in his memoirs, is forced to work within the very categories that decide who is, and is not, human. At one point in *The Periodic Table* he views himself again from a 'distance of thirty years':

I find it difficult to reconstruct the sort of human being that corresponded, in November 1944, to my name or, better, to my number: 174517. I must then overcome the most terrible crisis, the crisis of having become part of the *Lager* system, and I must have developed a strange callousness if I then managed not only to survive but also to think, to register the world around me, and even to perform rather delicate work, in an environment infected by the daily presence of death. (Levi 1975: 139–40)

The 'strange callousness' that Levi needs to survive as part of the '*Lager* system' also enables him to write his memoirs. For this reason, he tells the story of someone who understands, only too well, his own potential to dehumanize. In this sense, Levi is in thrall to his memory – and his need to bear witness – but, at the same time, his 'delicate work' of testimony is also a betrayal of his humanity. Such is Levi's impure scepticism, which contrasts with Améry's purifying victimhood. In fact, Levi charts the moment when he is transformed from a solitary traumatized figure writing 'bloody poems', in the guise of the Ancient Mariner, and becomes the ostensibly rational observer of his time in Auschwitz: 'My writing became a different adventure, no longer the dolorous itinerary of a conva-lescent, no longer a begging for compassion and friendly faces, but a lucid building, which now was no longer solitary: the work of a chemist who weighs and divides, measures and judges on the basis of assured proofs, and strives to answer questions' (153). Outside the irrationality of the camps ('there is no why here'), Levi was able to strive to answer questions. Améry, on the other hand, remained the 'solitary' figure in the guise of the 'dolorous' Ancient Mariner. His was the story of the exiled and trauma-tized seafarer. Never quite as measured as Levi, Améry resented the very words that he put on the page: 'What dehumanized me has become a commodity, which I offer for sale' (Améry 1966: 80). Always more equiv-ocal than his unbending interlocutor, Levi understood both the necessity and the danger of ordering and commodifying his memories so as to reach the broadest possible audience.

But this was not a straightforward matter. Levi's scepticism towards even his most dearly held beliefs eventually resulted in an abiding suspi-cion that his words on the page could no longer do justice to his memories because they stereotyped them. One should note here that the original meaning of the word 'stereotype' was associated with the printing press, and Levi sometimes seems to draw on this etymology of the word. After evoking quite magnificently the life of Sandro Delmastro, a fellow student and the first man to be killed in the Piedmontese anti-fascist resistance, Levi ends the 'Iron' chapter of *The Periodic Table* in despair:

> Today I know that it is a hopeless task to try and dress a man in words, make him live again on the printed page, especially a man like Sandro. He was not the sort of person you can tell stories about . . . he lived completely in his deeds, and when they were over nothing of him remains – nothing but words, precisely. (Levi 1975: 48–49)

This bleak sense of the limitations of language is explicitly articulated, in the spirit of a man who lived 'completely in his deeds', in Levi's essay on Améry. Referring once again to the Dante chapter in *If This Is a Man*, Levi makes an extraordinary comment: 'I really would have given bread and soup – that is blood – to save from nothingness those memories which today with the sure support of printed paper I can refresh gratis whenever I wish, and which therefore seem of little value. Then and there they had great value' (Levi 1986: 112). Once fixed on the printed page, Levi's memories are of little value as he is recounting nothing more than a commodified text. His memories, therefore, become reduced to a stereotype. Like Améry, who also valued his 'deeds' above all else, Levi was to recognize increasingly that using the language of reason to create a mass readership could mean that he was accounting for the death camps in the conventions of a culture that had also given birth to them. Such was the danger of being a normalizer, returning home in the guise of Ulysses, to recount his 'story' of the camps.

Alongside *If This Is a Man*, Levi co-wrote *The Auschwitz Report* (1946), a scientific report on his time in Auschwitz-Monowitz, as well as a series of 'bloody' and enraged poems for his friends and family. At about the same time, Améry also wrote a series of fictions, quasi-fictions and diaries, all of which recounted his experience of torture. Améry's biographer has noted the astonishing consistency in these writings, over two decades, culminating in *At the Mind's Limits*.[44] Like all of the figures writing immediately after the war and during the period of decolonization, Levi and Améry needed to find a language in which to understand what they had gone or were going through. Whereas Améry attempted to hold open as contradictions the extremities of torture and the language of the Enlightenment, Levi's writing is deceptively fluid, negotiating a range of irreconcilable narratives in his essays, memoirs, poetry and fictions. In the end, one survivor goes the way of a disciplined Manichaeism, the other the way of a messy and uncertain greyness. That is why Levi concludes *The Drowned and the Saved* with a direct challenge to Améry:

> More often and more insistently as that time recedes, we are asked by the young who our 'torturers' were, of what cloth they were made. The term torturers alludes to our ex-guardians, the SS, and is in my opinion inappropriate: it brings to mind twisted individuals, ill-born, sadists, afflicted by an original flaw. Instead they were made of the same cloth, they were average human beings . . . they were not monsters, they had our faces. (Levi 1986: 169)

This was also Hannah Arendt's conclusion in *Eichmann in Jerusalem: A Report on the Banality of Evil* (1963) which, along with Levi's memoirs, was for Améry a 'double provocation' (Heidelberger-Leonard 137). Levi both recognized his own potential to dehumanize and combated it in *The Periodic Table* with a surreal combination of chemical insight and metaphorical game-playing and by embracing his own only too human impurity. He ends the book by noting that he could 'tell innumerable other stories' but decides to 'tell just one more story, the most secret, and I will tell it with the humility and restraint of him who knows from the start that his theme is desperate, his means feeble, and the trading of clothes in words is bound by its very nature to fail' (Levi 1975: 232). Such 'humility and restraint' undoubtedly contrast with Améry's unsatiated rage and resentment, but are no less suspicious of the 'trading of clothes in words'.

In the end, Levi's ethical uncertainty allows the imagination to play with his traumatized past in a way that was not possible for Améry. This is why Levi, by the 1980s, thought of himself primarily as a writer of 'stories' rather than 'accounts' who was fortunate enough to give a few of the 'voiceless mass of the shipwrecked . . . the ambiguous perennial existence of literary characters' (Levi 1981: 10). These stories, attempting to give a voice to those who can no longer speak for themselves, were also histories (in Italian, *storia* conveys both meanings). The imaginative writers discussed in the next part of the book all attempt to reclaim a past and sense of self where diverse histories intertwine metaphorically and, as in Levi's fictions, poetry, essays and testimonies, are not eclipsed by a unique sense of victimization.

PART TWO

4

Diaspora, 'Race' and Redemption
Muriel Spark and the Trauma of Africa

'[Job] not only argues the problem of suffering, he suffers the problem of argument.' Muriel Spark, 'The Mystery of Job's Suffering' (1955), p. 7.

'It was Edinburgh that bred within me the conditions of exiledom; and what have I been doing since then but moving from exile into exile? It has ceased to be a fate, it has become a calling.' Muriel Spark, 'What Images Return' (1970), p. 151.

'We see and hear everywhere the representation of the victim against the oppressor, we have a literature and an artistic culture, one might almost say a civilization, of depicting suffering whether in social life or in family life. We have representations of the victim-oppressor complex, for instance, in the dramatic portrayal of the gross racial injustices of our world, or in the tyrannies of family life on the individual. . . . I am going to suggest that [the victim-oppressor complex] isn't achieving its end or illuminating our lives any more, and that a more effective technique can and should be cultivated.' Muriel Spark, 'The Desegregation of Art' (1971), p. 23.

Muriel Spark's 'The Desegregation of Art', a lecture delivered to the Blashfield Foundation in New York in May 1970 and published the following year, is both a literary manifesto and a refutation of past suffering. She gave the lecture when she was at the height of her powers, a decade after the international success of *The Prime of Miss Jean Brodie* (1961) and at the end of a period of extraordinary creativity that saw the publication of *The Public Image* (1968), *The Driver's Seat* (1970) and *Not to Disturb* (1971). The lecture, implicitly at least, refers to these three novellas, which were the closest that Spark came to the French *nouveau roman* and, as a result, were the least messy, the least emotionally invested, of her fictions. Spark consistently regarded *The Driver's Seat* as her best work.[1] It was not until *The Takeover* (1976) that she was once again to utilize material – either historical or personal – that could not be completely ordered and contained within a tight formal straitjacket. These novellas signalled a distinct shift from actuality to artifice, from the past to the present, and to a pitiless tone that has been rightly described by Angus Wilson, in relation to her earlier fiction, as 'machine made'.[2] Spark was quite explicit in her lecture about reinforcing a novel form where the author was at her most imperious, constructing her characters *sub specie aeternitatis*. After living in New York in the early 1960s and being rebuffed after the publication of *The Mandelbaum Gate* (1965), Spark moved to Italy in 1966.[3] She could now champion the cold eye of the permanent exile in her Blashfield lecture:

> the art and literature of sentiment and emotion, however beautiful in itself, however striking in its depiction of actuality, has to go. It cheats us into a sense of involvement with life and society, but in reality it is a segregated activity. In its place I advocate the arts of satire and ridicule. And I see no other living art form in the future.

According to Spark, the prevailing 'cult of the victim' was at the heart of the 'literature of sentiment and emotion' and resulted in a banal emotional catharsis disconnected from 'life and society' (Spark 1971b: 24). This was a combustible statement to make in the United States in the 1970s. As her biographer notes, 'the Vietnam conflict was raging, anti-war demonstrations and race riots [were] tearing American cities apart' (Stannard 2009: 370) and, as a result, there was a heightened sense at the time of who the victims of racism and colonialism were. What is more, terms like 'segregation' and 'desegregation' in the United States were far removed from Spark's championing of the 'arts of satire and ridicule'.

Not unlike Hannah Arendt's disastrous intervention in 'Little Rock', Spark's 'The Desegregation of Art' imposed her own rather idiosyncratic preoccupations onto the racial politics of the United States. To this extent she could be said to have followed Arendt – her fellow resident at the *New Yorker* and attendee at the Eichmann trial – by refusing to limit her work, in stark contrast to the growing canon of Holocaust testimony, to the sphere of suffering and victimization. In a 1970 interview, reprinted in *The Hothouse by the East River* (1973), Spark states that she does not 'believe in good and evil so much anymore' but in 'absurdity and intelligence'.[4] Perhaps for this reason Spark edits out any references in the final version of *The Hothouse by the East River* to what she calls, in an earlier version, 'the draft riots in the Civil War when black men were hung from the lamp posts' (quoted Stannard 2009: 318). These reconstructions of 'gross racial injustices' (Spark 1971b: 23) in *The Hothouse by the East River* were originally intended to follow *The Mandelbaum Gate* (1965), which included an account of the Eichmann trial. Spark's use of the *nouveau roman* was a direct response to her prolonged exploration of the past, especially her Jewishness, in this rather baggy novel. By the time of 'The Desegregation of Art', Spark was no longer interested in the life-story of the individual (herself included) or in the virtues of historical reconstruction. By the 1970s, only 'absurdity and intelligence' were 'illuminating', even in relation to the rise of Nazism:

> We have all seen on the television those documentaries of the thirties and of the Second World War, where Hitler and his goose-stepping troops advance in the course of liberating, as they called it, some

country or other; we have seen the strutting and posturing of Mussolini. It looks like something out of comic opera to us. If the massed populations of those countries had been moved to break up in helpless laughter at the sight, those tyrants wouldn't have had a chance. And I say we should all be conditioned and educated to regard violence in any form as something to be ruthlessly mocked. (24)

Spark worked as a 'black propagandist' in the last year of the Second World War, when she helped to present a subversive version of the war to the German people via a fake German radio station. Her lecture to the Blashfield Foundation seems to follow this activity by assuming that the populations of Germany and Italy could potentially have been 'moved' by the mocking intelligence of the authors of such black propaganda. But the idea of coaxing the populations of Italy and Germany into 'helpless laughter' at the sight of Hitler and Mussolini can be said, to put it mildly, to be a utopian version of this wartime activity. 'The Desegregation of Art' championed the redemptive powers of art over historical suffering, an idea that was to harden into a form of Sparkian orthodoxy. But this orthodoxy meant that the 'only problem' after the Second World War, the problem of suffering, had to be transcended.[5] In short, Spark championed satire so as to ensure that the 'ghastly objects of investigation no longer [had] the capacity to hurt' (Stannard 2009: 129), which was the implicit message of 'The Desegregation of Art'.

The redemptive power of absurdity and intelligence was also to become an originary myth in Spark's 'The First Year of My Life' (1967), which elided the date of her birth with the birth of the artist in the story. In this part autobiographical, part apocryphal story, Spark presents the First World War through the eyes of a newborn child since 'babies, in their waking hours, know everything that is going on everywhere in the world' (Spark 1994: 301). These supernatural powers of perception, a kind of innocent omniscience akin to the omniscience of the Sparkian narrator, are supposedly 'brainwashed out of us' (301) after our first year. Like Spark, who also came into a blood-ridden world in 1918, the baby 'had been born into a bad moment in the history of the world' and is rendered glum-looking as it witnesses 'infinite slaughter' (303). Only after a fatuous speech by Herbert Asquith in the House of Commons, about the 'cleansing and purging' (307) effects of the war, does the baby smile. It is typical of Spark that she compares a false form of purgation with the power of humour to redeem even the slaughter of the First World War. Here the omniscient, all-knowing baby is not unlike the impersonal artist (*pace* T.S. Eliot) who, in these terms, is also merely a conduit for a series of voices from the radically fallen world of the twentieth century.[6]

The fraught relationship between suffering and rebirth, in the form of both irredeemable trauma and redemptive comedy, is, I shall argue, in tension in the fiction and theological preoccupations of Muriel Spark. At this heightened stage in her career, Spark wished to declare the power of the artist to control and expunge suffering which she had experienced first-hand and which she characterized as her 'wasted years' in a well-known interview with Frank Kermode.[7] In that interview, Spark describes her turn to fiction from poetry, after she converted to Catholicism, as 'probably just a justification for the time I wasted doing something else'. She goes on to say that her novels are an attempt to 'redeem the time' so that her years before *The Comforters* (1957), her first novel, 'won't be wasted – it won't be wasted until I'm dead' (Kermode 1984: 132). In these redemptive terms, her first forty years became the waste material for much of her subsequent fiction. As late as *Loitering with Intent* (1981) and *A Far Cry from Kensington* (1988), Spark was to reinvent her past selves imaginatively and to reclaim her wilderness years for the artistic sphere. But, as we will see, the suffering that Spark experienced during her 'wasted years' – such as her husband's violent 'nervous disorder' in southern Africa (Spark 1992: 127) or her poverty and breakdown in London in the 1940s and '50s – was not so easily redeemed, and has a wider historical resonance, which is perhaps why she continually draws on these experiences in her fiction.

What I want to show is that Spark's fiction precisely evokes the trauma of madness and unrestrained emotion as a counternarrative that challenges the assumption that a life-story, also part of the histories of colonialism and fascism, can be converted easily into an untroubled redemptive narrative. That Spark settled on a particular voice and style to counter the 'politics of victimhood' (Stannard 2009: 65) in 'The Desegregation of Art' and her novellas of this period is therefore only one part of the story. To gain the level of detachment from both personal and historical suffering, which is most apparent in Spark's version of the *nouveau roman*, meant that she had to treat one part of herself 'as though she were dead', and it is the distance from a 'dead' version of the self that 'generated her pleasure in the world, beat back its terrors' (Stannard 2009: xxiv). But the one part of herself that could not be dispatched, or completely redeemed, was that which was so traumatized that it continually returned throughout half a century of writing fiction.

Between Spark and Africa

Muriel Camberg set sail for Cape Town in August 1937, at the age of nineteen, to marry her fiancée, Sydney Oswald Spark, who was teaching in Southern Rhodesia and whom she found 'interesting'. As she notes in her autobiography, she 'longed to leave Edinburgh and see the world' and to have an 'adventure in a strange continent' (Spark 1992: 116) as part of a long line of Scottish travellers and explorers. She left Scotland as a 'minor', needing her father's permission to marry, and returned to Britain in March 1944 as an adult, having given birth to a son, Robin, a year after her arrival in 1938 and nearly dying in the process. On discovering that her husband had a 'severe nervous disorder' (127), which could take a 'violent' form (130), she began divorce proceedings. Before leaving southern Africa in February 1944 on a troop ship, she left her son in a Dominican convent school in Gwelo (now Gweru). After returning to England, she contributed to the war effort as a 'black propagandist' for the Foreign Office. In her autobiography, Spark begins her chapter on Africa with a neat summary of her later orthodoxies:

It was in Africa that I learned to cope with life. It was there that I ↓
learned to keep in mind – in the front of my mind – the essentials of
our human destiny, our responsibilities, and to put in a peripheral
place the personal sorrows, frights and horrors that came my way. . . .
There was an element of truth and wisdom, in that existence in a great
tropical zone of the earth, that gave me strength. (Spark 1992: 119)

The stress here on the African landscape as imparting a quasi-religious
'element of truth and wisdom' to the young Spark speaks to its supposed
redemptive qualities, with 'personal sorrows, frights and horrors' pushed
to the margins and given a wider extrahuman perspective. Spark is referring to her earliest published short story, 'The Seraph and the Zambesi'
(1951), which, significantly, brings together an Old Testament Seraph
and the Zambesi river so that they are eventually indistinguishable: 'by the
mute flashes of summer lightning, we watched [the angel Seraph] ride
the Zambesi away from us, among the rocks that look like crocodiles and
the crocodiles that look like rocks' (Spark 1994: 93). As has been rightly
argued, 'the true Seraph belongs to Africa', which is why Spark finally
makes it indistinguishable from the landscape.[8] The story ends on the
transfigurative and spiritual qualities of the African landscape – later
conflated as 'the seraphic river' (Stannard 2009: 51) – which also transformed Spark's career as a writer. The story won the *Observer* Christmas
short-story prize of 1951; without this considerable fillip, she might well
have continued as a critic and poet. The success of 'The Seraph and the
Zambesi' literally changed her life. After the story was published, Spark
was immediately introduced to the editor of the *Observer* and began
writing occasionally for the newspaper. Her story also attracted the attention of the fiction editor at Macmillan, who commissioned her to write a
novel and collection of short stories, which became *The Comforters* and
The Go-Away Bird and Other Stories (1958). Such was Spark's meteoric rise
as a writer of fiction.

   That 'The Seraph and the Zambesi' should have unlocked her career as
a novelist is worth noting because, as she later stated, the African context

showed her for the 'first time [that] life and death came very close together' (Stannard 2009: 45). The traumatic 'personal sorrows, frights and horror[s]' of her time in Africa could only be lessened by embracing 'life' or a redemptive outlook. This doubleness characterizes Spark's Africa stories, collected in *The Go-Away Bird and Other Stories* and *Voices at Play: Stories and Ear-Pieces* (1961), which construct Africa as a territory of savagery and violence – preoccupied with the murder of women in Africa by white men – as well as a landscape of potential birth and rebirth.[9] Samuel Cramer, the anti-hero of 'The Seraph and the Zambesi', first appeared in 'The Ballad of the Fanfarlo', collected in Spark's *The Fanfarlo and Other Verse* (1952), and refers back to Baudelaire's story 'La Fanfarlo' (1848). Cramer is described, after Baudelaire, as 'the contradictory off-spring of a pale German father and a brown Chilean mother', words used as the epigraph to the poem. He is the first of Spark's racially indeterminate, exilic anti-heroes, but, unlike those who follow him, Cramer reappears, a century after his first incarnation, and has mysteriously hardly aged in Spark's account. In the story, Cramer has 'the look of north and south, light hair with canvas-coloured skin' – which Spark later described as 'racially different' – and he is also, more mundanely, 'half poet, half journalist' (Spark 1994: 86).[10]

Cramer as poet/journalist is the first of Spark's writer manqués with a limited imagination who attempt to shape reality according to their abiding myths. His romanticism results in an artistic ego that is unbounded and out of control (insisting on taking the part of the First Seraph in his masque); because of this egotism, he mistakes fiction for reality like many of Spark's subsequent mythomaniacs such as the quasi-fascist Jean Brodie. The point of the poem, more successful rendered in prose, is to contrast Cramer's bogus version of the Nativity masque with the real thing. In the poem, Cramer ends up in No-Man's Sanatorium, a place that conflates sickliness with the dangers of unbelonging, a conflation that was used elsewhere in Spark's fiction. When, in the story, an actual Seraph appears in his masque, Cramer, lacking a dimension outside the self, fails to recognize the angel and insists on playing the part anyway. His solipsism and empty individualism make the world unreal. Cramer's romantic no-man's-land exposes this unreality, which is why a Neoclassical view of art, taken especially from T.S. Eliot, prevails as indicated by the distinct 'outline' of the Seraph. In stark contrast to the flawed Cramer, the Seraph 'lacked the signs of confusion and ferment which are commonly the signs of living things, and this was also the principle of its beauty' (90).

After this story, the racial indeterminacy of Spark's heroines tends to give them a singular ability, as exiles, to understand the 'truth and wisdom' of the African landscape and to stand outside the race-thinking that saturates its colonial inhabitants. But this does not apply to Cramer, who, instead, anticipates the violence and unthinking racism of the men in the colonies as he shouts 'at someone, in the attitude of his dealings with the natives' (90) and also calls for a gun to shoot the Seraph. The narrator characterizes Cramer initially as a 'Belgian from the Congo' (86), and Spark, not unlike Arendt, does at times view Africa through the eyes of Conrad's *Heart of Darkness* (1899).[11] Cramer, as writer manqué, is the first of many exponents of such colonial brutalities who, not unlike the other 'European residents', is 'irresistibly prompted to speak kitchen kaffir to anything strange' (91). It is worth noting that the story was written in the year when *The Origins of Totalitarianism* (1951) was published, which is perhaps why Spark was to describe Cramer as 'representative of a mechanised, totalitarian age' (quoted Stannard 2003: 92). But while this characterization anticipates Spark's version of Eichmann, it differs from Arendt's humanism precisely because Spark rejected the individualistic limitations of a Cramer for that which goes beyond materialistic or mechanized rationality such as the six-winged Seraph.

It has been rightly argued that the story is best read as part of Spark's nascent search for a settled religious perspective, which was eventually signalled by her conversion to Roman Catholicism three years after its publication (Stannard 2003: 91–105). The story, in this regard, has a strong emphasis on birth and rebirth, with the narrator parodying the Nativity: 'it was Christmas week and there was no room in the hotel'. In this reading, the Christian subtext of the story, which takes place on Christmas Eve, is paramount, with the Seraph distinguishing between 'the Beginning [which] began first' as compared to Cramer being present at the 'start [of] my show' (Spark 1994: 86). But such births and rebirths also took a secular form, such as the birth of Spark's 'authentic voice as a writer' (Stannard 2003: 103) which the story enabled. As I will argue, Spark's eventual conversion also held in tension secular and religious versions of redemption.

Spark's later African stories, collected seven years later in *The Go-Away Bird and Other Stories*, also conflate the African landscape with spiritual experience. But, unlike the earlier story, they are written from the perspective of the victims of violence rather than the proponents such as Cramer. In fact, the murder of white women in Spark's Africa is such a commonplace that it later becomes the main theme of 'Bang-Bang You're Dead' (1961) where a friend, who resembles the narrator, is accidentally shot in her place. This fear of being shot pervades the story:

> There had been an outbreak of popular headlines about the shooting affairs in the Colony. Much had been blared forth about the effect, on the minds of young settlers, of the climate, the hard drinking, the shortage of white women. The Colony was a place where lovers shot husbands, or shot themselves, where husbands shot natives who spied through bedroom windows. (Spark 1994: 64)

Here 'the climate' of Africa, rather than leading to a quasi-religious experience, is a cause of various kinds of neuroses ('on the minds of young settlers') that can take a violent form. These 'shooting affairs' are repeated in Spark's African stories and radio dramas, such as 'The Curtain Blown in the Breeze' (1961), where a husband shoots a 'native' who 'spied through bedroom windows' and *The Dry River Bed* (1961), which concerns the slaying of two white women. Such 'shooting affairs' are also recounted in *Curriculum Vitae* in a reprise of the plot of 'Bang-Bang You're Dead':

When Nita McEwan, a friend from school, was killed that night by her husband in the hotel [in Rhodesia] where I was staying, I got seriously frightened. My husband had a small revolver, a 'baby Browning', which he liked to fire off in corridors and courtyards. I hid it and refused to hand it over when he demanded it. (Spark 1992: 130)

Here Spark identifies quite explicitly with her characters who are victims of these 'shooting affairs', although she is no less explicit in her memoir about the 'spiritual strength' that she gained from the African landscape: 'I knew my married life was over. Strangely the experience of the Victoria Falls gave me the courage to endure the difficult years to come. The falls became to me a symbol of spiritual strength' (128). As has been rightly noted, Spark's fiction and autobiography 'weave in and around each other' with regard to these 'affairs' (Byrne 116–18) and, I would add, in relation to the 'spiritual strength' of the African landscape such as her formative visit to Victoria Falls. Unusually, Spark's memoir seems to be quite happy to make 'seemingly straightforward relationships between her experiences and artistic intentions' (116) and, in so doing, it makes a crucial connection between the African landscape as a source both of redemptive spirituality, and of violence and mental breakdown. The conflation of violence and spirituality was also a key aspect of Spark's narrative of conversion, which similarly brings together the ideal of redemption with the fear of mental breakdown. An early articulation of this doubleness can be found in the poem 'On Africa' (1948), where the continent of Africa (again in the guise of the Zambesi river) is elided with a deranged form of masculinity:

He is like Africa and even
The dangerous chances of his mind
Resemble the precipice whereover
Perpetual waterfalls descend.

The double-edged quality of the African landscape (embodying both male insanity and female transcendence) can be seen in 'The Curtain Blown by the Breeze', where 'the curtain was fluttering at the open window, letting in wafts of the savage territory beyond the absurd drawing-room. The people were getting excited; I thought soon they might scream, once or twice like birds, and then be silent' (Spark 1994: 35). The 'savage territory' transforms men into beasts, not unlike Conrad's Kurtz in *Heart of Darkness*, and results equally in mindless violence and spiritual enlightenment. The commonplace lourie or 'Go-Away Bird' is, for instance, heard uniquely by Spark's heroine, Daphne, and unites her with the primitive truths of her surroundings. As Daphne comments, there is always a danger that the landscape might not be controllable: 'We are getting control over malaria. But we haven't got *the savage in ourselves* under control. This place brings out the *savage in ourselves*' (264). The fear of racial degeneration refers again to Kurtz and the need to order and contain the border between that which is considered 'savage' and that which is considered 'civilized'. The African landscape made such distinctions well-nigh impossible: 'This was a territory where you could not bathe in the gentlest stream but a germ from the water entered your kidneys and blighted your body for life; where you could not go for a walk before six in the evening without returning crazed by the sun' (23). The diseased landscape, in a kind of anti-baptism, resists the civilizing mission associated with the colonial settlement of Africa. The '*savage in ourselves*' is something that has to be overcome but is also embraced by Spark's heroines, who commune with the landscape and thereby subvert the opposition between savagery and civilization at the heart of British colonial discourse. What is more, the 'shooting affairs', which were mainly an extension of anti-black racism, undermine any pretensions to 'civilization' on the part of the white settlers. This is particularly illustrated in 'The Curtain Blown by the Breeze', which begins with the shooting of a twelve-year-old 'piccanin' who accidentally sees Sonji Van der Merwe 'suckle her child'. Jannie Van der Merwe, her husband, is jailed for the murder and Sonji, as a result, 'chang[es] her character' (23). After Jannie is jailed, she grows in confidence and independence, encouraged by her female friends, and converts to the Church of England rather than the 'Dutch Reformed persuasion of her forefathers'. In this state of liberation, Sonji (now 'Sonia') redecorates her bedroom so that it is 'black-and-white' and covers her chaise longue with 'black-and-white candy-striped satin' (28). As with so many of Spark's racially indeterminate heroines, it turns out that she has 'some coloured blood', which is reflected in her increasingly 'glamorous' (30) character. The contrast between the unremitting masculine violence of Jannie and the creative singularity of Sonji/Sonia is reinforced starkly at the end of the story when Jannie, after leaving jail on parole, shoots his wife when he sees her with another man.

Stannard, following Spark in her memoir, has described the African stories as a 'fragmented, abstracted autobiography', creating a 'landscape of neurosis' (Stannard 2009: 46). Many of the short stories of this period, beginning with 'The Girl I Left Behind Me' (1957), include characters who are so radically divided between body and soul that they are transformed into apparitions that haunt the page, a more extreme form of the *luftmensch*. The girl 'left behind' embraces her own dead body 'like a lover' (Spark 1994: 360) and, in a parody of spiritual renewal, jettisons a 'dead' self so as to breathe life into the ghostly narrator. 'The Portobello Road' (1958) similarly includes a female murder victim who returns to haunt her killer. This story, collected in *The Go-Away Bird and Other Stories*, moves between Britain and Africa, and is narrated by the ghostly victim. She argues that she travelled to Africa because of her 'inconsequential life': 'During my lifetime, I was a drifter, nothing organized' (5). Although her friends admire her as a free spirit and describe her as 'lucky', the narrator, known as 'Needle', is much less sanguine: 'There were times when, privately practising the writings of my life, I knew the bitter side of my fortune. When I failed again and again to reproduce life in some satisfactory and perfect form, I was the more imprisoned for all my carefree living for this satisfaction' (10). In the story, Needle sees a friend with a 'coloured' wife in Africa and threatens to betray him when he wants to marry again in London. That is why Needle is murdered and inevitably ends up, in a shameless quip, in a haystack. All of these early stories construct Africa as a traumatic space, especially for the young white women who visit, and this is why Needle wants to redeem the time (or 'wasted years') by reproducing her 'life in some satisfactory and perfect form'. In Spark's early sonnet 'The Victoria Falls' (1948), this perfect form is associated with the African landscape – 'Wrapped in this liquid turmoil who can say/ Which is the mighty echo, which the spray?' – which prefigures the ending of 'The Seraph and the Zambesi'. But, just as 'The Portobello Road' is predicated on the split between mind and body, there are dangers in associating Africa and Africans purely with the bodily realm. In her autobiography, Spark seems innocent of such difficulties:

> It struck me right away what good-looking people the blacks of that area were. It was rightly said that education could give whites an intellectual advantage over blacks, but what was never mentioned, never breathed, was that . . . the African natives of Southern Rhodesia were, as physical examples of the human race, vastly superior to the average white men and women around them. A great many of the Rhodesian blacks were magnificent. (Spark 1992: 125)

Spark's version of the Noble Savage is predicated on what she calls repeatedly the 'aridity of the white people there' (128), which threatened to 'enter one's soul' (127) and corrupt it. This aridity, or lack of spirituality, was associated with what she called the 'atmosphere of unreality' in apartheid South Africa: 'The [Cape Town] community was divided into three: coloured, black and white. . . . There were three entrances to the cinemas, and other public places labelled "Coloured", "Black" and "White". I thought this quite amusing when I didn't think it tragic' (139–40). Such unreality can be seen especially in 'Bang-Bang You're Dead', where Sybil's Africa is distanced both in time and in space as it is depicted in a film shown many years later in London. Sybil concludes the story by asking: 'am I a woman . . . or an intellectual monster?' (Spark 1994: 85) to indicate the limitations of an ordering authorial voice in search of the 'perfect form' characterized by the mind alone. Her singular vision, which defies 'tidy categor[ies]'

(73), means that she is all too aware of the dangers of coldly expunging an 'African' bodily realm which is the locus of an otherworldly spirituality. In Spark's African stories as a whole, the disembodied minds of her heroines (not least when they take the form of spectral or cinematic images or are characterized by their unique capacity to hear the faint sounds of the 'Go-Away Bird') contrast starkly with the 'magnificent' physicality of Africa and of Africans. But the Noble Savage, in these terms, can easily descend into a form of degenerative primitivism. One of Spark's narrators, for example, speaks of a native, echoing *Heart of Darkness*, with 'huge ape-like hands' (29). Nonetheless, the unreality of a society organized along racial lines did not leave Spark and became the means by which she began to understand her own sense of racial difference.

Between Spark and Conversion

In her autobiography, Spark tells the story of her search for a job in 1942 as a single parent with her soon-to-be-ex-husband in a 'nervous disorders hospital' (Spark 1992: 133). She makes an impression on the mother superior of an Anglican convent school in Bulawayo who, Spark is told, 'loves your complexion and your golden hair'. During the interview for the job, however, the mother superior comments: 'You see . . . the trouble with this war is the Jews. We need more people like you . . . Hitler's quite right. . . . The war is all the fault of the Jews' (134). In preparing to meet the mother superior for a fourth time, Spark informs her friend; ' "Today's the day. I'll tell her I'm a Jew". . . . This I did. I didn't say part-Jew or any other sort of Jew. I just said, "Of course, I'm a Jew." ' She concludes the story with the proud refrain; 'I took my fair skin and my golden locks right out of there' (135).

There is obviously a stark contrast between the colonial racism of the white settlers in southern Africa, written on the 'magnificent' black body, and Spark's deceptive 'Jewish' body, which was only superficially Aryan ('people like you'; 'fair skin and . . . golden locks'). That the paranoid anti-Semitism of the mother superior was merely a figment of a distorted imagination places her firmly on the side of Spark's unreal mythomaniacs. To combat her, Spark had to become a 'Jew' in recognition that the mother superior's paranoia was currently writ large on the European continent ('Hitler's quite right'). That Spark had the freedom to choose to be a 'Jew' (not 'part-Jew or any other sort of Jew') in a colonial context obviously contrasts with the fixity of the black body, whose visibility in Spark's 'shooting stories' led to lethal violence. Her sense of game-playing as a shape-shifter (looking Aryan when in fact a 'Jew') informs Spark's sense of Jewishness long after the war. Her time in Africa meant that she was both golden-haired and 'white', and, equally, in relation to European anti-Semitism which was exported to southern Africa, the dark or shadowy cause of the world's unrest.[12]

Spark's experience of colonial racism meant that she refused to play the victim as a Jew (away from a European context). This refusal to claim an unearned victimhood was a theme in her first novel. In *The Comforters* (1957), Caroline connects her own 'rapacity for suffering' (Spark 1957: 38) with her Jewish past and clearly wishes to transcend this Job-like condition so that it does not become unreal and insular. She rejects Mrs Hogg, a Catholic figure, who 'could easily become an obsession, the demon of that carnal hypocrisy which struck her mind whenever she came across a gathering of Catholics or Jews engaged in their morbid communal pleasures' (40). These hypocritical and 'morbid communal pleasures' turn out to be an exaggerated sense of suffering, which Caroline dismisses as 'an insult' when the armchair 'mock martyrs' are compared with the 'real ones' (39).

A decade after her return from Africa in 1944, Spark embraced the Roman Catholic faith. She converted from being a self-designated 'Gentile Jewess' and thereby attempted to contain and transcend an identity that was, in large part, conceived of in racial and victimized terms. That Spark chose the path of redemption rather than victimhood has led to a reductive reading of her fiction. Those critics who have noted Spark's double conversion to both Roman Catholicism and the art of the novel have argued mistakenly that these coexisting and redemptive transformations are somehow equivalent.[13] Instead of assuming that there is an organic coherence between Spark's religion and art, Gauri Viswanathan has maintained that religious conversion, far from being a unitary form of exchange, is a model of 'dissent'. In her reading, conversion is primarily a form of doubleness that 'destabilises' modern society as it 'crosses fixed boundaries between communities and identities'.[14] According to this argument, the mixing of two different cultures, not least in a colonial context, inevitably creates a sense in which any one ideology can be viewed from an estranged perspective. Far from merely superseding the past, conversion is seen primarily as an interpretative act that perceives one world through the eyes of another. Spark's fiction, for instance, reinterprets the secular novel as a parodic form of spiritual transfiguration, while her Catholicism is observed with an artist's sceptical eye. Rather than being an all-encompassing orthodoxy, conversion for Viswanathan becomes a form of heterodoxy that offers a plurality of interpretations rather than a single, dominant interpretation.

Although Viswanathan is correct to highlight the subversive potential within conversion, she overstates her case by focusing only on the question of heterodoxy, as opposed to religious orthodoxy, even in relation to a figure as contradictory as John Henry Newman.[15] Spark's poetry and fiction, crucially, illustrate both the authoritarian and the anarchic potential within the act of conversion. In fact, at the beginning of her career as a novelist, when she was most closely influenced by Newman, she was to reinforce the orthodox Catholic reading of conversion as a means of creating narrative and moral 'order' out of the waste and disorder of her early years. Here is Spark in 1961 talking about her conversion, describing Catholicism as a 'norm from which one can depart'.[16] She goes on to relate her reasons for conversion to her 'breakdown' at the time:

> The first reaction I had when I became a Catholic was that my mind was far too crowded with ideas, all teeming in disorder. This was part of my breakdown. The oddest, most peculiar variety of themes and ideas of all sorts teemed in my head. I have never known such mental

activity. It made me suffer a lot. But as I got better I was able to take them one at a time. . . . It was like getting a new gift. (Spark 1961a: 60)

In these orthodox terms, Roman Catholicism becomes an ordering principle as well as an act of faith: 'I used to worry until I got a sense of order, a sense of proportion. At least I hope I've got it now. You need it to be either a writer or a Christian' (63). Her conversion, according to religious orthodoxy, thus provided her with a renewed healthy identity and the ability to write in a controlled manner. This is why Spark's narrator in 'Portobello Road' speaks of her heroine's desire to 'reproduce life in some satisfactory and perfect form' (Spark 1994: 10). Conversion was understood by Spark both aesthetically and religiously, but it is a mistake to assume that these two realms were inevitably aligned in Spark's fiction.

Spark, for instance, was preoccupied with the relation between 'life' and 'perfect form' in the figures that she explored in her critical and biographical studies in the years leading up to her conversion to Roman Catholicism. Her study of John Masefield, published in 1953, notes 'those parts of his life story which the poet himself has written about' and which 'never fail to give the impression that life has always presented itself to him, as it were, in the narrative form' (Spark 1953b: x). In a 1961 interview, Spark says much the same thing in relation to her early work on Emily Brontë: 'For many years I was intensely occupied by Emily Brontë – almost haunted. What impressed me was the dramatic shape of her life. It's as if she had consciously laid out the plot of her life in a play called *Emily Brontë*. She might have been invented by Ibsen – a parson's daughter with a terrifying soul.'[17] In her *Emily Brontë: Her Life and Work* (1953), Spark meditates on the art of biography and asks, 'Which is the more accurate portrayal, that of the real man whom we chanced to meet, or that of our reconstruction – the legendary figure, in other words?', concluding characteristically that 'the second impression is more real. The first merely prefigured the legend.'[18] Here the mixture of the 'concrete' and the 'legendary' gives a 'true picture', and it is the transformation of a 'concrete' life into a dramatic or narrative form that was to become Spark's raison d'être. That is why Spark speaks of the imaginative possibility of Brontë self-consciously laying 'out the plot of her life' as if it were a drama by Ibsen. This mixture of the concrete and legendary, transforming a life into a narrative, takes both religious and aesthetic forms which often pull in different directions. This is evident especially with regard to Spark's Jewishness which, as we have seen, was open to imaginative play and transfiguration outside the context of European anti-Semitism.

At this stage in her career, Spark tended to construct Jews as figures of confusion and ambivalence when compared to the sanity and clarity of Christian culture. To be sure, such authoritarian thinking at first helped shape her identity as a Catholic writer, although such distinctions were quickly disrupted in her fiction. At the start of 'My Conversion', however, Spark characterizes the 'very peculiar environment' of her childhood which she states is 'difficult to locate': 'I am partly of Jewish origin, so my environment had a kind of Jewish tinge but without any formal instruc-tion' (Spark 1961a: 58). Later on, she speaks of the 'very indefinite loca-tion' (59) of her childhood as opposed to the clarity of her Catholic identity which enabled her to find 'one's own individual point of view' (61). As in T.S. Eliot's *Notes towards the Definition of Culture* (1948), which Spark had reviewed favourably, Christianity is seen as a means of imposing distinct boundaries on an excessively fluid and rootless identity. This inco-herent and unstable Jewishness, along with a sense of alienation and ill health, thus became a negative principle to set against a superior Christian aesthetics.[19]

It is in these authoritarian terms that Spark can be seen to have been especially influenced by Eliot, who particularly preoccupied her in the 1940s and '50s. This included her reading *The Dry Salvages* (1941) on the boat back to London from Africa and proposing a critical study of Eliot in the late 1940s, which was accepted by her publisher (Spark 1992: 204). Her neoclassical poetry, in particular, echoed Eliot's late poetry and often read like pastiches, which Spark eventually acknowledged when she self-consciously parodied his work in *The Symposium* (1990).[20] It was also significant that Eliot was a convert to Anglicanism, which was Spark's staging post on her way to Roman Catholicism. As her biographer notes, Eliot also played a strange role during Spark's lowest period, caused by an accidental overdose of Dexedrine which was contained in her diet pills. The overdose resulted in a paranoid episode where she suspected Eliot of sending her 'threatening messages': 'Obsessively she began to seek them out, covering sheet after sheet of paper with anagrams and cryptographic experiments' (Stannard 2009: 151). One of these messages, as recalled by Christine Brooke-Rose, was 'dirty Yid' (156).

Spark's critics have tended to underestimate the extent to which her conversion could take both an authoritarian and an anarchic form in her fiction. Her faith in a universal higher authority, in other words, is thrown into disarray by a fictional practice that is plural and partial and embraces a multiple sense of self. Here the Joycean embrace of the protean 'Jew' is worth placing next to Eliot's rejection of the same figure.[21] Joyce's Catholic authorial model, where the omniscient author is indifferent to his creation, 'paring his fingernails', which Spark is said to have adopted, is countered in *Ulysses* (1922) by the figure of Leopold Bloom. The Greek-Jewish Bloom represents ambivalence in extremis; the impossibility of imposing meaning on the world, however much his God-like author might wish to.[22] The ordering of reality in Spark's experimental fiction is similarly provisional and always open to question. That which she wishes to transfigure invariably proves to be uncontainable and returns to haunt her. Spark is never quite sure whether the quest for a redemptive ordering of reality, either aesthetically or theologically, is not itself a form of crazed unreality as it expunges an all too human 'confusion and ferment' (Spark 1994: 90) from the world.

There is always a problem for Spark in opposing human messiness ('confusion and ferment') with an otherworldly redemptive 'beauty'. In 'You Should Have Seen the Mess', written at the same time as her African stories, her deranged protagonist, in a parody of the omniscient God-like author, acts as if she can turn the messiness of life into a neatly ordered

narrative. In the orthodox language of the convert, she behaves as if
human dislocation and displacement can be easily tidied away. But, as this
story illustrates, Spark's critics have tended to underestimate the extent to
which her conversion not only unified a fragmented self, but also enabled
her to occupy more than one space in her fiction in an extension, rather
than a transcendence, of human messiness. Her faith in a universal higher
authority, in other words, is thrown into disarray by a fictional practice
that is plural and partial and embraces a multiple sense of self. This is
illustrated especially in a key story, 'Come Along, Marjorie' (1958), also
published at the same time as Spark's African stories. Set in a Catholic
retreat called Watling Abbey, all of the characters in the story are 'recovering from nerves' (Spark 1994: 163). But the narrator of the story, aptly
nicknamed Gloria Deplores-you, is alienated by the conformist demands
of her fellow neurotics:

> As we walked along with our suitcases I made note that there was little
> in common between them and me except Catholicism, and then only
> in a mystical sense, for their religious apprehensions were different
> from mine. 'Different from' is the form my neurosis takes. I do like the
> differentiation of things, but it is apt to lead to nerve-racking pursuits.
> On the other hand, life led on the different-from level is always an
> adventure. (161–62)

Her companion's neurosis, however, take the form of 'same as': 'We are all
the same, [Jennifer] would assert, infuriating me because I knew that God
had made everyone unique' (162). It was on these grounds that Spark
rejected a patriarchal conversionist orthodoxy. The impersonal and
universal higher order, which the convert is meant to assimilate into,
threatens to expunge individual difference and the ability to differentiate,
not least on the part of the writer of fiction. For this reason, the unbounded
singularity of Spark's heroines often takes a racial form, whether it be their
sense of not conforming to any national or ethnic category or their abiding
sense of 'exile' and estrangement.[23]

Daughters of Jerusalem

In 'The Gentile Jewesses' (1963), the 'nearly factual' account of her visits to her maternal grandmother in Watford (Spark 1992: 81), Spark describes her grandmother as a 'white negress' (Spark 1994: 309) who wears, symbolically, a 'white apron' over a 'black apron' (308). This black/white binary image-pattern is taken from Spark's earlier stories set in Africa, as is the undermining of 'black' and 'white' racial categories. Many of her African stories are, according to her memoir, about 'the great difficulties of mixed marriages' (Spark 1992: 135) and in this way relate to her sense of self as a 'Gentile Jewess'. 'The Black Madonna' (1961), most notably, concerns a white couple who give birth to a black baby unexpectedly. This story, although not set in Africa, is one of many examples of the return of the repressed in the early writings: a counternarrative that undermines both a redemptive account of conversion and the civilizing pretensions of colonialism. By bringing together the 'Gentile Jewess' with the 'white negress', Spark is demonstrating the extent to which these transgressive racial and gendered categories could be mapped onto each other. It is these metaphorical conjunctions that I will now explore in her work.

What is interesting about 'The Black Madonna' is the extent to which the characters are punished for refusing to take the question of racial difference seriously. Devoted Catholics Raymond and Lou Parker pray to the Black Madonna, recently installed with great pomp and circumstance at the Church of the Sacred Heart, to give them a much-desired child. Their reward is a 'darling black' baby (Spark 1994: 53), which is rejected in a self-conscious reference to Emily Brontë's *Wuthering Heights* (1847). The blackness of the baby, not unlike 'dark' Heathcliff who was similarly disowned, is said to be a result of Lou's 'obscure Liverpool antecedents' (54), echoing Heathcliff's mysterious origins.[24] Raymond and Lou have two Jamaican car workers as lodgers and their fear is that their neighbours will assume that Lou had slept with a 'nigger' (56). For much of the story, Raymond and Lou parade their 'colourful' (50) lodgers to a myriad of friends – 'accountants, teachers, packers and sorters' – in a bid to display their Christian decency or refined liberality. They are at pains throughout to correct the vulgar Tina Farrell for using racist language – 'They're no different from anyone else' (42) – although they eventually succumb to such racial disparagement themselves. In a typical Sparkian irony, only the coarse Farrell is prepared to consider keeping the baby: 'If that child was mine . . . I'ld never part with her. . . . She's the loveliest little darkie in the world' (56).

At one point in 'The Black Madonna', one of the Jamaican lodgers exclaims, 'I am black but comely, O ye daughters of Jerusalem' (47), and this playful reference to the Song of Songs is taken a stage further in 'The Gentile Jewesses'. The term 'Gentile Jewess', for instance, enables Spark to challenge, in her fiction of the 1960s, the universalizing promise of conversion which attempts to transcend the 'different-from'. She pointedly does not describe her characters as 'Christian Jews' or 'Jewish Christians', which would have reinforced a traditional Catholic view of the founders of the Church. Instead, the term 'Gentile' is deliberately ambiguous and suggests both a resonant paganism in relation to Judaism as well as a rather prim and comic Edinburgh gentility. Throughout its composition, *The Mandelbaum Gate* (1965) was called 'The Gentile Jewesses' although, in the end, only a short story emerged with this title. Like 'Bang-Bang You're Dead', 'The Gentile Jewesses' is a story about telling stories and is playfully self-conscious about its claims to authenticity. Spark is astutely aware of the extent to which identity needs to be performed and cannot be fixed by a patriarchal authority that lies outside the inner life of the individual. After recollecting her grandmother's shop in Watford, the Sparkian storyteller comments that the 'scene is as clear as memory to me' (308), which gives a flavour of the enticing ambiguities in the story. The clarity of Spark's memories is, after all, precisely what is open to question.

Told from the viewpoint of the granddaughter, the first-person narrator stresses throughout that this is just 'one telling of the story' (308) and that her memories have been changed and modified with constant retellings. What is more, the granddaughter often re-enacts, in retrospect, the stories told to her by her grandmother. After recalling a visit to a group of spiritualists, the granddaughter 'took my grandmother's hand to show me what spiritualists did' (311). Much of the story is performed in hindsight, as if Spark is deliberately going through the stages necessary to construct a singular history. Her grandmother's description of herself as a 'Gentile Jewess' is, in this way, enacted by the mother-figure and, eventually, by the Sparkian narrator herself. 'The Gentile Jewesses' thus holds in tension the fixity of mythmaking with the provisionality of storytelling.

Throughout the story, in fact, Spark's authorial voice stresses the extreme arbitrariness of her 'Gentile Jewish' identity. When told that she did not 'look like a Jew', she points to her small feet and claims that 'all Jews have little feet'. At another time, referring to her father's profession, she notes mischievously that 'all Jews were engineers'. The grandmother, on the other hand, dismissed as 'Pollacks' (313) a group of Polish-Jewish immigrants to Watford while embracing some Londoners of German descent as honorary Jews. Here the contrast is, once again, between a playful and fluid Jewish identity and the fixity of the 'black baby' in 'The Black Madonna' (53), which leads to the 'suffering' (54) of Raymond and Lou.

Rather than perceiving a sense of confusion that needed to be resolved, Spark's narrative voice locates her 'Gentile Jewish' identity as a creatively disruptive force. Much to the chagrin of her grandfather, her grandmother was an active suffragette who participated in women's marches down Watford High Street. In a development from her Africa stories, a distinctly feminine spirituality enables her heroines to challenge patriarchal authority of all kinds. Her mother's pagan ritual of bowing to the moon three times – a ritual that that the Sparkian narrator still continues 'for fun' (38) – is also related to the Judaic lunar calendar:

My mother never fails to bow three times to the new moon wherever she might be at the time of first catching sight of it. I have seen her standing on a busy pavement with numerous cold rational Presbyterian eyes upon her, turning over her money, bowing regardless and chanting, 'New moon, new moon, be good to me'. In my memory this image is fused with her lighting of the Sabbath candles on a Friday night, chanting a Hebrew prayer which I have since been told came out in a very strange sort of Hebrew. Still, it was her tribute and solemn observ-ance. She said that the Israelites of the Bible and herself were one and the same because of the Jewish part of her blood, and I did not doubt this thrilling fact. I thought of her as the second Gentile Jewess after my grandmother, and myself as the third. (314)

It is in relation to such pagan rituals that the Gentile Jewess and the 'white negress' are most closely aligned. Such paganism refers implicitly back to the primitive spirituality of the African landscape (which brings together the Hebraic Seraph with the Zambesi) and recalls key pagan figures in her longer fiction such as the 'half gipsy' Louisa Jebb in *The Comforters* (1957: 12) and January Marlow in *Robinson* (1958). Both of these characters offer an alternative vision to a patriarchal Catholic orthodoxy. January Marlow practises pagan ceremonies as the 'pagan mind runs strong in women' (Spark 1958: 8) and prefigures the part-pagan, part-Judaic rituals concerning the new moon in 'The Gentile Jewesses'. As early as *Robinson*, the Catholic Church was deemed to have become overly materialistic or masculinized and in need, above all, of feminine grace. Here it is Mariology that provides this alternative vision, although it is dismissed by more orthodox male Catholics as a form of idolatry that supposedly contains 'dangerous impurities' (79) and encourages the worship of a 'pagan goddess' (78).

But it is precisely such 'dangerous impurities', which Spark embraces in her novels, that counter a purifying conversion narrative. Towards the beginning of *The Girls of Slender Means* (1963), Spark imagines an 'organic' VE Day crowd made up of 'strange arms ... twined around strange bodies': 'Many liaisons, some permanent, were formed in the night, and numerous infants of experimental variety, delightful in hue of skin and racial structure, were born to the world ... nine months after' (Spark 1963: 17). In her African stories, these uncontrollable passions result in a violent response rather than a 'nerve-racking' 'differentiation of things', as Gloria Deplores-you puts it. The rejection of such 'dangerous impurities' by Raymond and Lou in 'The Black Madonna' exposes both their hypocrisy and the subversive power of the Madonna figure in relation to their rather prim and superficial orthodox Catholicism. In an echo of Spark's own experience of conversion, one of the Jamaican figures in the story 'took a tubercular turn which was followed by a religious one' (Spark 1994: 47). But, as we will see in relation to *The Mandelbaum Gate* (1965), the pilgrimage from sickness to spiritual transformation is not always that straightforward.

The Mandelbaum Gate, which includes a first-hand account of the Eichmann trial, is no less subversive than Spark's earlier encounters with white colonialists in Africa and religious orthodoxy in England. In this novel, it is the Nazi doctrine of expunging racial difference that is on the side of purity. Set in a divided Jerusalem, the book is unique among Spark's oeuvre in both its subject matter and its literary form. It is her only novel to contextualize broadly her Gentile-Jewish background, although this is alluded to in many of her other works. What is more, it is her longest, least serene and most ambitious novel of the 1960s and its poor reception in New York was probably a factor in her leaving the United States.[25] Spark clearly felt compelled to try to understand a key aspect of her past that had continued to haunt her a decade after her conversion to Catholicism. As she stated in an interview, the novel was designed to give her singular identity a much broader contextual reach: 'There were so many half-Jews that I knew and I thought this is a whole way of looking at life, a whole consideration worth writing about.' Perhaps for this reason, Spark's eighth novel has been described as heterodox and anarchic, with an 'untidy and crowded' cast of misfits.[26]

Unlike Spark's African stories, the dangerous autonomy of the heroine in the novel is curtailed by the weight of religious, racial and national history in Jerusalem in 1961, which includes the legacy of the British presence in Israel/Palestine.[27] On the one hand, Barbara Vaughan's Gentile Jewishness in *The Mandelbaum Gate* represents a kind of freedom, beyond a colonial Englishness, which is reflected in the unusual exuberance of

Spark's writing. But, in contrast to the cerebral detachment of her previous heroines, Barbara's identity is firmly rooted, from the beginning, in the physical realm. Within a few pages of the novel's beginning, Barbara argues that Jews 'believe with their blood. Being a Jew isn't something they consider in their minds, weigh up, and give assent to as one does in the Western Christian tradition. Being a Jew is inherent' (Spark 1965: 17). Seen through the eyes of the cheerfully anti-Semitic Freddy, Barbara's Jewish 'appearance' is characterized as 'something dark and intense beyond her actual shape and colouring' (18). A darkness that is not quite 'dark' goes back to the 'white negress' (Spark 1994: 309) and anticipates a sense of mixing the physical and spiritual (or the 'concrete' and 'legendary') that goes beyond 'actual shape and colouring'. This synthesis of inside and outside is characterized elsewhere as a form of Proustian sacrament that counters the prevailing 'dualistic attitude to matter and spirit'.[28] Barbara's 'mind is impatient to escape . . . memory [which] circulates like the blood-stream. May . . . it bring dead facts to life, may it bring health to whatever is borne' (Spark 1965: 31).

Appropriately enough, the second chapter of *The Mandelbaum Gate* is called 'Barbara Vaughan's Identity' and it is her self-confessed 'state of conflict' (23) that is writ large in the polarized history of Israel/Palestine and the bisected city of Jerusalem. The eponymous Mandelbaum Gate, which separates the Israeli and Jordanian sides of Jerusalem, makes it possible for Barbara to move within and between identities as a 'nun', 'spinster' and 'Gentile Jewess'. But as well as locating her 'mind' in the Jewish 'bloodstream' (since Jews 'believe with their blood'), Barbara also argues that 'the essential thing about herself remained unspoken, uncate-gorized, unlocated' (28). She later makes explicit her incommensurable identity: 'There's always more to it than Jew, Gentile, half-Jew, half-Gentile. There's the human soul, the individual. Not "Jew, Gentile" as one might say "autumn, winter". Something unique and unrepeatable' (37). In *The Comforters*, Jewishness is dismissed as one of Caroline Rose's 'half-worlds' (Spark 1957: 48) which need to be transfigured. Barbara Vaughan, a Gentile Jewess in the manner of Caroline Rose, moves beyond such 'half-worlds' by locating her sense of self in the world of 'Jerusalem, Old and New' (Spark 1965: 171). Unlike Caroline Rose, however, Barbara is aware that the too easy transcendence of racial difference is essentially fruitless in the Middle East as it does not take account of the irredeemable suffering of the Jews (which is in their bloodstream) as articulated in the Eichmann trial.

The presence of the Eichmann trial in *The Mandelbaum Gate* means that Barbara, unlike Caroline, is split between the redemptive promise of Christianity and the trauma of Jewish history. But as well as questioning a Christian version of redemption, there is also a critique of the Jewish version, which assumes that national redemption is an adequate response to the sufferings of the diaspora.[29] Much of the novel revolves around characters arguing about the 'rights and wrongs of [Barbara's] Jewish blood', which becomes most apparent when she is persuaded to take a 'pilgrimage' to the Eichmann trial. As her cousin Saul Ephraim argues, 'the trial is part of the [biblical] history of the Jews', and in this he follows Primo Levi's call for a 'new Bible' to take account of the stories arising from the camps.[30]

Barbara's 'pilgrimage' to the Eichmann trial is, in fact, one example of a number of set-piece pilgrimages in the novel, which range from her crossing through the 'no man's land' around the Mandelbaum Gate into Jordan dressed as a nun to her visiting the Holy Sepulchre site of Christian transfiguration. That is why she argues that 'everything's a subject for a Christian pilgrimage if you widen the scope enough' (175). What all of these pilgrimages have in common is that they take Barbara beyond the rational into another realm, which, needless to say, counters starkly the legalism of the trial and of Eichmann's banal testimony.[31] That is why Barbara visits the trial 'for no reason at all, for some reason she could not remember' (176). What is more, her response to the trial is to think of it as a 'familiar dream' or 'one of the new irrational films . . . one can neither cope with them or leave them alone' (177). All of these analogies, rather more than the economical Spark would usually make, are designed to illustrate the inability of Barbara's 'tidy mind' (175) to cope with the enormity of the trial: 'Barbara felt she was caught in a conspiracy to prevent her brain from functioning. . . . The man was plainly not testifying for himself, but for his pre-written destiny. He was not answering for himself or his own life at all, but for an imperative deity named Bureau IV-B-4, of whom he was the High Priest' (179). The well-known analogy that Barbara makes is with the *nouveau roman* or 'anti-novel', which underpins her response to the trial in its characteristic 'repetition, boredom, despair, going nowhere for nothing, all of which conditions are enclosed in a tight, unbreakable statement of the times at hand' (177). Earlier in the novel, Freddy has resisted being diagnosed by a Jewish doctor called Jarvis who Freddy immediately assumes is hiding something: 'his father must have been Jarvinsky' (122). The reason for Freddy's resistance to diagnosis, after his collapse, is his ironic fear that his symptoms are not merely physical: 'I don't believe there's such a thing as the Unconscious. . . . No one should submit their mind to another mind' (123). Perhaps this explains why Barbara responds to the Eichmann trial on the level of the unconscious – dreams, irrational films, the *nouveau roman* – all of which signify the extent to which her 'tidy mind' no longer functions. In the novel, as Freddy indicates, the unconscious is an alternative Jewish domain, which is why the judges presiding over the trial, in an anticipation of Hannah Arendt's account, all bear the 'recognizable scars of the western intellectual' (178): that is, the 'scars' of rationalism.[32] But the trial also indicates the limit of the unconscious, which is why the scenes concerning Eichmann include Spark's verbatim transcriptions, as if nothing can be added to the historical record.

In stark contrast to Barbara's 'unique and unrepeatable' sense of self, Eichmann represents the ultimate mythomaniac and false categorizer who drains people of their uniqueness. Barbara's response to the trial is to see Eichmann as essentially a false convert whose perverse beliefs are held with utter conviction. When pressed earlier to identify herself as a Jew by her Israeli tour guide, Barbara is determined to maintain a sense of a mysterious and uncategorizable identity. She states: 'I am who I am' (28), which ironically echoes God's answer to Moses from the burning bush on

Mount Horeb. And yet she soon becomes anxious at such 'mysterious truths', which 'were all right for deathbed definitions, when one's mental obligations were at an end' (29). Barbara's welcome scepticism can be contrasted with Father Jerome, the Catholic priest who, with God-like authority, tells Caroline in *The Comforters* that 'she was as she was' (Spark 1957: 62). Unlike Caroline, who welcomes the mystification of her iden-tity, Barbara is well aware that the effortless transformation of such ethnic, cultural and religious particularities, especially in the combustible context of the Middle East, is a too easy form of 'escape' (Spark 1965: 31). She questions an unthinking transcendence, as well as the Israeli tour guide's demand for definition which, she believes, resembles the false 'territorial consciousness' of other historically powerless peoples such as the Scots, Irish and Welsh (29).

By refusing either to territorialize her racial difference or to transcend it, Barbara Vaughan stands outside both Jewish nationalism and an orthodox Christian conversionism. Most importantly, her Gentile Jewishness becomes a model for other anarchic, unplaceable individuals throughout the novel. Barbara is attracted to her lover, Harry Clegg, for instance, because he eludes the unspoken assumption that pigeonholes him as an 'Englishman of lower-class origin' or 'red-brick genius'. The eroticizing of her Jewishness, not unlike the 'glamorous' 'coloured blood' of Sonia, similarly gives it a bodily dimension and complicates her role as an 'English spinster' (41). The novel is, in fact, stuffed full of people, such as Abdul and Suzi Ramdez, who cannot be addressed in a conventional mode and, not unlike the Gentile Jewess, are linked to a group of 'secret mixed-blood conclaves at Acre' (89). In the end, these identityless indi-viduals all seem to break down commonplace assumptions about nation, race, gender and class, and can be said to form an alternative community of exiles. Spark is quite explicit about this in her account of the blue-eyed, dark-skinned Palestinian brother and sister Abdul and Suzi Ramdez, who 'belonged to nothing but themselves' and yet, paradoxically, were part of a group made up of 'lapsed Jews, lapsed Arabs, lapsed citizens, runaway Englishmen, dancing prostitutes, international messes, failed painters, intellectuals, homosexuals. Some were silent, some voluble. Some were mentally ill, or would become so' (101). The warning at the end of this quotation that '[s]ome were mentally ill, or would become so' reminds the reader of the price that might be paid for such severe dislocation. At the same time, immediately after this paragraph, the narrative voice inter- venes to repeat unequivocally that 'others were not [mad], and never would become so; and would have been the flower of the Middle East, given the sun and air of the mind not yet available' (101). As the elusive 'air of the mind' indicates, not least in its vagueness, there is a thin line between madness and revolutionary change, derangement and enlighten- ment (and here we are reminded of the 'dangerous chances of his mind' in 'On Africa'). Earlier in the chapter, we are told that Abdul Ramdez catego- rized those in power as 'the System', which included 'fathers, the Pope, President Nasser, King Hussein, Mr Ben-Gurion, the Grand Mufti, the Patriarch of Jerusalem, the English Sovereign, the civil servants and upper militia throughout the world' (81). Later on, Eichmann's defence is said by Barbara to be predicated on the 'honour of the Supreme Being, the system, and its least tributary, Bureau IV-B-4' (179). The opposition to 'the System' – essentially patriarchal power, nationalist militarism and categorical thinking, which leads to dehumanization – is both a form of lunacy (in all of its meanings) and a revolutionary new way of imagining the Middle East. Spark, throughout *The Mandelbaum Gate*, is at pains to oppose orthodoxies of all kinds in these prophetic, anti-patriarchal terms.

Madness as a form of creative disordering refers back to the story 'The Gentile Jewesses', which opens with the grandmother frightening away a 'madman' from the local asylum who has threatened to murder her in her shop. The story of this lunatic in turn unlocks other, equally disruptive forms of anarchy and refers implicitly to her mother's devotion to the lunar calendar in 'The Gentile Jewesses', which foregrounds an alternative feminine spirituality. Uncontrolled passions in the African stories are equally murderous and cathartic. Barbara, importantly, 'caught some of Freddy's madness' when she eventually felt herself to be 'all of a piece; Gentile and Jewess, Vaughan and Aaronson . . . a private-judging Catholic, a shy adventuress' (164). All of the multiple identities in *The Mandelbaum Gate*, not unlike Barbara's, are caught between a liberating lunacy and a form of potentially disabling insanity. This is perhaps why there is a constant refrain in the novel, not least from Barbara, taken from the Book of Revelation: 'Being what thou art, lukewarm, neither cold nor hot, thou will make me vomit thee out of my mouth' (21, 127 and 185). Such uncategorizable or mixed identities are absolutely not conceived of as 'lukewarm', which is why Barbara's 'tidy' perspective is always open to a different 'air of mind'.

The Only Problem

Towards the end of *The Only Problem* (1984) Spark's Job-like protagonist, Harvey Gotham, is corresponding with his lifelong friend Edward Jansen about their mutual obsession, the nature of suffering. Harvey cites the advice from Prometheus: 'It's easy for the one who keeps his foot on the outside of suffering to counsel and preach to the one who's inside' (Spark 1984: 179). Harvey and Edward have long since discussed the Book of Job and are bound together by their 'deep old love of marvellous Job', whose story, they agree, is the 'pivotal book of the Bible'. After all, the Book of Job is about the 'only problem. The problem of suffering is the only problem. It all boils down to that' (29). Not unlike Spark, who wrote 'The Mystery of Job's Suffering' (1955) nearly three decades before the novel, Harvey has been thinking about the Book of Job since his student days and is writing a monograph on the subject nearly two decades later. *The Only Problem* turned out to be Spark's solitary full-length treatment of the 'problem of suffering' in lieu of her earlier promised study of the Book of Job (203).

At the beginning of her career as a novelist, Spark equated the difference between those who were 'inside' or 'outside' the experience of suffering with the difference between Job and his comforters. Caroline Rose in *The Comforters* had a 'rapacity for suffering' which she wished to distinguish clearly both from her family on her 'Jewish side' (Spark 1957:

38) and Georgina Hogg's 'fanatical moral intrusiveness' (147), which was associated with Hogg's Catholic orthodoxy. When Georgina Hogg recounts that she has known 'what persecution was', taking the role of a comforter or Bellovian reality instructor, Caroline immediately recalls 'her family on the Jewish side with their friends, so long ago left behind her': 'She saw them again, nursing themselves in a half-circle as they indulged in their debauch of unreal suffering; "Prejudice!" ". . . an outright insult!" Caroline thought, Catholics and Jews; the Chosen, infatuated with a tragic sense of themselves. They are tragic only because they are so comical. But the thought of those fireside martyrs, Jews and Catholics, revolted Caroline with their funniness' (38). The argument in 'The Desegregation of Art' – that the best response to the 'cult of the victim' is the 'arts of satire and ridicule' (Spark 1971b: 23–24) – is prefigured by Caroline Rose who distances her own 'suffering' when compared with the comic Catholic and Jewish 'fireside martyrs'. The only way to deal with the 'rapacity of suffering' is to get outside it rather than dwell constantly on a self-proclaimed victimhood. It is this characteristically Sparkian move that is her version of 'the only problem'.

The Only Problem is ostensibly about the question of theodicy or whether one can have faith in a divine providence that is the 'actual author' (Spark 1984: 19) of suffering in the world. It is this problem that obsesses Spark's protagonist, Harvey Gotham, a Canadian millionaire in his mid-thirties who uncannily relives the Book of Job. Not unlike Caroline Rose or Barbara Vaughan, Harvey is equally inside and outside the problem of suffering as a characteristic Sparkian persona who is both 'detached and involved at the same time' (28) and who dismisses his comforters as those who 'conspire . . . to estrange [him] from suffering' (64). He begins a study of the Book of Job after abandoning his wife, Effie, in Italy; Effie soon becomes linked with the terrorist activities of the Red Brigade. Wealthy and male, Harvey's surname associates him with the traditional foolish town of Gotham, and there are elements of his study, such as his research into the eyelids of crocodiles, that are absurdly literal. At the same time, many of his conclusions regarding the

Book of Job – that it is 'shockingly amoral' (67) and an unknowable 'poem' (132) – echo Spark's own essay, even, at one point, word for word: '[Job] not only argued the problem of suffering, he suffered the problem of argument' (30).

That Spark's version of Job endures the 'incurable' 'problem of argument' (30) indicates the extent to which she characterizes Job's (and Harvey's) suffering as a form of mental turmoil: 'How can you deal with the problem of suffering if everybody conspires to estrange you from suffering?' (64). The version of Job in the novel is, in fact, not unlike Spark's own history of nervous disorders in the 1940s and early '50s (which is also reflected in the babel of 'voices' that Caroline hears in *The Comforters*). Harvey believes, at various times, that Job was 'having a nervous crisis' (52) and was 'like a patient on the couch' (53), or that he 'had a sort of nervous breakdown' (68) that 'reduced' him to a 'mental and physical wreck' (78). When thinking of Job's three comforters, he imagines them taking 'turns as analyst' (53), which may be an implicit reference to Spark's own curative Jungian therapy in the 1950s. To this extent, Harvey's self-conscious parallels with the figure of Job – his temporary penury, the manifold sufferings caused by Effie's purported terrorist activities, his interfering 'comforters' (48) – eschew the bodily suffering of the biblical Job, who was, of course, afflicted with 'boils' (77).

From the beginning of her interest in it, Spark never wanted to turn the Book of Job into a specifically Christian allegory, which Carl Gustav Jung's *Answer to Job* (1952), in particular, was at pains to argue. Her essay on 'The Mystery of Job's Suffering' is, for the most part, an extended review of *Answer to Job*, Jung's implicit answer to the charge of anti-Semitism and Nazi collaboration levelled against him.[33] In her essay, Spark rejects as being 'far too anthropomorphic to be satisfying' Jung's belief that God's 'collision with Job' (Spark 1955: 7) is fulfilled in the Incarnation. This argument is repeated in *The Only Problem* when Harvey's 'puritanical' (Spark 1984: 179) Aunt Pet contends that there is a 'Christian message in the *Book of Job*'. Harvey objects to this statement with the following telling retort: 'but Job didn't know that' (136). In other words, Harvey, like Spark

before him, does not want to impose a redemptive narrative on the form-
less and unstructured Book of Job, which has, in turn, been rightly
described as a 'demonic parody' of Genesis. Harold Fisch is close to the
spirit of Spark's novel when he maintains that the Book of Job is haunted
by 'the image of a monstrous world . . . a world of eerie shapes and nightmares, of unimaginable gulfs, and of great creatures of the deep [that]
refuse to submit themselves to man'.[34] In these terms, the Book of Job is
resistant to exegesis of all kinds – 'beyond the reach of discourse' (Spark
1955: 7), as Spark puts it in her essay – with Job's comforters mistakenly
trying to make sense of the universe by anthropomorphizing it.

But there is an unresolved tension in the refusal to locate the causes of
suffering in the human realm given the overwhelming proximity of a
tormented world. Spark's particular investment in the nightmarish Book
of Job in the early 1950s, at the time of her conversion, is in response to
what Harvey calls the 'unspeakable sufferings of the world' (Spark 1984:
19). The stark disjunction between Spark's embrace of the Catholic faith,
shortly after the bloodshed and misery caused by the Second World War,
is a fraught aspect of a number of her earlier novels. *The Mandelbaum
Gate* evokes the unimaginable dimensions of the Holocaust, indicating the
severe limitations on the spiritual transfiguration of human suffering by
placing the actions of Eichmann in an untransformable realm as it
'revealed an empty hole in the earth, that led to a bottomless pit' (Spark
1965: 283). Part of Harvey's foolishness is to express a theory that can,
somehow, embrace misery on this vast historical scale and that, in the end,
is absurdly deterministic: 'the individual soul has made a pact with God
before he is born, that he will suffer during his lifetime. . . . Sufferers
would, in this hypothesis, be pre-conscious volunteers. The same might
apply to tribes or nations, especially in the past' (Spark 1984: 27). The shift
from the 'individual' to the 'tribe or nation' is particularly troubling for
Harvey as it confuses personal anguish with a much broader collective
history and is close to blaming the victims on a massive scale.

While Harvey recognizes that his 'distress' (180) does not make him a
'prophet' (124), he does play with the idea that he is able to take account

not only of his own suffering but of that of the world as a whole. In a key
scene in the book, he notices a 'lean-faced man with a dark skin' (152) who
appears to be a refugee from the Balkans. This figure enables him to get
outside his own dangerously self-centred sense of discomfort:

> It was not for the first time Harvey had noticed that poor people
> from Eastern Europe resembled . . . the poor of Western Europe years
> ago. . . . Patience, pallor and deep anxiety: there goes suffering, Harvey
> reflected. And I found him interesting. Is it only by recognising
> how flat would be the world without the sufferings of others that we
> know how desperately becalmed our own lives would be without
> suffering? . . . But *Job*, my work on *Job*, all interrupted and neglected,
> probed into and interfered with: that is experience, too. . . . To study, to
> think, is to live and suffer painfully. (153)

Significantly, Harvey attempts to conflate his own experiences with a
more widespread suffering and it is this conflation that troubles both
him and his author. He curiously leaves open the ways in which a writer's
life – rather 'flat' or 'desperately becalmed' without a certain amount of
distress – can be equated with the calamities of the world as a whole. One
should not underestimate, with regard to his solipsism, the connection
made between the poor of Eastern and Western Europe. The journey from
east to west, after all, recalls both the prewar migrations of European
Jewry – including Spark's paternal grandparents – as well as the struggle
of postwar Soviet Jewry to emigrate out of Stalinist Russia (which Spark
was actively interested in, to the extent that she attended a conference on
the topic).[35] Even the description of the refugee as having a 'dark skin'
relates to the Italian-Jewish Leo in *Territorial Rights* with his 'Afro-frizzed
hair' (Spark 1979: 92) as well as to Spark's 'white negress' (Spark 1994: 309)
and Barbara's unsettling 'darkness'. The historical resonances evoked by
the East European figure refer back to the 'Gentile Jewess' which, in turn,
speaks to the relationship between inner and outer, suffering then and
suffering now.

Some of Spark's readers, such as Gabriel Josipovici, have concurred fully with Harvey's belief that the torment of the writer is a form of combined suffering and joy that 'entails the daily struggle to shed cliché and habit'.[36] But there is a danger here of solipsism; stressing the inner life of the artist rather than the 'unspeakable sufferings of the world'. In Harvey's case, the world's media distort his theories concerning the Book of Job and his scholarly seclusion in the South of France is turned into a paranoid fantasy by his police interrogators. But his presumed empathy with historical misery, in the guise of his inner struggles, is in danger of becoming something of a romantic fallacy. Spark exposes this danger most forcefully with reference to the ghostly presence of his wife, Effie, who, although estranged from him, is in Harvey's thoughts almost as much as the figure of Job. Effie is an extreme example of a mythomaniac who wishes to turn her particular obsessions into an account of the world as a whole. Her insistence on linking petty theft to the search for global justice – 'the sufferings of the hungry' (Spark 1984: 26) – is symptomatic of this inflated desire which Harvey, at first, rejects completely (not least as Effie is eating when pleading on behalf of 'the hungry'). To this extent, she mitigates his facile shift from the self to the world and helps him to understand that he is not promoting an all-encompassing 'new religion' (136).

As both Josipovici and Frank Kermode have shown at some length, what is notable about Harvey's version of the Book of Job is the role played, compared to the original, by Job's wife, who is closely identified with Effie.[37] The reason why Harvey moves to the village of St Dié is that it is near to Epinal, which he visits frequently to see Georges de La Tour's 'sublime painting, *Job Visited by his Wife*' (75). His view of Effie's supposed terrorist activities is refracted through this painting to the extent that, after her death, he believes that she looks exactly like La Tour's wife of Job. Her death is objectified through this picture and helps Harvey to end his rather neurotic obsession with 'the only problem'. After all, Harvey's love for Effie has a supposed 'objective quality' (18), which enables him to move, not unlike the Sparkian novelist, from grand theories of the universe to a more profound exploration of the ambiguities of a single individual. The novel ends with the adoption of Effie's infant, and a new baby born to her sister Ruth, with Harvey, echoing the epilogue to the Book of Job, aiming to 'live another hundred and forty years [with his] three daughters, Clara, Jemima and Eye-Paint' (189). The ghostly Effie, a distinctly paradoxical version of feminine grace, enables Harvey to be once again on the side of life.

What is significant about the spiritual and aesthetic reclamation of Effie is that it does not result in a straightforward 'happy ending'. In fact, Harvey describes Job's epilogue as a 'tragedy' (186) as it finally removes suffering from the biblical story. Indeed, the possibility that Effie is living in a Californian commune, having avoided being killed in Paris, effectively illustrates the flattening consequences of a story without pain. In *Memento Mori* (1959), Henry Mortimer also recognized: 'Without an ever-present sense of death life is insipid. You might as well live on the whites of eggs' (Spark 1959: 150). But there is a difference, illustrated in *The Only Problem*, between the struggle with death and suffering in literature rather than in life. In these terms, Effie's mysterious state of grace cannot be said to bring Harvey any closer to the sufferings of the world at large. The figure of the immigrant 'with a dark skin' is in tension with this narrative of renewal, which is why the 'Gentile Jewess', akin to the 'white negress', is neither a figure who is facilely redeemed nor a figure who embraces a sense of victimhood, however great the sufferings of the Jewish or African peoples.

Epilogue: Out of Africa

At one point in *The Only Problem*, Harvey's anxiety at the police surveillance of his family and friends is exacerbated by a thought: 'Oh, God, will they shoot Ruth in mistake for Effie' (Spark 1984: 84). Ruth is very like her sister in appearance and Effie is, of course, a suspected terrorist. To make a police shooting less likely, Harvey hangs babyclothes on the line in his garden; this also ensures that he remains undisturbed by prospective suitors. But the fear that Ruth, whom he will eventually marry, will be shot by mistake takes the reader back to the 'shooting affairs' that are at the heart of Spark's African stories and her experience of southern Africa as recalled in *Curriculum Vitae*. In fact, 'Bang-Bang You're Dead' is precisely about two comparable women being in the firing line, with Sybil, an alter ego, narrowly avoiding being shot in the place of her friend. The murder at the end of the story recalls Sybil's parodic childhood game with the same friend where she is constantly shot only to 'resurrect herself' (Spark 1994: 63). This distinctive mixture of actual violence and anarchic playfulness (even towards her most sacredly held beliefs) characterizes Spark's fiction for over half a century.

While her time in Africa had a profound impact on Spark, it remains strangely absent, or displaced as in *The Only Problem*, up until the publication of *Aiding and Abetting* (2000). Spark's twenty-first novel returns the reader to the central preoccupations of her earlier work, especially the murderous husbands of her African stories (who now have something in common with Eichmann), the redemptive primitivism of the African landscape and the playful scepticism of her Gentile-Jewish heroines. The book begins sensationally with Lord Lucan, wanted for bludgeoning his children's nanny to death in 1974, visiting a psychiatrist, Dr Hildegard Wolf, in her Parisian offices. While this is startling in itself – the actual Lord Lucan has famously never been captured and is thought to have died in Africa some years ago – it is compounded by the bizarre fact that Hildegard Wolf already has a 'Lord Lucan' as a patient. What is more, it turns out that Hildegard has a wholly other history. She is an exemplary cosmopolitan heroine – she originally came from 'Bavaria, then Prague, Dresden, Avila, Marseilles, then London, and [is] now settled in Paris' (Spark 2000: 1) – and is not unlike Spark's earlier radically divided Gentile Jewesses.

Born Beate Pappenheim on a pig farm near Nuremberg, she managed to escape extreme poverty by becoming a 'fake stigmatic' who tricked thousands of impoverished Catholics into sending her 'many millions of marks' (16). After changing her identity, she became Dr Hildegard Wolf, a celebrated psychiatrist practising in the centre of Paris. It is no coincidence that her name is literally a beatification of Bertha Pappenheim, Freud's

'Anna O', one of his most famous patients. As is well known, Bertha Pappenheim appears in Joseph Breuer and Sigmund Freud's *Studies in Hysteria* (1895), and subsequently became the first social worker in Frankfurt-am-Main and the founder of the German-Jewish feminist movement. As Beate was born on a pig farm near Nuremberg, she could hardly be further removed from the biography of Bertha Pappenheim. But, at the same time, Beate and Bertha are brought together in relation to the scientific pretensions of psychoanalysis, which, not unlike the Catholic conversion narrative, is supposedly meant to be able to cure the diseased and unstable (or 'hysterical') Jewish mind.

Like Hildegard's dual self, the two Lord Lucans indicate the extent to which everything in *Aiding and Abetting* is doubled and redoubled. At first glance, there is something strangely plausible in the reptilian Lord Lucan seeking out Hildegard, even though he knows her to be a bogus (albeit highly successful) psychiatrist. Although Spark is at pains to differentiate her two main characters, it turns out that they are mirror images of each other. Both are fugitives from the law, who have been on the run for most of their lives, and both have been forced to assume alternative identities (Spark's Lucan undergoes plastic surgery). Beate Pappenheim's blood ritual, in particular, is dramatically related to Lucan's murder victim, Sandra Rivett, whose blood 'got everywhere. Pools of it' (36). Beate, the holy stigmatic, and another character based on an actual person, imitated one of the Five Wounds of Christ by covering herself in menstrual blood so that it would seep through her bandaged hands, feet or sides. These spurious 'wounds' were a sign of her 'healing powers' (23), which, in a typical Sparkian paradox, actually helped her perform minor 'miracles' (24). This interest in 'voodoo' and in 'blood cults' relates her to 'witch men' in central Africa whose similar use of 'fraudulent mystifications' (142) could also have a curative effect.

After the murder, Lucan was 'so covered in blood' (47) that bloodstains appeared on his clothes and letters sent to friends. By the end of *Aiding and Abetting*, in fact, Lucan makes the blood connection between himself and Hildegard explicit – 'we're both in this blood-business together, he seemed to say' (123) – although it is precisely these superficial similarities that are countered throughout the book. Spark's fiction invariably teases out the differences between ostensibly similar figures. Hildegard, as Beate becomes, and Lucan are both self-mythologizers, with links to Africa, and both are in the 'blood-business'. But they are also profoundly differentiated. The therapeutic 'Wolf method' allows Hildegard's voice to overwhelm her patients, with God-like narrative authority, for the first three sessions. Lucan, in stark contrast, is shown to be a bad writer in both aesthetic and moral terms since he believes that it is his 'destiny' to kill his wife. As a result of this mistaken belief, he constructs a storyline to make her murder look like the result of a robbery: '[Lucan] had thought his plan to kill his wife was watertight. Whereas, even if the nanny had taken her night off, even if he had murdered the countess, the plot leaked at every seam as truly as did the blood-oozing mailbag into which the body of Sandra Rivett was packed' (120). The sensational conflation of metaphor and reality at the end of this statement – which brings together the leaky plot of an ill-thought-out novel and a 'blood-oozing mailbag' – shows just how dangerous Spark's narrator regards Lucan as being. In her short story 'The Fortune-Teller' (1985), Spark distinguishes crucially between having a 'destiny' and a 'destination' (Spark 1994: 335). Once a life-story is thought of as a foregone conclusion, determined by a single destiny, then other possible destinations are of necessity excluded and diminished. It is Lucan's sense of 'destiny' that makes him the last of Spark's evil writers manqués who attempt to shape the world according to their own insane obsessions: 'Lucan believed in destiny. By virtue of destiny he was an earl. His wife had been destined to die, according to his mad calculation . . . he "needed" his wife dead, and it was his destiny'. His lack of 'imagination' (Spark 2000: 131), which prevents him from imagining other possible destinations, also relates him to both Spark's and Arendt's version of Eichmann.[38] While Hildegard, a version of the 'Gentile Jewess', is open to a myriad of different voices and destinations, Lucan only has a single sense of destiny, which is reduced ultimately to a bad fiction in which certain people 'need' to die.

What stops *Aiding and Abetting* from becoming overly moralistic or didactic is the exuberance of its storyline which means that the 'facts of blood' are not reduced to mere biology or racial determinism but are given a gloriously expansive set of meanings. As Hildegard's lover says of her past spoof activities: 'I don't blame her for doing something constructive with her own blood. What else should a woman of imagination do with her menstrual blood?' (158). While Hildegard's imagination is able to transform her personal circumstances, as well as the most mundane biological functions, Lucan, utterly devoid of imagination, fails to abolish the 'blood' and 'mess' that he had unleashed in 1974.

Lucan and Hildegard are brought together, however, in terms of their shared fear of the past, with Hildegard noting from the beginning: 'I am being threatened . . . about some past life of mine, something in another world. It's upsetting me. Not rationally, of course. But I don't know quite what to do' (18). Both are troubled by 'memories of the past' (51) and both have a 'blood secret' (41) which they attempt to expunge. Once again, Spark is preoccupied with those irredeemable traumatic aspects of her characters' past lives that haunt the present. At the same time, the novel's stress on the continual remaking of identity is clearly an implicit riposte to those who believe that they are merely determined by the past and cannot reinvent the self.[39] After they erase their personal histories, Spark seems to be arguing that the new-found identities of Hildegard and Lucan have a performative quality that is able to transcend the most rigid forms of determinism. To be sure, Hildegard is at pains to distinguish in moral terms between the real and false Lucans who consult her – after all, one is a murderer – but she can still argue of the Lucan impostor: 'after twenty-five years of playing the part of the missing Lord Lucan he surely is the part' (48). In a bid to avoid penury, thanks to the intervention of Karl Kanzia Jacobs, both Lucan and his double migrate to Kanzia to tutor the children of Chief Kanzia. The Chief argues that his many children will benefit from consuming one of the Lucans – since 'we become in some measure what we eat' (180) – and, while preferring the innocent double, they mistakenly devour the real Lord Lucan. This glorious parody of the transubstantiation results in Chief Kanzia's children being turned in part into 'little Lord Lucans' (181). Rather than a single act of sacramental redemption, Spark ends with an extraordinarily charged moment of comic playfulness and plurality.

The 'facts of blood' are finally thrown into disarray in the last chapter of *Aiding and Abetting*, with the tribe of Chief Kanzia, in a delightful instance of colonial mimicry, transformed bodily into members of the English aristocracy. Lucan's implacable sense of destiny is replaced by any number of possible racial destinations. But this is Spark's fiction at its most pleasurable, where the reader has to work out the ambiguities of such risk-taking on the part of the author. On the one hand, the myriad of African Lord Lucans is a typical instance of Sparkian poetic justice (Lucan finally gets his comeuppance). Such game-playing also recalls the parodies of fundamental Catholic tenets that had been an aspect of Spark's writing since 'Bang-Bang You're Dead' with its pastiche of the Resurrection. But the association of cannibalism with either Catholic ritual or African tribalism is, to say the least, combustible. *Aiding and Abetting* is thus both dangerously anarchic as well as straightforwardly moralistic – in distinguishing, say, between the blood of Christ (the blood of the Lamb) and Lord Lucan's daily diet of lamb chops.

Looked at from an African perspective – reminiscent of Evelyn Waugh's *Black Mischief* (1932) – the return to Catholic first principles assumes a completely different tenor.[40] On the one hand, the story of Lord Lucan is a refiguring of the 'shooting affairs' in Spark's early African stories. But it is characteristic of Spark that she is able to redeem the site of this abiding trauma by transforming it into the most subversive and playful element of her novel. By returning to the continent of Africa, Spark is able to deny the 'facts of blood' even when, as Barbara states in *The Mandelbaum Gate*, Jews 'believe with their blood' (Spark 1965: 17). Unlike her earlier fiction, where the desire to transcend racial difference is doomed to failure, Spark is finally able to make a systematic murderer, devoid of imagination, part of the landscape of Africa. *Aiding and Abetting* could not have taken Spark further from an identity based on victimhood. The preoccupation with

'Gentile Jewishness', as late as her twenty-first novel, illustrates perfectly the limitations of a redemptive conversionist narrative which, far from simply transfiguring her sense of difference, places her many contradictions in a sustained and creative dialogue.

But Spark does raise the question of the limits of metaphorical thinking in her fiction in so far as she loses control of her many imagined destinations. Hildegard is on the side of invention and performance when she says the Lucan impostor 'surely is the part' after 'twenty-five years of playing the part of the missing Lord Lucan' (48). But the abiding emphasis on the 'facts of blood', however subverted, disciplines such self-inventions and locates morality beyond the novel form. In a parallel literary career, Philip Roth has veered wildly in his fiction between literary game-playing and the 'facts' of history and identity. Never completely comfortable with metaphorical thinking (seeing 'similarities in dissimilars'), Roth, I will now argue, explores the boundaries of both nation and self, particularly in his late fiction.

5

The American Diaspora
Philip Roth and the National Turn

'Not to erase the contradiction, not to deny the contradiction, but to see where, within the contradiction, lies the tormented human being. To allow for the chaos, to let it in. You *must* let it in. Otherwise you produce propaganda . . . stupid propaganda for life itself – for life as it prefers to be publicized.' Philip Roth, *I Married a Communist*, p. 223.

'I wonder if you agree with this: if in writing about the bravery of the Jews who fought back, you felt yourself doing something that you *ought* to do, responsible to moral and political claims that don't necessarily intervene elsewhere [in your books], even when the subject is your own markedly Jewish fate.' Philip Roth to Primo Levi, *Shop Talk*, p. 15.

Philip Roth has recently returned to Newark as a conquering hero to celebrate his eightieth birthday after 'retiring' from writing fiction after the publication of *Nemesis* (2010).[1] That President Obama, as we saw in Chapter 1, singled out Roth, once the most transgressive and unconventional of novelists (whose fiction disdains 'moral and political claims' above all else), was part of a much wider canonization in the United States.

In 2001, *Time* magazine named Roth 'America's Best Novelist' and, in 2005, the *New York Times* asked hundreds of 'prominent writers, critics, editors and other literary sages' to identify the 'single best work of American fiction published in the past 25 years'. Roth, easily the most represented author, had six books in a list of twenty-five novels.[2] It may not be a coincidence that, a decade earlier, Harold Bloom's *The Western Canon* (1994) included nine Roth novels, more than any other living American author. In 2011, President Obama gave Roth a National Humanities Medal in a ceremony at the White House, which followed the National Book Foundation Medal for distinguished Contribution to American Letters in 2002. With Roth being only the third living author to have his work reprinted by the revered Washington-based Library of America (after Saul Bellow and Eudora Welty), President Obama was clearly on safe ground in highlighting him as a formative influence.

In outgrowing his role as the enfant terrible of postwar American letters, Roth has become, in his ninth decade, its éminence grise. *Our Gang* ('Starring Tricky and his Friends'), his 1971 satire on Richard Nixon, has as an epigraph a quotation from George Orwell: 'Political language . . . is designed to make lies sound truthful and murder respectable, and to give an appearance of solidity to pure wind' (Roth 1971: n.p.). By the time of his 'American Trilogy', presidents of the United States and their politics, rather than being castigated and demythologized, have become figures of epic comparison for Roth's tragic protagonists. In *The Human Stain* (2000), Coleman Silk is a 'great man brought low and suffering . . . like . . . Nixon at San Clemente' (Roth 2000: 18) and there are constant parallels in the novel with the attempt to impeach Bill Clinton. Seymour Levov in *American Pastoral* (1997) is known as 'our [Jewish] Kennedy' (Roth 1997: 83) and Ira Ringold in *I Married a Communist* (1998) is renowned for his close physical similarity to Abraham Lincoln, not unlike Barack Obama.[3] What is more, *The Plot against America* (2004) is explicitly concerned with the rise of a quasi-fascist US president. This focus on monumental history in the United States, as personified by its presidents, contrasts starkly with Roth as a diasporist writer, deeply influenced by European modernism, who is interested, above all, in the powerlessness and marginality of his protagonists in relation to the grand narratives of European history. This chapter will trace the 'national turn' in Roth's late work (from *Sabbath's Theater* onwards), whose universalizing focus on a postwar history of war and suffering in the United States contrasts starkly with a diasporic perspective where such history takes place elsewhere.

In increasingly celebratory readings of Roth, there is said to be a virtuous circle between his return to the United States as a historical subject (worthy at last of 'the Great American novel') and the best of 'democratic America', where both novels and society are distinguished by a creative appropriation and a 'turbulent', quintessentially American, pluralism.[4] Roth long since described the 'self-conscious and deliberate zigzag that my own career has taken, each book veering sharply away from the one before' (Roth 1975: 83–84). My argument, however, is that the remythologizing of postwar America as a locale of war and terror has finally brought to an end such internal dialectics. Roth, in his early and middle years, characterizes 'race', in the form of European anti-Semitism or the rage of African Americans, as the one discourse that limits the seemingly endless zigzagging of his fiction. By the time of his late work, as I will show, it is the monumental history of the United States that acts as a brake on his transgressive imagination.

The shift from diasporic to national history takes many forms in Roth's novels as there are different kinds of diasporic histories – 'there [in Eastern Europe] nothing goes and everything matters; here [in the United States] everything goes and nothing matters' (Roth 2001a: 53) – as well as the alternative national realms of the United States and the State of Israel. Part of his 'zigzagging' method is to contrast European and American versions of diaspora – one tragic, the other untragic – and, in his late work, to contrast a 'tragic' emplotment of American history with an earlier untragic version. By locating death and suffering at the heart of his idea of the nation, Roth both universalizes a victimized Jewish diaspora and ceases to be on the side of imaginative 'chaos' (223), as he puts it in *I Married a*

Communist (1998). I will begin with the counternational realm of the State of Israel where 'Roth' finally rejects his lifelong diasporism.[5]

The Death of George Ziad, or the End of Diasporism

Towards the beginning of *Operation Shylock: A Confession* (1993), we hear the radical Palestinian voice of Professor George Ziad, who had been a graduate student with 'Philip Roth' at the University of Chicago in the mid–1950s. Like all of the other 'real' figures and events in this novel – Roth's Halcion-induced depression, the Demjanjuk trial, Leon Klinghoffer's diary, the interview with Aharon Appelfeld – George Ziad is a fictionalized version of a 'real' person or happening – in this case Edward Said. As with Said, Ziad's name combines a king of England with an Arabic surname and, like his near-namesake, he is a Christian Palestinian who is a professor trained in an elite American university.[6] There is also some confusion (at least in *Commentary*-reading circles) concerning whether Said and Ziad were raised in Cairo or Jerusalem (Roth 1993: 120). But Ziad's family home in Jerusalem, like Said's, still exists. Roth's description of Ziad – 'with his wonderful manners and his refined virility not only masking the pain of dispossession and exile but concealing even from himself how scorched he was by shame' (123) – could easily be applied to Said. Ziad, in fact, turns out to be the eponymous Shylock-figure: 'at the core of everything was [Ziad's] hatred and the great disabling fantasy of revenge' (129). 'Roth's' supposed spying on the Palestine Liberation Organization in Athens, known as 'Operation Shylock', was only possible because of his friendship with his 'P.L.O. handler' Ziad (389). This fictionalized Mossad operation ends with Ziad's death.

Ziad, who in many ways is Roth's other double, echoes the two Roths in the novel in both his assimilationism of the 1950s ('[Jerusalem] was not something I talked about in 1955' [120]) and his diasporism of the 1990s ('There is more Jewish spirit and Jewish laughter and Jewish intelligence on the Upper West Side of Manhattan than in this entire country [of Israel]' [122]). His reading of Philip Roth's fiction, under the sign of postwar American exceptionalism, articulates the radical break in Roth's oeuvre, which structures this chapter, between what comes before and after *Operation Shylock*. Ziad, in a well-known summary of Roth's fiction since the 1950s, speaks of the 'pastoralization of the ghetto':

> Green lawns, white Jews – you [Roth] wrote about it. You crystallized it in your first book. That's what the hoopla was all about. 1959. The Jewish success story in its heyday, all new and thrilling and funny and fun. Liberated new Jews, normalized Jews, ridiculous and wonderful. The triumph of the untragic. Brenda Patimkin dethrones Anne Frank. (132)

Ziad's death as a supposed collaborator, caused presumably by his friendship with 'Philip Roth', anticipates the heroic anguish of the late work (especially the figure of Coleman Silk). This is also the death of an innocent diasporism that locates traumatic history ('Anne Frank') outside the American national realm. His brutal death and the suffering of Israelis and Palestinians – 'There is nothing in the future for these Jews and these Arabs but more tragedy, suffering and blood' (161) – is radically other to the life of American 'normalized Jews'. Indeed, Ziad is stabbed 'five times' by 'masked men' on the streets of Ramallah in front of his American-born son, who, after this experience, is 'accursed' and will 'never be free – of fealty to the father's quest' (389–90). At the same time, Roth celebrates the freedom inherent in a counterdiasporism ('Brenda Patimkin') that foregrounds the power of imaginative and social transformation ('Liberated new Jews'). Such celebratory diasporism is woven into the fabric of a fiction where everything is doubled and redoubled and becomes a form of theatrics or game-playing. It is the contrast between these two forms of history (one tragic, the other untragic) that separates Roth's early and late work.

My argument is that the Americanization of history, especially in the later work, appropriates a traumatic history (especially European-Jewish suffering) within the boundaries of the United States. But I want to distance myself from those critics who regard Roth's supposed diasporism rather too uncritically.[7] The diasporism in *Operation Shylock*, unlike its celebratory version in R.B. Kitaj's *First Diasporist Manifesto* (1989), drama-tizes an exhaustion with the diasporic fictions that have gone before. By returning to American history in the novels after *Operation Shylock* (Roth's 'national turn'), there is a universalization of a victimized Jewish diaspora within the US. If Roth's early fictions denote the 'triumph of the untragic', as Ziad among many others have argued, then the late fictions have precisely appropriated a tragic history (here in Palestinian guise) to shatter a naïve diasporism. What is more, as Ziad's lecture indicates, the question of 'race' ('white Jews') is deeply implicated in 'the triumph of the untragic'. After all, it was only by becoming 'white' that Jews could 'pasto-ralize the ghetto' and find a place in the United States outside the trau-matic history that had gone before. Within this logic, as I will show, the unwhitening of Roth's late protagonists is crucial to the tragic emplotment of contemporary America.

Operation Shylock and *The Counterlife* (1986), two of Roth's most playful fictions, are most often read together as 'Israel-centred novels' and, equally, as 'experimental' novels that destabilize the American diasporic experience in relation to a national centre.[8] Roth mischievously describes *Operation Shylock* as a 'nonfictional treatment' rather than a 'Zuckerman sequel to *The Counterlife*' (Roth 1993: 359). His diasporism, in these novels, has been characterized as a tension between the location of 'the real' in the State of Israel and the 'diasporic lure of the imagination' where narrative is unbounded.[9] In this reading, Roth is trapped in an endless dialectic between Zion and exile, mimesis and fiction, with his doubleness always excessive and therefore never quite reduced to a centre/periphery model of diaspora. Roth, at his most risk-taking, refuses such conven-tional dualities, as can be seen at the end of *The Counterlife* when he defines Nathan's predicament as being 'a Jew among Gentiles and a Gentile among Jews' (Roth 1986: 324). At its most disconcerting, his diasporism is disruptive rather than dialectical.[10]

To be sure, Roth's Israel is constructed self-consciously as a mimetic realm where perception and reality are equivalent and the uncertainties of diaspora are banished irrevocably. Towards the end of *Operation Shylock*, the Rothian narrator sums up the difference between his modernist diasporic imagination, which dwells in the 'house of Ambiguity' (Roth 1993b: 307), and the authoritative certainties of the Israeli Mossad agent known as 'Louis B. Smilesburger': 'my mind determines entirely how reality appears to me, but for you the mind works differently. You know the world as it really is, and I know it only as it appears' (392). Earlier, 'Roth' has summarized their differences as follows: 'he's swimming in the abrasive tragedies of life and I'm only swimming in art' (378). Nathan Zuckerman and 'Philip Roth' are able to imagine countless counterlives and counterselves in the performative space that is Roth's American diaspora, whereas the Israeli Jew has an ultimate reality, bounded by the fact of war, in which to situate an unambiguous sense of self. Henry Zuckerman summarizes such national singularity, as opposed to the 'oedipal swamp' of the diaspora, as having 'an *outer* landscape, a nation, a world! . . . [Israel] isn't some exercise for the brain divorced from reality' (Roth 1986: 140). In Roth's Israel, the diaspora is the natural home of the *luftmensch* ('brain divorced from reality').

According to this logic, the centring of Israel in these novels represents a national space, other than America, where reality is determined by the 'abrasive tragedies of life' rather than the vagaries of the untragic imagination. At the same time, both *Operation Shylock* and *The Counterlife* resist the idea that a Jewish national space purges 'Jewish experience of its ambiguity' and, so to speak, drains the 'oedipal swamp' of its messy uncertainties.[11] The redemptive or purifying role of the nation, which aims to subsume the individual within the collective, is merely an instance writ large of Roth's earlier travails with the American-Jewish community. But those critics who foreground Israel as a 'reality for which people gave their lives' tend to downplay the extent to which Roth has always disarticulated communal narratives.[12] In these terms, Roth constructs Europe – rightly characterized as the 'other Jewish diaspora' – as a disruptive third space

that throws into disarray the fixed points of Israel and the American-
Jewish diaspora, nation and exile.[13] The traumatic experience of the 'other
Jewish diaspora', Jewish racial persecution in Europe personified by the
figure of Shylock, is radically unassimilable and contrasts starkly with the
dream of assimilation in Israel and America. To make this point, 'Roth', in
Operation Shylock, explicitly compares his own authorial presence with
that of the novelist Aharon Appelfeld who, as a child, survived the Nazi
occupation in Eastern Europe by hiding in a forest:

> we are anything *but* the duplicates that everyone is supposed to believe
> you and me to be; because Aharon and I each embody the *reverse* of the
> other's experience; because each recognizes in the other the Jewish
> man that he is *not*; because of the all but incompatible orientations that
> shape our very different lives and very different books and that result
> from *antithetical* twentieth-century Jewish biographies; because we are
> the heirs jointly of a drastically *bifurcated* legacy. (200–01)

The 'distinctly radical *twoness*' (200) of 'Roth' and 'Appelfeld' fundamentally counters the notion of a unified Jewish self, moving smoothly between
the individual and the collective, or the imagination and reality. Appelfeld,
as a child survivor of the Holocaust, represents an insurmountable reality
in the novel which results in a tragic form of diaspora: 'Appelfeld is a
displaced writer of displaced fiction who has made of displacement and
disorientation a subject uniquely his own' (Roth 2001a: 20). The key point
is that the Holocaust, and by extension the history of European anti-
Semitism ('Shylock'), results in an abiding sense of traumatic history being
elsewhere and radically other to the experience of 'Philip Roth'. At the
beginning of *Operation Shylock*, the 'real' Roth precisely makes this
contrast in relation to his cousin Apter, a Holocaust survivor: 'The much
praised transfigurations concocted by Franz Kafka pale beside the unthink-
able metamorphoses perpetrated by the Third Reich on the childhoods of
my cousin [Apter] and my friend [Appelfeld], to enumerate only two'
(Roth 1993: 29). The last question 'Roth' asks Appelfeld, which remains

unanswered, is about the way Holocaust survivors have been 'ineluctably changed' (Roth 2001a: 214) by their experience. Here the unbridgeable gap between change as 'artistic transubstantiation' (Roth 1993: 361) and change as traumatic experience is paramount. The point is reinforced by Roth recalling his cousin Apter immediately after he hears from his 'Jerusalem counterself', whom he names comically Moishe Pipik. Pipik is the other Philip Roth in the novel and the very personification of the 'triumph of the untragic'. At the end of the novel, in fact, 'Roth' dismisses Pipikism as 'the untragic force that inconsequentializes everything – farcicalizes every-thing, trivializes everything, superficializes everything – our suffering as Jews not excluded' (389). Pipik's untragic version of diasporism, which aims to recreate a post-Holocaust Jewish diaspora in East-Central Europe, is bogus because it is a form of pastoralism that attempts to transcend reality through sheer willpower. His diasporism, in other words, is another version of the empty, merely aesthetic transformation of reality that the adolescent Roth and his Zuckermanic double once falsely believed in. In *Operation Shylock* 'Roth' repeatedly dismisses Pipik's 'dream' of resettling Israeli Jews of European origin back in East-Central Europe because it ignores the '*depths* of antipathy' (221) towards Jews: 'Of the numerous strong arguments against *his* [Pipik's] utopia, none is more of an impedi-ment than the fact that these are countries in which Jewish security and well-being would be perennially menaced by the continuing existence of European anti-Semitism' (104). As if Roth's 'numerous strong arguments' were not strong enough, we are later told that the '*depths* of antipathy' (221) towards Jews are not merely in 'bigoted, backwater, pope-ridden Poland' but even in 'civilized, secularized, worldly-wise England' (Roth reminds the reader that he 'lived eleven years in London' [221] and knows about these things). Here, needless to say, we have a reprise of *The Counterlife* where the anti-Semitism that he had experienced in England transformed Nathan Zuckerman into a *luftmensch* or weightless Sartrean Jew:

> 'England's made a Jew of me in only eight weeks, which, on reflection, might be the least painful method. A Jew without Jews, without

Judaism, without Zionism, without Jewishness, without a temple or an army or even a pistol, a Jew clearly without a home, just the object itself, like a glass or an apple' (Roth 1986: 324).

In both *The Counterlife* and *Operation Shylock*, to adapt a reading by Harold Bloom, ' "Philip Roth's" shadow self or secret sharer is not the wretched Moishe Pipik [or Henry Zuckerman] . . . it is Shylock.'[14] Bloom takes this assertion from Supposnik (a seller of rare books and possible Mossad agent), who argues that Shylock is the 'savage, repellent and villainous Jew, deformed by hatred and revenge', who has, over the past four hundred years, 'entered as our doppelgänger into the consciousness of the enlightened West' (Roth 1993: 274). 'Race', in this way, creates the *luftmensch* ('a Jew clearly without a home'). Such irreducible racial images, which culminate in European anti-Semitism, are the reason why the Holocaust cannot be simply transcended by resettling Jews back in Europe.

What has been hardly noticed, however, is that the history of European anti-Semitism is redoubled in the Shylockian figure of George Ziad – 'isn't a colossal, enduring injustice enough to drive a decent man mad?' (152) – who has settled 'the issue of self-division once and for all' by embracing 'immoderation with a vengeance' (151). Ziad, like Roth, moves from the untragic assimilationism of the 1950s to a tragic sense of his people's suffering and, in so doing, personifies both the endless splitting of the self in the novel and the violent resolution of such ambivalence through his insane 'hatred' (129). His transformations since the 1950s, the narrator tells us, embody the extent to which a 'tiny . . . self' contains 'contending subselves – and that these subselves should themselves be constructed of subselves, and on and on and on' (152). These splittings make the cosmopolitan Ziad, from a nationalist perspective, suspect as a collaborator and eventually lead to his death. But his self-divisions resonate in the doubling and redoubling of absolutely everything else in the novel: the Holocaust and the Intifada, the trial of Demjanjuk and the trial of unnamed

Palestinians, Zionism and Pipikism, 'Roth' and Appelfeld, and Wanda Jane
and Roth's first wife.

What is more, the redoubling of 'Roth' and traumatic Jewish history in
the figure of the radical Palestinian Ziad is part of the many 'contending
subselves' and distorting mirror images in the novel. As Morris Dickstein
has noted, Pipik's diasporism is a mirror image of Zionism since it similarly 'ignores the hostility of the indigenous population'. Other critics have
argued that Roth's nickname for Ziad, the letter 'Zee', also invokes the
'story of Z' or Zionism.[15] Both diasporism and Zionism, in these terms, are
forms of dangerously innocent pastoralism that attempt to transcend irredeemable historical reality. In the interview with Appelfeld, 'Roth' argues
that the 'coarse brutal, semisavage . . . goy' is 'rooted in real experience' as
opposed to the otherworldly 'Jewish imagination' (212): 'The most
imposing Gentile in all of Bellow's work . . . is Henderson – the self-
exploring rain king who, to restore his psychic health, takes his blunted
instincts off to Africa. For Bellow no less than Appelfeld the truly "earthly
soul" is not the Jew, nor is the search to retrieve primitive energies
portrayed as the quest of a Jew' (212–13). What is interesting about this
reading of Saul Bellow's *Henderson the Rain King* (1959), a novel that had
preoccupied Roth since his essay 'Writing American Fiction' (1960), is
that its version of Henderson – who attempts to restore his 'psychic health'
by taking his 'blunted instincts off to Africa' – echoes throughout Roth, as
I will show, from Alexander Portnoy to Henry Zuckerman. But where
Ziad differs most pointedly from Edward Said is that he gives up his
tenured professorship in Chicago and returns with his family to Ramallah
in a failed bid similarly to 'restore his psychic health'. His wife, Anna, a
Christian Palestinian raised in Lebanon, tries to protect their 'ahistorical
and free' (151) American-born son by sending him back to a New England
boarding school. She castigates her husband for returning to his roots:
'Roots! A concept for *cavemen* to live by! Is the survival of Palestinian
culture, Palestinian people, Palestinian heritage, is that really "a must" in
the evolution of humanity? Is all that mythology a greater must than the
survival of my son?' (161). Ziad's return changes him, in his wife's words,

into just 'another victim who can't forget' compared to his earlier American self, who had 'left all this victimization behind' (160).

Smilesburger's account of the death of Ziad stresses the endless permutations that surround his murder: 'maybe he was a collaborator who was murdered for the Israelis by Palestinians who are also collaborators – and then maybe not'. He describes this confusion as a deliberate policy towards the 'Arab population in the territories': 'the object is to create an atmosphere in which no Arab can feel secure as to who is his enemy and who is his friend'. This policy where *Nothing is secure*' (390) is later repeated as a way of summarizing diasporic fictions where similarly 'Nothing is secure. Man [is] the pillar of instability' (393). In an extraordinary twist, in the closing pages of *Operation Shylock*, the 'pervasive uncertainty' of Roth's fiction, keeping his readers in check, and the Israeli control of Palestinians, such as George Ziad, are seen as one and the same thing. Here the individual and the collective, imagination and reality, are finally unified. To enter the life-and-death realm of the Jewish nation, where 'Roth' is at last a good Jewish citizen, he has to give Smilesburger, in the role of Shylock, a 'pound of my flesh' (393). That is, he has literally to circumcise his book or edit out the notional last chapter concerning the PLO meeting in Athens. Such is the price that 'Roth' has to pay to unite his fiction with the collective.

In the last pages of the novel, 'Roth' has to decide whether to accept the Shylockian 'three thousand ducats' (395–96) that he receives in New York in payment for his supposed work for the Mossad. His first instinct is to pass the money on to a homeless 'black couple on the steps of [a] church' (395). He dubs this gesture 'The Mossad Fund for Homeless Non-Jews' (396), which is also, poignantly, a euphemism for the Palestinians ('Homeless Non-Jews'). In a summary of much of his previous fiction, it is poor African Americans, not unlike the dead George Ziad, who prick the 'Jewish conscience' (398). This 'real' suffering is the difference between the tragic and the untragic, or the Jewish-American and African-American version of the American diaspora. In the last pages of *Operation Shylock*, 'Roth' is asked to decide between his individual conscience and the power of the Jewish nation which, he is told, is able to destroy his reputation (in a reprise of the plot of *The Ghost Writer*). But *Operation Shylock*, I believe, dramatizes above all Roth's exhaustion with his previous fiction, which locates the tragedy of the Jewish diaspora, and the life-or-death normality of the Jewish nation, beyond the boundaries of the United States. We will now explore why Roth's diasporism, taken absolutely seriously by both the young Roth and the young Zuckerman, was eventually mocked and dismissed in the caricature of Moishe Pipik.

Roth, Race and Diaspora: History Elsewhere

It is no coincidence that *The Ghost Writer* (1979), the first part of *Zuckerman Bound: A Trilogy and Epilogue* (1985), begins where *Henderson the Rain King* leaves off, with Roth's alter ego, Nathan Zuckerman, imagining himself as a tabula rasa; the site par excellence of transcendent American self-creation. Arriving at Emanuel Isadore Lonoff's solitary New England home in December 1956, Nathan contemplates the fields of 'driven snow' that surround him: 'Purity. Serenity. Simplicity. Seclusion. All one's concentration and flamboyance and originality reserved for the gruelling, exalted, transcendent calling. I looked and I thought, this is how I will live' (Roth 1985: 5). Here we have the by now familiar pastoral realm on which Nathan will inscribe his new sense of self outside 'the world'. Unsurprisingly, given the imagery of frozen whiteness, Lonoff's working day is characterized by turning words around on a blank sheet of paper: 'I turn sentences around. That's my life. I write a sentence and then I turn it around. Then I look at it and turn it around again. Then I have lunch' (17–18). Detached from reality, the deracinated and ascetic Lonoff is viewed by Nathan as the 'Jew who got away' from history: 'You got away from Russia and the pogroms. You got away from the purges – and Babel didn't. You got away from Palestine and the homeland. . . . You got away from New York' (50). It is this ideal of the aesthetic transcendence of reality that the young Nathan, not unlike the young Roth, is initially attracted to. This is why Nathan, at the beginning of *The Ghost Writer*, imagines an alternative identity that does not originate in national and racial descent but is, instead, based on the power of the literary imagination. At the age of twenty-three, Nathan's homeland is the text: 'The pride inspired in my parents by the establishment in 1948 of a homeland in Palestine that would gather in the unmurdered remnant of European Jewry was, in fact, not so unlike what welled up in me when I first came upon Lonoff's thwarted, secretive, imprisoned souls' (12). Rather than a patriotism based on the formation of a Jewish nation in Palestine, Nathan's chest swells when he realizes that Lonoff (the 'most original storyteller since Melville and Hawthorne' [4]) has created a literature of 'wit and poignancy' out of an experience akin to that of his own 'striving, troubled father' (8). This is the source of Nathan's diasporism, which culminates in *The Counterlife* and is taken to an absurd extreme in *Operation Shylock*. In detaching himself from a collective identity based on national or communal pride, and the bloodline of fathers and sons, Nathan attempts to create an affiliative sense of self and paternal descent founded on the sanctity of art. This is, after all, the plot of *The Ghost Writer*. The young Nathan is in search of a surrogate literary father after being rejected by his actual father and the leaders of the Newark Jewish community for writing a short story based on a family scandal. In other words, *The Ghost Writer* is the beginning of a long and winding road on which 'Nathan Dedalus' searches for a history and a sense of self that escape the nets of religion, nation and community.

What is paradoxical here, as Clive Sinclair has argued, is that Nathan Zuckerman is constructed as 'the Semite-obsessed writer Roth's Jewish detractors imagine him to be'.[16] That is, Nathan is Philip Roth without his 'other books' or, more specifically, without any fiction apart from the Zuckermanic equivalent of *Goodbye, Columbus* ('Higher Education') and *Portnoy's Complaint* (*Carnovsky*). In confining Nathan racially to his 'Jewish' books, Roth turns him into a Sartrean Jew who is comically determined by the views of his communal readers. The inability of Nathan's readers to differentiate between different kinds of tragic and untragic histories means that the fears and desires of a relatively prosperous

postwar American Jewry are elided with the fears and desires generated by
the centuries-old 'imaginary Jew' ('Shylock') in Europe. Roth characterized the overdetermination of the 'imaginary Jew' in 1974 when he
described his 'novelistic enterprise' as 'imagining Jews *being* imagined by
themselves and others' (Roth 1975: 301). As he recounts in his autobiography, the 'fanatical security' of his lower-middle-class Newark childhood
has, in the monomaniacal misreading of his early fiction, been conflated
with the 'fanatical insecurity' engendered by the Holocaust. Here is his
account of when he was publicly vilified at Yeshiva University:

> This group whose embrace once had offered me so much security was
> itself fanatically insecure. How could I conclude otherwise when I was
> told that every word I wrote was a disgrace, potentially endangering
> every Jew? Fanatical security, fanatical insecurity – nothing in my
> entire background could exemplify better than that night [at Yeshiva
> University] how deeply rooted the Jewish drama was in this duality.
> (Roth 1988: 129–30)

This unresolved 'duality' entraps Roth's fictional alter ego since he has to
decide what credence to give to a metaphorical collective history of
suffering that results in a fanatical response to his fiction, even though this
history is clearly radically different from his own experience. The problem
for Nathan is that a vicarious Jewish victimhood, in evoking the trauma of
the Holocaust, subsumes the individual in the interests of the collective,
which leaves little space for his imagination. That Ralph Ellison came to
Roth's rescue with 'an eloquent authority' (128), and spoke on his behalf at
this public gathering, was a kindness that, as we shall see, was eventually
repaid in *The Human Stain* (2000).

The irony of *Zuckerman Bound* is that Jewish history, which supposedly determines Nathan (to the extent that his fiction is deemed to have
lethal consequences), happens elsewhere. The suffering of European Jews,
which the young Nathan feels compelled to take account of, is explored
initially through the ambiguous figure of Amy Bellette. Situated uneasily

between myth and history, Amy is a 'dark beauty' (Roth 1985: 17) who, like Roth's previous dark beauties such as the ironically 'Polynesian' (Roth 1959: 10) Brenda Patimkin, is a means through which Nathan can supposedly escape the narrow authorities who wish to determine his fate. She perceives herself – and is perceived by Zuckerman – as a reborn Anne Frank who has somehow survived Bergen-Belsen. As Hana Wirth-Nesher argues, Anne/Amy 'is the paragon of both Jewish suffering and of renunciation on the holy altar of art' who, more than anyone, is able to absolve Nathan of the guilt of 'betraying' his family and community.[17]

This metaphorical use of the history of Anne Frank by Nathan and also by Amy (in relation to Lonoff) and Judge Wapter (who recommends that Nathan see the Broadway production of *The Diary of Anne Frank*) points to the nature of the Holocaust 'ghosts' that haunt Nathan's quest for a transcendent aesthetic space. At the same time, the split between 'Anne Frank' and Amy Bellette indicates the general disparity between Nathan's Newark Jewish background and a victim-centred construction of Jewishness: 'Ma, you want to see physical violence done to the Jews of Newark, go to the office of the plastic surgeon where the girls get their noses fixed' (Roth 1985: 106). And it is 'girls get[ting] their noses fixed' that returns us to the world of Brenda Patimkin's nose job and the whitening of postwar American Jews. As the other books in *Zuckerman Bound* make clear, it is this process of whitening that determines Nathan's fate along with the suffering of European Jewry.

The ending of *Zuckerman Unbound*, where Nathan discovers himself to be truly alone, is pivotal in this regard: 'You are no longer any man's son, you are no longer some good woman's husband, you are no longer your brother's brother, and you don't come from anywhere, anymore, either' (404–05). The fantasy in the novel is that the bestselling *Carnovsky* (reminiscent of *Portnoy's Complaint*) is meant to have caused the death of his father, leaving Nathan bereft and devoid of family and community. But the reasons for Nathan no longer coming from 'anywhere' have as much to do with the depopulation of his birthplace as they do with *Carnovsky*:

The corner storefront, once a grocery, was now owned and occupied by the Calvary Evangelistic Assembly, Inc. Four stout black women with shopping bags were standing at the bus stop. In [Nathan's] early childhood, four black women at the bus stop would have been domestics . . . to clean for the Jewish women in the Weequahic neighbourhood. . . . Except for the elderly trapped in the housing projects, the Jews had all vanished. So had almost everyone white, including the Catholic orphans. The orphanage appeared to have been converted into some sort of city school. (402–03)

Instead of the conversion of American reality into the realm of storytelling – which is the dream of the twenty-three-year-old Nathan in *The Ghost Writer* – we have the transformation of Nathan's birthplace into an impoverished African-American neighbourhood, which means that Nathan no longer has a 'subject' (445). The powerlessness of art is revealed by irreconcilable social differences, with Catholic orphanages 'converted' into inner-city schools and a local synagogue transformed into an African Methodist Episcopal Church (405). As is common with Roth, it is the impoverished black cleaning women who represent a collective social reality that Jewish Americans have long since surpassed. Not that 'the Jews' are exactly synonymous with 'everyone white' in Roth's description. The view of the refashioned synagogue (where Nathan had his bar mitzvah lessons) ends *Zuckerman Unbound*, and this religious conversion is the final paradoxical proof (given Nathan's secularity) that Roth's alter ego is separated irrevocably from his birthplace. By the time of *The Anatomy Lesson*, the 'elfin elderly' (519) figure of Dr Kotler (with his 'nut-coloured face') links bathetically the loss of Jewish Newark to the loss of Jewish Europe:

Vanished now. Everything that happened to me down the twentieth-century drain. My birthplace, Vilna, decimated by Hitler, then stolen by Stalin. Newark, my America, abandoned by the whites and destroyed by the coloured. That's what I thought the night they set the fires in

1968. First the Second World War, then the Iron Curtain, now the
Newark Fire. (522)

Here Dr Kotler – 'Man in exile. Child of the times' (522) – articulates the
multiple losses (from Vilna to Newark) that make up his experience of the
twentieth century. Much of *The Anatomy Lesson* questions whether
Nathan can also lay claim to such a cosmopolitan perspective, the fruits of
metaphorical thinking, by including his 'exile' from Newark, which Alvin
Pepler in *Zuckerman Unbound* (1981) insists should be his subject, as part
of Kotler's wider history of exile.

As in his earliest stories and novels, Roth's protagonists are racially
indeterminate, which enables them to engage with an actual history of
racism in the United States rather than its fantasized counterpart (the
'imaginary Jew') which comically determines Nathan's fate. This racial
indeterminacy, neither black nor white, is figured through the antagonistic brothers, Nathan and Henry, in both *Zuckerman Bound* and *The
Counterlife*. When Henry is first introduced he is described as the 'tallest,
darkest, and handsomest by far of all the Zuckerman men, a swarthy,
virile, desert Zuckerman whose genes, uniquely for their clan, seemed to
have travelled straight from Judea to New Jersey without the Diaspora
detour' (368). The American diaspora makes Jews white, which is why
they are designated 'Caucasian' in *The Counterlife* (Roth 1986: 71), and
why Israel is 'only a stone's throw from Africa!' in *Portnoy's Complaint*
(Roth 1969: 286). By the time of *The Counterlife*, Nathan learns that
Israelis come from 'Tunis, Algiers, Casablanca' and that there are large
numbers of 'Jews from Ethiopia ... *black* Jews' beginning to migrate to
Israel (Roth 1986: 78). Not that being 'white' in the American diaspora is
necessarily the same thing as being 'white' per se as we see in the 'kinky
black Hebe hair' (Roth 1969: 183) of Alexander Portnoy and the 'swarthy'
Henry Zuckerman, who in turn recall the 'dark' Neil Klugman and the
'Polynesian' Brenda Patimkin.[18]

The reason for this abiding preoccupation with racial inbetweenness is
that, as we have seen with Hannah Arendt's inept intervention in Little

Rock, the history of slavery rightly defines the question of 'race' in the United States. In this context, Roth acknowledges a time when American Jews were not whitened and their voice was heard when they spoke about slavery.[19] This prehistory can be seen in the version of Nathan as the Ape in Kafka's 'A Report to an Academy' by André Schevitz in *Zuckerman Unbound*, who concludes that Nathan's four years of training in 'Advanced Humanistic Decisions' at the University of Chicago is rather like 'stealing a wild little baby baboon from the branches of the trees . . . and then, when he is big and hairy and full of himself, giving him a degree in Western Civilization and sending him back to the bush'. Schevitz, another cosmopolitan father-figure not unlike Dr Kotler, imagines Nathan as an 'enchanting little baboon' at the University of Chicago who 'won't ever be happy around the waterhole again'. Here Roth, through Kafka, is invoking the deeply troubling prewar racial images of European Jews as degenerate and primitive, not unlike Conrad's Africans in *Heart of Darkness*, who were unable to become 'white'. Although Henry is 'swarthy', the 'civilized' Nathan is described as a 'jungle baboon' who becomes a 'seminar baboon' (Roth 1985: 300). Here is an extreme version of Roth's sense of the 'cultural defection', 'miscegenation' and 'parasitism' caused by his pioneering generation of Jews who studied English in American universities in the 1950s (Roth 1975: 83). Such are the racialized images of inbetweenness and impurity that reach their apotheosis in *The Human Stain*.

The problem that Nathan has, however, is that he cannot lay claim to the European exilic cosmopolitanism of an André Schevitz or a Dr Kotler, nor can he write about an apocalyptic Newark, now lost as a 'subject' (Roth 1985: 445), in the compelling, albeit melodramatic, style of an Alvin Pepler. This results in a 'crisis of solipsism' (Roth 1975: 165), with Nathan, paralysed, undergoing a painful inner journey right to the tips of his 'frazzled Jewish' nerve-ends (Roth 1985: 501). At one point, he considers whether to make his lover Jaga, a Polish refugee, the material for an ameliorative novel, set in Eastern Europe, provisionally entitled *The Sorrows of Jaga*. But he drops the idea almost as soon as it is considered:

Hopeless – and not only because of the grass and the vodka. If you get out of yourself you can't be a writer because the personal ingredient is what gets you going, and if you hang on to the personal ingredient any longer you'll disappear right up your asshole. . . . You don't want to represent her Warsaw – it's what her Warsaw represents that you want: suffering that isn't semi-comical, the world of massive historical pain instead of this pain in the neck. War, destruction, anti-Semitism, totalitarianism, literature on which the fate of a culture hinges. . . . Chained to self-consciousness. Chained to retrospection. Chained to my dwarf drama till I die. (550–51)

In contrast to the figure of 'Anne Frank' in *The Ghost Writer*, who is potentially able to transport Nathan beyond his communal and familial 'dwarf drama', the suffering Jaga is unable to perform even this fantasized redemptive act. Nathan's would-be femme fatale is no longer the means by which he is able to commune with 'war, destruction, anti-Semitism, totalitarianism'. His 'crisis of solipsism' is caused by an inability to create a counterlife that can transcend his sense of constriction and insularity in the United States. For this reason, the focus for much of *Zuckerman Bound* is on Nathan's failure to connect with European suffering, crystallized in the word 'Holocaust', which his mother wrote and gave to her son while dying of a brain tumour. Zuckerman can look neither inwards ('Chained to self-consciousness') nor outwards ('the world of massive historical pain'). He thus embodies one extreme definition of the placeless and free-floating *luftmensch* who, in the mould of Lonoff, escapes history, especially traumatic history, which is located elsewhere.

By the time of *The Prague Orgy* (1985), however, Nathan is able to engage directly with European history in a bid to transcend his 'dwarf drama'. This novella, also based around a Jamesian novella, literally prefigures *The Ghost Writer* as it begins on 11 January 1976, before Nathan has supposedly written his earlier work.[20] The circular relationship of Roth's 'epilogue' with the beginning of *Zuckerman Bound* is reinforced by situating Nathan in Czechoslovakia in a redemptive search for the lost manuscripts of a Yiddish writer killed by the Nazis (based loosely on Bruno Schulz). Here the ideal of an imagined diasporism, first articulated in *The Ghost Writer*, is given a specific historical terrain which is eventually caricatured in *Operation Shylock*. In fact, many of the motifs of *The Ghost Writer* are reprised in *The Prague Orgy*. Instead of the redemptive 'Anne Frank', we have the 'ruined' (715) actress Eva Kalinova, who played Anne Frank on stage at the age of nineteen in 1956 and subsequently went on to play 'the Jewess on the stage' in Chekhov's *Ivanov*, followed by Jessica in *The Merchant of Venice* (712). Persecuted for her affair with a Czech Jew, the non-Jewish Eva is dubbed 'the Jew's whore' (711) and is eventually forced to emigrate to the United States. By the end of the novella, the Czech minister of culture thinks of Eva as one of a number of perverted Jewish artists who repel the 'ordinary hardworking Czech' as they are 'incorrigible deviants who propose to make their moral outlook the norm' (777).

For the adolescent Nathan, Kafka's Prague was 'the city I imagined Jews would buy when they accumulated enough money for a homeland' (761). Once again, it is an unbounded textual homeland rather than a limited and limiting national territory that offers a solution to Nathan's sense of internal exile and displacement:

> In this used city, one would hear endless stories being told – on benches in the park, in kitchens at night, while waiting your turn at the grocery store or over the clothes-line in the yard, anxious tales of harassment and flight, stories of fantastic endurance and pitiful collapse ... the mining and refining of *tons* of these stories [was] the national industry of the Jewish homeland (if not the sole source of satisfaction), the construction of narrative out of the exertions of survival. (761)

Rather than the otherworldly aesthetic transcendence of *The Ghost Writer*, the diasporist ideal in *The Prague Orgy* attempts to redeem the actual landscape of European Jewish suffering ('the construction of narrative out of the exertions of survival'). It is significant, in this regard, that the

'Semite-obsessed' (716) author in Roth's epilogue is not Nathan, wrestling the demons created by his 'Jewish' fictions, but the writer of lost Yiddish manuscripts shot by a chess-playing Gestapo officer. This shift from the paranoid imagination of Zuckerman to the historical terrain of *The Prague Orgy* takes place at breakneck speed in *The Counterlife*. At the end of *The Prague Orgy*, Nathan is forced to leave this 'nation of narrators' (781) and to return to his 'little world around the corner' (784). Here is the first of Roth's many arguments for the authenticity and weight of the European Jewish diaspora – at the heart of his storytelling – in comparison to either a weightless United States or a hyper-real State of Israel. After all, Nathan's designation as a 'Zionist agent' (784) on the final page of Roth's epilogue is no less part of a 'little world' than his self-characterization as an 'American citizen' (778).

   The Counterlife takes to an extreme the diasporism of *The Prague Orgy* as the rival insights of Nathan and Henry – whether situated in the United States, Israel or England – are skilfully undermined and transformed into a superabundance of possible stories. Up until the last pages of the novel, Roth constructs a bewildering series of potential 'selves' for Nathan and Henry based on deliberate and playful misreadings of texts that wilfully lack authority. His diasporism, once again, disrupts those who would want to confine narrative to family, community or nation. Such radical game-playing is resolved at the end of the novel not in relation to the authenticity of the nation but, instead, with recourse to the power of the 'imaginary Jew'. As in *The Prague Orgy*, 'race' in *The Counterlife* is meaningful in Europe rather than the United States or Israel. Nathan's sense of 'difference' is, pointedly, 'reactivated' not in Tel Aviv or New York but in London by 'sitting here beside the Thames' (Roth 1986: 324) near the Globe Theatre, where the figure of Shylock was first introduced to the world.

   One of the few indisputable facts of *The Counterlife* is the timeless tradition of English literary anti-Semitism in the 'Gloucestershire' and 'Christendom' sections of the novel and its present-day incarnations. In stark contrast to the manifold uncertainties of the novel as a whole, it is this age-old race-thinking that fixes Nathan as a Sartrean Jew. Not that *The Counterlife* ends with Nathan characterized merely in terms of the racial imagination. In a crucial conjunction, Roth contrasts England, as a place where Jews are still distinguished racially, with the act of circumcision, which 'confirms there is an us, and an us that isn't solely him and me' (324). The connection with a collective history is made in opposition to the 'mists and meadows of Constable's England' which mistakenly promotes the 'idyllic scenario of redemption through the recovery of a sanitized confusionless life'. England is, in other words, the ur-pastoral, an 'imagined world . . . often green and breastlike, where we may finally be "ourselves"' (322). For Nathan, the antidote to such Christianized and aestheticized notions of pastoralism, exported to the United States, is circumcision, which will force his newborn son to 'enter history': 'Circumcision is everything that the pastoral is not and, to my mind, reinforces what the world is about which isn't strifeless unity. Quite convincingly, circumcision gives the lie to the womb-dream of life in the beautiful state of innocent prehistory, the appealing idyll of living "naturally", unencumbered by man made ritual' (323). Through circumcision, and the sense of racial difference engendered by this act, Nathan Zuckerman separates his child from the history of European anti-Semitism and, equally, disrupts the pastoral myths exported from the mother country. But Nathan's alienation from the United States, and his strong identification with a Jamesian cosmopolitanism in this regard, is caused by a history of American racism rather than anti-Semitism. As a contributing editor of Philip Rahv's *Partisan Review*, Milton Appel was of the generation who fashioned themselves, and their literary subjects, by internalizing the vocabulary of European modernism: '*Alienated, rootless, anguished, bewildered, brooding, tortured, powerless.*' But Nathan promptly Americanizes (and thereby belittles) such self-characterizations: 'he could have been describing the inner life of a Mississippi chain gang' (Roth 1985: 477). Rather than the distant history of European anti-Semitism, Nathan compares Appel's fantasized suffering with the stark social realities of black America. By Americanizing such cosmopolitan self-fashioning – because of his overwhelming hatred of Appel – Nathan once again denies himself access to European history and a tragic sense of diaspora. This was to be Roth's revenge on Irving Howe (in the guise of Milton Appel) who, in this version, is also seen to have a 'thin personal culture'.[21] Caught between Europe and America, black and white, tragedy and untragedy, the only certainty that ends such indeterminacy is the certainty of anti-Semitism. But, when the European dead finally come home to America, the history of racism in the United States is entirely refashioned.

The National Turn: History Comes Home

Harold Bloom has argued that *Operation Shylock*, despite its extraordinary game-playing, is the third in a trilogy of 'autobiographical' works beginning with *The Facts: A Novelist's Autobiography* (1988) and *Patrimony: A True Story* (1991).[22] The supposed facticity of these books was, Roth has argued, a response to his endless transformations as a 'walking text' (Roth 1988: 162) in the guise of Nathan Zuckerman. After all, up until its last pages, *The Counterlife* shows the extent to which the transformative imagination can overcome even the death of its characters. In *The Counterlife* Roth describes pastoralism as a 'beautiful state of innocent prehistory' (Roth 1986: 323) which, in going beyond European history, constitutes a mythic United States as a tabula rasa where individuals are able to reinvent themselves endlessly. His later work, which turns to the United States as a 'factual' historical subject, has been rightly characterized as 'anti-pastoral', with Roth's characters subject to historical forces rather than being merely outside them.[23] These late novels follow Roth's permanent return to the United States in 1989 (after living eleven years mainly in London) with, in the same year, the death of his father and the author undergoing a quintuple bypass heart operation. No longer is Roth the innocent rebellious son, in voluntary exile from the United States, living in an utterly foreign country where he never 'felt more misplaced' (Roth 1990: 109). His late fiction, understandably preoccupied with death and dying, foregrounds many of the 'traumatic' historical events that affected the United States after 1945, as opposed to more remote European or Middle Eastern counterhistories.[24]

After *Operation Shylock*, the 'world of massive historical pain' finally comes home and shapes American history in a tragic rather than a non-tragic mode. That Roth elides personal and historical suffering in these late works goes back to the word 'Holocaust' which Nathan's mother highlights while dying of a brain tumour. According to Roth, the word 'Holocaust' structures *Zuckerman Bound* – as its necessary 'thematic architecture' (Roth 1975: 137) – and we have seen that this is true in so far as the word evokes the extent to which the Nazi genocide has haunted postwar American Jewry. But the word 'Holocaust' is ambiguous in these novels since it can also be applied (referring to its earliest usages) to people of Nathan's mother's generation, in the cancer wards, who are terminally ill. As Michael Rothberg notes in relation to *Patrimony*, Roth uses 'tropes of the Holocaust' with regard to his father's brain tumour which, not unlike the Nazis, is as 'merciless as a blind mass of anything on the march' (Roth 1991: 136).[25] There is perhaps an echo here of the final pages of *The Professor of Desire* (1977) when Kepesh hears the analogous 'dreadful sound' of a camp survivor, Barbatnik, and his fictionalized father 'lying alone and insensate' next door (Roth 1977: 263). But in this novel there is an insuperable division between metaphor and reality: Kepesh's 'dying' (261) passion for Claire Ovington and Barbatnik's survivor memoir, 'The Man Who Never Said Die'.

The Holocaust as an American 'archetype of innocent suffering', here in the guise of Barbatnik, is universalized in Roth's shorter works in this late period, such as *The Dying Animal* (2001) and *Everyman* (2006), which take as their subject the 'fact of death that overwhelms everything' (Roth 2006: 15) or the 'everyday fact that one's life is at stake' (Roth 2001b: 36).[26] In Roth's late work, the 'distance between history's victims and those who grow up in the relative peace and security of America' is radically eroded as Zuckerman's wartime generation is maimed or passes away en masse. But this is not the same as arguing that cancer in Roth's late work is 'deeply historical.[27] In fact, it is precisely the confusion between personal and historical suffering that is lost in the late work. Whereas the younger Kepesh searches in vain for something other than the 'discontinuous and provisional' (Roth 1977: 251–52), the elderly Kepesh is 'scared witless about death' (Roth 2001b: 153). The ironic distancing of European and American history in the earlier work, and the increasingly insurmountable gap between the postwar histories of Jewish and African Americans, has been replaced by the universalizing of death and torment within the United States.

Sabbath's Theater (1995) is the crucial transitional text in this regard, with Mickey Sabbath personified as 'America' (Roth 1995: 419–20) by his Croatian lover and, in a mock-obituary, shifting the national terrain from Israel to the United States ('Mr. Sabbath did nothing for Israel' [195]).[28] The elderly Kepesh argues that sex is 'the revenge on death' (Roth 2001b: 69), which is also, needless to say, a way of summarizing the plot of Sabbath's Theater, where the presence of death overwhelms the sixty-four-year-old protagonist. Whereas Portnoy's complaint is the fissure between mind ('ethical and altruistic impulses') and body ('extreme sexual long-ings' [Roth 1969: n.p.]), Sabbath's complaint is the failed attempt to over-come death via the diminishing sex drive. The epigraph of Sabbath's Theater – 'Every third thought shall be my grave' – is taken from Shakespeare's The Tempest, which rightly indicates that this novel is a late work. But Sabbath's Theater is Roth's least serene novel – with the focus on death, intransigence and irreconcilability, rather than the conventional harmonies of Shakespeare's late plays – which is a form of Saidian 'late style'.[29] Unlike Operation Shylock, with its 'Roth' figure who is radically removed from the experience of death and suffering, Sabbath's Theater (like Roth's late novels in general) is utterly saturated by the knowledge and experience of 'the grave'.

The key figure here is the Croatian Drenka Balich, Sabbath's female erotic double, who acts as a catalyst for his story and whose importance to the novel is not unrelated to the fact that she has died of ovarian cancer by the end of the first chapter. Here the sorrows of Drenka and the 'Sorrows of Jaga' (Roth 1986: 550) could not be more different, as one figure generates narrative while the other precludes it. As Frank Kelleter has argued, Sabbath's preoccupation with Drenka's death makes him one of the most 'death-plagued' characters in American literature.[30] In this reading, the death of his lover sends Sabbath on a journey into the underworld where he encounters those whom he has lost – his 'disappeared' (Roth 1995: 47) first wife, Nikki (whom Sabbath claims wilfully to have killed); Lincoln, Sabbath's New York friend, who commits suicide; and, most significantly (as this figure tends to be repeated throughout Roth's late fiction), Sabbath's brother, Morty (a little too obviously named), who is shot down as a bomber pilot over Japan during the Second World War. The loss of Morty has transformed Sabbath's mother, Yetta, into one of the living dead.

Roth's America in *Sabbath's Theater*, after Benedict Anderson, is a place of 'ghostly *national* imaginings', a domain of loss and anguish.[31] Following the death of Drenka, Sabbath appropriates her story in a reprise of her earlier perception of Sabbath as the very personification of America – 'To America. I was dancing with America' (419) – which, she believed, confirmed her own Americanization. There is an extraordinary episode in the novel when Sabbath discovers that he is not the only one of Drenka's former lovers masturbating by her graveside. After this realization, the narrator tells us that Sabbath 'did something strange, strange even for a strange man like him, [he] began licking from his fingers [Drenka's former lover] Lewis's sperm and, beneath the full moon, chanting aloud "I am Drenka, I am Drenka"' (142). As in the fiction of Muriel Spark, the full moon seems to transport Sabbath into a pre-social realm (before the pastoralization of the United States and the 'whitening' of the Jewish community). Here we have an image of Sabbath's appropriation of Drenka's death (of Drenka herself) which reverses her triumphant Americanization, in an anticipation of the novels to come. There is no longer the gulf between a Sabbath and a Drenka, or Europe and America, as there was once between a Nathan and a Jaga, or a Kepesh and a Barbatnik, or a 'Roth' and an 'Appelfeld'.

As Derek Parker Royal has argued, *Sabbath's Theater* 'helped pave the way for Roth's fuller treatment of national character in the American Trilogy'.[32] Roth's American Trilogy, also known as the Second Zuckerman Trilogy or the American Tragedies, are the novels that have, as we have seen, placed Roth right at the heart of the American postwar canon of letters. In this spirit, Greil Marcus has argued that Roth, in the second trilogy, has unshackled himself from the particularities of Zuckerman so that he can universalize himself through the mythic figures of the Swede, Iron Rinn and Coleman Silk in *American Pastoral* (1997), *I Married a Communist* (1998) and *The Human Stain* (2000) respectively. According to this argument, Roth, through Zuckerman, is able to commune directly with the country as a whole, with Roth taking the 'social history of postwar America into himself, or rather Zuckerman . . . in order to return it to America at large'. Through Zuckerman, Marcus believes, Roth is able to speak to and for an authentic America.[33]

What tends to be ignored in these celebratory readings of the American Trilogy, and Roth's late work in general, are the limits imposed on Roth's narratives by the tragic emplotment of postwar America. In *Operation Shylock*, as we have seen, the fictional 'Roth' speaks of having a 'drastically *bifurcated* legacy' (Roth 1993: 201) when compared with the biography of an 'Appelfeld'. Such extraterritorial comparisons are reduced to a national story in *The Human Stain*, where the word 'bifurcate' could not be used more differently: 'To become a new being. To bifurcate. The drama that underlies America's story, the high drama that is upping and leaving – and the energy and cruelty that rapturous drive demands' (Roth 2000: 342). Here, in short, is the radical revision of Roth's previous fiction, a move from the insurmountable ('bifurcated') gulf between different kinds of histories to the domestication of these counterhistories as part of an American story of individual bifurcation. This is not simply a question of historicizing 'possessive individualism' or demythologizing the exceptionalist myth that the United States has finally transcended (European) history.[34] To be sure, Nathan has long since claimed that 'the civility and security of South Orange' is a form of 'Jewish history' no less than 'world-historical event[s]' (Roth 1986: 146) taking place in the alternative national realm of Israel. By the time of *I Married a Communist*, however, such diasporic 'Jewish history' is universalized, with the young Nathan (not unlike the elderly Roth in many interviews) arguing: 'I didn't care to partake of the Jewish character ... I wanted to partake of the national character'.[35] With this distinction in mind, he characterizes the immediate postwar period, as encapsulated in the radio plays of Norman Cowen, in the following terms: 'History had been scaled down and personalized, America had been scaled down and personalized. ... You flood into history and history floods into you. You flood into America and America floods into you' (Roth 1986: 39). Greil Marcus lauds Roth's American Trilogy in exactly these terms, with Zuckerman universalized as the passive conduit of postwar American history. But what is missing from this account of Roth's engagement with the 'national character' is an acknowledgement of the reduced national stories that are allowed by Roth's 'tragic' vision. The kinds of stories that Roth tells are signalled at the beginning of *American Pastoral* when we are given a graphic account of the Depression-years baseball books that preoccupied the adolescent Nathan. These were, according to the elderly Zuckerman, akin to the Book of Job, as they were conceived out of the 'dark austerities' of the 1930s and above all dramatized the 'cruelty and injustice of life' (Roth 1997: 9). Such baseball books and contemporaneous works on 'American history' also open *I Married a Communist* where 'heroic suffering' is the young Nathan's 'speciality' (Roth 1998: 25), with an imaginary America, rather than imaginary Jews, being associated primarily with renunciation.

This refashioning of the national space with regard to suffering and injustice shapes Nathan's childhood memories of the Swede and Iron Rinn, who are both, in these terms, tragic heroes, with the Swede described as having a 'tragic fall' (Roth 1997: 88) and Iron Rinn as making a 'tragic mistake' (Roth 1998: 275). The 'blue-eyed blond' Seymour Irving Levov, known as the Swede, was 'born into our tribe' and was the 'household Apollo' of Weequahic Jews (Roth 1997: 3–4). This hero-worship is, we are told, best explained by the 'fears' fostered by the 'war against the Germans and the Japanese', which meant that the Swede was 'fettered to history, an *instrument* of history' (4–5). Whereas the 'fanatical insecurity' (Roth 1988: 129) of Newark Jewry alienated the earlier versions of Nathan Zuckerman, here the 'fears' generated by European anti-Semitism and the rise of fascism have produced the myth of the utterly whitened and Americanized Swede. His sporting prowess follows that of Ronald Patimkin in *Goodbye, Columbus* who, not unlike the Swede, is much more alive as a physical rather than a cerebral being: 'He gave one the feeling that after swimming the length of the pool he would have earned the right to drink its contents' (Roth 1959: 14). Such Americanization reaches its apotheosis with the Swede who, in the 'Paradise Remembered' section of the novel, is as unselfconscious about his godlike status as Milton's Adam and Eve.

The first two novels of Roth's American Trilogy repeat the narrative structure of *The Ghost Writer*, with the elderly Zuckerman looking back with irony at his younger self, but with one crucial difference. In both trilogies Zuckerman is a young aesthete who goes in search of authority figures who are characterized by their 'heroic purity' (Roth 1998: 54). But whereas Lonoff is in exile from monumental history ('the Jew who got away') and inspires the young Nathan's diasporism, the mythic heroes in the American Trilogy are tragic figures who evoke the monumental history of postwar America (Americanization, McCarthyism, the Vietnam, Korean and Second World wars, and American racial politics). Amy Bellette personifies this traumatic history in *The Ghost Writer* but, in contrast to the realism of the American Trilogy, her mythic Americanization (the shift from 'Anne Frank' to 'Amy Bellette') is deeply uncertain:

The [diary] came from Amsterdam, I opened it and there it was: my past, myself, my name, *my face intact* – and all I wanted was revenge. . . . It wasn't corpses I was avenging – it was the motherless, fatherless, sisterless, venge-filled, hate-filled, shame-filled, half-flayed seething thing. It was myself. I wanted their Christian tears to run like Jewish blood, for me. I wanted their pity – and in the most pitiless way. And I wanted love, to be loved mercilessly and endlessly, just the way I'd been debased. I wanted my fresh life and fresh body, cleansed and unpolluted. (Roth 1985: 153)

Such perverse purification makes a powerful statement about the connections, in *The Ghost Writer*, between writing, trauma, revenge, abjection and redemption. It is worth remembering that Jean Améry, not unlike Roth's 'Anne Frank', is similarly on the side of Shylock: 'I and others like me are the Shylocks, not only morally condemnable in the eyes of the nations, but already cheated of the pound of flesh too' (Améry 1966: 75). Roth is at his most courageous in unwriting, in the name of Shylockian vengeance, the humanized and universalized 'Anne Frank' who appeared on stage and screen in the 1950s and '60s.[36] He demythologizes an American 'Anne Frank' while retaining an abiding sense of uncertainty concerning the pointedly unresolved status of Amy Bellette, who may simply (or pathologically) be performing the role of her European counterpart. The split between Amy's 'sunny' (Roth 1985: 98) American disposition and her debasement as a 'half-flayed thing' (152) dramatizes this uncertainty without reducing it to the abjection of Roth's late work.

The perverse transfiguring power of Amy Bellette, who refashions the untragic Brenda Patimkin, is writ large in the American Trilogy, which is full of vengeful young women (reversing the Shylockian stereotype of the transformative 'dark beauty') in the guise of Meredith Levov, Sylphid Frame and Delphine Roux. Outside the context of the Holocaust, all of these 'venge-filled, hate-filled, shame-filled' figures are placed at the heart of postwar American history (whether it be the reactionary 1950s, the revolutionary 1960s or the puritanical 1990s), and all attempt to destroy the 'cleansed and unpolluted' world of their fathers. Each of these figures, in their different ways, causes the tragic fall of the novels' heroes by unwittingly exposing the spuriously innocent pastoralism of Roth's protagonists (whether it be the assimilationism of Levov or Coleman Silk or the utopianism of Iron Rinn). To this extent, Jerry Levov's description of his niece is representative: '[Meredith is] the daughter who transports [Seymour] out of the longed for American pastoral and into everything that is its antithesis and its enemy, into the fury, the violence, the desperation of the counterpastoral – into the indigenous American berserk' (Roth 1997: 86). According to the Shylockian stereotype, Jessica, the 'Jew's Daughter', represents the promise of Christian salvation (echoing Spark's Gentile Jewesses) and the transcendence of the grubby materialism and legalism that have led to her father claiming his pound of flesh.[37] Roth's daughters, in stark contrast, could not be less transcendent. When Jerry Levov castigates his brother for living an assimilationist fantasy he states that 'the reality of the place is right up in your kisser now. With the help of your daughter you're as deep in the shit as a man can get, the real American crazy shit. America amok! America amuck!' (277). Such excremental imagery is first introduced when Seymour confronts his daughter, who smells like 'a human being who grubs about for pleasure in its own shit ... a human mess stinking of human waste' (265). Sylphid also 'gives a dose of life's dung' to her mother, which is described pointedly as 'her deepest daughterly inclination' (Roth 1998: 179). One reason why both of these daughters are caricatured is that they have a strong symbolic function, following Amy Bellette, in representing an irredeemable impurity that is most usually associated with the trauma of the Holocaust ('half-flayed'), but that is here associated with the 'counterpastoral' or the 'American berserk'.

Towards the beginning of *American Pastoral*, Zuckerman explicitly articulates the version of impure 'dirty realism' that encompasses the form and content of his 'counterpastorals'. He is imagining giving a speech at his forty-fifth high school reunion where he will once again meet up with the Swede but decides that the speech is too 'ruminative' (Roth 1997: 44). He compares his Weequahic neighbourhood, hyperbolically, with Renaissance Florence to the extent that both domains overwhelm their children with the 'fullness of life'. The 'ocean of details' (42) that results from such an intense upbringing ('Let's remember the energy' [40]) also becomes the raison d'être for Roth's turn to dirty realism in the American trilogy: 'The *detail*, the immensity of detail, the force of the detail, the weight of the detail – the rich endlessness of detail surrounding you in your young life like the six feet of dirt that'll be packed on your grave when you're dead' (42–43). Here, in short, is the narrative method of the trilogy, which contains a wealth of loving detail (remaking Newark in all of its glory, not unlike Joyce remaking Dublin), but whose stories all pointedly conflate 'dirt' with 'detail'. It is, after all, the death of Roth's main protagonists ('the grave') that inspires the elderly Zuckerman to tell his stories. Once again, *Patrimony* gives a clue to Roth's 'dirty realism', where the marshalling of detail to make a book is said to be akin to filling a grave full of dirt. When his father's incontinence causes him to 'beshat [him] self' (Roth 1991: 172), Roth, who 'smelled the shit halfway up the stairs' (171), is overwhelmed by the spread of his father's faeces over everything in the bathroom (172). As he begins to clean, he thinks: 'It's like writing a book . . . I have no idea where to begin' (173). In going beyond his 'disgust' and 'nausea', Roth concludes that there is 'an awful lot of life to cherish' in his father's 'heroic, hapless struggle to cleanse himself' (175). Writing a novel is akin to bringing some kind of order to the stain of life, and it is the conjunction between Jews, impurity and the heroic struggle to 'cleanse' oneself that is Roth's characterization of the untragic diaspora. Perhaps that is why saying the word 'shit' in England is the way 'most people say "Jew"' (Roth 1990: 83).

One of the unusual characteristics of English anti-Semitism in *The Counterlife* is the *foetor judaicus* (or 'Jewish stench'), which has been associated with Jews since the medieval period and influenced *The Merchant of Venice*, reaching its apotheosis in the poetry of T.S. Eliot and Ezra Pound (where Jews, excrement and sliminess are often combined). Such olfactory thinking in the American Trilogy reclaims this history of anti-Semitism and places it on the side of 'life' and 'impurity'.[38] In his interview with Primo Levi, Roth focuses on Levi's description of his Jewishness as a form of 'impurity' and asks if there is a tension between Levi's 'rootedness' and 'impurity' (Roth 2001a: 13) in relation to Italy's wartime racial laws. Levi responds by asking if Roth does not himself feel 'rooted' in the United States while simultaneously saying that he perceives a 'sharp mustard flavour' in his books that he associates with belonging to a 'minority' (13). One of the reasons why *The Human Stain* is the most compelling part of the trilogy is that the associations between Jews, impurity and life ('life, in all its shameless impurity' [Roth 2000: 3]) are both universalized in the figure of Coleman Silk and complicated when Roth, in the 'guise of telling a Jewish story . . . also tells an African American one'.[39]

There are two models of racial discourse in *The Human Stain*, which broadly follow two widely acknowledged but dissonant presences in the novel, Anatole Broyard and Ralph Ellison.[40] The first model, following Broyard loosely, is based on what has been described as 'the great narrative of American impersonation known as racial passing'. This is, needless to say, essentially a 'black and white' story, which, in its earlier incarnations, most often takes a 'tragic' form.[41] This passing narrative of exposure by concealment is summarized by Zuckerman when he notes, on discovery of Coleman Silk's 'real' identity as an African American, that his 'unmasking' makes him 'more of a mystery' than anything else (Roth 2000: 333). But clashing with this tragic narrative is a reprise of the 'inbetween' Jewish identities in Roth's earlier diasporic novels. Here a creative in-betweenness takes the form of Iris Gittelman, Silk's wife, whose 'thicket of important hair' (12) makes her not unlike the hirsute Jews who preceded her, such as Portnoy with his 'kinky black Hebe hair' (Roth 1969: 183). In *American Pastoral* we are told that the hair of Angela Davis, the radical black philosophy professor, 'reminds the Swede of Rita Cohen' (Roth 1997: 157). Iris's hair similarly acts as a bridge between blacks and Jews: 'that sinuous thicket of hair that was far more Negroid than Coleman's' (Roth 2000: 136). Such racialized affiliations can also be found in the figure of Ellison, an important influence on Roth, who welcomed the designation 'black Jew'. While Iris is 'jewishblack', the 'crimped-haired' Coleman is 'blackjewish': 'the small-nosed Jewish type . . . of a light yellowish skin pigmentation . . . of the ambiguous aura of the pale blacks who are some-times taken for white' (15–16).[42]

If Roth were writing in a diasporic mode, then such ambiguities would be, after Joyce, a cause for celebration: 'jewishblack is blackjewish.' Such doubleness goes back to 'Eli, the Fanatic' in *Goodbye, Columbus*, whose eponymous protagonist, when he dons the traditional gabardine worn by the refugees from the Displaced Person Camps, literally '*smelled* the colour of blackness' (Roth 1959: 206). Iris, to be sure, is closely identified with Coleman's pastoral ideal of postethnicity: 'To be two colours instead of one? To walk the streets incognito or in disguise, to be neither this nor that but something inbetween?. . . To her there was nothing frightening about such seeming deformities' (Roth 2000: 130). But Roth, writing in the mode of dirty or tragic realism, places such life-enhancing impurities on the side of death. Jerry, in *American Pastoral*, is utterly dismissive of the Swede's transcendence of race and religion: '[The Swede's wife is] post-Catholic, he's post-Jewish, together they're going to . . . raise little post-toasties' (Roth 1997: 73). In *The Human Stain* such postethnicity, in the figure of Iris, is dismissed as the 'pinnacle' of New York 'Jewish self-infatuation' (Roth 2000: 131) after the Second World War, which Roth also associated with Milton Appel and the *Partisan Review* (Roth 1985: 477). That Iris is 'murdered' (Roth 2000: 12) by the accusation of racism (when Coleman uses the word 'spooks' with regard to two absent black students in his class) demonstrates the time-bound nature of such postwar cosmo-politan self-fashioning.[43] The olfactory thinking, which Roth reclaims, where the impurity of diaspora Jews is universalized as 'the human stain', is here bounded not by the fears generated by European anti-Semitism but by the realities of American racism (the 'smell' of blackness).

From first to last, words kill in *The Human Stain*. This is in stark contrast to *Zuckerman Bound*, which spent nearly a thousand pages demonstrating the ironic distance between Zuckerman's books and the fears generated by them. One cannot take seriously the accusation that Zuckerman has murdered his father by writing *Carnovsky* or has caused a rise in anti-Semitism with the publication of his early stories. The plot of *The Human Stain*, on the other hand, is generated by the lethal use of words, which begins with 'spooks' and ends with Zuckerman being forced to move (before publishing his account of Coleman Silk) lest the murderous Les Farley discover his whereabouts ('I knew that my five years alone in my house here were over' [360]). Playing the role of 'the Jew' in *The Human Stain*, in stark contrast with the game-playing in *Operation Shylock* or *The Counterlife*, has lethal consequences. Silk, Zuckerman concludes, was 'killed as a Jew. Another of the problems of impersonation'

(325). What once was merely theatrical and provisional is here aligned with European histories of anti-Semitism and the traumatic consequences of the Vietnam War.

The final setting of *The Human Stain* goes back to *Henderson the Rain King* and the canonical American fiction that offered an 'arcadian' (Roth 2000: 361) vision of 'serenely unspoiled' (345) whiteness: 'On this empty, ice-whitened stage, the *only* enemy' (346). This 'pure and peaceful' (361) vision, the frozen lake where Farley is ice-fishing, is nonetheless bitterly ironic as Farley ('the *only* enemy') is, as Posnock rightly argues, the pathological version of Coleman Silk's radical individualism going back to Emerson.[44] In the final refiguring of the novel's black/white binaries, Farley, seen from a distance, appears to be a 'tiny spot' on the 'icy white of the lake' (361), not unlike the black hole that he has made in the lake so that he can fish. He tells Zuckerman, in a 'chilling resonance', that it is '*real dark*' (358) under the lake and, in doing so, replaces the promise of an American tabula rasa with an inexorable inner darkness.

The blackening of the 'ice-whitened stage' at the end speaks especially to the unpacking of the novel's title by Faunia Farley: 'we leave a stain, we leave a trail, we leave our imprint. Impurity, cruelty, abuse, error, excrement, semen – there's no other way to be here' (242). The impurities ('excrement') hitherto associated with Jews under the gaze of anti-Semitism are here displaced onto a black and white passing narrative that above all else concerns Coleman Silk's aim to eradicate a racialized blackness: 'to identify himself as white . . . was the most natural thing for someone of his outlook and temperament and skin colour to have done' (120). On the one hand, the slipperiness and emptiness of Coleman Silk, who like Faunia is just 'a blank' (213), align him with the diasporic Zuckerman as a *luftmensch* who is able endlessly to recreate himself. By the end of *The Human Stain*, however, Coleman's story is reduced to a tragic passing narrative, with pointed reference to Classical Greek sources ('the purifying ritual'), and Coleman unable to reveal the one truth (his African-American family) that would exonerate him from the charge of racism. These two competing narratives – one triumphant, one tragic; one Jewish, one black

– are finally resolved by the history of American racism rather than anti-Semitism.

The black and white passing narrative, which ends the novel and replaces the narrative of postwar Jewish self-fashioning, is conveyed to Zuckerman in the earnest and didactic voice of Silk's sister, Ernestine. That she speaks in her father's precise English, taken from 'Chaucer, Shakespeare and Dickens' (92) (each of whom, as we know from *The Counterlife*, is tainted with anti-Semitism), means that the novel ends rather tamely in the form of 'a history lesson', as Jonathan Freedman has argued.[45] The literalism of *The Human Stain*, where words and reality are one and the same, is enacted by Zuckerman at Coleman's graveside when he tells us that he is 'completely seized by [his] story' (Roth 2000: 337) and that 'Coleman Silk's life had become closer to me than my own' (344). Unlike the perversity and vengeance of Meredith Levov, Sylphid Frame and Delphine Roux, Ernestine tells the story of her brother all too conventionally in her father's precise English.

In contrast, *American Pastoral* dismisses Meredith's perverse revolutionary pretensions as a form of 'idiocy' when compared to the actual site of revolution in Fanon's Algeria: '*there is . . . continuity between the woman and the revolutionary. The Algerian woman rises directly to the level of tragedy*'.[46] Meredith, by contrast, merely rises to the 'level of psychosis' (Roth 1997: 261) and such psychosis is associated, dubiously, in the novel with both the anti-Vietnam War protests and the 'purifying' and 'transmogrifying' of Newark in the 1968 riots which leave 'Nothing. Nothing in Newark ever again' (268–69). But if Meredith, Sylphid and Delphine fail to rise to the level of tragedy, unlike their mythic father-figures, Ernestine's story of her brother reinforces the power of narrative realism by blurring life and art: 'the book was [Coleman's] life . . . [his] art was being a white man' (Roth 2000: 345).

As Eric Sundquist has argued, Roth's American Trilogy deliberately reverses the Fanonian binaries between black and Jew, mind and body, ego and id.[47] Roth begins with the whitening of Jews in *American Pastoral*, contrasts this with the victimization of 'blacken[ed]' Jews (Roth 1998: 12) in *I Married a Communist*, and concludes the trilogy with the figure of Coleman Silk, who troubles these Fanonian oppositions (as a 'black' boxer and a 'white' professor of classics). Although *The Human Stain* does complicate a standard passing narrative, Ernestine's unanswerable history of American racism illustrates the inherent difficulties in writing about American anti-Semitism in equivalent terms. The abiding problem that Roth has in his earlier novels is that the history of slavery in the United States, rather than an indigenous American anti-Semitism, is the true analogy to European anti-Semitism. By reimagining American anti-Semitism as the dominant racism in the United States in *The Plot against America* (2004), Roth ignores the implicit question in his diasporic fiction: 'what's the meaning of Jews without anti-Semitism?'[48]

In his second trilogy, Roth Americanizes the monumental history that, in his earlier fiction, is elsewhere. All three novels include 'war, destruction, anti-Semitism, totalitarianism', which finally enables Zuckerman to go beyond his 'dwarf drama' and enter the 'world of massive historical pain' (Roth 1985: 550–51). The abiding problem with this national turn, however, is that Roth cannot decide what kind of American history he is writing. On the one hand, Herman Roth, a fictionalized version of Roth's father, offers an interpretation of history as a universal in *The Plot Against America*: 'History is everything that happens everywhere. Even here in Newark' (Roth 2004a: 180). At the same time, history is particularized by the Rothian narrator as a form of 'terror': 'The terror of the unforeseen is what the science of history hides, turning a disaster into an epic' (114). Unlike the historical chronicler, the novelist focuses on the 'terror of the unforeseen' or the 'disaster' that is Roth's version of pathological 'normalcy' (53) in the form of the pro-Nazi Charles A. Lindbergh as president. Is the history of the United States the same as everywhere else, as Roth argues ('History claims everybody, whether they know it or not and whether they like it or not') or is it that which is truly terrible?[49]

Roth resolves this dilemma by foregrounding a counterfactual history of American anti-Semitism on European lines in *The Plot against America* which, in effect, universalizes American history as a form of terror. When the fictionalized Herman Roth is abused as a 'loudmouth Jew' at the Lincoln Memorial, his embarrassed guide quickly moves him on to the Gettysburg Address where he points to an 'angel of truth freeing a slave'. The young Philip notes that 'my father could see nothing' as he was 'quivering with indignation' (Roth 2004a: 65) at such a public expression of anti-Semitism. After *The Human Stain*, there is clearly a problem with privileging a fantasized history of American anti-Semitism over an actual history of racism and slavery. With the 'race-haters . . . running the show', the radical radio commentator Walter Winchell asks: 'who's next . . . the long-suffering Negroes? The hard-working Italians? . . . Who else among us is no longer welcome in Adolf Lindergh's Aryan America?' (229). But it is precisely such a hierarchy of suffering that Roth avoided in *The Human Stain*, where the marriage between Iris and Coleman 'made sense' as a 'hitherto unknown amalgam of the most unalike of America's historic undesirables' (Roth 2000: 132).

The difference between fantasized and actual suffering, as I have argued, is at the heart of Roth's diasporic fiction, which has rightly been described as 'demystifying the pieties of Jewish American culture'. To this extent, *The Plot against America* 'overturn[s] Roth's entire oeuvre' by taking to an extreme the tragic national narrative in his late fiction.[50] When Alvin loses his leg during the war he distinguishes between two kinds of pain: 'there's pain where you are . . . and there's pain where you ain't' (154). His 'stump', to be sure, is written on the body not unlike the 'half-flayed' Amy Bellette, although this may merely be prosthetic pain. Such ambiguities run counter to the abiding sense of 'catastrophe' (188) or 'perpetual fear' (1) that overwhelm the Roth family. As we have seen, the reason why the ending of the film *Home of the Brave* (1949) made Fanon 'weep' is the too easy universalization of victimhood when a shell-shocked black soldier befriends a white compatriot who has lost a leg: 'The crippled veteran of the Pacific war says to my brother, "Resign yourself to your colour the way I got used to my stump; we're both victims"' (Fanon 1952: 140). To this extent, Alvin's 'stump' universalizes the endless 'torment' (154) of all of America's racial victims which so enraged Fanon.

After his 'bruising' public exchange at Yeshiva University, with Ralph Ellison speaking on behalf of a fellow beleaguered author, Roth comments that this exchange 'constituted not the end of my imagination's involvement with the Jews, let alone an excommunication, but the real beginning of my thralldom ... I was branded' (Roth 1988: 129–30). In a perverse parody of the history of slavery in America, Roth, after his early short stories, is 'branded' and becomes in thrall to his Jewishness ('it was the luckiest break I could have had' [130]). It is perhaps not a coincidence that, when Roth announced his 'retirement' from writing fiction, he argued: 'I don't wish to be a slave any longer to the stringent exigencies of literature.'[51] But such solipsistic imagery merely throws into relief actual histories. *The Plot against America* could not be less transgressive in dutifully bringing the Holocaust home to the United States in the form of an American Kristallnacht and the radical assimilationist programme of the Office of American Absorption. As Clive Sinclair has argued, Roth's intense encounters with Appelfeld and Primo Levi were to act as a brake on his imagination in *The Plot against America*.[52] From a European perspective, these events left 'the Jews essentially unharmed' (324), apart from the loss of an idealized pluralism: 'Something essential had been destroyed and lost, we were being coerced to be other than the Americans we were' (108). Such are the limits of the nation when it is merely a site of appropriation.

Rather than a divide between European and American history, in relation to the Jewish diaspora, history returns to the United States in the guise of an abiding and universalized 'trauma'. One only need compare the bloodshed caused by the Korean War in *Indignation* (2008) with 'The Defender of the Faith' (1959) in *Goodbye, Columbus* to gauge just how far Roth's characters have travelled as traumatized war victims. In the climax to *Indignation*, for instance, the student generation of *Goodbye, Columbus* are told quite explicitly that 'warfare, bombings, wholesale slaughter' will eventually find them out: 'Beyond your fraternities, history unfolds daily – warfare, bombings, wholesale slaughter, and you are oblivious of it all. Well, you won't be oblivious for long! . . . history will catch you in the end. Because history is not the background – history is the stage! And you are *on* the stage' (Roth 2008: 222). In *The Plot against America* the young Philip, up to his neck in history, learns to value family, community and nation, and concludes that 'motherless and fatherless you are vulnerable to manipulation, to influences – you are rootless and vulnerable to every-thing' (Roth 2004: 358). The orphans and isolates in this novel are rootless and vulnerable because the history of suffering and trauma has finally come home to deform the nation and family, with the United States trans-formed into a motherless and fatherless 'stump'. To this extent, *The Plot against America* is rightly described as a post–9/11 novel and, unlike the American Trilogy, it became a bestseller in the United States. The main reason for this popularity, I suspect, reinforced by Roth's canonization and embrace by President Obama, is that the mood of a traumatized body politic after 9/11 is unfortunately captured in his late fiction. These novels are chock-full of deformed bodies, from Consuela Castillo in *The Dying Animal* to Bucky Cantor in *Nemesis* (2010), who return the reader – quite literally in *Exit Ghost* (2007) – to the original 'half-flayed' Amy Bellette and the possibility of individual and national redemption through suffering.

But the rise of an authoritarian and racist American government in *The Plot against America* leaves 'undramatized the effects on blacks', which reinforces a model of 'white' European history, and post-Holocaust European trauma, not least in the maimed Jewish and Hispanic bodies that populate the late fictions.[53] In this spirit of unironic appropriation – from medieval Christendom to contemporary Europe – Roth's late work enacts repeatedly the replacement of pastoral innocence (in its many forms) by an overwhelming sense of Holocaust-inflected suffering and anguish. *Nemesis*, Roth's supposed last novel, subtly refigures the history of anti-Semitism as the polio epidemic of 1941, which precisely unites the fate of European and American Jews, according to the polio-ridden narrator, in a single tragedy: 'Because this was real war too, a war of slaughter, ruin, waste, and damnation, war with the ravages of war – war upon the children of Newark' (Roth 2010: 132). As with Roth's version of anti-Semitism as a *foetor judaicus* or 'Jewish stench' in *The Counterlife* and beyond, we are told that polio 'gets in the air and you open your mouth and breathe it in' (59), which is why the 'anti-Semites are saying that it's because they're Jews that polio spreads there' (193). Here the impurity of the diaspora, where stories collide and plural versions of history compete with each other, is replaced by the traumatized nation where, finally, the air that you breathe is indistinguishable from the 'disease' that once infected the continent of Europe. As we will now see, Salman Rushdie has also breathed this impure air in his fiction and, like Roth, has never been quite sure whether the power of his imagination could overcome such a stench.

6

Diaspora and Postcolonialism
Salman Rushdie and the Jews

'NO PARTITION OR ELSE PERDITION! MUSLIMS ARE THE JEWS OF ASIA!' Salman Rushdie, *Midnight's Children* (1981), p. 72.

' "You're Jewish", he pointed out. "I was brought up to have views on Jews." ' Salman Rushdie, *The Satanic Verses* (1988), p. 60.

A few months after the fatwa calling for his assassination as an apostate, there was a large demonstration in Hyde Park urging Salman Rushdie and his publishers to withdraw *The Satanic Verses* (1988). Alongside the banners abusing him as a 'devil' or 'son of Satan' there was an effigy of Rushdie 'affixed to the body of a pig'.[1] This grotesque figure wore devil horns, was placed next to a gallows and had a Star of David around its neck. As Malise Ruthven has noted, the 'Star of David testified to the view . . . that the whole Rushdie affair was a Zionist plot to undermine Islam' (Ruthven 2). According to this 'international capitalist-Jewish conspiracy' (Rushdie 1991: 393), the governments of Europe and the United States colluded with the so-called 'Jewish' publisher, Penguin Books, to pay Rushdie to denigrate Islam.[2] Radio Tehran reported Ayatollah Khomeini's view that *The Satanic Verses* was the 'result of years of effort by American, European and Zionist so-called experts on Islam' to find the 'best way to insult and undermine Islam's highest values and traditions' (Appignanesi and Maitland 206). Such conspiratorial thinking, combined with the transformation of Rushdie into a pig and a devil-figure in London's Hyde Park, represents a surprisingly comprehensive rehash of the motifs that make up the history of European anti-Semitism.[3] Rushdie's *Joseph Anton: A Memoir* (2012), an account of his 'wasted' ten years in hiding after the fatwa, shows the extent to which these discourses were to shape his experience.[4]

But it would be a mistake to assume that the racialization of Rushdie as a Jew is the result of a 'widely-held' Muslim anti-Semitism, in response to the fatwa, as Ruthven contends (Ruthven 2). From the earliest critical reception of his work, Rushdie has been characterized crudely as a deracinated cosmopolitan – one of Frantz Fanon's 'race of angels' (Fanon 1961: 167) – who, in stark contrast to Fanon, has supposedly refused the role of the revolutionary 'organic intellectual'.[5] As we have seen in the case of Fanon, the accusation of being 'colourless, stateless, rootless' (Fanon 1961: 167) was imbricated with the figure of the cosmopolitan Jew. Such itinerant figures, detached from an anti-colonial national struggle, were to be routinely castigated by one strand of postcolonial criticism, using the Orwellian distinction between the principled 'exile' and depthless 'vagrant', to denigrate Rushdie (and elsewhere Edward Said) as 'vagrants'.[6] Only since Khomeini's death sentence has Rushdie's 'vagrancy' 'turned, paradoxically and tragically, into full-scale exile' (Ahmad 157). But even after this lethal turn, Rushdie's 'inability to believe in any community of actual praxis' (159), his rootlessness, is still condemned as unprincipled and weightless. In the wake of such attacks, Rushdie comments bitterly that two 'socialist intellectuals', John Berger and Paul Gilroy, had blamed the victim and accused him of creating his own 'tragedy' as he had 'misjudge[d] the people' (Rushdie 2012: 179) or, as Gilroy put it quaintly, the 'world of ordinary folk'.[7]

The characterization of Rushdie as a 'self-hating, deracinated Uncle-Tom' (Rushdie 1991: 393), devoid of any historical, political or communal depth, is not unlike the dismissal of Philip Roth's 'thin personal culture' by Irving Howe.[8] One way of reading Roth's 'tragic' (pre- and post-9/11) version of American history is as a means of overcoming Howe's charge of being deracinated and self-hating in the 'diasporic' fictions. It is not a coincidence, in this regard, that the first public words that were heard from Rushdie after going into hiding, which were not a direct response to the fatwa, turned out to be a review of Philip Roth's *The Facts: A Novelist's Autobiography* (1988). Published in the *Observer* newspaper, twelve days after the fatwa, this review was subsequently reprinted in *Imaginary Homelands* and was Rushdie's first literary reappearance following the international maelstrom caused by the call for his assassination.[9] In the review, Rushdie identifies himself with Roth at the moment when, at the conference at Yeshiva University in New York, Roth realized that he was 'not just opposed but hated' (Roth 1988: 127) after the publication of *Goodbye, Columbus* (1959). In an unusually personal note, Rushdie writes as a 'similarly beleaguered writer' who finds it 'very moving, even helpful', to read Roth's 'responses to being so vilified'. The extent to which Rushdie channels his own experience through that of Roth is obvious from the review:

> I was able to recognize in myself the curious lethargy, the soporific torpor that overcomes Roth while he is under attack; to recognize, too, the stupid humiliated rage that leads him to cry: 'I'll never write about Jews again!' And when the anger passes, and he understands the 'most bruising public exchange of my life constituted not the end of my imagination's involvement with the Jews, let alone an excommunication, but the beginning of my thraldom. . . . My humiliation was the luckiest break I could have had. I was branded' – then there, too, he seems to speak directly, profoundly, not only to, but *for*, me. (Rushdie 1991: 347)

Roth, unsurprisingly, has pointed out that the 'tiny turbulence' caused by *Goodbye, Columbus* is hardly comparable with the international crisis precipitated by the publication of *The Satanic Verses* nearly three decades later.[10] Nonetheless, what is interesting about the review is Rushdie's willingness to let Roth speak *for* him, as he puts it, and to identify with Roth as a Jewish writer under attack by his own ostensible community of readers. It is perhaps not a coincidence, in this regard, that the earliest version of *Midnight's Children*, as a 'vulgar' satire of Indira Gandhi, was based loosely on Roth's *Our Gang* (1971), a scurrilous caricature of Richard Nixon ('Tricky and his Friends') (Rushdie 2012: 51). What I want to show in this chapter is that these forms of imaginative crossovers (seeing similarities in dissimilars) can be traced back to Rushdie's earliest fiction and essays and forward to his later novels.

The Limits of the Imagination: Rushdie's *Grimus*

Rushdie's first novel *Grimus* (1975), a work of science fiction, is rightly regarded as an 'allegorical narrative of how the imagination can seek to detach itself from reality and create a "world" of its own'.[11] In these terms, Grimus is a writer manqué whose use of the Stone Rose to create 'Calf Island' out of his own consciousness exposes the limits and abuses of the imagination. Following Naipaul in *The Mimic Men* (1967), and here also in a mode that refuses a too easy identification, Rushdie evokes recent events in Europe through the eponymous 'prisoner of war' who, after being captured, feared 'every day . . . I would be killed. . . . It was an expert torture' (Rushdie 1975: 238). By his 'accents' Grimus was 'evidently Middle-European, a refugee no doubt' (208), and the link between his traumatic wartime experiences and his overweening imagination are made explicit in a final summation:

> The undermining horror of [the] prison camp, the destruction of his
> human dignity, of his belief in the whole human race; the subsequent
> burrowing away, away from the world, into books and philosophies
> and mythologies, until these became his realities, these his friends and
> companions, and the world was just an awful nightmare; the monkish
> man finding beauty in birds and stories. (243)

One of the main lessons that Grimus learnt after his experience in the camps, and which helped him to survive, is that he 'wanted to be the one to organize my life' (238), and it is the Stone Rose that enables him to 'shape a world and a life and a death exactly as he wanted' (243). There is a strand of Rushdie criticism that has read Grimus's sterile 'country of the mind',[12] known as Calf Island, as speaking for Rushdie himself: 'It would be hard to find a novel that demonstrated better the truth of Fanon's claim that a culture that is not national is meaningless' (Brennan 70).But what is missing from this dismissal of Rushdie's non-national fiction (as if Fanon were an unthinking nationalist) is any sense of the novel itself challenging an utterly constructed 'Grimushome' where 'Grimus-consciousness' is confused with 'self-consciousness' (Rushdie 1975: 222) or where the world is merely an extension of the imagination.

The novel's protagonist 'Flapping Eagle' precisely resists the 'Grimus Effect' (177) while simultaneously being portrayed as Grimus's double ('grim-us'), to the extent that he has also been compared to a Wandering Jew (Grant 2012: 35). When they finally meet, in the last section of the book, Flapping Eagle is told: 'Your face is as like the face of Grimus as his own reflection. Younger-looking, paler, but so, so similar. Did you not know that was what attracted him to you in the first place?' (Rushdie 1975: 205). That Grimus and Flapping Eagle are doubles structures the novel, which begins with Flapping Eagle attempting suicide; after he is saved and guided by the aptly named Virgil Jones, he is known initially as Born-From-Dead. As an American Indian or 'Axona', he is, like the European-Jewish Grimus, part of a people who have recently been very nearly annihilated. Both figures are shape-shifters – Grimus a 'master of disguise' (206); Flapping Eagle a *'chameleon'* (31) – and are thus fantastically hybridized. Flapping Eagle, known at this point as 'Joe-Sue', is described as unusually pale-skinned ('the Axona are a dark-skinned race') and a freakish 'hermaphrodite' who was 'an exile in an isolated community'. The *'whiteness'* (18) of Flapping Eagle is contrasted with the darkness of Grimus, who changed his name from 'something unpronounceable' (209) when he migrated over thirty years ago.[13] The latter's adopted name derives anagrammatically from the Simurg, a mythical bird that originates from Sufism, a branch of Islamic mysticism: 'There is a Sufi poem in which thirty birds set out to find the Simurg on the mountain where he lives. When they reach the peak, they find that they themselves are, or rather have become, the Simurg. The name, you see, means Thirty Birds. Si, thirty. Murg, birds. . . . The name of the Mountain of Kaf' (209). Brennan rightly notes that Calf Island (an extension of the Mountain of Kaf) is located 'between Orient and Occident' which, given the Western and Eastern influences of the novel, becomes a 'symbolic typography' (Brennan 70). After all, the Mountain of Kaf (using the Arabic and Hebraic letter Kaf) is 'bastardize[d]' (Rushdie 1975: 211) to Calf ('Fatted? Golden?') and also becomes the City of K (which Grimus invents) and relates back to Kafka and a Middle European modernist tradition. Both Flapping Eagle and Grimus are *looking for a suitable voice to speak in*' (32) or have the 'memory of a man searching for a voice to speak in' (236), which is why Flapping Eagle is part of Grimus's 'grand design': 'by shaping you to my grand design I remade you completely as if you had been unmade clay.' To this end, Grimus rewrites the myth of the Simurg so that it becomes a Phoenix myth – 'Through death, the annihilation of the self, the Phoenix passes its selfhood on to its successor' (233) – and so Grimus tricks Flapping Eagle into replacing him after he dies.

The final part of *Grimus* charts the struggle of Flapping Eagle to retain a sense of selfhood and autonomy in the face of Grimus's 'grand design', which is why it is a mistake to reduce Flapping Eagle metaphorically to the figure of the Wandering Jew. Flapping Eagle refuses to succumb to Grimus's stratagems as they are utterly cerebral: 'You are so far removed from the pains and torments of the world you left and the world you made that you can even see death as an academic exercise. You can plan your own death as a perfect game of chess' (236). In his defence, Grimus recounts his wartime experiences (and the reasons for creating a city of immortals) but Flapping Eagle significantly refuses to be assimilated into

Grimus's particular European history of suffering which overdetermines the mind and eschews the body:

> The mind of Grimus, rushing through. The mandarin monk released into me an orgasm of thinking. The halfbreed semi-semitic prisoner of war and his contradictions, the aportance of self-coexisting with the utter necessity of imparting that self, cruel necessity, ineluctable, the mind of Grimus rushing through. Like a beating of wings his self flying in. *My son, my son, what father fathered a son like this, as I do in my sterility.* (243)

The merging of Grimus and Flapping Eagle highlights paradoxically a dominant Judaeo-Christianity made up of the 'halfbreed semi-semitic prisoner of war', constructed as a Hebraic God, and the Christ-like son played by Flapping Eagle: '*My son, my son, what father fathered a son like this, as I do in my sterility.*' By the time of *Midnight's Children*, Saleem Sinai embodies a Judaeo-Christian tradition originating on Mount Sinai in a less oppositional fashion. In this novel, the Judaeo-Christian synthesis prefigures the hoped-for peaceful coexistence of Hindus and Muslims after Indian independence in 1947 (with Saleem's name echoing the Urdu, Arabic and Hebrew words for 'peace'). In *Grimus*, however, the Judaeo-Christian synthesis unravels as it is the Hebraic God, rather than the Christian son, who speaks. But Flapping Eagle resists such silencing by destroying the Stone Rose (the source of Grimus's power) and by foregrounding the body over the mind in making love as Calf Mountain de-evolves.

One way of reading *Grimus* is as a Fanonian allegory that, in the end, privileges the body over the mind or a concrete sense of place (subject to the forces of history) over a 'sterile' ahistorical imaginary homeland. Such an allegory also privileges colonial histories of suffering (located spatially) over indigenous European histories (located temporally) and enacts the kinds of anxieties that we have seen in the formation of postcolonial studies while excluding the colonized figure of 'the Jew'.[14] That Flapping

Eagle refuses to be assimilated into Grimus's traumatic post-Holocaust creations refers, implicitly at least, to the postcolonial rethinking of the history of ghettoization, minoritization and diaspora beyond its Jewish antecedents. Not unlike Flapping Eagle, Rushdie, in his essays and interviews, describes himself as both 'pale-skinned' – 'my freak fair skin' (Rushdie 1991: 18) – and as an internal exile: 'a member of an Indian Muslim family in [largely Hindu] Bombay, then part of a "mohajir" – migrant family – in Pakistan, and now as a British Asian'. It was from this minority perspective (in a 'minority group all my life' [4]) that Rushdie delivered his literary manifesto, 'Imaginary Homelands'. But Rushdie's fiction, unlike his essays, tends to question, rather than merely celebrate, such imaginary homelands.

To be sure, as Brennan has argued, *Grimus* lacks a '*habitus*' (Brennan 70), or concrete locale, but it is precisely this lack that Rushdie explores, most especially through the figure of the Gorfs who are unable to go beyond word-play ('The gorfic obsession with anagram-making') and who attempt to control Flapping Eagle through the 'Divine Game of Ordering' (Rushdie 1975: 64). That the novel interrogates the Eurocentric limits of such imaginative game-playing, divorced from actuality, makes possible *Midnight's Children* (1981) and *Shame* (1983), which are both 'handcuffed to history' (Rushdie 1981: 11). It is for this reason that Rushdie, as he puts it, 'had to reject *Grimus* to write *Midnight's Children*'.[15] But if Saleem Sinai follows Flapping Eagle, the first of Rushdie's 'mental travellers' (Grant 2012: 29), then Grimus, a Jewish patriarch and victim of European barbarity who embraces unequivocally the power of world-making divorced from reality, will also reappear in *The Satanic Verses* (1988), *The Moor's Last Sigh* (1995) and *Shalimar the Clown* (2005). That Grimus is murdered brutally in Rushdie's first novel, and denied a death of his own choosing, signifies the limits of an overweening (albeit traumatically induced) imagination. Taking Grimus's experiences as a 'Middle-European refugee' as his starting point, Rushdie, I will now argue, both doubles and redoubles the minority history of his Indian migrants by juxtaposing it with that of their Jewish 'secret sharers'.

'It was next best to Kosher': *The Satanic Verses*

To mark the publication of *The Satanic Verses*, Rushdie talked to Sean French about the differences between his latest novel and his previous two novels:

> *The Satanic Verses* is very big. There are certain kinds of architecture that are dispensed with. *Midnight's Children* had history as a scaffolding on which to hang the book; this one doesn't. And since it's so much about transformation I wanted to write it in such a way that the book itself was metamorphosing all the time. Obviously the danger is that the book falls apart. (quoted Appignanesi and Maitland 8)

While much of *The Satanic Verses* is about the transformation of the two migrants at the heart of the book, Rushdie, as he indicates in this interview, is aware of the dangers of being consumed by the incoherence of these transformations. This check on the ideal of limitless diasporic transfiguration, as against grave histories of suffering and victimhood, is particularly embodied in the ancient and contemporary Cone (Cohen) family in the novel. This 'Jewish strain' (Goonetilleke 82) has tended to be downplayed in most readings of the book, which are, understandably, shaped by the 'Rushdie Affair' (the global response to the novel). The main problem with this, as others have argued, is that the novel has tended to be reduced to a work about Islam, as if this had been Rushdie's prime concern.[16] What is more, Rushdie's response to the purifying rage that surrounded the novel tended to be equally reductive in its own terms, stressing the novel as a paean of praise to 'our mongrel selves':

> *The Satanic Verses* celebrates hybridity, impurity, intermingling, the transformation that comes of new and unexpected combinations of human beings, cultures, ideas, politics, movies, songs. It rejoices in mongrelisation and fears the absolutism of the Pure. Melange, hotchpotch, a bit of this and a bit of that is *how newness enters the world*. It

is the great possibility that mass migration gives to the world, and I
have tried to embrace it. . . . It is a love song to our mongrel selves.
(Rushdie 1991: 394)

Rushdie's celebratory reading of *The Satanic Verses* is understandable as a
response to the wilful misreadings or misrepresentations of his novel that
constituted the Rushdie Affair. But his counterreading ignores precisely
his sense of 'danger' in embracing 'hybridity, impurity, intermingling' as
absolutes and as the only possible response to mass migration. Here I
agree with Robert Eaglestone who has argued that there are two unresolved narrative in Rushdie's fiction – one 'bleak, rooted conservative',
the other open and liberal, 'hybrid [and] migrant' – which explore the
tensions between exile and diaspora, an imaginative embrace of the
weightlessness of migrancy and a countervailing understanding that foregrounds the determining gravity of history.[17] What makes *The Satanic
Verses* such an important novel is that it, precisely, questions Rushdie's
own stated assumptions and offers competing versions of migration and
the migrant which are not as easily resolved as his authorial reading would
allow.

At the beginning of the Ayesha section of the novel, the narrator distinguishes crucially between 'an exile' and 'all the other words that people
throw around: "émigré, expatriate, refugee, immigrant"': 'Exile is a dream
of glorious return. Exile is a vision of revolution: Elba, not St Helena'
(Rushdie 1988: 205). It is the Imam, in these terms, who is the quintessential exile: 'His home is a rented flat. It is a waiting room, a photograph,
air' (206). Rushdie shapes *The Satanic Verses* around the contrast between
the migrant and the exile and a host of distinctions taken from these two
differing conditions. While the exile dreams of a 'glorious return' to an
autochthonous homeland, the migrant is a 'vagabond, wandering, unsettled condition' as suggested in the epigraph to the novel. This is why the
epigraph is taken from Daniel Defoe's *The Political History of the Devil*
(1726), which describes Satan (not unlike the Marxian caricature of
Rushdie) as the quintessential 'vagrant': 'he is . . . without any fixed place,

or space, [that] allowed him to rest the sole of his foot upon.' What is more, while the exiled Imam can make a temporary 'home' out of 'air', Satan, as a consequence of his 'angelic nature', creates a 'kind of empire in the liquid waste or air' (Rushdie 1988: n.p; Defoe 58). Both exile and migrant are, in other words, *luftmenschen* or air-men, which is where, of course, *The Satanic Verses* begins.

The literal and metaphorical *luftmenschen*, Gibreel Farishta and Saladin Chamcha, are introduced floating through the air, after their Boeing aircraft explodes, which signifies memorably their historical weightlessness. The free-floating doubled and redoubled protagonists are initially merged into one ('Gibreelsaladin Farishtachamcha') and are condemned to an 'endless but also ending angelicdevilish fall' (5). This is, we are told, the first of their many transmutations caused by their enforced migration from Bombay to London.[18] As the novel progresses, these characters become radically individualized as polar opposites – angel and devil, purity and impurity, exile and migrant:

> Should we say that these are fundamentally different *types* of self? Might we not agree that Gibreel ... has wished to remain, to a large degree, *continuous* – that is, joined to and arising from his past ... whereas Saladin Chamcha is a creature of *selected* discontinuities, a *willing* re-invention; his *preferred* revolt against history being what makes him, in our chosen idiom, 'false'? ... While Gibreel, to follow the logic of our chosen terminology, is to be considered 'good' by virtue of *wishing to remain*, for all his vicissitudes, at bottom an untranslated man. (427)

As the devilish narrative voice makes clear, such distinctions rest on the 'fantastic notion' of a 'homogenous, non-hybrid, "pure"' (427) self as fundamentally unchanging. This is why Gibreel, as exile, is 'continuous' with the past but embraces a deadening form of truth. Saladin, on the other hand, is a weightless migrant whose partial and plural transformations are merely aesthetic or 'false'. Unlike Gibreel, who reasserts the authority of the father, Saladin's slimy presence disrupts all certainties. Rushdie, as we have seen, celebrates such cultural transformations, brought about by mass migration, as a homage to our impure 'mongrel selves' (Rushdie 1991: 394). But when Saladin is transformed into a cloven-hoofed devil, he appears to return to the distinction between Lucretius and Ovid evoked by Rushdie in the novel. Here Lucretius is on the side of metamorphosis (where the self is split into old and new) whereas Ovid stands for a sense of the essential, immutable self that cannot, fundamentally, be transfigured. This is a reworking of the tension between religious and aesthetic forms of conversion in Muriel Spark's fiction, although the unresolved nature of these radically different types of transformation throws Saladin into despair: 'This is pretty cold comfort. ... Either I accept Lucretius and conclude that some demonic and irreversible mutation is taking place in my inmost depths, or I go with Ovid and concede that everything now emerging is no more than a manifestation of what was already there' (Rushdie 1988: 277). But the distinction in the novel, between Ovidian essence and Lucretian plurality, purity and impurity, religious and secular ways of perceiving the world, is not straightforwardly 'mapped' onto the novel (Eaglestone 2004: 97). On the one hand, we have the underlying contrast between Gibreel as an angelic 'untranslated man', whose exile is '*continuous*' (Rushdie 1988: 427) with the past, and Saladin, whose enforced metamorphosis into a devil-figure, reflecting the racism of English society, is, finally, just one of his many transfigurations as a migrant. While the exile of Gibreel, following the figure of the Imam, leads him unconsciously to the origins of Islam, Saladin remains the eternal migrant who, not unlike Defoe's history of the devil, is 'without any fixed place, or space'. But these somewhat comforting oppositions are also disrupted by the novel's devilish narrator.

Building on the deep Western cultural linkages between Jews and devils, *The Satanic Verses* inserts the experience of Jewish migration and persecution into the binary account of contemporary Indian migration and the origins of Islam.[19] This takes a variety of forms, focusing on the Jewish migratory presence in London and Jahilia, the post-Holocaust perspective of Otto Cone and his wife, Alicja, and the desirability of two Jewesses, Alleluia Cone and Mimi Mamoulian. This 'Jewish strain' is highlighted at a key moment in the novel, also a focus of intense controversy, when the author Salman the Persian 'pollut[es] the word of God with my own profane language' (Rushdie 1988: 367) by replacing the word 'Christian' with the word 'Jew' (before their utopian synthesis as 'Judeo-Christian') in the 'satanic verses' of the Koran (368). This 'devilment, changing verses' (367), remains unnoticed by 'Mahmoud' and is therefore proof positive that Islam was authored and interpreted by man rather than God. It is well known that this reimagining was the catalyst for the 'Rushdie Affair' and for the enforced exile of Salman Rushdie. But that the 'satanic verses' foreground the relationship between Muslims and Jews (anticipating *The Moor's Last Sigh*), rather than Muslims and Christians, is much less discussed.[20] In this extraordinarily transgressive reading, 'the Jew' is on the side of the devil – the migrant, the impure, the unhoused – and this reading remains radically unresolved in the novel.

It is the figure of Otto Cone who, paradoxically, bridges the ancient and contemporary worlds by rejecting the 'idea of the continuum' as the 'most dangerous of all the lies we are fed'. Anyone, he argues, who believes that this 'most beautiful and most evil of planets is somehow homogenous, composed only of reconcilable elements, that it *all adds up*', needs a 'straightjacket tailor': 'The world is incompatible, just never forget it. . . . Ghosts, Nazis, saints, all alive at the same time; in one spot, blissful happiness, while down the road the inferno. You can't ask for a wilder place.' Cone, like Grimus, is a 'survivor of a wartime prison camp whose name was never mentioned' (295), who thus embodies the utter powerlessness of the victimized migrant. His wife comments to their daughter: 'you could say your father's life didn't go to plan. . . . In this century . . . character isn't destiny any more. Economics is destiny. Ideology is destiny. Bombs are destiny. What does a famine, a gas chamber, a grenade care how you lived your life?' (432). In one reading of *The Satanic Verses*, the perspective of Otto Cone, arising from his historical experience, can be placed at the heart of the book. After all, his belief that the 'modern city is the locus classicus of incompatible realities' (314) is writ large in the novel, which, from the beginning, attempts to lessen the distance between two incompatible modern cities, London and Bombay ('the distance between cities is always small' [41]). What is more, his rejection of the idea of a 'continuum' between place (nation and exile) or across time (the belief that timeless religious values exist outside history) places him firmly on the side of modernist fragmentation, as opposed to ancient continuities, and against the idea of an Ovidian essential self.

But, almost as soon as Otto Cone is introduced, Rushdie ruthlessly undermines him, even though he champions Otto's anti-essentialist credo in his essays.[21] Not unlike Grimus, who advocates the impure imagination above all else, Otto represents the 'mongrel self' taken to its deranged limits. The frequently 'appalling' (296) Otto turns out to resolve his sense of unchecked rootlessness by becoming a 'melting-pot man' (298) who, echoing Saladin's attempted acculturation into Englishness, is utterly assimilationist. He changes his name from Cohen to Cone and rejects his Polish mother tongue, which he believes, following George Steiner in relation to the German language, to be 'irredeemably polluted' after the camps.[22] The result is that he turns into a 'pantomime member of the English gentry' who, with his strong East European accent, sounds not unlike Rushdie's Anglo-Indian migrants: 'Silly mid-off? Pish-Tush! Widow of Windsor! Bugger all' (297). He celebrates the 'English rite' of Christmas by dressing up as a 'pantomime Chinee' crying 'Father Christmas is dead! I have killed him!' (296). The repetition of the adjective 'pantomime' indicates the limits of Otto's heterogeneous credo where the self is caricatured and is nothing more than parody.

But, soon after this caricature, we learn that 'Otto Cone as a man of seventy-plus jumped into an empty lift-shaft and died' (298). This is a clear reference to the not dissimilar suicide of Primo Levi, who died a year before the publication of The Satanic Verses.[23] Otto's hybrid self is either utterly lampooned or associated with an overwhelming grief. To this extent, he is the very personification of irreconcilability as he, paradoxically, does not allow the novel to rest (pace Rushdie's essays) on the professed values of intermingling and discontinuity that he articulates so forcefully.

That the Jewish migrant, and his experience of the camps, should expose the limits of a celebratory postmodernism (a 'society capable only of pastiche') is reinforced throughout the novel by the death of his daughters, Allie and Elena Cone, and the scepticism of another Jewish woman Mimi, who comments to Saladin: 'We had exploitation when you – plural were running round in skins. Try being Jewish, female and ugly sometimes. You'll beg to be black. Excuse my French: brown'. That these Jewish characters are overwhelmed by death and suffering, against the 'flattened' world of 'postmodernist critiques of the West' (261), acts as an important break on the authorial argument that the novel concerns just devil-may-care impurity. Allie Cone enacts this distancing from the novel's moralized oppositions by climbing Mount Everest, where she can 'escape from good and evil', in the belief that 'all the truth' will float up to the top of the mountain: '[the truth] just upped and ran away from those cities where even the stuff under our feet is all made up, a lie. . . . It's up there all right. I've been there. Ask me' (313). Not unlike Grimus, who attempts to shape reality while sitting on top of a mountain, Allie, according to Robert Clark, 'stands for a meaning which lies beyond the arguments and manipulations of the satanic narrator'.[24] Her search for truth, beyond the merely imaginary, is redoubled after her father's 'betrayal of his own act of survival' (Rushdie 1988: 299) but ends similarly with her death.

This search for authenticity is reinforced by Allie's mother who, soon after her husband's suicide, rejects his superficial 'imitation of life': 'After his death she went straight back to Cohen, the synagogue, Chanukah and Bloom's' (298). What is more, Alicja recedes into a 'kind of Singer Brothers dybbukery, and her mysticism never failed to exasperate her pragmatic, mountain-climbing daughter' (301). Rushdie had reviewed Isaac Bashevis Singer, in an essay collected in *Imaginary Homelands*, and refers to him again towards the end of the novel as a writer who had rejected 'angels and devils – who needed them?' (408). This strain of Jewish mysticism, or

Kabbalism, which informed Singer's fiction and is closely related to
Rushdie's beloved Sufism, is earlier compared with a more Manichaean
version of Islam:

> light versus dark, evil versus good, may be straightforward enough in
> Islam ... but go back a bit and you see it's a pretty recent fabrication.
> Amos, eighth century BC, asks: 'Shall there be evil in a city and
> the Lord hath not done it?' Also Jahweh, quoted by Deutero-Isaiah
> two hundred years later, remarks: 'I form the light, and create
> darkness; I make peace and create evil; I the Lord do all these things.'[25]
> (323).

Not unlike Bellow, Paley, Roth and Singer, who provided Rushdie with a
contemporary model of Jewish literature that was also secular and univer-
salistic, the ancient Judaic Kabbalistic tradition is taken as a means of
throwing the more recent Manichaean foundations of Islam (as opposed
to the Sufist version of Islamic mysticism) into disarray.[26] The opposition
between Gibreel and Saladin can be said to be inflected by this mystical
Judaizing ambivalence, going back to Salman the Persian and his
foregrounding of 'Jew' over 'Christian'. On the one hand, we have
Gibreel's search for clarity and redemption which returns us to the
purifying Islam of the Imam: 'No more of these English-induced ambiguities, these Biblical-Satanic confusions! – Clarity, clarity, at all costs
clarity!' (353). His plea for unbiblical clarity is aimed especially at the
acculturating Saladin, a mimic man who has failed to decolonize his mind
and has become 'self-hating, constructing a false ego, autodestructive'. To
this end, Gibreel evokes Frantz Fanon – 'The native is an oppressed person
whose permanent dream is to become the persecutor' – but finds that
Fanon does not offer enough clarity: 'It occurred to [Gibreel] that he
was forever joined to the adversary [Saladin], their arms locked
around one another's bodies, mouth to mouth, head to tail, as when they
fell to earth, when they *settled*' (353). No longer able to separate angel and
devil, light from dark, inside from outside, Fanon is read, once again, as a

troubling, migrant cosmopolitan who can no longer offer the desired clarity.

Steven Connor has argued influentially that at this point in the novel the 'very distinction between distinction (Gibreel) and indistinction (Saladin) is compromised' (Connor 119). The novel's third way takes the form of Allie Cone. Following her 'father's faith in the myriad and contradictory possibilities of life' (Rushdie 1988: 302), Allie acts as a bridge between Gibreel and Saladin, to the extent that she is described as the 'third point in the triangle of fictions' (437). She becomes increasingly important in the novel as an object of female desire and as an alternative to the masculine certainties that perpetuate a foundational Islam. For all her dislike of her mother's mysticism, Allie thinks of the 'goddess-mountain' Everest in Kabbalistic terms: 'the mountain was diabolic as well as transcendent, or, rather, its diabolism and transcendence were one'. Just as her father was on the side of discontinuity, where opposites collide, Allie thinks of Everest as the 'land's attempt to metamorphose into sky; it is grounded flight, the earth mutated – nearly – into air, and become, in the true sense, exalted' (303). But, as with Otto, this sense of exaltation ('Allelulia, her very name an exaltation' [458]) is undermined when she falls to her death from the roof of a skyscraper. Unlike Gibreel and Saladin, Allie is an unlucky 'faller' (546) who lacks the weightlessness of the postcolonial migrant.

Throughout the novel Allie's extravagant whiteness ('the miracle of her skin' [195]) acts as a tabula rasa on which the fantasies of Gibreel and Saladin can be projected. Known as the 'snow maiden' or 'icequeen', Allie is an abiding figure of desire who is 'invented', not unlike the Sartrean Jew, so as to become the 'fiction's antagonist' (428). The Cone family are examples of previous British migrants successfully making things anew: 'not all migrants are powerless. . . . They impose their needs on their new earth, bringing their own coherence to the new-found land, imagining it afresh.' But soon after this celebratory account of migration, the narrator sounds a note of alarm: 'But look out, the city warns. Incoherence, too, must have its day' (458). Rushdie's London ('Ellowen Deeowen') is divided between the 'purifying' (468) riots of Brickhall and the cosmopolitan admixture of the East End of London, where a Muslim migrant is described as 'a brown Jew' (300) and where Halal food is the 'next best to Kosher' (184). After Otto's death, Alicja spends a great deal of time in Bloom's Kosher restaurant in East London but, rather than resolving the city's incoherence (by reconstructing a purely Jewish sense of identity), she merely throws the confusion of London into relief. After all, if 'Nazis' and 'saints' exist simultaneously, as Otto above all maintained, then it makes no sense for her just to focus on one side of this divide.

The deaths of Otto and Allie make it impossible to offer a merely celebratory account of a cosmopolitan Englishness, as many critics have argued.[27] While the avenging Gibreel enacts the 'exile' and return to the father(land), he follows Otto and Allie by putting a 'barrel of the gun into his mouth and pull[ing] the trigger; [he] was free' (546): 'if the old refused to die, the new could not be born' (547). Gibreel ends with two models of how 'newness enters the world' (272) that are overdetermined by his final vision of Alleluia Cone in the 'hotel lobby' (545). On the one hand, we have the ancient Christian ideal of newness superseding (or killing) the Jewish father (echoing Lucretius), which is figured in the desire to embrace the Jewish daughter.[28] On the other, we have the contemporary European Jewish experience (as embodied in Otto Cone, a Holocaust survivor who is also an art historian), where the ambivalence of the diasporic migrant produces both modernist art and culture as well as quintessentially modern forms of racism – what Cone calls 'Nazis' and 'saints'.[29] Saladin, a mimic man and devil-figure invented by the English racist imagination and turned into a 'Jew', embodies this historical incoherence, originating in Europe. His final transformation is figured as a 'chimeran graft' that had notably been the 'pride' of Otto Cone's garden and lives on: 'a chimera with roots, firmly planted in and growing rigorously out of a piece of English earth' (406). Such are the unresolved oppositions that characterize Cone as both authentic cosmopolitan and counterfeit assimilationist; doyen of hybridity and Jewish-Anglian.[30]

The Moor's Last Sigh: Rushdie and the Elephant Question

There are a great many elephants in *The Moor's Last Sigh*, Rushdie's sixth novel and the first to be published after the maelstrom that surrounded the publication of *The Satanic Verses*. As this novel is in part about the rise of a quasi-fascist Hindu fundamentalism in India, it is appropriate that the elephant-headed Hindu god Ganesh, who was at the wise heart of *Midnight's Children* as the 'god of literature', appears in a more 'brutal' guise here (Goonetilleke 29 and 136). After Abraham and Aurora Zoigoby move from Cochin to Bombay, they live in a house that is perversely called 'Elephanta' (after Elephanta Island) even though Aurora regularly mocks Hindu triumphalism by dancing on her balcony, muttering the family curse '*mashed white elephants*', as the hordes of Dancing Ganeshes pass her by (Rushdie 1995: 127). The novel is full of 'fabulous elephant-tales' (135). Ganesh, after all, recorded the *Mahabharata* and his popularity is associated especially with the city of Bombay: 'in the days before men there were elephants sitting on thrones and arguing philosophy.' This is a city and novel with 'elephants on the brain'. But, as Ganesh also records financial accounts, putting him at the centre of commerce in the city, the narrator is less enthusiastic about elephants than his fellow Bombayites: 'Elephanta was anything but a fantasy island.' While Elephanta was commonly thought of as 'the land of milk and honey' (127), the reality turns out to be the 'Place of Elephants', which is merely a 'large and hideous fountain' (396).

At a crucial point in his story Moraes Zogoiby (known as 'Moor') pauses after recounting his family's plural history (which spans multicultural Goa in southern India and Muslim Spain) and comments: 'Christians, Portuguese and Jews; Chinese tiles promoting godless views; pushy ladies, skirts-not-saris, Spanish shenanigans, Moorish crowns . . . can this really be India?' The paternal Zogoiby family stem from the Jews of Cochin, who were exiled from either Palestine or Moorish Spain, and the maternal de Gama family stem from fifteenth-century spice-traders who, as part of Portuguese Goa, helped to establish Cochin. But Moraes insists that this is an 'Indian yarn' and that the '[Hindu] Majority, that mighty elephant, and her [Muslim] side-kick, Major-Minority, will not crush my tale beneath her feet' (87). This is a determinedly minority story rather than the grander national narratives that shaped *Midnight's Children* and *Shame*. Rushdie's alter ego, Joseph Anton, has recounted the origins of this novel as follows: 'In 1982 he had visited the old synagogue in Cochin, Kerala. . . . The story of an almost-extinct community of Keralan Jews caught his imagination.' But when Rushdie spoke to the caretaker of the synagogue about possibly writing a novel which included the history of Keralan Jews, the caretaker responded by saying: 'there is no need . . . we already have a leaflet' (Rushdie 2012: 428).

In stark contrast to the nation-formation inherent in Rushdie's best-known novels, Moraes's parents are described as 'the tiniest of the tiny . . . no more than flies upon the great diamond of India. . . . They were asking to be squashed' (Rushdie 1995: 98). That Rushdie, after *The Satanic Verses*, chose to write a novel about flies rather than elephants is perhaps understandable given his inevitable sense of being 'squashed' in the aftermath of the Rushdie Affair.[31] Moraes is quite explicit about not recounting a national tale from under the feet of elephants, as it were, which is in stark contrast to the second-rate artist Vasco Miranda, who paints a 'full-grown elephant from underneath' (325). Only Moraes is on the side of the flies or minorities rather than the elephantine majority. He is a self-described 'jewholic-anonymous, a cathjew nut, a stewpot, a mongrel cur . . . a real Bombay mix'. He goes on to embrace the word 'bastard' as his Jewish and Catholic parents remained unmarried: '*Baas*, a smell, a stinky-poo. *Turd*, no translation required' (104). Such is the place where impure, mixed-up and smelly flies feel most at home.

Aamir Mufti has emphasized the extremity of Rushdie's 'irreducibly minor' protagonist who, not unlike Joyce's 'greekjewish' Leopold Bloom, experiences a newly formed nation as if he were positioned as a 'minority of one' (Rushdie 2012: 294).[32] It is from this liminal position that *The Moor's Last Sigh* decentres the elephantine Hindu/Muslim ascendancy which, from Rushdie's minority perspective, deformed Pakistan and India after partition. The novel can be read in these terms as a type of precolonial nostalgia. After all, the famous sigh to which the title refers was breathed in 1492 by Boabdil, the last Moorish king of Granada, as he looked back at the city before going into exile in Africa, ending Arab-Islamic rule in Iberia. This fateful year also coincided with the expulsion of the Jews of Spain and the ending of a culture where Muslims, Catholics and Jews flourished together. This moment of partition, and the violent purification of culture (reflected in Columbus's discovery of the United States in the same year), is read back into post-partition India. To this extent Rushdie echoes Amitav Ghosh's *In an Antique Land* (1992), which, in the name of an Indian multiculturalism, also evokes those 'small, indistinguishable, intertwined histories, Indian and Egyptian, Muslim and Jewish, Hindu and Muslim', that had been 'partitioned long ago'.[33]

In *The Moor's Last Sigh*, the 'golden age' of a lost multicultural India ('Jews, Christians, Muslims, Parsis, Sikhs, Buddhists, Jains') is vividly depicted in the 'Moor Paintings' of Aurora Zogoiby, which attempt to 'create a romantic myth of the plural hybrid nation' by 'using Arab Spain to re-imagine India' (Rushdie 1995: 227). These paintings are described by Rushdie as 'palimpsest-art', a place where 'worlds collide . . . where an air-man can drowno in water, or else grow gills' (226). Unlike Allie's vision at the summit of Mount Everest, where land and air meet, Aurora's version of the 'intermingling of land and water' is a self-described 'metaphor' (226–27). To confirm that this rather defensive 'hybrid fortress' is a mere construction, she names her mythic nation 'Mooristan' or 'Palimpstine' (227). As J.M. Coetzee first noted, Rushdie's use of these paintings is a form of *ekphrasis*, or the 'conduct of narration through the description of imaginary works of art'.[34] This estranging technique, where Rushdie's 'plural hybrid nation' is doubly mythologized as a 'golden age' in an imagined painting, indicates a twofold distancing from such secular, democratic Nehruvian ideals.

While Aurora's paintings seemed 'more like [Moraes's] autobiography than the real story of my life' (Rushdie 1995: 227), and are said to invoke actual Jewish and Christian histories in Cochin (the birthplace of Aurora and Abraham), this portrait of 'the Moor' is not the only possible version of his 'mongrel' past. Aurora's 'Moor Paintings' change considerably throughout the novel, reflecting the deformation of post-independence India and the brutalization of the narrator. Although they begin with a vision of a 'golden age' where 'worlds collide', creating new versions of history and contemporary reality, the paintings gradually become less vivid, until Aurora is '*working only in black, white and occasional shades of grey*' (259). The 'Moor in Exile' sequence rejects the Moor's previous symbolic portrayal as a 'unifier of opposites, a standard bearer of pluralism' for the 'new nation', and now finds that he 'contained a potential for darkness as well as light'. The 'black moor' was a 'new imagining of the idea of hybrid' (303) and one way of reading this novel is as a sustained engagement with this 'new imagining'. The final 'Moor Painting' has Moraes fully humanized but 'lost in limbo like a wandering shade: a portrait of a soul in Hell' (315). Here the Satanic associations with the wandering 'air-man' (227) or *luftmensch* are reinforced but, unlike *The Satanic Verses*, are far from celebratory.

What the fluid, darkening paintings of Aurora demonstrate is how unstable her use of 'palimpsest-art' is. The idea of palimpsest is absolutely central to the novel – 'The city [Bombay] itself, perhaps the country, was a palimpsest' (184) – but it works on a range of contradictory levels. Rushdie has a long investment in the idea of palimpsest, which was at the heart of *Shame*, where his narrator's 'palimpsest-country' (Rushdie 1983: 88) is compared with the actual formation of Pakistan: 'A palimpsest obscures what lies beneath. To build Pakistan it was necessary to cover up Indian history, to deny that Indian centuries lay just beneath the surface of Pakistani Standard Time. The past was rewritten; there was nothing else to be done.' Here the difference between an artistic 'vision of the world' and 'Pakistan, the peeling, fragmentary palimpsest', is described as the 'failure of the dreaming mind'. All migrants, the narrator claims, are fantasists who 'build imaginary countries and try and impose them on the ones that exist' (87). It is this self-confident, imposing version of 'palimpsest-art' that Rushdie tests to destruction in *The Moor's Last Sigh*. While Aurora's 'palimpsest-art' represents this early ideal, she is tellingly marginalized and, finally, killed off.

Moraes, like Saleem Sinai in *Midnight's Children*, personifies the nation as a whole and gradually succumbs to the elephantine forces of majoritarian history which is his misfortune (the literal translation of his surname, 'Zogoiby'). Aurora's art, not unlike the novel, attempts to respond to an India trampled by elephants by transcending the brutalities of the present in a bid to reveal a more open and plural past.[35] This version of palimpsest was prefigured in Rushdie's 1994 essay 'Bosnia on my Mind':

> There is a Sarajevo of the mind, an imagined Sarajevo whose ruination and torment exiles us all. That Sarajevo represents something like an ideal; a city in which the values of pluralism, tolerance and coexistence have created a unique and resilient culture. In that Sarajevo there actually exists that secularist Islam for which so many people are fighting elsewhere in the world.[36]

As D.C.R.A. Goonetilleke has noted, Rushdie's 'Sarajevo of the mind', a place where secular Islam could coexist with other cultures and religions, is the model for the version of Bombay and Granada in *The Moor's Last Sigh* (Goonetilleke 143). But these imaginary homelands fall far short of this ideal as they make an 'exile' of the novel's protagonist. The self-confident aestheticizing palimpsest, taken from *Shame*, is replaced by an utterly '*worldly*' (Rushdie 1995: 318) version utilized by Abraham, who succumbs completely to a majoritarian national history: 'Under World beneath Over World, black market beneath white; when the whole of life was like this ... how could Abraham's career have been any different?' (184). In these terms, the Hindu ultra-nationalist Raman Fielding argues that he is merely defending himself from 'the culture of Indian Islam that lay palimpsest-fashion over the face of Mother India' (299). Moraes is trapped between these two versions of palimpsest – one fluid and mobile (artistic, transformational and utopian), the other bleak and frozen (rigid, materialistic and hate-ridden). Abraham, flattened by the elephantine forces of the nation-state, reduces absolutely everything to a Manichaean allegory. He demonstrates above all, in the words of Alicja Cone, that 'character isn't destiny any more. Economics is destiny. Ideology is destiny. Bombs are destiny' (Rushdie 1988: 432).

At an early stage in the novel we learn that Abraham's rather carica-tured role as a browbeaten Jewish husband is nothing more than a 'cover' (Rushdie 1995: 107) for his nefarious underworld activities. As a black marketeer, Abraham will be a 'formidable antagonist in the coming war of the worlds' between commerce and religion: 'Under versus Over, sacred versus profane, god versus mammon, past versus future, gutter versus sky' (318). To this extent, both Abraham and Moraes embody the nation, as opposed to Aurora who, as an artist, merely depicts it. The club hand of Moraes and his speeded-up growth rate are often read as exemplifying the potential for both violence and the hyper-modernization of post-independence India. Abraham's Manichaeism similarly personifies the 'struggle between the two layers of power' that has trapped 'Bombay, and even India itself . . . like dust between coats of paint' (318). Unlike the open-ended palimpsest-art of Aurora, Abraham's distorted version of palimpsest is stuck at the moment when there is nothing more than 'dust between coats of paint'. His vast and secretive commercial empire is 'submerged below the surface of things' (341). By the end of the novel we learn that Abraham, who began by dealing in drugs and prostitution, is attempting to manufacture a 'secret nuclear device' (335), a 'so-called Islamic bomb' (341).[37]

After he moves to Bombay, Abraham unites the 'Muslim gangs' (331) of the city against the religious-nationalist Hindu movement led by Raman Fielding. It is this conflict between rabid versions of capitalism and religion that structures the novel as a whole and represents the 'war of the worlds' (318) in post-Emergency India. Raman Fielding is based on the leader of the Shiv Sena, Bal Thackeray, and his regional organization ('Mumbai's Axis') is described in quasi-fascist terms in the novel: 'these Mainduck-style little Hitlers . . . must reclaim [the true nation] from beneath the layers of alien empires' (297–99). As the good-luck swastika of Ganesh was used prominently by this movement (it adorned the editions of Kipling's writings up until 1933), it is significant that Rushdie was to caricature Mumbai's Axis (evoking the 'Axis Powers' during the Second World War) as a form of quasi-fascism. The reason why Moraes, at his lowest point, agrees to be an enforcer for Fielding and to spy against his father is telling in this regard. At this point in the novel Moraes revels, above all, in being part of the majority: 'I found, for the first time in my short-long life, the feeling of normality, of being *nothing special . . .* that is the defining quality of home' (305).

Moraes's move from minority to majority, or from exile to home, echoes the experience of the Indian nation which has, in similar fashion, been transformed from colonized exile to majoritarian statehood. For this reason, the association of a national home with violence (or the violence of the majority) is particularly reinforced in the novel. Rushdie's narrative of the decline of postcolonial India, and especially the corruption of Nehru's utopian idealism, begins with Indira Ghandi's 1975 Emergency and culminates with the destruction of the sixteenth-century mosque in Ayodha in 1992 by supporters of the Bharatiya Janata Party (BJP) (a Hindu nationalist party formed in the wake of the Emergency). By the time of *The Moor's Last Sigh*, the decline of Nehruvian Indian pluralism parodies the rise of fascism in Europe: 'After the Emergency people started seeing through different eyes. Before the Emergency we were Indians. After it we were Christian Jews'. Told to 'Go find Palimpstine; go see Mooristan' (235), the Jews of India are placed in the same position as the Jews of Europe.

In *Joseph Anton*, Rushdie tends to take these parallels rather seriously. After meeting an extreme Hindu nationalist in India in 1986, he comments that the 'festival in honour of the elephant-headed Ganesh, which was once a day of celebration for all religious backgrounds, had been reduced to a fist-pumping, neo-Nazi assertion of Hindu power' (Rushdie 2012: 82). In contrast, a younger Rushdie argued famously in *Midnight's Children* that 'Europe repeats itself, in India, as farce' (Rushdie 1981: 185). While Fielding's quasi-fascist 'anti-Abrahamic tirade[s]' (Rushdie 1995: 295) are equally anti-Muslim, anti-Christian and anti-Jewish, Moraes does not become a 'Jew' merely in response to the extremes of Hindu nationalism. It is, rather, the machinations of his father that make him a 'Jew'. After hearing about the true extent of Abraham's nefarious activities, Moraes challenges his stony-faced father, who replies: 'I am a business person. . . . What there is to do, I do.' Moraes regards this statement as YHWH-like ('*I am that I am*' [336]) and connects it to the Satanic imagery that surrounds Abraham throughout the book: ' "To my astonishment," I told this shadow-Jehovah, this anti-Almighty, this black hole in the sky, my Daddyji, "excuse me, but I find that I'm a Jew" ' (336–37). Rushdie's narrator, however, frames this confrontation by secularizing it rather than locating it in the theological realm: 'Why not God and the Devil and the whole blest-damned thing? If so much revelation, why not Revelation? – *Please*. This is no time to discuss theology. The subject on the table is terrorism, and a secret nuclear device' (334–35). In stark contrast to *The Satanic Verses*, where the secular, the Satanic and the cosmopolitan are placed on the side of the angels, *The Moor's Last Sigh* moves radically away from this position. In an interview with Maya Jaggi, given to mark the publication of his sixth novel, Rushdie makes this reversal quite explicit:

> I was interested to try and suggest there's a flip side to pluralism; the down side can be confusion, formlessness, chaos, a lack of vision or singleness of purpose. There are some very strong, monolithic, brutal views around, and sometimes those who have a clearer view get further.[38]

All of the major characters in *The Moor's Last Sigh* can be said to personify the 'flip side of pluralism'. Aurora's art is ineffective against the violence of Hindu nationalism which she attempts to contain, following her son, by getting into bed (perhaps not literally) with Raman Fielding. In the hands of Abraham, Aurora's cosmopolitanism quickly becomes corrupted into a form of rapacious global capitalism. The vacuum left by the failure of Nehruvian plural democracy is filled equally by Hindu ultra-nationalism and by Abraham's rapacious financial empire. Rushdie includes two key second-generation characters, Uma Saraavati and Adam Sinai, who precisely embody the 'flip side of pluralism' and a pessimistic sense of the future. The betrayal of Uma, whom Moraes loves, is said to lead to the 'defeat for the pluralist philosophy on which we had all been raised': 'Uma with her multiple selves, her highly invented commitment to the infinite malleability of the real, her modernistically provisional sense of truth . . . had turned out to be a bad egg' (Rushdie 1995: 272). Moraes's sense of being ruined, after Uma tries to kill him, is described as a 'fall from grace', a shattering of the self not unlike a piece of broken glass: 'one thousand and one fragmented images of myself, trapped in shards of glass' (279).

In his famous manifesto, defining the 'shards of memory' as a form of archaeological remains that were to be reassembled capriciously in his fiction, Rushdie maintained that the excavation of such 'broken glass' was a 'useful tool with which to work in the present' (Rushdie 1991: 12). Such fragmentation was self-consciously incomplete and characterizes Rushdie's revision of modernism in *Midnight's Children* and *Shame*. By the time of *The Moor's Last Sigh*, such 'modernist cosmopolitanism' – and the plural and partial selves of its main characters – is regarded as a 'trap' leading to mere 'confusion' (Rushdie 1995: 276) or a 'tangled mess' (277).[39] With Uma turning out to be 'evil' (268), Aurora 'fries' the 'bad egg' (272) in her 'black Moor' paintings. In these paintings, 'ideas of impurity, cultural admixture and mélange' are reimagined as a 'Baudelairean flower', the '*fleur du mal*', which circulates a degenerate version of hybridity and plurality as a form of airborne 'decay' (303). Uma, after all, 'infect[ed], like a disease, all those with whom she came into contact' (266). Like all 'bad eggs' her stench, once associated with European Jews, contaminates absolutely everything.[40]

Moraes's fall from grace, after he is accused of the murder of Uma, leads him into the arms of Raman Fielding, which eventually results in him challenging his father's corrupt version of cosmopolitanism. Adam Sinai, the fully grown son of Saleem Sinai and his hope for the future in *Midnight's Children*, quickly learns to manage Abraham Zogoiby's Sidicorp Corporation. Adam is adopted as Abraham's 'beloved son' (349) and is

rejected by Moraes as he had 'fallen for such an act once' although Uma
had been a 'far greater practitioner of the chameleon arts'. Adam's response
to the hostility of Moraes is to belittle his Jewishness: 'Damn unusual for
you Jew boys. I thought you were all book-nosed, four-eyed members of
the international world-domination conspiracy' (354). What is interesting
here is the separation of Adam's shape-shifting cosmopolitan 'chameleon
arts' from the Jewishness of Moraes. It is the ethical content of Moraes's
imaginary Jewishness ('I find that I'm a Jew'), in relation to a potentially
genocidal global capitalism (the 'Islamic bomb'), that leads him to reject
his father's embrace.

Moraes, above all, writes *The Moor's Last Sigh* from the minority position of a suffering 'Jew'. As in so much of Rushdie's fiction, he is a
Scheherazade-figure whose story, his family saga, is told under threat of
death. His migration to 'Little Alhambra' at the end of the novel is both a
reverse Zionism, a profound rejection of secular postcolonial nationalism,
and a return to the precolonial history of intermingling diasporas that had
hitherto shaped the novel. He ends up a prisoner in Vasco Miranda's
house, which is modelled on Aurora's early 'Moor Paintings', and imagines
that he is living in a 'palace set by a mirage of the sea; part-Arab, part-
Mughal'. Moraes quotes his mother's earlier description of her paintings as
depicting a place 'where an air-man can drown in water, or else grow
gills' (408) as he perceives himself to be bringing the metaphorical *luftmensch* ('air-man') to life. Rushdie not only refers to a myriad of literary
and cinematic texts in *The Moor's Last Sigh*, including his own fiction, the
novel also, finally, quotes itself. But, in referring back to Aurora's exemplary palimpsest-art, *The Moor's Last Sigh* overlays (palimpsest-like) these
earlier celebratory visions in a tragic mode. While Moraes believes that he
has 'truly found Mooristan' he finally understands his mother's art
sequence in terms of one 'uniting principle': 'the tragedy of multiplicity
destroyed by singularity, the defeat of the Many by One' (408).

During his exile in 'Little Alhambra', the suffering, Christ-like Moraes
imagines that he is living in a fictionalized 'Indian country' but as the
'wrong sort of Indian': 'In Indian country, there was no room for a man

who didn't belong to a tribe, who dreamed of moving beyond; of peeling off his skin and revealing his secret identity – the secret, that is, of the identity of all men – of standing before the war-painted braves to unveil the flayed and naked unity of the flesh' (414). The image of being 'flayed', which we have already seen in the fiction of Philip Roth (and which is especially prevalent in *Shame* and at the end of *Midnight's Children*), is thought of by Moraes, in one version, as a form of postracial transcendence: 'When I was young I used to dream . . . of peeling off my skin plantain-fashion, of going forth naked into the world . . . set free from the otherwise inescapable jails of colour, race and clan' (136). This is not merely a 'psychedelic trip' (Grant 2012: 113) but rather a more extreme and bleak version of palimpsesting that, we have seen, shapes the novel as a whole. While in jail, Moraes feels his skin coming away from his body in a place where 'roaches crawled and mosquitoes stung'. His 'peeling skin', in this context, symbolizes not the 'naked unity of flesh' but that he was 'becoming nobody, nothing' and that he was reduced to the smelly 'turd' ('baas-turd') of his earlier incarnation: 'what my nose smelled on my body, what the rats were beginning, with growing enthusiasm, to approach', was that he was 'scum' (Rushdie 1995: 288). But it may also be a self-image of the suffering novelist who, in one version, is 'perpetually naked and alone' (Rushdie 2012: 410). By the end of the novel, Moraes 'still dreamed of being skinned' (Rushdie 1995: 425) – '*if my skin was falling from me at last, I was happy to shed that load*' (433) – but it is unclear whether this is transformative or merely a form of unredeemed affliction.

Coetzee is only half-right when he argues that Rushdie's implicit turn to the Holocaust, in finally depicting Moraes as a suffering, exiled Jew, means that he is asserting, 'however symbolically, solidarity with persecuted minorities worldwide' (Coetzee 211). The question here is what weight Rushdie gives to the symbolic in evoking such historical suffering. Throughout these final chapters we are told that his 'nutty cathjew confusions persisted right to the end!' (Rushdie 1995: 428). But it is precisely these confusions that complicate such easy identifications. Moraes, in exile from everything apart from the capacity to narrate a story ('naked and alone'), is no longer able to champion the transformative power of the artistic imagination to make such identifications. While his position, as others have argued, is analogous to Rushdie's own exile after the fatwa, his final sense of the possibility of transcendence – '[I] hope to awaken, renewed and joyful, into a better time' (434) – is predicated on his making the 'last sigh' before his death. He is, par excellence, Rushdie's 'last Jew', who in evoking the passion of Christ has to transcend his Jewish self to achieve the universality of love: 'our need for flowing together, for putting an end to frontiers, for dropping the boundaries of the self' (433). Moraes, in either his 'black' or his 'white' form, remains 'nobody, nothing', a mere vagrant, but defined above all by his suffering. Both the hope of imaginative transformation ('renewed and joyful') and a new historical context (in a 'better time') can act as a counterweight to his sense of being utterly crushed by the elephantine forces which have placed him in exile and made him weightless.[41]

Rushdie's Last Jew: *Shalimar the Clown* (2005)

The last words of *The Moor's Last Sigh* – 'our need for flowing together, for putting an end to frontiers, for dropping boundaries of the self' – are taken up again at the beginning of *Shalimar the Clown*, but to very different effect. According to his daughter, the dream of Maximillian Ophuls, after his parents had died in the death camps during the Second World War, was to build a 'new world in friendship, a world without walls, a frontierless newfound land of infinite possibility' (Rushdie 2005: 20). The difference between Max and Moraes, however, could not be starker. Moraes is the exiled minority Jew, ultimately defined by his powerlessness and suffering, whereas Max Ophuls is the American-centred, irresistible Jewish 'billionaire power-broker, the maker of the world!' who is also a 'resistance hero' and 'philosopher prince' (27). What is more, while Moraes is the quintessential son of Abraham, in the mould of Rushdie's other beloved son, Saleem Sinai, Max is the quintessential 'mountain-father' (20), following in the footsteps of Rushdie's other patriarchs,

Grimus, Otto Cone and, above all, Abraham Zogoiby. Like Abraham, Max enters the 'house of power' and understands that 'power does its work by stealth' (179).

Shalimar the Clown begins with the murder of Max Ophuls by the eponymous anti-hero, whose 'signature trick' on the high wire, as part of a circus troupe in Kashmir, was to 'lean out sideways . . . until he seemed he must fall, and then, with much clownish playacting of terror and clumsiness, to right himself with gravity-defying strength and skill' (93). At first Shalimar, born Noman Sher Noman, seems to be a typical Rushdian *luftmensch* whose father initiates him into a 'mystery': 'A rope could become air. A boy could become a bird. Metamorphosis was the secret heart of life' (56). In this spirit of metaphorical transfiguration, Max was known famously as the 'flying Jew' (158) as he had dramatically escaped the Nazi occupation in a Bugatti Racer. Shalimar's dream, in the first flush of love, is similarly to do away with the tightrope and hang in 'empty air' like a 'cosmonaut without a suit' (57). But his eventual metamorphosis, far from being life-giving, results in his transformation into an Islamic terrorist who no longer merely performs 'terror'. And, by the end of his life, Max's daughter, India Ophuls, describes Max's postwar belief in a 'frontierless newfound land of infinite possibility' as a 'utopian fallacy' that made him look like a 'tightrope walker trying to keep his balance even though there was no longer a rope beneath his feet' (20).

Max and Shalimar are mirror figures – both are *luftmenschen* who aspire initially to a utopian 'world without walls' – and are mature versions of Grimus and Flapping Eagle in Rushdie's first novel. They also both emerge from border territories – Alsace and Kashmir – exactly the kind of places that have, historically, eschewed national boundaries. Max is a 'Frenchman with a German name' and his family are influenced equally by both nations as 'in civilization there are no borderlines' (141). The novel is dedicated to Rushdie's 'Kashmiri grandparents' and, from the beginning, 'Kashmiriness' is described as a culture where a 'common bond . . . transcended all other differences' (110). In this place, 'Hindu' and 'Muslim' were 'descriptions, not divisions', as 'the frontiers between the words, their hard edges, had grown smudged and blurred' (57). This blurring of word-boundaries meant that the Muslim Shalimar was allowed to marry a Hindu, Bhoomi Kaul or Boonyi, hence the reference to *Romeo and Juliet* in the novel's epigraph. Max Ophuls is said to understand Kashmir because 'where he was raised had also been defined and refined for many centuries by shifting frontiers, upheavals and dislocations, flights and returns, conquests and reconquests' (138). Whereas India and Pakistan both claimed Kashmir, France and Germany, historically, both claimed Alsace.

The novel spends a great deal of time comparing the histories and experiences of Max and Shalimar, who are both resistance fighters and weightless shape-shifters who, in Rushdie's vocabulary, witness and respond to different versions of the 'holocaust' (88). Some of these comparisons are made through the eyes of Max, who flees the 'exterminating angel, just as the Kashmiri palace servitors would abandon the royal Desserha banquet' (141–42). When he first visits Kashmir as an ambassador from the United States, he universalizes these tragic histories: 'Each tragedy belongs to itself and at the same time to everyone else. What diminishes any of us diminishes us all' (138). Nazi-occupied Alsace and Kashmir (which is made up of 'no more than five million souls' [253]) are also brought together by an impersonal narrator who, in describing unimaginable atrocities committed by the Indian army in Kashmir, speaks of the 'pogrom of the pandits' (296) rotting in their 'slum camps' and their 'dream of return'. Echoing Primo Levi's 'here is no why here', used as a chapter heading in Martin Amis's *Time's Arrow* (1991), Rushdie ends the account of the Kashmiri 'holocaust' with the pained 'why was that why was that why was that why was that why was that' (297).[42]

Rushdie tends to displace the language of holocaust atrocities and representations from the Holocaust in Europe to the Kashmiri 'holocaust' in Southeast Asia. This is in part because Max Ophul's parents were 'wealthy, cultured, conservative, cosmopolitan' and acted as if 'they could behave the Nazis out of existence' (150). The contrast here is with the three 'dancing Jews' from Shalimar's Kashmiri village who are murdered with the blunt conclusion, echoing *The Satanic Verses*, that 'their characters were not their destinies' (Rushdie 2005: 304 and Rushdie 1988: 432). As Max is a quintessential 'faker' (Rushdie 2005: 140), whose 'gift for forgery' enabled him to forge a 'new self, one that resisted, that pushed back against fate, rejecting inevitability, choosing to remake the world' (148), there is a sense in which he challenges this dictum. But Rushdie is at pains also to associate Max with the triple destinies of 'economics', 'ideology' and 'bombs'.

On the one hand, Max becomes a 'metaphor for the Liberation' (160), rather than an actual fighter, and spends most of the war years creating 'false identities' (162). It is the link between metaphor and reality that is crucial in this narrative as false identities are said to save some French children from being deported to Auschwitz (163). Max's parents are also, with bitter irony, 'killed' by 'scholarship' as they had been 'used for medical experimentation' (157). For Max, 'entering the Resistance' was 'a kind of flying. . . . One took leave of one's name, one's past, one's future, one lifted oneself away from one's life . . . borne aloft by necessity and fatalism' (166). Such was the weightlessness at the heart of his experience of resistance. Max thinks of his 'reinvention of the self' during the war as a 'classic American theme' (162), thus linking his wartime experiences and the desire to 'remake the world' in the image of American individualism. It was in these terms that Max moved to the United States after the war, 'choosing the burnished attractions of the New World over the damaged gentility of the Old'.

With his 'movie-star good looks' (161), Max is suitably named after the German-Jewish émigré filmmaker and, not unlike his fiction-creating Hollywood namesake, engages in fakery on a worldwide stage.[43] In this he is a Grimus-figure, a bogus artist who, after the trauma of the Holocaust, detaches his imagination from reality so as to create a solipsistic 'new world'. Not unlike his prototype, Max's life after the Holocaust is 'empty', an 'open grave' (33), and this vacuum is filled by world-making. But, in contrast to *Grimus*, Rushdie's more mature novel focuses on the politics of being a 'maker of the world' (27). Max, we are told, was privy to the proposals to bring the Council of Europe, the International Monetary

Fund and the World Bank into being after the Second World War. The narrator comments pointedly that the 'future was being born' and Max was 'being asked to be its midwife' (173). But this future world was utterly American-centred, which is said to result in a 'new captivity' (170), with the 'cycle of violence' (173) remaining unbroken. By the end of the novel, the political consequences of Max's world-making are made apparent: 'He had been a dealer in the dangerous, hallucinogenic narcotic of the future, offering it at a price to his chosen addicts, the reptilian cohorts of the future which his country [the United States] had chosen for itself and for others; Max . . . the invisible robotic servant of his country's overweening amoral might' (336). Whereas the world-making of Grimus exposes, rather abstractly, the limits and abuses of the imagination, Max's delusions, his complicity in shaping geopolitical reality in the image of the United States, take the form of an unreal power politics. Both are dangerous world-makers and both are exposed as weightless Holocaust survivors, driven by their imaginations, in contrast to their postcolonial counterparts mired in a sorrowful reality. This is quite explicit in *Shalimar the Clown*, where Max, in his role as an American ambassador to the region, is characterized as 'supporting terror activities while calling himself an ambassador for counterterrorism' (272) and, finally, as 'part terrorist' (335). Here the narrator is thinking of American support for the Indian 'ethnic cleansing' (295) of Kashmir, and the 'militarization of the Kashmir valley' (197), in a bid to defeat 'Islamist terror international' (291). The brutality of Indian 'storm troopers' who invade and decimate 'town by town, hamlet by hamlet' (292) is what is meant by the Kashmiri 'holocaust' (88). Such complicity can be seen when Max visits Kashmir and watches Boonyi Noman dance and is reminded of the 'feathered dead-eyed showgirls wreathed in Nazi cigar smoke'. This memory is quickly qualified: 'I'm not a Nazi . . . I'm for God's sake one of the Jews who lived'. But the reason why he doubts himself is because he is now the 'American ambassador, the guy in the white hat' (141).

The plot revolves around this chance meeting of Max and Boonyi. Max, needless to say, proves to be irresistible to Boonyi and, although she is married to Shalimar, Max is an ideal means for her to escape the poverty and suffering of Kashmir. But, as a result of this love affair, Max is characterized as a 'sexual predator' by the Indian government, drawing on a tradition of Jewish 'alien enchanters' going back to the character of Svengali or, as Rushdie put it, 'lust-crazed wogs' (Rushdie 1991: 101).[44] In this way, India presents itself as the defender of Kashmir against 'marauders of all types' (Rushdie 2005: 206) and attacks Max who is known to have 'expressed horror at the slaughter of innocent Muslims' (29). But it is paradoxical that the main experience of state-sponsored anti-Semitism in the novel, which Max experiences, is provided by the Indian government. As we have seen, Rushdie's depiction of the Holocaust is rather sanitized and, for the most part, so is his representation of European anti-Semitism. That Max and his first wife are known throughout the novel, after wartime slang, as 'Rat and her Mole' (187) (or 'ratty' and 'ratteta') ultimately domesticates the Nazi depiction of Jews as subhuman rats and returns such racialized images to the Edwardian innocence of Kenneth Grahame's *The Wind in the Willows* (1908).

But such innocence, in general, is also dismantled in Rushdie's ninth novel. Most reviewers have read *Shalimar the Clown* as reinforcing benignly the credo stated at the outset: 'Everywhere was now part of everywhere else. Russia, America, London, Kashmir. Our lives, our stories, flowed into one another's, were no longer our own, individual, discrete. This unsettled people. There were collisions and explosions. The world was no longer calm' (37). Here the contrast is with *Haroun and the Sea of Stories* (1990), where stories flowed into one another as an unequivocal good. But, at the end of *Shalimar the Clown*, Rushdie concludes quite differently: 'Everywhere was a mirror of everywhere else. Executions, police brutality, explosions, riots: Los Angeles was beginning to look like wartime Strasbourg; like Kashmir' (355). On one level, this is the familiar Rushdian story of 'shattered idylls' – California, Alsace, Kashmir – which is reinforced throughout the novel since Kashmir, we are told repeatedly, means paradise.[45] Such mirroring, rather than aiding identification or understanding leads to violence ('collisions and explosions'), however.

This is, after all, the story of Max and Shalimar, who, in his role as Max's chauffeur and murderer, is described as his 'shadow-self' (322). The familiar credo of mixing stories, finding impure, 'smudged and blurred' (57) words to describe an intertwined world, leads only to death and destruction.

Rushdie emphasizes that Shalimar kills Max not for ideological reasons but due to his jealous rage at losing Boonyi.[46] This loss leads Shalimar to question radically all of his previous beliefs and to join the Islamic resistance in the Kashmiri mountains: 'By crossing the mountains . . . [he] stood now on the threshold of the world of truth, which was invisible to most men' (266). Shalimar's search for truth in the mountains, which takes the form of religious fundamentalism, could not be more different from Allie Cone's search for 'truth' on Mount Everest, which goes beyond 'good and evil' (Rushdie 1988: 313).[47] On her discovery that Shalimar has killed her father, the renamed Kashmira Ophuls becomes a 'black scheherazade' (Rushdie 2005: 374) and writes to Shalimar every day in jail so that the dead are 'not gone not forgotten. They live on in me' (379). Shalimar's village, after the rampages of the Indian army, similarly 'ceased to exist anywhere else, except in memory' (309). All of the foundational terms that Rushdie articulates in *Imaginary Homelands* – impurity, storytelling, 'shards of memory', cosmopolitanism and an imaginative space beyond 'good and evil' – fail utterly in this book. Max and Shalimar, figures who survive the most ferocious forms of repression, are as bad as each other in embracing, however equivocally, a form of 'terrorism'. Their mirror lives lead not to a shared understanding but merely add to the world's 'brutality'. No wonder *Shalimar the Clown* has a rather despairing epigraph: '*A plague on both your houses*.'

Conclusion: Joseph Anton or Moses Herzog?

As is well known, Joseph Anton was the codename that Rushdie chose for himself while in hiding and was based on a hyper-canonical combination of Joseph Conrad and Anton Chekhov. This nom de guerre, needless to say, has reinforced the critique of Rushdie as an elitist, preoccupied with the literary canon above all else rather than the 'world of ordinary folk' or, more seriously, the 'wretched of the earth'.[48] Not unlike Roth, Rushdie is now an éminence grise and this shift into mainstream respectability is usually framed in two ways. His acceptance of a knighthood ('Sir Salman versus Salman') and the shift from an anti-American to a pro-American stance (Grant 2012: 123–25) as seen in the essays in *Step Across This Line* (2002) (many of which were written initially for an American readership after his move to New York in 2000).[49] To be sure, one way of reading Rushdie's memoir, *Joseph Anton*, is as a paean of praise to the freedom that he was given in the United States, rather than in European countries, during his 'plague years' (Rushdie 2002: 229). But the attack on Rushdie on the grounds that he is a rootless cosmopolitan (in this guise, endlessly crossing the Atlantic to mix with celebrities), who does not speak for 'ordinary folk', predates the fatwa by many years.

In his 1990 defence of *The Satanic Verses*, 'In Good Faith', Rushdie is well aware of the caricature of him as a 'self-hating, deracinated Uncle Tom' and argued that the novel was instead written from the experience of 'uprooting, disjuncture and metamorphosis . . . that is the migrant condition' and was a 'metaphor for all humanity' (Rushdie 1991: 393). The migrant as metaphor was most clearly expressed, although not as a universal, in *Shame*:

> I, too, know something of this immigrant business, I am an emigrant from one country (India) and a newcomer in two (England, where I live, and Pakistan, to which my family moved against my will). And I have a theory that the resentments we *mohajirs* engender have something to do with our conquest of gravity. We have performed the act of which all men anciently dream, the thing for which they envy the birds; that is to say, we have flown.

Rushdie's persona is resented, in a form of proteophobia, because he has 'floated upwards from history, from memory, from Time' (Rushdie 1983:

87). Such weightlessness, at this point, was celebrated by many readers as it was considered disruptive politically. In *Shame*, for instance, Rushdie's Pakistan is 'two countries, real and fictional, occupying the same space' (29), making his migrant metaphors tangible in relation to national narratives to the extent that the novel was banned in Pakistan. As Susheila Nasta has argued, Rushdie maps out 'the imaginative territory of the novel as an arena where some of the unresolved and perhaps unresolvable political ambiguities of his diasporic location might be addressed'.[50] But, in recent years, and particularly since *Joseph Anton*, Rushdie has moved from political ambiguities to political certainties (not least in relation to Islam) and, in so doing, he can be said to have narrowed the perspective of his metaphorical *luftmenschen*.

At one point in *Joseph Anton*, Rushdie evokes Otto Cone's philosophy that we live in an age where 'incompatible realities frequently collided with one another . . . Israel and Palestine, for example' (Rushdie 2012: 534). But he then goes on to compare his own plight with such 'incompatible realities', 'in which he was a decent, honourable man and a good writer' who had 'collided with another reality in which he was a devil creature and a worthless scribe. It was not clear that both realities could coexist' (534–35). But the analogy here with Israel/Palestine is more than a little troublesome. In his essay on Said's memoir *Out of Place* (1999), Rushdie notes that 'Said is a passionate advocate of reconciliation between Jews and Palestinians' (Rushdie 2002: 318–19), which rightly assumes that 'both realities could coexist'. What is more, the analogy between Israel and Palestine and the 'good writer' and 'devil creature' does not work unless Rushdie is prepared to place Israel and Palestine on either side of his moral divide. Unlike many of his earlier accounts on the response to *The Satanic Verses*, much (but not all) of *Joseph Anton* is written from a moralizing post-9/11 perspective which takes as read Samuel P. Huntington's 'clash of civilizations' thesis: 'Let's start calling a spade a spade. Of course this is "about Islam"' (Rushdie 2002: 395). As Kenan Malik has argued, the idea of a 'civilizational struggle' between Islam and 'the West' began with the battle over *The Satanic Verses* and has ended with the 'war on terror'.[51]

But, in stark contrast to such Manichaeism, Rushdie in *Joseph Anton* also regularly channels Moses Herzog, the central character in Saul Bellow's *Herzog* (1964) (whose name was in turn taken from Joyce's *Ulysses*). The suffering, isolated Herzog on the verge of insanity – 'If I am out of my mind, it's all right with me' – proves to be a more sustained analogy with Joseph Anton in hiding and under a death sentence than the geopolitical example of Israel/Palestine.[52] In fact, soon after completing *The Satanic Verses*, Rushdie writes that he was trying to 'kick-start his imagination' and, among other books, read '*Herzog* for the umpteenth time' (Rushdie 2012: 106). To be sure, at this point in the memoir, Rushdie is at pains to distance himself from the 'book's attitude to women [which] really grated' (107) but nonetheless, and perhaps with some self-irony, he goes on to channel his experiences through Herzog, a Bellovian 'dangling man' (Rushdie 1991: 349). As has already been noted, Rushdie was well aware that, as part of the attack on *The Satanic Verses*, he was Judaized as a 'devil creature' and was, in turn, seen as part of an elaborate Jewish conspiracy to undermine Islam.[53] But my focus here is on the extent to which Rushdie, in the spirit of his fiction, reclaimed this Semitic discourse through Bellow's Herzog both to exemplify a secular Jewish literature (as a model for his own secular Islam) and to challenge such crude and 'routine' (Rushdie 2002: 394) conspiratorial thinking made in the name of religious purity.[54]

At the beginning of the memoir, Rushdie is contemplating how best to defend himself and notes that, among many others, 'Jewish community leaders required protection from time to time after receiving credible Islamist threats' (Rushdie 2012: 96) and this would be a precedent for him. Such an analogy leads naturally to Rushdie assuming the guise of Herzog at some of his lowest moments: 'He found himself composing a thousand letters in his head and firing them off into the ether like Bellow's Herzog, half-deranged, obsessive arguments with the world that he could not actually send on their way' (185). One of the first of these 'letters' was to the British chief rabbi, Lord Immanuel Jakobovits, written as if he were the actual Herzog rather than a mere simulacrum. Lord Jakobovits had written to *The Times* to lend his support to those who were against the publication of *The Satanic Verses* and to call for draconian laws 'prohibiting the publication of anything likely to inflame, through obscene defamation, the feelings of any section of society'.[55] Rushdie replies at length (in his head). Here is an extract:

> 'Both Mr Rushdie and the Ayatollah have abused freedom of speech', you say. Thus a novel which, love it or hate it, is in the opinion of at least a few critics and judges a serious work of art is equated with a naked call for murder. This ought to be denounced as a self-evidently ridiculous remark; instead, Chief Rabbi, your colleagues the Archbishop of Canterbury and the Pope of Rome have said substantially the same thing. . . . Why this strange unanimity between apparent irreconcilables? (186–87)

Such letters are repeated throughout *Joseph Anton* – 'blasting his words into empty space' (305) – and all in Herzog's intransigent and irascible 'late style', which Edward Said characterized as 'apartness, exile, and anachronism'.[56] There is also some of Bellow's aestheticism ('*a serious work of art*'), with his novel defended on purely artistic grounds, and the pessimism of Otto Cone ('irreconcilables'). But the alternative to Herzog is his 'reality instructors', who attempt to discipline Bellow's eponymous anti-hero throughout *Herzog* and who give Rushdie an education in 'worthlessness': 'the media pundit who suggests that a manly death would be better than hiding like a rat; the letter writer who points out that the trouble is that I *look* like the Devil, and wonders if I have hairy shanks and cloven hooves' (Rushdie 1991: 432–33).[57] Such is Rushdie's construction as a racialized 'Jew': both ratlike (going back to *Shalimar the Clown*) and devil-like (going back to *The Satanic Verses*). No wonder he chose to be a 'last' Jew, a 'minority of one' (Rushdie 2012: 294), like Moraes Zogoiby: 'I ask the reader to imagine how it might feel to be intellectually and emotionally bludgeoned, from a thousand different directions, every day for a thousand days and more' (Rushdie 1991: 433). As always, his essays and memoir privilege his impure imagination (to commune with the suffering of others) whereas his novels, especially after the fatwa, are rather less optimistic. Nonetheless, the credo that ends *Joseph Anton* could not be more apposite for this book, which does, after all, evoke Rushdie's 'Indias of the mind' (Rushdie 1991: 10): 'Yet this is an age in which men and women were being pushed towards ever narrower definitions of themselves, encouraged to call themselves just one thing, Serb or Croat or Israeli or Palestinian or Hindu or Muslim or Christian or Baha'i or Jew, and the narrower their identities became, the greater was the likelihood of conflict between them.' For Rushdie, literature and the imagination are the antidote to such identity politics (although less straightforwardly so in his novels) since they 'encouraged understanding, sympathy and identification with people not like oneself' while the world was 'pushing everyone in the opposite direction' (Rushdie 2012: 628). It is with this clash between the world and the imagination, rather more productive than the 'clash of civilizations', that *Diasporas of the Mind* now concludes.

7

Conclusion
Diaspora and Postethnicity

'I feel disinherited even from my childhood memories, so that I stand before you as a writer without any ground of being out of which to write: really blown about from country to country, culture to culture until I feel – until I am – nothing. I'm not complaining – this is not a complaint, just a statement of fact.' Ruth Prawer Jhabvala, 'Disinheritance' ('The 1975 Neil Gunn Lecture'), p. 4.

Ruth Prawer Jhabvala was born in Germany in 1927 to a Polish-Jewish father and German-Jewish mother. She left Cologne in 1939 at the age of twelve with her parents and brother, Siegbert Prawer, who became a well-known comparative literary critic. They were among the last Jewish families to leave Nazi Germany for England. Her father, Marcus Prawer, committed suicide in 1948 after hearing of the death of more than forty friends and relatives in the camps. In 1951, she married Cyrus Jhabvala and moved with him to Delhi, where she remained until 1975. It is no coincidence that Prawer Jhabvala delivered the Neil Gunn Lecture in the year in which she finally became disillusioned with India, because of the extent of the human misery in her adopted homeland, and decided to go into exile once more. By 1975 she was able to travel as a writer after gaining international recognition for *Heat and Dust* (1975), including the Booker Prize, and her screenplays. For the next four decades, until her death in April 2013, she divided her time mainly between New Delhi and New York.[1] Anita Desai's *Baumgartner's Bombay* (1988) is, in one way, an act of imaginative appropriation of her friend's traumatic past focusing on Kristallnacht, which frames Desai's novel, and the silence of her protagonist. As Prawer Jhabvala stated in her 1975 lecture, this was the first time that she had spoken about the years 1933–39, in stark contrast to much of her brother's work, which implicitly addressed these years through his accounts of German-Jewish literature (especially Heine) and European anti-Semitism. As Primo Levi has noted, there are two kinds of survivors, those who 'remain silent and those who speak'.[2]

Salman Rushdie invokes Prawer Jhabvala so as to challenge the early disciplinary boundaries of 'Commonwealth Literature' which, as he understood it, was made up of a series of unrelated postimperial national literatures: 'looked at from the point of view that literature must be nationally connected and even committed, it becomes simply impossible to understand the cast of mind and vision of a rootless intellect like Jhabvala's' (Rushdie 1991: 68). Here is the figure of 'the stranger' who contaminates with uncertainty nationally connected ways of thinking.[3] But Rushdie also argues that the image of the *luftmensch* or rootless intellect ('without any ground of being ... blown about from country to country, culture to culture') is perceived (or feared) differently depending on whether this figure is located on the European continent, in Southeast Asia or in the United States. On the European continent, compared to Southeast Asia, there are 'enough instances of uprooted, wandering writers and even peoples to make Jhabvala's work readily comprehensible' (Rushdie 1991: 68). The danger is that individual exile and estrangement have been universalized in a European context so that they speak only to the post-Holocaust history of the West.[4]

Prawer Jhabvala's sense of nothingness ('until I feel – until I am – nothing') is the starting point for *Diasporas of the Mind* and is a void that is filled both by disciplinary and metaphorical thinking. At one end of the spectrum we have the 'statelessness' of Hannah Arendt or Jean Améry after the Holocaust (Rushdie's 'wandering peoples') and, at the other, a sense of a global 'tabula rasa' shared by Frantz Fanon and Aimé Césaire in the postwar years of mass (but not universal) decolonization. As Fanon emphasizes at the end of *The Wretched of the Earth* (1961), which is echoed by Arendt at the end of *The Origins of Totalitarianism* (1951) and throughout her other work, what is needed is a 'new start' – a 'new way of thinking' (Fanon 1961: 239). Writing from a similar position to Prawer Jhabvala in 1943, as a migrant from Nazi Germany, Arendt rejects the old assimilatory language of 'refugees' (as she would have it) and prefers the racially neutral term 'newcomers', which became the subject of Anita Brookner's *Latecomers* (1988).[5] The term 'newcomers', Arendt argues, indicates that her fellow exiles and émigrés merely 'wanted to rebuild our lives' (Arendt 1943: 264), although not without qualification:

> But the recovering of a new personality is as difficult – and as hopeless – as a new creation of the world. Whatever we do, whatever we pretend to be, we reveal nothing but our insane desire to be changed, not to be Jews. All our activities are directed to attain this aim: we do not want to be refugees; we pretend to be English-speaking people, since German-language immigrants of recent years are marked as Jews; we don't call ourselves stateless, since the majority of stateless people in the world are Jews; we are willing to become loyal Hottentots, only to hide the fact that we are Jews. We don't succeed and we can't succeed; under the cover of our 'optimism' you can easily detect the hopeless sadness of assimilationists. (271–72)

That Arendt in 1943, at the height of the Nazi extermination programme, regards any possible change from Jewishness as an 'insane desire' is obviously understandable but it does contrast starkly with Fanon, two decades later, who precisely wanted to create a 'new species' of humanity after decolonization, to accompany, as he hoped, the end of colonial racism.

Characteristically Arendt brings together different versions of racial difference ('loyal Hottentots') while making her Jewishness the limit case of the
impossibility of individual or social transformation. *Diasporas of the Mind*
begins at a time when the transcendence of racial difference was desired
universally but was quickly disrupted by the dispossessed and rootless
remnants of the camps and of colonialism that haunt all the figures in this
book. With 'the Jews' appropriated as world-historical victims – as if the
European Jewish diaspora no longer existed – there has been a simultaneous urge either to supersede or to universalize the 'classic' diaspora or,
alternatively, to connect with 'other others', in the phrase of Jonathan
Freedman, in the contexts of Europe, Africa, the United States and
Southeast Asia.[6] Desai's *Baumgartner's Bombay* and Zadie Smith's *White
Teeth* (2000) both illustrate the tensions between universalizing the *luftmensch* – a 'metaphor for all humanity' (Rushdie 1991: 393) – and
exploring that figure's limitations: in the case of Desai, he is so traumatised
that he can only connect with the animal world and, in the case of Smith,
he has finally and smugly come home.

Anita Desai: Broken Mirrors

'Mystifying and alarming were the three-piece mirrors that sat on the
dressing tables and showed you unfamiliar aspects of your head,
turning you into a stranger before your own eyes as you slowly rotated
to find the recognizable.' (Desai 1988: 26)

Baumgartner's Bombay is one of a large number of books on the history of
Jews in Southeast Asia, on the links between Indians and European Jews,
and on coexistent precolonial cosmopolitan communities.[7] At one extreme,
readings of the novel have argued, in the name of authenticity, that the
brutal partition of Southeast Asia is the 'proper setting' for a discussion of
the European Holocaust. But Desai has also been accused of merely replicating the figurative Wandering Jew or the *luftmensch* and of writing a
particular kind of middlebrow fiction for an American readership.[8] That

the novel can be read equally as a product of historical authenticity and inauthentic racial discourse indicates the uncertainty generated by the global figure of the metaphorical Jew. I want to suggest that Desai claims both sides of this argument as she attempts to universalize the *luftmensch* as a metaphor for humanity and also to connect Jewish and postcolonial histories.

Her claim for historical authenticity can be found in a review essay on 'Jews, Indians and Imperialists' where she summarizes much of the history of the Cochin Jews and Bene Israel in India (based on two recent accounts) and, interestingly, relates this history to the arrival of European Jewish refugees in 1933 which she witnessed in her adolescence: 'Indian Jews might have continued to think of the Holy Land as a distant mirage had European Jewish refugees not begun to arrive in 1933 and talk of pogroms, discrimination, and anti-Semitism of a kind they themselves had not experienced in India.'[9] Such was the 'talk' that became the topic of Prawer Jhabvala's 1975 lecture. In *Baumgartner's Bombay*, and much of her previous fiction, Desai is preoccupied with the continued violence inherent in the partition of India and Pakistan. Anticipating Rushdie and Amitav Ghosh, she also associates this enforced partition with the destruction of a lost historic pluralism as represented by the Jewish communities in India and Pakistan:

> In Pakistan anti-Jewish riots took place [in 1947] during demonstrations in favour of Arab Palestine and Jewish refugees streamed into Bombay from where they were helped to go to Israel. . . . Baghdadi Jews were the first to leave India . . . while Cochin Jews and Bene Israel lingered only to find that when they applied for jobs the answer was often: 'We're reluctant to hire you because . . . you'll leave for Israel.' (Desai 1990: 56)

It is in the context of the partition of Hindus, Muslims and Jews after 1947 that Desai inserts her *luftmensch*, neither east nor west, black nor white, who does not fit into an increasingly narrowly defined India as represented by the ruthless son of Chimanlal, a mirror image of Kurt, the murderous son of Germany. While Chimanlal's son dismisses Hugo Baumgartner as a 'filthy foreigner' (Desai 1988: 226), it is significant that Baumgartner's one Indian friend and supporter, Farrokh, is a Parsi, who is outside the religious and national divides that reverberate through the novel. Farrokh belongs to a minority religious community who, as Homi Bhabha has reminded us, are known as the 'Jews of the East'.[10] While Farrokh, for pragmatic reasons, wishes Baumgartner to befriend Kurt (so as to remove him from his café), Baumgartner is embarrassed that 'anyone should think he ought to or would try to protect the white man' (17). The one thing that defines Baumgartner, it seems, is that he is not white.

After the novel's publication Desai moved to the United States for part of the year: 'I suppose *Baumgartner's Bombay* was the beginning of my move away from India. . . . Now I have things to compare it with which I didn't earlier.'[11] Her subsequent novels, such as *Journey to Ithaca* (1995), *Fasting, Feasting* (2000) and *The Zigzag Way* (2004), have all been comparative, connecting the Americas and India, which indicates the extent to which her ninth novel acted as a gateway into American culture. But the consequences of moving to the United States meant that *Baumgartner's Bombay* was read entirely differently from the way her previous work had been received by a predominantly British and Indian readership, which was, hitherto, the more natural audience for her fiction:

> every book of mine has received a great deal of notice in England. Not as much in America. That's because America hasn't the same interest in India as England has. . . . The reason that *Baumgartner's Bombay* has had any success [in the United States] is not because of the Indian material but because of the Jewish material. It aroused a great deal of curiosity and interest amongst Jewish readers. It won a Jewish prize, in fact, the Hadassah prize, and people are interested in the element of the war, the Nazis and then the Holocaust. India is really superfluous as far as American readers are concerned.[12]

Desai's denationalized reception in the United States, as a result of her 'Jewish' material, is particularly ironic as she has often stated that in making Baumgartner a Jew she wanted to 'generalize his isolation' so that his 'suffering fits into the general scheme of things' (Bliss 522). For this reason, Desai in interview is at pains to universalize Baumgartner, beyond the particularities of his German-Jewish upbringing, to the extent that she regards him as a 'representative not of the Jewish race but of the human race, of displaced and dispossessed people and tribes all over the world' (523). To this extent, as J.M. Coetzee notes in his review of *The Moor's Last Sigh*, Desai's turn to the Holocaust was another instance of a writer asserting, 'however symbolically, solidarity with persecuted minorities worldwide'.[13] For Desai, the Holocaust was 'neither new nor unique' but it was 'the scale that was unprecedented and appalling' (Bliss 531). Baumgartner is therefore seen by Desai as part of a long line of 'failures and wrecks', as she puts it, who are all, in their very different ways, victims of historical circumstance:

His life had no pattern; the pattern had been blown to bits by history. In India this happened to Muslims, in Pakistan to Hindus, and it is still happening – people are being victimized because of their religion, or caste, because of war and history. In literature you can construct the gigantic movements of history stampeding through the world, or the frantic scurrying and fleeing of the people like ants in its way. They have no control over such things. All they can do is blunder through the wreckage and the chaos with their wretched belongings, hoping to escape the notice of history. (523)

This strong universalizing impulse, with regard to the Holocaust and Baumgartner's Jewishness, is tempered throughout the novel where warped reflections of India in Germany and Germany in India proliferate and are embodied in Baumgartner's flight in 1938 from Berlin to Bombay after Kristallnacht. Desai constructs *Baumgartner's Bombay* around parodic versions of European and Indian history as seen through each

other's distorting lenses. Thus, the ethnic cleansing that accompanied
Indian independence – with Habibullah forced to flee to Dacca from
Calcutta – repeats the forms of racialized partition in Europe that drove
Baumgartner out of Germany and resulted in his father's suicide after his
internment in Dachau. His imprisonment in a British anti-alien camp in
Ahmednagar, near Bombay, is turned into a domestic version of the
concentration camp where his mother died. What is more, the extreme
poverty that Baumgartner encounters in Bombay is a constant reminder
of the suffering of German Jewry under the Nazis. Along with these
historic mirror images, the plot also revolves around Baumgartner's brutal
murder by Kurt, a German backpacker, who engages in a tragicomic reca-
pitulation of the paranoid fantasies of European fascism. To this extent, a
mirror that transforms its viewers into 'a stranger before your own eyes' is,
in miniature, the imaginative method of Desai's ninth novel.

It is characteristic of Desai's subtlety that a novel so full of doublings
and historical comparisons eschews facile mirror images by showing how
distorted and limiting such reflections can be. As Judie Newman has
argued, it is the gap between discourse and history, or between fantasy
and reality, rather than mere historical comparisons, that structures the
novel.[14] Because Baumgartner left for Bombay soon after Kristallnacht,
the early part of the novel is full of mirrors that are broken and fragmented. Desai juxtaposes the shattering of mirrors with the break-up of
language and identity by refracting Baumgartner's childhood memories
through untranslated German nursery rhymes and the memory of his
father's suicide. For Rushdie, the 'broken mirror' (Rushdie 1991: 11) corresponds to a modernist refashioning of India and Pakistan, whereas for
Desai the shattering of mirror images represents the limits of her universalizing intentions and her protagonist's ability to connect with other
histories.

Although Desai is certain in interview that there is a straightforward
shift from Baumgartner's Jewish rootlessness to persecuted minorities in
general, this is much less clear in the novel. The shattering and estrangement of all mirror images point to an alternative narrative that eschews

overt comparisons between east and west, India and Germany. Baumgartner copes with his abiding ambivalence by embracing the 'stratagems of silence and evasion', which is a response, above all, to the fate of his mother and other German Jews:

> Although part of him greedily, hungrily took in every morsel of information that came his way of the situation of the Jews in Germany . . . another part frantically built a defensive barrier against it. It was as if his mind were trying to construct a wall against history, a wall behind which he could crouch and hide, holding to a desperate wish that Germany were still what he had known as a child and that in that dream-country his mother continued to live the life they had lived there together. (118)

Baumgartner's 'wall against history' and his 'dream-country' are brought together as they prevent him from being 'plunged once more into chaos' after the war.[15] His abiding silence, which structures the novel in implicit homage to Prawer Jhabvala, is contrasted starkly with a wide variety of competing texts and discourses – from nursery rhymes to high culture, Nazi-sanctioned postcards to German Orientalism, the fiction of Kafka and Forster to memoirs of alien internment in India during the war. But all of these intertexts, in ironic juxtaposition with the novel's assured title, are unable to name either an incommensurable India or an unknowable Baumgartner.[16] In interview, Desai has argued that she wanted *Baumgartner's Bombay* to contain a 'certain mystery, a puzzle at the heart of it' (Bliss 530), which is signified by the cryptic postcards, sent by his mother from a concentration camp, that begin and end the book. The silence of the Holocaust, concerning the exact fate of his mother, is the empty signifier in the novel on which Desai projects the violence of partition and the death and displacement of hundreds and thousands of individuals.

The tension between Baumgartner's inauthentic ambivalence, neither black nor white, east nor west, and the supposedly authentic humanizing impulse in the novel is played out with reference to images of fragmentation and wholeness. The opposite of the shattered mirror image in *Baumgartner's Bombay* is the images of harmony and completeness where racial and national differences are transcended. This can be seen most clearly in Baumgartner's short sojourn in Venice after he leaves Berlin for Bombay. His idealized memories of Venice are derided throughout the novel, reaching a climax when Kurt dismisses Venice as 'only drains' (Desai 1988: 160). Before his encounter with Kurt, Baumgartner tells Julius that he is reminded of a 'glass bowl' he 'saw in a window in Venice once', and Julius responds equally scornfully: 'you look like a beetroot farmer. . . . In Venice, he says!' (122). This memory of the glass bowl – a benign version of the humiliating glass ball that is given to him from a Christmas tree in his youth in lieu of a real present – is also associated with Baumgartner's fantasies about the young wife of the missionary Bruckner which take place in the British anti-alien internment camp: 'When had they set about converting the natives? He made up a picture of her touching the bowed heads of the tribal men and women in grass skirts, and at night holding a great glass globe between her fingers in which candlelight was reflected and flickered' (128). Here the unfragmented 'great glass globe between her fingers' is part of a chain of images – from glass bowl to glass globe – with Venice as the quintessence of a harmonizing Christian civilization. As I have noted elsewhere, this version of Venice is famously summarized in E.M. Forster's *A Passage to India* (1924), where Fielding regards the city as the epitome of 'the harmony between the works of man and the earth that upholds them, the civilisation that has escaped muddle, the spirit in a reasonable form with flesh and blood subsisting'.[17] Venice as an idealized Christian locale – precisely because of its sacramental balance of body and spirit – is contrasted in *A Passage to India* with the muddle and confusion of India. Desai's Venice, in a pointed rewriting of Forster, becomes less a place of harmony than a city of strangers or 'fair-skinned' (60) Orientals that allows Baumgartner, after drifting around in search of the Jewish quarter, to feel at home at last:

He stood there, as entranced as he was alarmed. Venice *was* the East, and yet it was Europe too; it was that magic boundary where the two met and blended, and for those seven days Hugo had been a part of their union. He realised it only now: that during his constant wandering, his ceaseless walking, he had been drawing closer and closer to this discovery of that bewitched point where they became one land of which he felt himself the natural citizen. (63)

By thinking of Venice as a blend of Europe and Asia, Baumgartner imagines himself to be a 'natural citizen' of this dream-city where he can begin to feel at ease with his strangeness. At the same time, Desai is careful not to simply make Baumgartner's homelessness a facile diasporic homeland constructed primarily through the literary imagination. Because Baumgartner moves between such radically different historical circumstances there is no attempt simply to elide the fantastically divergent racial and national contexts in which he finds himself. For this reason, Desai characterizes his Jewishness as 'both in [the East] and travelling to it, at a distance and yet one with it' (64). In a telling lack of closure, Baumgartner never quite manages to enter the Jewish ghetto in Venice as this would have been a far too easy resolution of his incommensurable identity. Unlike Forster's *A Passage to India*, which echoes slyly throughout the novel, the strangeness of Venice becomes a utopian space that enables Desai to universalize India and Europe, Bombay and Berlin, in the figure of Baumgartner.

Desai has spoken of her unease at turning a figure who is so radically indeterminate into a symbol of suffering humanity: 'I'm really not sure how successful a character he is in subjective terms. There's too great a distance between Hugo and myself, Hugo and society, Hugo and all the historical events around him. I'm not sure that I haven't allowed him to drift too far apart, become disassociated' (Bliss 526). That Baumgartner errs on the side of fragmentation rather than uniting the dispossessed is obviously in keeping with Desai's skilful and convincing characterization of his abiding trauma. But his failure to represent humanity in general means that Baumgartner is frequently described in animal terms, as a 'crustacean – crab – ungainly turtle' (Desai 1988: 11), as a 'mournful turtle' (109) or as being as 'slow as a snail, slow as a turtle' (194), which chimes with the fact that he has given his life over to the animal realm in Bombay by collecting stray cats. Such are the limitations of Desai's postethnic humanizing ideals.

The animal realm is first associated with the Aryan 'Gentleman from Hamburg' (51) – named after Isaac Bashevis Singer's equally sinister story 'The Gentleman from Cracow' (1957) – who describes Baumgartner's parents as 'obstinate mice who turned up their noses at the cheese' (54). The two horse races that unify the novel, and provide Baumgartner with intense adolescent frustration in Germany and unique periods of happiness in India, also bring Baumgartner's many lives together: 'the circular track that began in Berlin and ended here in Bombay' (194). It is therefore fitting that the last few pages of *Baumgartner's Bombay* are a reworking of Franz Kafka's novella *Metamorphosis* (1915), when the 'cockroach' Gregor Samsa, not unlike Baumgartner, is cleared away with unseemly haste so as to usher in a supposedly rosier future. The novel ends with the recognition that Baumgartner was unable to escape the violence that forced him to migrate to India in the first place. But his displaced sympathy for the animal world in Bombay finally signifies his inability to commune with the wretched of the earth within his adopted country. In contrast to her many proclamations that Baumgartner represented suffering humanity as a whole, Desai's novel complicates such universalizing by revealing just how difficult and painful it was for her traumatized protagonist to make connections with others.

Epilogue: Zadie Smith's Neutral Ground

A neutral place. The chances of finding one these days are slim. . . . The sheer *quantity* of shit that must be wiped off the slate if we are to start again as new. Race. Land. Ownership. Faith. Theft. Blood. And more blood. And more. And not only must the *place* be neutral, but the

messenger who takes you to the place, and the messenger who sends
you the messenger. (Smith 2000: 291–92)

In her essay on Zora Neale Hurston's *Their Eyes Were Watching God*
(1937), Zadie Smith recalls her younger, teenage self endeavouring to find
a 'neutral universal' (Smith 2009: 11) as a reader beyond 'genetic or socio-
cultural reasons' (3): 'I disliked the idea of "identifying" with the fiction I
read. . . . I want my limits to be drawn by my own sensibilities, not by my
melanin count' (7–10). At one point in the essay she compares Hurston's
'soulfulness' with Philip Roth's notion of the 'romance of oneself' but then
goes on, in a long end-note, to contrast Hurston's 'black woman-ness' with
Roth's Jewishness: 'In literary terms, we know that there is a tipping point
at which the cultural particular – while becoming no less culturally particular – is accepted by readers as the neutral universal. The previously
"Jewish fiction" of Philip Roth is now "fiction". We have moved from the
particular complaints of Portnoy to the universal claims of Everyman'
(13).[18] That Roth's fiction shifts from the particular to the universal, in the
guise of a refashioned Nathan Zuckerman in the late American Trilogy, is
an argument made in this book. But it is crucial, I believe, to see this shift
as a deliberate strategy of Roth's to speak with a national voice and, as he
put it in his younger days, to aspire to write the 'great American novel'.
That Roth, as an American novelist, is confused with the universal is, of
course, not unusual but this slippage should not be generalized to include
all 'Jewish fiction'. Earlier in her essay Smith defines both blackness and
Jewishness, in relation to Kafka and Hurston, as a product of the 'build-up
of a cultural residue' (12) that does offer an alternative viewpoint. As we
will see, Smith's first two novels also shift between associating Jews with
the 'neutral universal' (echoing Desai's intentions for Baumgartner) and
placing them on the same footing as their black counterparts.

The association of contemporary Jews with a privileged neutral ground
is a narrative strategy that is repeated in *White Teeth* (2000) in the guise of
the Chalfen family. Throughout the novel, the teenage Irie veers between
her own ethnic and racial difference and a desire to acculturate into the

'neutral universal', not unlike Smith's version of herself as a fourteen-year-old in the Hurston essay. This is, as we have seen, a story that has been told many times before, beginning with Fanon's younger self in *Black Skin, White Masks* (1952) who initially craves assimilation into the French variation of universalism. Her desire to assimilate is at its most painful and uncomfortable when Irie attempts to have her hair straightened. The aspiration to be part of the Chalfen family is a comic variant of this assimilatory desire, which is made clear when she compares her own family with the Chalfens after coming across a 'small slice of the Chalfen family tree, an elaborate oak that stretched back into the 1600s and forward to the present day': 'The differences between the Chalfens and the Jones/ Bowdens were immediately plain. For starters, in the Chalfen family everybody seemed to have a normal number of children. More to the point, everybody knew whose children were whose. . . . Dates of birth and death were concrete. And the Chalfens actually *knew* who they were in 1675' (Smith 2000: 290). For Irie, the Chalfens represent that 'strange and beautiful thing, the *middle class*' (277), which is why she focuses on their supposed normality, certainty and concreteness, and compares them to an elaborate English oak. But, as the narrator notes, the teenage Irie's desire for the 'Englishness' of the Chalfens – 'the *purity* of it' – ignores the fact that they were, 'after a fashion, immigrants too (third generation, by way of Germany and Poland, née Chalfenovsky)', which discounts the concreteness of the Chalfen family in prewar Poland and Germany at least. What is more, when Irie 'stepped over the threshold of the Chalfen house' she felt an illicit thrill, like a 'Jew munching a sausage', which positions her as the transgressive and impure 'Jew' in stark contrast to the Chalfens who are, pointedly, 'more English than the English' (283).[19] The Chalfens' version of immigration ('after a fashion') is the complete opposite of the Caribbean and Asian versions of immigration in the book, which are disorderly and disconnected, not unlike earlier constructions of unassimilated and unassimilable Jewishness. But the Chalfens are said to deal 'in the present' and, unlike Archie and Samad, do not 'drag ancient history around like a chain and ball' (281).[20]

Zadie Smith has acknowledged in an interview that she is now embarrassed by her caricatural portrayal of the Chalfens – 'even hearing the name the Chalfens make me want to writhe' – but they clearly have a pivotal function in the novel as an individualistic and narcissistic variant of the multicultural hybridity that Smith has been falsely said to champion.[21] Joyce Chalfen describes her 'varied off-spring' as a form of 'cross-pollination between a lapsed Catholic horticulturist feminist and an intellectual Jew' (Smith 2000: 267) and writes bestselling books on cross-breeding. Marcus Chalfen, equally crudely, is a geneticist who believes in the '*perfectability* of all life' and attempts to achieve this via gene transfer, creating 'mice with rabbit genes' which 'his God's imagination . . . could not conceive of' (269). In this parodic world of overdetermined hybridity, Irie '*wanted* to merge with the Chalfens, to be of one flesh; separated from the chaotic, random flesh of her own family and transgenically fused with another' (295). While her family are 'chaotic' and 'random', the Chalfens are on the side of rationality and order, with Marcus's gene therapies designed specifically to eliminate the 'random', ushering in 'a new phase in human history' so that humanity can be 'directors and arbiters of our own fate' (370). For Irie, it is precisely their rationality, embodied in their superior whiteness, Englishness and rather 'smug' middle-class identity, that makes the Chalfens the very epitome of postethnic assimilationism. They represent, above all else, a utopian ideal of the 'neutral universal' to go along with the other religious and secular versions of utopianism in the novel.

Irie's preoccupation with this idealized neutrality begins with her quest to find a 'neutral place' for the twins Millat and Magid to meet so as to bridge their differences – one on the side of religious fundamentalism, the other on the side of liberal secularism. The failure of this project becomes a motif in the final chapters of the novel: 'The brothers begin to argue and they make a mockery of that neutral place . . . they take what was blank and smear it with the stinking shit of the past like excitable excremental children' (397). Irie repeats much the same argument, especially her sense of an excremental past, when she explodes at the Iqbals and the Joneses on

a bus because they are arguing loudly much to her embarrassment: 'Not
everyone in the *universe* wants to listen to you lot . . . did you know how
other families are? They're *quiet*' (439): 'What a *joy* their lives must be.
They open a door and all they've got behind it is a bathroom and lounge.
Just neutral spaces. And not this endless maze of present rooms and past
rooms . . . and everybody's old historical shit all over the place' (440). Here
Irie's multiple associations of her family with disorder, loud voices, impurity and, above all, an excremental past evoke a whole series of racial
images that, as we have seen throughout *Diasporas of the Mind*, have
historically been associated with Jews. By claiming these characteristics
for her family and newer Asian families – the Iqbals and the Joneses – Irie
finally rejects her desire for a 'neutral space', otherwise known as 'Happy
Multicultural Land':

> Mr Schmutters and Mr Banajii will merrily set upon another, weaving
> their way through Happy Multicultural Land. Well, good for them. But
> Magid and Millat couldn't manage it. They left the neutral room as they
> had entered it: weighed down, burdened, unable to waver from their
> course. . . . (398)

Smith goes back to an older type of Jewish immigrant in recalling the
Yiddish-inflected Mr Schmutters (the name literally means 'a rag man' and
is evocative of a first generation of Jewish migrant tailors making cheap
clothes) in stark contrast to the bourgeois Chalfens. Here there is an
equivalence with Mr Banajii (pointedly not a caricature name), with both
figures aiming to 'merge' with the 'oneness of this greenandpleasantliber-
tarianlandofthefree' (398). The issue here is not Jewishness per se but
liberal assimilation as personified by Marcus Chalfen, who recalls Otto
Cone in *The Satanic Verses* – described as a 'pantomime member of the
English gentry' (Rushdie 1988: 297) – and Mr Shylock in Naipaul's *The
Mimic Men*. But where these figures differ from Marcus is that they are
both associated with the Holocaust (Otto with Primo Levi's suicide and
Mr Shylock with 'recent events in Europe'), whereas Marcus could not be

more distant from the camps despite his German and Polish antecedents. This is made clear in the comic dénouement of the novel which is designed specifically to associate the 'loyal' (Smith 2000: 92) Nazi-inspired eugenicist Perret (whom Archie and Samad failed to kill during the war) with Marcus Chalfen's research into animal genetics. After all, Marcus launches his 'FutureMouse' at the Perret Institute ('The Final Space'), with Dr Marc-Pierre Perret himself in the audience and Archie and Samad re-enacting farcically their failure to kill him.

That Marcus's work is associated with Nazi eugenics remains undisturbed by his Jewishness, even when, not unlike the demonization of Rushdie during the *Satanic Verses* affair, he is known by Millat as the 'scientist Jew' (397) and racially Judaized by the comically named Islamic group KEVIN: 'It's Chalfen's head with mouse ears attached to a goat's torso, which is attached to a pig's arse' (422). Nonetheless, the Chalfens are the *luftmenschen* (or 'Mr Schmutters') come home to liberal England, which means that the Holocaust, an excremental past par excellence, is barely acknowledged. This can be seen when Clara and Alsana fall silent in the local park as they discuss their husbands' twin obsessions with the past. The reason for the silence is the appearance of the figure of Sol Jozefowitz, who continues to look after the park long after his salary has been stopped, and who may be a camp survivor. Once Sol disappears from view, the two women resume their 'talk, talk, talk', with Alsana concluding: 'I cannot be worrying-worrying all the time about the *truth*. I have to worry about the truth that can be *lived with*' (69). At this point she unknowingly evokes Kafka in describing their husbands, Archie and Samad, as 'daddy-long-legs': 'One leg in the present, one in the past' (70).[22] Ironically, given Alsana's disdain for the Chalfens, they are an ideal form of ethnic identity, in these terms, as they are disconnected from a traumatized past and, in somehow transcending their Jewish family's history in Germany and Poland, embody a 'truth that can be *lived with*'.

There is a split in *White Teeth*, not only between Marcus Chalfen and Sol Jozefowitz, but also between the Chalfens and the Iqbals and the Chalfens and the Joneses. All of the Chalfens' supposedly 'Jewish' characteristics are displaced onto other, more recent migrant families in the novel, which is why they are more 'English than the English' and represent the normative ideal of liberal assimilationism. Only Josh Chalfen, in betraying his father, makes sense of his non-Jewish Jewish family and in so doing prefigures a younger generation in *The Autograph Man* (2002). Josh is described as 'the last man standing' (414), as he is a member of the animal rights group FATE ('Fighting Animal Torture and Exploitation') and is able to get close enough to his father to release the experimental mouse. Josh is Zadie Smith's 'last Jewish intellectual' and is part of the eschatological discourses in *White Teeth* parodying Francis Fukuyama's *The End of History and the Last Man* (1992).[23] That the child betrays the father is a central feature of Christian constructions of Jews – going back to *The Merchant of Venice* and medieval mystery plays – which is why Joshua is valued by FATE as '*the convert from the other side*'.[24]

Josh joins FATE after a 'conversion' when he realizes that the 'largest community on earth, the animal kingdom, were oppressed, imprisoned and murdered on a daily basis' (412), which, not unlike Baumgartner, turns out to be his way of engaging with the Holocaust. Whereas his father sides with a former Nazi sympathizer, Josh frees the experimental mouse, which, as we have seen in *Baumgartner's Bombay* (and know from Art Spiegelman's *Maus*), is also a metaphor for the victims of the camps. Throughout the novel Josh is characterized by his 'Jew-fro' hair and is a mirror image of Irie as a continually insulted 'nerd-immigrant', which made her '*one of his own*' (256). That Irie wants to straighten the hair that characterizes Josh's ethnic Jewishness also speaks to his 'immigrant' credentials. His understanding of the nature of blackness, with reference to Shakespeare's 'dark lady' (234–35), as opposed to his mother's insensitive references to 'brown strangers' (281), also draws Irie to him. That Irie finally understands that immigrants 'cannot escape their history any more than you yourself can lose your shadow' (398) speaks to Josh's rejection of his father's 'enlightenment' (372) values, which abolish the past in the name of animal experimentation. Unlike the Chalfens, who need no one except themselves – and attempt to remake Millat and Magid in their own image – Josh engages with his past so that he can relate to other migrants in northwest London.

Unlike Desai, whose post-partition fictional world is further brutalized in the hands of the ruthless son of Chimanlal and Kurt, the murderous son of Germany, Josh and Irie are writ large in *The Autograph Man* in the guise of Alex-Li Tandem and Adam Jacobs (who are a younger generation on the side of mixed-up thinking of all kinds). Alex and Adam are teenagers and ethnic hybrids – Chinese/Jewish and black/Jewish – who spend most of the novel negotiating between the actual and the metaphorical, like John Middleton Murry, to retain a sense of sanity.[25] The central concern of the novel, Alex's inability to mourn (say *Kaddish*) for his Chinese father, contrasts starkly with the presentation of Josh in *White Teeth*, where he engages with a wider community of suffering through his animal rights activism. *The Autograph Man*, not unlike *White Teeth*, wishes to supplement ethnic hybridity with other values – in this case, spiritual belief rather than class difference. But what is startling about Smith's second book is that it is a postethnic novel that eschews universalism, determinedly mixing and intertwining racial differences of all kinds, and that uses Jewishness as a metaphor to understand the pitfalls of a too easy transcendence of 'race' and ethnicity. For all its undoubted engagement with the Kabbalah and Buddhist spirituality (representing Alex's father and mother), the novel is most concerned with the performative or gestural, which is why Alex deals in autographs and is preoccupied with popular culture.[26] In this sense Alex is a Chalfenist as he is located only in the present and is an empty signifier (James Wood calls him a 'dreary blank') on which the anxieties of the other characters are projected. That he is more concerned with keeping figures alive metaphorically, by collecting the ephemera of dead celebrities, rather than commemorating his actual father or mother, characterizes his priorities.[27] He regards the memorabilia from his mother's Jewish relatives who perished in the camps, for instance, as merely 'tiring': 'Everyone in these photographs is dead, thought Alex wearily' (Smith 2002: 92–93).

In keeping with the vacant figure of Alex (who is stoned or drunk for much of the novel), *The Autograph Man* sets up Jewishness as an empty signifier, based on Lenny Bruce's comically capricious distinctions between Jewishness and Goyishness, and attempts to understand the value of an ethnicity that is completely without foundation. For most of the novel Alex is working on a manuscript that divides the world up into Jewishness and Goyishness, which 'gave him a simple pleasure. He did it because he did it' (88). Such distinctions enable him to expand Jewishness into a signifier for the world at large, which both mimics racial discourse and also undermines it. Smith seems to have written a novel precisely to make it impossible to universalize ethnicity. *The Autograph Man* finally resolves this conundrum by combining the mystical traditions that surround the Kaddish with the purely gestural in an uneasy synthesis of the actual and the metaphorical, the traumatic and the ephemeral, in a bid both to contain and to transcend historical suffering. But this experimental novel proved to be a dead end for Zadie Smith.

After the critiques of James Wood in particular, Smith 'changed her mind' about the efficacy of her postethnic fictions and retreated into the discipline of the canon (Forster in particular) as a neutral place where black and white differences could be explored with clarity and certainty. Desai's gentle undermining of Forster's *A Passage to India* in *Baumgartner's Bombay* contrasts interestingly with Smith's endorsement of Forster in both *On Beauty* (2005) and her critical essays.[28] Wood's critique of Smith's 'hysterical realism' is based on her presumed lack of aesthetic command of her material, which is, crucially, associated with her subject matter. The excess of belonging of her *luftmenschen* – being simultaneously everywhere and nowhere – is critically related to the supposed unshaped verbosity of her written style, which is described as 'excessively centripetal': 'The different stories all intertwine, and double and triple on themselves. Characters are forever seeing connections and links and hidden plots, and paranoid parallels.'[29] For Wood, the Forsterian project of finding 'connections' is 'essentially paranoid', hence the term 'hysterical realism': 'There is something essentially paranoid about the idea that everything connects with everything else' (Wood 2011: 170). This lack of discrimination means that Smith's black, Jewish and Asian characters are impossible to represent with clarity as they confuse language (words abound) and they are a part of 'life' (the world of reportage), not 'art' (where the autonomy of her characters is paramount).

Such critiques stung Smith into writing more formally exact and much less verbose fictions, as can be seen in *NW* (2012) in particular. This novel exposes the false 'neutral universalism' of 'white' fictions which enables her to explore 'NW' not merely as a multicultural locale in northwest London but also as 'nowhere', a tabula rasa where it is not racial but class differences that count. Smith is an interesting case study for this book as her fictions veer between the dangerous freedoms inherent in her first two experimental novels, which foreground a metaphorical Jewishness as a means of speaking about ethnicity in general, and, in contrast, the more disciplined and therefore more reductive novels that she has written subsequently and that are 'black and white'. As with Desai, there is a tension in Smith's work between superseding the 'classic' expression of diaspora and victimhood and, at the same time, recognizing diaspora Jewishness as a living history that can enable it to make connections across histories and communities. The dismissal of this project as 'paranoid' gives a sense of how threatening it is to move beyond disciplinary thinking – whether it be in relation to nation, community or the literary canon – to open up the novel form so that it can connect with dissimilarities. *Diasporas of the Mind* is on the side of such metaphorical thinking while acknowledging that it is not without risks and may fail aesthetically (in Wood's terms). But these risks are worth taking if the alternative is a diminished capacity to enlarge our sense of self so as to include 'other others' in the pantheon of what it is to be human.

Notes

Chapter 1

1. http://www.salon.com/topic/ireland/, accessed 6 June 2012.
2. Remnick is referring in particular to Obama's response to the arrest of Henry Louis Gates in his house on July 2009.
3. A working title of *Changing my Mind* was *Between Black and White*.
4. In March 2012, after the shooting of Trayvon Martin in Florida, Obama responded by saying, 'If I had a son, he'd look like Trayvon', raising the issue of racial profiling. He was understandably more playful in an Irish context.
5. Ishmael Reed et al., 'Is Ethnicity Obsolete?', in Werner Sollors (ed.), *The Invention of Ethnicity* (New York: Oxford University Press, 1989), pp. 226–36.
6. Remnick, *The Bridge*, p. 190, argues that Obama chose 'his racial identity', and David Maraniss, *Barack Obama: The Making of the Man* (New York: Atlantic Books, 2012), follows this postethnic narrative.
7. For a recent discussion of the authenticity of Alex Haley's bestselling *Roots: The Saga of an American Family* (1976), see Marianne Hirsch and Nancy K. Miller, *Rites of Return: Diaspora Poetics and the Politics of Memory* (New York: Columbia University Press, 2011), pp. 1–2 and ch. 4.
8. For a discussion of Zadie Smith and supposed racial neutrality, see the epilogue to this book, pp. 255–64 below.
9. The figure of the 'tragic mulatto' will reappear in the guise of Coleman Silk in Philip Roth's *The Human Stain* (2000).
10. For Remnick's description of Obama as a 'shape-shifter', see Stephanie Clifford, 'Making It Look Easy at *The New Yorker*', *New York Times* (4 April 2010), B1.
11. See, for instance, President Obama's speech to the Hebrew University in Jerusalem (21 March 2013), where he spoke of the celebration of Pesach (Passover) in the White House and the analogous experience of blacks and Jews being freed from slavery.

12. See, for example, Sander Gilman, *Smart Jews: The Construction of the Image of Jewish Superior Intelligence* (Lincoln, Nebr.: University of Nebraska Press, 1996). Philip Roth describes himself as a 'walking text' in *The Facts: A Novelist's Autobiography* (New York: Farrar, Straus & Giroux, 1988), p. 162.

13. See Fanon 1961: ch. 6 for a new global humanism.

14. See, for example, David Cesarani, *Eichmann: His Life and Crimes* (London and New York: William Heinemann, 2004), p. 325, and Dan Stone and Richard King (eds), *Hannah Arendt and the Uses of History: Imperialism, Nation, Race and Genocide* (New York: Berghahn Books, 2007), p. 2. See also Shoshana Felman, *The Juridical Unconscious: Trials and Traumas in the Twentieth Century* (Cambridge, Mass.: Harvard University Press, 2002), ch. 3, and Tony Kushner, *The Holocaust and the Liberal Imagination: A Social and Cultural History* (Oxford: Basil Blackwell, 1994).

15. For the Francophone tradition, see Michael Rothberg, *Multidirectional Memory: Remembering the Holocaust in the Age of Decolonization* (Stanford, Calif.: Stanford University Press, 2009), and Max Silverman, *Palimpsestic Memory: The Holocaust and Colonialism in French and Francophone Fiction and Film* (New York: Berghahn, 2013).

16. See, in particular, Susannah Young-ah Gottlieb (ed.), *Hannah Arendt: Reflections on Literature and Culture* (Stanford, Calif.: Stanford University Press, 2007).

17. The phrase 'thinking without a banister' is cited in Richard Bernstein, *Hannah Arendt and the Jewish Question* (New York and Oxford: Polity Press, 1996), p. 41.

18. See also Arendt's *The Human Condition* (1958), p. 184.

19. Bryan Cheyette, *Constructions of 'the Jew' in English Literature and Society: Racial Representations, 1875–1945* (Cambridge: Cambridge University Press, 1993).

20. 'The Jew as Pariah: A Hidden Tradition' (1944), in Jerome Kohn and Ron H. Feldman (eds), *Hannah Arendt: The Jewish Writings* (New York: Schocken Books, 2007), pp. 275–97.

21. Seyla Benhabib, *The Reluctant Modernism of Hannah Arendt* (New York: Rowman and Littlefield, 2000), pp. 173–75, points out the ambiguity of the word 'thoughtlessness', which veers between an inability to be ethical and an inability to think critically.

22. See, for example, Ross Posnock, *Color and Culture: Black Writers and the Making of the Modern Intellectual* (Cambridge: Harvard University Press, 1998), p. 2, and Jacqueline Rose, *Proust among the Nations: From Dreyfus to the Middle East* (Chicago: Chicago University Press, 2011), ch. 1.

23. Stephen J. Whitfield, *Into the Dark: Hannah Arendt and Totalitarianism* (Philadelphia: Temple University Press, 1980), p. 183 and ch. 6.

24. Benhabib, *The Reluctant Modernism of Hannah Arendt*, p. 155, and Margaret Canovan, *Hannah Arendt: A Reinterpretation of her Political Thought* (Cambridge and New York: Cambridge University Press, 1992), ch. 5.

25. Benhabib, *The Reluctant Modernism of Hannah Arendt*, p. 149, and Cheyette, *Constructions of 'the Jew' in English Literature and Society.*

26. See also 'Law's Necessary Forcefulness: Ralph Ellison vs. Hannah Arendt on the Battle of Little Rock', in Anthony Simon Laden and David Owen (eds), *Multiculturalism and Political Theory* (Cambridge: Cambridge University Press, 2007), ch. 7, and Emily Miller Budick, *Blacks and Jews in Literary Conversation* (Cambridge: Cambridge University Press, 1998), pp. 73–78.

27. Robert Bernasconi, 'When the Real Crimes Began', in *Hannah Arendt and the Uses of History*, ch. 3 and pp. 62–64. But see Eyal Weizman, *The Least of All Possible Evils: Humanitarian Violence from Arendt to Gaza* (London and New York: Verso, 2012), ch. 2, for the relevance of Arendt to an understanding of contemporary Africa.

28. Chinua Achebe, 'An Image of Africa: Racism in Conrad's *Heart of Darkness*', in *Hopes and Impediments: Selected Essays, 1965–1987* (New York: Random House, 1988), ch. 1.

29. See King and Stone (eds), *Hannah Arendt and the Uses of History*, for the centrality of Arendt to this comparative work. The exception to this rule is Mark Mazower,

Hitler's Empire: Nazi Rule in Occupied Europe (London and New York: Penguin Books, 2008), p. 9 and pp. 602–04, who rejects the influence of Arendt (via the 'totalitarian paradigm') while also providing exhaustive historical evidence for the 'colonial turn'. As I argue below, this may be an example of the 'anxiety of appropriation'.

30. For this argument in a different context, see Sidra Dekoven Ezrahi, *Booking Passage: Exile and Homecoming in the Modern Jewish Imagination* (Berkeley: University of California Press, 2000).

31. As Lyndsey Stonebridge shows, Arendt began by not even being able to name her status as a refugee. See her *The Judicial Imagination: Writing after Nuremberg* (Edinburgh: Edinburgh University Press, 2011), ch. 4.

32. For a recent discussion focusing on contemporary literature, without the aid of Arendt or Murry on metaphor, see Jonathan P.A. Sell (ed.), *Metaphor and Diaspora in Contemporary Writing* (New York: Palgrave Macmillan, 2012).

33. Gauri Viswanathan confirmed in conversation that Said requested that the interview be the last word in the volume.

34. Lecia Rosenthal, 'Between Humanism and Late Style', in Adel Iskandar and Hakem Rustom (eds), *Edward Said: A Legacy of Emancipation and Representation* (Berkeley, Calif.: University of California Press, 2010), p. 483, describes the interview as 'somewhat legendary'.

35. See, for instance, Steven Aschheim, *Beyond the Border: The German-Jewish Legacy Abroad* (Princeton, N.J.: Princeton University Press, 2007), pp. 81–82 and ch. 3.

36. For a set of rather arbitrary and polarized differences between exile and diaspora, see Nico Israel, *Outlandish: Writing between Exile and Diaspora* (Stanford, Calif.: Stanford University Press, 2000), p. 8 and pp. 5–18. In this reading 'diaspora' (on the side of postmodernity) has superseded 'exile' (on the side of modernity) and the terms are therefore in unresolved tension.

37. King and Stone (eds), *Hannah Arendt and the Uses of History*, p. 2. See also Judith Butler, *Parting Ways: Jewishness and the Critique of Zionism* (New York: Columbia Unversity Press, 2012), and the critique of *Parting Ways* by Seyla Benhabib in *Constellations*, 20: 1 (2013), pp. 150–63.

38. Aamer Mufti, *Enlightenment in the Colony: The Jewish Question and the Crisis of Postcolonial Culture* (Princeton, N.J.: Princeton University Press, 2007). For a summary of this recent work, see my special issue of *Wasafiri*, 57 (winter 2009), on Jewish/postcolonial diasporas.

39. See also Said's introduction to *Mimesis* collected in *Humanism and Democratic Criticism* (London and New York: Palgrave Macmillan, 2004), p. 97 and ch. 4.

40. Emily Apter, *The New Translation Zone: A New Comparative Literature* (Princeton, N.J.: Princeton University Press, 2006), ch. 3.

41. Bryan Cheyette, 'A Glorious Achievement: Edward Said and the last Jewish Intellectual', in Tobias Döring and Mark Stein (eds), *Edward Said's Translocations: Essays in Secular Criticism* (London and New York, 2012), pp. 74–97.

42. On the American critic as self-fashioned alienated cosmopolitan, see Jonathan Freedman, *The Temple of Culture: Assimilation and Anti-Semitism in Literary Anglo-America* (New York and Oxford: Oxford University Press, 2000).

43. Ezrahi, *Booking Passage*, pp. 11–15, also has a critique of Steiner in these terms.

44. See also his *Feeling Global: Internationalism in Distress* (New York: New York University Press, 1999), ch. 6.

45. Bryan Cheyette, 'White Skin, Black Masks: Jews and Jewishness in the Writings of George Eliot and Frantz Fanon', in Keith Ansell Pearson, Benita Parry and Judith Squires (eds), *Cultural Readings of Imperialism: Edward Said and the Gravity of History* (London: Lawrence and Wishart, 1997), pp. 106–26.

46. For an important rereading of this manifesto, see Susheila Nasta, *Home Truths: Fictions of the South Asian Diaspora in Britain* (London and New York: Palgrave, 2002), ch. 4.

47. Patrick Williams, 'Naturally, I Reject the Term "Diaspora": Said and Palestinian Dispossession', in Michelle Keown, David Murphy and James Proctor (eds), *Comparing Postcolonial Diasporas* (Basingstoke: Palgrave Macmillan, 2009), pp. 83–103.

48. The contrast is with Nico Israel, *Outlandish: Writing between Exile and Diaspora*. Perhaps the focus on historical and political difference, missing from Israel's account, explains these differing versions.

49. Salman Rushdie, *The Satanic Verses* (London: Viking, 1988), pp. 205 and 427.

50. Bill Ashcroft and Kadhim Hussein (eds), *Edward Said and the Postcolonial* (Huntington: Nova Science, 2001).

51. 'Classical Notions of Diaspora: Transcending the Jewish Tradition', in Robin Cohen, *Global Diasporas: An Introduction* (London: Routledge, 1997), pp. 1–29.

52. Chana Kronfeld, *On the Margins of Modernism: Decentering Literary Dynamics* (Berkeley, Calif.: University of California Press, 1996), for 'minor' Jewish cultures.

53. Bernstein, *Hannah Arendt and the Jewish Question*, pp. 108–10, and Jacqueline Rose, *The Question of Zion* (Princeton, N.J.: Princeton University Press, 2005), ch. 2. See also David Herman, 'Edward Said (1935–2003)', *Salmagundi* (summer 2004), 76–88, who makes a case for Said's 'tragic' vision in relation to the binational ideal (pp. 87–88).

54. Terry Eagleton, *Exiles and Emigrés: Studies in Modern Literature* (London: Chatto and Windus, 1970).

55. Catherine Rainwater and William J. Scheick, 'An Interview with Cynthia Ozick', *Texas Studies in Literature and Language* (1983), pp. 254–65. The contrast here is with George Steiner, 'The Long Life of Metaphor: An Approach to the "Shoah"', in Berel Lang (ed.), *Writing and the Holocaust* (New York: Holmes and Meier, 1988), ch. 11, which confines metaphor to the metaphysical realm.

56. A London death actually means a Jewish death (according to Jewish practice), hence its speed and 'secrecy'.

57. 'Rachmanism' has entered the English language as a particularly pernicious form of exploitation of Caribbean migrants but it is by no means certain that Rachman was any worse than the London rentier class in general. The best-known literary representations of Rachman can be found in Peter Flannery's *Singer* (London: Nick Hern, 1992) and Linda Grant's *The Clothes on their Backs* (London: Virago, 2008). For a history of these perceptions, see Tony Kushner, *We Europeans? Mass-Observation, 'Race' and British Identity in the Twentieth Century* (London: Ashgate, 2004).

58. See also Stephen Clingman, 'Other Voices: An Interview with Caryl Phillips', *Salmagundi* (summer 2004), 113–40.

59. Paul Gilroy, 'Not Being Inhuman', in Bryan Cheyette and Laura Marcus (eds), *Modernity, Culture and 'the Jew'* (Oxford: Polity Press, 1998), p. 287 and pp. 282–97; *The Black Atlantic: Modernity and Double Consciousness* (Cambridge, Mass.: Harvard University Press, 1993), ch. 6; and *Between Camps*, which is Gilroy's most comprehensive account of this comparative project. Clingman, *The Grammar of Identity*, pp. 73–75, rightly notes the links between the work of Phillips and Gilroy.

60. Hanif Kureishi, 'We're Not Jews', in *Love in Blue Time* (London and New York: Faber, 1997), pp. 41–51, and Sander Gilman, *Jewish Frontiers: Essays on Bodies, Histories and Identities* (London and New York: Palgrave Macmillan, 2003), ch. 7. See also Wendy Zierler, ' "My Holocaust Is Not your Holocaust": "Facing" Black and Jewish Experience in *The Pawnbroker, Higher Ground*, and *The Nature of Blood*', *Holocaust and Genocide Studies* 18: 1 (spring 2004), 46–67.

61. See also David Macey, *Frantz Fanon: A Life* (London and New York: Granta Books, 2000), p. 449, and Martin Evans, *Algeria: France's Undeclared War* (Oxford and New York: Oxford University Press, 2012), p. 324.

62. There are two forms of uniqueness discourse that this book resists. The first reduces the comparative and connected histories and literatures that are discussed to the question of anti-Semitism or racism, and the second treats the 'classic' Jewish diaspora as a unique case. My work, in this latter regard, differs from the otherwise stimulating Vijay Mishra, *The Literature of the Indian Diaspora: Theorizing the Diasporic Imaginary* (London and New York: Routledge, 2007).

Chapter 2

1. David Macey, *Frantz Fanon: A Life* (London: Granta Books, 2000), p. 28 and ch. 1, is the best recent summary of the reception of Fanon after his death.
2. For a discussion of this split in Fanon Studies, see the introduction to Lewis R. Gordon et al., *Fanon: A Critical Reader* (Oxford: Blackwell Publishers, 1996).
3. Homi Bhabha, 'Remembering Fanon: Self, Psyche and the Colonial Tradition', is the foreword to the 1986 Globe edition of *Black Skin, White Masks*. The best-known critique of this approach is Benita Parry, 'Problems in Current Theories of Colonial Discourse' (1987), collected in her *Postcolonial Studies: A Materialist Critique* (London and New York: Routledge, 2004), ch. 2. See also Neil Lazarus, *Nationalism and Cultural Practice in the Postcolonial World* (Cambridge: Cambridge University Press, 1999), ch. 2.
4. Henry Louis Gates, 'Critical Fanonism', *Critical Inquiry* (spring 1991), 457–58 and 457–70.
5. Black Cat was a popular imprint of Grove Press in the 1960s and '70s.
6. Ross Posnock, *Color and Culture: Black Writers and the Making of the Modern Intellectual* (Cambridge, Mass.: Harvard University Press, 1998), p. 45.
7. Albert Memmi, 'The Impossible Life of Frantz Fanon', *Massachusetts Review* (winter 1973), 9–39.
8. Robert J.C. Young, 'Sartre the "African Philosopher"', in Jean-Paul Sartre, *Colonialism and Neocolonialism* (1964) (London and New York: Routledge, 2001), p. xxiii.
9. Albert Memmi, *The Pillar of Salt* (1955) (Boston, Mass.: Beacon Press, 1992), p. x and Prologue. During this period Fanon also wrote a number of unpublished plays in a similar search for a new evocative language close to storytelling.
10. David Marriott, 'Whither Fanon', *Textual Practice* (Feb. 2011), 64 and 33–69.
11. There is some confusion concerning Fanon's pan-Africanism. See, for instance, Robert J.C. Young's *Postcolonialism: An Historical Introduction* (Oxford and New York: Blackwell, 2001), p. 276, where he argues that Fanon was not a pan-Africanist, and 'Fanon and the Turn to Armed Struggle in Africa', *Wasafiri* (spring 2005), 38 and 33–41, where he argues for a Fanonian version of pan-Africanism.
12. Albert Memmi, *Dominated Man: Notes towards a Portrait* (Boston: Beacon Press, 1968), p. 16.
13. Ann Pellegrini, *Performance Anxieties: Staging Psychoanalysis, Staging Race* (London and New York: Routledge, 1997), p. 110 and ch. 6. See also Richard H. King, *Race, Culture and the Intellectuals* (Baltimore, Md. and London: Johns Hopkins University Press), ch. 9, for a discussion of Memmi, Fanon and Negritude.
14. See also Peter Geismar, *Frantz Fanon* (New York: Dial Press, 1971), pp. 133–34.
15. Aimé Césaire, 'The Revolt of Frantz Fanon', *Jeune-Afrique* (Dec. 1961), 24.
16. Daniel Boyarin, 'Homophobia and the Postcoloniality of "Jewish Science"', in Daniel Boyarin, Daniel Itzkovitz and Ann Pellegrini (eds), *Queer Theory and the Jewish Question* (New York: Columbia University Press, 2003), pp. 175 and p. 168–98.
17. Homi Bhabha, 'Preface: Framing Fanon', in Frantz Fanon, *The Wretched of the Earth* (New York: Grove Press, 2004), pp. xix–xx.
18. The combustible context for these quotations, where Fanon notoriously describes the Holocaust as a 'little family quarrel', is probably the reason for this elision, but it also

indicates the slipperiness of Fanon's characterization of the racialized person. For a fuller discussion of this quotation, see pp. 67–69 below.

19. Martin Evans, *Algeria: France's Undeclared War* (Oxford and New York: Oxford University Press, 2012), p. 322 and pp. 322–25.

20. In general, Azzedine Haddour recognizes the importance of Memmi's version of Fanon, while disagreeing with Memmi's approach, as can be seen from his foreword 'Postcolonial Fanonism', to his *The Fanon Reader* (London: Pluto Press, 2006), pp. vii–xxv, and his 'The Importance of Sartre in Fanon', *New Formations* (summer 2002), 34–38. See also his introduction, 'Remembering Sartre', to Jean-Paul Sartre's *Colonialism and Neocolonialism*, pp. 1–21.

21. Albert Memmi, *Jews and Arabs* (New York: J. Philip O'Hara, 1975), pp. 209–15.

22. For the best account of Sartre's 'Zionism' and support for the Palestinians, see Jonathan Judaken, *Jean-Paul Sartre and the Jewish Question: Anti-Antisemitism and the Politics of the French Intellectual* (Lincoln, Nebr.: University of Nebraska Press, 2006), ch. 6.

23. Macey, *Frantz Fanon: A Life*, pp. 466–68.

24. A recent example is Nigel C. Gibson, *Fanon: The Postcolonial Imagination* (Cambridge: Polity, 2003), ch. 1. But most received accounts, such as this, assume a simple equivalence between anti-black and anti-Jewish racism, which, I argue, is a reductive reading of Fanon's work.

25. Memmi distances himself from Sartre's conception of 'the Jew' as a product of anti-Semitism most explicitly in *Portrait of a Jew* (New York: Orion Press, 1962) and *The Liberation of the Jew* (New York: Orion Press, 1966). See Hannah Arendt, *The Origins of Totalitarianism* (1951) (New York: Schocken Books, 2004), pp. 8–9, for Arendt's 1967 preface where she distances herself from Sartre on the same grounds as Memmi. See also Richard Bernstein, *Hannah Arendt and the Jewish Question* (New York and Oxford: Polity Press, 1996), pp. 195–97.

26. Posnock, *Color and Culture*, rightly constructs a long intellectual tradition of black thought that counters the racialized associations of blacks with irrationality and the body.

27. I am grateful to Pellegrini, *Performance Anxieties*, p. 106, for this point.

28. Robert J.C. Young, *White Mythologies: Writing History and the West* (London and New York: Routledge, 1990), p. 8.

29. See Michael Rothberg, *Multidirectional Memory: Remembering the Holocaust in the Age of Decolonization* (Stanford, Calif.: Stanford University Press, 2009), chs 2 and 3, for contrasting 'boomerang effects' in the work of Hannah Arendt and Aimé Césaire. Rothberg does not, however, include Sartre's preface to *The Wretched of the Earth*, which articulates a similar effect.

30. Aimé Césaire, *Discourse on Colonialism*, pp. 59–62, also has an extended critique of Mannoni that influenced Fanon.

31. Rothberg, *Multidirectional Memory*, pp. 7–11, is an excellent recent account of the limitations of a uniqueness discourse.

32. Young, *Postcolonialism: An Historical Introduction*, p. 422, and Parry, *Postcolonial Studies*, p. 16.

33. David Marriott, *On Black Men* (Edinburgh: Edinburgh University Press, 2000), p. 67 and ch. 4.

34. Parry, *Postcolonial Studies*, pp. 48–49.

35. Jock McCulloch, *Black Soul, White Artifact: Fanon's Clinical Psychology and Social Theory* (Cambridge: Cambridge University Press, 1983), p. 214.

36. Paul Gilroy, *Between Camps: Nations, Cultures and the Allure of Race* (Harmondsworth: Penguin Books, 2000), p. 1, and Caryl Phillips, *The European Tribe* (London: Faber and Faber, 1987), p. 54.

37. McCulloch, *Black Soul, White Artifact*, p. 80.

38. For evidence that Sartre drew on anti-Semitic wartime sources, see Susan Rubin Suleiman, 'The Jew in Sartre's *Réflexions sur la question juive*: An Exercise in Historical Reading', in Tamar Garb and Linda Nochlin (eds), *The Jew in the Text* (London: Thames & Hudson, 1995), pp. 201–18.

39. Pellegrini, *Performance Anxieties*, p. 122.

40. Here my disagreement is with Boyarin, 'Homophobia and the Postcoloniality of "Jewish Science"', who assimilates Freud a little too easily into his reading of Fanon.

41. See Michael Rogin, *Blackface, White Noise: Jewish Immigrants in the Hollywood Melting Pot* (Berkeley: University of California Press, 1996), ch. 7, and Marriott, *On Black Men*, pp. 72–79, for excellent readings of this film.

42. Donald Bogle, *Toms, Coons, Mulattoes, Mammies and Bucks: An Interpretive History of Blacks in American Films* (New York: Continuum Books, 1989), p. 145.

43. For this argument in relation to contemporary Hollywood, see Michael Rogin, *Independence Day* (London: BFI Publishing, 1998).

44. David Cesarani, *Eichmann: His Life and Crimes* (London and New York: William Heinemann, 2004), pp. 333–34.

45. Parry, *Postcolonial Studies*, pp. 53–54.

46. Hannah Arendt, *On Violence* (New York: Harcourt Brace and Co., 1970), p. 12.

47. As Macey notes, *The Wretched of the Earth* would have been much less contentious, and less open to the polemics of Sartre and Arendt, if Fanon had spoken about an 'armed struggle' in Algeria rather than abstracted 'violence' (Macey 2000: 475).

Chapter 3

1. Alexander Stille, 'What the Holocaust Meant: The Thinking of Primo Levi and Jean Améry', *Dissent* (summer 1990), p. 361 and pp. 361–66. See also Judith Woolf, *The Memory of the Offence* (Market Harborough: Troubadour, 2001), ch. 6, and Nancy Wood, *Vectors of Memory: Legacies of Trauma in Postwar Europe* (Oxford and New York: Berg, 1999), ch. 3.

2. Irène Heidelberger-Leonard, *The Philosopher of Auschwitz: Jean Améry and Living with the Holocaust* (London: IB Taurus, 2010), p. 65.

3. The Italian translation of *At the Mind's Limits* uses Levi's essay title *The Intellectual in Auschwitz*, which would have reinforced Améry's sense of being eclipsed by Levi.

4. Ian Thomson, *Primo Levi* (London: Hutchinson, 2002), pp. 395–96.

5. The original title of Améry's work was *Jenseits von Schuld und Sühne* (Beyond Guilt and Atonement), which echoes Nietzsche's *Jenseits von Gut und Böse* (*Beyond Good and Evil*).

6. Robert S.C. Gordon, ' "How Much Home Does a Person Need?" Primo Levi and the Ethics of Home', *Annali d'Italianistica* 19 (2001), pp. 215–34, is the best account of Levi and Améry in relation to home and homelessness. For Levi as a diasporist, see also Amira Hass, 'Between Two Returns', in Marianne Hirsch and Nancy K. Miller (eds), *Rites of Return: Diaspora Poetics and the Politics of Memory* (New York: Columbia University Press, 2011), ch. 11.

7. Eugene Goodheart, 'The Passion of Reason: Reflections on Primo Levi and Jean Améry', *Dissent* (autumn 1994), 525 and 518–27.

8. Philip Roth, *Shop Talk: A Writer and his Colleagues and their Work* (London: Jonathan Cape, 2001), p. 4 and pp. 1–17.

9. Gordon, ' "How Much Home Does a Person Need?" ', and see also his *Primo Levi's Ordinary Virtues: From Testimony to Ethics* (Oxford: Oxford University Press, 2001).

10. Ariella Lang, 'Reason as Revenge: Primo Levi and Writing the Holocaust', *Symposium* (winter 1999), 255–68.

11. For writing as rebirth in Levi, if a little overstated, see Daniel R. Schwarz, *Imagining the Holocaust* (New York: St Martin's Press, 1999), pp. 75–99.
12. George Steiner, 'Our Homeland the Text' (1985), in *No Passion Spent: Essays 1978–1996* (London: Faber and Faber, 1996), pp. 304–27.
13. See, for example, Susan Neiman, 'Jean Améry Takes his Life', in Sander Gilman and Jack Zipes (eds), *Yale Companion to Jewish Writing and Thought in German Culture, 1096–1996* (New Haven, Conn. and London: Yale University Press), pp. 775–82.
14. Cited in Heidelberger-Leonard, *The Philosopher of Auschwitz*, p. 76.
15. Walter Benjamin, 'The Storyteller: Reflections on the Work of Nikolai Leskov', *Illuminations* (London: Jonathan Cape, 1970), pp. 84–85 and pp. 83–109.
16. Jean Améry, *Radical Humanism: Selected Essays*, edited and translated by Sidney and Stella P. Rosenfeld (Bloomington: Indiana University Press, 1984), p. vi.
17. For Primo Levi's equally fraught relationship to the values of European humanism, see Jonathan Druker, *Primo Levi and Humanism after Auschwitz: Posthumanist Reflections* (New York: Palgrave Macmillan, 2009).
18. Simon Wiesenthal (ed.), *The Sunflower: On the Possibilities and Limits of Forgiveness* (New York: Schocken Books, 1979), p. 192.
19. Thomson, *Primo Levi*, pp. 326–99, charts this correspondence, which was partly fictionalized in *The Periodic Table*, in detail.
20. Berel Lang, *The Future of the Holocaust: Between History and Memory* (Ithaca, N.Y. and London: Cornell University Press, 1999), pp. 142–60.
21. Bryan Cheyette, 'Appropriating Primo Levi', in Robert S.C. Gordon (ed.), *The Cambridge Companion to Primo Levi* (Cambridge: Cambridge University Press, 2007), ch. 5.
22. For a general discussion of forgiveness that alludes briefly to both Levi and Améry, see Charles L. Griswold, *Forgiveness: A Philosophical Exploration* (Cambridge: Cambridge University Press, 2007).
23. Paul Gilroy, *Between Camps: Nations, Cultures and the Allure of Race* (London and New York: The Penguin Press, 2000), p. 90.
24. Heidelberger-Leonard, *The Philosopher of Auschwitz*, p. 70, who also notes Améry's growing disillusionment with Third World politics by the 1970s.
25. Gordon, *Primo Levi's Ordinary Virtues*, ch. 5, is the best account of Levi's political pragmatism. For a travesty of Levi's politics, see Judith Butler, *Parting Ways: Jewishness and the Critique of Zionism* (New York: Columbia Unversity Press, 2012), ch. 7.
26. W.G. Sebald, 'Jean Améry and Primo Levi', in Irène Heidelberger-Leonard (ed.), *Über Jean Améry* (1990), p. 119 and pp. 115–23, quoted in Heidelberger-Leonard, *The Philosopher of Auschwitz*, pp. 70–71.
27. Thomson, *Primo Levi*, p. 532. Cynthia Ozick, 'Primo Levi's Suicide Note', *Metaphor and Memory* (New York: Alfred A. Knopf, 1989), reads *The Drowned and the Saved* back from Levi's suicide and has proved to be a malign influence in this regard.
28. Giorgio Agamben, *Remnants of Auschwitz: The Witness and the Archive* (New York: Zone Books, 1999), p. 162. In his *The Search for Roots* (*La ricerca delle radici*) (1981), p. 98, Levi also notes pointedly that 'Death Fugue' is the 'exception' to Celan's poetry, which he contends was written only 'for the few'. Nonetheless, he wears 'Death Fugue' 'inside me like a graft'.
29. Lawrence Langer, *Preempting the Holocaust* (New Haven, Conn. and London: Yale University Press, 1998), p. 42.
30. W.G. Sebald, 'Against the Irreversible: On Jean Améry', *On the Natural History of Destruction* (London: Hamish Hamilton, 2003), p. 160 and pp. 147–71.
31. For a contrasting perspective, see Michael Rothberg, *Multidirectional Memory: Remembering the Holocaust in the Age of Decolonization* (Stanford Calif.: Stanford University Press, 2009), pp. 47–54.

32. See also Wood, *Vectors of Memory*, p. 74, for Nietzsche and Améry.

33. See James Young, *Writing and Rewriting the Holocaust* (Bloomington: Indiana University Press, 1988), ch. 5.

34. See Druker, *Primo Levi and Humanism after Auschwitz*, for Levi's self-identification with Ulysses, although he assumes incorrectly that the figure of Ulysses is synonymous with a dominating European culture.

35. Gordon, '"How Much Home Does a Person Need?"', p. 230.

36. Carole Angier, *The Double Bond: Primo Levi, a Biography* (London: Viking, 2002), p. 253.

37. Mirna Ciciona, *Primo Levi: Bridges of Knowledges* (Oxford: Berg, 1995), p. 126, and Sander Gilman, *Inscribing the Other* (Lincoln: University of Nebraska Press, 1991), p. 300.

38. Eric J. Sundquist, 'Silence Reconsidered: An Afterword', in David Cesarani and Eric J. Sundquist (eds), *After the Holocaust: Challenging the Myth of Silence* (London and New York: Routledge, 2012), p. 212.

39. Marco Belpoliti and Robert Gordon (eds), *Voice of Memory: Interviews 1961–87* (Cambridge and New York: Polity Press, 2001), pp. xx and xxiv. See also Massimo Giuliani, *A Centaur in Auschwitz: Reflections on Primo Levi's Thinking* (New York: Lexington Books, 2003), and Anthony Rudolf, *At an Uncertain Hour: Primo Levi's War Against Oblivion* (London: Menard, 1990).

40. Cited in Gilman and Zipes, *Yale Companion*, p. 779.

41. Gordon, *Primo Levi's Ordinary Virtues*, ch. 10.

42. Paul Gilroy, *Darker Than Blue: On the Moral Economies of Black Atlantic Culture* (Cambridge, Mass.: Harvard University Press, 2010), pp. 76–78.

43. Robert Eaglestone, *The Holocaust and the Postmodern* (Oxford and New York: Oxford University Press, 2004), pp. 322–23.

44. The *Auschwitz Report* (1946) was written with Leonardo De Benedetti, and many of the poems in *Shema* (1948), Levi's first anthology of poetry, were written on his return from Auschwitz. Heidelberger-Leonard, *The Philosopher of Auschwitz*, ch. 4, is a comprehensive account of Améry's writings in the 1940s and '50s.

Chapter 4

1. Ian Rankin, 'The Deliberate Cunning of Muriel Spark', in Gavin Wallace and Randall Stevenson (eds), *The Scottish Novel since the Seventies: New Visions, Old Dreams* (Edinburgh: Edinburgh University Press, 1993), pp. 43–44 and ch. 3.

2. Angus Wilson, 'Journey to Jerusalem', *Observer* (17 Oct. 1965), p. 28.

3. Martin Stannard, *Muriel Spark: The Biography* (London and New York: Weidenfeld and Nicolson, 2009), ch. 13.

4. *Guardian* (30 Sept. 1970), p. 8, cited in Rankin, 'The Deliberate Cunning of Muriel Spark', p. 41, and Lyndsey Stonebridge, *The Judicial Imagination: Writing after Nuremberg* (Edinburgh: Edinburgh University Press, 2011), ch. 3.

5. Muriel Spark, 'The Mystery of Job's Suffering: Jung's New Interpretation Examined', *Church of England Newspaper* (15 April 1955), 7.

6. In her preface to *Voices at Play: Stories and Ear-Pieces* (London: Macmillan, 1961), p. v, Spark states that she 'turned my mind into a wireless set and let the characters play on my ear'.

7. Frank Kermode, 'The House of Fiction: Interviews with Seven Novelists', in Malcolm Bradbury (ed.), *The Novel Today: Contemporary Writers on Modern Fiction* (London: Fontana Paperbacks, 1977), p. 132.

8. Abdel-Moneim Aly, 'The Theme of Exile in the African Short Stories of Muriel Spark', *Scottish Studies Review* 2: 2 (2001), 95 and 94–104.

9. Eleanor Byrne, 'Muriel Spark Shot in Africa', in Martin McQuillan (ed.), *Theorizing Muriel Spark: Gender, Race, Deconstruction* (New York: Palgrave, 2002), p. 118 and ch. 6, although the focus here is on the question of male violence.

10. Martin Stannard, 'Nativities: Muriel Spark, Baudelaire and the Quest for Religious Faith', *Review of English Studies* 218 (2003), 92 and 91–105.

11. January Marlow is pointedly the heroine of Spark's second novel, *Robinson* (London: Macmillan, 1958).

12. Stannard, *Muriel Spark: The Biography*, pp. 270–71, notes Spark's commitment to combating anti-Semitism, which, she stated, 'fairly curdles the Jewish part of my blood'.

13. Malcolm Bradbury, 'Muriel Spark's Fingernails', in *No, Not Bloomsbury* (London: Arena, 1987), pp. 268–78, and Peter Kemp, *Muriel Spark: Novelists and their World* (London: Paul Elek, 1974), p. 158. For a critique of this widespread assumption, see Bryan Cheyette, *Muriel Spark* (Plymouth: Northcote House Press, 2000).

14. Gauri Viswanathan, *Outside the Fold: Conversion, Modernity and Belief* (Princeton, N.J.: Princeton University Press, 1998), pp. xvii and ch. 1.

15. Viswanathan, *Outside the Fold*, ch. 2, for a view of Newman as a contradictory figure.

16. Muriel Spark, 'My Conversion', *The Twentieth Century* (autumn 1961), p. 60 and pp. 58–63. While Spark's 'My Conversion' is referred to extensively in many previous critical studies of her fiction, it has at times been repudiated by Spark herself. For an annotated version of the essay, in a bid to expose its inaccuracies, see the Muriel Spark Manuscript Collection in the University of Tulsa, McFarlin Library, item 53:3.

17. 'At Emily Brontë's Grave, Haworth, April 1961', cited in Michael Gardner and Willy Maley (eds), *The Edinburgh Companion to Muriel Spark* (Edinburgh: Edinburgh University Press, 2010), p. 24 and ch. 2.

18. Muriel Spark and Derek Stanford, *Emily Brontë: Her Life and Work* (London: Peter Owen, 1953), p. 15 and ch. 1.

19. Muriel Spark, 'The Poet in Mr. Eliot's Ideal State', *Outposts* 14 (summer 1949), pp. 26–28, and Bryan Cheyette, *Constructions of 'the Jew' in English Literature and Society: Racial Representations, 1875–1945* (New York and Cambridge: Cambridge University Press, 1993), pp. 264–67 for a discussion of *Notes towards the Definition of Culture* in these terms.

20. See also Stannard, *Muriel Spark: The Biography*, p. 116.

21. Cheyette, *Constructions of 'the Jew' in English Literature and Society*, ch. 6.

22. My argument here is with Bradbury, 'Muriel Spark's Fingernails', pp. 268–78.

23. Aly, 'The Theme of Exile in the African Short Stories of Muriel Spark', for the conjunction of Africa and exile.

24. Spark and Stanford, *Emily Brontë: Her Life and Work*, ch. 9.

25. Stannard, *Muriel Spark: The Biography*, pp. 318–19 and ch. 13, and Stonebridge, *The Judicial Imagination*, p. 74.

26. Ruth Whittaker, *The Faith and Fiction of Muriel Spark* (London: Macmillan Press, 1982), p. 78, and McQuillan, *Theorizing Muriel Spark*, p. 215.

27. Jacqueline Rose, *States of Fantasy (Clarendon Lectures in English Literature)* (Oxford: Oxford University Press, 1996), ch. 3.

28. 'The Religion of an Agnostic: A Sacramental View of the World of Marcel Proust', *Church of England Newspaper* (27 Nov. 1953), 1.

29. Esther Benbassi, *Suffering as Identity: The Jewish Paradigm* (London: Verso, 2010).

30. Primo Levi, *If This Is a Man* (1947) (London and New York: Abacus Press, 1969), pp. 71–72.

31. Stonebridge, *The Judicial Imagination*, ch. 3.

32. Hannah Arendt, *Eichmann in Jerusalem: A Report on the Banality of Evil* (Harmondsworth: Penguin Books, 1977).

33. Aryeh Maidenbaum and Stephen A. Martin (eds), *Lingering Shadows: Jungians, Freudians and Anti-Semitism* (Boston and London: Shambhala, 1991), pp. 10–11, 83–86.

34. Harold Fisch, *A Remembered Future: A Study in Literary Mythology* (Bloomington: Indiana University Press, 1984), pp. 164–65.

35. Stannard, *Muriel Spark: The Biography*, pp. 270–71, has an account of Spark attending a conference with Lionel Trilling in 1962 on the plight of Soviet Jewry.

36. Gabriel Josipovici, 'On the Side of Job', *TLS* (7 Sept. 1984), 989.

37. Josipovici, 'On the Side of Job', and Frank Kermode, 'Old Testament Capers', *London Review of Books* (20 Sept.–3 Oct. 1984), 10–11.

38. Arendt, *Eichmann in Jerusalem*, pp. 287, and pp. 9–10 of this book.

39. This is probably an implicit reference to Spark's public dispute in the first half of 1998 with her son, Robin, who claimed to have a marriage certificate that proved that his grandparents had wedded in a synagogue and that he was, therefore, 'fully Jewish'. For a summary of this controversy, see Martin Stannard, 'The Letter Killeth', *The Spectator* (6 June 1998), 36–37. See also Samuel Robin Spark, 'Life with the Cambergs', *The Edinburgh Star* (Feb. 1999), 13–17, and Stannard, *Muriel Spark: The Biography*, pp. 518–19.

40. See my forthcoming Oxford University Press World's Classics edition of Evelyn Waugh's *Black Mischief* (1932) for this argument in full.

Chapter 5

1. See http://rothsociety.org/philip-roths-birthday-and-media-fenzy for an account of these celebrations (last accessed 7 April 2013). These celebrations also included a full-length Public Broadcasting Service documentary on Roth in the American Masters series and innumerable public events in the United States marking the occasion. See also Nelly Kaprièlian, 'In Which Philip Roth Announces his Retirement', *Paris Review* (13 Nov. 2012), 1.

2. http://www.nytimes.com/ref/books/fiction-25-years.html, last accessed 7 April 2013. For President Obama on Roth, see p. 5, above.

3. David Brauner, *Philip Roth* (Manchester and New York: Manchester University Press, 2007), 180.

4. Ross Posnock, *Philip Roth's Rude Truth: The Art of Immaturity* (Princeton, N.J. and Oxford: Princeton University Press, 2006), pp. 6 and 100. See also Jonathan Freedman, *Klezmer America: Jewishness, Ethnicity, Modernity* (New York: Columbia University Press, 2008), ch. 4, and Greil Marcus, *The Shape of Things to Come: Prophecy and the American Voice* (London and New York: Faber and Faber, 2006), pp. 40–100.

5. Roth most probably took the term 'diasporism' from R.B. Kitaj's *First Diasporist Manifesto* (New York: Thames & Hudson, 1989). Kitaj was a friend of Roth's.

6. Edward Said, *Out of Place: A Memoir* (London: Granta Books, 1999), pp. 3–4.

7. See, for example, 'Philip Roth's Diasporism: A Symposium', *Tikkun* 8:3 (May 1993), pp. 41–45.

8. Emily Budick Miller, 'Roth and Israel', in Timothy Parrish (ed.), *The Cambridge Companion to Philip Roth* (New York and Cambridge: Cambridge University Press, 2007), p. 71 and ch. 5. See also Brauner, *Philip Roth*, p. 51, and Ranen Omer-Sherman, *Diaspora and Zionism in Jewish American Literature* (Hanover and London: Brandeis University Press, 2002), ch. 5.

9. Sidra Dekoven Ezrahi, *Booking Passage: Exile and Homecoming in the Modern Jewish Imagination* (Berkeley: University of California Press, 2000), p. 225.

10. For this distinction, see Rebecca L. Walkowitz, *Cosmopolitan Style: Modernism beyond the Nation* (New York: Columbia University Press, 2006), p. 6. See also Sander Gilman, *Jewish Frontiers: Essays on Bodies, Histories and Identities* (London and New York: Palgrave Macmillan, 2003), for a critique of the centre/periphery model of diaspora.

11. Josh Cohen, 'Roth's Doubles', *The Cambridge Companion to Philip Roth*, p. 89 and ch. 6.

12. Budick Miller, 'Roth and Israel', p. 72. For a counterreading, see Andrew Furman, 'A New Other Emerges in American-Jewish Literature: Philip Roth's Israel Fiction', in Harold Bloom (ed.), *Philip Roth: Modern Critical Views* (Philadelphia: Chelsea House Publishers, 2003), pp. 145–62.

13. Vivian Liska and Thomas Nolden (eds), *Contemporary Jewish Writing in Europe: A Guide* (Bloomington: Indiana University Press, 2008), p. xix.

14. Harold Bloom, 'Operation Roth', *New York Review of Books* (April 1993), 48.

15. 'Philip Roth's Diasporism', *Tikkun*, pp. 41–45, and see also Debra Shostak, *Philip Roth: Countertexts, Counterlives* (Columbia: University of South Carolina Press, 2004), p. 142.

16. Clive Sinclair, 'The Son Is Father to the Man', in Asher Z. Milbauer and Donald G. Watson (eds), *Reading Philip Roth* (Basingstoke: The Macmillan Press, 1988), p. 169.

17. Hana Wirth-Nesher, 'From Newark to Prague: Roth's Place in the American-Jewish Literary Tradition', in Milbauer and Watson (eds), *Reading Philip Roth*, p. 26.

18. For other accounts of Roth and Race, see Dean J. Franco (ed.), *Philip Roth Studies* (fall 2006) and his *Race, Rights, and Recognition: Jewish American Literature since 1969* (Ithaca, N.Y. and London: Cornell University Press, 2012), ch. 1.

19. Freedman, *Klezmer America*, pp. 1–38.

20. Sinclair, 'The Son Is Father to the Man', p. 170, rightly argues that 'since *The Ghost Writer* takes place in December 1956 and was composed more than twenty years later, it is clear that Zuckerman must have written it some months after the eponymous visit to Prague'.

21. Irving Howe dismissed *Portnoy's Complaint* (1969) because of the 'thin personal culture' of the author in his 'Philip Roth Reconsidered', *Commentary* (Dec. 1972), pp. 69–72. See also David Gooblar, *The Major Phases of Philip Roth* (London and New York: Continuum, 2011), ch. 3 and pp. 204–05 below.

22. Bloom, 'Operation Roth', p. 48. Roth reinforced the impression that the novel was an actual 'confession' by claiming to be a Mossad agent: 'A Bit of Jewish Mischief', *New York Times Book Review* (7 March 1993), 20. The preface to *Operation Shylock* is also supposedly drawn from 'notebook journals', p. 13.

23. Brauner, *Philip Roth*, pp. 148–49.

24. For a view of American history as 'trauma' in Roth's novels, see Aimee Pozorski, *Roth and Trauma: The Problem of History in the Later Works (1995–2010)* (New York and London: Continuum Books, 2011).

25. Michael Rothberg, 'Roth and the Holocaust', in Timothy Parrish (ed.), *The Cambridge Companion to Philip Roth* (Cambridge: Cambridge University Press, 2007), p. 60 and ch. 4.

26. See Nelly Kaprièlian, 'In Which Philip Roth Announces his Retirement', where Roth argues that he groups his last four novels (*Everyman, Indignation, The Humbling* and *Nemesis*) as 'Nemeses' because 'each one deals with the subject of death from a different point of view'. See also Rothberg, 'Roth and the Holocaust', p. 60.

27. Rothberg, 'Roth and the Holocaust', p. 61, and Shostak, *Philip Roth: Countertexts, Counterlives*, p. 249.

28. The influence of Kitaj's biography as a merchant sailor on this novel is yet to be studied. But I believe that it is significant that an Americanized, rather than diasporized, Kitaj influenced the work.

29. Edward Said, *On Late Style: Music and Literature against the Grain* (London and New York: Bloomsbury, 2006), pp. 7–17.

30. Frank Kelleter, 'Portrait of the Sexist as a Dying Man: Death, Ideology and the Erotic in *Sabbath's Theater*', in *Philip Roth: Modern Critical Views*, 179 and 163–98.

31. Benedict Anderson, *Imagined Communities* (London and New York: Verso, 1983), p. 9.

32. Derek Parker Royal (ed.), *Philip Roth: New Perspectives on an American Author* (Westport, Conn.: Greenwood Press, 2005), p. 186 and ch. 13.

33. Marcus, *The Shape of Things to Come*, p. 62.

34. Posnock, *Philip Roth's Rude Truth*, p. 138.

35. Roth stated in 1997: 'Jew is just another way of being an American'. Cited in Shostak, *Philip Roth: Countertexts, Counterlives*, 236.

36. Barbara Kirshenblatt-Gimblett and Jeffrey Shandler (eds), *Anne Frank Unbound: Media, Imagination, Memory* (Bloomington: University of Indiana Press, 2012).

37. Nadia Valman, *The Jewess in Nineteenth-Century British Culture* (Cambridge and New York: Cambridge University Press, 2007).

38. Bryan Cheyette, 'English Anti-Semitism: A Counter-Narrative', *Textual Practice* 25:1, 2011, pp. 18–34.

39. Parker Royal, *Philip Roth: New Perspectives*, p. 211 and ch. 14.

40. Eric J. Sundquist, *Strangers in the Land: Blacks, Jews, Post-Holocaust America* (Cambridge, Mass., and London: Harvard University Press, 2005), pp. 512–23. See also Posnock, *Philip Roth's Rude Truth*, pp. 88–100, and Brett Ashley Kaplan, 'Anatole Broyard's Human Stain: Performing Postracial Consciousness', *Philip Roth Studies* (fall 2005), pp. 125–44.

41. Shostak, *Philip Roth: Countertexts, Counterlives*, p. 153.

42. Posnock, *Philip Roth's Rude Truth*, p. 99. See also Adam Zachary Newton, *Facing Black and Jew: Literature as Public Space in Twentieth-Century America* (New York and Cambridge, Cambridge University Press, 1999), ch. 1.

43. There is also an implicit reference to Kitaj, who accused his London critics of 'murdering' his wife in 1994 after a retrospective of his work was poorly received and who returned to the United States as a result. See David Brauner, *Contemporary American Fiction* (Edinburgh: Edinburgh University Press, 2010), pp. 130–32.

44. Ross Posnock, 'Purity and Danger: On Philip Roth', *Raritan* 21:2, 2001, pp. 85–101.

45. Freedman, *Klezmer America*, pp. 171–72.

46. This quotation is taken from Frantz Fanon, *Studies in a Dying Colonialism* (1959) (London: Earthscan, 1965), p. 50.

47. Sundquist, *Strangers in the Land*, p. 515.

48. Walter Benn Michaels, 'Plots against America: Neoliberalism and Antiracism', *American Literary History* 18:2 (2006), 296 and 288–302.

49. Philip Roth, 'The Story behind *The Plot against America*', *New York Times Book Review* (19 Sept. 2004), 12 and 10–12.

50. Michael Rothberg, 'Against Zero-Sum Logic: A Response to Walter Benn Michaels', *American Literary History* 18:2 (2006), 305 and 303–11.

51. *Le Monde* (14 Feb. 2013), 1.

52. 'Matthew Asprey Interviews Clive Sinclair', *Los Angeles Review of Books* (18 Dec. 2012), http://lareviewofbooks.org/article.php?id=1257&fulltext=1, last accessed 11 April 2013.

53. Sundquist, *Strangers in the Land*, p. 36.

Chapter 6

1. Malise Ruthven, *A Satanic Affair: Salman Rushdie and the Rage of Islam* (London and New York: Hogarth Press, 1991), p. 2.

2. Lisa Appignanesi and Sarah Maitland (eds), *The Rushdie File* (London: Fourth Estate, 1989), pp. 2–4, 85–86 and 203–07.

3. Isaiah Shachar, *The Judensau: A Mediaeval Anti-Jewish Motif and its History* (London: Warburg Institute, 1974), and see also Irving M. Zeitlin, *Jews: The Making of a Diaspora People* (New York and Cambridge, Polity Press, 2012), p. 177.

4. Salman Rushdie, *Joseph Anton: A Memoir* (London and New York: Jonathan Cape, 2012), p. 129: '*The Jews made him do it*, they said. *His publisher was a Jew and paid him to do it. His wife, a Jew, put him up to it.*' See also pp. 96, 115, 121, 127, 150, 210, 255, 329, 362 and 625 and the conclusion to this chapter. Marianne Wiggins, who spent the first few months in hiding with Rushdie, has a 'Zelf-Portret' of Anne Frank in *Bet They'll Miss Us When We're Gone* (New York and London: HarperCollins, 1991), pp. 59–76.

5. Timothy Brennan, *Salman Rushdie and the Third World* (London: Macmillan Press, 1989), pp. 55–58.

6. Aijaz Ahmad, *In Theory: Classes, Nations, Literatures* (London: Verso, 1992), p. 157. See also pp. 22–23 above.

7. This is taken from Paul Gilroy, 'Frank Bruno or Salman Rushdie?', *Small Acts: Thoughts on the Politics of Black Cultures* (London and New York: Serpent's Tale, 1993), p. 88 and ch. 5. See also his *Between Camps: Nations, Cultures and the Allure of Race* (Harmondsworth: Penguin Books, 2000), pp. 246 and 378–79, for a more nuanced reference to the Rushdie Affair.

8. 'The cruelest thing anyone can do with *Portnoy's Complaint* is to read it twice': Irving Howe, 'Philip Roth Reconsidered', *Commentary* (Dec. 1972), 74 and 69–77.

9. For an account of how this review came to be written, in extraordinarily difficult circumstances, see *Joseph Anton*, p. 166.

10. Bryan Cheyette, 'Rewriting Rushdie', *The Jewish Quarterly* 36:3 (autumn 1989), 3–4.

11. Damian Grant, *Salman Rushdie* (Plymouth, Devon: Northcote House Press, 2012), p. 11.

12. Victoria Glendenning, 'A Novelist in the Country of the Mind', *Sunday Times* (25 Oct. 1981), p. 38.

13. It may be significant, in this regard, that Rushdie noted he could 'pass' for white in his early years in England. See Susheila Nasta, *Home Truths: Fictions of the South Asian Diaspora in Britain* (London and New York: Palgrave, 2002), p. 148.

14. Jonathan Boyarin, *Storm from Paradise: The Politics of Jewish Memory* (Minneapolis: University of Minnesota Press, 1992), p. 82.

15. Cited in D.C.R.A. Goonetilleke, *Salman Rushdie* (London: Macmillan Press, 1998), p. 15.

16. Steven Connor, *The English Novel in History: 1950-1995* (London and New York: Routledge, 1996), pp. 112–27. See also Youssef Yacoubi, *The Play of Reasons: The Sacred and the Profane in Salman Rushdie's Fiction* (New York and Berlin: Peter Lang, 2012).

17. Robert Eaglestone, 'Salman Rushdie: Paradox and Truth', in Philip Tew and Rod Mengham (eds), *British Fiction Today* (London and New York: Continuum, 2006), pp. 94–6 and ch. 8.

18. As Rushdie notes in *Joseph Anton* (p. 69), Chamcha echoes Gregor Samsa, 'Kafka's poor metamorphosised dung beetle', the anti-hero of Kafka's novella *Metamorphosis* (1915).

19. Joshua Trachtenberg, *The Devil and the Jews* (New York: Jewish Publication Society of America, 1995).

20. See, for example, Yacoubi, *The Play of Reasons*, p. 140, although this book does recognize in general the porous boundaries between Jews, Muslims and Christians.

21. In *Joseph Anton*, p. 534, Rushdie champions Otto Cone's sense of 'incompatible realities' colliding with one another.

22. George Steiner, 'The Hollow Miracle', in *Language and Silence: Essays 1958-1966* (London and New York: Faber and Faber, 1967), pp. 136–51.

23. Levi 'stepped out of the third floor landing and pitched himself over the railing of the marble staircase': Ian Thomson, *Primo Levi* (London: Hutchinson, 2002), p. 536.

24. Roger Y. Clark, *Stranger Gods: Salman Rushdie's Other Worlds* (Montreal and London: McGill-Queen's University Press, 2001), p. 132.

25. Salman Rushdie, 'The Indian Writer in English', in Maggie Butcher (ed.), *The Eye of the Beholder: Indian Writing in English* (London: Commonwealth Institute, 1983), p. 79 and pp. 77–82. See also Clive Sinclair's *The Brothers Singer* (London: Allison and Busby, 1983), which was a key influence on Rushdie in this regard. Both Rushdie and Sinclair were on the Granta list as two of the 'top twenty British novelists' in 1983.

26. See the essays in *Imaginary Homelands*, for instance, on the American-Jewish writers E.L. Doctorow, Isaac Bashevis Singer, Philip Roth, Saul Bellow and Grace Paley.

27. For a nuanced reading of *The Satanic Verses* that complicates the usual pieties, see Nasta, *Home Truths*, ch. 4.

28. Nadia Valman, *The Jewess in Nineteenth-Century British Culture* (Cambridge and New York: Cambridge University Press, 2007).

29. The dialectic between barbarism and civilization, suggested here, goes back to Walter Benjamin. For a version of this dialectic, see, in tandem, Zygmunt Bauman's *Modernity and the Holocaust* (Cambridge and New York: Polity Press, 1989) and his *Modernity and Ambivalence* (Cambridge and New York: Polity Press, 1991).

30. Here I follow Rushdie's self-designation in *Imaginary Homelands* (1991), where he speaks of his fellow 'Indo-Anglians' on pp. 1, 3 and 69.

31. Hillel Halkin, 'Salman Rushdie Surrenders', *Commentary* 102 (7 Jan. 1996), 55–59.

32. Aamer Mufti, *Enlightenment in the Colony: The Jewish Question and the Crisis of Postcolonial Culture* (Princeton, N.J.: Princeton University Press, 2007), pp. 246–47, and see also Stephen Morton, *Salman Rushdie: Fictions of Postcolonial Modernity* (London and New York: Palgrave, 2007), ch. 5.

33. Amitav Ghosh, *In an Antique Land: History in the Guise of a Traveller's Tale* (London and New York: Vintage Books, 1992), p. 339. See also Shaul Bassi, 'Mooristan and Palimpstine: Jews, Moors, Christians in Amitav Ghosh and Salman Rushdie', in David Brauner and Axel Staehler (eds), *The Edinburgh Companion to Modern Jewish Fiction* (Edinburgh: Edinburgh University Press, 2015).

34. J.M. Coetzee, *Stranger Shores: Essays 1986–1999* (London and New York: Secker & Warburg, 2001), p. 202 and ch. 16. See also Rushdie, *Joseph Anton*, p. 463.

35. For a corrective to such precolonial nostalgia, see Richard Fletcher, *Moorish Spain* (London and New York: Weidenfeld and Nicolson, 1992).

36. Salman Rushdie, 'Bosnia on my Mind', *Index on Censorship* (May–June 1994), 17–18.

37. See also Rushdie, *Joseph Anton*, p. 86.

38. Maya Jaggi, 'The Last Laugh', *New Statesman and Society* (8 Sept. 1995), 20.

39. Rebecca L. Walkowitz, *Cosmopolitan Style: Modernism Beyond Nation* (New York: Columbia University Press, 2007), ch. 5, although there is unfortunately no discussion of *The Moor's Last Sigh* as a counter to her characterization of Rushdie's 'mixed-up' 'modernist cosmopolitanism'.

40. There is an obvious link here with the *foetor judaicus* discussed in relation to Roth.

41. In *Joseph Anton*, p. 441, Rushdie notes that he had Moraes's 'graveyard requiem for himself', which concludes the book, 'almost from the beginning' of writing it.

42. Earlier in *Shalimar the Clown*, p. 145, the title of Levi's novel *If Not Now, When?* (1981), which is based on a well-known Talmudic saying, is also evoked by Rushdie.

43. Max Ophüls was a German-Jewish émigré filmmaker whose first Hollywood film was *The Exile* (1947).

44. Daniel Pick, *Svengali's Web: The Alien Enchanter in Modern Culture* (New Haven, Conn. and London: Yale University Press, 2000).

45. Peter Kemp, 'Shattered Idylls', *Sunday Times* (11 Sept. 2005), 27.

46. For a critique of the novel as 'depolitical', see Rehana Ahmed, Peter Morey and Amina Yaqin (eds), *Culture, Diaspora and Modernity in Muslim Writing* (London and New York: Routledge, 2012), ch. 13.

47. Clark, *Stranger Gods*, pp. 176–81, and Eaglestone, 'Salman Rushdie: Paradox and Truth', p. 99.

48. Gilroy, *Small Acts*, p. 88, and see, for example, Zoe Heller, 'The Salman Rushdie Case', *New York Review of Books* (20 Dec. 2012) and Pankaj Mishra's review of *Joseph Anton* for the *Guardian* (18 Sept. 2012).

49. See, for instance, Ruvani Ranasinha, 'The Fatwa and its Aftermath', in Abdulrazak Gurnah (ed.), *The Cambridge Companion to Salman Rushdie* (Cambridge and New York, 2007), ch. 4.

50. Nasta, *Home Truths*, p. 153.

51. Kenan Malik, *From Fatwa to Jihad: The Rushdie Affair and its Legacy* (London and New York: Atlantic Books, 2009), p. x and *passim*. See also Peter Morey and Amina Yaquin, *Framing Muslims: Stereotyping and Representation after 9/11* (Cambridge, Mass. and London: Harvard University Press, 2011).

52. Saul Bellow, *Herzog* (London: Weidenfeld and Nicolson, 1964), p. 7.

53. See note 4 above, and also Shabbir Akhtar, who argued that had British Muslims 'been a powerful, well-organised lobby like the Jews, Rushdie's outrages would never have got into print', quoted in Ruthven, *A Satanic Affair*, p. 128.

54. In 'One Thousand Days in a Balloon' (1991), added to the paperback edition of *Imaginary Homelands*, Rushdie is quite explicit about developing the 'nascent concept of the "secular muslim", who, like the secular Jews, affirmed his membership of the culture while being separate from the theology', p. 436.

55. Cited in Cheyette, 'Rewriting Rushdie', p. 3.

56. Edward Said, *On Late Style: Music and Literature against the Grain* (London and New York: Bloomsbury, 2006), p. 17.

57. See also Clive Sinclair, 'That's what we do . . . We Show each other our Cloven Hooves', 'Bulgarian Notes', *TLS* (14 Dec. 1990), 1357 for the association of Jews and cloven hooves.

Chapter 7

1. Ronald Shepherd, *Ruth Prawer Jhabvala in India: The Jewish Connection* (Delhi: Chanakya Publications, 1994).

2. Primo Levi, 'Beyond Judgement', *New York Review of Books* 34:20 (17 Dec. 1987), 20, and S.S. Prawer, *Heine's Jewish Comedy: A Study of his Portraits of Jews and Judaism* (Oxford and New York: Oxford University Press, 1983).

3. Georg Simmel, 'The Stranger' (1908), in Donald N. Levine (ed.), *George Simmel: On Individuality and Social Forms* (Chicago: Chicago University Press, 1972), pp. 143–49.

4. Nico Israel, *Outlandish: Writing between Exile and Diaspora* (Stanford, Calif.: Stanford University Press, 2000).

5. Hannah Arendt, 'We Refugees' (1943), in Jerome Kohn and Ron H. Feldman (eds), *Hannah Arendt: The Jewish Writings* (New York: Schocken Books, 2007), p. 264 and pp. 264–74. See also Vivian Liska and Thomas Nolden (eds), *Contemporary Jewish Writing in Europe: A Guide* (Bloomington: Indiana University Press, 2008), p. 92 and pp. 98–99, and Lyndsey Stonebridge, *The Judicial Imagination: Writing after Nuremberg* (Edinburgh: Edinburgh University Press, 2011), ch. 4.

6. Jonathan Freedman, *Klezmer America: Jewishness, Ethnicity, Modernity* (New York and Chichester: Columbia University Press, 2008), p. 140.

7. See Bryan Cheyette (ed.), *Wasafiri* 57 (winter 2009), on Jewish/postcolonial diasporas, and Shaul Bassi, 'Mooristan and Palimpstine: Jews, Moors, Christians in Amitav

Ghosh and Salman Rushdie', in David Brauner and Axel Staehler (eds), *The Edinburgh Companion to Modern Jewish Fiction* (Edinburgh: Edinburgh University Press, 2015).

8. Aamer Mufti, *Enlightenment in the Colony: The Jewish Question and the Crisis of Postcolonial Culture* (Princeton, N.J.: Princeton University Press, 2007), p. 255, and Anne Guttman, Michel Hockx and George Paizis (eds), *The Global Literary Field* (Newcastle: Cambridge Scholars Press, 2006), ch. 4.

9. Anita Desai, 'Jews, Indians and Imperialists', *New York Review of Books* 37:19 (6 Dec. 1990), 56 and 53–56.

10. Homi Bhabha, 'Joking Aside: The Idea of a Self-Critical Community', in Bryan Cheyette and Laura Marcus (eds), *Modernity, Culture and 'the Jew'* (Oxford: Polity Press, 1998), p. xv and pp. xv–xx.

11. Corinne Demas Bliss, 'Against the Current: A Conversation with Anita Desai', *The Massachusetts Review* 19:3 (fall 1988), 537 and 521–37.

12. Feroza F. Jussawalla and Reed Way Dasenbrock, *Interviews with Writers of the Post-Colonial World* (Jackson: University Press of Mississippi, 1992), p. 169.

13. J.M. Coetzee, *Stranger Shores: Essays 1986–1999* (London and New York: Secker & Warburg, 2001), p. 211.

14. Judie Newman, *The Ballistic Bard: Postcolonial Fictions* (London and New York: Arnold, 1995), ch. 4.

15. Shirley Chew, 'Life on the Periphery', *TLS* (July 1988), 787.

16. Newman, *The Ballistic Bard*, pp. 58–60.

17. E.M. Forster *A Passage to India* (Harmondsworth: Penguin Books, 1924), p. 278, and see also Bryan Cheyette, 'Venetian Spaces: Old-New Literatures and the Ambivalent Uses of Jewish History', in Susheila Nasta (ed.), *Reading the 'New' Literatures in a Postcolonial Era* (Cambridge: Boydell & Brewer, 2000), pp. 53–72.

18. Smith also has a chapter on Kafka in *Changing my Mind* (pp. 57–70) which is pointedly entitled 'F. Kafka, Everyman'.

19. This is, of course, ambiguous as the assumption is that the sausage is not kosher.

20. Unlike the United States, Jews are not necessarily a model minority to be emulated by other ethnicities in this novel. See the contrast in Freedman, *Klezmer America*, ch. 6.

21. David Sexton, 'Zadie Smith's Mistake Radio', *Sunday Telegraph* (9 Jan. 2005), 7.

22. As Kafka put it in a letter to Max Brod, 'their hind legs were still mired in their father's Jewishness and their thrashing fore legs found no new ground', cited in Zygmunt Bauman, *Modernity and Ambivalence* (Cambridge and New York: Polity Press, 1991), pp. 86–87.

23. Francis Fukuyama's *The End of History and the Last Man* (1992), which popularized Nietzsche's notion of the 'last man'.

24. These conversionist discourses, as we have discussed in relation to Muriel Spark's and Philip Roth's fiction, usually apply to the 'Jew's daughter'.

25. J. Middleton Murry, *Countries of the Mind: Essays in Literary Criticism* (Oxford: Oxford University Press, 1931), p. 1 and pp. 1–17. See also Andrew Furman, 'The Jewishness of the Contemporary Gentile Writer: Zadie Smith's *White Teeth* and *The Autograph Man*', *MELUS* 30:1 (spring 2005), 3–17.

26. Jonathan Sell, 'Chance and Gesture in Zadie Smith's *White Teeth* and *The Autograph Man*: A Model for Multicultural Identity?', *The Journal of Commonwealth Literature* 47:27 (2006), 27–44.

27. James Wood, 'Fundamentally Goyish', *London Review of Books* 24:19 (3 Oct. 2002), pp. 17–18.

28. See for example, *Changing my Mind*, ch. 2.

29. James Wood, *The Irresponsible Self: On Laughter and the Novel* (London and New York: Jonathan Cape: 2004), p. 170 and pp. 167–83.

Bibliography

Primary Texts

Jean Améry, *Radical Humanism: Selected Essays*, edited and translated by Sidney and Stella P. Rosenfeld (Bloomington: Indiana University Press, 1984).

—— 'In the Waiting Room of Death: Reflections on the Warsaw Ghetto' (1969), *Radical Humanism: Selected Essays*, edited and translated by Sidney and Stella P. Rosenfeld (Bloomington: Indiana University Press, 1984), pp. 21–36.

—— *At the Mind's Limits: Contemplations by a Survivor on Auschwitz and its Realities* (1966) (Bloomington: Indiana University Press, 1998).

—— *On Suicide: A Discourse on Voluntary Death* (1976) (Bloomington: Indiana University Press, 1999).

—— 'The Birth of Man from the Spirit of Violence: Frantz Fanon the Revolutionary' (1971), *Wasafiri* 44 (spring 2005), 13–18.

Hannah Arendt, *The Origins of Totalitarianism* (1951) (New York: Schocken Books, 2004).

—— *The Human Condition* (1958) (Chicago: University of Chicago Press, 1999).

—— *Eichmann in Jerusalem: A Report on the Banality of Evil* (Harmondsworth: Penguin Books, 1965).

—— *Men in Dark Times* (New York: Harvest, 1968).

—— *On Violence* (New York: Harcourt Brace and Co., 1970).

—— *The Life of the Mind* (New York: Harcourt, 1971).

—— 'Reflections on Little Rock' (1959) in Jerome Kohn, ed, *Hannah Arendt: Responsibility and Judgement* (New York: Schocken Books, 2003), pp. 193–213.

—— 'We Refugees' (1943) in Jerome Kohn and Ron H. Feldman, eds, *Hannah Arendt: The Jewish Writings* (New York: Schocken Books, 2007), pp. 264–74.

—— 'The Jew as Pariah: A Hidden Tradition' (1944) in Jerome Kohn and Ron H. Feldman (eds), *Hannah Arendt: The Jewish Writings* (New York: Schocken Books, 2007), pp. 275–97.

Saul Bellow, *Herzog* (London: Weidenfeld and Nicolson, 1964).

Aimé Césaire, 'The Revolt of Frantz Fanon', *Jeune-Afrique* (Dec. 1961), 13–19.

—— *Discourse on Colonialism* (1955) (New York: Monthly Review Press, 2000).

Anita Desai, 'Jews, Indians and Imperialists', *New York Review of Books*, 37:19 (December 6 1990), 53–6.

—— *Baumgartner's Bombay* (1988) (London: Vintage, 1998).

—— *Fasting, Feasting* (London: Vintage, 2000).

—— *Journey to Ithaca* (1995) (London: Vintage, 2001).

—— *The Zigzag Way* (2004) (London: Vintage, 2005).

Frantz Fanon, *Black Skin, White Masks* (1952) (New York: Grove Press, 1967).

—— Studies in a Dying Colonialism (1959) (London: Earthscan, 1965).

—— *The Wretched of the Earth* (London and New York: Penguin Books, 1961).

—— *Toward the African Revolution* (1964) (New York: Grove Press, 1994).

Ruth Prawer Jhabvala, *Heat and Dust* (London: Abacus, 1975).

Jerome Kohn and Ron H. Feldman, eds, *Hannah Arendt: The Jewish Writings* (New York: Schocken Books, 2007).

Hanif Kureishi, *Love in a Blue Time* (London and New York: Faber and Faber, 1997).

Primo Levi, *If This Is a Man* (1947) (London: Abacus, 1987).

—— 'The Jewish Question' (1961) in Marco Belpoliti and Robert Gordon, eds, *Voice of Memory: Interviews with Primo Levi, 1961–87* (Cambridge and New York: Polity Press, 2001), pp. 179–83.

—— *The Truce* (1963) (London: Abacus, 1987).

—— 'Preface to L. Poliakov's *Auschwitz*' (1968) in *The Back Hole of Auschwitz* (Cambridge and New York: Polity Press, 2005), pp. 27–29.

—— *The Periodic Table* (1975) (New York: Schocken Books, 1984).

—— 'A Self-Interview: Afterword to *If This is a Man*' (1976) in Marco Belpoliti and Robert Gordon, eds, *Voice of Memory: Interviews with Primo Levi, 1961–87* (Cambridge and New York: Polity Press, 2001), pp. 184–207.

—— 'Jean Améry, Philospher and Suicide' (1978) in *The Back Hole of Auschwitz* (Cambridge and New York: Polity Press, 2005), pp. 48–50.

—— *The Wrench* (London: Abacus, 1978).

—— *If Not Now, When?* (1982) (London: Abacus, 2000).

—— 'Note to Franz Kafka's *The Trial*' (1983) in *The Back Hole of Auschwitz* (Cambridge and New York: Polity Press, 2005), pp. 140–41.

—— *Other People's Trades* (1985) (London: Abacus, 1991).

—— *The Search for Roots* (1981) (London: Allen Lane, 2001).

—— *The Drowned and the Saved* (1986) (London: Abacus, 1989).

—— 'Beyond Judgement', *New York Review of Books* (17 Dec. 1987), 10–14.

—— *Collected Poems* (London: Faber and Faber, 1988).

—— and Leonardo de Benedetti, *Auschwitz Report* (1946) (London: Verso Books, 2006).

Albert Memmi, *The Pillar of Salt* (1955) (Boston, Mass.: Beacon Press, 1992).

—— *The Colonizer and the Colonized* (1957) (Boston, Mass.: Beacon Press, 1967).

—— *Portrait of a Jew* (New York: Orion Press, 1962).

—— *The Liberation of the Jew* (New York: Orion Press, 1966).

—— *Dominated Man: Notes Towards a Portrait* (Boston: Beacon Press, 1968).

—— 'The Impossible Life of Frantz Fanon', *Massachusetts Review* 14 (winter 1973), 9–39.

—— *Jews and Arabs* (New York: J. Philip O'Hara, 1975).

V.S. Naipaul, *The Mimic Men* (London and New York: Vintage, 1967).

Caryl Phillips, *The European Tribe* (London: Faber and Faber, 1987).

—— *The Nature of Blood* (1997) (London: Vintage, 2008).

—— *Higher Ground* (London: Faber and Faber, 1989).

—— *A New World Order: Selected Essays* (London: Secker & Warburg, 2001).

Philip Roth, *Goodbye, Columbus* (London: Vintage, 1959).

—— 'Writing American Fiction', *Commentary* (1960).

Philip Roth, *Portnoy's Complaint* (London: Vintage, 1969).
—— *Our Gang* (London: Vintage, 1971).
—— *Reading Myself and Others* (1975) (London and New York: Penguin, 1985).
—— *The Professor of Desire* (London: Vintage, 1977).
—— *Zuckerman Bound: A Trilogy and Epilogue* (London: Vintage, 1985).
—— *The Counterlife* (London: Vintage, 1986).
—— *The Facts: A Novelist's Autobiography* (New York: Farrar, Straus & Giroux, 1988).
—— *Deception: A Novel* (New York: Simon and Schuster, 1990).
—— *Patrimony: A True Story* (London: Vintage, 1991).
—— *Operation Shylock: A Confession* (London: Vintage, 1993).
—— *Sabbath's Theater* (London: Vintage, 1995).
—— *American Pastoral* (London: Vintage, 1997).
—— *I Married a Communist* (London: Vintage, 1998).
—— *The Human Stain* (London: Vintage, 2000).
—— *Shop Talk: A Writer and his Colleagues and their Work* (London: Jonathan Cape, 2001a).
—— *The Dying Animal* (London: Vintage, 2001b).
—— *The Plot Against America* (London: Vintage, 2004a).
—— 'The Story behind *The Plot against America*', *New York Times Book Review*, 19 Sept. 2004b, 10–12.
—— *Everyman* (London: Vintage, 2006).
—— *Exit Ghost* (London: Vintage, 2007).
—— *Indignation* (London: Vintage, 2008).
—— *Nemesis* (London: Vintage, 2010).
Salman Rushdie, *Grimus* (London: Vintage, 1975).
—— *Midnight's Children* (London: Vintage, 1981).
—— *Shame* (London: Vintage, 1983).
—— *The Satanic Verses* (London: Viking, 1988).
—— *Haroun and the Sea of Stories* (London: Penguin, 1990).
—— *Imaginary Homelands: Essays and Criticism 1981–1991* (London and New York: Granta Books, 1991).
—— 'Bosnia on my Mind', *Index on Censorship* (May–June 1994) 16–20.
—— *The Moor's Last Sigh* (London: Vintage, 1995).
—— *Step Across This Line: Collected Non-Fiction, 1992–2002* (London: Vintage, 2002).
—— *Shalimar the Clown* (London: Vintage, 2005).
—— *Joseph Anton: A Memoir* (London and New York: Jonathan Cape, 2012).
Edward W. Said, *Beginnings: Intention and Method* (New York: Columbia University Press, 1975).
—— *Orientalism* (London: Penguin Books, 1978).
—— *The Question of Palestine* (New York: Random House, 1979).
—— *The World, the Text and the Critic* (London: Faber and Faber, 1984).
—— 'Intellectuals in the Post-Colonial World', *Salmagundi*, 70–71 (spring–summer 1986), 44–64.
—— *Culture and Imperialism* (New York: Vintage, 1993).
—— *Representations of the Intellectual* (New York: Random House, 1994a).
—— *The Politics of Dispossession: The Struggle for Palestinian Self-Determination, 1969–1994* (London: Chatto, 1994b).
—— *Out of Place* (London: Granta, 1999).
—— *The End of the Peace Process: Oslo and After* (London: Granta, 2000).
—— *Reflections on Exile and Other Literary and Cultural Essays* (London: Granta, 2001).
—— *Freud and the Non-European* (London: Verso Books, 2003).
—— *Humanism and Democratic Criticism* (London and New York: Palgrave Macmillan, 2004).
—— *On Late Style: Music and Literature against the Grain* (London: Bloomsbury, 2006).
Jean-Paul Sartre, *Anti-Semite and Jew: An Exploration in the Etiology of Hate* (1946) (New York: Schocken Books, 1976).

—— 'Introduction', *The Colonizer and the Colonised* (1957) (Boston, Mass.: Beacon Press, 1967), pp. 19–28.

—— 'Preface', *The Wretched of the Earth* (London and New York: Penguin Books, 1961), pp. 7–26.

—— *Colonialism and Neocolonialism* (1964) (London and New York: Routledge, 2001).

Zadie Smith, *White Teeth* (London: Penguin, 2000).

—— *The Autograph Man* (London: Penguin, 2002).

—— *On Beauty* (London: Penguin, 2005).

—— *Changing my Mind: Occasional Essays* (New York: Penguin Press, 2009).

—— *NW* (London: Penguin, 2012).

Muriel Spark, 'The Poet in Mr. Eliot's Ideal State', *Outposts* 14 (summer 1949), 26–28.

—— 'The Religion of an Agnostic: A Sacramental View of the World of Marcel Proust', *Church of England Newspaper* (27 Nov. 1953a), p. 7.

—— *John Masefield* (London: Peter Nevill, 1953b)

—— 'The Mystery of Job's Suffering: Jung's New Interpretation Examined', *Church of England Newspaper* (15 April 1955), 7.

—— *The Comforters* (London: Macmillan, 1957).

—— *Robinson* (London: Macmillan, 1958).

—— *Memento Mori* (London: Macmillan, 1959).

—— *The Ballad of Peckham Rye* (London: Macmillan, 1960).

—— *The Bachelors* (London: Macmillan, 1960).

—— 'My Conversion', *The Twentieth Century* 170 (autumn 1961a), 58–63.

—— *Voices at Play: Stories and Ear-Pieces* (London: Macmillan, 1961b).

—— *The Prime of Miss Jean Brodie* (London: Macmillan, 1961c).

—— *The Girls of Slender Means* (London: Macmillan, 1963).

—— *The Mandelbaum Gate* (London: Macmillan, 1965).

—— *The Public Image* (London: Macmillan, 1968).

—— *The Driver's Seat* (London: Macmillan, 1970).

—— *Not to Disturb* (London: Macmillan, 1971a).

—— 'The Desegregation of Art', *American Academy of Arts and Letters* (New York: The Blashfield Foundation, 1971b), 21–7.

—— *The Hothouse by the East River* (London: Macmillan, 1973).

—— *The Abbess of Crewe* (London: Macmillan, 1974).

—— *The Takeover* (London: Macmillan, 1976).

—— *Territorial Rights* (London: Macmillan, 1979).

—— *Loitering with Intent* (London: The Bodley Head, 1981).

—— *The Only Problem* (London: The Bodley Head, 1984).

—— *A Far Cry from Kensington* (London: Constable, 1988).

—— *Symposium* (London: Constable, 1990).

—— *Curriculum Vitae: A Volume of Autobiography* (London: Constable, 1992).

—— *The Collected Stories of Muriel Spark* (Harmondsworth: Penguin Books, 1994).

—— *Reality and Dreams* (London: Constable, 1996).

—— *Aiding and Abetting* (London and New York: Viking, 2000).

—— and Derek Stanford, *Emily Brontë: Her Life and Work* (London: Peter Owen, 1953).

Secondary Texts

Chinua Achebe, *Hopes and Impediments: Selected Essays, 1965–1987* (New York: Random House, 1988).

Giorgio Agamben, *Homo Sacer: Sovereign Power and Bare Life* (Stanford, Calif.: Stanford University Press, 1998).

—— *Remnants of Auschwitz: The Witness and the Archive* (New York: Zone Books, 1999).

Aijaz Ahmad, *In Theory: Classes, Nations, Literatures* (London: Verso, 1992).

Rehana Ahmed, Peter Morey and Amina Yaqin, eds, *Culture, Diaspora and Modernity in Muslim Writing* (London and New York: Routledge, 2012).

Abdel-Moneim Aly, 'The Theme of Exile in the African Short Stories of Muriel Spark', *Scottish Studies Review* 2 (2001), 94–104.

Benedict Anderson, *Imagined Communities* (London and New York: Verso, 1983).

Carole Angier, *The Double Bond: Primo Levi, a Biography* (London: Viking, 2002).

Keith Ansell Pearson, Benita Parry and Judith Squires, eds, *Cultural Readings of Imperialism: Edward Said and the Gravity of History* (London: Lawrence and Wishart, 1997).

Kwame Anthony Appiah, *In my Father's House: Africa in the Philosophy of Culture* (Oxford and New York: Oxford University Press, 1992).

Lisa Appignanesi and Sarah Maitland, eds, *The Rushdie File* (London: Fourth Estate, 1989).

Steven Aschheim, *Beyond the Border: The German-Jewish Legacy Abroad* (Princeton, N.J.: Princeton University Press, 2007).

Bill Ashcroft and Kadhim Hussein, eds, *Edward Said and the Postcolonial* (Huntington, N.Y.: Nova Science, 2001).

——, Gareth Griffiths and Helen Tiffin, *Post-Colonial Studies: The Key Concepts* (London and New York: Routledge, 2007).

Matthew Asprey, 'Matthew Asprey Interviews Clive Sinclair', *Los Angeles Review of Books*, 18 Dec. 2012, http://lareviewofbooks.org/article.php?id=1257&fulltext=1, last accessed 11 April 2013.

Eric Auerbach, *Mimesis* (1946) (Princeton, N.J.: Princeton University Press, 2003).

Shaul Bassi, 'Mooristan and Palimpstine: Jews, Moors, Christians in Amitav Ghosh and Salman Rushdie', in David Brauner and Axel Staehler (eds), *The Edinburgh Companion to Modern Jewish Fiction* (Edinburgh: Edinburgh University Press, 2015).

Zygmunt Bauman, *Modernity and the Holocaust* (Cambridge and New York: Polity Press, 1989).

—— *Modernity and Ambivalence* (Cambridge and New York: Polity Press, 1991).

—— 'Allosemitism: Premodern, Modern, Postmodern', in Bryan Cheyette and Laura Marcus, eds, *Modernity, Culture and 'the Jew'* (Stanford, Calif.: Stanford University Press, 1998), pp. 143–56.

Simone de Beauvoir, *The Force of Circumstance* (New York: Paragon House, 1992).

Marco Belpoliti and Robert Gordon, eds, *Voice of Memory: Interviews with Primo Levi, 1961–87* (Cambridge and New York: Polity Press, 2001).

Esther Benbassi, *Suffering as Identity: The Jewish Paradigm* (London: Verso, 2010).

Seyla Benhabib, *The Reluctant Modernism of Hannah Arendt* (New York: Rowman and Littlefield, 2000).

Walter Benjamin, *Illuminations* (London: Jonathan Cape, 1970).

Walter Benn Michaels, 'Plots against America: Neoliberalism and Antiracism', *American Literary History* 18:2 (2006), 288–302.

Robert Bernasconi, 'When the Real Crimes Began', in Richard King and Dan Stone, eds, *Hannah Arendt and the Uses of History: Imperialism, Nation, Race, and Genocide* (New York: Berghahn Books, 2007), pp. 54–67.

Richard Bernstein, *Hannah Arendt and the Jewish Question* (New York and Oxford: Polity Press, 1996).

Homi Bhabha, 'Framing Fanon', preface to Frantz Fanon, *The Wretched of the Earth* (New York: Grove Press, 2004).

—— 'Remembering Fanon: Self, Psyche and the Colonial Tradition', foreword to Frantz Fanon, *Black Skin, White Masks* (New York: Grove Press, 2006).

David Biale, *Power and Powerlessness in Jewish History* (New York, Schocken Books, 1986).

—— Michael Galchinsky and Susannah Heschel, eds, *Insider/Outsider: American-Jews and Multiculturalism* (Berkeley: University of California Press, 1998).

Corinne Demas Bliss, 'Against the Current: A Conversation with Anita Desai', *The Massachusetts Review* 19:3 (fall 1988), 521–37.

Harold Bloom, 'Operation Roth', *New York Review of Books* (22 April 1993), 45–8.

—— ed., *Philip Roth: Modern Critical Views* (Broomall, Pa: Chelsea House Publishers, 2003).

Donald Bogle, *Toms, Coons, Mulattoes, Mammies and Bucks: An Interpretive History of Blacks in American Films* (New York: Continuum Books, 1989).

Paul A. Bové, ed., *Edward Said and the Work of the Critic: Speaking Truth to Power* (Durham, N.C. and London: Duke University Press, 2000).

Daniel Boyarin, Daniel Itzkovitz and Ann Pellegrini, eds, *Queer Theory and the Jewish Question* (New York: Columbia University Press, 2003).

Jonathan Boyarin, *Storm from Paradise: The Politics of Jewish Memory* (Minneapolis: University of Minnesota Press, 1992).

—— *Thinking in Jewish* (Chicago: University of Chicago Press, 1996).

—— and Daniel Boyarin, *Powers of Diaspora: Two Essays on the Relevance of Jewish Culture* (Minneapolis: University of Minnesota Press, 2002).

Malcolm Bradbury, ed., *The Novel Today: Contemporary Writers on Modern Fiction* (London: Fontana Paperbacks, 1977).

—— *No, Not Bloomsbury* (London: Arena, 1987).

David Brauner, *Philip Roth* (Manchester and New York: Manchester University Press, 2007).

—— *Contemporary American Fiction* (Edinburgh: Edinburgh University Press, 2010).

—— and Axel Staehler, eds, *The Edinburgh Companion to Modern Jewish Fiction* (Edinburgh: Edinburgh University Press, 2015).

Timothy Brennan, *Salman Rushdie and the Third World* (London: Macmillan Press, 1989).

Maggie Butcher, ed., *The Eye of the Beholder: Indian Writing in English* (London: Commonwealth Institute, 1983).

Judith Butler, *Parting Ways: Jewishness and the Critique of Zionism* (New York: Columbia Unversity Press, 2012).

Eleanor Byrne, 'Muriel Spark Shot in Africa', in Martin McQuillan, ed., *Theorizing Muriel Spark: Gender, Race, Deconstruction* (New York: Palgrave, 2002), pp. 113–26.

Margaret Canovan, *The Political Thought of Hannah Arendt* (London: J.M. Dent, 1974).

—— *Hannah Arendt: A Reinterpretation of Her Political Thought* (Cambridge and New York: Cambridge University Press, 1992).

David Cesarani, *Eichmann: His Life and Crimes* (London and New York: William Heinemann, 2004).

—— and Eric J. Sundquist, eds, *After the Holocaust: Challenging the Myth of Silence* (London and New York: Routledge, 2012).

Shirley Chew, 'Life on the Periphery', *Times Literary Supplement* (July 1988), 787.

Bryan Cheyette, 'Rewriting Rushdie', *The Jewish Quarterly* 36:3 (autumn 1989), 3–4.

—— *Constructions of 'the Jew' in English Literature and Society: Racial Representations, 1875–1945* (Cambridge: Cambridge University Press, 1993).

—— *Muriel Spark* (Tavistock, Devon: Northcote House Press, 2000).

—— 'Venetian Spaces: Old-New Literatures and the Ambivalent Uses of Jewish History', in Susheila Nasta, ed, *Reading the 'New' Literatures in a Postcolonial Era* (Cambridge: Boydell & Brewer, 2000), pp. 53–72.

—— 'Appropriating Primo Levi', in Robert S.C. Gordon (ed.), *The Cambridge Companion to Primo Levi* (Cambridge: Cambridge University Press, 2007), pp. 67–85.

—— ed., *Wasafiri* 57 (winter 2009).

—— 'English Anti-Semitism: A Counter-Narrative', *Textual Practice* 25 (2011), 18–34.

Bryan Cheyette, 'A Glorious Achievement: Edward Said and the Last Jewish Intellectual', in Tobias Döring and Mark Stein (eds), *Edward Said's Translocations: Essays in Secular Criticism*, (London and New York: Routledge, 2012), pp. 74–97.

—— and Laura Marcus, eds, *Modernity, Culture and 'the Jew'* (Stanford, Calif.: Stanford University Press, 1998).

Mirna Ciciona, *Primo Levi: Bridges of Knowledges* (Oxford: Berg, 1995).

Roger Y. Clark, *Stranger Gods: Salman Rushdie's Other Worlds* (Montreal and London: McGill-Queen's University Press, 2001).

Stephanie Clifford, 'Making It Look Easy at *The New Yorker*', *New York Times* (5 April 2010), B1.

Stephen Clingman, 'Other Voices: An Interview with Caryl Phillips', *Salmagundi* 143 (summer 2004), 112–40.

—— *The Grammar of Identity: Transnational Fiction and the Nature of the Boundary* (Oxford and New York: Oxford University Press, 2009).

J.M. Coetzee, *Stranger Shores: Essays 1986-1999* (London and New York: Secker & Warburg, 2001).

Robin Cohen, *Global Diasporas: An Introduction* (London: Routledge, 1997).

Steven Connor, *The English Novel in History: 1950-1995* (London and New York: Routledge, 1996).

Daniel Defoe, *The Political History of the Devil* (1726).

Arik Dirlik, 'The Postcolonial Aura: Third World Criticism in the Age of Global Capitalism', *Critical Inquiry* 20 (winter 1994), 328–56.

Tobias Döring and Mark Stein, eds, *Edward Said's Translocations: Essays in Secular Criticism* London and New York: Routledge, 2012).

Jonathan Druker, *Primo Levi and Humanism after Auschwitz: Posthumanist Reflections* (New York: Palgrave Macmillan, 2009).

Robert Eaglestone, *The Holocaust and the Postmodern* (Oxford and New York: Oxford University Press, 2004).

—— 'Salman Rushdie: Paradox and Truth', in Philip Tew and Rod Mengham (eds), *British Fiction Today* (London and New York: Continuum, 2006), pp. 91–102.

Terry Eagleton, *Exiles and Emigrés: Studies in Modern Literature* (London: Chatto and Windus, 1970).

Martin Evans, *Algeria: France's Undeclared War* (Oxford and New York: Oxford University Press, 2012).

Sidra Dekoven Ezrahi, *Booking Passage: Exile and Homecoming in the Modern Jewish Imagination* (Berkeley: University of California Press, 2000).

Shoshana Felman, *The Juridical Unconscious: Trials and Traumas in the Twentieth Century* (Cambridge, Mass.: Harvard University Press, 2002).

Alain Finkielkraut, *The Imaginary Jew* (1980) (Lincoln, Nebr.: University of Nebraska Press, 1994).

Harold Fisch, *A Remembered Future: A Study in Literary Mythology* (Bloomington: Indiana University Press, 1984).

Peter Flannery, *Singer* (London: Nick Hearn, 1989).

Richard Fletcher, *Moorish Spain* (London and New York: Weidenfeld and Nicolson, 1992).

E.M. Forster, *A Passage to India* (Harmondsworth: Penguin Books, 1924).

Dean J. Franco, ed., *Philip Roth Studies* (fall 2002).

—— 'Philip Roth and Race', *Philip Roth Studies* 2 (2006), 83–85.

—— *Race, Rights, and Recognition: Jewish American Literature since 1969* (Ithaca, N.Y. and London: Cornell University Press, 2012).

Jonathan Freedman, *The Temple of Culture: Assimilation and Anti-Semitism in Literary Anglo-America* (New York and Oxford: Oxford University Press, 2000).

—— *Klezmer America: Jewishness, Ethnicity, Modernity* (New York and Chichester: Columbia University Press, 2008).

Francis Fukuyama, *The End of History and the Last Man* (London: Penguin, 1992).

Andrew Furman, 'The Jewishness of the Contemporary Gentile Writer: Zadie Smith's *White Teeth* and *The Autograph Man*', *MELUS* 30:1 (spring 2005), 3–17.

Tamar Garb and Linda Nochlin, eds, *The Jew in the Text* (London: Thames & Hudson, 1995).

Michael Gardner and Willy Maley, eds, *The Edinburgh Companion to Muriel Spark* (Edinburgh: Edinburgh University Press, 2010).

Henry Louis Gates, 'Critical Fanonism', *Critical Inquiry* 17 (spring 1991), 457–70.

Peter Geismar, *Frantz Fanon* (New York: Dial Press, 1971).

Amitav Ghosh, *In an Antique Land: History in the Guise of a Traveller's Tale* (London and New York: Vintage Books, 1992).

Nigel C. Gibson, *Fanon: The Postcolonial Imagination* (Cambridge: Polity, 2003).

Sander Gilman, *Inscribing the Other* (Lincoln, Nebr.: Nebraska University Press, 1991).

—— *Smart Jews: The Construction of the Image of Jewish Superior Intelligence* (Lincoln, Nebr.: University of Nebraska, 1996).

—— *Jewish Frontiers: Essays on Bodies, Histories and Identities* (London and New York: Palgrave Macmillan, 2003).

—— and Jack Zipes, eds, *Yale Companion to Jewish Writing and Thought in German Culture, 1096–1996* (London and New Haven, Conn.: Yale University Press, 1997).

Paul Gilroy, *Small Acts: Thoughts on the Politics of Black Cultures* (London and New York: Serpent's Tale, 1993a).

—— *The Black Atlantic: Modernity and Double Consciousness* (Cambridge, Mass.: Harvard University Press, 1993b).

—— *Between Camps: Nations, Cultures and the Allure of Race* (London and New York: The Penguin Press, 2000).

—— *Darker Than Blue: On the Moral Economies of Black Atlantic Culture* (Cambridge, Mass.: Harvard University Press, 2010).

Massimo Giuliani, *A Centaur in Auschwitz: Reflections on Primo Levi's Thinking* (New York: Lexington Books, 2003).

Victoria Glendinning, 'A Novelist in the Country of the Mind', *Sunday Times* (25 Oct. 1981).

David Gooblar, *The Major Phases of Philip Roth* (London and New York: Continuum, 2011).

Eugene Goodheart, 'The Passion of Reason: Reflections on Primo Levi and Jean Améry', *Dissent* (autumn 1994), 518–27.

D.C.R.A. Goonetilleke, *Salman Rushdie* (London: Macmillan Press, 1998).

Lewis Gordon, T. Denean Sharpley-Whiting and Renee T. White, eds, *Fanon: A Critical Reader* (Oxford: Blackwell Publishers, 1996).

Robert S.C. Gordon, *Primo Levi's Ordinary Virtues: From Testimony to Ethics* (Oxford: Oxford University Press, 2001a).

—— '"How Much Home Does a Person Need?" Primo Levi and the Ethics of Home', *Annali d'Italianistica* 19 (2001b), 215–34.

—— ed., *The Cambridge Companion to Primo Levi* (Cambridge: Cambridge University Press, 2007).

Damian Grant, *Salman Rushdie* (Tavistock, Devon: Northcote House Press, 2012).

Linda Grant, *The Clothes on their Backs* (London: Virago, 2009).

Sue Greene, 'The Use of the Jew in West Indian Novels', *World Literature Written in English* 26 (1986), 150–69.

Charles L. Griswold, *Forgiveness: A Philosophical Exploration* (Cambridge: Cambridge University Press, 2007).

Abdulrazak Gurnah, ed., *The Cambridge Companion to Salman Rushdie* (Cambridge and New York, 2007).

Anne Guttman, Michel Hockx and George Paizis, eds, *The Global Literary Field* (Newcastle: Cambridge Scholars Press, 2006).

Azzedine Haddour, 'The Importance of Sartre in Fanon', *New Formations* 47 (summer 2002), 34–38.

—— ed., *The Fanon Reader* (London: Pluto Press, 2006).

Alex Haley, *Roots: The Saga of an American Family* (New York: Vintage, 1976).

Hillel Halkin, 'Salman Rushdie Surrenders', *Commentary* 102 (7 Jan. 1996), 55–59.

Stuart Hall, 'Culture Identity and Diaspora', in J. Rutherford (ed.), *Identity: Community, Cultural Difference* (London: Lawrence and Wishart, 1990), pp. 222–37.

Amira Hass, 'Between Two Returns', in Marianne Hirsch and Nancy K. Miller, *Rites of Return: Diaspora Poetics and the Politics of Memory* (New York: Columbia University Press, 2011), pp. 173–84.

Irène Heidelberger-Leonard, *The Philosopher of Auschwitz: Jean Améry and Living with the Holocaust* (London: IB Taurus, 2010).

Zoe Heller, 'The Salman Rushdie Case', *New York Review of Books* (20 Dec. 2012).

David Herman, 'Edward Said (1935–2003)', *Salmagundi* 143 (summer 2004), 76–88.

Marianne Hirsch and Nancy K. Miller, eds, *Rites of Return: Diaspora Poetics and the Politics of Memory* (New York: Columbia University Press, 2011).

G.Z. Hochberg, 'Edward Said: "The Last Jewish Intellectual": On Identity, Alterity, and the Politics of Memory', *Social Text* 24 (summer 2006), 47–65.

David Hollinger, *Postethnic America: Beyond Multiculturalism* (New York: Basic Books, 1995).

Nubar Hovsepian, 'Connections with Palestine', in Michael Sprinker, ed., *Edward Said: A Critical Reader* (Oxford: Blackwell, 1992), pp. 5–18.

Irving Howe, 'Philip Roth Reconsidered', *Commentary* 54 (Dec. 1972), 69–77.

Adel Iskandar and Hakem Rustom, eds, *Edward Said: A Legacy of Emancipation and Representation* (Berkeley, Calif.: University of California Press, 2010).

Nico Israel, *Outlandish: Writing between Exile and Diaspora* (Stanford, Calif.: Stanford University Press, 2000).

Maya Jaggi, 'The Last Laugh', *New Statesman and Society* (8 Sept. 1995), 20–21.

Gabriel Josipovici, 'On the Side of Job', *TLS* (7 Sept. 1984), 989.

Jonathan Judaken, *Jean-Paul Sartre and the Jewish Question: Anti-Antisemitism and the Politics of the French Intellectual* (Lincoln: Nebraska University Press, 2006).

Feroza F. Jussawalla and Reed Way Dasenbrock, *Interviews with Writers of the Post-Colonial World* (Jackson: University Press of Mississippi, 1992).

Brett Ashley Kaplan, 'Anatole Broyard's Human Stain: Performing Postracial Consciousness', *Philip Roth Studies* (fall 2005), 125–44.

Nelly Kaprielian, 'In Which Philip Roth Announces his Retirement', *Paris Review* (13 Nov. 2012).

Frank Kelleter, 'Portrait of the Sexist as a Dying Man: Death, Ideology and the Erotic in *Sabbath's Theater*', *Contemporary Literature* 39 (summer 1998), 262–302.

Peter Kemp, *Muriel Spark: Novelists and their World* (London: Paul Elek, 1974).

—— 'Shattered Idylls', *Sunday Times* (11 Sept. 2005), 27.

Michelle Keown, David Murphy and James Proctor, eds, *Comparing Postcolonial Diasporas* (Basingstoke: Palgrave Macmillan, 2009).

Frank Kermode, 'The House of Fiction: Interviews with Seven Novelists', in Malcolm Bradbury, ed., *The Novel Today: Contemporary Writers on Modern Fiction* (London: Fontana, 1977).

—— 'Old Testament Capers', *London Review of Books* (20 Sept.–3 Oct. 1984), 10–11.

Richard King and Dan Stone, eds, *Hannah Arendt and the Uses of History: Imperialism, Nation, Race and Genocide* (New York: Berghahn Books, 2007).

Richard H. King, *Race, Culture and the Intellectuals: 1940–70* (Baltimore, Md. and London: Johns Hopkins University Press, 2004).

Barbara Kirshenblatt-Gimblett and Jeffrey Shandler, eds, *Anne Frank Unbound: Media, Imagination, Memory* (Bloomington, Ind.: Indiana University Press, 2012).

R.B. Kitaj, *First Diasporist Manifesto* (New York: Thames & Hudson, 1989).

Chana Kronfeld, *On the Margins of Modernism: Decentering Literary Dynamics* (Berkeley, Calif.: University of California Press, 1996).

Tony Kushner, *The Holocaust and the Liberal Imagination: A Social and Cultural History* (Oxford: Basil Blackwell, 1994).

—— *We Europeans? Mass-Observation, 'Race' and British Identity in the Twentieth Century* (London: Ashgate, 2004).

Anthony Simon Laden and David Owen, eds, *Multiculturalism and Political Theory* (Cambridge: Cambridge University Press, 2007).

Ariella Lang, 'Reason as Revenge: Primo Levi and Writing the Holocaust', *Symposium* 52 (winter 1999), 255–68.

Berel Lang, ed., *Writing and the Holocaust* (New York: Holmes and Meier, 1988).

—— *The Future of the Holocaust: Between History and Memory* (Ithaca, N.Y. and London: Cornell University Press, 1999).

Lawrence Langer, *Preempting the Holocaust* (New Haven, Conn. and London: Yale University Press, 1998).

Neil Lazarus, *Nationalism and Cultural Practice in the Postcolonial World* (Cambridge: Cambridge University Press, 1999).

Donald N. Levine, ed., *George Simmel: On Individuality and Social Forms* (Chicago: Chicago University Press, 1972).

Vivian Liska and Thomas Nolden, eds, *Contemporary Jewish Writing in Europe: A Guide* (Bloomington: Indiana University Press, 2008).

David Macey, *Frantz Fanon: A Life* (London and New York: Granta Books, 2000).

Aryeh Maidenbaum and Stephen A. Martin, eds, *Lingering Shadows: Jungians, Freudians and Anti-Semitism* (Boston and London: Shambhala, 1991).

Kenan Malik, *From Fatwa to Jihad: The Rushdie Affair and its Legacy* (London and New York: Atlantic Books, 2009).

Octave Mannoni, *Prospero and Caliban: The Psychology of Colonization* (1950) (Ann Arbor: University of Michigan Press, 1990).

Hilary Mantel, 'Black Is Not Jewish', *Literary Review* (Feb. 1997), 140.

David Maraniss, *Barack Obama: The Making of the Man* (New York: Atlantic Books, 2012).

Greil Marcus, *The Shape of Things to Come: Prophecy and the American Voice* (London and New York: Faber and Faber, 2006).

David Marriott, *On Black Men* (Edinburgh: Edinburgh University Press, 2000).

—— 'Whither Fanon', *Textual Practice* 25 (Feb. 2011), 33–65.

Mark Mazower, *Hitler's Empire: Nazi Rule in Occupied Europe* (London and New York: Penguin Books, 2008).

Jock McCulloch, *Black Soul, White Artifact: Fanon's Clinical Psychology and Social Theory* (Cambridge: Cambridge University Press, 1983).

Martin McQuillan, ed., *Theorizing Muriel Spark: Gender, Race, Deconstruction* (New York: Palgrave, 2002).

Asher Z. Milbauer and Donald G. Watson, eds, *Reading Philip Roth* (Basingstoke: Macmillan Press, 1988).

Emily Miller Budick, *Blacks and Jews in Literary Conversation* (Cambridge: Cambridge University Press, 1998).

Pankaj Mishra, 'Joseph Anton', *Guardian* (18 Sept. 2012).

Vijay Mishra, *The Literature of the Indian Diaspora: Theorizing the Diasporic Imaginary* (London and New York: Routledge, 2007).

Peter Morey and Amina Yaqin, *Framing Muslims: Stereotyping and Representation after 9/11* (Cambridge, Mass., and London: Harvard University Press, 2011).

Stephen Morton, *Salman Rushdie: Fictions of Postcolonial Modernity* (Palgrave: London and New York, 2007).

Aamer Mufti, 'Auerbach in Istanbul: Edward Said, Secular Criticism, and the Question of Minority Culture', in Paul A. Bové, ed., *Edward Said and the Work of the Critic: Speaking Truth to Power* (Durham, N.C. and London: Duke University Press, 2000), pp. 229–56.

—— *Enlightenment in the Colony: The Jewish Question and the Crisis of Postcolonial Culture* (Princeton, N.J.: Princeton University Press, 2007).

J. Middleton Murry, *Countries of the Mind: Essays in Literary Criticism* (Oxford: Oxford University Press, 1931).

Susheila Nasta, ed., *Reading the 'New' Literatures in a Postcolonial Era* (Cambridge: Boydell & Brewer, 2000).

Judie Newman, *The Ballistic Bard: Postcolonial Fictions* (London and New York: Arnold, 1995).

Adam Zachary Newton, *Facing Black and Jew: Literature as Public Space in Twentieth-Century America* (New York and Cambridge: Cambridge University Press, 1999).

Barack Obama, *Dreams from My Father: A Story of Race and Inheritance* (1995) (Edinburgh: Canongate, 2007).

Cynthia Ozick, 'A Liberal's Auschwitz', *Confrontation* 10 (spring 1975), 125–29.

—— *Metaphor and Memory: Essays* (New York: Knopf, 1989).

Derek Parker Royal, ed., *Philip Roth: New Perspectives on an American Author* (Westport, Conn.: Greenwood Press, 2005).

Timothy Parrish, ed., *The Cambridge Companion to Philip Roth* (New York and Cambridge: Cambridge University Press, 2007).

Benita Parry, *Postcolonial Studies: A Materialist Critique* (London and New York: Routledge, 2004).

Ann Pellegrini, *Performance Anxieties: Staging Psychoanalysis, Staging Race* (London and New York: Routledge, 1997).

Daniel Pick, *Svengali's Web: the Alien Enchanter in Modern Culture* (New Haven, Conn, and London: Yale University Press, 2000).

Ross Posnock, 'Purity and Danger: On Philip Roth', *Raritan* 21:2, 2001, 85–101.

—— *Color and Culture: Black Writers and the Making of the Modern Intellectual* (Cambridge, Mass.: Harvard University Press, 1998).

—— *Philip Roth's Rude Truth: The Art of Immaturity* (Princeton, N.J. and Oxford: Princeton University Press, 2006).

Aimee Pozorski, *Roth and Trauma: The Problem of History in the Later Works (1995–2010)* (New York and London: Continuum Books, 2011).

S.S. Prawer, *Heine's Jewish Comedy: A Study of His Portraits of Jews and Judaism* (Oxford and New York: Oxford University Press, 1983).

Catherine Rainwater and William J. Scheick, 'An Interview with Cynthia Ozick', *Texas Studies in Literature and Language* 25 (summer 1983), 255–65.

Ian Rankin, "The Deliberate Cunning of Muriel Spark", in Gavin Wallace and Randall Stevenson (eds), *The Scottish Novel Since the Seventies: New Visions, Old Dreams* (Edinburgh: Edinburgh University Press, 1993), pp. 43–56.

Ishmael Reed, et al., 'Is Ethnicity Obsolete?', in Werner Sollors, ed., *The Invention of Ethnicity* (New York: Oxford University Press, 1989), pp. 226–36.

David Remnick, *The Bridge: The Life and Rise of Barack Obama* (New York: Knopf, 2010).

Bruce Robbins, 'Secularism, Elitism, Progress and Other Transgressions', in Keith Ansell Pearson, Benita Parry and Judith Squires, eds, *Cultural Readings of Imperialism: Edward Said and the Gravity of History* (London: Lawrence and Wishart, 1997), pp. 67–87.
—— *Feeling Global: Internationalism in Distress* (New York: New York University Press, 1999).
Michael Rogin, *Blackface, White Noise: Jewish Immigrants in the Hollywood Melting Pot* (Berkeley, Calif.: University of California Press, 1996).
—— *Independence Day* (London: BFI Publishing, 1998).
Jacqueline Rose, *Proust Among the Nations: From Dreyfus to the Middle East* (Chicago: Chicago University Press, 2011).
Michael Rothberg, 'Against Zero-Sum Logic: A Response to Walter Benn Michaels', *American Literary History* 18 (2006), 303–11.
—— *Mutidirectional Memory: Remembering the Holocaust in the Age of Decolonization* (Stanford, Calif.: Stanford University Press, 2009).
Jonathan Rutherford, ed., *Identity: Community, Culture, Difference* (London: Lawrence and Wishart, 1990).
Malise Ruthven, *A Satanic Affair: Salman Rushdie and the Rage of Islam* (London and New York: Hogarth Press, 1991).
Daniel R. Schwarz, *Imagining the Holocaust* (New York: St Martin's Press, 1999).
W.G. Sebald, *On the Natural History of Destruction* (London: Hamish Hamilton, 2003).
Jonathan P.A. Sell, 'Chance and Gesture in Zadie Smith's *White Teeth* and *The Autograph Man*: A Model for Multicultural Identity?', *The Journal of Commonwealth Literature* 47 (2006), 27–44.
—— ed., *Metaphor and Diaspora in Contemporary Writing* (New York: Palgrave Macmillan, 2012).
David Sexton, 'Zadie Smith's Mistake Radio', *Sunday Telegraph* (9 January 2005), 7.
Isaiah Shachar, *The Judensau: A Mediaeval Anti-Jewish Motif and Its History* (London: Warburg Institute, 1974).
Ronald Shepherd, *Ruth Prawer Jhabvala in India: The Jewish Connection* (Delhi: Chanakya Publications, 1994).
Debra Shostak, *Philip Roth: Countertexts, Counterlives* (Columbia, S.C.: University of South Carolina Press, 2004).
Max Silverman, *Palimpsestic Memory: The Holocaust and Colonialism in French and Francophone Fiction and Film* (New York: Berghahn, 2013).
Clive Sinclair, *The Brothers Singer* (London: Allison and Busby, 1983).
—— 'Bulgarian Notes', *Times Literary Supplement* (14 December 1990), 1357.
Werner Sollors, ed., *The Invention of Ethnicity* (New York: Oxford University Press, 1989).
Samuel Robin Spark, 'Life with the Cambergs', *Edinburgh Star* (February 1999), 113–17.
Gayatri Chakravorty Spivak, *Death of a Discipline* (New York: Columbia University Press, 2003)
Michael Sprinker, ed., *Edward Said: A Critical Reader* (Oxford: Blackwell, 1992).
Martin Stannard, 'The Letter Killeth', *The Spectator* (6 June, 1998), 36–37.
—— 'Nativities: Muriel Spark, Baudelaire and the Quest for Religious Faith', *Review of English Studies* 218 (2003), 91–105.
—— *Muriel Spark: The Biography* (London and New York: Weidenfeld and Nicolson, 2009).
George Steiner, *Language and Silence: Essays 1958–1966* (London and New York: Faber and Faber, 1967).
—— *Extraterritorial: Papers on the Literature and the Language Revolution* (New York: Atheneum, 1971).
—— *No Passion Spent: Essays 1978–1996* (London: Faber and Faber, 1996).

Alexander Stille, 'What the Holocaust Meant: The Thinking of Primo Levi and Jean Améry', *Dissent* 37 (summer 1990), 361–66.

Lyndsey Stonebridge, *The Judicial Imagination: Writing After Nuremberg* (Edinburgh: Edinburgh University Press, 2011).

Eric J. Sundquist, *Strangers in the Land: Blacks, Jews, Post-Holocaust America* (Cambridge, Mass. and London: Harvard University Press, 2005).

Philip Tew and Rod Mengham, eds, *British Fiction Today* (London and New York: Continuum, 2006).

Ian Thomson, *Primo Levi* (London: Hutchinson, 2002).

Joshua Trachtenberg, *The Devil and the Jews* (New York: Jewish Publication Society of America, 1995).

Nadia Valman, *The Jewess in Nineteenth-Century British Culture* (Cambridge and New York: Cambridge University Press, 2007).

Gauri Viswanathan, ed., *Power, Politics, and Culture: Interviews with Edward W. Said* (New York: Pantheon Books, 2001).

Rebecca L. Walkowitz, *Cosmopolitan Style: Modernism Beyond the Nation* (New York: Columbia University Press, 2006).

Gavin Wallace and Randall Stevenson, eds, *The Scottish Novel Since the Seventies: New Visions, Old Dreams* (Edinburgh: Edinburgh University Press, 1993).

Eyal Weizman, *The Least of All Possible Evils: Humanitarian Violence from Arendt to Gaza* (London and New York: Verso, 2012).

Stephen J. Whitfield, *Into the Dark: Hannah Arendt and Totalitarianism* (Philadelphia: Temple University Press, 1980).

Ruth Whittaker, *The Faith and Fiction of Muriel Spark* (London: Macmillan, 1982).

Simon Wiesenthal, ed., *The Sunflower: On the Possibilities and Limits of Forgiveness* (New York: Schocken Books, 1979).

Marianne Wiggins, *Bet They'll Miss us When We're Gone* (New York and London: Harper Collins, 1991).

Patrick Williams, 'Naturally, I Reject the Term "Diaspora": Said and Palestinian Dispossession', in Michelle Keown, David Murphy and James Proctor, eds, *Comparing Postcolonial Diasporas* (Basingstoke: Palgrave Macmillan, 2009), pp. 83–103.

Angus Wilson, 'Journey to Jerusalem', *Observer* (17 October 1965), 28.

James Wood, 'Fundamentally Goyish', *London Review of Books* (3 October 2002), 17–18.

—— *The Irresponsible Self: On Laughter and the Novel* (London and New York: Jonathan Cape, 2004).

Nancy Wood, *Vectors of Memory: Legacies of Trauma in Postwar Europe* (Oxford and New York: Berg, 1999).

Judith Woolf, *The Memory of the Offence* (Market Harborough: Troubadour, 2001).

Youssef Yacoubi, *The Play of Reasons: The Sacred and the Profane in Salman Rushdie's Fiction* (New York and Berlin: Peter Lang, 2012).

James Young, *Writing and Rewriting the Holocaust: Narratives and the Consequences of Interpretation* (Bloomington, Ind.: Indiana University Press, 1988).

Robert J.C. Young, *White Mythologies: Writing History and the West* (London and New York: Routledge, 1990).

—— *Postcolonialism: An Historical Introduction* (Oxford and New York: Blackwell, 2001).

—— 'Fanon and the Turn to Armed Struggle in Africa', *Wasafiri* 20 (spring 2005), 33–41.

—— 'Edward Said: Opponent of Postcolonial Theory', in Tobias Döring and Mark Stein, eds, *Edward Said's Translocations: Essays in Secular Criticism* (London and New York: Routledge, 2012), pp. 23–43.

Susannah Young-ah Gottlieb (ed.), *Hannah Arendt: Reflections on Literature and Culture* (Stanford, Calif.: Stanford University Press, 2007).

Elisabeth Young-Bruehl, *Hannah Arendt: For Love of the World* (New Haven, Conn. and London: Yale University Press, 1982).

Irving M. Zeitlin, *Jews: The Making of a Diaspora People* (New York and Cambridge: Polity Press, 2012).

Wendy Zierler, '"My Holocaust Is Not Your Holocaust": "Facing" Black and Jewish Experience in *The Pawnbroker*, *Higher Ground*, and *The Nature of Blood*', *Holocaust and Genocide Studies* 18:1 (spring 2004), 46–67.

Index

Holocaust (*cont.*)
    identification with Jews 35–36; Jewish
      and Palestinian suffering 19, 23–24,
      27–28, 170
    Arendt on European imperialism as
      prelude to 15, 16
    argument for uniqueness 6, 39, 57, 88
    and Fanon 69
    and India in Desai's *Baumgartner's
      Bombay* 249–53
    and Postcolonial Studies 24–25
    Philip Roth: suffering of Jews in work
      175–76, 179–80, 184–85, 201; and
      tragic diaspora 168–70, 184–202
    and Salman Rushdie's work 206–07,
      234–35
    and Zadie Smith's work 260, 261,
      262
    see also Eichmann, Adolf; Nazism
Holocaust Studies 6, 7, 19
    'colonial turn' 16
home: in the work of Primo Levi and
    Jean Améry 81–83, 98–99
Home of the Brave (film) 71, 72–73, 199
homosexuality and Frantz Fanon 68–69,
    70, 71
Howe, Irving 184, 205
humanism
    Jean Améry and Primo Levi 76, 83, 84,
      87, 96–97, 105–06, 108; and 'humane
      vengeance' 93–94, 96, 97, 100; Primo
      Levi and dehumanized *Muselmann*
      108–10
    barbarity of European humanism 56–57,
      58, 73–75, 77
    Central European 21, 26–27, 206
    Frantz Fanon's 'new humanism' 6, 45,
      75–76
    and Albert Memmi 52
    Edward Said's humanism 20, 31
    and Muriel Spark 125
Huntington, Samuel P. 240
Hurston, Zora Neale: *Their Eyes Were
    Watching God* 255–56
hybridity
    and Stuart Hall's definition of 'diaspora'
      28–29
    and multi-ethnicity 3–4, 5–6
    and Salman Rushdie's work 211–12, 220,
      222, 223–24, 229
    and Edward Said 20, 23–24, 29,
      30–31
    and Zadie Smith's work 258, 262

identity
    Jean Améry and Jewish identity as racial
      construct 80, 83, 103
    black appropriation of Jewish identity
      32–37
    Jewish identity and Philip Roth's writing
      173–84
    Jewishness and Goyishness in Zadie
      Smith's *Autograph Man* 263
    Jewishness in Muriel Spark's work
      131–32, 135, 138, 139–48, 152
    Salman Rushdie: minority perspective
      25–26, 210, 222–23, 227–28; self and
      other in work 207–10, 233, 237–38
    Edward Said and 'Jewish identity' 30–31
'imaginary Jews' 39–40, 175
imagination and storytelling
    Hannah Arendt and metaphorical
      thinking 7–18, 28–29; lack of
      imagination and evil 9–10
    differences of exile and diaspora 26–8
    and history xii–xiii, 17–18
    Primo Levi and overcoming experience
      101, 107–08, 112–13
    literature and understanding of world
      7–9, 10
    Salman Rushdie: aestheticization of
      diaspora 26–27; imagination in
      Grimus 206–10
    see also literature; metaphorical thinking
immigrants
    black appropriation of Jewish history
      32–37
    see also migrants
imperialism
    Hannah Arendt and European
      imperialism 15–16
    European colonialism and Nazism 15,
      16, 56, 57–59
    see also colonialism
impurity xiii, 6, 18
    and blackness 55
    foetor judaicus ('Jewish stench') 193,
      202, 229, 279n40
    Primo Levi on 78, 100, 102, 104,
      105–06, 110, 112
    migrant as disruptive presence 28
    Philip Roth's 'dirty realism' 192–94,
      195, 196
    in Salman Rushdie's work 211–12, 213,
      214, 215, 216, 217, 222, 229, 238
    and Zadie Smith's *White Teeth* 257,
      259